MORAL REASONING

Ethical Theory and Some Contemporary Moral Problems

SECOND EDITION

VICTOR GRASSIAN

Harbor College
Wilmington, California

PRENTICE HALL, Englewood Cliffs, New Jersey 07632

Library of Congress Cataloging-in-Publication Data

Grassian, Victor.
  Moral reasoning : ethical theory and some contemporary moral
problems / Victor Grassian.—2nd ed.
      p. cm.
  Includes bibliographical references and index.
  ISBN 0-13-601378-3
  1. Ethics. 2. Social ethics. I. Title.
BJ1012.G68   1992   91-9032
170—dc20   CIP

Editorial/production supervision
  and interior design: *Robert C. Walters*
Cover design: *Lundgren Graphics, Ltd.*
Prepress buyer: *Herb Klein*
Manufacturing buyer: *Dave Dickey*
Acquisitions editor: *Ted Bolen*

 © 1992, 1981 by Prentice-Hall, Inc.
A Simon & Schuster Company
Englewood Cliffs, New Jersey 07632

Printed in the United States of America

10 9 8 7 6 5 4 3 2 1

ISBN 0-13-601378-3

Prentice-Hall International (UK) Limited, *London*
Prentice-Hall of Australia Pty. Limited, *Sydney*
Prentice-Hall Canada Inc., *Toronto*
Prentice-Hall Hispanoamericana, S.A., *Mexico*
Prentice-Hall of India Private Limited, *New Delhi*
Prentice-Hall of Japan, Inc., *Tokyo*
Simon & Schuster Asia Pte. Ltd., *Singapore*
Editora Prentice-Hall do Brasil, Ltda., *Rio de Janeiro*

To my parents
David and Ann Grassian
who toiled so their sons would have
the opportunities they never did

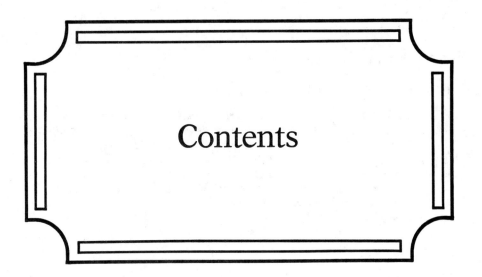

Contents

3
Morality, Self-Interest, Free Will, and Moral Responsibility   141

6
Euthanasia   268

7
Racial and Sexual Discrimination and the Problem of "Reverse Discrimination"   300

x   **Contents**

. . . all our dignity lies in thought. Let us strive, then, to think well.

PASCAL

What good fortune for those in power that people do not think.

HITLER

Preface

I have attempted to provide an ethics text which is readable and enlighteningly relevant to the philosophical novice without being superficial to the more sophisticated reader. It is roughly equally divided between issues in ethical theory and contemporary moral issues. It is my foremost hope that the text can, by its example, encourage students to think more clearly and critically about abstract and practical moral questions. In this analytic spirit, the success of this text should be measured by the degree to which it leads students toward the Socratic ideal of critical thinking which strives to dig beneath the surface of the often passionate though logically hollow rhetoric of popular moral reasoning.

The impetus that propelled me about a decade ago to write the first edition of this text has not changed. Introductory ethics texts and anthologies tend to be either too analytically abstract or not challenging enough for most beginning students, who should be exposed to the traditional questions of ethical theory as well as to contemporary moral issues. Texts and anthologies devoted to philosophical discussions of contemporary moral issues are usually not preceded by comprehensive discussions of the issues of ethical theory. Students are exposed to arguments on contemporary moral issues without any general consideration of the nature of moral reasoning and the theoretical perspectives that can serve to organize moral thinking. Anthologies, while useful in providing a diversity of points of view, are often too difficult for the novice, since the selections are usually extracted from philosophy journals directed to the philosophically sophisticated.

In addition, discussions of contemporary moral issues by philosophers are rarely presented in historical perspective or related to contemporary psychological and sociological perspectives or to the complex practical concerns of the law which can infuse these problems with greater meaning. For example, questions of the morality of affirmative action programs can be made more significant to introductory students when they are related to specific cases and to the conflicting judicial decisions that such cases have generated. Similarly, a discussion of the morality of homosexuality should presuppose some understanding of psychological theories about the nature and causes of homosexuality. Traditional ethical questions relating to human motivation and moral responsibility are also made more meaningful and engaging by being related to psychological theories. Consequently, in the discussions of psychological egoism and the free will controversy the student is made aware of how the resolution of these traditional philosophical concerns depends on the resolution of scientific questions.

Those familiar with the first edition of this text will notice extensive substantive and stylistic changes. In particular, the second edition differs from the first in providing a fuller treatment of the nature and pitfalls of moral reasoning and in providing sections on natural law and social contract theory which were lacking in the first edition. A new section on the boundaries of a moral community and the rights of animals has also been added, providing background for the discussion of the moral status of a human fetus, the central philosophical issue in the abortion controversy. The sections on contemporary moral issues have been updated to reflect recent developments, especially in the law. The text's detailed discussions of the Supreme Court's course on affirmative action should provide students with a sense of the tentative and on-going quality of judicial reasoning on divisive social issues which mirrors the model of moral reasoning presented in this text.

A tension between the desire for rationality and a realization of its limits is a distinctive thread that unifies this text. While rationally irreconcilable moral tension is at times unavoidable, reason can most certainly clear away the intellectual rubbish, and there will always be plenty of that around. It can also do much more, and, by so doing, justify the special dignity that moral philosophers have traditionally confired upon the human capacity to act as rational moral agents.

Victor Grassian

I

ETHICAL THEORY

Reason is, and ought only to be the slave of the passions...

DAVID HUME

...the will is a faculty of choosing only that which reason, independently of inclination, recognizes...as good.

IMMANUEL KANT

The foundations of morality are like all other foundations: if you dig too much about them the superstructure will come tumbling down.

SAMUEL BUTLER

A philosophy is characterized more by the formulation of its problems than by the solution of them.

SUSANNE LANGER

The Nature
of Moral Reasoning

1

1. INTRODUCTION

What Is Ethics?

Ethics may be defined as the philosophical study of morality—that is, of right conduct, moral character, obligation, and responsibility, social justice, and the nature of the good life. The philosophical study of morality should be distinguished from its descriptive or scientific study. It is not the philosopher's task, as it is that of the anthropologist, sociologist, or psychologist, to describe the various positions individuals and societies take on questions of morality nor to devise explanations as to why they have those views. Although philosophers make use of descriptive and scientific studies of morality, their tasks are different. Philosophers attempt to provide some theory of the *right* answers to moral questions. Yet this does not uniquely identify the philosophical study of morality, for such great literary figures as Shakespeare and Dostoyevsky have also enriched our lives with insight into the answers to moral questions, as have psychologists who grasp the psychological consequences of various moral positions. What distinguishes a philosophical account of morality is its generality, its systematic nature, and above all its attempt to prove through arguments that a proposed morality is indeed ideal.

The attempt to provide systematic and justifiable answers to moral questions is called *normative ethics* and is distinguished from the second task of the philosophical study of morality, *metaethics,* which consists of an inquiry into the meaning and logic of moral language. First, metaethics attempts to supply an account of the nature of morality and of the meanings and interrelationships of the fundamental concepts of moral language, answering such questions as the following: "How does a moral principle differ from a nonmoral one—such as a principle of etiquette?'' ''What do we mean when we say that an act is right?'' ''Can the notion of 'right conduct' be defined in terms of the notion of what is 'good' (that is, worth seeking) and can this notion in turn be defined in terms of some nonmoral quality such as 'pleasure'?'' ''What do we mean by saying that one has 'free will' or is 'morally responsible' for one's actions?'' Second, metaethics attempts to supply an account of the nature of moral reasoning, and considers questions such as the following: ''How does moral reasoning differ from scientific reasoning?'' ''In what sense, if at all, can a moral claim be said to be 'true' or 'false'?'' ''Is there such a thing as moral knowledge or is morality, in the last analysis, simply a 'matter of taste'?''

Why Study Ethics?

Although a study of ethics will not in itself make one into a good person, it can provide us with more than knowledge of abstract philosophical theories and terminologies that are incapable of aiding us in the solution of our own practical moral problems. A study of ethics can help us better understand and classify our own moral principles; most of all, it can help refine, develop, and sometimes change these principles. Beginning students of ethics come to this study laden with beliefs on many moral issues, but rarely have they adequately thought about the implications of these beliefs and whether they are consistent.

The study of ethics can lead one from blind and irrational acceptance of the moral dogma one has assimilated without logical scrutiny into the development of a critical reflective morality of one's own. Certainly, all reflective people at some time in their lives have been struck by the vagueness and inconsistencies of conventional morality, where moral principles are called upon in one context only to be conveniently forgotten in others. Who has not on occasion suspected that some cherished moral belief was simply a deeply felt prejudice? Aware of the many apparently divergent moralities that coexist in the world around us, many of us wonder whether our moral beliefs can be rationally justified. Are they nothing more than a reflection of the prevailing mores of our culture—no more right or wrong than those of other cultures? Some of us may shudder to think that a future student of anthropology may laugh as he reads about the strange moral beliefs that we now hold, just as many of us now laugh at those of certain ancient cultures. It is in the face of such intellectual uneasiness that philosophical inquiry often begins. By studying the arguments that philosophers give for their ethical positions and the objections they pose to the views of others, the ability to defend one's own position and to recognize its shortcomings will be sharpened. This is by far the most important benefit that the study of ethics has to offer.

Socratic Method and the Ideal of Consistency

As the ancient Greek philosopher Socrates noticed long ago, most of us have strong opinions on moral matters, but are neither capable of adequately justifying these opinions nor of defining their key concepts. Philosophical reflection begins, as it began for Socrates, with the questioning of one's own beliefs. Socrates is remembered today not for his philosophical positions (he claimed he had none), but for his method of doing philosophy—the Socratic Method. As he walked the streets of Athens, conversing on philosophical topics, Socrates did not play the advocate, attempting to convince others of the correctness of his views. Instead, he simply questioned them as to the presuppositions and implications of their opinions. In the process, he uncovered the logical weaknesses of those opinions.

When you subject your moral beliefs to Socratic scrutiny, you may be embarrassed to discover that the moral principles you claim to hold and act upon are unclear, difficult to justify, and have contradictory implications. As we shall discuss, although there may be rationally irreconcilable differences in moral views, rationality demands that one strive to make one's moral principles clear and consistent.

Each of us comes to the study of ethics with a multitude of judgments on concrete moral questions, such as, Should X lie in situation Y? Should homosexuality be illegal? Are abortions morally justified? The task of philosophical reflection is to unify these particular moral judgments into some systematic and consistent whole. As you attempt to discern *general* underlying moral principles that can account for your particular moral judgments, you may find that a principle accepted in one concrete situation appears unacceptable in another. Unless you can point to some morally relevant difference in the two situations, the ideal of consistency demands that you either modify your commitment to the general moral principle or revise your moral judgment of the concrete situation. The difficulty of developing a unified and consistent system of underlying moral principles to guide you in the resolution of concrete problems can be clearly seen in moral dilemmas that arise when moral principles to which you feel allegiance are in conflict. Let us turn to some examples of such moral dilemmas.

2. SOME MORAL DILEMMAS

In each of the following cases try to extract the underlying moral principle that justifies the position you take. Be on guard for a principle that you are inclined to use in one example but not in another. When this happens, ask yourself what differences there are in the two cases that incline you to treat them differently.

As you proceed, see if there are some general moral principles on which you consistently rely. Is it possible for your moral principles to be arranged in hierarchical order where certain *basic* general principles are used to justify derivative ones but cannot be justified in terms of some higher level principle? Do you accept more than one basic moral principle? If so, can they conflict? How would you choose among them in such a case. Can you *justify* your choice of basic moral principles? Ponder these questions as you consider the moral dilemmas. After we have studied the general theories of normative ethics of some famous philosophers, we can consider how these philosophers would resolve our dilemmas. Most important, after having subjected your own moral views to reasoned criticism, you may find that your reactions to these dilemmas have themselves changed or developed.

1. The Overcrowded Lifeboat

In 1842, a ship struck an iceberg and more than 30 survivors were crowded into a lifeboat intended to hold 7. As a storm threatened, it became obvious that the lifeboat would have to be lightened if anyone were to survive. The captain reasoned that the right thing to do in this situation was to force some individuals to go over the side and drown. Such an action, he reasoned, was not unjust to those thrown overboard, for they would have drowned anyway. If he did nothing, however, he would be responsible for the deaths of those whom he could have saved. Some people opposed the captain's decision. They claimed that if nothing were done and everyone died as a result, no one would be responsible for these deaths. On the other hand, if the captain attempted to save some, he could do so only by killing others and their deaths would be his responsibility; this would be worse than doing nothing and letting all die. the captain rejected this reasoning. Since the only possibility for rescue required great efforts of rowing, the captain decided that the weakest would have to be sacrificed. In this situation it would be absurd, he thought, to decide by drawing lots who should be thrown overboard.

As it turned out, after days of hard rowing, the survivors were rescued and the captain was tried for his action. If you had been on the jury, how would you have decided? Why?

2. A Father's Agonizing Choice

You are an inmate in a concentration camp. A sadistic guard is about to hang your son who tried to escape and wants you to pull the chair from underneath him. He says that if you don't he will not only kill your son but some other innocent inmate as well. You don't have any doubt that he means what he says. What should you do?

3. The Fat Man and the Impending Doom

A fat man leading a group of people out of a cave on a coast is stuck in the mouth of that cave. In a short time high tide will be upon them, and unless he is unstuck, they will all be drowned except the fat man, whose head is out of the cave. There seems no way to get the fat man loose without using dynamite which will inevitably kill him; but if they do not use it everyone will drown. What should they do?

4. The Costly Underwater Tunnel

An underwater tunnel is being constructed despite an almost certain loss of several lives. Presumably the expected loss is a calculated cost that society is prepared to pay for having the tunnel. At a critical moment when a fitting must be lowered into place, a workman is trapped in a section of the partly laid tunnel. If it is lowered, it will surely crush the trapped workman to death. Yet, if it is not and a time-consuming rescue of the workman is attempted, the tunnel will have to be abandoned and the whole project begun anew. Two workmen have already died in the project as a result of anticipated and unavoidable conditions in the building of the tunnel. What should be done? Was it a mistake to begin the tunnel in the first place? But don't we take such risks all the time?

5. Involuntary Euthanasia
and the Common Good

Most of us would feel great moral repugnance at the Nazi program of involuntary euthanasia of the chronically and hopelessly ill, the insane, the senile, and congenital idiots. The rationale given by the Nazis was that the immense amount of money it cost to care for such people could be better spent on social programs for those with great capacities for meaningful lives. Indeed, with current technology, the bodies of the victims of involuntary euthanasia would provide "spare parts," saving lives or increasing the quality of life of others. Most of us will say, "It is wrong to sacrifice people for the common good like this." Yet if this is so, how can we feel justified in sacrificing innocent lives for the greater good in a war. What, if any, are the relevant moral differences in these cases?

6. The Musings of Desperation

Bob's son has a rare form of cancer for which only one treatment has proven successful. It is very costly, however, and Bob, even with the help of friends, cannot afford it. In desperation, he thinks of stealing the money from a miserly and eccentric old woman who is known to hoard great wealth in her home. If only he could get the money from her, she wouldn't even miss it! Sure, she has a right to her property, but his son's right to life is so much more important. If I could rob her with impunity, I would, Bob muses, and I wouldn't feel guilty. It's really the right thing to do . . .

   Is Bob correct? Why?

7. Sherman McCoy's Dilemma

In Tom Wolff's *The Bonfire of the Vanities,* the hero, Sherman McCoy, finds himself in the midst of a political firestorm, that makes it difficult for him to get a fair trial in a case of vehicular homicide. His attorney obtains someone else's surreptitiously recorded tape of Sherman's conversation with a woman. The tape can serve to exonerate him, but the attorney tells Sherman that such a tape would be admissable only if he had recorded it himself. Sherman is furious and decides to lie, claiming that he made the recording. At the moment of his perjury, Sherman feels acute discomfort. Torn between his ingrained sense of his obligation to obey the law and his desire to use the truth to save himself, Sherman agonizes:

> I'm doing something illegal. Yes, but in the name of truth. This is the subterranean path to the light. This is the actual conversation we had . . . for this to be suppressed

that would be the greater dishonesty, wouldn't it? Yes, but I'm doing something illegal. Around and around it went in his mind.... As the tape rolled on... Sherman McCoy discovered what many had discovered before him. In well reared boys and girls guilt and the instinct to obey the rules are reflexes, ineradicable ghosts in the machine...

Was Sherman right in resisting the "reflex" to abide by the law? In general, when is it right to disobey the law?

8. Jean Valjean's Conscience

In Victor Hugo's *Les Miserables,* the hero, Jean Valjean, is an ex-convict, living illegally under an assumed name and wanted for a robbery he committed many years ago. Although he will be returned to the galleys—probably for life—if he is caught, he is a good man who does not deserve to be punished. He has established himself in a town, becoming mayor and a public benefactor. One day, Jean learns that another man, a vagabond, has been arrested for a minor crime and identified as Jean Valjean. Jean is first tempted to remain quiet, reasoning to himself that since he had nothing to do with the false identification of this hapless vagabond, he has no obligation to save him. Perhaps this man's false identification, Jean reflects, is "an act of Providence meant to save me." Upon reflection, however, Jean judges such reasoning "monstrous and hypocritical." He now feels certain that it is his duty to reveal his identity, regardless of the disastrous personal consequences. His resolve is disturbed, however, as he reflects on the irreparable harm his return to the galleys will mean to so many people who depend upon him for their livelihood—especially troubling in the case of a helpless woman and her small child to whom he feels a special obligation. He now reproaches himself for being too selfish, for thinking only of his own conscience and not of others. The right thing to do, he now claims to himself, is to remain quiet, to continue making money and using it to help others. The vagabond, he comforts himself, is not a worthy person, anyway. Still unconvinced and tormented by the need to decide, Jean goes to the trial and confesses. Did he do the right thing?

9. A Callous Passerby

Roger Smith, a quite competent swimmer, is out for a leisurely stroll. During the course of his walk he passes by a deserted pier from which a teenage boy who apparently cannot swim has fallen into the water. The boy is screaming for help. Smith recognizes that there is absolutely no danger to himself if he jumps in to save the boy; he could easily succeed if he tried. Nevertheless, he chooses to ignore the boy's cries. The water is cold and he is afraid of catching a cold—he doesn't want to get his good clothes wet either. "Why should I inconvenience myself for this kid," Smith says to himself, and passes on. Does Smith have a moral obligation to save the boy? If so, should he have a legal obligation as well? Why?

10. A Poisonous Cup of Coffee

Tom, hating his wife and wanting her dead, puts poison in her coffee, thereby killing her. Joe also hates his wife and would like her dead. One day, Joe's wife accidentally puts poison in her coffee, thinking it's cream. Joe has the antidote, but he does not give it to her. Knowing that he is the only one who can save her, he lets her die. Is Joe's failure to act as bad as Tom's action? Why?

11. The Torture of the Mad Bomber

A madman who has threatened to explode several bombs in crowded areas has been apprehended. Unfortunately, he has already planted the bombs and they are scheduled to go off in a short time. It is possible that hundreds of people may die. The authorities cannot make him divulge the location of the bombs by conventional methods. He refuses to say anything and requests a lawyer to protect his fifth amendment right against self-incrimination. In exasperation, some high-level official suggests torture. This would be illegal, of course, but the official thinks that it is nevertheless the right thing to do in this desperate situation. Do you agree? If you do, would it also be morally justifiable to torture the mad bomber's innocent wife if that is the only way to make him talk? Why?

12. Political Assassination

You are the director of the C.I.A. A mentally unstable tyrant is in control of a small nation and is ruthlessly killing his real and imagined opposition. He has, however, assumed control legally. You are presented with a plan to assassinate him which that you think has a good chance of succeeding. Should you go ahead? On what does it depend?

13. The Cog in an Unjust System

You have just been offered a high position in your corrupt city government. If you attempt to buck the system, you will be thrown out at once and a person with fewer scruples will take your place. Would it be right to accept the position, going along with the corrupt system when you must but trying to do as much good as you can?

14. The Principle of Psychiatric Confidentiality

You are a psychiatrist and your patient has just confided to you that he intends to kill a woman. You're inclined to dismiss the threat as idle, but you aren't sure. Should you report the threat to the police and the woman or should you remain silent as the principle of confidentiality between psychiatrist and patient demands? Should there be a law that compels you to report such threats?

15. The Partiality of Friendship

Jim has the responsibility of filling a position in his firm. His friend Paul has applied and is qualified, but someone else seems even more qualified. Jim wants to give the job to Paul, but he feels guilty, believing that he ought to be impartial. That's the essence of morality, he initially tells himself. This belief is, however, rejected, as Jim resolves that friendship has a moral importance that permits, and perhaps even requires, partiality in some circumstances. So he gives the job to Paul. Was he right?

16. The Value of a Promise

A friend confides to you that he has committed a particular crime and you promise never to tell. Discovering that an innocent person has been accused of the crime, you plead with your friend to give himself up. He refuses and reminds you of your promise. What should you do? In general, under what conditions should promises be broken?

17. The Reluctant Voter

You have always been a conscientious voter, but on this national election day, it would be especially inconvenient for you to take the time to vote. You convince yourself that doing so would not serve any useful purpose, for a single vote certainly will not make a difference in this election. To avoid criticism, you decide not to tell anyone you didn't vote. The more you think about it, the more convinced you become that it is foolish for people to vote when they know that their refusal to vote will not affect the outcome or the voting behavior of others. What, if anything, is wrong with this sort of reasoning?

18. The Soft-Hearted Professor

You are a professor of philosophy. A student who is doing D work comes to you just before the final and explains that he needs a C to be admitted next semester to a business school. He claims that he's been working hard in your class but just doesn't seem to understand what is going on. You offer to help him, but soon discover that there isn't much you can do short of giving him the questions and answers to the final. He seems quite sincere, however, and you would hate to have his admission rejected on the basis of your grade. You're very tempted to give him the C and attempt to justify this to yourself by reflecting that "a good business administration major doesn't have to have any aptitude for philosophy." But then again, you think, "It would be unfair to the other students." What should you do?

3. THE NATURE OF MORAL VALUES

What Is Morality?

As discussions of moral dilemmas such as the preceding amply illustrate, moral opinions often differ. Is there some way to resolve these differences, some way to distinguish true moral opinions from false ones? Are these opinions merely a matter of taste, and whatever agreement exists, merely a matter of social convention? We cannot adequately tackle this central issue in metaethics without considering, at least briefly, the meaning of the concept of morality. At the very beginning of this text, it was said that *ethics* may be defined as the philosophical study of morality. In ordinary usage, however, the concept of ethics is often used interchangeably with that of morality. For this reason, when people speak of *moral and ethical* principles, it is not clear what distinction, if any, they attribute to these two concepts.

As we shall see throughout this text, the first step in resolving a philosophical issue is coming to grips with the meaning of the key concepts involved. Yet, as we shall also constantly see, ordinary language is often frustratingly vague or ambiguous. Consequently, philosophers must often clarify the meanings of concepts rather than simply report their established meanings in the manner of a compiler of a dictionary. In doing this, philosophers supply *explicative* or *stipulative* definitions. An explicative definition is one that clarifies by making more precise the scope of application of a vague term. (How much hair can a "bald" man have?) Stipulative definitions are often required when we are dealing with ambiguity rather than vagueness—i.e., with a term that has different meanings rather than one that has a single imprecise meaning. The latter is the case with the concept of ethics. That is why we said not that ethics *is* but rather *may* be defined as the philosophical study of morality, stipulating a meaning of this term that would be useful in the discussion that followed. Ethics, in this sense, is synonymous with the more precise term, *ethical theory,* widely used by moral philosophers.

Ethics, we have stipulated, is the philosophical study of morality. But what is morality? To say, as the first sentence of this book does, that it is concerned with "right conduct, moral character, obligation and responsibility, social justice, and the nature of the good life" helps by distinguishing different spheres of morality. But what do all these spheres have in common? Why are they classified together as elements of the broader sphere called morality? The answer to this question is itself a point of contention among moral philosophers; entire books have been written on it. So, it is impossible to do justice to this issue in a cursory way. However, let us try at least to begin untangling the complexities of meaning that surround this fundamental concept that will occupy us throughout this text.

We may begin by observing that we do not normally speak of (nonhuman) animals as having a morality. Why is that? Is it not because we do not think of animals as rational beings who need to structure and curb their desires with rules, principles, and ideals that take priority over the promptings of momentary desires or more lasting nonreflective moods? As James Madison said, a society of perfectly good angels would not need a government. For the same reason, they would not need a morality, for they would not have to place restraints on their behavior as we do. They, unlike us, would not have to be concerned with reflecting upon their behavior, personality, and life, and with measuring them against rational standards, principles, or ideals. Many see these standards as emanating from God, an innate conscience, or society. Others see them as demands of "a higher self" that guides the often fickle, inconsistent, and short-sighted promptings of our complex psychological natures. Western religious tradition sees the human capacity for moral reflection as what distinguishes human beings from other animals. Feelings of integrity, remorse, self-reproach, guilt, and shame are the psychological capabilities that confer *dignity* upon people.[1]

The moral point of view, we have said, is directed to rational creatures who can act in accord with the principles and rules which structure behavior. But this does not distinguish morality from other principled or rule-governed behavior such as law and etiquette. How, for example, would an anthropologist studying a strange culture distinguish the principles of morality of that culture from its legal principles and from its principles of etiquette? As with the concept of morality, books have been written on the concept of law and there is philosophical debate about the relationship between morality and law.[2] Suffice it to say for our purposes here that, law, unlike morality entails specific procedures for recognition, enactment and response to violators. Laws, unlike morality, can be purposely changed from one day to the next by those in *authority*. In this respect, rules that govern games like baseball are more like laws than moral principles or principles of etiquette. How does etiquette differ from morality? Certainly, moral matters are more important than matters of etiquette. But why? First, rules of etiquette are essentially matters of convention, like whether one drives on the right or left side of the road or whether one wears a suit or less formal attire. But most of us think and behave as if morality has an *objective* justification and unity that is not found in variable social conventions. Unlike the specific demands of etiquette, we expect that specific moral demands derive from general moral demands that transcend the issue at hand.

Clearly, the social importance attached to morality and the relative seriousness of response that awaits its transgressors reside in its attempt to harmonize the interests of individuals in order to reduce social conflict. Nevertheless, morality, as commonly understood, has a personal dimension as well, for conflicts arise not only among the desires of different people, but also within the psyche of an individual. For this reason, people often impose personal ideals of integrity on themselves which, unlike the social demands of morality, are theirs alone. Our

---

[1]If, as the evidence seems to suggest, some nonhuman animals are capable of such feelings, they too are worthy of respect and recognition as members of a moral community. And we are treating them unjustly if we refuse to consider their interests as well as our own.

[2]For example, some legal philosophers say that it is essential to distinguish the claim that a law is legally valid (e.g., unconstitutional law is not legally valid within the United States) from whether it is morally correct or wise. Others, however, claim that adherence to certain general principles of morality are required before one can properly speak of the existance of a legal system. As Saint Augustine provocatively put it, "What are states without justice, but robber bands enlarged."

social morality demands a general respect for the interests and dignity of others; it does not demand the self-sacrifice of a Saint Francis or a Mother Theresa. Although, as we shall later discuss, many have argued that it is wrong to consider purely self-regarding practices that do not cause harm to others to be immoral, let alone illegal, this is an ideal to which no society consistently adheres. For example, according to Roman Catholic morality, some sexual practices such as masturbation and homosexuality are wrong regardless of whether such practices cause social harm. While one can give grounds for rejecting conceptions of morality that see actions as evil regardless of their social consequences, such grounds presuppose controversial normative stands on what morality ought to be. However liberal we may be as to nonharmful and mutually consenting sexual behavior, we all have our limits. What would you think, for example, of a man who routinely had sex with his willing dog or who occasionally obtained sexual gratification by urinating on his willing spouse? Some of us may simply register our disgust with such practices, while refraining from any moral judgment: the majority of us, however, would see such behavior as a blot on one's moral character. For we would see such people as less than fully adequate human beings—as people who fall seriously short of ideals that we have of what it is to be a properly functioning human being—a central part of the concerns of morality.

Is Morality Objective?

The demands of morality, we have said, are directed to creatures who are capable of curbing and structuring their desires by *rational* principles. But we know that rational people often disagree about moral principles. Is there some way to resolve this conflict, or must we ultimately resort to purely emotional techniques of molding behavior which are deceptively clothed in the garb of impersonal demands of an objective morality?

Intuitionism

According to one tradition in ethics, there are certain self-evident general moral principles from which all specific moral principles can be deduced. This point of view is called *intuitionism* and is well-expressed by the eighteenth-century philosopher Thomas Reid who wrote:

> All reasoning must be grounded on first principles... There must, therefore, be in morals... first or self-evident principles, on which all moral reasoning is grounded. From such self-evident principles, conclusions may be drawn... But without such principles, we can no more establish any conclusion in morals, than we can build a castle in the air, without any foundation.

Intuitionists disagree, however, as to the self-evident foundations of moral knowledge. Such disagreement gives credence to the cynical observation that intuitionists are simply trying to get others to adopt their own moral preferences. Intuitionists speak of those who do not accept their intuitions as "morally blind," but, unlike the color-blind, the morally blind are not compelled to accept the existence of a capacity in others that they lack themselves.

If some features of morality are self-evident it is only because they are built into our definition of morality. For example, the influential philosopher Immanuel Kant (1724–1804), whose ethical theory we will later study, claimed that the notions of autonomy, objectivity, impartiality, and universalizability are necessary features of *any* morality. As Kant saw it, there is a supreme moral principle, the categorical imperative, built upon these notions, which must be regarded as correct if *any moral discourse is to be possible at all.* Yet the meaning and implications of this allegedly self-evident supreme moral principle have been the subject of heated debate among philosophers. Other philosophers, like the utilitarians Jeremy Bentham (1748–1832) and John Stuart Mill (1806–1873), would claim that the concept of morality, if it is to be objective, must be tied to the notion of rational benevolence, and must be concerned with the reconciliation of the interests of members of a moral community. Yet philosophers who accept this point of view differ in their conception of how one ought to reconcile the interests of others.

The Divine Command Theory

Despairing of the limitation of the human mind to discern self-evident moral truths, some philosophers have turned to God, seeing the ultimate source of morality in his commands. A right act, on this view, consists of obedience to God's will; this is the only genuine basis for morality. Atheists may live according to the moral point of view, but if their behavior is to have any objective justification, it must come from God. As Dostoyevsky's Ivan Karamazov puts it, "If there is no God, then anything is permissible." Let us briefly consider this view.

Assuming that we were created by God, there are two different claims that can be made about the connection between God and morality. First, one may claim that though we can understand what morality demands of us without relating it to the will of God, the existence of God gives the only adequate reason for being moral at all times. Second, one may claim that morality must *be defined* in terms of God's will. The first view usually involves an eventual day of moral reckoning, when the virtuous will be rewarded and the wicked punished. This view, which we shall not pursue here, appeals to one's self-interest as a reason for being moral. The second view, however, is relevant to our interest at this point not in why one ought to be moral, but in the logically more basic question of what counts as moral behavior.

The question of the legitimacy of defining morality in terms of God's will is the subject of an early Platonic dialogue called the *Euthyphro.* In this dialogue, representative of Socratic method, Socrates discusses the meaning of morality with Euthyphro. As in other dialogues, Socrates acts as an interrogator who points out logical weaknesses in his opponent's view. Euthyphro, accepting the Greek belief in many gods, claims that morality is defined as the will of the gods. Leaving aside the question of how Euthyphro can know when the gods agree and what we are to say when they disagree (as they allegedly did), Socrates attempts to make Euthyphro distinguish between the claim that an act is right because the gods will it and the claim that the gods will an act because it is right. This distinction can also be applied to Judeo-Christian monotheism.

Is an act right because God wills it or does God will it because it is right? According to the former, right action must be defined in terms of God's will, while according to the latter, there is some logically independent standard of right action to which God's will adheres. It is the former claim that Socrates finds objectionable. Why should the fiat of any being, even God, in itself make an act right? Is it because God is our creator and as such has the right to demand our total obedience? Bishop Robert C. Mortimer advocates this view, writing,

> God made us and all the world. Because of that he has an absolute claim on our obedience. We do not exist in our own right, but only as His creatures, who ought therefore to do and be what He desires.

This, however, seems inadequate, for is it not conceivable that we were created by an evil deity for some malevolent purpose. Were we to do what such a being wants, it would not be out of respect, but simply out of fear for the consequences of his power, should we disobey. "This is absurd!" a critic is bound to retort. "We were not created by such a God, but a morally perfect one—to suggest otherwise is to blaspheme the Judeo-Christian God." This is so, but it also brings out the circularity of attempting to define morality in terms of God's will. It is precisely because the Judeo-Christian God is defined partially in terms of moral perfection that a denial of God's goodness is itself a rejection of the Judeo-Christian God. The traditional Judeo-Christian answer to the question "Why ought we to worship and obey God?" is that "God *deserves* our worship and obedience *since* he is morally perfect." Such a claim can only make sense if we understand the notion of moral perfection before we relate it to God. The very fact that we refuse out of hand to consider the possibility of a fiendish creator reflects the fact that we are employing some logically independent standard in morally judging the appropriateness of respecting the God in whom we were taught to believe. We may have faith in the morality of an act, which we would otherwise think of as immoral, because we believe it to be willed by God; however, this is not a result of a complete abandonment of independent moral appraisal.

Consider, for example, the biblical story of Abraham's willingness to sacrifice his son Isaac to God. Did not Abraham have faith that God had good reasons for requesting such a sacrifice? Should it have been morally acceptable to Abraham, had he sacrificed his son, to find that God simply enjoyed causing anguish to his fatherly heart and abusing the vulnerability of his innocent faith? It would appear that while we may have faith that God has reasons that we cannot understand due to our ignorance of his purposes or our muddled thinking, we, should nevertheless, believe that God has reasons which are worthy of respect.[3] Consequently, it is not the fiat of God that makes an act right, but the reason that God, whom we believe to be good, would give for his actions. These reasons would have their logical force (if not practical efficacy) *even if God did not exist,* and can be studied in their own right.

The considerations that lead us to reject blind acceptance of the will of God should lead us equally to dismiss the view that *conscience* is the correct standard. Suppose we assume, what secular psychologists would strongly contest, that one's conscience reflects the inborn knowledge of "moral law" instilled in us by God. There is no sure means to distinguish the notoriously divergent promptings of conscience as correct or incorrect. The conscience of a religious pacifist, for example, tells him that war is contrary to the moral law, whereas the consciences of his non-pacifistic brethren speak with a different voice.

If we are to distinguish *enlightened* consciences from *misled* ones or from the disguised promptings of some other source, we must have some standard. If, as often suggested, the mark of an enlightened conscience is its correspondence with the revealed word of God as found in the Bible, we must have some standard for choosing the *right* bible and its *proper* interpretations. The widespread disagreement of theologians is ample testimony that the words of a given holy book are open to differing interpretations (and even disagreements as to translation). More fundamentally, there is no agreement as to which book of allegedly divinely inspired writings should be accepted. Should we turn to the Christian Bible? If so, which version? Should we, perhaps, restrict our attention to the Old Testament as Judaism does? Or should we turn to the Koran or the holy writings found in Eastern religions? The lessons to be learned will differ depending on where we turn. Again, there is no way to escape using our own independent moral standards as at least a partial standard for the acceptance or rejection of the divinely inspired nature of some religious writing. If we picked up an alleged bible to find that it seemed to have been written by the Marquis de Sade, we would dismiss it as not inspired by the good Judeo-Christian God.

Ethical Relativism

If we cannot establish what is right or wrong by turning to our intuitions or to God, and if, as we shall soon see, there are incompatible ethical theories as to the standard to be used in resolving moral disputes, perhaps these disputes are, in the last analysis, nonrational and can only be decided on the basis of one's emotional preferences or commitments. Perhaps, ethical choice is more like choosing the flavor of ice cream than discerning the objective size of an object, for there are no correct

---

[3]This is denied by the Danish philosopher Kierkegaard (1813–55) who claimed that religious faith involves the acceptance of beliefs that are absurd or immoral by rational standards. Kierkegaard contends in his book *Fear & Trembling* that Abraham was "the knight of faith" precisely because he was willing unquestioningly to obey God's outrageous command without trying to understand and justify it. In making this claim, Kierkegaard severs the connection between religion and ethics that is central to the Judeo-Christian tradition.

answers as to which flavor is best. This is the position of ethical relativism which claims that there is no way to pick out a specific morality as correct. The belief in ethical relativism is often based on the observation that, as a matter of fact, different societies or cultures have fundamentally different moral beliefs. This doctrine is called *sociological* or *cultural relativism* and has been held by many students of anthropology to be obviously true. Not all cultural relativists, however, have been ethical relativists. One may accept cultural relativism, while taking the metaethical position that only one morality can be justified as correct.

According to cultural relativists, the fact of cultural moral variability has been conclusively established. All educated people are aware of the abundant differences in the mores of different cultures, the changing mores of a given culture through time, or of a pluralistic society like ours where varieties of life-styles coexist at a given time. Furthermore, the cultural relativist will assert that moral beliefs are neither inborn nor the result of logical reasoning but are rather the *internalized* reflection of the views of our culture transmitted to us by our parents and other influences. The acquisition of moral beliefs is an unconscious psychological process based not upon our capacity for reasoning but on our emotional natures. The result is in an essentially emotional nonreasoning acceptance of the norms of one's culture. These norms, which are explained and reinforced by a society's religious beliefs and practices, maintain social coherence. It is precisely the human desire to cling to one group and to reject others as inferior that explains the tendency to believe that the moral norms of one's culture are the only true ones, and those of other cultures false. This ethnocentric (group centered) feeling, based as it is primarily on nonreasoning emotion, often causes people to be narrow-minded in their ethical outlook and afraid to subject their moral beliefs to logical scrutiny. This, in brief, is the case presented for sociological relativism, and by inference, ethical relativism, by their adherents.

Sociological relativism is, however, open to challenge. No doubt different societies have different attitudes concerning the morality of specific practices and place different degrees of emphasis upon such possibly conflicting principles as individual freedom and social welfare. It is open to question, however, whether these different attitudes on specific issues reflect deeper differences in ultimate moral perspectives or are instead reflections of differing circumstances or factual or religious beliefs. Perhaps, if agreement could be obtained on these nonmoral factors, there would be agreement on moral issues as well.

It is quite conceivable that all societies share the same *basic* moral principles (i.e., those used to justify derivative principles though incapable of justification by more fundamental moral principles). Consider, for example sexual morality. Let us assume that in society *A* premarital sex and polygamy are encouraged, whereas they are condemned in society *B*. Clearly, we have moral disagreements here—but they need not be ultimate. Perhaps both societies are committed to the same basic moral principle that "one should always do what is conducive to the general happiness." The differences in the two societies' positions on sexual morality may stem from differences in their circumstances and factual beliefs. Perhaps women in society *A* greatly outnumber men and most people in that society believe that sexual experience in general and with one's prospective spouse in particular, is necessary for maximum human happiness. Similarly, a given society may approve of cannibalism while we condemn it only because it accepts what is to us the erroneous belief that eating the flesh of one's enemy is necessary for the survival of one's group. Likewise, we may morally condemn the practice during the Inquisition of burning people at the stake, but this does not imply that our disagreement is over basic moral principles. Perhaps the disagreement stems from a change in religious belief. During the Inquisition, there was greater fear of eternal damnation than there is today. It was generally fervently believed that burning people at the stake was the only way to save them from that far worse fate. If we shared the same religious belief, would we not also approve this distasteful and desperate action?

Granted then that a mere difference in moral position need not reflect disagreement on a basic ethical principle, is there any reason to think that all cultures actually do share the same basic moral principles? Some people, perhaps in over-reaction to thoughtless defenses of sociological relativism, point to the underlying similarities of human beings the world over and of the conditions necessary for mutual cooperation and survival as sufficient to disprove this doctrine. For example, the psychologist S. E. Asch writes, "We do not know of societies in which bravery is despised and cowardice held up to honor, in which generosity is considered a vice and ingratitude a virtue." Even if this were true, Asch neglects the fact that different cultures have different conceptions of bravery and generosity. Similarly, one may accept that no society tolerates the indiscriminate killing of its members but distinguishes between justifiable and unjustifiable homicide. Yet the nature of this distinction may be quite different in different societies.

Why, assuming Asch is right, do all societies consider bravery and generosity virtues? As Asch recognizes, the answer would have to be sought in universal features of human nature and social conditions. Given human selfishness and the struggle for survival that the world we inhabit imposes upon us, societies are invariably governed by principles which restrain human selfishness for the common good. All societies recognize that there are times when abiding by the moral and legal principles of the group is very difficult; there also are times when the common good requires individual sacrifices that go beyond normal moral obligations. Consequently, societies may inevitably have the concepts of bravery and generosity which are used to describe people who act beyond the calls of ordinary duty, and societies will naturally support and encourage such behavior. Yet societies may have very different conceptions of the common good and of the degree of adversity or sacrifice that is required for an act of bravery or generosity.

Given invariable features of human psychology, viable moralities may have to have a similar structure and content. These similarities would naturally come to be considered essential to the very concept of morality. Any morality must take into consideration that human beings tend to be partially selfish and partially altruistic; they are vulnerable to others and need the cooperation of others; they have limited understanding and strength of will; and to live together harmoniously, they need to see their society as built on the foundation of fair mutuality of benefit and burden.

It is important to see the worldwide similarities of the human condition, but one should not neglect differences which may well lead to fundamental divergence in moral outlook. It is one thing to say that all societies encourage cooperation, have some notion of property, rules prohibiting theft and distinguishing permissible from impermissible homicide, and have procedures for recognizing the legal consequences of sexual unions.[4] It is, however, something quite different to say that this similarity negates the thesis of sociological relativism. The mere fact that human beings share similar emotions, such as love, hate, happiness, sadness, pride, and shame, does not establish a similar basic moral outlook. Clearly, it makes a difference, for example, whether one takes pride in the number of people one helps or in the number of people one kills.

As we will see in our discussion of specific ethical theories, moral principles, such as "always act to maximize human happiness" and "always act to preserve the value of human freedom," can take on quite different meanings depending on the meanings attributed to the key notions of "happiness" and "freedom." Thus, two societies committed to a moral principle like the "maximization of human happiness," may be committed to quite different moral ideals. Similarly, while all societies may condemn theft and incest, they may have very different notions of these acts, reflecting different moral outlooks on *legitimate* property relationships and *appropriate* sexual relationships. Indeed, some cultural relativists have claimed that two cultures may inhabit such differing moral universes that it is impossible to translate moral categories of one into those of the other. Different cultures, we may want to say, do *see the world differently*. But are ways of seeing the world reflective of differences in *factual* or *moral* belief? The source may not be clearly distinguishable in some cases, for the conceptual difference between moral and factual beliefs is itself problematic. So, it is not at all easy to appraise the contention of sociological relativism's critics that all moral differences between cultures can be traced back to some difference in nonmoral belief.

Furthermore, even if it could be shown that two societies, whose external ways of life appear very different, actually share the same basic moral principles, they could still disagree morally if they differed on the *ranking* of these moral principles in cases of conflict. For example, two societies might share a basic commitment to individual liberty and general happiness, but disagree on when society may make people happy *in spite of themselves*. Similarly, a society might accept some basic moral principle conferring rights to animals, but this principle may be much lower in the hierarchy of this society's values than it is in another. In addition, it is possible for two societies to agree on a basic moral principle but to disagree on its range of application. (Does the principle of "the greatest happiness for the greatest number" include the happiness of animals? If it is only to apply to people,

---

4Indeed such notions are built into the very definition of "society." Thus, a claim such as "All societies encourage cooperation and prohibit indiscriminate deception, violence, and theft" is true by definition.

does it apply to everyone in the world or to a more specific group? Does it apply to future generations?)

The truth of sociological relativism does not establish the truth of ethical relativism. It is possible that there is a single correct morality even though few societies, or perhaps none, accept it. Is there any good reason for believing this? Many philosophers have thought so. For example, W. T. Stace (1886–1967), in a widely reprinted section of his book *The Concept of Morals,* argues against ethical relativism and for the existence of a single correct morality. Although one would expect a person who takes such a view to present us with a moral code and then some argument supporting this morality as the sole correct one, Stace does not. Instead, he argues for his position indirectly by pointing out what he sees as the highly undesirable consequences of accepting ethical relativism. Counting on us to see these consequences as undesirable and inevitable implications of ethical relativism, Stace assumes that to avoid them, we will reject the doctrine that must lead to them. As Stace puts it:

> Ethical relativity can only end in destroying...morality altogether, in undermining its practical efficacy,...in robbing human beings of any incentive to strive for a better world, in taking the life-blood out of every ideal and every aspiration which has ennobled the life of man.

This criticism is inadequate. First, one should notice that even if Stace were right that ethical relativism does lead to such consequences, this does not show that it is false. The truth, after all, need not be pleasant. Stace's argument here is reminiscent of the argument for belief in God often used in the nineteenth century. The idea was not that one should believe in God because such a belief was true or at least probably true; one should believe in God because the consequences would be better if one did so. In particular, it was argued that one would be happier or more inclined to accept conventional moral standards if one thought that God existed. The attitude that we ought to believe things simply because they make us feel better or have better social consequences—regardless of their truth—will be strongly opposed by those moralists who believe that knowing the truth is a basic value. It is clearly not the attitude a philosopher should take who is seeking the truth. Second, Stace is unjustified in claiming that individuals would cease to strive for the realization of their moral principles, unless they thought that they were the only reasonable ones. It is possible for a person to *feel* strongly enough about ideals and to strive for others to accept them, while admitting that people equally reasonable can accept conflicting ideals and that there is no way to prove them wrong. Nevertheless, one might convince others to accept one's ideals by making them *care* about the things one cares about; many try very hard to do precisely that. Does not the "life-blood of our ideals" come from the strength of our feelings about them rather than from the possibility of their objective justification?

As Stace sees it, if there were no single correct morality, then moral ideals would be purely arbitrary and incapable of any rational justification. These are not, however, the only two possibilities. Although there may be no way to pick one morality as the sole correct one, there may be principles which allow us to dismiss some views as inadequate—that is, there may be necessary factors that any adequate morality must possess, even though different moralities may possess them all. Exactly what these factors are is a controversial philosophical issue, but logical consistency definitely is one of them. In addition, moral beliefs should certainly be informed. A moral belief can be criticized as based on a misapprehension of circumstances, facts, scientific theories, or ideological or religious doctrine. Perhaps, in addition, all justified moral beliefs must pass some test of generalizability and impartiality similar to the golden rule or Kant's categorical imperative, which we shall later discuss. If this is true, there is much that can be said in criticism of a person's alleged moral stand, even if individuals can hold fundamentally different moral outlooks that can never be reconciled by reason alone. Yet, this might happen much less often than Stace suggests.

When we have reached this fundamental impasse, the French existentialist Sartre is correct when he emphasizes that one's ultimate moral values and the ranking of these values in cases of conflict must be based on a *choice* of a particular way of life for which no full agreement is possible and no single choice objectively right. We may be guided to some extent by our knowledge of the sort of persons we are and the sort of life we can best live with; but there will sometimes be a choice between conflicting, though equally compelling, values which determine the sort of person we are to become.

Whether ethical relativism is true or false depends on the exact meaning one assigns to this concept. As is often the case with philosophical concepts, philosophers have attributed different meanings to it. Thus, philosophers debating its merits can become engaged in a *merely verbal dispute* that is not based on any substantial disagreement. Indeed, a philosopher may use apparently different definitions in his discussion of this topic, without resolving the question of whether these definitions are equivalent in meaning or implication. When philosophers inquire into the justification of certain basic beliefs underlying our understanding of things, it becomes necessary to clarify (analyze) the meaning of these beliefs. As we progress through our study of ethics, we shall see that the meaning that should be attributed to key moral concepts is often at issue when philosophers discuss such questions as the truth of the doctrine of ethical relativism, the *subjectivity of values,* whether everyone is or ought to be *selfish,* or whether anyone has *free will* or is *morally responsible* for his actions.

The definition previously attributed to ethical relativism is the most defendable. Moreover, if we use this definition, ethical relativism can be contrasted with its denial, the view often called ethical absolutism, which asserts that there is a single correct morality that can be used to determine which acts are (really) right, regardless of prevalent moral standards. Very often, however, ethical relativism is defined as the view that "whatever a given society's (culture's) moral beliefs are, these moral beliefs are correct for them and are logically immune from rational criticism"—that is, whatever a society *believes* is right *actually is* right for them. Behind such a view is often the metaethical assumption that the logic of proper moral reasoning varies from society to society and that there are no universal principles of moral reasoning which must be assumed by anyone, in any culture, who thinks reasonably about moral matters.

The definition of ethical relativism as the view that whatever a society believes is right actually is right for them breaks down as inadequate under analysis. First, according to this definition, all moral reformers who revolt against the established morality of their society must be taken as mistaken when they are rebels, although if they succeed in converting the members of their culture to their beliefs, their beliefs will then become correct. Consequently, the correctness of a moral view is to be understood in terms of its shifting acceptability, regardless of the *grounds* for that acceptability. For example, if some mad scientist were capable of involuntarily manipulating the minds of members of a society so that they would all come to share the most preposterous of ungrounded moral beliefs (such as, brown-eyed people are less worthy than blue-eyed ones), these moral beliefs would be correct for the members of such a society and nonmembers of that society would have no basis for criticizing the correctness of such a morality. Any doctrine that leads to such a conclusion should certainly be rejected.

Furthermore, this definition does not tell us what is to count as a "society" or "culture" and does not stipulate how this definition is to be applied when, as is often the case, we find a group of people who, though certainly united into what we would reasonably want to call a culture or society, tolerate great divergence in moral beliefs. This is, after all, the case here in the United States where many different subcultures coexist, with importantly different standards of morality. Since there does not seem to be anything that can be described as the morality of the United States, are we to speak instead of the moralities of a rural community, of an inner city ghetto minority, of religious fundamentalists, or of liberal Protestants? However morally homogeneous and small we make the groups we are to consider, we will still find some divergence in moral opinion. Are we then to take the view of the majority of some group, assuming that the will of the majority is always correct while the minority always mistaken? It would appear that the definition of ethical relativism under discussion would best be amended to refer to individuals rather than to societies or cultures, and consequently be taken to state that "whatever an individual believes is right is right for that individual." But according to such a view, an individual would be speaking in a logically incoherent manner were he to say "I thought about the issue of abortion more deeply and have come to the opinion that my previous beliefs on this issue were *mistaken*." According to our amended definition of ethical relativism, when an individual changes his moral opinions, he cannot reasonably make judgments about their relative justifiability. This is a mistake.

The Roles of Reason and Feeling
in Moral Judgment

Underlying Stace's rejection of ethical relativism is undoubtedly his belief that if there were no single objective rational standard for appraising moral judgments, they would become totally capricious and subjective—a reflection of feelings formed on the shifting sands of constitutional predisposition and social conditioning rather than based on the invariable and durable dictates of reason. There can be no doubt that both reason and feeling play a part in our moral judgments—morality is something most of us deeply care about and argue about. In this respect, moral judgments are quite unlike purely subjective preferences, such as one's choice of ice cream flavors. Preferences in ice cream flavors, we would all agree, are appropriately described as subjective for they cannot meaningfully be said to be either true or false, but are instead merely reflections of one's own feelings.

A perennial question of ethical philosophy concerns the proper classification of moral judgments as either objective or subjective. For some philosophers, such as Plato, just as there are scientific facts waiting in the world to be discovered by ordinary sense perception or by the discerning scientist, there is also a moral order in the world waiting to be discovered either by the average person's ordinary moral sense or by that of a penetrating moralist. As we have discussed, some philosophers who hold this objective view of morality identify this moral order with the revealed commands of a God; others, like Plato, believe that there is some faculty of reason which can reveal immutable moral facts which allow us to discover what is good and right and to regulate our desires and emotions accordingly.

Many contemporary philosophers have rejected this view and have pointed with approval to the moral writings of the Scottish philosopher David Hume (1711-1776). According to Hume's classical statement on the bearing of reason and feeling to moral judgment, although reason is necessary to guide and direct our sentiments (feelings) in such a way that we may best achieve our objectives, it is ultimately sentiment itself and not reason which moves us to judge things as good, bad, right, or wrong. It is our feelings of approval or disapproval toward things, Hume contends, that determine our moral judgments and not the other way around. On this perspective, since morality is a function of temperament, it becomes logically possible that individuals of fundamentally different temperaments may reach a point of *ultimate moral disagreement*—that is, a disagreement which would persist even with total agreement on all possibly relevant nonmoral facts.

For example, there would appear to be an ultimate moral disagreement, irreconcilable by reason alone, between the ethical philosophies of the English philosopher Jeremy Bentham (1748-1832) and the German philosopher Friedrich Nietzsche (1844-1900) which reflects the irreconcilable differences in the feelings of these two men. Focusing upon the similarities in the abilities of all human beings to experience happiness and pain, and feeling a certain universal benevolence toward all mankind, Bentham afforded all human beings an equal moral importance. Nietzsche, on the other hand, did not share Bentham's basic benevolent feelings toward all humanity, and a different ethical perspective was the result. Deriding the virtues of self-sacrifice and equality that Bentham preached, Nietzsche turned instead to the virtue of individual self-assertion, or, as he called it, "the will to power." Superior people, he claimed, are those who have the courage to master their passions so as to maximize their individual power, regardless of their exploitation of others. On the other hand, those who follow the universalistic ethics of benevolence are in reality weak people who lack the courage to assert themselves. Unable to grasp for themselves the self-fulfillment that life has to offer, they cravenly cling to the virtues of consideration and compassion, virtues which in reality, Nietzsche claimed, are rationalizations masking a basic cowardice and resentment toward the selfishly self-assertive who alone are worthy of respect. Persons sharing the sentiments of Bentham may shake their heads in moral disagreement, but rational means alone can never generate the feeling for the happiness of the average human being that is required to cause a Nietzschian to chance his views.

On a personal note, I remember myself, as a student at the height of the Vietnam war, listening to a defense of the war by the then Secretary of State, Dean Rusk. I remember being struck by the realization that the disagreement between Rusk and the antiwar movement reached a fundamental impasse which went deeper than their obvious disagreements over beliefs as to the likely effects and bearing of our actions in Vietnam upon our own national interests. At that moment, it appeared to me that the Secretary of State simply did not *feel* sufficient sympathy for the vast suffering of human beings who were being sacrificed for unclear ideals of American security. As I listened to Rusk, my predominant reaction was not to argue with him rationally, but in some sense to shake him into an emotional realization of the enormity of human suffering we as a nation were creating in Vietnam. An emotional conversion was required here, not simply cold rational arguments, for there are no rational arguments or calculations that can tell us how much human suffering should be allowed for the achievement of certain desired ends.

Hume's insight that ultimate moral disagreements are possible is a sound one. One must admit that human desires are various, widely adaptable, and often conflicting and that this plurality of desires can generate a plurality of human ideals. Where there is no background of mutually accepted ideals, rational argument reaches an impasse and the various techniques of emotional arousal are our only recourse. Yet it is equally a mistake to overplay the importance of emotion in moral assertions as did the twentieth century ethical disciples of Hume, the emotivists.[5] One must realize to begin with, that it is quite unlikely that those who engage in moral disputes will not share certain moral feelings or attitudes which can provide some basis for rational argument. Furthermore, even though there is an irreducible element of feeling in moral judgment, a moral judgment is more than the mere reflection of strong and transitory feelings. One must use reason to organize one's desires into some coherent whole (one's *reasoned preferences*) which can withstand rational scrutiny and embody those feelings one chooses to be guided by when momentary feelings are at less than their best. Although Hume was right that the ultimate source of our moral principles resides in our feelings, one should

---

[5]According to emotivists, ethical assertions are nonfactual ones which cannot meaningfully be said to be either true or false. Emotivists do not, however, agree on the proper analysis of ethical assertions. They have been analyzed as (a) expressions of feelings or attitudes, (b) linguistical devices for arousing feelings of approval or disapproval, (c) commands, and (d) universal prescriptions (that is, recommendations that *everyone* ought to behave in a given way in a given situation).

not assume that we must be slaves to our feelings. One cannot only change one's principles when they conflict intolerably with one's natural feelings, one can also attempt to adjust one's feelings when they conflict with one's reasoned preferences.[6] The moral life is a constant interplay between reason and feeling.

Since reason and feeling are both essential to the moral life, it is a mistake to make it appear, as some philosophers do, that one must choose between the view that morality is objective in the sense that moral judgments are true or false, depending upon the objective nature of things, independent of considerations of human psychology, and the view that morality is subjective in the sense that moral claims are nothing more than nonrational emotional responses or mere expressions of capricious and arbitrary taste. Although these two views may be presented as mutually exhaustive (that is, if one rejects one view, one must accept the other), this is not so, since morality is neither objective nor subjective in the above senses. In choosing between competing ethical views, an essential part of one's task is *to clarify and refine the philosophical choices that are possible.*

In addition, as we have mentioned before, one should always be on the alert to the possibility that philosophers may be attributing different meanings to the key concepts they employ. As such, philosophical labels can at times cause more confusion than understanding. This is the case with the familiar distinction often presented between "moral objectivism" and "moral subjectivism." It is a fundamental mistake to assume that these, as well as other basic philosophical concepts, have a single clear meaning and that learning philosophy consists of placing philosophical theories in the right conceptional pigeon hole. On the contrary, quite often sophisticated philosophical views straddle the simple classifications that are presented to us and, indeed, at times, the very objective of philosophical reflection involves molding new and more enlightening ways of classifying things.

---

[6]The Humean insight that our morality should not be seen as something external to our feelings, but rather as an attempt to organize feelings into some coherent whole, is lost on Twain's Huck Finn when he helps his slave friend Jim escape Although Huck's natural sympathies are clearly with Jim, his socially conditioned conscience tells him that he is acting wrongly. Incapable of realizing that he can and should reconsider the promptings of his socially conditioned conscience in the light of his natural sympathies and criticize the morality of his day as a bad one, Huck sees himself as a person of weak moral will who is sacrificing an objective morality for the promptings of his own personal feelings. Consider, for example, the following passage:

Jim was saying how the first thing he would do when he got to a free state, he would go to saving up money...and when he got enough he would buy his wife....and then they would both work to buy the two children, and if their master wouldn't sell them, they'd get an Ab'litionist to go and steal them.

It most froze me to hear such talk....Thinks I, this is what comes of my not thinking. Here was this nigger, which I had as good as helped to run away, coming right out flat-footed and saying he would steal his children—children that belonged to a man I didn't even know; a man that hadn't ever done me no harm. I was sorry to hear Jim say that, it was such a lowering of him. My conscience got to stirring me up hotter than ever....

...I go aboard the raft, feeling bad and low, because I knowed very well I had done wrong. ...Then I thought a minute, and says to myself, hold on;' s'pose you'd 'a' done right and give Jim up, would you felt better than what you do now? No, says I, I'd feel bad....

DISCUSSION QUESTIONS

1. Consider the following dialogue:

   A: I admit that conventional morality requires that I keep my promise in this situation and I accept that demand as correct. Nevertheless, I do not intend to keep my promise and furthermore do not think that I ought to. Other considerations override the moral ones for me in this situation. Although breaking my promise is morally wrong according to the morality I accept, it is not wrong for me, all things considered.

   B: What you say makes no sense. If you accept conventional morality's demand that one keep one's promises in situations such as yours, then you must logically admit that you will be acting wrongly when you break your promise—not just according to conventional morality, but from your own point of view as well. If you do not think that you are acting wrongly, then you must really be rejecting conventional morality's demand that one keep one's promises in such situations. You cannot have it both ways.

   Whose side would you take in this debate? Why? Do you think that *A* and *B* are attributing the same meaning to the concept of morality?

2. Consider the following dialogue:

   A: One can discover people's moral beliefs only through honest conversation and not simply by observing their behavior, for some people consistently act contrary to their moral principles.

   B: People who consistently act contrary to the moral beliefs they profess cannot meaningfully be said to accept those principles. People, after all, sometimes lie to themselves about what they believe.

   What do you think of *B*'s reply? Is there some essential connection between behavior and moral belief?

3. Practically all of us would consider it morally reprehensible to kill our aged parents when their care creates hardship for others. Yet Eskimos used to consider it proper to kill aged parents who would endanger their tribe in their nomadic journey from winter to summer quarters. Do you think this fact provides a good example of a cultural disagreement in basic moral principle?

4. Do you see the disagreement between principled vegetarians who believe that animals have a right not to be killed by humans for food and those who do not believe that animals have such a right as one that would be resolved if the disputants agreed on all their nonmoral facts?

5. After claiming that there is no inconsistency in believing that moral judgments ultimately are based on human feeling, while at the same time expressing emphatic opinions on moral questions, Bertrand Russell, the famous twentieth century philosopher, goes on to admit,

   Certainly there seems to be something more. Suppose, for example, that someone were to advocate the introduction of bull-fighting in this country. In opposing the proposal, I should *feel*, not only that I was expressing my desires, but that my desires in the matter are *right*, whatever that may mean. As a matter of argument, I can, I think, show that I am not guilty of any logical inconsistency in holding to . . . [a subjective] interpretation of ethics and at the same time expressing strong ethical preferences. But in feeling I am not satisfied.

   What conclusion do you draw from this?

6. Are there some actions or general moral principles that are self-evidently wrong? If so, is there some general reason why they are self-evident?

7. Some philosophers have suggested the following definition of what it *means* to say that an act is right:

    "X is right" means that an ideal observer would approve of it. An "ideal observer" is defined to be impartial, fully informed and vividly aware of the relevant facts, and in a calm frame of mind.

    Supporters of this definition have suggested that its acceptance makes moral judgments capable of being confirmed or disconfirmed by scientific observation. What do you think of this claim and the preceding analysis of what it means to say that an act is right?

8. Solomon Asch, a social psychologist, writes,

    If...we are to speak of relativism with reference to infanticide we must assume that the *same* action which is tolerated under one set of conditions is outlawed under other conditions. This assumption is...dubious....In the first few days of life, an infant may be regarded as not yet human....Therefore, the act of killing will not have the same meaning....

    Asch claims that disagreement as to the morality of infanticide is not indicative of a difference in basic moral value if there is disagreement as to the humanity of an infant. For example, a society that prohibits infanticide may see an infant as a human being, while a society that tolerates it may see the same infant as less than a human being. Is Asch right in his apparent assumption that one's perception of the nature of an infant is a nonmoral perception that determines one's moral attitude toward infanticide or is this perception itself a moral one? If so, is it simply true by definition that "Whenever individuals disagree as to the morality of an action, there is a difference in *the meaning* they attribute to this action," as Asch claims?

9. How do rational moral judgments differ from mere prejudices? Indeed, can a mere prejudice be called a moral judgment, at all?

10. How would you resolve the following issue?

    Principled Vegetarian: How can you eat meat with a clear conscience? Don't you realize that a conscious, feeling creature had to be killed so that you could gratify your carnivorous appetite?

    Meat Eater: There you go again with your obsessive concern about the killing of animals for food. It might be wrong for you to eat meat, but it's not wrong for me. Let's leave it at that.

    Principled Vegetarian: You can call my concern obsessive, but I think your lack of concern is improper and your belief that it's all right to eat meat a prejudice that allows you to do as you like with a clear conscience.

    Meat Eater: Look, you and I have an ultimate moral disagreement in this matter that reflects differences in our attitudes toward animals. Since such differences are not over facts, you have no right to call my attitude toward animals a prejudice. I know you don't like my attitude, but there's no way you can prove it to be mistaken, just as I can't prove your opposed attitude mistaken. That's the way it is when you come to basic moral commitments.

    Principled Vegetarian: That's not so. If I told you that people with brown eyes should be afforded less respect than people with blue eyes and that this was a basic moral principle with me, you'd think me crazy. Basic moral principles must themselves be rational.

11.   Consider the following quotation from the anthropologist Ruth Benedict:

> From all that we know of contrasting cultures it seems clear that. . .there is an ascertainable range of human behavior that is found [in every society]. . . . But the proportion in which behavior types stand to one another in different societies is not universal. The vast majority of the individuals in any group are shaped to the fashion of that culture. In other words, most individuals are plastic to the moulding force of the society into which they are born. . . .The deviants, whatever the type of behavior the culture has institutionalized, will remain few in number. . . .The small proportion of the number of the deviants in any culture is not a function of the sure instinct with which that society has built itself upon the fundamental sanities, but of the universal fact that, happily, the majority of mankind quite readily take any shape that is presented to them. . .

Do you agree with Benedict? Do you think that the divergent behavior patterns of different cultures reflect divergent moral outlooks, as Benedict does? If so, is it unreasonable, as Benedict claims, to distinguish correct from incorrect moral outlooks? Why?

4. MORAL ARGUMENTS

Since reasoning is essential to moral evaluation, arguments play a central role in the resolution of moral issues. In general, an argument consists of a set of statements, one of which, the *conclusion,* is supported by the others, the *premises.* Arguments are further distinguished by logicians as *deductive* or *inductive,* depending on the degree of support the premises are alleged to confer upon the conclusion. A deductive argument is one in which it is claimed that the premises offer conclusive support for the conclusion (i.e., it is claimed that if the premises are true, the conclusion must be true). For example the argument "Since 2 is an even prime number and all even numbers are divisible by 2, it follows that there is one and only one even prime number" is a deductive argument. Inductive arguments, on the other hand, are arguments in which the premises are claimed to offer less than conclusive support for the conclusion. For example, weather forcasts are based on inductive arguments which rely on the probabilities that certain current atmospheric conditions will result in specific future weather conditions. Unlike deductive arguments in which the conclusion either does or does not follow from its premises, inductive arguments can be said to have varying degrees of support. While the notion of a valid argument is often used in ordinary language to describe any good argument, most logicians for the sake of clarity, restrict the notion of validity to that of deductive arguments, defining a valid deductive argument as one in which the conclusion actually does follow conclusively from its premises. Since one can argue validily from false premises, logicians define sound deductive arguments as valid ones, all of whose premises are true. Valid deductive arguments need not have true conclusions, but sound deductive arguments must.

Deductive arguments play an essential role in justifying *specific* moral positions as the following imaginary dialogue illustrates:

A: Abortion is wrong.

B: Why?

A: Because it is the killing of an innocent person and it's always wrong to kill an innocent person.

B: But do you really believe that it's always wrong to kill an innocent person? Are you
against wars, for example, which involve the killing of innocent persons?

Notice the procedure here. First A presents an argument consisting of two premises.
The first premise is a general moral principle that asserts that all things that have
a particular property are wrong. The second premise asserts that abortions have
this property. The conclusion is then validly drawn that abortions are wrong. B then
proceeds to challenge the soundness of the argument by challenging the truth of
the general principle. He does this by offering an alleged *counterexample* to the
principle which he hopes A will accept as a counterexample (i.e., as something
that has the property in question, but is not wrong). The alleged counterexample
B chooses in the preceding dialogue is the death of innocent people in wars. At
this point, A could accept the conclusion that if abortion is wrong because it involves
the death of innocent people then, for the same reason, so are wars (at least modern
ones), which also involve the death of innocent people. B could then proceed to
question A as to whether there are any conceivable circumstances in which it would
be right to kill an innocent person, in wars or elsewhere. If A is willing to make
exceptions to his principle, B can then attempt to draw an analogy between these
exceptions and the case of abortion, and the argument will continue.

Let us assume, however, that A does not take this line but continues as
follows:

A: No, I think wars are sometimes morally justifiable, even though they involve the
death of innocent persons. This case is, however, different from that of abortions.

B: How is it different?

A: Well, one may rightfully fight a war knowing that innocent people are going to die,
as long as one does not intend these deaths, but simply accepts them as a by-product
of one's action which is motivated by some good intention. In abortions, however,
one intends the death of a fetus.

B: So the principle you hold is not "It is always wrong to perform an action which in
point of fact will result in the death of an innocent person," but rather the principle
that "It is always wrong to act with the intention (purpose) of causing the death of
an innocent person."

A: Yes, that's what I believe.

B: But is it not possible to perform an abortion, knowing that a fetus will die, without
intending that death, no less than it is possible to engage in a war, knowing that
innocent people will die, but not intending their deaths. For example, imagine a three-
months pregnant woman with cancer of the uterus. She has her uterus removed with
the intention of protecting herself from cancer, knowing that the fetus she is carrying will die as a result, but not intending (wanting) this death.

A: Yes, I see what you mean. I didn't think of that before. I suppose there are some
abortions—if by "abortion" one means "any medical intervention with a pregnancy
that will reesult in the death of a fetus"—that can be morally justified. On the other
hand, I don't think I would want to call such procedures as the removal of a pregnant

woman's cancerous uterus an "abortion." I would prefer to define an "abortion" as "an action whose purpose is the death of a fetus," in which case I would maintain my absolute moral prohibition against abortion.

Notice that in this dialogue A initially appears willing to accept the counter-example to his moral principle and attempts to circumvent it by *refining his moral principle* so that a relevant moral distinction can be drawn between the cases of abortion he judges to be wrong and the wars he judges to be right. Notice, too, in A's last remark how an alleged counterexample can be absorbed by a modification in the meaning of a key concept as well as by a modification of a moral principle. Moral arguments often involve disagreements as to the meaning of key concepts. For example, the debate over the morality of abortion often hinges on the meaning to be attributed to the concept of a "person." Consequently, instead of pressing A on his acceptance of the principle that "It is always wrong to kill an innocent person," B could have pressed A to defend his characterization of a fetus as a person.

As we have seen, it is essential that those who make specific moral judgments believe that there are reasons supporting these judgments and acknowledge as appropriate the demand for them. These reasons will involve appeals to general moral principles from which the specific moral principles are claimed to follow. The quest for justification can thus continue to even more general moral principles, until we arrive at our basic moral principles. Whether, and how, these basic moral principles can themselves be known to be true is a subject of philosophical controversy as is the issue of whether there is a single basic moral principle and, if not, whether it is possible to have rationally irreconcilable conflicts among basic moral principles.

It was suggested that there would appear to be an ultimate moral disagreement, irreconcilable by reason alone, between the universalistic ethics of Bentham and the supremist ethics of Nietzsche. Nevertheless, supporters of these very different ethical views will most likely share certain moral sentiments which can provide some basis for rational argument. For example, while many of Nietzsche's claims (e.g., "You want to decrease suffering; I want precisely to increase it") will, *if taken in isolation,* be repulsive to our moral sensibilities, such remarks were not made in isolation but within the contest of a comprehensive world view and way of thinking about the value of human life. The value Nietzsche placed on suffering was not an end in itself but a means to such noble virtues as strength rather than weakness and to individuality rather than "sheeplike conformity." These values are, of course, values we all profess to share. Consequently, to reject Nietzsche's ethical philosophy, one must either find some flaw in the arguments he presents for connecting moral values as he does or, if one accepts these connections, one must take the moral stand that the Nietzschean view of morality exacts too high a price from other moral values. Whether the price of a particular moral view is "too high" is a question that cannot always be resolved by an appeal to immediate intellectual perception or logical argument, untainted by psychological bias. This is the core of truth in subjectivistic views of morality.

5. SOME PITFALLS OF MORAL REASONING

The existence of rationally irreconcilable differences in moral perspectives leads to disagreements as to what counts as a *good* moral argument. As such, there is no list of fallacies that we can mechanically apply to test the correctness of a person's moral reasoning.

Nevertheless, there are certain pitfalls of moral reasoning to which the uninitiated can easily fall victim. It is important that these stumbling blocks be pointed out at the very outset of our philosophical inquiry into moral issues. Let us then consider:

1. The failure to recognize the vagueness of moral concepts
2. The failure to recognize the value-laden nature of many concepts which appear value-free
3. The uncritical use of emotive terms
4. The tendency to dilute moral principles into tautologies
5. Hasty moral generalizations
6. Faulty causal reasoning
7. Uncritical use of analogical reasoning
8. Rationalization
9. The dismissal of moral positions on the basis of their origin
10. The confusion between what one would be inclined to do and what one morally ought to do

The Problem of Vagueness

It is common to find people defending moral principles without any clear understanding of their meanings. Consider, for example, the moral principle "never lie." What is a lie? "A false statement that is made with the intention of deceiving," one might answer. Is this adequate? Is it possible to lie without making any statement at all? For example, suppose I am asked if I agree with a statement and refuse to answer, knowing that my silence will be taken as a tacit affirmation of that statement. Assuming that I know that statement to be false but want to mislead others into believing it's true, have I lied? Similarly, have I lied when someone asks me to lend him a $10 bill and I say, "Sorry, I don't have it," and although it is true that I don't have a $10 bill, I do have a couple of $20 bills and know that I can easily get change? Have I lied, too, when in response to my spouse's inquiry into my faithfulness, I loudly respond, "I haven't committed adultery," then, in order to make my statement true, add in an inaudible whisper "not today"? If these examples should count as instances of lying, perhaps we should revise our definition to cover "all that one says or does with the intent of misleading." But, this definition appears too broad. Do we really want to say, for example, that a person who intentionally misleads a friend into thinking that he is far more successful than he really is, through a lavish show of generosity that he can ill-afford, has lied to his friend, even though he never said anything that was false? As you can see, the concept of a lie is a vague one which does not sharply limit the range of things that fall within its definition. Consequently, the claim that "lies are always wrong" does not clearly specify which things are wrong.

The same can be said for the concept of killing. What is it to kill someone? That seems easy. "You have killed someone," you might say, "when he dies as a result of what you have done to him." This definition can be applied with no problem in many cases. For example, if you shoot someone directly in the heart and he dies immediately as a result, you have obviously killed him. But, imagine that, intending to merely scare him, you point a gun at him and pretend you are going to shoot him, and as a result he dies of a heart attack. Have you killed him? Similarly, in which of the following cases do you think that the accused person can be said to have killed (that is, *caused* the death of someone)?

1. Accused gravely injures his victim. The victim is taken to a hospital where he dies as a result of negligent medical treatment. Given proper medical treatment, he would most likely have survived.
2. Accused gravely injures his victim who is hospitalized with almost no chance of survival. While lying in his hospital bed, the victim is stabbed by a maniac.
3. Accused brutally rapes X who, distracted by intense pain and grief, jumps into a creek and drowns.
4. Accused throws a live grenade into X's room, intending to kill him. X seizes it and throws it out of his window where it falls to the crowded street below, exploding and killing several persons.
5. Accused engages in an armed robbery, not intending to kill anyone. However, in the course of his apprehension by the police, a policeman accidentally kills an innocent bystander.
6. Accused negligently strikes X with his automobile, throwing him about 20 feet and breaking his thighbone. Soon afterward, X dies from delirium tremens which was precipitated by his injury. The injury would not have led to delirium tremens, however, if X were not an alcoholic.

In addition to facing the problem of how far back we should go in a causal chain of events (this problem is reflected in the legal distinction between *proximate* and *remote* causation), we must also face the problem of when one can be said to have caused the death of another through some omission. Everyone will agree that if parents let a newborn baby die by refusing to feed it, they have *caused* the death of the baby (that is, has killed it) by their omission. But if failure to do something can be called killing, aren't we in the affluent part of the world guilty of killing starving people in other parts of the world whose lives could be saved if we were more willing to share our wealth with them? Again, we can see that the concept of killing is not the sharply defined one that many people seem to think it is.

The Conflation of Factual and Value Judgments

It is tempting to think that the question of whether an omission is *really a cause* of a given event or whether a given event in a causal chain is *the true cause* of a resulting event is a purely factual one. This is not so. The decision as to whether a given event should be picked out as a cause or the cause of a given event is often based on some moral judgment. Consider, for example, a two car automobile accident that would not have occurred but for the convergence of several independent factors (that is, these factors were all necessary conditions for the accident). Let us say that the accident would have been avoided if

1. there had been better street lighting
2. the brakes on one of the cars had been in better condition
3. the driver of the other car had reacted with quicker reflexes

Since all three features were equally necessary ingredients in causing the accident, the question of which of these factors should be singled out as the cause of the accident is not a factual one but rather one concerning where we choose to place the responsibility for this accident. It is for this reason that the question "What caused X?" is often equivalent to the question "What ought we to consider responsible for X?" The answer to this question might in turn reflect some general social policy decision as to how we ought best to attempt to control the occurrence of X.

There are many concepts that misleadingly appear to be value-free which turn out under closer inspection to presuppose a particular moral standpoint. For example, many philosophers have claimed that "a voluntary act" should be defined as "an act which is not a result of coercion." One problem with this definition is that the notion of coercion is itself in need of clarification. Indeed, after seeing the differing uses make of this concept, one may come to realize that the question of what counts as *coercion* is not a purely factual one, but reflects a commitment to moral standards which distinguish *proper* from *improper* causal influence. If this is true, then it is a mistake to think that the judgment of whether an act is voluntary is a purely factual matter that justifies the moral stands we take (since his action is involuntary, he ought not to be held responsible) rather than a reflection of our moral judgment (since I do not believe that it would be morally proper to hold him responsible for his action, I judge his action to be an involuntary one).

The concepts of mental health and mental illness are also good examples of concepts that can often be used to present particular moral commitments under the guise of value-free diagnoses. Consider, for example, the following definition of mental health given by the noted psychiatrist Karl Menninger:

> Mental health is the adjustment of human beings to the world and to each other with a maximum of effectiveness and happiness. Not just efficiency or just contentment—or the grace of obeying the rules of the game cheerfully. It is all of

these together. It is the ability to maintain an even temper, an alert intelligence, socially considerate behavior, and a happy disposition. This, I think, is a healthy mind.

Though Menninger offers this definition is his capacity as a psychiatric expert, such a definition does not rely upon a psychiatric insight but reflects value judgments that Menninger is no more qualified to make than any of us. In effect, Menninger, by conceiving of mental health in terms of adjustment, prescribes that we come to terms with our culture and its institutions, making a claim which reflects a conservative political bias. It is a question open to moral debate, after all, whether one *ought to* adjust to a given society and accept life in that society with a happy disposition.

As many sociologists have pointed out, when some psychiatrists classify behavior as a manifestation of mental health or mental illness, they are at the same time labelling that behavior as, at least to some extent, morally desirable or morally undesirable. Two psychiatrists, fully agreeing on the nature and causes of a given pattern of thought, feeling, and behavior, might disagree as to whether this pattern should be described as a mental illness (is homosexuality a mental illness?), precisely because of their differing judgments as to the moral desirability of that pattern of thought, feeling, and behavior. In calling someone mentally ill, one is often not merely describing the facts but taking a moral position on these facts. People, unfortunately, are often not aware of this, camouflaging their moral positions behind the facade of terms that give the mistaken impression of being value-neutral.[7]

It is often simpler in theory than in practice to separate facts from values; for our values can permeate how we classify *or see* the facts. For example, it would be logically clearer if we could separate the question of what pornography means from that of when, if ever, it should be made illegal. Yet, people differ greatly in the meaning they attribute to this notion. For some, it is clearly a moral term and is used synonymously with that of either immoral or indecent portrayals of sexual behavior. Since people differ in what they perceive as immoral or indecent portrayals of sexual behavior, there is naturally disagreement on what counts as pornography. For example, the feminist Helen E. Longino (*Women and Values,* p. 168) defines pornography as "verbal or pictorial explicit representations of sexual behavior that have as a distinguishing characteristic the degrading and demeaning portrayal of the role and status of the human female as a mere sexual object to be exploited and manipulated sexually." From such a perspective, Longino distinguishes pornography from sexually explicit erotic material. This definition

---

[7]Freud himself was quite aware of this problem. The concept of mental health, he once wrote, is "a purely conventional practical concept and has no real scientific meaning. It simply means that a person gets on well; it doesn't mean that the person is particularly worthy." Freud's disavowal of the scientific nature of the distinction between health and illness anticipated the contemporary sociological view that a diagnosis of mental illness is best conceived as a negative cultural judgment of a person's social performance (for a person may get on well in one culture, but not in another). From such a perspective, though the question of whether a pattern of behavior should be classified as a mental illness is not a scientific question, once a person is so classified, one must turn to science to discover the causes and methods of altering that person's maladaptive behavior.

of pornography is reflective of Longino's feminist orientation, but not of ordinary usage. After all, many women as well as men, profess to enjoy certain sorts of "pornography" which they see as compatible with feminist values. Clearly, a less biased definition than Ms. Longino's would admit that pornography *can be* degrading to men as well as women and that the wanton violence that is sometimes found in sexually explicit material can be the element that makes such material offensive and, perhaps, worthy of legal restriction.

For those, like Ms. Longino, who equate pornography with immoral portrayals of sexual behavior, pornography is *by definition* wrong. It may be surprising, however, to discover that apparently morally neutral definitions of "pornography" often contain terms which can be interpreted in a morally loaded way. For example, the *American Heritage Dictionary* defines pornography as "written, graphic, or other forms of communication intended to excite lascivious feelings." This, of course, invites us to look up "lascivious" which the same dictionary defines as "characterized by lust." Well, "lust" isn't always bad, is it? Let's see what the same dictionary has to say about the meaning of "lust." It is, it tells us:

1. Sexual craving, especially excessive or unrestrained.
2. Any overwhelming desire or craving...to have an inordinate or obsessive desire, especially sexual desire.

The dictionary, understandably, does not attempt to tell us what standards to employ in determining when a sexual desire is "inordinate" or "obsessive"—an issue that generates moral disagreement. Clearly, the standards utilized by a libertine such as *Playboy's* Hugh Hefner would greatly differ from those of the fundamentalist preacher Jerry Falwell!

The reader may at this point cry out in exasperation, this is "just semantics." Of course it is, but semantics are very important. From a practical point of view, the question of how we are to define pornography is not important, what is important is the arguments we can give for declaring certain sexually explicit material to be immoral or undesirable (and the logically separate) arguments we can give for making such material illegal. Given the tendency to use the notion of pornography in a morally loaded way, clarity of thought might best be served by avoiding the use of this term in such discussions. Nevertheless, such a way of sidestepping the semantic issue of an emotionally loaded term is not open to those who adhere to rigid moral principles that claim that a particular form of behavior is always wrong. For example, it is Roman Catholic doctrine that *divorce* and *adultery* are always wrong. Such apparently rigid principles can, however, be softened by semantic considerations. For example, the current Roman Catholic notion of annulment has been broadened to include most, if not all, of what non-Catholics would call divorce.

"Adultery" too poses its conceptual difficulties. When one thinks of this concept, one imagines a married person having sexual relations with someone other than his or her spouse for self-seeking and (usually) erotic reasons. Implicit in our concept of adultery is that the act be voluntary. For example, a married woman who, without putting up a fight, allows a man to have sexual intercourse with her for fear that she will be killed if she does not, has been raped and has not committed adultery. Indeed, the use of the term "allows" in the situation of a woman who for fear of her safety refuses to put up a fight is itself questionable. But what if a man threatens to kill the child of a married woman unless she *allows* him to have intercourse with her? What if a very poor married woman *allows* a rich man to have intercourse with her for a sum of money that is desperately needed for the very survival of a member of her family? Is she an adulteress? The line, as you can see, is not easy to draw.

The Uncritical Use Of Emotive Terms

The tendency of apparently morally neutral factual terms to camouflage implicit moral judgments is amusingly captured in the twentieth-century philosopher Betrand Russell's quip: "I am firm, you are stubborn; he's a pig-headed fool." In these descriptions, we are referring to a person whose behavior or principles are not easily subject to change. This is the *cognitive meaning* of the three expressions, but the *moral attitude* these expressions convey as to the appropriateness of such behavior is quite different. To describe a person as *firm* tends to convey our approval of this behavior, while the other two expressions convey our disapproval. This difference in attitudinal meaning naturally leads to *special pleading* where one unfairly, and often surreptitiously, utilizes different standards to appraise the actions of different people. For example, while Jones may criticize Smith's child for lying or having no respect for the facts. When he is told that his own child has a tendency to lie, he might very well dismiss such a complaint, by saying that his child just has a playful and vivid imagination.

Such special pleading permeates moral arguments that attempt to sway public opinion. For example, many moralists have claimed that only wars to repel aggression are morally justified. Nevertheless, much disagreement exists over the standards to be utilized in determining what is to count as an act of aggression. Consider, for example, the Six Day War between Israel and its Arab enemies. At the U.N., defenders of the Arab countries used all their rhetorical skills to denounce the *aggression* of their *hostile* Israeli neighbors. The Israelis, they pointed out, struck the first blow. It was their planes that destroyed the defenseless Arab planes in their airfields. Surely, they were the aggressors, it was claimed. The Israelis, of course, did not think so, pointing to the *provocation* that preceeded their *preemptive strike*.

Consider too, the notions of democracy and freedom. As children, we in the West have been taught (subject to propaganda?) to contrast Communism with freedom and democracy. What we are not taught, unfortunately, is that children in the Communist world have been taught (notice how much easier it is to call this propaganda) that our democracy and the freedom we cherish are shams. The concept of democracy can for the Communist be as highly charged a positive evaluative term as it is for his Western counterpart. Both may accept the definition of "democracy' as "government by the people," but differ greatly in their interpretation of what sort of government this notion implies. Similarly, when we speak of freedom in the West, it is what philosophers call *negative freedom* that we have in mind—i.e., the freedom to be left alone to express our views, live the lives we choose, and to compete fairly within the confines of a free marketplace. For the Communist, howver, such negative freedom is of secondary importance to the *positive freedom* to cultivate one's potential—a freedom which, they would claim, entails the right to such things as food, shelter, employment, medical care, and education. A right which, as they see it, is seriously denied those who through no fault of their own are born into poverty in capitalist countries. As the Frenchman Anatole France (1844–1924) once put it, in relation to the "freedom" then offered the French, "The law in its majestic equality forbids the rich as well as the poor to sleep under bridges, to beg in the streets, and to steal bread." Certainly, without *at least* some right to adequate physical, emotional, and educational sustenance, one's freedom is severely limited. In this the Communists are right. But, as the competing and also compelling picture of freedom that is advocated in the West demonstrates, this is not enough. Unfortunately, the key question of the relative moral importance of *different sorts of freedom* is often disguised in the emotionally loaded words we throw around, giving vent, no doubt to deep visceral feelings of approval or disapproval, but throwing little or no light on the important underlying moral issues.

In this regard, consider the term "racist" which is so often bandied about in contemporary discussions of programs that involve "preferential treatment." As we shall see, the supporters of such programs claim that they are required to erase *racism*. No, say their opponents, you can't oppose *racism* by *racism*. No, the supporters, say in rejoinder, such programs are not really *racist* because. . . .and the debate continues, often distorted by a term with more emotive than cognitive meaning.

Moral Principles Can Be Reduced To Tautologies

The tendency people have to accept or reject certain terms because of their strong emotive content leads to another recurring pitfall of moral reasoning. In the course of defending a moral principle, the principle is diluted into a tautology—that is, a statement that might appear to be informative but is merely true by definition. For example, a person, after initially claiming that lying is always wrong, may be forced to admit that it is sometimes right to say things that are false with the intention of deceiving. For example, he may admit that it would be right to lie to a maniac who, with the intention of killing someone, asks you where that person is. It is right, too, he admits, to tell a gracious hostess untruthfully that you enjoyed the meal she prepared. But he is still unwilling to abandon his principle that lying is always wrong. Instead, he claims that such lies are merely "white lies," and he did not mean to include them in his principle. When we press him to be specific as what should count as a white lie, however, he seems unable to give us any specific definition and finally says that a white lie is a morally justifiable lie. But if he accepts this definition of a white lie, his principle that all lies, except white lies, are always wrong, reduces to the empty tautology that all lies which are not morally justifiable are wrong. This statement is no more informative than Calvin Coolidge's famous remark that "when large numbers of people are out of work, unemployment results," for it too, is simply true by definition.

Similarly, a person who bases his morality on the Ten Commandments might initially claim that it is always wrong to kill. But upon being pressed to consider various possible counterexamples to his principle, he admits that it is not wrong to kill animals or kill human beings in self-defense or as a just punishment for their criminal deeds. It may be right, he now says, to kill, but it is never right to *murder* human beings. When asked to define what he means by "murder," he initially says that murder is the intentional taking of a human life neither in self-defense nor as a just punishment.[8] But under questioning, he is willing to grant that it is also morally permissible to kill a person if this is essential to prevent him from killing innocent people and that it may be morally permissible as well for a spy to kill himself rather than to divulge vital information to the enemy. As other cases are thrust before him (such as hastening the death of someone who is bound to die in a short time, in order to ease his excrutiating pain), he admits that there are various exceptions to the prohibition against the taking of human life. Believing now that there is no simple way to exhaustively classify these exceptions, he suggests that murder should be defined as the unjustifiable taking of human life. But if this definition is accepted, the principle that murder is always wrong turns into a tautology.

As we shall see in our discussions of moral issues, assertions that may appear to be telling us something about the world or making some substantial moral point may turn out to be disguised tautologies that reflect a particular stipulation as to how a concept is to be used. For example, many philosophers have claimed that the plausibility of the view that all voluntary human actions are selfishly motivated comes from the tendency of its adherents to use the concept of selfishness with such an expanded meaning as to make it synonymous with the notion of a voluntary action, rendering their view into a tautology.

Hasty Moral Generalizations

The process of extracting moral principles from concrete cases, such as those on our list of moral dilemmas, requires great care. As you reflect upon a concrete moral problem that you are inclined to evaluate in a particular way and search for some underlying general principle that can justify your particular evaluation, you may find yourself embracing some generalization which you would be inclined to reject upon consideration of a wider spectrum of cases. Since all concrete moral problems possess many features, it is quite possible that you may have focused on a given feature as the solely morally relevant one (say F_1) when other features $(F_2 \ldots F_n)$ may be having an unconscious effect upon your moral appraisal. Consequently, given another situation which possesses F_1, but not $F_2 \ldots F_n$, you may

[8]Notice that one could pursue the question of why the death penalty is a *just* punishment, as well as the question of what excatly should count as an act of *self-defense.*

find your moral reaction to be quite different. If this happens, you must reconsider your generalization as to the importance of F_1 when taken in isolation. Perhaps, F_1 is morally relevant to you only when it is combined with some other feature or combination of features, or perhaps you may even find that F_1 is a morally irrelevant feature, focusing your attention now on the moral relevance of other features, previously neglected.

Let us consider, for example, the case of the poisonous cup of coffee (see p. 9). It is my experience that most people will claim that Joe's action is as morally wrong as that of Tom. Yet Tom's action must be described as one of *killing* his wife, whereas many will claim that it is improper to so describe Joe's action which should be seen as one of *letting* his wife *die*. Some will disagree, however, claiming that in this case Joe's letting his wife die is a way of killing her. The claim that an act of letting die is conceptually equivalent to that of killing reflects the fact, previously discussed, that the description of an action as one of killing may reflect a decision as to how the facts are to be morally evaluated. Regardless of how one chooses to describe Joe's action, most people will perceive Joe's action as morally equivalent to that of Tom's. Consequently, one may hastily conclude that there is no morally relevant distinction between the notion of killing and that of letting die, dismissing the contention of some that this distinction has great moral weight. (As we shall see in our discussion of the euthanasia issue, it has been claimed that although we have no justification to kill the hopelessly dying, we do have a right to let them die. We may feel confirmed in this appraisal when we compare allowing an infant to die by the refusal to feed it with that of directly killing it by a lethal injection. Although cases such as these may indicate that letting someone die in some situations is morally equivalent to killing that person, one would be rash to jump to the conclusion that this distinction has no moral relevance whatsoever.

For example, practically everybody would agree that there is a tremendous moral difference between killing a child with a gun so that one may be freed of the burden of its support and the situation of letting many children die in the poverty stricken parts of this world by our refusal to donate the funds necessary to feed them. Certainly, in this case, most of us would claim that killing is worse than letting die. We would also accept this appraisal in considering the case of a great surgeon who is contemplating killing a bum, who is useless to himself and others, in order to obtain a kidney and heart which are required to keep two highly productive and well-loved human beings alive—one of whom is dying of heart failure, the other of kidney failure. Even if we were convinced that these two human beings would certainly die unless the surgeon obtained the needed organs in such a manner, most of us would condemn such action. The surgeon, we will say, must not kill the bum, but must let the others die. In the light of such cases, we may now reconsider our claim that these two notions are morally equivalent, claiming instead that killing is generally, though not always, worse than letting die.

Maybe so, but one can also point to cases where killing seems to be preferable to letting die. Consider, for example, our case of the fat man (p. 6). If the dynamite is not used, one will certainly be letting many people die, yet if one uses it, one will be killing the fat man. Yet many people who would consider it morally reprehensible for the surgeon to kill the bum will claim that the dynamite should be used in this situation. Consider, as well, the situation of a President who is told that a missile carrying an atomic bomb has been launched and is aimed towards New York City. The only way this bomb can be prevented from striking New York City and killing millions, the President is told, is by deflecting it toward the Atlantic Ocean; but unfortunately the bomb will still have a devastating effect on the tip of Long Island, killing thousands. Considering the savings of life and the importance of New York City to the economic well-being of the nation, the President decides to deflect the bomb. Most of us will agree with his action. Yet his action can be described as one of choosing to kill rather than letting die. The conclusion that must be drawn from a consideration of these various cases of choosing between killing and letting die is that this distinction will not form the foundations of some general and simple moral principle which can mechanically yield conclusions about specific moral problems, as some think it can. One must delve deeper than this distinction in order to obtain some insight into the factors that motivate us to make the moral distinctions that we do.

Why, for example, do so many of us believe that Joe's action is as wrong as Tom's in the case of the poisonous cup of coffee? There seem to be several factors that determine our judgment. First, Joe's motive is morally relevant, for we are assuming that he hates his wife and wants her dead, and this is a black mark against him. But more important is the great ease with which he could save his wife, coupled with the fact that he alone can help her. Similar remarks can be made of the refusal to feed a newborn infant. Our judgment that such an omission is the moral equivalent of directly killing the infant stems both from the fact that feeding an infant requires so little effort and from the special responsibility that we place upon parents and doctors for the care of the newborn. Clearly, we believe that there is a marked difference in the degree of responsibility parents and doctors have for the children in their care than we have for starving children who bear no special relationship toward us. Why is this so? The best way to answer this question is to consider what would happen if all human beings were considered to have an equal claim to our aid. This would so diffuse our responsibilities that we would become incapable of ever fully discharging them, for it is impossible to aid everyone who might profit from our aid. Furthermore, why should we assume the burden of helping individuals to whom we have no special responsibilities when others, who could equally assume this obligation, refuse? Does not this fact to some extent explain why we often consider the distinction between taking life and not saving it to be a very important one?

Do we not also draw this distinction because of an underlying belief that individuals have *rights* to noninterference which should not be violated out of a belief that by so doing greater general happiness or welfare will be created? Is it not for this reason that practically all of us recoil with horror at the contemplation of the surgeon killing individuals in order to save others whose potential for happiness or social productivity is greater? Perhaps, our reaction here stems from our fear of living in a society where individuals do not have rights to noninterference that can override the demands of the common good. We fear that human beings would prove incapable of wisely and impartially judging both the demands of the common good and the necessity for sacrificing innocent individuals to meet its demands.

How can those many individuals who believe that it would be morally permissible to use the dynamite on the fat man distinguish this case from other cases of sacrificing innocent individuals for the common good, such as that of the surgeon, which they would strongly condemn? It would appear that the *causal responsibility* of the fat man for the plight of the others determines our moral judgment. Even though the fat man may have no moral responsibility for the sad predicament of his companions, he is causally responsible for it, whereas the surgeon's contemplated victim, we may assume, has no connection to those who would profit by his sacrifice.

In the case of the President deflecting the bomb from New York City to the tip of Long Island, this distinction does not play a role. It has been suggested that the relevant consideration here is that the President is not *creating a threat* but *deflecting an already existing threat*. In addition, the more momentous nature of the consequences for the general good and a President's special responsibility to consider these consequences, and even to decide to sacrifice innocent human lives if necessary in an act of war, leads us to allow the President to act on a principle which we would preclude from the surgeon.

As you can see, the factors that motivate us to make moral distinctions are complex. After studying various theories of normative ethics which attempt to unify and criticize the various factors that form our collective moral beliefs you might feel that philosophers should give more attention than they often do to understanding the interrelationships of diverse and conflicting moral considerations instead of pursuing the task of providing a specious sense of unity to diverse and independent moral factors. This is a central criticism you will find threaded through the critical evaluation of various theories of normative ethics in this book.

Faulty Causal Reasoning

Causal judgments permeate moral reasoning. For example, a Presidential commission appointed by President Nixon to study the issue of pornography claimed that there is no evidence of a causal link between pornography and crimes of violence. This contention was challenged by a more recent Presidential commission, headed by Attorney General Edward Meese, which studied the same issue. The very different conclusion arrived at by the majority of the Meese commission was not due to new scientific findings unavailable to the Nixon commission. On the contrary, this disagreement was a result of differing causal analyses of ambiguous statistical data. Consider, for example, the warning on cigarette packages that "The surgeon general has determined that cigarette smoking is harmful"—i.e., that it *causes* such diseases as lung cancer and heart disease. While this is now widely accepted, the cigarette industry resisted this alleged causal connection for some time and some people still do.

Similarly, there is debate today over the causal connection between coffee drinking and disease. Those who claim a causal connection point to the statistical significance of the percentage of those who drink coffee, as opposed to those who don't, developing heart disease and cancer. Is drinking coffee bad for your health? The question is simple enough and of wide interest to the multitude who would rather forego breakfast than the several cups of coffee they have in the morning. How much coffee, we reasonably ask, is *too* much? Scientists do not know. While there have been many medical studies of the link between coffee drinking and disease, their conclusions have been tentative and conflicting. The strongest link, apparently, is between coffee drinking and heart disease. Such studies employ statistical inferences from samples of coffee drinkers who drink at least a certain number of cups of coffee (say five) per day to samples of those who do not. Yet, it is often very difficult to separate the many specific factors that are involved in a statistical correlation and arrive at some conclusion concerning causation. For example, if some occurrence A were found to uniformly precede another occurrence B, we might naturally jump to the conclusion that "A causes B," but this might be a mistake. Once we come to understand the *causal mechanism* behind the uniform correlation between A and B, we may find that there is some other event C, which *independently* causes both A and B. For example, in the coffee and heart disease example, it is possible that heavy coffee drinking is not directly causally related to heart disease which instead is caused by certain underlying psychological or physiological characteristics of the typical heavy coffee drinker. In addition, it may be discovered that a much higher percentage of heavy coffee drinkers are smokers, as compared to nonheavy coffee drinkers. Perhaps, then, a statistically significant correlation between heavy coffee drinking and heart disease is really due to the smoking behavior of those in the sample of heavy coffee drinkers.

In light of such considerations, one should be wary of the causal pronouncements of those, like the Meese Commision, who see causal connections that the more acute observer would be wary of asserting on the basis of *mere statistical correlations*. For example, critics cogently point out that the sort of pornographic material the Meese Commission focused upon in their conclusions was violent in nature. Perhaps then, if there is a causal connection between pornography and acts of violence, it is the *violence* and not the erotic element of pornographic material that is the causal culprit. Yet the majority report of the Meese Commission does not distinguish different sorts of pornography and draw different conclusions as to their likely effects on crimes of violence. Consequently, as the dissenting minority opinion points out, the majority opinion of the Meese Commission suffers from serious logical flaws.

Since so many of the moral issues that are subject to contemporary debate hinge over differing views as to causal connections, one should be wary of drawing hasty causal conclusions that conveniently allow one to believe what one would like to believe. For example, there is much debate over whether the death penalty causes a decrease in homicides and whether the tolerance of homosexuality has undesirable causal effects upon established "family values" or, in some sense "leads to general social disintegration." As always, while clarity of thought, devoid of facts, cannot answer such questions, facts, without clarity of thought, are worthless in the achievement of an understanding of causal connections.

The Uncritical Use Of Analogical Reasoning

The premises of an inductive argument, it has been noted, are claimed to support a given conclusion with less than the certainty of a deductive argument. Many logic texts, influenced by the model of science with its concern for predicting the future, define inductive arguments as arguments where the conclusion is claimed to *probably* (but not certainly) follow from the premises. The notion of probability, however, has its place in verifiable predictions and not in moral and legal arguments. Just as a skillful attorney can forcefully argue both sides of a legal controversy, so, too, one can often find merit in both sides of a controversial moral issue. This is the case with the controversial moral issues we shall be discussing in the second part of this book. For example, good arguments can be given for and against liberal abortion laws. While one can debate the relative merits or weight of such arguments, one cannot meaningfully speak of the "probabilities" such arguments confer upon their competing conclusions, for there is no unique and single dimensional scale for weighing the merits of such arguments. Ultimately the manner in which we weigh competing moral and legal arguments reflects commitments to possibly competing policies or principles. The specific competing principles which can underlie moral and legal arguments can, in turn, often be traced to commitments to competing normative ethical theories—for example to those that are built upon a respect for human rights or those that are built upon an attempt to maximize the satisfaction of human desires.

Our underlying commitment to certain policies or principles can serve to determine the manner in which we choose to classify things and argue analogically from a given case to one that is similar to it. Analogical reasoning plays a central role in the legal and moral arguments that surround us. For example, an Alabama court decision claimed that many science textbooks advocated the *religion* of secular humanism when they attempted to explain things without reference to a divine creator. In reply, many criticized this decision, claiming that such explanations should not be seen as religious, but as scientific. Those who agreed with the decision, on the other hand, claimed that some alleged scientific beliefs presuppose an atheistic world-view which functions as a mode of organizing thought and attitude no less than supernaturalistic world-views and as such should be seen as religious in nature (consider in this regard that atheistic Marxism has been called a religion). In deciding whether to classify certain secular teachings as religious for the purpose of determining whether the promulgation of such teachings by a state supported educational institution infringes on the Constitutional provision of separation of church and state, a court must turn to its understanding of the meaning and purpose of this Constitutional provision—a controversial issue involving a consideration of policy and principle.

As this is written, the New Jersey Supreme Court has just ruled in the "Baby M" case that the contract between the surrogate mother, Mary Beth Whitehead, and the biological father, William Stern, and his wife was null and void since it amounted to baby selling, prohibited by the state of New Jersey. In so ruling, the New Jersey Supreme Court overturned a lower court decision which upheld the contract between the Sterns and Ms. Whitehead. The legal arguments on both sides centered on the appropriateness of describing the case in various ways—which in turn hinged on the appropriateness of different analogies. This case, some said, should be seen as one in contract law. No, said others, it should be seen as one in adoption law which makes baby selling illegal. No, rejoined those who advocated the contract view, the contract between the Sterns and Ms. Whitehead did not involve baby selling, but the purchase of the personal services of Mary Beth Whitehead. Yet others pointed to the lack of rights of sperm donors to claim their biological offspring, claiming that the fact that William Stern was the biological father of Baby M should be as irrelevant as it would be were he an anonymous sperm donor. Some who took this position referred to the importance of respecting the autonomy of a pregnant woman. If Ms. Whitehead could by signing a contract forfeit any subsequent claim to the child she pledged to bear for someone else, should surrogate motherhood not be seen as akin to slavery? If a prgenant woman has a right to an abortion, this right cannot be denied to a surrogate mother, without forcing her to sell herself into a type of slavery that would clearly be unconstitutional. But if a surrogate mother has the right to kill the fetus she is carrying, would it not be bizzare to prevent her from keeping the child and abrogating her prior agreement to give it up? Such an argument would be countered by claiming that the analogies of surrogate motherhood with slavery and the forfeiture of basic constitutionally protected rights suffers from serious deficiencies.

As we shall see in our discussion of specific contemporary controversial moral issues, the claim that "this case is in all morally relevant respects just like..." often elicits the response, "No, it is not, for this case differs in the respect that...." A sensitive legal or moral judgment on how a specific case is to be classified requires an awareness of the plausibility of different analogies that underlie competing arguments, an awareness that is often lacking when, motivated by strong commitments to specific policies or principles, we choose the analogy that will best achieve a desired result. Wisdom in making moral and legal decisions on how to perceive a particular case demands awareness of what we lose as well as what we stand to gain when we choose certain analogies over others and the realization that in making such choices normative concerns become interwoven with linguistic ones.

Rationalization

While people often quite knowingly act in ways they believe to be wrong, it is perhaps even more common for people to convince themselves that what they want to do is what they ought to do. Since it is very important to most of us to have a moral self-image of ourselves, there is a marked human tendency to engage in a process of self-deception in which one devises justifications for actions which are motivated by other factors. Psychiatrists call this process rationalization. Since rationalizations are merely rational cover-ups of one's true and often unflattering motives which are devised after one has already arrived at some decision, one is apt to conveniently forget these same reasons when it is in one's interest to so forget. For example, when Jones cheats on an important test, he will say that "everyone does it sometimes" or that "the test was unfair anyway"; but if Smith should cheat when Jones doesn't, Jones will be morally indignant and accuse Smith of "not having any personal integrity" or of "being unfair to those who are honest." Similarly, if Brown is reprimanded by his boss for being late, he might very well think ill of him for his "stern and inhumane attitude" and for his refusal "to give a guy a break once in a while," but if his wife is late with the supper, he will quickly and sternly reproach her for her "lack of consideration" or "laziness." The human capacity for inconsistency and self-deception is certainly staggering at times. Indeed, one of the greatest virtues of subjecting one's own moral beliefs to philosophical scrutiny is that under the light of such scrutiny, such self-deception and inconsistency can be brought to consciousness and dealt with rationally.

The Genetic Fallacy

As the common tendency toward rationalization demonstrates, the reasons people give for their beliefs are often quite different from the factors that actually motivate or cause them to have these beliefs; or, as it is often put, they are not their "real reasons." It is, however, misleading to equate the notions of a *cause* and a *reason,* as this common figure of speech does. The causes of a person's beliefs may not be reasons in the logical sense of rational considerations that are taken as supporting these beliefs. For example, although Jack may be capable of giving arguments for believing in the Judeo-Christian God, his belief in God may not have been influenced by these arguments. Instead, this belief may have been motivated purely by his needs and fears.

Since people often arrive at their moral beliefs as a result of nonrational factors of which they are not aware, it is tempting for us not to pay any heed to the reasons they give for their nonrationally motivated moral beliefs—assuming, quite mistakenly, that these reasons cannot be good reasons. Although people may be mistaken in their self-knowledge of why they hold the moral beliefs they do, they may, nevertheless, be capable of rationally defending them. For example, although Mary may believe that abortion is wrong as a result of nonrational factors, she may still be capable of giving good arguments in defense of her belief. If Mary's position on the abortion issue is not a result of her consideration of these reasons, we have grounds for challenging the rational self-image she may have of herself, but we have no justifiable basis for dismissing her belief about abortion as unwarranted unless we can counter the arguments she presents. Consequently, when one assumes that a belief is false or unjustifiable because of its causal origin (that is, its genesis) one has committed a fallacy—*the genetic fallacy* or, as it is often called, the fallacy of *argumentum ad hominem* (literally: an argument directed to the man; that is, to the *source* of the argument rather than to the argument itself).

It is important that we realize that the reasons people offer in support of their beliefs must always be evaluated on their own merits, even if these reasons did not motivate (cause) the acceptance of these beliefs. We must not lose sight of the fact that although people will often search for good reasons to justify their nonrationally preconceived beliefs, they may very well find that justification.

Although people may have plausible reasons for a belief that is arrived at on nonrational grounds, if these reasons are sufficient to justify acceptance of their belief and if they are truly rational people who are motivated to act by the reasons they give, they should continue to find these reasons sufficient to motivate their acceptance of the belief they support even without the further impetus of the non-rational factors that motivated them previously. This is, unfortunately, often not the case, and consequently, we are right in being suspicious of the motivating power of the reasons people often give in defense of their moral postions. As psychiatrists stress, human beings are often much less rational in their behavior than their rational self-images of themselves would have them believe.

The Confusion Between What One Ought to Do and What One Would Be Inclined to Do

Although the distinction between what one morally ought to do and what one would be inclined to do is an obvious one, in a debate over the resolution of specific moral dilemmas, such as those on our list, it is quite common for a person to challenge the worth of this enterprise, claiming that most of us simply do not know how we would react in the situations described. No doubt, this is very often true. Our quest, however, is not the psychological one of what an individual would as a matter of fact be inclined to do in a given situation but, rather, the normative one of what he morally ought to do. The mere fact that an individual might be inclined to act in a particular way does not show that that is the way he should act. Once pointed out, this is obvious, and most will be satisfied with such an answer, especially when it is suggested that we are more apt to make rational moral judgments about what is right when we are not personally involved in a situation. For example, one would not expect most pepole to do their best moral deliberation in great stress and very limited time. Nevertheless, this response is not completely adequate. If moral judgments were objective in the sense that they could be said to be true or false, independently of the way human beings happen to *feel* about things, then one would be more apt to arrive at correct moral judgments when one detaches oneself from the corrupting influence of emotional factors which cloud one's moral reason. On the other hand, if one takes the subjective view that moral judgments are ultimately dependent on human feelings, the value of armchair moral speculation, as opposed to moral reflection made in the heat of action, becomes a more difficult question. A person who takes the subjective view of moral judgments, in response to a request to give his view of what he thinks is right in a complex moral situation might reply as follows:

> I dont' know what I think is right here, and I don't think I would know until I were in such a situation myself and discovered how much certain things meant to me or how vividly I would empathize with certain individuals if I were involved in their situation. Without this knowledge of what my own subjective feelings would be

in the situation described, I don't know what *I think* is right in this situation. Indeed, if I were in this situation, forced to choose between different options, I would probably discover something about my own true moral values and their relative importance that I am ignorant about now.

DISCUSSION QUESTIONS

1. Which of the following do you think turn out to be tautologies? Why?
   a. A person should always do what is best.
   b. A person should always do as he thinks best.
   c. Cowardice is always wrong.
   d. Selfishness is not a desirable moral trait.
   e. It is always unjust to punish the innocent.
   f. It is always wrong to punish the innocent.
   g. When a person makes a promise, she has an obligation to keep it.
   h. When a person makes a promise, she ought to keep it.
   i. One always likes those whom one loves.
   j. Equality of opportunity allows for differences of opportunity unless these differences are deemed unfair.

2. Consider the following case:

   Jones is driving a tram in a crowded amusement park. Seeing two little children darting in front of the moving tram, Jones quickly slams his foot on the brake, but there is no response. Frantic, he looks quickly to his left and right, noticing to his left a lone pedestrian and to his right a crowd of them. Jones realizes that the tram is bound to hit, and most likely kill, someone regardless of what he does. Attempting to minimize the number of people who will be hit, Jones steers the tram in the direction of the lone pedestrian who is critically injured as the tram finally comes to a halt.

   a. Did Jones do the right thing?
   b. In what morally relevant ways, if any, does Jones' decision to sacrifice one to save two differ from the surgeon who also decides to sacrifice one to save two? (See p. 39.)

3. Your author suggests that an important reason for our tendency to assume responsibility to specific children to whom we have a special relationship, but not to all the starving children of the world stems from the impossibility of ever fully discharging so diffuse a responsibility. Is this response adequate? While a given person in the affluent world cannot save all the starving children in the world, each of us can save some, if we make some sacrifice. Consider, for example, a neighbor's child who is so neglected by her parents that we fear for her life. To no avail, we seek governmental intervention and plead with the parents to take care of their child. They tell us to mind our own business and that they're willing to give "the little brat to us, if we think we can do a better job with her." Do we have a moral obligation to accept that offer, if we can take care of the child without any severe hardship? Would we not feel guilty, if we turned our backs? Should we feel guilty? If we should, should we feel less guilty as we eat at fancy restaurants while so many poor people are dying of starvation? Can we not imagine a more humane society of the future where people are considered to have an obligation to all suffering human beings, where a person who did not voluntarily make sacrifices

to help strangers would be considered a callous moral outcast? Would such a society be better than ours? Would the same be true of a society of principled vegetarians who look with moral revulsion at the brutal meat-eating practices of our culture which raises animals, oblivious of their welfare, to fatten them up as quickly as possible in order to eat them? Would they be justified in seeing us as "cannibals?" Critically discuss.

4. Critically analyze the issues involved in the following dialogue.

A: Alcoholism, unlike moderate drinking, is a disease.
B: No, it is not. It is a result of moral indulgence that can be corrected by an act of moral will.

FURTHER READINGS

General Reference Sources

The Encyclopedia of Philosophy (Macmillan, 1967) is an excellent general reference source. Articles especially relevant to this chapter are: "Ethical Relativism," "Ethical Objectivism," "Ethical Subjectivism," "Ultimate Moral Principles: Their Justification," and "Emotive Theory of Ethics." *The Dictionary of the History of Ideas* (Scribners, 1973) is another excellent reference source for broad general surveys of philosophical ideas which, unlike *The Encyclopedia of Philosophy,* does not contain entries on particular philosophers. Two articles especially relevant to this chapter are "Relativism in Ethics" and "Moral Sense."

Hume on Reason and Sentiment, and the Emotivists

Hume's most provocative presentation of his thesis that moral questions are decided by sentiment and not reason is found in Book II, Part III, Section III of his *A Treatise of Human Nature.* It is in this section that Hume makes his famous remark that "reason is...the slave of the passions," and that as long as a "passion is neither founded on false suppositions, nor...[chooses] means insufficient for the end...[reason] can neither justify nor condemn it. 'Tis not contrary to reason to prefer the destruction of the whole world to the scratching of my finger." Disapppointed by the poor literary reception of the *Treatise,* Hume reformulated his ideas on ethics into the more popular form of his *Enquiries Concerning the Principles of Morals.* Hume's treatment of the relationship between reason and feeling is found in Appendix I of this work. While Hume is one of the most readable of classical philosophers, he does employ technical philosophical terms in this work which would make it hard going for students not familiar with his general philosophy.

Hume's identification of morality with subjective feelings was strongly criticized by Immanuel Kant who, as we shall see, saw morality as a demand of objective reason. In the twentieth century, Humean subjectivism was embraced by the logical positivists who incorporated it with their general theory that only verifiable assertions are meaningful. Claiming that moral asssertions are not verifiable, the emotivists dismissed them as meaningless. A very brief expression of this point of view is found in A. J. Ayer's 1936 positivist classic *Language, Truth and Logic.* More refined and detailed positions are found in C. L. Stevenson's *Ethics and Language* (1944) and R. M. Hare's *The Language of Morals* (1952).

Books by Specific Authors

Of the many philosophy books that delve into the issue of ethical relativism, Richard Brandt's very clear and philosophically rigorous *Ethical Theory* (Prentice-Hall, 1959) is the one I recommend the most for students who would like to pursue this issue more deeply. Brandt enriches his discussion of ethical relativism with a knowledge of anthropology and with his own first-hand experiences of the Hopi Indian culture. A good discussion of the issue of ethical relativism as well as the meaning of morality is found in Tom L. Beauchamp's *Philosophical Ethics* (McGraw-Hill, 1982) which also contains readings.

W. T. Stace's view, discussed in this chapter, can be found in his *The Concept of Morals* (Macmillan, 1937). Stace believes that there is a single correct morality for human beings based on a universal human nature which is not a function of cultural factors. Stace calls this position "ethical universalism," and not "ethical absolutism" which he defines to be the view that moral judgments are "valid independently of all conditions." Since Stace believes that morality depends on human nature and would be different if human nature were different, he rejects ethical absolutism.

Anthologies

Selections of material on ethical relativism can be found in many anthologies of readings in general philosophy, as well as those devoted to ethics. The short paperback *Right and Wrong* (Harcourt Brace Jovanovich, 1986) edited by Christina Sommers has a good selection on this topic for beginning students. It begins with a brief passage from the first Western historian Herodotus (485–430 B.C.) in defense of ethical relativism. This is followed by the widely reprinted defense by the twentieth century anthropologist Ruth Benedict which is in turn followed by brief criticisms, including Stace's. Wilfred Sellars and John Hospers (eds.) *Readings in Ethical Theory*, Second Edition (Prentice-Hall, 1970) provides an extensive collection of more technical selections. John Ladd (ed.) *Ethical Relativism* (Wadsworth, 1973) is devoted exclusively to selections for and against ethical relativism.

Citations

The quotation from Robert Mortimer appears in an excerpt from his book *Christian Ethics* (1950), included in the anthology *Ethics for Modern Life* (St. Martins Press, 1975), edited by R. Abelson and M. Friquegnon. The quotations from Solomon Asch appear on p. 378 and 376–7 of his book *Social Psychology* (Prentice-Hall, 1952). The quotation from Stace appears on p. 45 of his *The Concept of Morals*. The quotation from Ruth Benedict originally appeared in her article "Anthropology and the Abnormal" in the *Journal of General Psychology*, 1934.

Theories
of
Normative Ethics
2

6. THE TERMINOLOGY OF
NORMATIVE ETHICS

It may be helpful to begin our study of normative ethics with a discussion of some of the key concepts philosophers employ in this area of study. A preliminary acquaintance with these concepts will help us to perceive in broad outline the issues and conflicting positions we will be discussing in this chapter.

The question that has preoccuped moralists most is, as one would expect, the question of what actions are morally right or obligatory. General answers to this question are provided in what philosophers call *theories of moral obligation.* Moral judgments can also be made about the intentions, motives, and character of moral agents, such as whether they are good, bad, praiseworthy, blameworthy, or morally responsible. The perspectives philosophers provide for answering such questions are called *theories of moral value.* Moral questions also arise as to what things in life are worthwhile or desirable. In discussing this issue, philosophers make a distinction between those things that are *instrumentally good* (that is, good because of their consequences) and those things which are *intrinsically good* (that is, good in and of themselves). For exmaple, unless a person has masochistic desires, having a dentist drill one's teeth to fill a cavity is merely instrumentally good, not intrinsically good; the drilling is not good in and of itself, but rather for its consequences. Similarly, if we ask a person why he works, he might reply that he works for the money he can earn. If we go on to ask why he wants money, he might say that it is necessary in order to buy the things that he wants, and if we pursue the questioning further and ask him why he wants to buy things, he might reply that it gives him pleasure. If we then ask him why he desires pleasure, there would seem to be no answer he could give, for he does not seek pleasure in order to gain something else—that is, pleasure is intrinsically good. Philosophers have had different views concerning what is intrinsically good. The most famous view is *hedonism* which asserts that pleasure is *the only* intrinsic good. For example, according to the hedonist, knowledge has value, not as an end in itself, but only as a means for obtaining pleasure—that is, knowledge is only instrumentally good.[1]

Theories of normative ethics have been distinguished as *teleological* or *deontological*. Both concepts have Greek derivations, teleological deriving from the Greek concept *teleos* which means goal or purpose and deontological deriving from the Greek concept *deontos* which means duty. A normative theory of ethics is said to be teleological if it claims that right conduct is determined solely by what is achieved by the conduct, i.e., by the intrinsic good it brings into the world. Consequently, a teleological theory of moral obligation is dependent upon some theory of intrinsic good. Although teleologists have often been hedonists, this has not always been the case. Some have identified intrinsic good with power, knowledge, self-realization, or several distinct qualities. Teleologists have differed not only on the question of what is intrinsically good, but also on the question of whose intrinsic good should be sought. *Ethical egoism* holds that one should always do what will promote one's own greatest good, while *utilitarianism* holds that one should always do what will promote the greatest good for everyone. Since the most famous utilitarians, Jeremy Bentham and John Stuart Mill, were also hedonists, the principle of utilitarianism is often given as the principle of "the greatest happiness for the greatest number."

Teleologists are also divided on the issue of whether or not intrinsically good things are *commensurable,* that is, whether or not there is some common unit by which they can be compared and ranked in terms of relative value. Those teleologists who believe this is possible are *consequentialists* who identify rightness with the maximization of intrinsic value. Utilitarianism is a consequentalist theory for its central concept of "the greatest good" (or "best consequences") tacitly assumes that there is some common unit by which competing values can be compared and ranked. On the other hand, Natural Law Theory, the foundation of traditional Catholic morality, is a nonconsequentialist theory, for one of its basic assumptions is that there are several independent intrinsic goods which are incommensurable. For example, natural law theorists have claimed that such intrinsic goods as life, health, procreation, and friendship cannot be traded off for one another on the basis of some common scale of comparison. Consequently, the notions of maximizing value or obtaining the best consequences—notions central to utilitarianism—are sometimes senseless from a natural law perspective. Similarly, while

---

[1]Since many philosophers have identified the intrinsic good with those things that are *worthwhile apart from any moral consideration,* theories of intrinsic value are sometimes called theories of *nonmoral value.* Not all philosophers, however, have identified intrinsic good with nonmoral qualities. Some, for example, have claimed that certain qualities of moral character—such as honesty, integrity, and conscientiousness—are intrinsic goods. In addition, considerations of justice (such as, that the good should prosper and the wicked suffer) have been taken by some philosophers to be intrinsic goods.

utilitarianism naturally leads to the judgment that, everything else being equal, two human lives are more valuable than one human life, such a judgment is alien to the natural law perspective, which sees each human life as *uniquely valuable,* and, as such, morally incapable of being traded off for other human lives.

Deontologists deny what teleologists affirm—that right conduct is determined solely by the intrinsic good that is brought into being by such conduct. Some deontologists have claimed that what is right does not depend at all upon notions of intrinsic good and the consequences of actions. Other more moderate deontologists see such factors as relevant, but not decisive. For example, in deciding whether to keep a promise, one should consider the consquences, either good or bad, of keeping the promise; nevertheless, it is sometimes right to keep a promise even though the consequences in balance would be worse if one does so. Deontologists also disagree as to the role that general rules should play in determining what is right. At one extreme, there are those who believe that since each situation of moral choice is unique, we must intuit or decide separately in each particular situation the right thing to do without any appeal to general rules or to the consequences of our actions. At the other extreme, there are those deontologists who claim that the ultimate standard of right conduct consists of allegiance to one or more rules. These rules may be either very concrete ones such as "Always keep promises," "Never lie," and "Never kill innocent people," or abstract ones such as Kant's categorical imperative which asserts (in one of its formulations) that one should "act only on that maxim which you can at the same time will to be a universal law." By reducing all of morality to this single basic moral rule, Kant avoids the difficulty that besets those deontologists (*ethical pluralists*) who accept more than one basic rule and have no rule for resolving conflicts among them.

The disagreement between teleologists and deontologists is the most basic one in normative ethics. Teleologists will look ahead to the consequences of actions, whereas deontologists will look back upon the nature of the act itself, seeing it within the context of the duties and obligations one has either simply by virtue of being a human being (such as the duty to be just, honest, or benevolent) or by virtue of the specific personal and social relationships that one assumes (such as the duty of being a parent, of citizenship, or of one's profession). The moral life for most of us is a mixture of deontological and teleological considerations, and that, as it shall later be argued, is the way it should be.

7. THEORIES OF INTRINSIC GOOD:
HEDONISM AND SELF-REALIZATION

The most profoundly personal question that each reflective person can face is the question of how he or she ought to live. Socialization teaches us all as young children that some of our desires must be curbed if we are to live harmoniously with others. But apart from the constraints imposed by the need to resolve disputes among people, each of us makes choices that determine the direction of our personal lives. While Western philosophers, from Socrates to the present, preach the value of calm, reflective self-examination of the direction of our lives, most of us do not reflect upon this matter until we are faced with some momentous choice between competing values or goals. Indeed, most people associate the search for wisdom, that is, according to its original Greek meaning, the quest of philosophy, with precisely the search for an answer to the question of how we are to live. The *depth* of such a question (another characteristic of philosophy) comes from the fact that any reflective answer to this question must either explicitly or implicitly come to grips with central metaphysical and psychological questions as to the nature of the universe and the place and needs of human beings within that universe. For the ancient Greeks, man was by nature a social animal. As Aristotle put it, "He who is unable to live in society, or has no need because he is sufficient for himself, must be either a beast or a god." From such a perspective, the concept of human happiness was, for Aristotle, necessarily social. The ideal of individualism, with its emphasis upon *individual autonomous* self-development that is so central to current Western civilization was an alien one to the Greeks, as was the concept, also central to individualistic theories of political obligation, that the ultimate source of social authority derives from individual consent. From this perspective, which is the foundation of social contract theories of political obligation, human beings have basic needs which can be identified apart from the societies in which they live. Foremost in influence among these individualistic conceptions of the good life are those of hedonism and self-realization—the former assumed by classical utilitarianism and the latter by modern natural law theory, theories we shall later discuss.

In this section, we will discuss the doctrine of hedonism. As is often the case with central ethical concepts, the more we delve into this concept, the more complicated it will become. Indeed, as we shall see, a refined hedonistic perspective can become indistinguishable from one of self-realization.

Hedonism

A Question of Definition

"Hedonism" was defined on p. 51) as the doctrine that pleasure is the only intrinsic good. More precisely, hedonism may be defined as the doctrine that *all and only* pleasure is intrinsically good. The technical difference here is that if one accepts the former definition, it is possible to claim that some pleasures (e.g., the pleasure obtained by a sadist) is not intrinsically good. According to the second formulation, however, any pleasure, in and of itself, is intrinsically good. (According to this view, the pleasure obtained by the sadist can be criticized only on the basis of its undesirable consequences—i.e., because it conflicts with the pursuit of other pleasures.) The second formulation is preferable, for, if we accept the first and stipulate that some pleasures are not intrinsically good, we are forced to introduce some nonhedonistic notion to distinguish good from bad pleasures and in effect we will have abandoned the view that pleasure *alone* is the standard for determining what is intrinsically good.

Some Historical Background

The hedonistic point of view has been embraced by many philosophers. Its roots can be traced back to Aristippus (435–350 B.C.) who was an older contemporary of Plato and, like him, a student of Socrates. The most famous supporter of hedonism was Epicurus (342–270 B.C.), the founder of the school of philosophy known as epicureanism. Ironically, this word has now come to describe a view of the good life against which Epicurus would strongly protest. As it is currently used, an epicurean is a gourmet whose main delights consist in the enjoyment of exquisite food and drink. Epicurus was anything but an epicurean in this sense. He is said to have suffered from stomach trouble and to have subsisted on the blandest of food and drink.

While embracing the hedonistic view that pleasure alone is good, Epicurus viewed pleasure more as the absence of painful wants or longings than as the positive gratificaiton of longings. From this perspective, he made a central distinction in his philosophy between those pleasures that have painful consequences and those that do not. A life devoted to the gratification of bodily sensations was bound to prove unsatisfying eventually, he believed, since the price of such pleasures is often greater pain in the long run. For example, sexual love, he warned, often proves unsatisfying since it is usually "accompanied by fatigue, remorse, and depression." Similarly, gluttony and indulgence in alcoholic beverages are unsatisfying in the long run since they lead to indigestion and hangovers. Since the good life, as Epicurus saw it, was essentially a life containing as few painful experiences as possible, such a life, he believed, could not be achieved if one turned to the physical pleasures for gratification. One should turn instead, he preached, to the more tranquil modes of enjoyment which are not accompanied with the unpleasant side effects of the bodily pleasures. These modes of enjoyment included the joys of friendship, good conversation, and philosophical and artistic contemplation.

Epicurus' advocacy of the tranquil pleasures that come to those who are free of strong passions has not been shared by all hedonists. For example, Aristippus claimed that the aim of life should not be tranquility but the maximization of as many particular pleasures as our intelligence can procure and assimilate. Very intense pleasures, Aristippus claimed, are to be sought even when they are the occasion of considerable pain, for a life without excitement would be dull and uninteresting.

Since the word "pleasure" often suggests bodily or physical enjoyment that many hedonists such as Epicurus do not advocate, some have preferred substituting the term "happiness" for that of "pleasure" in expressing their hedonistic commitment. They have preferred this concept since it suggests longer lasting enjoyment which need not refer to specific bodily pleasures. Not all philosophers, however, have been willing to identify pleasure with happiness. According to Aristotle, for example, the good should be identified with happiness, but not with pleasure. As he perceived it, happiness refers to "activity in accordance with the moral and intellectual virtues," and not to a particular sensation such as that of pleasure. Although pleasure accompanies such activities, Aristotle believed, it is not the proper end of our desires but simply a by-product.

There have been many other philosophers who have refused to accept the hedonistic thesis that pleasure alone is intrinsically good. The good has been equated by nonhedonistic philosophers with such things as knowledge, moral virtue, beauty, self-realization, power, friendship, communion with God, and the just apportionment of happiness to desert. Many philosophers have also accepted a pluralistic view of intrinsic good, taking the position, shared by Plato, that the good life is "a mixed life" consisting of various different intrinsically good things. The hedonist, one should realize, will not deny that there are many different things—such as knowledge and moral virtue—which are desirable; what he will deny is that anything other than pleasure is intrinsically good. The things in life that are good other than pleasure are merely instrumentally good as means for obtaining pleasure, he will say. For example, knowledge, the hedonist would say, is generally valuable because it enables us to understand and satisfy the needs of individuals and, consequently, is a source of pleasure. In addition, the very pursuit of knowledge is for many a very pleasurable activity in itself. In those situations, however, where knowledge does not lead to human pleasure, the hedonist would claim that it has no value. The same is true, he would say, of the various moral virtues, such as benevolence and courage, for the only justifiable moral virtues are those which promote human pleasure. Similarly, the hedonist would contend, it is not the existence of beauty, friendship or self-realization in some impersonal and unexperienced (and, perhaps, meaningless) sense that is of value, but rather the satisfactory or pleasurable experience that human beings obtain from such things as aesthetic experience, having friends, and realizing their potentialities.

If the hedonist is also a utilitarian who places equal value on the pleasures of others, he will stress that a person's pursuit of a given pleasure can be bad not only when it leads in the long run to greater dissatisfaction for himself, but also when it causes greater dissatisfaction for others. It is for this reason, the hedonistic utilitarian would say, that many pleasures are to be condemned. The cruel man, for example, may obtain pleasure from his cruelty, but his cruelty is to be condemned for it is likely to cause greater pain to others and indeed possibly to himself in the long run. Any pleasure, however, revolting we may find it (such as the pleasures of sadomasochists) is never to be condemned in and of itself, but only for its consequences (that is, on the grounds that it leads to greater human dissatisfaction than satisfaction in the long run), the hedonist contends.

Bentham's Quantitative Hedonism

As we shall see in the next section, the doctrine of hedonism was presupposed by Jeremy Bentham (1748–1832), the founder of the classical school of utilitarianism. It was Bentham's ideal that ethics could be made into a science whose subject matter would be capable of quantitative measure. Born into an age that had witnessed rapid development in the mathematical sciences, it was Bentham's hope that, just as scientists could measure the quantities of physical properties such as heat and sound, it should also be possible to measure the quantities of pleasure and pain.

In arriving at a judgment of a pleasure's worth, it would be necessary, Bentham believed, to measure the following seven features of pleasure:

1. intensity (how strong or weak it is)
2. duration (how long it lasts)
3. certainty (the degree of probability that it will occur)
4. propinquity (how soon it will be fulfilled)
5. fecundity (its ability to lead to other pleasures)
6. purity (the likelihood that it will not be mixed with or followed by pain)
7. extent (the number of people who will experience it—a reflection of Bentham's utilitarian commitment).

If these features could prove quantifiable and capable of being incorporated into a mathematical formula, moral reasoning could become a type of "hedonistic calculus" capable of giving exact guidance to action and legislation. Although Bentham assumed that this was theoretically possible, he did not suply a method for computing the quantity of a given pleasure. As Bentham's critics have pointed out, while it may be possible to roughly rank pleasures according to their relative strength, exact mathematical measurement seems out of the question. Indeed, different sorts of pleasures often appear incommensurate. How can we, for example, compare the relative amount of pleasure that one obtains from a good meal as opposed to pleasure obtained from an invigorating and relaxing swim or from a good book? Indeed, does it really make sense to attempt to compare in any exact manner the relative amount of even similar sorts of pleasures? (Did the hamburger I had for lunch give me 1/10, 1/4, or perhaps 1/2 of the pleasure of yesterday's steak?) Furthermore, pleasures, unlike calories, change their amounts when they are combined with other pleasures. For example, the pleasure one obtains from a good dinner, wine, and the company of some loved one in romantic surroundings could be considerably greater when these pleasurable elements are taken together than they would be if they were experienced separately and then added together. Finally, as we shall discuss later, Bentham's attempt to quantify pleasures may be based on the error of assuming that the concept of pleasure refers to specific identifiable sensations or feelings. Perhaps, as behavioristic psychologists have suggested, the concept of pleasure should be taken to refer instead to dispositions (tendencies) to behave, think, and feel in certain general ways which render inappropriate any type of exact quantitative measure.

In addition to assuming that pleasures were capable of quantitative measure, Bentham also firmly held the view that pleasures should be ranked only on the basis of the seven features previously mentioned. Bentham rejected the view that some pleasures, apart from their quantity, were of a "higher level" or "quality" than others. If pleasures were to be said to differ in quality as well as quantity, Bentham feared, the result would be unresolvable debates as to the "true worth" or "level" of a given pleasure, where conflicting statements of personal preference would falsely be made to appear to be dictated by impersonally justifiable standards of value. Such, of course, would make a shambles of his attempt to reduce ethics to "moral arithmetic." Bentham's view that pleasures should not be said to differ in quality as well as quantity was summed up in his famous remark that "quantity of pleasure being equal, pushpin [an old English table game] is as good as poetry."

Bentham's refusal to rank pleasures according to their quality as well as quantity led many of his critics to describe his hedonistic utilitarianism as "a philosophy fit only for pigs." Such critics shared Plato's disdain for the "lower" bodily pleasures that human beings share with other animals and his view that there are distinctively human sorts of pleasures that are more worthwhile apart from their amount or consequences. Bentham's reply was that even though a life limited to the bodily pleasures would be as good as one devoted to intellectual sorts of pleasures *if* their quantities were the same, as a matter of fact, the latter sort of life allows for a more varied and complex level of enjoyment which generally results in a far greater amount of pleasurable experience in the long run.

Mill's Qualitative Hedonism

This reply did not seem sufficient to John Stuart Mill (1806–73), Bentham's foremost disciple, who introduced a qualitative element into Bentham's quantitative hedonism. "It is better to be a human being dissatisfied than a pig satisfied, better to be Socrates dissatisfied than a fool satisfied," he asserted. According to Mill, "there is but one possible answer" to the question of the relative ranking of different pleasures, and he gives it as follows:

> ... of two pleasures, if there be one to which all or almost all who have experience of both give a decided preference, irrespective of any feeling of moral obligation to prefer it, that is the more desirable pleasure. If one of the two is, by those who are competently acquainted with both, placed so far above the other that they prefer it, even though knowing it to be attended with a greater amount of discontent, and would not resign it for any quantity of the other pleasure which their nature is capable of, we are justified in ascribing to the preferred enjoyment a superiority of quality, so far outweighing quantity as to render it, in comparison, of small account.
>
> Now it is an unquestionable fact that those who are equally acquainted with, and equally capable of appreciating and enjoying both, do give a most marked preference to the manner of existence which employs their higher faculties. Few human creatures would consent to be changed into any of the lower animals, for a promise of the fullest allowance of a beast's pleasures; no intelligent human being would consent to be a fool, no instructed person would be an ignoramus, no person of feeling and conscience would be selfish and base, even though they should be persuaded that the fool, the dunce, or the rascal is better satisfied with his lot than they are with theirs.

According to Mill, then, the relative qualities of two different pleasures are to be determined by asking those who have experienced both to rank them. Mill's account is inadequate. First, individuals who are familiar with different sorts of pleasures will rarely come close to a unanimous agreement on their ranking. In addition, it is no more adequate to claim that the pleasure preferences of "most" people is the ultimate standard of the quality of a pleasure than it is to say that the standard for determining what is right is what most people think is right. Clearly, the vast majority of people can sometimes be very wrong. For example, as many a frustrated teacher of literature or art will confirm, many, and perhaps even most, individuals who are exposed to great literature of art do not prefer it to simpler and less demanding forms of literary or artistic enjoyment. It is not the preferences of all those who have been exposed to literature and art which should be used as the standard of literary or artistic value, but the preferences of those who are competent to judge. The same is true of the relative qualities of different sorts of pleasures. Yet, as Bentham rightly saw, there are no clear, agreed-upon standards for determining who is and is not competent to make such judgments.

One should also consider that if we were to employ Mill's test of quality, then most of us would apparently have no right to judge the quality of pleasure experienced by such individuals as the guilt-free psychopathic killer whose mode of enjoyment we have not experienced. In addition, it is possible that the intellectual pleasures that Mill advocates act to dull one's former appreciation of the simpler less cerebral type of pleasure. At any rate, unlike Mill, Tolstoy and other thinkers have expressed a preference for these simpler pleasures over the more intellectual ones. Furthermore, it is one thing to say that a human being capable of reason, aesthetic satisfaction, and complicated feeling would not want to be turned into an animal who is incapable of these experiences; it is something else to say that the pleasures we share with animals are less valuable than those we uniquely enjoy. Some would claim that although intellectual and aesthetic experiences help to "enhance" the bodily ones, it is, nevertheless, the bodily ones that are more valuable in and of themselves.

Such a view cannot be refuted simply by pointing out that it is a minority opinion. Those of us who reject a life primarily devoted to the titillation of the bodily senses have to base our objection either on the claim that such a life does not usually produce as much pleasure in the long run as other forms of life or be forthright and renounce the hedonistic point of view that pleasure alone is intrinsically good, as Mill should have done. Does it really make any difference, after all, to say that "two pleasures can be equal in amount and consequences and yet one can be 'better' than the other" instead of saying that "pleasure is not the only intrinsic good"?

The Marxist Challenge:
Which Pleasures Are Really Satisfying?

Even if one accepts the hedonistic thesis that pleasure alone is intrinsically good, it is clear that the various objects of human desire vary greatly in their capacity to generate lasting pleasure or happiness. If people seeking advice as to the proper end or ends of the good life, were told nothing more than "seek pleasure," this advice would not in itself inform them as to which of the multitude of possibly pleasurable activities they could seek would most likely prove satisfying in the long run. Indeed, according to the *hedonistic paradox,* those who aim directly at pleasure rarely achieve it, while those who direct their attention to other pursuits more often do. We may, like Bentham, be committed to the maximization of human pleasure or happiness, but without specific goals and some insight into human nature we will have no specific view of the good life. As we have seen, philosophers have been committed to very different types of hedonistic views. Each specific view is built upon assumptions as to the nature of human beings and their place in the universe they inhabit, as well as upon value judgments based on those assumptions. For example, a value judgment must be made as to whether it is better to live dangerously, risking great pain as a price for great happiness, or to play it safe, seeking the tranquility of the perhaps less intense but more pain-free pleasures.

Often these assumptions and value judgments, while exerting their strong influence on a given ideal of the good life, are not fully brought to consciousness and subjected to scrutiny. This is the criticism Karl Marx (1818–83) directed towards Bentham's hedonistic utilitarianism. Given Marx's view that ethical philosophies are often *ideologies* in which naked power clothes itself in the robes of legitimate authority, Marx looked with suspicion at the pronouncements of Bentham and his followers. Referring to Bentham's principle of the greatest happiness for the greatest number, Marx contemptuously wrote, "at no time and in no country has the most trivial commonplace ever before strutted about with such appalling self-satisfaction." In a similar vein, Marx went on to remark that this principle is quite useless apart from a definite conception of the nature of man:

> To know what is useful for a dog, we must study dog nature. This nature cannot be excogitated from the "principle of utility." If man is in question, human nature and its historical transformations must be studied. But Bentham makes short work of it. In his arid and simple way, he assumes the modern petty bourgeois, and above all the modern English petty bourgeois, to be the normal man. Whatever seems useful to this queer sort of normal man and to his world is regarded as useful in and by itself.

Marx, we should note, is not criticizing Bentham as many others did, for identifying the good with pleasure, but is rather willing to take this as a "trivial commonplace." The real question to answer, Marx tells us, is which pleasures are truly satisfying to human beings. This cannot be discovered by an appeal to the principle of utility, but requires understanding of the psychological nature and social conditions of mankind. Bentham, however, Marx says, neglects any such explicit considerations and when one reads between the lines to discover which sorts of activities he focuses upon as pleasurable, one finds him taking it for granted that the good life is a life which satisfies the desires of the English middle class. But the real unanswered question here, as Marx perceived it, was whether these desires are truly satisfying in the long run or are merely *false needs* created by a capitalistic society. According to Marx, it is a fundamental mistake to take an individual's desires as given and unchallengeable, as Bentham so readily did, for these desires can be the reflection of social conditioning that does not reflect the true psychological nature of man. To understand the nature of the good life, one must understand human psychology, and for Marx this in turn meant that one must understand sociology, since an individual's psyche is molded by social forces. Accepting Montesquieu's insight that "institutions form men," Marx, in his many writings, presented a theory of how social institutions are themselves rooted in economic conditions. The capitalistic economic system, he believed, produces as a chief motivating factor the desire for money and property, while other economic systems can produce quite different desires. Some of these desires, such as those generated by capitalism, Marx claimed, create false needs that are not psychologically satisfying in the long run. On the other hand, the communist society he envisioned would cater only to man's true needs.[2] Regardless of the inadequacies in Marx' conception of the nature of man and society, his criticism is sound that philosophical inquiry as to the nature of the good life is useless apart from a commitment to some general conception of human nature.

Theories of Self-Realization

Once hedonists accept the necessity of formulating a specific conception of human nature, their theory can become indistinguishable from the various, historically competing, theories which have identified intrinsic good with human self-realization. Such theories, which can be traced back to the ancient Greek philosophers, notably Aristotle, are united in their view that the good life for an individual is one in which one strives to realize one's potential. Such an unrefined view is open to the obvious objection that human beings have many, often conflicting, potentialities which we neither could nor would want fully realized. If one asserts that each of us should develop his own special talents, we must face the sad fact that some predominant potentialities (such as brutality, greed, and dishonesty) should never be fully realized. Philosophers and psychologists have often camouflaged their own personal preferences as to the ideals that we should strive to realize by speaking of *true self-realization* or of what it is to be *genuinely human*—conveniently using these terms to describe those human potentialities of which they approve. Nevertheless, those human tendencies of which they disapprove are just as real and human as those they admire. Even though many theories of self-realization are nothing more than statements of personal preference, others provide us with great insight into human nature and those things that are necessary for long-range human satisfaction.

The Lilnguistic Challenge: What Is "Pleasure"?

Marx' criticism that hedonism is not so much a mistaken doctrine as it is an empty one has been further strengthened by contemporary analyses of the concept of pleasure by psychologists and philosophers. Like many other philosophers of his day who were under the influence of the philosopher Descartes, Bentham believed that the most certain knowledge possible is that which results from the introspection of the workings of one's mind. From this perspective, Bentham assumed that "pleasure" was the name of a single distinctly introspected feeling that every human being could easily identify. Is this, however, true? Is there some common element

[2]Although Marx makes it appear that his conception of man's true needs is purely scientific, and does not reflect his own basic value preferences, this is open to serious question.

present in the various activities that we describe as pleasurable or enjoyable? As I focus on some of the things that give me pleasure, I cannot find a common felt quality that they all share. Indeed, although some pleasurable activities are accompanied with discernable sensations, this does not always seem to be the case. If "pleasure" is not the name of the sensation, what then is it? Contemporary philosophers are not universally agreed, but many would accept the view that to say, "*X* is pleasurable" means "*X* is an experience that one would rather have than not have, apart from any considerations as to its morality or possible consequences." Similarly, to say, "*X* is more pleasurable than *Y*" does not mean "the sensations of pleasure accompanying *X* are greater than those accompanying *Y*," but rather, "One would prefer *X* over *Y* if one were asked to choose between them without regard to consequences or moral considerations." If we accept this general conception of the meaning of "pleasure," we can easily understand why a person who says, "I find *X* pleasurable but see no reason to do it," seems to be talking nonsense, and we can see, too, why we often discover what things really give us pleasure only when we compare our preferences for different things. Consider, for example, the following analysis of the concept of pleasure that is found in Gilbert Ryle's (1900–76) *The Concept of Mind:*

> The words "pleasure" and "desire" play a large role in the terminology of moral philosophers and of some schools of psychology. It is important briefly to indicate some of the differences between the supposed logic of their use and its actual logic.
>
> First, it seems to be generally supposed that "pleasure" and "desire" are always used to signify feelings. And there certainly are feelings which can be described as feelings of pleasure and desire....
>
> ...But there is another sense in which we say that a person who is so absorbed in some activity, such as golf or argument, that he is reluctant to stop, or even to think of anything else, is "taking pleasure in" or "enjoying" doing what he is doing, though he is in no degree convulsed or beside himself, and though he is not, therefore, experiencing any particular feelings.
>
> Doubtless the absorbed golfer experiences numerous flutters and glows of rapture, excitement, and self-approbation in the course of his game. But when asked whether or not he had enjoyed the periods of the game between the occurrences of such feelings, he would obviously reply that he had, for he had enjoyed the whole game. He would at no moment of it have welcomed an interruption: he was never inclined to turn his thoughts or conversation from the circumstances of the game to other matters....
>
> In this sense, to enjoy doing something, to want to do it and not to want to do anything else are different ways of phrasing the same thing.

The essential point Ryle is making here is that when we say that we are getting pleasure from something, we usually mean not that we are dong that thing and experiencing something else, but that we are doing it "wanting to do it and not wanting to stop." Since we may want to do things as a means to other things or on the basis of a sense of moral obligation, and since we may be willing to stop engaging in some pleasurable activity out of a sense of moral obligation or because an even more pleasurable activity can be pursued, the initial definition of "pleasure" provided is a better one. So let us assume now that "*X* is pleasurable to *A*" means

"*X* is an experience that *A* would rather have than not have, apart from any considerations as to its morality or possible consequences." This would seem to be just another way of saying "*X* is an experience that *A* would desire to prolong for its own sake." But if this definition is accepted, the hedonistic view that "pleasure alone is intrinsically good" would reduce to the view that "something is intrinsically desirable to a person only if it is an experience that that person would want to prolong for its own sake." Such a definition invites the Marxist challenge that hedonism is a "trivial commonplace." Since not all philosophers have identified intrinsic good with states of consciousness, hedonism is informative, even though many would consider it beyond question that the only things human beings ought to seek are states of consciousness that can be experienced as satisfactory.

The actual desires and preferences of human beings are the province of the science of psychology. The scientific study of psychological phenomena can also provide insight into the causal connections among our desires, providing us with knowledge of the coherence of our desires and their capability of providing long-range satisfaction. This is very important, for as the philosopher Morris R. Cohen (1880–1947) rightly observed:

> One of the obvious facts of human nature is that our unhappiness comes not only from the fact that we cannot have what we want, but very often we are most miserable because we succeed in getting what we thought we wanted. Wisdom, therefore, consists in surveying our various conflicting desires with a view to the attainment of a harmony, or a maximum happiness. A man may prefer a short but a merry life. Another may prefer suicide. But, if we regard our life as a continuing one, that is, if we have some regard for our own personality, we must integrate all of our desires into one coherent system, so that we can attain self-respect. Just as all of our judgments of perception of nature can be integrated by physical science into a view of the world, so may our judgments of preference be integrated with them into a view of the most desirable mode of life.

While psychologists today differ in their conceptions of the exact interrelationships of our desires, there is general acceptance of the Platonic view that the only satisfactory type of life is a mixed one devoted to the pursuit of a plurality of things which are intrinsically valuable. Furthermore, there is general consensus that the realization of one value is often achieved only at the price of another. Psychologists can help us to realize the price we must pay for a way of life, but ultimately each of us must choose for ourselves whether the price is one we are willing to pay. There is no way of life that has no cost and no single right price to pay. There is no reason to believe that rationality demands that all people choose the same way; what it does demand is that we know what we are choosing. When we attempt, as hedonists do, to reduce all desires to the common denominator of pleasure we run the risk of deceiving ourselves, through a linguistic trick, into believing that human desires are more unified than they really are.

DISCUSSION QUESTIONS

1. According to G. E. Moore, an undesirable consequence of Bentham's hedonism is that:

   ...The state of mind of a drunkard, when he is intensely pleased with breaking crockery, is just as valuable in itself—just as well worth having, as that of a man who is fully realizing all that is exquisite in the tragedy of *King Lear,* provided only that the mere quantity of pleasure in both cases is the same.

   How would a defender of Bentham reply? What do you think of this reply?

2. The philosopher Bertrand Russell was once asked whether criminals sentenced to life imprisonment (without chance of parole) should be sent to the South Sea Islands instead, if they could be equally as well removed from society that way. Russell claimed that this would be fine as long as the South Sea Islanders' security was not endangered and it was kept secret. (If it weren't kept secret, such treatment would not serve as a deterrent to would-be criminals.) Do you agree with Russell that convicted criminals should be allowed to experience as much pleasure as possible as long as no hedonistic utilitarian purpose can be served by making them suffer pain? Do you accept the hedonistic view that the experience of pleasure is always in itself good?

3. In Mark Twain's *The Mysterious Stranger,* an angel promises an unhappy old man that he will make him happy. He accomplishes this by making the old man insane. Deluded into thinking that he is very rich, the old man takes great joy in giving away things that he doesn't possess to his friends and relatives. Wouldn't a hedonist have to claim that this old man is better off insane than sane? Do you agree? Why? If you disagree, do you think a person can ever be said to be better off if, after taking a drug, he finds himself much happier than he was before, although not as intellectually capable?

4. Assuming that a community of sadomasochists would maximize their pleasure (in the long run) by indulging their sadomasochistic desires, without this having any adverse effect upon individuals outside of their community, a hedonist would be committed to the view that the good life for them is one in which they satisfy these desires. Do you agree? If not, why not? (Do not claim that they could not "really" be happy or that they would be happier if they did not possess their sadomasochistic desires, for we are to accept as a premise of this case that this is simply not so. If you refuse to make this assumption about human beings, imagine it to be true of creatures from some strange world.)

5. Aldous Huxley depicts a society committed to the hedonistic ideal in his novel *Brave New World.* In this society, people are immunized from all diseases and are genetically engineered and behaviorally conditioned so that they quite naturally do as they ought to do. The euphoric drug *soma* is used to combat any depression in life and to create the most pleasurable of sensations. The merits of Huxley's imagined society are debated within the novel by the "Controller," Mustapha Mond, who directs the society and a "Savage" who

has not yet been "civilized." Consider the following excerpt from this dialogue:

The Savage nodded. . . "Yes, that's just like you. Getting rid of everything unpleasant instead of learning to put up with it. Whether 'tis better in the mind to suffer the slings and arrows of outrageous fortune, or to take arms against a sea of troubles and by opposing end them. . . . But you don't do either. Neither suffer nor oppose. You just abolish the slings and arrows. It's too easy. . . . Isn't there something in living dangerously?"

"There's a great deal in it," the Controller replied. "Men and women must have their adrenals stimulated from time to time. . . . It's one of the conditions of perfect health. That's why we've made the V.P.S. treatments compulsory."

"V.P.S.?"

"Violent Passion Surrogate. Regularly once a month. We flood the whole system with adrenin. It's the complete physiological equivalent of fear and rage. . . without any of the inconveniences."

"But I like the inconveniences.". . . .

"In fact," said Mustapha Mond, "you're claiming the right to be unhappy. . . . Not to mention the right to grow old and ugly and impotent; the right to have syphilis and cancer; the right to have too little to eat. . . the right to live in constant apprehension of what may happen tomorrow. . . the right to be tortured by unspeakable pains of every kind."

There was a long silence.

"I claim them all," said the Savage at last.

Mustapha Mond shrugged his shoulders. "You're welcome," he said.

Do you agree with the Savage that there is something seriously lacking in Huxley's imagined society? If so, what is it?

6. It is now possible to implant electrodes in a region of the brain (the septal region) which can be electrically stimulated to cause very pleasurable sensations. One can consequently imagine a "Brave New World" of the future where individuals spend their leisure time stimulating their implanted electrodes, and thoroughly enjoying themselves. Let us take this a step further and imagine a "dream machine" to which people can connect themselves to create the most vivid and coherent of dreams. While one is connected to this machine, one's experiences appear as real as they do when one is awake. There is no sensory, physical, or psychological experience that the dream machine is incapable of reproducing. Furthermore, it is possible to individually program the dream machine to cater to the differing psychological needs of people. Now, let us imagine someone who is dissatisfied with his experience of the real world and decides to opt out by having himself connected to the dream machine for the remainder of his life. (Let us assume that he can be kept physically healthy this way—that is, he will be fed intravenously, his body wastes removed, etc.—and that the efficient society of the future has no need for his labor.) What do you think of the desirability of such a life? What, if anything, is missing from it?

FURTHER READINGS

Bentham's version of hedonistic utilitarianism is found in chapters 4 and 5 of his *An Introduction to the Principles of Morals and Legislation* (Hafner), and Mill's account in chapters 2 and 4 of his much more readable *Utilitarianism* (Bobbs-Merrill). J.J.C. Smart, the foremost contemporary defender of the utilitarian view that the rightness of an action depends solely on its consequences, presents his hedonistic view in section 3 of his essay "An Outline of a System of Utilitarian Ethics" in *Uilitarianism: For and Against* (Cambridge University Press), coauthored by Bernard Williams.

In chapter VII of his *Principia Ethica* (Cambridge University Press), the influential twentieth century utilitarian, G. E. Moore rejects hedonism and with it the view that there is only one intrinsic good. In his article "Pleasure" which appears in *The Encyclopedia of Philosophy,* William Alston critically discusses different analyses of the concept. Gilbert Ryle's behavioristic analysis of the concept of pleasure is found in chapter IV, section 6, of his influential *The Concept of Mind* (Harper & Row, 1949). It would be worthwhile also to read the first chapter for background. In this chapter, Ryle expresses his central thesis that most mental terms do not refer to mental events that occur in immaterial things called minds. In later chapters, Ryle defends his view that most mental terms including those relating to knowledge and emotion refer, instead, to behavioral dispositions.

Aldous Huxley presents an unsympathetic literary portrayal of a futuristic society dedicated to the hedonistic ideal in his classic *Brave New World* (Harper & Row, 1949).

In chapter 6 of his *Reasons for Living* (Macmillan, 1988), Burton F. Porter discusses various interpretations of the goal of self-realization and its relationship to hedonism. Porter includes quotations from the writings of the twentieth-century self-realizationist psychologists Abraham Maslow and Carl Rogers. He then turns to the Hegelian idealistic notion of self-realization which was embraced by the British philosopher F. H. Bradley (1846–1924). He includes a long quotation from Bradley's *Ethical Studies* which he then evaluates. Porter next turns to an evaluation of a long passage from Aristotle that focuses on the goal of self-realization.

Chapter 2 of John Hosper's introductory ethics text *Human Conduct,* second edition (Harcourt Brace Jovanovich, 1982) provides an engaging discussion of hedonism and pluralistic theories of intrinsic good that would be helpful to beginning students.

The quotation from J. S. Mill appears on p. 12 of the Bobbs-Merrill edition of *Utilitarianism.* The quotation from Karl Marx appears on p. 671 of Volume III of *Capital,* translated by F. Engels (Kerr, 1909). The quotation from Morris R. Cohen appears on p. 170 of *A Preface to Logic* (Holt, Rinehart and Winston, 1944). The quotation from G. E. Moore appears on p. 147 of *Principia Ethica.* The quotation from Aldous Huxley appears on pp. 286–88 of *Brave New World* (Harper & Row, 1932) and is quoted with the permission of the publisher.

8. NATURAL LAW

As Marx claimed in his criticism of hedonism, views of the good life presuppose views of human nature. At the very least, one's view of human nature sets limits on one's conception of moral obligation. Can a complete account of moral obligation be derived from an understanding of human nature? According to one school of normative ethical theory, called *natural law theory,* the answer is yes. As is the case with ethical theories that have deep historical roots, there is no single unequivocal meaning of the concept of natural law. Again, its roots go back to classic Greek philosophy. For example, in Plato's *Republic* "justice" is defined as "conforming to nature." The identification of morality with nature continued and was refined by Aristotle. Aristotle's view, in turn, was incorporated into the medieval theological viewpoint of St. Thomas Aquinas and today forms the cornerstone of Roman Catholic moral theory. It also played a prominent role in Roman law when Roman jurists sought legal concepts that they could apply throughout the vast Roman empire, with its diversity of specific moral and legal practices. Looking for common features that underlied the apparent diversity of moral and legal customs, Roman jurists sought to find a common human nature and values that all human beings share.

Historically, the concept of natural law developed in conjunction with the growing human awareness of the regularity of natural phenomena. The quest for order in the external phenomena of nature led the Greek philosophers to a general belief that all phenomena, including moral ones, are rationally ordered. Disagreeing with those who proclaimed that all morality is convention, Plato and Aristotle claimed that there is an objective moral truth, discernable to human reason, that can be used to criticize transitory and culturally instilled values. The facts of human nature, they believed, determine the basic prescriptive laws which are binding on *all* human beings, irrespective of cultural heritage. It is a common human nature that causes people to naturally pursue certain goals, such as procreation and the preservation of life, that reflect basic human *functions*. These natural functions are good, while interfering with them is unnatural and bad. Consequently, a corollary of natural law theory was the view that individuals have *natural rights* which take precedence over the demands of any social order. If a social order violates these basic human rights, and by so doing *violates the dignity of man,* it forfeits its right to obedience. This notion of natural rights played a pivotal role in the political philosophy of John Locke (1632–1704) and in the American Declaration of Independence (1776) and French Declaration of Rights of Man (1789). As the Declaration of Independence put it:

> We hold these truths to be self-evident, that all men are created equal, that they are endowed by their Creator with certain unalienable Rights, that among these are Life, Liberty, and the pursuit of Happiness.

The Declaration of the Rights of Man echoes similar sentiments when it proclaims:

> The aim of every political association is the consecration of the natural and inalienable rights of man. These rights are freedom, property, security, and the right of resistance to oppression.

Aristotle's Teleological Perspective

Aristotle's view of morality followed from his general metaphysical emphasis upon purpose and function. Unlike contemporary science which seeks explanations for natural phenomena in prior causes, Aristotle sought explanations in the purposes or goals of objects. In Aristotle's view, there was an order of increasing comprehensiveness in the goals and corresponding functions of natural objects, including living creatures. The function of plants, for example, was growth and reproduction. These functions were shared by (nonhuman) animals, who also shared the functions of locomotion and sensation. Human beings also had these functions, but their distinctive function was their capacity for reason. The goal of each thing, including living creatures, was to act in accordance with its distinctive function. Consequently, the goal of human beings, according to Aristotle, was "a life concerned with action, belonging to the rational part of life." Yet, Aristotle did not neglect the reality of human emotional and physical needs. As he saw it, human happiness requires health, friendship, financial security, and other material goods. Aristotle's acceptance of the necessity of material goods was rejected by the *Stoics*, a school of ethical thinking that began in ancient Greece and flourished during the waning days of the Roman Empire. Unlike Aristotle, the Stoics downplayed the biological and emotional nature that human beings shared with animals and the importance of material goods. Human dignity, from the Stoic perspective, came not from success in the world, but from the ability to develop a mental fortitude that could withstand the vicissitudes of an uncertain world. With their denial of worldly concerns, the Stoics, unlike Aristotle, downplayed the need of socialization into a particular cultural milieu. Instead they presented a cosmopolitan view of the universal fellowship of man. This Stoic ideal, along with the Stoic insistence that the distinctive *dignity* of human beings derived from their *freedom* to cultivate their minds and free them from worldly concerns, had a great influence on St. Thomas Aquinas who attempted to unify Christian theology with the Aristotelian and Stoic concepts of natural law.

Thomistic Natural Law

Like Aristotle, Aquinas accepted a *teleological* world-view, seeing objects as regularly moving toward certain natural ends which were taken as the ultimate standard of goodness—i.e., what regularly occurs was seen as what ought to occur. Again, like Aristotle, Aquinas saw the moral life as a life lived "according to reason." Aquinas, however, anchored these notions to his Christian belief in God as a supreme law-giver. According to the Thomistic world-view, the universe was governed by eternal natural laws which are a reflection of divine reason. These eternal laws included the *purely descriptive* laws that governed the regular and inevitable behavior of all objects and make knowledge of the world possible (e.g., the daily rising of the sun, the melting of water at a particular temperature). Such regularities would, with the advent of the Scientific Revolution, be given a precise mathematical formulation. But, as Aquinas saw it, along with the descriptive laws of nature that report unbroken regularities, God also ordained laws of behavior directed exlusively at human beings who had the free choice either to obey or disobey them. Such natural laws governing proper behavior were not, however, alien constraints that God imposed upon us, for he so constructed our natures that we would naturally find fulfillment only through the pursuit of these laws. Consequently, as rational creatures we would want to obey these laws for our own fulfillment, apart from a sense of obligation to God. Utilizing the reason given to us by God, human beings can distinguish the natural and proper ends of human behavior from their unnatural and improper counterparts. The basic moral obligations revealed to reason were necessary for the realization of the fundamental human values of life, health, procreation, knowledge, and sociability. Like Kant, who would later concur, Aquinas placed a greater stringency on *negative* duties not to violate natural human values than on *positive* duties to promote them. For example, according to Thomistic moral theory, we have an obligation not to interfere with procreation, but we do not have a duty to procreate.

Also, according to Thomistic moral theory, the basic values of natural law are incommensurable and consequently cannot be compared on a common scale; that is one value cannot be traded off for another. This, as we have seen, is a fundamental difference between natural law theory and utilitarianism. Natural law theory also differs in a fundamental way from utilitarianism in its emphasis upon the motives of an action. While utilitarians distinguish the rightness of an action from the motives behind that action which are reflective of the moral character of a person, natural law theory (like Kantian ethics, which we shall later discuss) considers the motives of an action in determining the rightness of an act. According to natural law theory, an act is always wrong if a person *intends* to violate a basic prohibition of natural law.

If it is always wrong to violate a basic prohibition of natural law—such as the sanctity of life—what are we to do when basic values conflict? For example, what are we to do when in order to preserve our own lives we are forced to resort to lethal force that will kill someone else? Natural law theorists have introduced two principles that qualify their insistance on the absoluteness of the values they claim derive from the dictates of natural law—the principle of *forfeiture* and the principle of the *double effect*. For example, according to the principle of forfeiture, while it is never right to intentionally kill an innocent person, regardless of the consequences, it is permissible to use lethal force against an aggressor who through a voluntary action of his own has forfeited his right to life, if such force must be taken to prevent his aggression. Similarly, natural law theorists utilize the principle of forfeiture as a justification for capital punishment.

The principle of double effect serves to clarify and soften the Thomistic injunction that "evil is not to be done that good may come of it" (i.e., good consequences cannot justify the violation of a basic human value). According to this principle, it is morally permissible to perform an action that has two effects, one good and the other bad if:

1. The bad effect is unavoidable if the good effect is to be achieved.
2. The intent of the action is to obtain the good result and not the bad result.
3. The bad result is not a means to the good result.
4. The good result is proportionate to the bad result.
   (Thus, consequentialist considerations are relevant to Thomistic natural law theory. Nevertheless, they are relevant only when the prior three conditions are met.)

Underlying this principle is the common distinction we make between what we intend to do and what we know will happen as a result of what we do, *without directly intending it*—i.e., what happens as a *by-product* of our actions. In Thomistic moral thinking, the latter is described as the indirect intentions of one's actions. The distinction between direct and indirect intention plays a central role in Roman Catholic thinking about abortion, euthanasia, and the morality of war. Consider, for example, the issue of abortion. According to Roman Catholic doctrine, it is always wrong to directly intend the death of a fetus, but it is permissible to perform a medical procedure (for example, the removal of a three-month pregnant woman's cancerous uterus) which one knows will result in the fetus' death, as long as one is acting to save the mother's life and not to kill the fetus. If one defines an abortion as the voluntary act which results in the death of a fetus, then according to traditional Roman Catholic morality, it is always wrong to perform direct abortions—i.e., ones in which the death of a fetus is either intended as an end in itself or as a means to some other end. But it is permissible to allow indirect abortions—i.e., ones in which the death of the fetus, while foreseen, is neither one's purpose nor a means to one's purpose.

The doctrine of the double effect is frought with many conceptual difficulties. Consider again the issue of abortion. According to Catholic moralists who employ the doctrine of the double effect, it would be wrong for a doctor to perform a craniotomy in which the skull of the fetus in the process of being born is crushed in order to save the life of its mother—a direct abortion. It is a direct abortion, it is claimed, because the death of the fetus is a means to the desired end of saving the mother. But, it has been suggested by critics that this case can be redescribed so as to make it an indirect abortion. What is wanted as a means, it may be said, is not the death of the fetus, but the removal of an obstruction. The death of the fetus is a foreseen but unwanted by-product. A Catholic moralist will reject this description as improper. Since the removal of the obstruction in this case *is* the crushing of a human skull, it is absurd to claim that what is directly desired as a means is the crushing of a skull, not the death of a person, it will be said. But why cannot one say equally as well in the case of the cancerous uterus that it is absurd to claim that what is directly desired as a means is the removal of a cancerous uterus, but not the death of the fetus enclosed within it, when its death is as medically certain in this case as in the former? Cannot one plausibly say that in this case the *means* to the good result of saving the mother's life *involves* the death of a fetus? Intuitively, the difference in these two cases resides in the greater ease with which we can conceptually separate the death of the fetus from the removal of the uterus than from the crushing of the fetus' skill. But exactly how is this distinction to be understood? While there is a much greater possibility that medical technology will one day devise a technique for removing a very young fetus from its mother's womb and keeping it alive in an artificial incubator, it is at least *logically possible* and *consistent with the laws of nature* to imagine a fetus surviving the crushing of its skull and its later reconstruction through greatly advanced medical technology. How then can we justify the description of the craniotomy as one of directly causing the death of a fetus and the removal of the cancerous uterus as indirectly causing it? Unfortunately, it is not at all clear how proper descriptions of acts are to be distinguished from improper ones—a distinction that is essential in applying the doctrine of the double effect. The fact that acts can be described in more than one way poses a serious difficulty for applications of the principle of the double effect.

Furthermore, even if the distinction between direct and indirect intention can be made sufficiently clear, so that it can, in most cases, be unambiguously applied, the notion of proportionality is also frought with difficulties. For example, Aquinas claimed that wars to repel aggression are justified if the means employed to wage the war are proportionate to the ends to be achieved. Yet, the notion of proportionality in debates over the morality of war has proved to be a very flexible one that has been used to justify and condemn the same actions.

Critical Comments

The strength of natural law theory lies in its claim that an understanding of human nature limits the content that any morality must have if it is to function as an adequate guide to human flourishing. The problem, however, is that a complete account of morality cannot be derived from an understanding of human nature alone. In practice the specific directives that are supposed to follow in some objective way from a knowledge of natural law incorporate subjective moral preferences which tend to be conservative in reflecting moral tradition. This is the case with current official Roman Catholic moral teaching. Evidence of this can be found when one reads dissenting contemporary Catholic moralists like Father Charles E. Curran, who argue from the natural law standpoint for a liberalization of rigid Catholic moral teachings. For example, Father Curran claims that the Church should not see the primary function of sex as a purely biological procreative act, but should take as equally primary the capacity of the sex act to be an expression of love. Such a point of view allows Father Curran to dissent from the Roman Catholic view that homosexuality per se is wrong, for homosexuals, no less than heterosexuals, can express love through a sex act. The debate between liberal Catholic moralists like Father Curran and the conservative Roman Catholic leadership cannot be settled by a study of human nature alone. Our view of human nature, as Marx saw, is socially conditioned. One needs a standard to distinguish proper from improper human functioning. It would appear that unless one turns to a god who designed us for a purpose and accepts the divine command theory, this distinction has no meaning. While we are never totally free of biological and social programming in choosing what we want to be, we are at least partially free to do so.

In addition, natural law theory has rightly been criticized as too rigidly absolutist. How many of us would be willing to say—in the context, let us assume, of a war—that it is never right to directly intend the death of an innocent person even if that is necessary to save thousands of other innocent people? Similarly, how many of us would say that it is never right to perform a direct abortion in order to save the mother when both will die if the abortion is not performed? Yet both positions are official Roman Catholic doctrine, allegedly derived from natural law. Of course, a Roman Catholic moralist can claim that even though a majority of people would strongly reject some of their conclusions, they are nevertheless right. But when a moral theory deviates too far from commonly accepted moral beliefs, one seeks very strong reasons to accept the theory and dismiss as mistaken one's prior moral beliefs—strong reasons that cannot be given in contemporary Roman Catholic applications of natural law theory. Indeed, while the doctrine of the double effect is supposed to serve to soften the absolutist and rigid prohibitions of the dictates of natural law, it is not at all clear that this doctrine does the job well. As we have seen, the manner in which the doctrine of the double effect is to be applied in specific cases is often unclear. In addition, while natural law theory's emphasis upon the intentions of actions captures an important element of everyday moral thinking, it is highly questionable whether it captures that element in the right way. As our discussions of contemporary moral issues will make clear, there are diverse specific moral principles relating to intention utilized in our moral reasoning that cannot be captured in a single underlying moral principle.

DISCUSSION QUESTIONS

1. What does the Declaration of Independence mean when it asserts that all human beings have certain *unalienable* rights?
2. According to the doctrine of the double effect, was it right to use the dynamite on the fat man stuck in the mouth of the cave (see p. 6) Do you agree with this mode of reasoning?

FURTHER READINGS

Excellent analytic and historical surveys of the natural law tradition in ethics can be found under the entries of "Natural Law" and "Nature" in both *The Encyclopedia of Philosophy* and *The Dictionary of the History of Ideas.* Extensive bibliographies are included.

Artistotle's natural law perspective is found in his *Nichomachean Ethics,* Aquinas' in his *Summa Theologica,* and Locke's in his *Second Treatise of Government.* There are several editions of these works. Lucid criticisms of the natural law tradition are found in John Stuart Mill's essay "Nature" included in his *Three Essays On Religion* (1874) and in chapter 9 of H.L.A. Hart's *The Concept of Law* (Oxford University Press, 1961).

The first chapter of Michael D. Bayles and Kenneth Henley (eds.) *Right Conduct,* second edition (Random House, 1989), has selections on natural law, including excerpts from Aquinas and Locke.

9. THE UTILITARIAN THEORY

Like natural law theory, the roots of utilitarianism can be traced back to ancient Greek philosophy. Nevertheless, the term "utilitarianism" is used today to refer to the specific systematic ethical theory of Jeremy Bentham who was the first to coin this term and to the later refinements of his theory at the hands of his many disciples, in particular, John Stuart Mill. Although Bentham was primarily a moral reformer bent on criticizing and changing the existing legal and social institutions of the England of his day, he also believed, as did many of his disciples, that the utilitarian perspective was implicit in the generally accepted moral common sense or intuitions of the average person insofar as this common sense or intuition was justifiable. Seeing his utilitarian theory as the *only* defensible moral theory, it was

Bentham's belief that those who accepted moral beliefs inconsistent with his utilitarian theory would under more careful analysis renounce these beliefs as either unintelligible or unjustified and come to accept the utilitarian theory as the ultimate theoretical underpinning of their own moral reasoning.

Bentham's Criticism of Intuitionism in Ethics

Trained as a lawyer at Oxford under the tutelage of the famous legal theorist and constitutional scholar Sir William Blackstone, Bentham found himself dissatisfied with both the pratical operations of the law of his day and its theoretical justification by Blackstone and others, a justification which Bentham saw as no more than elaborate and ultimately indefensible rationalizations for the status quo. The prevalent legal theory of his day was that the ultimate standards for the moral appraisal of law were certain clearly recognizable natural laws engrained upon the consciences of mankind by God. In order to discover whether a given act was right or wrong, a person was not supposed to inquire as to its effects, but rather to consult the inner moral light of conscience whose pronouncements were seen as self-evident. It was this aspect of the ethical philosophy of his predecessor John Locke, the philosophical force behind the American Declaration of Independence, that Bentham scorned. Locke's notion of self-evident natural rights Bentham dismissed as nothing but "nonsense on stilts." When Locke and other moral and legal philosophers turned to intuited moral rules and principles, they inevitably, Bentham believed, turned to their own learned, and often irrational, moral feelings.

Similarly, when legislators felt greatly revolted by certain actions, they would punish them heavily, even when these actions caused little or no suffering to anyone (such as certain sexual offenses). On the other hand, if legislators did not have strong feelings of repugnance toward actions, they were either left unpunished or punished lightly, regardless of their capacity to cause human suffering (such as certain business practices). But the legislator, faithful to the obscure philosophy of his day, would not admit that the ultimate source of his moral sentiments were certain visceral feelings and would instead describe these feelings in a way which made them unjustifiably appear to have some objective basis. (For instance, it was not said that homosexuality should be condemned because most people felt revolted by the practice, but that it should be condemned since "the clear light of moral conscience reveals the self-evident unnaturalness of homosexuality.") The moral intuitionism of philosophers such as Locke seemed to be nothing more than an appeal to sentiment—or as Bentham called it, to "the principle of sympathy and antipathy"—which by some verbal magic exalted prejudices into seeming eternal and immutable principles. Bentham wanted to do away with such rationalization. It must be recognized, he argued, that the sole aim of morality and law is to maximize human happiness, not to intuit certain unchangeable moral laws that stigmatize actions as bad in themselves, without regard to their consequences.

It was not only the criminal law that Bentham saw infected with this error in moral theory; the civil law was equally a victim, for the generally accepted pronouncement of conscience was that one's moral obligations, such as the obligation to keep one's promises, were absolutely binding. For example, since a contract is a legally enforceable promise, the view was that contracts, once made, should always be kept. Occasionally, however, those who enforced the law were unwilling to enforce a contract that clearly seemed to go against the public interest, but instead of admitting that contracts were not absolutely binding but subordinate to the general public interest, it would be said that the contract was null and void—that there never was a valid contract. In other words, the facts would be distorted to save a mistaken moral theory.

The Universalistic Element
of Bentham's Utilitarianism

As well as criticizing the legal theorists of his day for unjustifiably elevating the status quo into immutable dictates of reason, Bentham criticized them for blinding themselves to the widespread exploitation of the new and burgeoning class of city workers that resulted from the Industrial Revolution. Torn from the security of the English countryside and herded into factories, this new class found itself exposed to inhumanly long days, and grueling working conditions for a pay scarcely adequate to maintain a bare subsistence. Sheltered from the cruelty of this sort of life, legal theorists spoke complacently of the natural and inalienable rights of property of the privileged class, blinding themselves to the legalized inequalities and exploitation that the exercise of these rights entailed. As Bentham saw it, some kind of universal principle of moral criticism was needed that could cut through the partiality of the status quo and the abstract talk of natural rights that supplied its moral rationale. This principle Bentham saw as that of "the greatest happiness for the greatest number"—or, as he also called it, "the principle of utility." This principle had, he thought, two great virtues. First, it was a universalistic one that referred equally to all human beings and not just to some. As such, it could be utilized as a principle for criticism of the partiality of the status quo. As he passionately wrote:

> Government has, under every form comprehending laws and institutions, had for its object the greatest happiness not of those over whom, but of those by whom, it has been exercised; the interest not of the many, but of the few, or even of the one, has been the prevalent interest; and to that interest all others have been at all times sacrificed. To these few, or to this one, depredation has everywhere been the grand object.

Second, equating morality with the maximization of happiness which Bentham saw as a determinable "real entity" capable of scientific measure, afforded morality the objective status that the purely subjective intuitionistic view lacked.

The Attack on Fictitious Entities

Armed with the principle of utility, Bentham attempted to cut through the obscure ethical and legal theory of his day and the undefined abstract terms in which it was formulated. When theorists spoke of the existence of obligations and rights as if these words referred to specific *things* that people had or did not have, Bentham rejected such talk which he dismissed as a belief in "fictitious entities." If abstract moral terms are meaningful, they must, he believed, be translated into concrete terms that have some real reference. As Bentham saw it, the abstract notion of an individual's obligations to behave in particular ways must, in order to be made meaningful, be translated into talk about the concrete feelings of pleasure and pain. As Bentham put it "An obligation...is incumbent on a man...insofar as, in the event of his failing to conduct himself in that manner, pain, or loss of pleasure, is considered as about to be experienced by him." Consequently, for Bentham, the notion of an obligation was to be defined in terms of the notion of a sanction— that is, on the pain or loss of pleasure that normally resulted from its neglect. Legal and moral obligations, as he saw it, differed only in the types of sanctions they involved. If the sanction was a physical, political or economic one that officials of government are able and disposed to inflict, the obligation was a legal one. If the pain was the loss of others' or one's esteem, the obligation was a moral one. (Such a view of legal obligation was later developed by John Austin, the famous legal theorist and disciple of Bentham.)

Similarly, as Bentham saw it, when we say that an individual has a political or moral right, we are speaking of "a general disposition, on the part of those by whom the powers of government are exercised, to cause him to possess...the benefit to which he has a right." Since no such disposition to confer benefits exists in the case of alleged natural rights, this notion has no definite sense, Bentham declared. (Notice that a religious moralist can claim that such a disposition exists in God. Indeed, Locke, himself, believed that natural rights were derived from God.) The most that one can be taken to mean by asserting that someone has a natural right to something, Bentham wrote, is that "I am of the opinion that he ought to have a political right to it; that...he ought to be protected and secured in the use of it"; in other words, that "the ideas of his being so is pleasing to me, and the idea of the opposite result displeasing."

Bentham's Utilitarian Perspective

With this criticism as a backdrop, Bentham developed his hedonistic utilitarian theory. The goal of life, as he saw it, was to create as much human happiness as possible. Those religious moralists who condemned the gratification of certain desires as inherently evil were mistaken. A human desire should only be condemned when it comes into conflict with other desires which promise to create greater human happiness in the long run. Morality should not be perceived as a conflict between inclination and an abstract duty having nothing to do with human happiness, but rather as an attempt to arbitrate between conflicting inclinations so as to maximize happiness. Either in a situation of individual moral choice or in the legislative task of deciding between conflicting laws, the right act or law to choose was that which among all the alternatives produced the greatest happiness for the greatest number. Perhaps in overreaction to what he saw as the unscientific method of his intuitionistic opponents, Bentham assumed that the concepts of happiness (pleasure) and unhappiness (pain) could be measured and compared in quantitative terms. For each alternative, one would add up the sum of pleasure that would likely be experienced and subtract from it the amount of likely pain, choosing that alternative with the greatest net sum. From such a perspective, Bentham envisioned moral reasoning as a type of "moral arithmetic" or "moral accounting." In this type of moral arithmetic, all individuals would be treated equally, no indiviudal's pleasure or pain counting more heavily than another's. In addition, since for Bentham the rightness of an act depends on its never fully foreseeable consequences, moral judgment is always subject to correction as new and unforeseeable consequences come into focus. Given the possibility of unforseeable consequences and the difficulty of estimating the probability of foreseeable ones, even the most widely made moral judgments are subject to error. This is the inevitable price one must pay for the finiteness of human foresight.

Since in the utilitarian view the rightness of an action depends solely on its consequences, it followed, Bentham believed, that there could be no absolute exceptionless moral rules other than the principle of utility. It seemed clear to Bentham that in certain circumstances the consequences of lying, breaking promises, stealing, and even killing the innocent, might be more desirable than refraining from these actions. Consequently, conventional moral rules, such as "never lie," "never break promises," "never steal," and "never kill the innocent" had exceptions. Bentham did not, however, totally reject these rules of conventional morality. Many of them, he argued, were useful rules of thumb which served in most cases to maximize human happiness. Given the difficulty of foreseeing possible consequences, one has need for moral guides other than the principle of utility. The rules of conventional morality often provide these guides. Furthermore, they provide a background of stability which enables us to better anticipate the actions of others and to plan our own actions accordingly. Nevertheless, Bentham believed, these rules should not be used blindly. Given important choices or a conflict in the conventional rules themselves, one should always resort to the principle of utility itself in deciding what to do.

In deciding whether a conventional moral rule should be violated, it was essential, Bentham claimed, to consider the long-range consequences of such a violation. Quite often, even though the short-range consequences of breaking a rule may be advantageous, its long-range consequences may be undesirable. For example, even though in the short run, a refusal to keep a promise to repay a debt of money to a wealthy friend may have a utilitarian justification if this money is used instead to help a more needy person, this may not be so in the long run. Among the long-range consequences, are the effects of one's actions on people's confidence in one's reliability and on the general practice of promise-keeping which serves the general interest. The short-range beneficial consequences to be gained in a particular instance of breaking a promise may be more than offset by such undesirable long-range effects.

Criticisms and Modifications
of Bentham's Utilitarianism

Bentham's utilitarian theory has been subjected to much criticism both by those fundamentally opposed to it as well as by those sympathetic to its main tenets who sought to refine it. Let us briefly consider some of these criticisms.

The Truth of the Principle of Utility

Although Bentham saw the principle of utility as a *true* principle and not a mere statement of his own personal commitment, it is not clear how it can be known that our sole basic moral obligation is to maximize human happiness. In one of his writings, Bentham is willing to concede that he cannot prove the principle of utility to be correct since "it is used to prove everything else and a chain of proofs must have their commencement somewhere." At this point, it is open to a utilitarian to say, as the early twentieth century utilitarian Henry Sidgwick said, that this principle is known by intuition or is self-evident. This view, however, was not open to Bentham who saw such notions as rationalizations for one's prejudices.

Bentham and Mill attempted in some of their writings to anchor the principle of utility to the doctrine of psychological egoism which asserts that the pursuit of individual pleasure is, as a matter of fact, the *sole* human motive. (We shall discuss the adequacy of this theory in section 17.) According to this theory of motivaiton, people seek only to maximize their own pleasure. From this pesrspective, one is concerned about the pleasures of others only insofar as they are seen *as means* to the satisfaction of one's own pleasure. But individuals do not always, as a matter of fact, feel concern or sympathy for others or see the pleasure of others as means to their own pleasure. Indeed, both Bentham and Mill stress the need to *induce* people (especially children) through sanctions to develop such feelings and to associate the pleasure of others with their own pleasure. Consequently, they both seem to admit that there is no guarantee that self-interest would naturally lead one inevitably to a concern for the interests of others or more specifically to consider all human beings equally, whether they be oneself, one's family, or total strangers. Indeed, even if one could be conditioned to feel this way, some have questioned its desirability. Consequently, there is a fundamental logical gap between the doctrine of psychological egoism and the principle of utility. This gap is not explicitly bridged by Bentham who never explains the source of our ultimate moral obligaiton to maximize human happiness, especially when this obligation seems to conflict with our own interests. While Bentham does not make this claim himself, perhaps implicit in his thinking is the assumption made by his contemporary, the philosopher and economist, Adam Smith, that in the nature of things, the purely self-seeking pursuit of pleasure will tend in the long run to coincide with the general interest. According to Adam Smith's classical laissez-faire theory of economics, a situation of unfettered economic competition, where each producer attempts to sell his own products and maximize his own profit, leads in the long run *without any conscious intention* to the most efficient economic system for all concerned. Adam Smith's faith in the ultimate convergence of self and community interest would, however, be widely rejected today as overly optimistic.

Utilitarianism and the Need for Specific Moral Rules

Some philosophers sympathetic to the utilitarian point of view have been reluctant to accept Bentham's claim that all moral principles, other than the principle of utility itself, are subject to exceptions. For example, G. E. Moore, an influential British utilitarian argued in his *Principia Ethica* (1903) that there are certain moral rules whose violation so regularly leads to bad consequences that one would be mistaken in violating them in any given situation. As Moore saw it, even though from a utilitarian perspective there are justified exceptions to such moral rules, a person will never have sufficient information in a concrete situation of moral choice to know that in *this* situation breaking such a rule will have the best consequences. Experience has often shown that the expected good consequences that are utilized as a justificaiton for breaking moral rules often turn out to be unattainable or are outweighed in the long run by the evil means employed in obtaining them. Furthermore, when one assumes that moral rules can always be broken as long as it appears that human happiness will be maximized by so doing, one often becomes a victim of selfishly motivated rationalization. We may find ourselves breaking rules for selfish reasons and then conveniently weighing the consequences in such a way as to justify the actions we desire. In addition, even if we are correct in a given situation that the violation of a conventional moral rule is justified on utilitarian grounds, breaking the rule might be a dangerous example to ourselves in future, less clear, cases and to other individuals, less scrupulous and impartial in weighing the consequences.

Moore's fear of individuals taking upon themselves the task of weighing the consequences of obeying deeply cherished conventional moral rules is justified. It is plausible to believe that a constant reliance upon the principle of utility in deciding what one ought to do is likely in practice to produce a greater threat to the utilitarian ideal than that of individuals blindly following moral rules which generally serve the common good. Nevertheless, if the stakes are high enough, it is not plausible to contend that those completely committed to the utilitarian point of view will consider any moral rule, other than the principle of utility itself, totally inviolate. For example, consider the sad situation facing the President of the United States in the novel *Fail Safe*. One of his nuclear bombers is mistakenly on its way to bomb Moscow. Certainly as we read the novel (or watch the movie), we tend to agree with the President's decision to attempt to shoot down his own plane. (He fails.) Yet this would seem to be a violation of the moral rule forbidding us to kill the innocent. It certainly is a colossal violation of this principle when the President, in desperation, decides to drop a nuclear bomb on New York City as a price the Soviets will accept for the now unavoidable bombing of Moscow. This is a horrible choice, but it seems the only way to avert a far worse nuclear confrontation. Most of us will accept the President's decision as justified on utilitarian grounds. Even though the President cannot be absolutely sure that the consequences of his decision will be as he anticipates, he has good reason to believe this and good reason to believe that any other choice will have the most tragic of consequences. He must, most of us believe, attempt to avoid these tragic consequences in a way that minimizes human misery, regardless of the moral rules he breaks in the process.

Similarly, if it seemed quite clear that the tragedy of a nuclear war could be averted only by torturing one or several innocent people, such an action would also seem to be justifiable from a utilitarian perspective. Granted that one should never do such things in doubtful or insignificant cases, nevertheless, sometimes the situation does appear clear or the consequences so momentous that such a painful choice seems required from a utilitarian perspective. If actions are to be evaluated solely by their consequences, it seems inescapable that, given the complexities and tragedies of this world, all conventional moral rules will, as Bentham saw, be subject to exceptions. If one does not want to accept this conclusion, one must either reject the principle of utility as the sole basic moral standard, or claim, as some contemporary philosophers have, that although the principle of utility should be used to justify moral rules which should then be used to justify particular acts, it is wrong to justify particular acts directly by an appeal to the principle of utility. (We shall discuss this modern view called *rule utilitarianism* is section 12.)

Utilitarianism and Special Responsibilities

As critics of utilitarianism have often pointed out, a commitment to the utilitarian point of view would seem to lead us in some situations to justify actions that would go contrary to most people's intuitive moral reactions. For example, in our relationships with people, we naturally feel *special moral obligations* to people to whom we have special relationships, such as family and friends. Traditional utilitarianism is, however, silent about the notion of special responsibilities. On the face of it, our common belief that we have special moral obligations to particular individuals seems quite foreign to utilitarianism, which claims that in attempting to maximize the total good in the world we should consider everyone equally. Although it is open for a utilitarian to claim that human happiness can only be maximized in the long run if individuals assume special moral responsibilities to each other, the specific nature and force of such special responsibilities has never been worked out by any utilitarian. The utilitarian neglect of special moral obligations has been considered by many to be a serious failure of utilitarianism as a comprehensive ethical theory.

Utilitarianism and the Principles
of Distributive Justice

Bentham's utilitarian theory suffers from an inherent ambiguity in its formulation. According to Bentham's formula, the right act or rule in a given situation is that act or rule which produces "the greatest happiness for the greatest number," counting each person's happiness equally. There are, however, two notions conflated into this formula, the maximization of both the *total happiness* for all individuals and the *total number of individuals* who share in that happiness. Bentham and Mill did not distinguish these two factors, nor realize the possibility of conflict when one must choose between a greater total amount of happiness for those involved or a wider distribution of it. Since Bentham often spoke of "the greatest happiness" principle, deleting reference to "the greatest number," it would appear that the meaning he intended for his formula was that one should always attempt to maximize the amount of happiness, regardless of its method of distribution. This is clearly inadequate. The same quantity of happiness can be distributed in many different ways. One arrangement might give all, or most, of that happiness to a relatively small number of people who do not especially *deserve* it while other arrangements might spread it more evenly or in accord with desert. In morality, one cannot do without principles of distributive justice, which Bentham and Mill do not supply. Certainly it is possible that an act which maximizes the sum of human happiness is nevertheless wrong if that happiness is unjustly distributed.

For example, today most of us will readily condemn the institution of slavery as unjust, even if its existence can in some situations maximize human happiness, as some historians have suggested. To use a more frivolous example, most of us would condemn a group of sadists for inflicting pain on some unwilling innocent victims even if we were convinced that the sum of happiness the sadists were experiencing outweighed the sum of the pain of their victims. Consider, as well, the Russian Communist practice, under Stalin, of repressing civil liberties and unjustly imprisoning or executing individuals who were seen as a threat to the social order. All this was justified as a necessary means to the maximization of the general happiness for this and future generations. Yet even if this were true, it would not guarantee that such practices were right. Granted that justice should at times be sacrificed for the common good (such as, killing innocent people in war), the point is that there are different, and possibly conflicting, principles involved here—general utility versus individual justice. Bentham and Mill did not recognize this. Similarly, although Mill attempted to reconcile the utilitarian desire to maximize the general happiness with a very liberal principle of individual liberty in his essay *On Liberty,* there is no guarantee that these values will always coincide. Given today's more pessimistic view of human rationality, one may reject Mill's essential assumption that individuals tend to be the best judges of their own happiness. If this assumption is not made, utilitarian thinking may lead us to force people to be happy *in spite of themselves* an extent to which Mill would have been aghast. The conflict between governmental paternalism and individual freedom is for most of us a conflict over differing principles and not a question of the proper application of the single utilitarian principle, as Mill suggested. Similarly, although Bentham and Mill were strong proponents of greater equality, particularly of plans for the more even distribution of wealth, their theoretical justification for this aim was that a more equal distribution of goods was the most likely *means* toward a greater total happiness for society as a whole. There is again no good reason to believe that these two values will necessarily coincide. When they do not, some of us will choose to sacrifice some degree of equality to achieve a greater total of happiness, whereas others will choose to accept a smaller sum of happiness for a more equal distribution of it. Such situations of moral choice seem to involve a conflict of independent basic moral principles that cannot be resolved by an appeal to a higher moral principle.

DISCUSSION QUESTIONS

1. Consider the following criticism of utilitarianism by the American philosopher William James:

    If the hypothesis were offered us of a world in which Messrs. Fourier's and Bellamy's and Morris's utopias should be all outdone, and millions kept permanently happy on the one simple condition that a certain lost soul on the far-off edge of things should lead a life of lonely torture, . . . [would we not] immediately feel, even though an impulse arose within us to clutch at the happiness so offered, how hideous a thing would be its enjoyment when deliberately accepted as the fruit of such a bargain.

    Do you agree with James? If you do, what is your reaction to the following claim by the American philosopher Morris R. Cohen:

    Moral feelings are very strong, but this does not prevent them from appearing as irrational taboos to those who do not share our conventions. This should warn us against the tendency to make ethical philosophy an apology or justification of the conventional customs that happen to be established. Suppose that someone were to offer our country a wonderfully convenient mechanism, but demand in return the privilege of killing thousands of our people every year. How many of those who would indignantly refuse such a request will condemn the use of the automobile now that it is already with us?

    Can you see any relevant moral differences between the cases James and Cohen mention?

2. No doubt, most of us feel strongly that our obligation not *to harm* people is much more stringent than our obligation *to help* people. Can a utilitarian give any justification for this moral distinction? Similarly, do you think a utilitarian could give a plausible defense of our tendency to distinguish such claims as, "It would be *morally ideal* for Jones to do X" from "Jones is *morally obligated* to do X"? If so, how do you think a utilitarian would analyze the different meanings of these two claims?

3. There is an unresolved problem that utilitarians must face of the scope of the principle of utility. Should it apply only to human beings and not to animals? only to presently existing human beings or to future generations as well? If we are to consider future generations, how are we to weigh the interests of an indefinite posterity against the interests of the existing generation?

How do you think we should weigh the rights of animals against those of human beings? If, let us imagine, beating animals before killing them resulted in making the animals' meat far more tender and succulent, would we be morally justified in this sort of action? If not, what justifies us in eating them at all? If you think we are justified in using animals for our benefit as we do, would it be morally correct for beings from some other part of our universe whose abilities are vastly superior to ours to use us in a similar manner?

4. According to the principle of utility, our concern should always be with the maximization of *the sum* of happiness in this world. Assuming then that a world filled with ten billion marginally happy people yields more happiness in sum than a world filled with three billion individuals who are individually far happier, does this mean that the more populated world even with its more thinly distributed happiness is a better world? If not, how should a utilitarian handle this situation?

5. According to the principle of utility, one should always attempt to maximize the general happiness. Does this imply that promises can be broken and debts unpaid whenever such actions maximize happiness? Can you accept as proper an ethic that is *always* willing to renounce our special obligations to particular individuals in behalf of the general happiness? In addition, if you were committed to the view that the right thing to do is always to act so as to maximize the general happiness, would you be acting immorally whenever you spent money on some personal luxury for yourself when this same money would create greater happiness if given to the poor? If so, is the principle of utility a principle that the average person can reasonably be expected to follow or is it one only for saints?

6. Consider the following quotation from Ayn Rand's *Atlas Shrugged:*

"the good of others" is a magic formula that transforms anything into gold....your code hands out, as its version of the absolute, the following rule of moral conduct: if *you* wish it, it's evil; if others wish it, it's good; if the motive of your action is *your* welfare, don't do it; if the motive is the welfare of others, then anything goes....For those of you who might ask questions, your code provides a consolation prize and boobytrap: it is your own happiness, it says, that you serve the happiness of others, the only way to achieve your joy is to give it up to others...and if you find no joy in this procedure, it is your own fault and the proof of your evil....a morality that teaches you to scorn a whore who gives her body indiscriminately to all men—this same morality demands that you surrender your soul to promiscuous love for all comers.

To what extent does Rand misinterpret the utilitarian point of view? To what extent to you agree with her?

7. In upholding the involuntary sterilization of a retarded 16-year-old girl, a 1925 Michigan court (*Smith v. Command*) claimed in justification that "No citizen has any right superior to the common welfare." First argue for or against this general principle and then consider its application to the particular question of the involuntary sterilization of the mentally retarded.

8. Evaluate our list of moral dilemmas from the utilitarian point of view. In which cases, if any, do you find this point of view inadequate? Why? In particular, focus on the utilitarian relevance of the secrecy of one's act in the

cases of "The Reluctant Voter," and The Soft-Hearted Professor."

9. A popular objection to utilitarianism is that it can lead to the punishment of the innocent. If we are to assume, as Bentham did, that the main aim of punishment is deterrence (that is, frightening people into obeying the law through the fear of punishment), law enforcement officials, it has been claimed, would be justified in particular situations in framing innocent individuals as a deterrent to future crimes when the guilty parties cannot be found and the framing can be kept secret. Yet such a practice is clearly wrong, it is claimed. What is the most plausible reply a utilitarian could make to this criticism? Does it convince you?

10. In the last chapter of his book *Utilitarianism,* John Stuart Mill writes:

> Justice is a name for certain moral requirements which, regarded collectively, stand higher in the scale of social utility, and are therefore of more paramount obligation, than any others.

Do you think it is plausible to claim, as Mill does, that *all reasonable* principles of justice can be derived from the principle of utility? Similarly, do you agree with Mill when he writes the following?

> To have a right . . . is, I conceive, to have something that society ought to defend me in the possession of. . . . If the objector goes on to ask me why [society ought to accord me rights], I can give him no other reason than general utility.

Critically discuss.

FURTHER READINGS

Jeremy Bentham presents his version of utilitarianism in *An Introduction to the Principles of Morals and Legislation,* first published in 1789 and reprinted in 1948 by Hafner Press. This long and involved book is not for casual reading, but its detailed table of contents makes it a good reference source. In his brief and clearly written book *Utilitarianism,* first published in 1863, and reprinted by Bobbs-Merril (1957) with an introduction by Oskar Piest and by Hackett (1979) with an introduction by George Sher, John Stuart Mill, Bentham's foremost disciple, presents his version of utilitarianism. (Sher's seven-page introduction would prove more useful to students than the one-and-a-half-page introduction supplied by Piest.) The most thorough attempt at developing a hedonistic utilitarian philosophy is found in Henry Sidgwick's *The Methods of Ethics,* seventh edition (Macmillan, 1907). While Sidgwick writes clearly, this 528 page book is directed to the philosophically sophisticated. J.J.C. Smart is the foremost contemporary defender of the utilitarian view that the rightness of an action is determined solely by its consequences. *Utilitarianism: For and Against* (Cambridge University Press, 1973) consists of an essay by Smart defining and defending a utilitarian point of view and one by Bernard Williams in criticism.

D. H. Monro provides an excellent brief summary of Bentham's ethical philosophy in his article "Bentham" appearing in *The Encyclopedia of Philosophy.* Excellent short surveys of utilitarianism can be found in *The Encyclopedia of Philosophy* and *Dictionary of the History of Ideas* by J.J.C. Smart and D. H. Monro, respectively. Michael Bayles (ed.) *Contemporary Utilitarianism* (Doubleday, 1968) is a good collection of essays pro and con on utilitarian ethical theory by contemporary philosophers.

The quotation from Bentham that appears in this chapter comes from the preface of his *The Theory of Legislation.* The quotation from William James comes from *The Will to Believe and Other Essays in Popular Philosophy* (Longman, 1896), p. 188. The quotation from Morris Cohen comes from *Studies in Philosophy and Science* (Ungar, 1949), pp. 24–25. The quotation from Ayn Rand comes from *Atlas Shrugged* (Random House, 1957), pp. 1030, 1031, 1033.

10. KANTIAN ETHICS

Introduction

The ethical theory of the influential philosopher Immanuel Kant (1724–1804) stands in marked contrast to that of the utilitarians. Unlike the utilitarians, Kant did not think that people needed guidance in arriving at enlightened moral judgments. The central question of morality for Kant was not, "What would be the right thing for a person to do in this specific situation?" The answer to this question, he assumed, would usually be perfectly clear to every decent human being. Perhaps due to his deeply religious background, discerning the right was not a major problem for Kant; the problem was maintaining the self-control to do what is right. As a result, Kant does not dwell upon the type of moral perplexity, emphasized by the existentialist Sartre, that arises from confusion as to what is right when one feels oneself torn between conflicting obligations.

From such a perspective, the task Kant set for himself was not one of demonstrating that the ordinary person's moral intuitions made sense; this he assumed. His task was to formulate some comprehensive theory of the nature of morality, human beings, the physical world, the after-life, and God, which could explain *how* mortality, as the common person understood it, was possible and rational. In particular, Kant was struck by the apparent incompatibility of human free will and the assumption of the developing deterministic sciences of his day that every event, including human behavior, could in principle be predicted from a knowledge of scientific causal laws. It seemed clear to Kant that if moral actions were entirely governed by causes, as the deterministic view seemed to entail, then free will would be an illusion. Since it makes sense to tell people what they morally *ought* to do only when we believe that they *can* do it, morality presupposes the existence of free will, which determinism seems to deny. In order to remove the apparent inconsistency between freedom and determinism, Kant made a radical distinction between that part of people—their sensual or animal natures—that is fully determined by causes capable of scientific understanding and prediction, and their distinctive part—their natures as rational moral beings—which stands outside of the stream of these causes. Consequently, for Kant, our uniqueness among the animals resides in our capacity for rational moral choice; it is this that gives us our special dignity.

Kant's ethical theory can be best undersood as a reaction to what he saw as the two fundamental inadequacies of hedonistic utilitarianism: its reliance upon the notion of happiness as the ultimate ground of morality and its potential for injustice. First, Kant rejected the utilitarian assumption that morality is nothing more than a maximization of human desires, such as the desire for happiness. From this point of view, human reason must be subservient to one's desires or passions. As the philosopher David Hume expressed it, "Reason is the slave of the passions." Kant rejected this view. As he saw it, morality should be grounded in a value which gives human beings their distinctive worth. Such a value cannot be a desire such as that for happiness which is grounded in human psychology. People may desire happiness, but they do not derive their dignity or worth as persons from desiring it. According to Kant, they derive this dignity from their freedom and ability to reason, the characteristics which distinguish human beings from other animals. People alone can act from reasons, as opposed to being acted upon by external causes; people alone can act freely. Morality, then, as Kant saw it, must be based on the values of rationality and freedom. Only by acting as a free and rational human being would act, Kant believed, do people reveal their dignity and assert that autonomy of action that distinguishes them from the brutes. Believing, as Hume before him believed, that there was an unbridgeable gap between reason and desire—that desires could never in themselves be said to be reasonable—the way Kant saw it, one cannot be acting morally when one justifies one's actions by an appeal to one's desires.

Second, Kant feared that a complete commitment to the principle of utility could lead to grave injustices. As we have seen, a glaring inadequacy of the traditional utilitarian theory developed by Bentham was its neglect of distributive justice. In his preoccupation with the maximization of happiness, Bentham neglected the principles that should be utilized to assure that the distribution of that happiness be fair. It is his fear that utilitarian ethics could lead one to sacrifice justice for the maximization of happiness, a sacrifice that he thought should never be made, that led Kant to speak warningly of "the serpent windings of utilitarianism." As Kant saw it, legal systems exist in order to secure the value of justice. Justice, in turn, demands that each person enjoy the fullest possible liberty compatible with a like liberty for all. The law can legitimately interfere with a person's freedom only when that person illegitimately interferes with the liberty of others. It is improper for the law to interfere with a person's liberty to enforce the nebulous goal of the common good which is subject to conflicting interpretations and has the potential for gravely interfering with individual liberty—the very value that gives human beings their dignity.

Although Mill argues in his famous essay *On Liberty* that the principle of utility implies a commitment to the value of freedom which allows individuals to make their own decisions as to what is best for themselves, there is no guarantee that these two values will always coincide. It is not hard to imagine, as Aldous Huxley did in his novel *Brave New World*, a society of happy, though minimally free, individuals. The widely felt revulsion towards Huxley's envisioned totalitarian society stems not from the belief that the people in such a society cannot really be happy but from the fact that they are not allowed the freedom to make their own decisions as to how to find their happiness. Perceiving the potential conflict between freedom and utility and seeing the dignity of man in his freedom, Kant attempts to solidly anchor the value of freedom to an absolute principle of justice.

In his emphasis upon justice, the basic human rights that justice demands, and the rationality of human beings that makes morality possible, Kant's moral thinking was closely attuned to the natural law tradition. There are, however, important differences. Unlike classical natural law theorists who derived their concept of morality from a biological and social view of human nature, Kant attempts to free moral theory from such considerations. The basic principles of morality, from his perspective, are binding upon all rational persons, regardless of their psychological desires. Like the upright moral person that he was, Kant emphasized that morally good people act according to moral principles that bind them to act in a certain way, regardless of whether or not they desire to act that way—that is, moral principles act as rational curbs upon our desires. Moral principles, he claimed, are not prudential means to the satisfaction of the desires that we happen to have, as Hume claimed, or derivable from some allegedly objective conception of human nature, as the natural law theorists claimed, but are demands that any rational person would see as implicit in the idea of morality.

In his belief that the foundations of moral thinking consisted of self-evident moral truths, Kant's moral theory was similar to that of ethical intuitionists like Thomas Reid (see p. 13). Unlike Reid and other moral intuitionists, however, Kant did not intuit moral truths in a philosophical vacuum but attempted to provide some comprehensive theory of the nature (meaning) or morality. As Kant saw it, the concept of morality is inextricably connected to the concepts of impartiality, rationality, and respect for the autonomy of persons.

Unlike the utilitarians who did not have much to say about the principles to be utilized in the evaluation of moral character,[3] Kant provides us not only with a theory of moral obligation (that is, a theory of how we should determine when an act is right), but also with a theory of moral value (that is, a theory of how we should determine when a person is morally good). Let us turn to a consideration of the main elements of these two theories.

Kant's Theory of Moral Value

How do we determine if a person is morally good? Clearly, it is insufficient to look at the person's actions and their consequences without considering motives and intentions. Indeed, actions may give no indication about moral character. A bad person may do right things for wrong reasons, and a good person, having only good intentions, may nevertheless do bad things. According to Kant, the only motive that should be taken as a sign of good character is the motive of conscientiousness (that is, acting from duty). A morally good person (or as he prefers to put it, a person with good will) is a person "who intends to do his duty because it is his duty and summons all the means in his power to do that duty." It is this, and this alone, which determines a good will, Kant declares. A person who does his duty for any other reason does not have a good will and is consequently unworthy of moral praise. As an example, Kant mentions a shopkeeper who is honest, not because he believes that it is his moral duty to be so, but because he believes

[3]Like many philosophers of his age, Jeremy Bentham was committed to the doctrine of psychological egoism which asserts that all (voluntary) human motives are ultimately selfish. Given this assumption, Bentham understandably felt little impetus to delve into the subtleties of human motives. Instead, his concern with human motivation centered on the problem of how to motivate rational self-interested people to obey moral and legal rules which aim at the general interest.

that honesty pays off by giving him a good reputation which in turn brings him more customers and more profit. Such a person, who is fortunate to find himself motivated by self-interest to do as duty demands, does not have a good will and is unworthy of moral praise, Kant says. In addition, Kant asserts, the naturally good person who does what is right out of natural inclination without any moral consideration also does not have a good will and is unworthy of moral praise. For example, if Jones helps others, not out of a sense of moral duty, but simply out of his kindly nature, Kant would not consider him worthy of moral praise.

Is it reasonable to ignore inclination in determining a person's moral goodness? Critics of Kant have contended that the sign of moral maturity is when one does what is right without being tempted to do otherwise, and consequently without having to think about duty. For example, imagine that at first you want very much to steal, but, recognizing your duty to refrain, you don't. After awhile, however, you find yourself no longer even tempted to steal. Many philosophers have claimed that it is quite unreasonable to say as Kant does, that your action is now no longer a morally praiseworthy one.

Kant would have a reply. He would agree that it is best for people not to always have to think about their duty and to train themselves into developing habits of restraint. The important thing, as he saw it, was that one have *a disposition to act from duty* (that is, that one would do what is right out of a sense of duty *even if* one had no natural inclination to do so). Morally good persons are not necessarily persons who always act from duty; they are rather persons who *would* choose duty over inclination *if* they had to make such a choice. As Kant saw it, we should not get credit for our natural inclincations, since they are largely determined by heredity and environment over which they have no control.

An adequate criticism of Kant's position here would involve coming to grips with the philosophical problem of determinism and free will which we shall tackle in section 18. For our purposes at this point, it will suffice to mention that critics of Kant would say that he is fundamentally mistaken in claiming that human freedom is best manifested in choices involving moral duty. The disposition to do one's duty, the critics would say, is as much determined by hereditary and environmental factors as are other inclinations. If people do not have free choice in determining whether they should have a kindly or courageous character, for example, why should they be said to have free choice when it comes to their disposition to act from duty? After all, a person's sense of duty might be as much a result of childhood training as another person's kindness. If, on the other hand, people are properly subject to moral praise or blame for the choices they make between the demands of duty and conflicting natural inclinations, why can't they equally as well be subject to moral praise or blame for choosing between these inclinations themselves and for the temperament they develop through their choices.

Regardless of the inadequacies of Kant's view of moral character, this view does bring out the important point that human beings have less control over their temperament than they do over the principles under which they choose to act. In addition, it also makes us consider the fact that some people find it much easier than others to do their duty as a result of hereditary and environmental factors that they had no hand in choosing. If, for example, Jones has a much less violent and imperturbable nature than Smith, it will be easier for Jones than for Smith to control himself from reacting with unjustified violence to strong provocation. If we can ultimately trace the difference between Jones' and Smith's nature to hereditary or early environmental factors over which neither had control, it is not to Jones's moral credit that he is a more self-controlled individual than Smith. Indeed, is it not the case that if Smith and Jones both restrain themselves equally well, Smith's behavior would be more to his moral credit and consequently more worthy of praise than Jones' since it involved more moral effort? It is the virtue of Kant that he makes us think about such issues.

Another problem with Kant's view of moral character relates to the fact that he rivets his attention upon people who not only act from duty but are also correct in their appraisal of what duty demands. Consequently, he does not tell us whether people who act from a *mistaken* conception of duty are worthy of moral praise. In judging moral character, must we not consider what a conscientious person is conscientious about? As we have mentioned, Kant did not focus on this problem, for he thought that the demands of duty were usually clear. But people often profoundly disagree as to the demands of duty. Consider, for example the following two cases:

> Mr. and Mrs. Jones are Jehovah's Witnesses who believe that blood transfusions are morally wrong. Their son, whom they love dearly, is involved in a serious accident. The doctors say that without a blood transfusion he will die. Even though it strongly goes against their natural inclination, Mr. and Mrs. Jones say no, for they see such treatment as contrary to the will of God.

> Mr. Smith is a very angry person who constantly refers to passages in the Bible and to the wrath of God. The world, he says, is corrupt to its core. People need stern discipline, and if they do not respond to it, they should be pruned away like weeds. Some groups of people would be best weeded out entirely to prevent their polluting influence. It would take moral courage to do so, but we must stand with God against these instruments of the devil. Mr. Smith also treats his children very harshly, beating them regularly. It hurts me more than you, he tells them, but sparing the rod spoils the child. It is God's way; he is stern, but he is just. It is our duty to do as he wills.

Assuming that the Jones' are mistaken about what their duty demands, what should our judgment be of their moral character? If we are to consider them praiseworthy for their conscientiousness, it is doubtful that we would feel the same way about Mr. Smith. What is the morally relevant difference in these two cases? Does the difference reside in the fact that we are willing to accept the Jones' conflict between duty and inclination as a real one, but are not apt to do the same with Mr. Smith? We may sympathize with the Jones', seeing their choice as a genuine case of self-sacrifice. We may shake our heads in sadness over their ignorance, but feel that they cannot reasonably be blamed for it. When we turn to Smith, however, we are apt to distrust his claim that it hurts him more than it hurts them. We suspect that he is lying to himself, that he is rationalizing. We suspect that deep down he wants to hurt others and then conveniently convinces himself that his duty demands that he do what he is inclined to do anyway. Consider, for example, the following imaginary dialogue:

X: People who always act on principle are much more to be trusted than people who act on the basis of feelings. Such people can be counted on, regardless of how they might happen to feel at a given moment. We all know how fickle one's feelings can be.

Y: No doubt people's feelings are often fickle, but one's sense of duty can be equally fickle. It is quite common for the person of principle to trim and interpret his principles in such a manner that he can justify doing exactly what he wants to do, with a good conscience.

Y is right. One's sense of duty can be a convenient rationalization for doing as one would want to do apart from any moral consideration. Holden Caulfield, the hero of J. D. Salinger's *The Catcher in the Rye* reflects on this possibility when he says:

> Even if you did go around saving guys' lives and all, how would you know if you did it because you really wanted to save guys' lives, or whether you did it because what you really wanted to do was be a terrific lawyer, with everybody slapping you on the back and congratulating you in court when the goddam trial was over, the reporters and everybody...How would you know you weren't being a phony?

Is one, however, "being a phony" if one helps others when one gets something out of helping them, or is one being a phony when one does something out of a sense of duty that does not reflect one's own desires? Ayn Rand the foremost contemporary advocate of the virtue of selfishness, would claim that it is the second, and not the first, person who is the true phony. As she puts it in her novel *Atlas Shrugged:*

> If you wish to save the last of your dignity, do not call your best actions a 'sacrifice': that term brands you as immoral. If a mother buys food for her hungry child rather than a hat for herself, it is not a sacrifice if she values the child higher than the hat; but it is a sacrifice to the kind of mother whose higher value is the hat, who would prefer her child to starve and feeds him only from a sense of duty.

Kant's Theory of Moral Obligation

Fundamental to most conceptions of morality is a commitment to the value of justice. Although, like the utilitarians, we are all concerned with maximizing the good in society, most of us would not consider this alone as right. It is an efficient society, we are apt to say, that is most capable of maximizing the good of its citizens, but such a society is not a moral one unless its goods are justly distributed. Clearly, for most of us, any adequate moral theory must find a central place for the notion of justice. It is this notion that forms a cornerstone of Kant's theory of moral obligation. In this theory, the notion of justice is inseparably tied to the notions of freedom and rationality. As Kant saw it, justice in its most basic respect involves treating individuals fairly, and this in turn involves considering them as rational moral agents who have the right to make their own choices unless these choices interfere with the freedom of others. From such a perspective, it is fundamentally wrong to *use* individuals, as the utilitarian scheme would invite us to do, as mere means to be manipulated in our quest for the maximization of human happiness. To treat individulas in such a way, Kant would claim, is to treat them as less than *persons* that is, as less than free rational moral agents.

The demands of morality, Kant claimed, are *categorical* and not *hypothetical,* that is, they are not means for achieving our desires but are independent of any desire we may happen to have. For example, if one wants to lose weight, then it is rational for one to eat less. The imperative (command) to eat less, Kant would say is hypothetical in that it will bind us only insofar as we accept the end of losing weight. If we reject this end, the command "to eat less" will have no force for us. A demand of morality, on the other hand, Kant asserts, is categorical in the sense that it presents "an action as of itself objectively necessary, without regard to any other end" (that is, it constitutes a rational principle of action even in the absence of any desire in that direction). For example, according to Kant, our moral obligation to keep our promises in no way depends upon whether or not we desire to keep them.

Kant claims that the various specific categorical demands of morality follow from a supreme categorical moral principle which he calls the categorical imperative. The categorical imperative, Kant believed, is so basic to moral thinking that all rational persons who understand what it means would accept it as binding, regardless of their specific psychological idiosyncracies. Kant presents five formulations of this supreme moral principle which he claims are equivalent in meaning. According to one of these formulations, the categorical imperative enjoins you to "act in such a way that you always treat humanity, whether in your own person, or in the person of any other, never simply as a means, but always at the same time as an end." This formulation of the categorical imperative expresses Kant's view that individuals who are treated simply as means are not treated with respect as persons, as morality demands they should. Individuals are treated simply as means when our responses to them are motivated not by their choices, but by ours in disregard of theirs. As Kant saw it, since the very dignity of human beings resides in their freedom and rationality, human beings are treated with respect only when they are treated as rational moral agents who are given the freedom to set their own goals. To be *treated as a person* is simply to be afforded this respect.

According to Kant's first and most widely discussed formulation of the categorical imperative, you should "act as if the maxim of your action [the subjective principle under which you act] were to become through your will a universal law of nature [i.e., that everyone follow that maxim]." In telling you to perform the thought experiment of imagining everyone doing as you contemplate doing, Kant is giving sophisticated expression to the idea, central to the concept of morality, that morality demands impartiality. The idea of impartiality is at the heart of the Golden Rule of Christian ethics which commands that you "Do unto others as you would have them do unto you," and it is the same idea, stated in a less demanding and more passive way, that is expressed in the Confucian rule to "Do not do unto others as you would not have them do unto you." When people act on moral principles, they must, we tend to believe, be willing to accept the right of everyone else to act on the same principle—that is, they must be willing to accept the *universalization* of the rule under which they act. The categorical imperative was Kant's attempt to formulate in a more precise manner the spirit behind the Golden and Confucian Rules, without their implicit reference to the variable subjective tastes of human beings.

With their apparent reference to the subjective preferences of human beings, the Golden and Confucian rules would appear, if taken literally, to lead to absurd consequences. For example, if Jones is a sadomasochist who enjoys being hurt and hurting others, we would certainly think that Jones is violating the spirit behind the Golden Rule, if not its letter, when he hurts Smith and justifies it by saying that he is merely doing unto Smith as he would have Smith do unto him. As George Bernard Shaw, the English literary figure, once remarked, the Golden Rule seems to neglect the fact that people's tastes may be different. Given this observation, one can either reject the Golden Rule as a useless guide to moral conduct (some have) or try to dig more deeply into the ideas that underlie it. This is what Kant attempted. It is, however, far from clear if Kant's first formulation of the categorical imperative is any clearer than the Golden Rule it so much resembles.

When Kant tells us that we should do only what we *can* will that everyone else do, what exactly is the force of the "can" here? Does it mean what we can *logically* will (that is, what it is possible to conceive), or what is *scientifically possible* for us to will (that is, what is consistent with the laws of nature), or what we can *rationally* will, or merely what we would *desire* as a matter of psychological fact. Kant himself does not clearly say and what he does say points in different directions. Consequently, Kantian scholars disagree as to the precise meaning that should be attributed to the categorical imperative.

Whatever else Kant might have meant when he tells us that we should only act according to maxims that we can *universalize,* he meant to exclude actions that it would be logically impossible for everyone to follow. For example, it would be logically impossible for everyone to act in accordance with the maxim "Never offer to contribute to projects in the common good, instead let your neighbors make the necessary sacrifices, while you share in the benefits these sacrifices make possible." Obviously, a person who acts under such a maxim assumes that not everyone will, for it is logically impossible for everyone to follow it. A person who reaps the benefits of a community without assuming the burdens that make them possible is a parasite who counts on others not acting the way he acts.

An example Kant himself gives of a maxim that it would be logically impossible to universalize is the following one: "When I think myself in need of money, I shall borrow and promise to repay, although I know that I can never do so." Although Kant says this is the maxim he is considering, it would appear that the maxim he actually is focusing upon is the broader one, "Whenever necessary to obtain the things that I desire, I shall make promises that I know I cannot keep." So let us consider this maxim. The way Kant sees it, it is logically impossible to universalize this maxim since if everyone were to follow it, promises would cease to have any force and the institution of promise-keeping would be destroyed. As Kant puts it, "There would be no promises at all. . . . Thus my maxim would necessarily destroy itself as soon as it was made a universal law." Notice that, unlike the preceding example, the universalization of the maxim in question does not destroy itself in the straight-forward logical sense that the preceding maxim did. Certainly, like Kant, we realize that if everyone were always willing to make promises they knew they could not keep in order to obtain things they desired, the institution of promise-keeping would soon be destroyed. But it would be destroyed only if we make the *factual assumption* that people often find themselves in situations where they desire things that can be obtained only by making promises that cannot be kept and that the frequency of dishonest promise-making would lead people to refuse to accept promises. This is, no doubt, true; it is not, however, logically true but involves some assumptions about the nature of people and the world they inhabit.

While one can see the categorical imperative in the preceding two examples as a demand that the universalization of one's maxims of action be neither logically impossible nor self-defeating of one's purposes in acting, it is not clear what the force of the categorical imperative is in examples Kant himself gives of its use. He tells us that it would be contrary to the categorical imperative for us

1. not to help individuals who are in need of help, whenever we find it inconvenient
2. not to develop our special talents
3. to commit suicide if life's prospects include more pain than pleasure

What are we to say to such examples?

According to a common interpretation, the categorical imperative should be taken to prohibit not only those maxims which it is logically impossible to universalize, but also those which one would not *choose* to have universalized after one had *impartially* thought through what such a universalization would involve. According to this view, even though there is no inconsistency involved in everyone acting under the maxim "Don't help others who need help when you find it inconvenient," it would be wrong for us to act under this maxim if we would be unwilling to live in a world where this maxim was universally followed. What Kant is claiming, these interpreters suggest, is that since we all realize that we may one day desire help from others, none of us would want to live in such a world. Consequently, Kant concludes that it would be wrong for us not to help those in need. But, one may protest, it is possible that a person sure of his own material and psychological resources may have no fear at all of ever needing help from anyone else. It has been suggested that Kant would insist at this point that an individual must be willing to accept a situation where everyone follows the same principles of behavior even if he did not know what he would stand to gain or lose in such a situation. He must be willing to empathize with all who stand to be affected by the universalization of his act and be willing to accept the desirability of that universalization without taking advantage of his own specific psychological attributes and specific social role. Would a person, for example, be willing to live in a society where no one helped those in need, even if, by some magic, a cosmic roulette wheel were to randomly spin and he were to find himself occupying someone else's body and someone else's social role?

Even on this fanciful assumption, it seems that some people might very well be willing to live in a world where everyone follows the principle "Look out for yourself, give no help to others and expect none in return." A rugged and selfish individualist might be willing to take his chance on the spin of the wheel, hoping to fare well but willing to accept the consequences if he does not. It would seem that if an act is right as long as one is psychologically capable of willing its universalization, Kant's standard is a subjective one which makes the rightness of an action a function of one's desires. Yet this is clearly what Kant wanted to avoid. As Kant most likely saw it, the selfish individualist, the person who refuses to cultivate his special talents, and a person contemplating suicide could not will that everyone else act as they are acting *if they were fully rational*. But it is not clear how Kant can justify the "irrationality" of those whose views of the good life differ from his own.

Although Kant claimed that utilitarian considerations should have no bearing on the determination of one's moral obligations, it has been suggested by some philosophers that, in deciding which maxims a rational person would be willing to see universalized, the standard Kant appears to use in some of his examples concerns itself with the *desirability* of the consequences of the universralization of that maxim. This, as we shall see, is the position of *rule-utilitarians* who assert that an act is right if and only if it falls under a moral rule whose general observance has the best consequences—that is, the question is not "What will the consequences be if I do this?" but rather "What would the consequences be if everyone were to do it?" Most Kantian scholars would dismiss this interpretation of Kant as inconsistent with his intention. One may, however, grant this and nevertheless claim that some of Kant's examples of non-universalizable maxims can be made intelligible only from a rule-utilitarian point of view.

Aside from the unresolved question of the force of the word "can" in Kant's first formulation of the categorical imperative, there are other serious problems involved in interpreting the meaning of the categorical imperative. Kant, in some of his writings, contends that the categorical imperative would lead one to embrace all sorts or exceptionless moral rules—such as, "never break promises and never lie, regardless of the circumstances." For example, in an article entitled "On the Supposed Right to Lie from Benevolent Motives," Kant claims that it would always be wrong for an individual to lie since, if everyone did so, the very purpose of communication would be defeated. This argument seems absurd. Certainly, common sense would reply that there are all sorts of lies. Although one can reject with Kant the universalization of the maxim "Lie whenever it suits your purpose," why cannot one accept more specific maxims such as "Lie whenever it is necessary to save an innocent human life," or more generally, "To prevent great harm" or "To help others in distress"? The same can be said for promises. Although one would not will the universalization of the maxim "Break your promises whenever it suits your purpose," there seems to be no problem in willing the universalization of more specific maxims which allow the breaking of promises in particular circumstances. Kant ignored the fact that acts do not come with ready labels. The very same act can, for example, be described as a lie which suits one's purpose, an unselfish lie, or a lie which is necessary to save an innocent human life. Each of these different descriptions generates a different maxim. Following Kant, one will not want to universalize the first maxim, but practically all of us will want to universalize the last. Although Kant categorizes his actions very broadly, he fails to give any justificaiton for rejecting a narrower categorization. A principle for deciding upon the proper categorization of an act is lacking in Kantian ethics.

As critics of Kant have pointed out, without such a principle a person can always categorize his action so narrowly that his maxim covers only his own specific case. For example, even if we assume that no rational person would want to live in a world where everyone lied whenever they wanted to, it might very well be quite rational for Jones to want to live in a world where "all five-foot-eleven inch Los Angeles stockbrokers with two-inch scars over their right temples lie whenever they want to,"knowing he is most likely to be the only one that would fit such a description. No doubt, such a flagrantly narrow maxim would be dismissed as morally absurd.[4] But without some principle for determining how to properly categorize one's act, an individual can always try to build enough specific details into his maxim of action so that he has no compunction at all in willing its universalization.

Although rules can at times be qualified and interpreted in such a manner as to render them capable of justifying almost anything, there is no way to escape the need for qualifying and interpreting such rules as "never lie," "never break promises," and "never steal" that Kant takes to be absolute. Without a principle for qualifying such rules, there will be no way to resolve possible conflicts in duty. For example, what is one to do when one must lie in order to keep a promise? Kant gives us no clue as to how such conflicts of duty are to be resolved. Similarly, Kant is much too uncritical in his acceptance of such concepts as lying, promising, and stealing.

As discussed in the section on the pitfalls of moral reasoning, it is often difficult to pin down the meanings of the vague and morally-loaded concepts we employ so readily. For example consider the concept of stealing. Although this concept might have been unproblematic to Kant, people can disagree as to what should count as an act of stealing. For example, to many socialists, the inheritance

---

[4]Certainly, we would not believe that our stockbroker actually had such a maxim in mind when he acted. It is important to realize that the Kantian view that the rightness of an action is to be judged by the maxim under which one acts makes it impossible to judge the rightness of an act apart from an agent's perception of what he is doing. In this respect, Kant's first formulation of the categorical imperative is quite unlike the principle of utility which judges the rightness of actions in terms of what actually will (or is likely to) contribute to the greatest good and not in terms of whether an act is motivated by such a belief. For the utilitarian, questions of motivation, while irrelevant to the question of the rightness of an action, find their proper place in judgments as to a person's moral character. According to the first formulation of the categorical imperative, however, the rightness of one's action logically depends on one's motive. In addition, the first formulation of the categorical imperative neglects the fact that people often act impulsively under no maxim at all. Yet, such actions are ordinarily subject to moral judgment as right or wrong.

of wealth is a type of stealing. Consequently, for such socialists, strict adherence to the command "never steal" should rule out the inheritance of wealth. Kant did not think about this, assuming quite uncritically that stealing is what the common person sees as stealing. Yet, as a Marxist would be quick to point out, one often sees things through an ideological structure of beliefs that serves as a rationalization for the self-interest of a particular class of people.

Kant, unfortunately, never came to grips with the legitimacy of the underlying institutions that are unquestioningly assumed by our familiar moral intuitions. Instead, the way Kant tended to see it, a person who acted to destroy these institutions was always acting immorally. For example, Kant would most likely accuse a poor person who steals from the rich as acting immorally since, if everyone were to steal from those who had more than they, the entire institution of private property would be destroyed. Yet this might be exactly what the poor man wants.

While it has been suggested that the problem here is not with the categorical imperative but with Kant's application of it, the problem is deeper than this, for there is no agreement among philosophers as to what the categorical imperative should be taken to mean. For example, many scholars have rejected Kant's claim that his various formulations of the categorical imperative are equivalent in meaning. As some see it, the essence of Kantian morality is not its insistence on universalizability but its emphasis upon human *autonomy* and its insistence that individuals have *rights* that protect them from being paternalistically treated and from being used as mere instruments in the quest for the maximization of the common good. From this perspective, it is Kant's claim that the categorical imperative demands *respect for persons* by enjoining us "never to treat individuals as mere means" which best expresses the spirit of Kantian morality. Yet there is wide disagreement as to what "respect for persons" specifically entails. If, on the other hand, Kant's insistence on universalizability is to be taken as the essence of the categorical imperative, as it often is, we run into the problem of how an act is to be categorized.

As we have seen, the more narrowly one perceives one's act, the easier it is to accept "everyone's doing the same." How is one to decide upon an act's proper categorization? How is one to distinguish the actions of a moral saint from those of a moral fanatic, for both may accept the universalization of their principles of action. While Kant's view of morality reflects our intuitive sense that morality strives to be impartial, universal and rational, there is more to the moral point of view than Kantian ethics is willing to grant.

Reflections on Kantian Ethics

Kant's ethical theory has an importance which transcends the difficulties of his formulations of specific ethical principles. It provides us with a conceptual framework for the solution of moral problems, deeply reflected in ordinary moral thinking and especially in the Judeo-Christian religious tradition. The central moral concept in Kant's theory of social obligation was not, as it was for Bentham, Mill, and the socialistic thinkers who followed them, the maximization of human happiness or the common good, but rather the maximization of human freedom. The language of Kantian social morality is the deontological one of rights and obligations. Within this moral framework, our obligation to respect the rights of others to be left alone always overrides our obligation to provide positive assistance to those to whom we have no specific obligation. As Kant saw it, while we ought to attempt to contribute to the general happiness, no one can demand *by right* that we do so. On the other hand, people can demand *by right* that they be given the freedom to work out their lives as they see fit. Since the distinctive nobility of human beings lies in their capacity to govern themselves by freely chosen principles of reason, a respect for humanity requires the right to freedom of choice. As Kant saw it, a rational person's right to noninterference by others can only be forfeited when that individual has himself interfered with the legitimate rights of others. In particular, we cannot violate his right to be left alone on the grounds that we believe that we can make him happier or provide for a greater common good.

As Kant clearly saw, of all tyrannies, a tyranny exercised for the good of its victims may be the most oppressive, for those who have power over us can strip us of our freedom and dignity as persons with a clear conscience that they are helping us when, in reality, they are doing nothing of the kind. The development of more and more effective and sophisticated techniques of behavioral control testifies to the potential tyranny of a utilitarian commitment to the common good which is unlimited by a Kantian concern for the rights of indiviudals and their dignity as persons. As we shall see in our discussions of the moral issues of punishment, abortion, euthanasia, and war, the Kantian way of thinking permeates influential views of these problems. According to these views, central distinctions must be made between our duties of noninterference and benevolent aid and between the direct intentions of our acts and their likely consequences. As our discussions of these moral issues will indicate, for most of us the moral life is an uneasy balance between the utilitarian and Kantian moral perspectives.

DISCUSSION QUESTIONS

1. Evaluate the following disagreement:

    Kantian: Man's greatest moral virtue is his capacity to be rational and to be self-governing. It is this capacity which enables him to adopt moral principles and to live by them, regardless of the contingencies of his feelings.

    Utilitarian: The most important moral virtue is the capacity to feel sympathy for one's fellow creatures. Conscientiousness itself is unimportant. What is important is that one be conscientious about the right things and this requires that one be motivated by feelings of benevolence.

2. What is the most plausible meaning that can be attributed to the Golden Rule?

3. Evaluate the following disagreement:

    A: I know it would be right for me to lie in these circumstances, but I don't know if it would be right for anyone else in the same circumstances.

    B: What you say makes no sense. If you really thought that *all* the relevant circumstances were the same, you would have to make the same moral judgments; otherwise, you're misusing moral language. What is right for one person cannot be wrong for someone else unless there is some relevant difference in their circumstances. The very meaning of moral language requires this.

4. Kant tells us that we should never treat individuals as mere means. Are soldiers who are drafted into the army treated as mere means? Are criminals who are punished? Explain.

5. Critically consider the following claim:

Kant's picture of human beings as autonomous rational moral agents unfortunately does not fit most human beings who tend to be quite irrational. Although Kant says that human beings should be respected as persons, most human beings should be treated as children.

6. Argue as forcefully as you can either for or against the claim "Let justice be done though the heavens fall" (in less poetic language: "When justice and utility conflict, as they may, always choose justice over utility").

FURTHER READINGS

Kant's writings on ethics are difficult and obscure. They also contain conflicting strands which make it impossible to provide a single coherent account of Kantian ethics. Elementary expositions, such as the one in this chapter, are necessarily incomplete. More comprehensive ones, on the other hand, are usually written for the philosophical scholar, and beginning students of philosophy will have a difficult time with them. In reading Kant's own works (translated from the German), it is very helpful to read the introductions by the editors.

Kant's Main Writings on Ethics

Kant's most abstract, comprehensive, and difficult ethical writing is the *Foundations* (or *Groundwork* or *Fundamental Principles,* depending on the translation) of *the Metaphysics of Morals* (1785). There are several translations of this classic work. The one I recommend is by the Kantian scholar H. J. Paton which is preceded by Paton's own section-by-section short summary and analysis of the work—*Groundwork of the Metaphysics of Morals* (Harper & Row, 1964). Another widely used translation is by the Kantian scholar Lewis White Beck—*Foundations of the Metaphysics of Morals* (Bobbs-Merrill, 1959). This same translation is also included in Robert Paul Wolff's *Foundations of the Metaphysics of Morals: Text and Critical Essays* (Bobbs-Merrill, 1969). The nine critical essays included with Kant's work, with the exception of the article, "The Categorical Imperative," by Jonathan Harrison, are too difficult for beginning students.

    In *The Metaphysics of Morals,* Kant applies the categorical imperative to derive more specific moral directives. Its two parts have been translated and printed separately, the first as *The Metaphysical Elements of Justice,* (John Ladd, Trans., Bobbs-Merrill, 1965) and the second as *The Metaphysical Principles of Virtue* (James Ellington, Trans., Bobbs-Merrill, 1964) or as *The Doctrine of Virtue* (Mary Gregor, Trans., Harper & Row, 1964). In *The Metaphysical Elements of Justice,* Kant is concerned with the notions of legality and rights and the general question of the state's moral right to use coercion to limit the freedom of individuals. The view of Kantian morality emphasized in this section comes from this work. While Kant is concerned with the question of external legal compulsion in *The Metaphysical Elements of Justice,* in *The Metaphysical Principles of Virtue* he turns his attention to those moral virtues that he claims should be enforced from within by one's sense of duty. Kant considers duties to oneself as well as duties to others. In this work, the ends of happiness to others and one's own perfection are the central concepts, whereas the maximization of freedom is Kant's central concept under his theory of justice, expressed in *The Metaphysical Elements of Justice.* Kant's application of his general ethical theory is also found in his *Lectures on Ethics* (Louis Infield,

Trans., Hackett, 1963) which consists of the lecture notes of three of his students. This work, along with *The Metaphysics of Morals,* helps put flesh on the bare bones of Kant's theoretical discussion of ethics in the *Foundations of the Metaphysics of Morals.*

Commentaries on Kant

A good short account of Kant's ethical theory in *The Foundations of the Metaphysics of Morals* and its application to *The Metaphysical Elements of Justice* which would be helpful to beginning students is Jeffrie Murphy's *Kant: The Philosophy of Right* (Macmillan, 1970). More difficult expositions of *The Foundations* are found in H. J. Paton's *The Categorical Imperative* (Harper & Row, 1967), Robert Paul Wolff's *The Autonomy of Reason* (Harper & Row, 1973), and Onora Nell's *Acting on Principle: An Essay on Kantian Ethics* (Columbia University Press, 1975).

Jack Glickman (ed.), *Moral Philosophy* (St. Martin's Press, 1976) contains a good selection of critical articles by contemporary philosophers on various aspects of Kantian ethics as well as Kant's own *Fundamental Principles of the Metaphysics of Morals.*

Influential Contemporary Works Which Center on the Notion of Universalization

In his book *The Moral Point of View* (Cornell University Press, 1958), Kurt Baier, following Kant, claims that the moral point of view logically requires that one act from rational principles which in turn requires universalization. Baier specifies conditions which he sees as elements of the type of universalization that is logically required for moral rules. For example, he claims that moral rules must be "universally teachable" and cannot be "self-frustrating" or "self-defeating."

In his article "Universalizability" in *Proceedings of the Artistotelian Society,* 55 (1954), R. M. Hare defends the thesis that moral judgments must *by definition* be universalizable. Hare incorporates his view that universalization is a necessary condition of the moral point of view with the subjectivistic view that one must choose one's moral principles and not discover them, in his influential book, *The Language of Morals* (Oxford University Press, 1952). In this respect, Hare's point of view is quite different from that of Baier.

Citations

The quotation from Salinger's *The Catcher in the Rye* appears on p. 172 of the Bantam 1964 edition, and the quotation from Rand's *Atlas Shrugged* appears on p. 1029 of the Random House 1957 edition.

11. SOCIAL CONTRACT THEORIES OF MORAL AND POLITICAL OBLIGATION

If the fundamental dictates of justice cannot, as Kant assumed, be derived from a consideration of the very meaning of the moral point of view, can they be derived in some other way? According to *social contract* theories of moral obligation, they can be derived from a model of the sort of moral code and political system a society of rational self-seeking individuals would agree upon as the best means of preserving their liberty and obtaining the goods in life that they seek. This point of view is found in the writings of Plato, Hobbes, and Locke and is suggested in one of Kant's formulations of the categorical imperative. It is also central to the competing influential theories of justice of the contemporary Harvard philosophers John Rawls and Robert Nozick.

Historical Background

As we have discussed in the section on natural law theory, for the ancient Greek and Roman philosophers, human beings are by their very natures social animals bound to each other through relations of mutual dependence, respect, and sympathy. Since from this perspective, a society is as much an organic whole as human beings are themselves, the need for some central authority coordinating the parts of an organic group of human beings called a society is as obvious as is the need for the human body to be subjected to the central control of human reason. This *organic* view of social relations finds its classic expression in Plato's (427?–347 B.C.) most famous dialogue, *The Republic,* and is echoed in his student Aristotle's (384–322 B.C.) writings on political philosophy. Taking for granted the legitimacy of governmental authority, Plato and Aristotle turned their attention to the questions of who should exercise that authority, under what conditions, and within what limits.

In the theological world view of the Middle Ages, which saw all authority deriving ultimately from God, secular governmental authority was naturally seen as a trust from God, whether that authority be the power of a feudal lord over his serf or an absolute monarch over his subjects. As absolute monarchy became the mode of government in Western Europe, the brute physical power that brought such monarchies into power was legitimized through the general belief in the divine right of kings to rule. As a result of both the decline of the Church's influence in the fifteenth century and the Protestant Reformation (i.e., the religious movement that resulted in the establishment of the various sects of Protestantism) in the sixteenth century, a new *liberal* tradition of political philosophy emerged, a tradition greatly influenced by the new Protestant doctrine of the equal priesthood of all believers before God and of equal access to divine revelation and moral truth. At the core of this new liberal political philosophy was a commitment to individualism. Unlike the organic political theorist, who saw human beings as inherent parts of a greater social whole, the individualistic political theorist saw government and law as instruments for the satisfaction of private human needs that are independent of a specific social setting. Influenced by the new ideology of individual freedom that justified the growing power of the new middle class, the liberal political theorist, unlike his organic predecessor, saw the coercive power of government that curbs individual freedom as an intrinsic evil that cried out for justification. The central question from the liberal perspective was how human beings could justify the loss of freedom entailed by submission to governmental authority. As Jean-Jacques Rousseau (1712–78) put it at the very beginning of his treatise on political philosophy, *The Social Contract,* "Man is born free, and everywhere he is in chains." Can such chains be justified? political theorists now asked. Indeed, are they really chains, or is submission to authority self-imposed, that is, a result of some type of mutual consent.

The idea that the legitimacy of a state derives from the mutual consent of the governed is the key idea of various *social contract* theories of political obligation, which attempt to answer the central question posed by political liberalism.

As the words of the American Declaration of Independence state, "Governments are instituted among men, deriving their just powers from the consent of the governed...." The Declaration's assumptions of a social contract view of political obligation and of the doctrine of *natural rights* ("We hold these truths to be self-evident, that all men...are endowed by their Creator with certain unalienable rights...") reflect the intellectual debt its author Thomas Jefferson (1743–1826) owed to the political philosophy of the social contract theorist John Locke (1632–1704), as expressed in his famous *Two Treatises of Government* (1690). This classic of Western political liberalism was in turn greatly influenced by Thomas Hobbes' (1588–1679) classic of political theory *Leviathan* (1651), of which Locke was highly critical. Beginning with the same view that the legitimacy of government derives from the consent of the governed, Hobbes saw the necessity for unlimited and undivided sovereignty while Locke saw the necessity for limited powers of government and for the checks and balances that so strongly motivated the framers of our American Constitution.

Hobbes: The Classical Social Contract Justification for Unlimited Sovereignty

Hobbes' *Leviathan* was written in a period of great political unrest and discussion in England. While other social contract theorists attempted to undercut the power of the English monarchy, Hobbes employed the social contract perspective to argue for the unlimited sovereignty that defenders of the monarchy argued for on the grounds of tradition and divine right. As is the case in all classics of political philosophy, underlying the arguments of *Leviathan* is a particular theory of human nature. Committed to a deterministic, materialistic world view, Hobbes painted a very bleak and pessimistic picture of human nature. According to this picture, human beings are complex causal mechanisms, motivated exclusively by self-interest and never by impersonal moral principle. Consequently, *the state of nature* (i.e., conditions in the world prior to the institution of government) is for Hobbes an amoral condition in which all attempt to satisfy their purely selfish appetites. Alas, however, the realities of limited resources make this impossible and human beings come into conflict. The result is a jungle-like existence that is, in Hobbes' memorable words, "solitary, poor, nasty, brutish and short." Given the fact that human beings are equal enough in physical strength, mental shrewdness, and vulnerability to render negligible the strengths of others, everyone is dissatisfied with this state of affairs. Wanting above all else the security and freedom from fear that is impossible in a state of nature, human beings desperately seek an alternative to their miserable state of existence. Since they are fortunately rational as well as selfish, human beings realize that peace with their fellows is necessary for a tolerable existence. As Hobbes saw it, it is precisely our overriding fear of the insecurity of the state of nature that prompts us to accept the civilizing coercion of an external government. Revealingly, Hobbes jested that "fear and I were born twins," referring to his premature birth brought on by his mother's great fear of the approach of the menacing Spanish Armada.

As Hobbes saw it, the insecurity of the state of nature can be eliminated only when human beings submit to absolute and undivided governmental power. If human beings were morally perfect, a mutual promise to refrain from violence would suffice to provide the security which human beings are so desirous of obtaining, but given their amoral nature, "covenants, without the sword, are but words, and of no strength to secure man at all." Given the total selfishness of human beings, matters must be so arranged that it will never be to anyone's advantage to break his promise. This is possible, Hobbes believed, only if there is an absolute and unlimited government to enforce the promise. Anything less, he believed, would invite anarchy. While Hobbes himself was a strong defender of a monarchy (a view, it has been suggested, he may have adopted to curry favor with the king), what was essential, as Hobbes saw it, was that sovereignty be unlimited and undivided and not that it be given to a single individual rather than to a group of individuals. Nevertheless, it seemed to Hobbes that if the power of government were in the hands of more than one person, it would be much more difficult to assure the secrecy and constancy of policy that effective government requires, and the ever-present possibility of disagreement among the rulers would provide the potential for civil war and the dreaded anarchy that government was meant to eliminate.

Having consented (or having agreed that it would be rational to so consent[5]) to absolute sovereignty, citizens can justifiably revolt, Hobbes believed, only when the sovereign can no longer protect their lives and physical security. As Hobbes was well aware, a government's ability to provide its citizens with security is consistent with great tyranny; nevertheless, Hobbes believed that the tyranny of a government that assures its citizens physical protection is less obnoxious than the tyranny of the amoral law of the jungle and its resultant anarchy.

Locke: The Classical Social Contract Justification of Limited Sovereignty and the Separation of Powers

Like Hobbes' *Leviathan,* Locke's *Two Treatises of Government* (1690) was written in a time of political turmoil. This work served as a philosophical justification for the middle-class-inspired Glorious Revolution (Bloodless Revolution) of 1688, which increased the power of the English parliament relative to that of the monarchy. Locke's arguments for limited government had great influence in the United States and France as well as in Great Britain. Locke's influence upon such

---

[5]It is unclear whether Hobbes believed that the agreement of human beings to abide by the directives of an absolute sovereign actually occurred or was rather a *hypothetical* account of the rationality of such an agreement. The first view, as Hume sharply pointed out in his criticism of social contract theories, is in practically all cases refuted by the historical facts. According to the second view, however, the actual genesis of government is not at issue. What is at issue is whether it would be rational for a person to consent to his government. If we answer this question in the affirmative, then, it is claimed, we have the same moral obligation to abide by the directives of our government that we would have had if we had actually promised to so abide. Such a view was explicitly held by Spinoza, who was influenced by Hobbes.

American political theorists as Jefferson and Paine was reflected in the Declaration of Independence and the United States Constitution, which accepted all of Locke's major proposals for an ideal government. In France, Locke's influence was reflected in the political writings of Montesquieu and Rousseau, which in turn provided the philosophical justification for the French Revolution (1789–99).

Rejecting Hobbes' bleak picture of human nature, Locke saw human beings as motivated by feelings of benovolence and empathy as well as by self-interest. Most important, he believed that people have the capacity to renounce their selfish interests for the demands of an objective morality that could be used as a standard for judging the legitimacy of the actual laws of a society. At the core of Locke's political philosophy was his commitment to the *natural law* tradition which saw all existing laws as subject to appraisal by an objective and self-evident code of morality that is inherent in the rational fabric of the universe. Accepting the theological underpinning for this point of view (widely held in the Middle Ages) Locke saw the Judeo-Christian god as the ultimate source of natural law and the natural rights which flowed from it. As he saw it, human beings are God's property. Because of this, no human being can rightfully have complete control over another human being, who has such natural rights as the right to life, liberty, and property. It is these natural rights which provide God's ordained limits to the power of any government over its subjects, Locke believed.

Like Hobbes before him, Locke built his political philosophy upon the foundations of his conception of human beings in a state of nature. Locke's natural man, unlike Hobbes' natural man, recognizes the moral legitimacy of the natural rights of other people. In particular, he recognizes their right to life and to the ownership of those goods with which he "has mixed his labor."[6] In addition, he recognizes that he has a natural, God-given right to punish transgressors of the natural law. Indeed, as Locke saw it, there are actually two distinct rights here, "the one of punishing the crime, for restraint and preventing the like offense, which right of punishing is in everybody; the other of taking reparation, which belongs only to the injured party." While painting a much more optimistic picture of the state of nature than Hobbes, Locke too saw such a state as one that rational people would find less desirable than the institution of governmental authority for protecting life and property and punishing transgressions of the natural law. This is so, Locke claimed, because in a state of nature, there is no uniform and impartial administration of the natural law and often inadequate force for punishing its transgressors. In order to remedy the inadequacies of the state of nature, a government is required to lay down uniform and specific laws which follow from the laws of nature, to interpret and administer these laws, and to enforce them. In short, a legislature, judiciary and executive are required. Realizing the need for these governmental functions, human beings in a state of nature would find it reasonable to

---

[6]It is interesting to note that Locke's strong emphasis upon the natural right to property provided a philosophical justification for the legitimacy of the growing English middle class and the Whig party, which reflected its interests. As Karl Marx would later provocatively charge, Locke's political theory may be seen as an attempt *after the fact* at philosophical justification for a change in social relations actually caused by underlying economic currents.

delegate their own natural right of enforcing the natural law to some centralized government, as long as no single branch of government is given absolute power, for absolute power, Locke believed, is an invitation to tyranny. Ridiculing Hobbes' contention that individual security requires absolute government, Locke wrote:

> ...The hypothesis is that the timid individual would exchange the possible threat to life presented by 100,000 men, all of whom individually might attack him, for the threat to his life made possible by the authority of one man, who has 100,000 men under his command and can do anything he pleases, without fear...

A firm believer in majority rule, Locke saw the contractual surrender of individual authority to centralized government as a two-step procedure. First, there is the commitment to abide by the will of the majority. Second, the specific features and relative powers of the various branches of government are decided upon by the will of the majority. Insisting only on governmental "checks and balances" and on the separation of powers, Locke did not think it essential that the majority choose a specific form of government. For example, Locke was not in principle opposed to putting the power to make law into the hands of one or a very small number of people. Influenced by the British form of government, however, Locke expressed his preference for dual legislatures, consisting of "an assembly of hereditary nobility" and "an assembly of representatives chosen pro tempore by the people" and for a "single hereditary person having the constant, supreme, executive power." As Locke saw it, the supreme branch of government should be the legislature. The executive branch, he believed should be extremely limited, its principle function being to act in national emergencies.

The Primacy of Natural Rights

The notion of natural rights plays a central role in social contract theories as it did in natural law theory. In classical Greek and Thomistic natural law theory, this notion was perceived as derivable from some general concept of human nature. With the advent of individualistic moral and political thinking, as exemplified in the writings of Hobbes and Locke, the notion of natural rights took on an individualistic character that detached it from a comprehensive theory of the good life. For the new natural rights theorists, natural rights, and not utility or self-realization, were taken as the primary starting point for moral reasoning. Once rights and not values are seen as primary, the fundamental question is not how to achieve certain ends, but rather how to best preserve the fundamental rights to which human beings are *entitled* and from which they derive their *dignity* as equal members of a moral community. In this respect natural rights theory is similar to Kantian moral thinking. It would be a mistake, however, to assimilate modern natural rights theory with Kantian ethics, as some commentators do. Although the notion of rights plays a central role in Kantian ethics, Kant's view of morality is much broader in scope than that found in modern natural rights theory. Like the utilitarians, Kant in his discussion of the categorical imperative was concerned with the broad question of "how one is to act." In attempting to answer this question, Kant distinguishes (as other moral thinkers before him did) *perfect duties* which are *always* morally obligatory from *imperfect* duties which are not. According to Kant, one's duty to keep one's promises is a perfect one (Kant called it a *necessary* or *rigorous* duty), i.e., promises are always morally obligatory, regardless of the circumstances. On the other hand, Kant claimed that the duty to be benevolent was an imperfect one (or as he called it a *contingent* or *meritorious* duty), that is, although it is our duty to be benevolent to other human beings, one does not have a duty to be benevolent to *any* human being who would benefit from an act of benevolence. While one has a general duty to be benevolent, it is not one's duty to be benevolent in all circumstances, Kant believed. While a good man will give to charity, a poor person does not have a right to demand charity. On the other hand, once a promise is made to someone, that person has a right (is entitled) to expect that the person who made that promise will attempt to fulfill it. Unlike Kant, modern natural rights theorists narrow their focus to the obligations we have that are based on a person's rights or entitlements; yet, as we shall see in our discussion of Rawls and Nozick, their views of entitlements can be quite different.

Rawls and Nozick: Two Competiting Contemporary Theories of Justice in the Kantian and Social Contract Traditions

The Kantian and social contract traditions of moral reasoning have exerted great influence upon contemporary philosophers. Two competing theories of justice, the liberal welfare-state theory of John Rawls and the libertarian theory of Robert Nozick are deeply Kantian in outlook. Fundamental to both theories is an acceptance of the Kantian view of human beings as autonomous rational moral agents and a rejection of the utilitarian view of them as mere pleasure seekers. Following Kant, both Rawls and Nozick see justice and not utility as the primary moral value. Like Kant, they see justice as the cornerstone of human dignity and self-respect. Yet their theories of justice are very different and reflective of contemporary disagreements over the proper scope of government. Do poor people, for example, have a *right* to adequate food, housing and medical care, and to a job, if they are capable of socially productive work? Yes, say social welfare liberals; no, say their libertarian conservative counterparts. In defense of their position, libertarian conservatives often claim that since they have a *right* to what they have earned *legitimately* within our free economy, no one else has a right to confiscate these earnings through redistributive taxation. On the other hand, social-welfare liberals focus on the *undeserved inequalities* in the distribution of income, wealth and opportunities and on the grave and *unfair* difficulties the poor often have to break out of the cycle of poverty that engulfs them. Consequently, social-welfare liberals naturally support a greater degree of redistributive taxation which will reduce what are, to them, obviously unfair social inequalities. Yet to libertarian conservatives, these inequalities are not *unfair* at all. This disagreement at the heart of our political alliegences is reflected at a theoretical level in the writings of Nozick and Rawls. For Nozick, and less reflective conservative voters, principles of just acquisition and entitlement set limits to redistributive economics. If gross inequalities result from just acquisitions, *justice* demands that we pay this price, they claim. For Rawls, and less reflective liberal voters, principles of socialistic distribution set limits, if not define, legitimate entitlements. If the creation of a society whose goods are justly distributed results in massive interference with traditional notions of legitimate acquisition within the free market system, justice demands that we pay this price, they claim. So, as we see, although using the same word, Nozick and Rawls ground their concept of justice in different places.

The central notion in Robert Nozick's theory of justice is that of *entitlement*. Like Locke and Kant before him, Nozick equates justice with an absolute (inalienable) respect for certain basic human rights. As he sees it, people's rights are respected only when they are allowed to keep and control that to which they are *entitled*. An individual is entitled to those things which he has acquired without resort to force, theft, and fraud within a free marketplace. This is all one can demand *by right*. Although individuals can demand by right that they be left alone to make their own decisions as to how they are to live their lives, they cannot demand by right that the state provide them with assistance in the pursuit of their ends, Nozick declares, echoing Kant. Such positive interferences by the state are illegitimate impositions upon personal autonomy since the state can help some only by violating the entitlements of others. From this perspective, Nozick argues for a *minimum state* which is limited to the narrow passive functions of protection against force, theft, and fraud, and the enforcement of contracts. Nozick argues first that a minimum state would naturally arise out of an association of human beings "even though no one intended this or tried to bring it about, by a process which need not violate anyone's rights." He then goes on to argue that a more extensive state cannot be justified. In particular, he argues that a state is not justified in redistributing the wealth of its citizens or in paternalistic legislation (which aims at protecting people from themselves). Consequently, such things as the progressive income tax, publicly supported education and welfare, and mandatory seat-belts in automobiles are all unjustified infringements of human liberty for Nozick. If people want such things as education and health or unemployment insurance, they will be free in Nozick's minimal state to voluntarily contract for them. Nozick's extreme libertarianism is shared today by members of the Libertarian Party who are united in their commitment to individual freedom and opposition to the welfare state.

Unlike Nozick, Rawls is quite concerned with human welfare in his theory of justice. Nevertheless, like Nozick, he accepts the Kantian view that individual liberty takes precedence over the utilitarian concern with the common good. As Rawls puts it,

> Each person possesses an inviolability founded on justice that even the welfare of society as a whole cannot override. For this reason justice denies that the loss of

freedom for some is made right by a greater good shared by others...the rights secured by justice are not subject to political bargaining or to the calculus of social interests.

In the social contract tradition, Rawls tries to derive principles of morality from a hypothetical consideration of the moral principles that purely self-interested rational people would unanimously choose to regulate the practices of their society. Believing that fully knowledgeable self-interested people seeking to maximize their own interests would be unable to unanimously agree on any specific principles, Rawls hypothesizes that they are ignorant of their individual mental and physical attributes, their conceptions of the good life and of the particular places they will occupy in society. Furthermore, he assumes that, while the framers of his hypothetical social contract do not know the particular economic or political circumstances of their own society, they do "know the general facts of human society," and, in particular, "understand political affairs and the principles of economic theory; they know the basis of social organization and the laws of human psychology." Subject to certain other constraints, Rawls argues that, given this *veil of ignorance,* rational and purely self-interested persons would choose certain principles of justice to rule their lives over utilitarian principles and would commit themselves to abide by these principles when the veil of ignornace is lifted. According to Rawls, the participants would accept the following two principles:

1. *First Principle:* Each person is to have an equal right to the most extensive total system of equal basic liberties compatible with a similar system of liberty for all.
2. *Second Principle:* Social and economic inequalities are to be arranged so that they are both:
   (a) to the greatest benefit of the least advantaged, consistent with the just savings principles [which obligates us to deal justly with future generations by, for example, conserving natural resources], and
   (b) attached to offices and positions open to all under conditions of fair equality and opportunity.

According to Rawls, the first principle has priority over the second. Liberty can legitimately be infringed only for the sake of greater liberty, and not for the sake of utility. Having agreed upon the basic principles of justice that are to be the foundation of society, Rawls envisions the veil of ignorance slowly being lifted to allow more facts to be known as they are relevant to decisions concerning the application of the basic principles to concrete realities and for choices between alternative secondary moral principles. Yet faithful to his Kantian perspective, Rawls assumes that the veil of ignorance would always prevent a participant in his hypothetical social contract from knowing their own particular interests, assuring the impartiality and universality which he takes as presupposed by the moral point of view.

According to Rawls' second principle, inequalities of power, wealth, and other resources are justifiable only if they work out to the advantage of the worst-off members of society. No greater disadvantage, however small, for the worst-off members of society can justify a greater advantage, however large, for those better-off. From this perspective, Rawls views rational people acting under the constraint of the veil of ignorance as very cautious people who plan their lives on the basis of the least favorable possibility about how things will turn out.

Critical Comments

Rawls' and Nozick's theories of justice are works of intellectual brilliance. But perhaps, like Kant, they overplay the role of reason in moral judgment and underplay the role of feeling. Neither Rawls nor Nozick seems willing to accept the existence of conflicts of basic moral principles, irreconcilable by reason alone. As such they construct elaborate moral systems that do justice to some of our moral intuitions only at the expense of conflicting ones that most of us are unwilling to abandon. For example, Nozick in his preoccupation with individual freedom and entitlement to the goods and services that one produces in a free market, finds no central place for the concepts of need and benevolence in his scheme. Like Locke before him, Nozick claims that our basic right to engage in economic exchanges that take place without force, theft, and fraud is inalienable, but he cannot provide a logically compelling argument for this controversial position as well as for his general view that entitlement claims always have priority over those based on need. Equally fundamental, while admitting that currently legitimate acquisitions within the free marketplace cannot always be traced back to legitimate acquisitions, Nozick conveniently sidesteps the issue of the rectification of previous injustice. This creates a major gap in Nozick's theory, for history attests to the central role that deceit, robbery, and violence have played in creating the status quo. Consider, for example, the plight of American Indians and Blacks in the United States today. Certainly, Nozick's implicit acceptance of the justness of the status quo will rightly be hotly contested by those who have suffered the legacy of previous injustices and cry out for reparation or compensation. As we shall see, such claims permeate contemporary arguments for preferential treatment. Nozick, however, conveniently neglects them, as he neglects the fact, stressed by Marx, that present patterns of distribution tend to trap the poor in a cycle of poverty that is not easily broken while those who are lucky enough to inherit great wealth can, if they so choose, sit back and leisurely allow their wealth to beget greater wealth. Yet if we trace back the origin of this wealth, we often find that it was "earned" only by the exploitation of others whose current descendents suffer from the legacy of that exploitation. On the other hand, Rawls, in his preoccupation with freedom and equality, finds no place for an individual's right to control that which he has produced. As Nozick rightly points out, Rawls presents his view as if the goods of society had suddenly rained down haphazardly upon us as an undeserved gift from God. Conveniently, Rawls sidesteps the question of how those in grave need came to be in grave need. In the real world, however, as arguments over issues of welfare indicate, such questions are quite important, for the injustice and ultimate disutility of rewarding the lazy is not easily forgotten when individuals are asked to sacrifice some of their earnings to help those in grave need. Both Nozick's and

Rawls' moral systems are inadequate to the complexity of the moral life and for that reason do not provide a pattern for living to which most of us would be willing to fully commit ourselves. Indeed, perhaps the truth for most of us is that the principles we choose to live by cannot be reconciled into a single coherent moral system.

DISCUSSION QUESTIONS

1. If you were to detach yourself from your own present vested interests, what basic principles to govern social life would you advocate? Why? How does our present society fall short of your ideal?
2. Do you agree with Nozick that the poor do not have *a right* to welfare? On what basis, if any, does the government have a right to tax individuals to pay for social services to which they would not themselves voluntarily consent? On what grounds, if any, can it be said to be *just* that the rich should pay a higher percentage of their earnings in taxes than the poor? Should the government guarantee everyone a minimum standard of living and/or impose a limit on what one can earn? Could such governmental intervention in the free marketplace reasonably be seen as demands of justice?
3. Evaluate the following claim:

    When Rawls speaks of "our intuitive conviction of the primacy of justice," he is speaking for himself and not for the majority of human beings. For them, it is security and not justice which is the most important virtue of social systems.

FURTHER READINGS

Thomas Hobbes' social contract view is found in his *Leviathan*. The Bobbs-Merrill (1958) edition with a seven-page introduction by Herbert W. Schneider modernizes the seventeenth-century English in which it was written, making it easier to read than the Pelican Classics (1951) edition with a 154-page introduction by C. B. MacPherson. John Locke's view is found in his *Second Treatise of Government,* which was reprinted in 1952 by Bobbs-Merrill with a 16-page introduction by Thomas P. Peardon and in 1968 by Hackett with a 14-page introduction by C. B. MacPherson. Peter Laslett supplies an introduction of over 100 pages in the 1960 Cambridge University Press edition, which was reprinted by The New American Library in 1963. J. W. Gough's *John Locke's Political Philosophy,* second edition (Oxford University Press, 1973) consists of eight of Gough's clear and nontechnical essays on aspects of Locke's political philosophy, including its historical influence. Jean-Jacques Rousseau expresses his view in his *The Social Contract,* translated from the French by Maurice Cranston for Penguin books (1968) and by Judith R. Masters for St. Martin's Press (1978). Both translations are good and preceeded by good introductions. David Hume's "Of The Original Contract" is a classic criticism of the idea of a social contract. This essay, along with the essays by Locke and Rousseau, are found in Ernest Barker (ed.), *The Social Contract* (Oxford University Press, 1960) and are preceeded by an editorial introduction.

In his *The Social Contract,* second edition (Greenwood Press, 1957), J. W. Gough traces the historical development of the social contract idea from its roots in ancient Greek philosophy, through its development in the Middle Ages, and in the political writings of Hobbes, Spinoza, Rousseau, Kant, and Hegel. Gough's primary concern, however, is critical analysis and not historical exposition. The book is well-written, but detailed and philosophically involved.

John Rawls' elaborate development of the idea of arriving at principles of political justice through a social contract is found in his *A Theory of Justice* (Harvard University Press, 1970) and Robert Nozick's contrasting view is found in his *Anarchy, State and Utopia* (Basic Books, 1974).

12. RULE UTILITARIANISM

"Rule utilitarianism" refers to a cluster of theories developed and supported by twentieth-century philosophers dissatisfied with the potential injustice of traditional utilitarianism and the Kantian attempt to detach the foundations of morality from a consideration of consequences and human psychology. Although utilitarian in its ultimate concern with beneficial consequences, rule utilitarianism incorporates this concern with a Kantian requirement either that actions should be capable of universalization or that they should be guided by specific moral rules and not by a direct appeal to the principle of utility. The simplest version of this cluster of theories employs the Kantian notion of universalization. As this theory sees it, in determining how one is to act, the relevant moral question is not "What would the likely consequences of *this act* be?" but "What would the likely consequences be if *everyone* were to do the same?"—that is, according to this view, the morality of an individual act is to be judged by the utility of the general performance of acts relevantly similar to it. For convenience, let us label this view of moral obligation *general-rule-utilitarianism.*

While general-rule-utilitarianism makes the rightness of an action depend on the consequences of its universalization (philosophers call this *utilitarian generalization*) and not on its correspondence to independently specifiable moral rules, this is not the case with other rule-utilitarian theories. These theories draw a distinction between the procedures to be employed in justifying specific actions and moral rules. As these theories see it, when determining how one ought to act, one should not appeal directly to the principle of utility, focusing on whether a specific action is likely to have the best consequences. Instead, one should determine what one ought to do on the basis of specific moral rules which are themselves justified in terms of their utility. Some of these theories claim that actions should be justified in terms of the actual and recognized rules of a given society, while others claim that actions should be justified in terms of moral rules which would be ideal for a given society, from a utilitarian point of view. For convenience, let us call the former class of theories of moral obligation *actual-rule-utilitarianism*[7] and the latter class *ideal-rule-utilitarianism*, and let us call the traditional utilitarian theory, which claims that the rightness of an action should be judged by its consequences, *act-utilitarianism.*[8]

[7]There are different forms of *actual-rule-utilitarianism*. According to some forms, a person has an obligation to abide by the moral code of his society only if it is, in some loose sense, *reasonable* from a utilitarian point of view—even if it is less than *ideal* from that point of view. More commonly, however, actual-rule-utilitarianism is used to refer to that theory of moral obligation that asserts that a person has no moral obligations apart from the obligations imposed on him by the moral code of his society. Consequently, this theory is quite anti-utilitarian in its conception of an individual's moral obligations. It is utilitarian, however, in asserting that it is utility that justifies decisions as to whether a moral code is itself justifiable or ought to be changed. In this section, actual-rule-utilitarianism shall be used to refer to this theory.

[8]The distinction between act and rule utilitarianism is a twentieth century one which was not made by Bentham and Mill. Given Bentham and Mill's concern with amending the laws of England into greater conformity with the principle of utility, they naturally focused on justifying rules of conduct rather than specific acts. Indeed, it has been suggested that Mill's utilitarianism, unlike Bentham's, is more attuned to rule than act utilitarianism.

The merits of the various theories of rule-utilitarianism over act-utilitarianism have been a subject of controversy among contemporary philosophers. Such theories are not as much in vogue today as they once were. First, it is not clear how general-rule-utilitarianism is to be distinguished from act-utilitarianism, and if it can be distinguished, how it can be justified. Second, if, as actual- and ideal-rule-utilitarians claim, the principle of utility is the sole standard to be used in justifying moral rules, then these rules would seem to allow unjust social practices that most of us would consider wrong. Consequently, it would seem that, utilitarianism, in any of its forms, must be supplemented by independent and possibly conflicting principles of justice. Let us explore these contentions.

The difficulty in distinguishing general-rule-utilitarianism from act-utilitarianism resides in the problem, mentioned in our discussion of Kantian ethics, of deciding upon the proper categorization of an act. To illustrate this problem, let us turn to the case of "the mad bomber" in our list of moral dilemmas. If we were to reason as act-utilitarians in deciding whether the mad bomber should be tortured, we would focus upon the likely consequences of this course of action as opposed to others. Certainly, immediate utility would be maximized by torturing the mad bomber as a necessary means for saving the lives of many innocent people. The perceptive act-utilitarian will also have to focus upon the more remote consequences of this act—in particular, the effect torturing the bomber will have upon general respect for law and upon those law enforcement officials who would violate their legal duty by so acting. Nevertheless, the monumental undesirable consequences of allowing the bombs to explode would seem to justify the act of torturing the mad bomber from a purely act-utilitarian point of view. Indeed, the act-utilitarian justification for this course of action would be greatly strengthened if it could be done in secret (perhaps by killing the bomber and falsely claiming that he died in an escape attempt).

Now, a general-rule-utilitarian will most likely claim that his standard does not lead to the same conclusion, morally repugnant to many of us. According to our general-rule-utilitarian, we must weigh the consequences, not of the specific act of torture against the refusal to so act in this case, but rather against the consequences of everyone taking the law into their own hands as a way of averting violence. Certainly, our general-rule-utilitarian will claim, the consequences of this becoming a general practice would be disastrous. Consequently, it is wrong for us to so act, even if in this particular situation such an act would have the best consequences. Since it would be wrong for everyone to act in such a manner, it is wrong for anyone to do so.

The reasoning here is unclear. According to our general-rule-utilitarian we must focus upon the consequences of *everyone* doing the *same*. But who is to count as "everyone"? All those in situations where it appears to them that breaking the law would have desirable consequences? All law enforcement officials who are inclined to break the law for altruistic reasons and risk undesirable consequences to themselves when this seems the only way to avoid great violence? Similarly, what is to count as a situation which is relevantly similar to the given situation? One where *violence* is threatened and *can be averted* by the use of *torture*? One where *mass murder* is threatened and *can be averted only by torturing the responsible party* in a situation where one can be reasonably assured that this action can be kept *secret*? It would appear that if we incorporate every relevant utilitarian consideration into our description of the act in question it would make no difference if we ask "What would happen if everyone did the same?" instead of "What would happen if this act were performed?" In our example, if one could be reasonably assured that the torture of the bomber could be kept secret and consequently not act as a precedent to be followed in less clear cases or lead to a more diffuse lessening of general respect for law, it would appear that a general-rule-utilitarian should incorporate this relevant utilitarian characteristic into his description of the act in question and conclude that the consequences of the general performance of such acts would have the best consequences.

Similarly, it would be absurd for a general-rule-utilitarian to abide by a "keep off the grass" sign that is posted to preserve a lawn *already* ruined by trampling and to justify the action by claiming that the consequences of general disregard for such signs would be undesirable. Certainly, a general-rule-utilitarian should narrow his or her focus to include all relevant utilitarian circumstances surrounding the situation and as such should focus upon the consequences of everyone disregarding "keep off the grass" signs that *do not serve the purpose for which they were intended*. But once all relevant utilitarian factors are incorporated into one's description of one's act, general-rule-utilitarianism will justify whatever traditional act-utilitarianism can justify and consequently is equally subject to the charge of being potentially unjust.

For example, consider a group of people engaged in some cooperative enterprise—let us say, preparing a cooperative vegetable garden, requiring the participation of most, but not all, of those who will benefit from this enterprise. Practically everyone is willing to do his share *out of a sense of justice*, but one general-rule-utilitarian is not. Realizing that his effort is not especially needed and that no one will even realize that he did not participate in the work, he decides to spend his time in a more personally enjoyable manner. Although he is acting *unfairly*, accepting the benefits of the vegetable garden without assuming the burden that others have assumed, he need not care if *everyone* who shares his reasoning does likewise if he knows that most people do not think that way and that the necessary work will be done. Supporters of the general-rule-utilitarian point of view will object that our reluctant gardener should not focus on the consequences of everyone who thinks like him not working on the garden, but rather on the consequences of absolutely everyone connected with the garden not working; but no utilitarian reason can be given for a rejection of the narrower categorization. It is our sense of justice, and not utility, that so strongly inclines us to reject it.

Let us turn our attention now to actual-rule-utilitarianism. Underlying this view is the assumption that it is for the greatest good for individuals to act on the basis of specific moral rules, less general in scope than the principle of utility itself. If individuals always felt justified in abandoning specific moral rules whenever it was believed that the consequences would be maximized by so doing, confusion, it is claimed, would be the natural result. The predictability and guidance that specific rules of conduct provide would be lost if the principle of utility itself could be directly appealed to as a justification of specific actions. The moral life requires individuals to subject themselves to established ways of doing things—that is, to practices—that are defined by rules and require abdication of full liberty to act on utilitarian grounds. To accept a practice is to commit oneself to follow the rules that define it. For example, to accept the practice of promising, one must abdicate the right to decide on particular occasions whether it would be best on the whole to keep the promise. To refuse to do so is to refuse to participate in the practice of promise-keeping. Similarly, to accept the practice of punishment that exists in this country is to accept a system for making and applying criminal laws defined by certain rules. Under these rules, legislators in deciding upon the justification of criminal laws are permitted to appeal to general utilitarian considerations which are precluded from the judge who is bound to abide by general rules of law which serve to guide and limit his discretion to act as he thinks best in a given situation.

Once one distinguishes between practices and acts falling within a practice, the actual-rule-utilitarian claims, it can be seen that utilitarian justifications should be reserved for decisions relating to the moral desirability of certain practices but, once a practice is instituted, they do not properly belong to questions of what one should do within that practice. Such questions are answered by reference to the rules defining the practice and not to the principle of utility itself. This view of the logically indispensable place of rules within the moral life stands in contrast to traditional act-utilitarianism. For traditional utilitarians, such as Bentham, specific moral rules of conduct were not logically indispensable to the moral life, but rather were needed as practical guides for conduct, necessitated only by the brute facts of man's finite knowledge of the consequences of his actions and of his tendency toward partiality and rationalization. If man were a god, endowed by perfect omniscience and concern for others, such rules could be discarded in favor of the principle of utility. Given man's limitations, however, specific moral rules are necessary as rules of thumb that experience has shown usually maximize utility. Nevertheless, one ought to break any such rule whenever it is clear that to do so will have greater utility in the long run than will abiding by it. As the foremost act-utilitarian of our day, J.J.C. Smart puts it,

> Suppose that there is a rule R and that in 99 percent of cases the best possible results are obtained by acting in accordance with R. Then clearly R is a useful rule of thumb; if we have not time or are not impartial enough to assess the consequences of an action it is an extremely good bet that the thing to do is to act in accordance with R. But is it not monstrous to suppose that if we have worked out the consequences and if we have perfect faith in the impartiality of our calculations, and if we know that in this instance to break R will produce better results than to keep it, we should nevertheless obey the rule? Is it not to erect R into a sort of idol if we keep it when breaking it will prevent, say, some avoidable misery? Is not this a form of superstitious rule-worship (easily explicable psychologically) and not the rational thought of a philosopher.

The actual-rule-utilitarian who denies the justification of breaking specified moral rules seems to be in an unstable position. If specific moral rules are, as he claims, means to the end of utility, why should they not be put aside when they fail that end? If utility can justify a rule, why not an act? As Smart suggests, the rule-utilitarian seems committed to a rule-worship that the principle of utility should disallow. It is one thing to point out the need for the stabiilty and guidance provided by moral rules and the practices they define; it is something else to say that the rules defining a practice, however good they may be in general, should never be violated regardless of the consequences.

For example, if the law enforcement officials in our mad bomber case decide to torture the bomber, they will be violating the rules defining the practice of punishment in this country. And, even if we assume that this practice can be justified on a purely utilitarian basis, it does not appear unreasonable for these law enforcement officials to consider their moral obligation to humanity as a whole to be of such overriding moment in this situation as to outweigh their obligations as defined by a practice to which they may have a deep commitment. Although breaking these obligations often would be logically incompatible with such a commitment, breaking them once or very infrequently would not. The commitment to any practice and to the roles defined by it should never be absolute and blind us to our foremost obligation to humanity as a whole.

Indeed, actual-rule-utilitarianism neglects the fact that our responsibilities, as defined by the different roles we occupy under different practices, can often conflict and that the rules that are supposed to guide the moral life will inevitably be incomplete and lead to conflicts. In such cases, the actual-rule-utilitarian would have to appeal directly to the principle of utility to determine what one ought to do. This may happen much more than he foresees.

Actual-rule-utilitarianism, like so many theories of normative ethics, captures something important about the moral life, but then goes on to overemphasize its importance. What this theory captures is our feeling that we usually have a moral obligation to abide by the rules and practices that actually exist in our society, even if they are less than ideal. Although irrational social conditioning no doubt plays a part, many of us recognize that it is usually *unfair* for one to accept the benefits that the rule-governed behavior of others makes possible while refusing, oneself, to submit to these same rules. As Kant before us, we are sensitive to the special *injustice* that such behavior usually involves. Nevertheless, while it is reasonable to claim that we have some obligation to abide by the moral code of our society, it is quite unreasonable to claim, as actual-rule-utilitarians do, that one cannot speak of one's moral obligations apart from the moral code of one's society. Clearly, most of us believe, as we should, that acts can be judged right or wrong apart from the prevalent moral standards of our society. If this were not the case, we would have had no moral right to try Nazis in Nuremberg for crimes against humanity, for they, after all, just went along with the moral code of their society. Clearly, we believe that the Nazis who went along acted wrongly, while those who refused to do so, acted rightly, regardless of what their society said. There is more to the moral life than actual-rule-utilitarianism is willing to allow. Recognizing this, many philosophers have turned to the ideal-rule-utilitarian point of view.

While there are different types of rule-utilitarian theories which relate the rightness of actions to possible as opposed to actual moral rules, the term ideal-rule-utilitarianism is usually reserved for the view that "an act is right in a given society if and only if it conforms to a moral code whose general acceptance in that society would maximize utility." The great virtue of this theory is that it allows us to judge the rightness or wrongness of actions independently of the moral standards that actually exist in a given society. On the other hand, it achieves this objective at the cost of providing a standard for judging the rightness of actions that is impractical and serves to distort the true nature of moral choice. According to this theory, a morally perplexed person is not supposed to ask, "Will my act have the best consequences," or "Does the moral code of my society allow me to do this," but rather, "What would the moral code of my society allow me to do in this situation if it were that code, among all possible moral codes, which would maximize utility in this society." It is difficult enough to know in many cases what the first two standards prescribe; the third, however, seems designed only for an omniscient god.

As those familiar with the law well know, legal theorists often disagree over which legal rules would exist in ideal utilitarian legal codes. At any rate, such questions, if they are to be useful, must take place within the context of proposals for specific changes within an ongoing complex legal system. According to the ideal-rule-utilitarian, however, moral questions are not to be related to a specific functioning legal system or to an existent moral code but to an ideal moral code that has never existed. In addition, underlying the ideal-rule-utilitarian view is the myth that in principle, if not in practice, there is an objective way to determine which moral code would be ideal for a given society. Utilitarians may speak as if all the various elements of the good life can somehow be reduced to a single scale and weighed objectively against each other, but, as suggested before, this may be an illusion. If this is so, the utilitarian quest, in whatever form, for the maximization of the good is a quest that can lead us in different directions. Given the apparent impossibility of objectively measuring the utility of things, one should be suspicious of the ideal-rule-utilitarian's claim that "an ideal moral code would allow (prohibit). . . ." While such claims are easy to make, it is quite another matter to justify them. Such claims often serve as convenient rationalizations for moral beliefs whose sources lie elsewhere. The true motives for defending a moral position of even the most rational of philosophers can often be hidden behind a self-deceiving and ultimately indefensible facade of rationality; it is just that the rational facades of philosophers are more abstractly and intricately woven.

Assuming, however, that we can attach some definite meaning to the notion of an ideal moral code and can agree on what such a code would prescribe in concrete situations, why ought we to follow this ideal moral code when we know that others will not and consequently that the good that general compliance would bring cannot be achieved? Using our "keep off the grass" sign as an example, is it wrong for one not to abide by the sign when practically no one else does and one's action will have absolutely no effect upon the grass? Similarly, and of more moment, one would certainly assume that it would be best for nations to accept a rule which foreswears the use of nuclear weapons. But ought a nation to do so when it is reasonably assured that others will not? The ideal-rule-utilitarian directive to always act in accordance with that set of rules whose general compliance would maximize utility, would seem to have a place only in a world where one could rely upon others to do similarly; yet this is a description of an ideal world sadly different from the world in which we find ourselves and in which we must make our moral decisions.

Some critics of ideal-rule-utilitarianism have suggested that it, no less than general-rule-utilitarianism, reduces to act-utilitarianism. As they see it, one of the rules of an ideal moral code would be always to do what will maximize utility, and another rule would be to appeal directly to the principle of utility when the rules of the ideal moral code conflict. If both these rules are accepted, the ideal moral code collapses into the act-utilitarian principle. Defenders of ideal-rule-utilitarianism have replied that no ideal moral code would have a rule allowing people to appeal directly to the principle of utility in deciding what act is right. Life, they have claimed, would be chaotic if such a rule were generally accepted and acted on by members of a given society. Such a claim is dubious. First of all, it is interesting to note that the influential American Law Institute accepts the principle of utility itself as a rule which supersedes all other rules in its (1958) Model Penal Code. According to the A.L.I.,

> Conduct which the actor believes to be necessary to avoid an evil to himself or to another is justifiable, provided that the evil sought to be avoided by such conduct is greater than that sought to be prevented by the law defining the offense charged....

Although the A.L.I. considered this rule to provide "a general justification for conduct that otherwise would constitute an offense," it obviously did not think that such a rule would lead to chaos. In the real world, the mere existence of a generally accepted moral or legal rule does not mean that people will tend to act on such a rule whenever they think that they are justified in doing so. In the case at issue, the A.L.I. expected that in unclear cases those who violate established legal rules on the grounds that utility demands such action would have the burden of defending their moral judgment in court. This is a powerful deterrent to acting lightly in such cases.

It is important that we draw a distinctinon between those moral rules that are incorporated in legal systems which function as constraints on human behavior and those rules that a person should appeal to in deciding how he morally ought to act in a given situation. Any rational person, of whatever ethical persuasion, would want the law to encourage people to follow specific rules and not to directly appeal to the principle of utility in most situations of moral choice. Similarly, any rational person would want a law that is effective in motivating people to comply with its directives. In addition, any rational person would want people to be morally trained to have respect for specific moral rules (such as, "keep your promises") and to feel guilty when these rules are broken. In the moral education of children, it must be specific rules and not their exceptions or abstract ones like the principle of utility that must first be impressed upon the developing moral conscience. If moral education succeeds, people will naturally be hesitant to appeal directly to the principle of utility instead of to the specific moral prohibitions which were so deeply engrained into them by their early moral training. It is because of this early moral training that people naturally feel guilty when they lie or break promises, but not when they violate the principle of utility.

But the question still arises: Is it right for a person to break a moral or legal rule when he is reasonably assured that this would have the best consequences? For example, should people keep promises when they are reasonably assured that doing so would not have the best consequences? The act-utilitarian would say yes. The ideal-rule-utilitarian will say no. But what justification can he give for his position. To say simply "the rules don't allow it" subjects him to Smart's charge that he is a rule worshiper, who follows rules as an end in itself. He can't say "it would be unfair (or dishonest)," for as a utilitarian, questions of justice (or honesty) that are not based on utilitarian considerations are not supposed to have any affect upon his rational moral decisions. So what can he say?

The most fundamental charge that can be made against ideal-rule-utilitarianism is that it fails in its underlying objective to avoid the charge leveled against act-utilitarianism—that it is an incomplete moral theory which neglects necessary and *independent* moral considerations, such as that of distributive justice. There is no guarantee that a single-minded pursuit of utility will not lead an ideal-rule-utilitarian to embrace moral rules which go against one's sense of justice. For example, our criminal justice system might very well be made more efficient, from a solely utilitarian standpoint, if harsher punishments, now considered inhumane, were instituted, if less due process of law were afforded criminals, if collective punishments were allowed (punishment of a group for the acts of one of its members), and if strict liability (liability without fault) were used much more than it is now. It is the *injustice* of these measures that leads us to reject them and not their ultimate disutility. Indeed, incorporated, in uneasy balance, within our criminal law are two conflicting models—the utilitarian one of maximizing the *efficiency* of our crime control procedures and the Kantian one of respecting *the rights* of individuals caught up within the criminal *justice* system. The proper balance that should exist in a functioning legal system between these two conflicting models is a perennial topic for debate, but practically all of us would shudder at the thought of a criminal law ruthlessly devoted to the general welfare and eradication of crime and unwilling to ever sacrifice that objective to even a small degree by a desire to protect the rights of individuals caught up in the criminal process.

It has been suggested by some utilitarians that although it is theoretically possible for justice to conflict with utility, this is impossible in practice, given a realistic knowledge of human nature. Injustice, it is claimed, will never lead to the maximization of human happiness in the long run. For example, Paul Taylor relates such an argument in his *Principles of Ethics*. He tells us to imagine a society which unfairly distributes its benefits and burdens. In such a society, the argument goes, an individual unfairly treated will not accept the rules of this society as fair and will conform to the rules only because he is forced to. Taylor continues the argument, writing,

...To make sure that social conflict will not get out of hand, let those who accept the rules establish a power structure which will ensure their domination over those who reject them.... To this the utilitarian replies, history has shown us that no such power structure can last for long; even while it does last, the effort spent by the "ins" on maintaining domination over the "outs" makes it impossible for the "ins" to obtain much happiness in life. A social system of this kind is constantly liable to break down. The need to preserve their position of power drives the "ins" to even greater measures of surveillance and repression. The society as a whole becomes a closed system in which the freedom of all individuals is diminished.... Inevitably, there develops an intolerance of diversity in thought, in speech, in styles of life. A narrow conformity of taste, ideas, and outward behavior becomes the main concern of everyone. What kind of "happiness" is this?

The upshot of the argument is now apparent: Given a clear-headed view of the world as it is and a realistic understanding of man's nature, it becomes more and more evident that injustice will never have, in the long run, greater utility than justice. Even if the two principles of justice and utility can logically be separated in the abstract and even if they can be shown to yield contradictory results in hypothetical cases, it does not follow that the fundamental idea of utilitarianism must be given up. For it remains the case that, when we are dealing with the actual practices of people in their social and historical settings, to maximize happiness... requires an open, freely given commitment on the part of *everyone* to comply with the rules for settling conflicts among them. Anyone who is coerced into following the rules when he, in good conscience, cannot accept them as being fair... will not consider himself morally obligated to abide by them.... From his point of view, he will have good reason to do what he can to change or abolish the rules. He will join with anyone else who rejects them as unfair, in an effort to overcome his powerlessness. Thus injustice becomes, in actual practice, a source of great social disutility.

Although this argument has merit, it does not support the contention that social injustice will never maximize utility in the *long* run. The unjustly treated may be so few in number or so powerless or fearful as to prove no threat to those who exploit them. More menacingly, the exploited could be brainwashed into accepting their plight. As Marx saw, those in power often do not need physical power to exploit others, but can more effectively achieve this end through the vast power of ideological or religious persuasion where they may cloak their vested interests in the garments of morality. This is precisely why Marx called religion "the opium of the people," for those in power can use religion as an instrument for perpetuating the injustice of the status quo. (Consider, for example, the American experience under slavery, where the Southern plantation owner often encouraged religion among his slaves as a vehicle for teaching them to accept their plight or, at least, not to revolt against it.)

History does support the contention that unjust power structures are inherently unstable or that societies which tolerate more individual freedom tend to be happier than those who do not. In addition, there is no invariable connection between democratic values, economic justice and the tolerance of diversity, as the argument Taylor presents suggests. A democratic society can be devoted to economic justice for all its citizens and yet be quite intolerant, by popular opinion if not criminal law, to divergent lifestyles. Conversely, a society can be undemocratic and economically unjust but allow its minorities great cultural freedom and diversity of lifestyles as long as this diversity does not threaten the political and economic order. It would be nice if this world were so constituted that injustice would always be unprofitable in the long run, even to those who initially profit from it, but this is simply not the way it is in this world. As Henry Fielding, the author of *Tom Jones* put it in a slightly different context:

> There are a set of...moral writers who teach that virtue is the certain road to happiness and vice to misery in this world. A very wholesome and comfortable doctrine, and to which we have but one objection, namely, that it is not true.

The fact that philosophers so often use arguments such as the one presented by Taylor is an indication of the tendency of some philosophers to distort the facts in order to save a moral theory which would otherwise run counter to strong moral sensibilities.

The ultimate failure of rule-utilitarianism in any of its forms is that it, no less than traditional act-utilitarianism, when unlimited by other moral principles, can justify more than most people's moral sensibilities are willing to allow. Rule-utilitarianism, with its emphasis on utilitarian generalization or the general following of moral rules, may give the appearance of preventing this from happening, but it does not. Certainly, as rule-utilitarians point out, many of us would feel that it is wrong not to vote for the candidate of our choice when we are assured that he will win without our vote. We feel this way, however, not because of some abstract commitment to general moral rules or to a nebulous principle of utilitarian generalization, but as a result of our realization that if others vote when we refrain, we are acting *unfairly* since we have no special claim to so act, and consequently our happiness is parasitic upon the efforts of others. Such notions are part of the general concept of justice and cannot be assimilated to that of utility. The moral life cannot be reduced to a purely teleological model and remain faithful to our deepest moral sensibilities. This is, indeed, the claim of David Ross, a twentieth century philosopher to whom we now turn.

DISCUSSION QUESTIONS

1. You are driving in a deserted area and have stopped at a red light. You are already late for a social engagement and are impatiently waiting for the light to change. You are absolutely positive that there are no vehicles coming, nor any pedestrians or policemen. (The visibility is excellent and unobstructed in every direction.) You want very much to run the red light, but you feel that it's wrong. Is it?

2. Evaluate our moral dilemmas as you think the different sorts of rule-utilitarians would, comparing their evaluation of these cases to those of an act-utilitarian.

FURTHER READINGS

Although J. S. Mill did not make this distinction himself, J. O. Urmson defends the view that Mill was a rule, and not an act, utilitarian in his article "The Interpretation of the Moral Philosophy of J. S. Mill" which appeared in *The Philosophical Quarterly,* 3 (1953). Urmson's contention is challenged in Brian Cupple's "A Defense of the Received Interpretation of J. S. Mill" which appeared in the *Australasian Journal of Philosophy,* 50 (1972).

In "Two Concepts of Rules," *Philosophical Review,* 64 (1955), John Rawls argues for the merits of a type of limited actual-rule-utilitarianism over act-utilitarianism. As he sees it, some of our actions (but not all of them) can only be morally evaluated in terms of certain rules or practices (which are justified in terms of their utility) that define these actions as the sorts of actions they are taken to be.

The most sophisticated defense of a version of ideal-rule-utilitarianism is found in Richard Brandt's *A Theory of the Right and the Good* (Oxford University Press, 1979). Brandt presents a less elaborate defense of the same view in his article "Some Merits of One Form of Rule-Utilitarianism," which originally appeared in *University of Colorado Series in Philosophy,* 3 (1967), and is reprinted in Joel Feinberg and Henry West (eds.) *Moral Philosophy: Classical Texts and Contemporary Problems* (Dickenson, 1977). This anthology also contains a discussion by the foremost contemporary defender of act-utilitarianism, J.J.C. Smart, of the place of rules in act-utilitarianism; this discussion is a section of his article "An Outline of a System of Utilitarianism" (his contribution to the book *Utilitarianism: For and Against,* coauthored by the utilitarian critic Bernard Williams).

Criticisms of ideal-rule-utilitarianism are found in J.J.C. Smart's "Extreme and Restricted Utilitarianism" which originally appeared in the *Philosophical Quarterly,* 6 (1956) and in H. J. McCloskey's "An Examination of Restricted Utilitarianism" which appeared in the *Philosophical Review,* 66 (1957). Both articles are reprinted in the excellent anthology *Contemporary Utilitarianism* edited by Michael D. Bayles (Doubleday, 1968). This anthology also contains the previously mentioned articles by Urmson and Rawls.

The classic treatment of "generalization arguments" (i.e., arguments of the form: "If everyone were to do that, the consequences would be disastrous (undesirable), therefore no one ought to do that") is found in Marcus G. Singer's *Generalization in Ethics* (Knopf, 1961). In this technical study, Singer attempts to distinguish legitimate from illegitimate generalization arguments. For example, in rejecting the argument: "Since if everyone were to produce food, the consequences would be disastrous, then no one should produce food" as an illegitimate generalization argument, Singer claims that all valid generalization arguments must be "invertable,"—that is, it cannot be the case that the consequences would be disastrous if no one did the thing in question, as well as if everyone did.

David Lyon's *Forms and Limits of Utilitarianism* (Claredon Press, 1964) is another technical analytic study of rule-utilitarianism. In this work, Lyons argues that general rule-utilitarianism reduces to act-utilitarianism and criticizes ideal-rule-utilitarianism. Excerpts from Lyons' and Singer's books are found in Wilfred Sellars and John Hospers (eds.), *Readings in Ethical Theory,* second edition (Prentice-Hall, 1970) which is directed to the analytically sophisticated reader.

The quotation from J.J.C. Smart is taken from his article "Extreme and Restricted Utilitarianism" in the 1956 *Philosophical Quarterly,* p. 348. The quotation from Paul Taylor comes from his *Principles of Ethics* (Dickenson, 1975), pp. 77–78 and is reprinted by permission of Wadsworth Publishing Company. The quotation from Henry Fielding is found on p. 672 of The Modern Library edition of *The History of Tom Jones.*

13. THE ETHICS OF W. D. ROSS

As we have seen, unrestricted utilitarian thinking would seem to have logical consequences which go contrary to most people's moral convictions. For example, most people believe themselves to have special obligations to particular individuals which should be put before their general obligation to aid mankind in general. Our moral obligations, it would appear, are often *past-looking* as well as *future-looking*—that is, some of our duties rest on our previous actions and not on the possible future good that their fulfillment will create.

Perhaps any adequate morality will have to incorporate elements of both utilitarianism and Kantian ethics. It would have to accept the Kantian view that the demands of justice are essential aspects of the moral life which are independent of the utilitarian commitment to the common good. Yet it would reject the Kantian view that considerations of justice can never be sacrificed for the common good. Similarly, it would accept the utilitarian view that the various specific duties that form the core of conventional morality—such as our duty to keep our promises and to be truthful—are not absolute. Nevertheless, it would reject the utilitarian view that one ought to consider only the consequences of one's action in deciding when a conventional duty should be kept. It may be wrong to assume, as both utilitarians and Kantians do, that moral reasoning must come to rest on a single basic moral principle. It would do more justice to the moral life if we were to assume, instead, that there are several independent and possibly conflicting moral principles. This is the position of the English philosopher W. D. Ross (1877–1971) in his influential book *The Right and the Good,* published in 1930.

According to Ross, utilitarianism in all its forms is an inadequate moral theory because it is inconsistent with the moral convictions of the ordinary man. The essential defect of utilitarianism, Ross writes,

> . . . is that it ignores, or at least does not do full justice to, the highly personal character of duty. If the only duty is to produce the maximum of good, the question of who is to have the good—whether it is myself, or my benefactor, or a person to whom I have made a promise to confer that good on him, or a mere fellow man to whom I stand in no such special relation—should make no difference to my having a duty to produce that good. But we are all in fact sure that it makes a vast difference. (p. 22)

Kant was also wrong, Ross claims, because he failed to distinguish absolute duties which we must always discharge, from *prima facie* duties which we must discharge if no other conflicting *prima facie* duties interfere. (The Latin term *prima facie* means "at first sight.") As Ross uses the term, a *prima facie* duty is a duty that can in certain circumstances be overridden by a more compelling conflicting duty. One's actual duty in a given situation, Ross claims, is determined by consulting one's *prima facie* duties. For example, according to Ross, we have a duty to produce the most good possible, as the utilitarians claimed, and, when this duty does not interfere with any other *prima facie duties*, it should be followed. Nevertheless, this duty can conflict with our other *prima facie* duties—such as the duty to keep one's promises. When this occurs, we have to choose between these *prima facie* duties. If breaking a promise will create only a slightly greater amount of good, the promise should be kept, but if the amount of good that can be created is very great, it should be broken. In describing our *prima facie* duties, Ross writes,

> (1) Some duties rest on previous acts of my own. These duties seem to include two kinds, (a) those resting on a promise or what may fairly be called an implicit promise, such as the implicit undertaking not to tell lies. . . . These may be called the duties of fidelity; (b) those resting on a previous wrongful act. These may be called the duties of reparation. (2) Some rest on previous acts of other men, i.e., services done by them to me. These may be loosely described as the duties of gratitude. (3) Some

rest on the fact or possibility of a distribution of pleasure or happiness (or of the means thereto) which is not in accordance with the merit of the persons concerned; in such cases there arises a duty to upset or prevent such a distribution. These are the duties of justice. (4) Some rest on the mere fact that there are other beings in the world whose condition we can make better in respect of virtue, or of intelligence, or of pleasure. These are the duties of beneficience. (5) Some rest on the fact that we can improve our own conditions in respect of virtue or of intelligence. These are the duties of self-improvement. (6) I think that we should distinguish from (4) the duties that may be summed up under the title of "not injuring others." No doubt to injure others is incidentally to fail to do them good; but it seems to me clear that nonmaleficience is apprehended as a duty distinct from that of beneficience, and as a duty of a more stringent character. (p. 21)

Ross admits that his list of *prima facie* duties may be incomplete. Believing that our *prima facie* duties are self-evident, Ross writes,

I should make it plain at this stage that I am *assuming* the correctness of some of our main convictions as to *prima facie* duties, or, more strictly, am claiming that we *know* them to be true. To me it seems as self-evident as anything could be, that to make a promise, for instance, is to create a moral claim on us in someone else. Many readers will perhaps say that they do *not* know this to be true. If so, I certainly cannot prove it to them; I can only ask them to reflect again, in the hope that they will ultimately agree that they also know it to be true. The main moral convictions of the plain man seem to me to be, not opinions which it is for philosophy to prove or disprove, but knowledge from the start; and in my own case I seem to find little difficulty in distinguishing these essential convictions from other moral convictions which I also have, which are merely fallible opinions based on an imperfect study of the working for good or evil of certain institutions or types of action. (p. 22)

It is indeed the case, as Ross asserts that making a promise "is to create a moral claim on us in someone else." This is what a *promise* means; it does not guide us in making moral choices. Even if one grants, along with Ross, that promises should be kept if no other *prima facie* duty conflicts, this does not tell us much. Indeed, some of the *prima facie* duties Ross sees as self-evident have been rejected as proper moral demands by others. It is open to debate, for example, that self-improvement should be considered a *moral* demand. And even if this is granted, the differing meanings that can be attributed to this obligation will generate different moralities. In addition, there are some possible moral duties that other moralists would consider legitimate that are absent from Ross' list of *prima facie* duties. For instance, under the first category of *prima facie* duties, duties based on our own previous actions. Ross lists two subdivisions, those based on past or implicit promises and those based on past wrongful acts—the first subdivision leads to duties of fidelity, the second to duties of reparation. Why, one may well ask, are there not two subdivisions also in the second category of *prima facie* duties, those based on previous acts of others? One might have expected this duty to be subdivided into the duties of gratitude for favors done us and that of retribution for wrongs done us, but the second of these subdivisions does not appear on Ross' list. Ross intuits that there is no *prima facie* retributive duty, but he gives no reason to reject the conflicting moral intuitions of retributivists such as Kant.[9] Similarly, Ross nowhere mentions as a possible candidate for a *prima facie* duty the duty not to participate in injustice even if less injustice will be done if one does participate. (Consider the moral dilemma of "The Cog in an Unjust System.") Again, Ross may intuit that such a duty does not exist, but others will disagree.

Even if most of us would accept Ross' list of *prima facie* duties, we would disagree to a very substantial extent when it comes to interpreting these *prima facie* duties and weighing them in cases of conflict. Apart from telling us that the duties of noninterference (nonmaleficence) and promise-keeping *normally* override the duty of benevolence, Ross does not place his *prima facie* duties in hierarchical order from the most to the least stringent. He does not supply us with any standard to aid us in determining what we ought to do when our *prima facie* duties conflict. Although he tells us, for example, that promises should sometimes be kept and sometimes broken, depending on the magnitude of the consequences, he does not give us any guidance as to how much good must be produced before we are justified in breaking a promise for its sake.

In response to the problem of weighing conflicting *prima facie* duties, Ross writes that in such cases

> ...while we can see with certainty that the claims exist, it becomes a matter of individual and fallible judgment to say which claim is in the circumstances the overriding one. (p. 189)

In this and in other passages, Ross admits that the certainty by which we can discern our *prima facie* duties does not carry over to our actual duties, when *prima facie* duties conflict. While he is not as explicit on this matter as one would have liked, Ross does not believe that judgments as to the comparative strength of *prima facie* duties are merely subjective personal preferences. By claiming that moral judgments of actual duty are fallible, Ross implies that one can be *mistaken* in one's weighing of conflicting *prima facie* duties. Ross attributes this fallibility to our partial knowledge, especially of consequences, and not to some inherent subjectivity of moral judgment. For example, he writes, "But suppose that from a state of partial knowledge in which I think A to be my duty, I could pass to a state of perfect knowledge in which I saw act B to be my duty..." In this passage, Ross suggests that to an all-knowing deity specific moral judgments would be as certain as *prima facie* ones are to human beings with limited knowledge. While equally reasonable people may have different opinions as to their moral obligations in complex situations, and at times must take "a moral risk" in acting as they do, Ross apparently

---

[9]Ross rejects that type of retributive theory of punishment, accepted by Kant, which asserts that criminals ought to be punished simply because they deserve it and that the degree of punishment should be proportionate to one's moral guilt. He also does not accept the utilitarian view that punishment can be justified simply by its beneficial consequences. As Ross sees it, society derives its right to punish from the *prima facie* duties of beneficence (that is, promoting the general interest), of justice (punishment should be proportional to the offense committed), and of fidelity to promises (the promise that criminals will be punished and the law-abiding will not). (pp. 56–64)

assumes that difficult specific moral judgments involving conflicts between *prima facie* duties are attempts to discern a realm of values that exists apart from the shifting sentiments of human beings and the social forces that help mold them. Even if Ross is mistaken in this assumption, his theory is not without value, for it makes us focus on a plurality of independent moral obligations and although this complicates the moral life it also does it greater justice.

Ideal Utilitarianism versus Rossian Ethics: How Rival Philosophical Theories Can Be Made to Converge

A central theme of Ross' *The Right and the Good* was that the utilitarian point of view in vogue during the early part of the twentieth century among English philosophers was inadeqauate. In particular, Ross meant to criticize the *ideal utilitarianiam* presented by his contemporary, the philosopher G. E. Moore, in his influential *Principia Ethica*. While accepting the utilitarian position that the right action to perform in a given situation is that act which maximizes intrinsic good, Moore was unwilling to embrace the hedonistic viewpoint of Bentham and Mill. While he accepted pleasure as an intrinsic good, he accepted other intrinsic goods as well. For example, he claimed that it is good in and of itself that the wicked be punished, writing:

> ...the infliction of pain on a person whose state of mind is bad may, if the pain be not too intense, create a state of things that is better on the whole than if the evil state of mind had existed unpunished. (p. 214)

Once one recognizes a plurality of intrinsic goods, as Moore did, an ideal utilitarian point of view can become indistinguishable from the Rossian point of view. All the ideal utilitarian has to do is to claim that all of Ross' *prima facie* duties are intrinsic goods—such as, that it is intrinsically good that one keep one's promises, that one make reparation for injuries done, etc. Since the list of intrinsic goods supplied by an ideal utilitarian can be identical to Ross' list of *prima facie* duties, such rival theories of normative ethics can be made to converge into the same theory, one formulated in a language of goods while the other is formulated in a language of duties. If this were to happen, the choice between a Rossian type of ethics and an ideal utilitarian one would become one of choosing a more preferable mode of expressing one's moral commitments and would not express differing moral commitments.

DISCUSSION QUESTIONS

In his book *Thinking About Ethics,* Richard Purtill suggests that "other things being equal" (such as, the needs of individuals), Ross' *prima facie* duties can be ranked in terms of their relative stringency as follows:

1. Not to harm others
2. To make reparations for harm done by us
3. To keep our commitments
4. To repay our benefactors
5. To treat people as well as they deserve to be treated
6. To do some good to some people, deserving or not
7. To improve ourselves in some ways

Do you agree with this ranking? If not, how would you change it? Would you want to make any changes, deletions, or additions to this list of our basic moral obligations? How useful do you think a list like this is in providing guidance to the solution of moral problems?

FURTHER READINGS

David Ross presents his ethical theory in *The Right and the Good,* published in 1930 by Oxford University Press. The quotation from G. E. Moore's *Principia Ethica* (which was first published in 1903) is taken from the 1959 Cambridge University edition. In his very readable introductory ethics text *Thinking About Ethics* (Prentice-Hall, 1976), Richard Purtill embraces the Rossian point of view. Beginning students would profit by comparing Purtill's treatment of Ross (chapter 4) with my own. It would also be worthwhile to consider Purtill's application of the Rossian point of view in his chapter on situation ethics. While reading these two chapters, focus on the points of disagreement between Purtill and myself. Does Purtill overemphasize the practical usefulness of the Rossian rules or do I underestimate it?

14. SITUATION ETHICS

As we have seen, Rossian ethics does not provide principles for determining the scope and relative strengths of our *prima facie* duties. Faced with a conflict of *prima facie* duties or moral perplexity over how a situation should be classified, Ross leaves us adrift. Yet it is precisely guidance in moral perception and the making of moral choices that we seek. For many, this guidance is provided by the rigid moral precepts of a religious ethics which shields us from the discomfort of moral uncertainty. While conservative religious moralists act as bastions of resistance to the winds of moral change, their liberal counterparts are often adroit at accommodating traditional moral principles to popular new moral perceptions. Such was the case, for example, in the 1960s when heated debates raged over the righteousness of the American intervention in Vietnam, over abortion, and over a permissive sexual morality. In the midst of this heated ferment, many sought a new liberal moral compass and found it in Joseph Fletcher's *Situation Ethics.*

Published in 1966, Fletcher's book immediately generated controversy among religious moralists. Some acclaimed it in such glowing terms as "a watershed in the history of moral theology," or as an "idea whose hour has come," while others denounced it as "frightening" or "shocking" in its implications. Unlike most expositions on normative ethics, however, Fletcher's book attracted a very wide lay audience, who, frustrated by the rigidity of more traditional religious ethics, were quite receptive to the liberal and permissive tone of *Situation Ethics* and the "new morality" which it exemplified. The great attraction they found in *Situation Ethics* was its central precept that the most important aspects of the moral life was not a blind adherence to the letter of the law, but rather to the spirit of loving concern which should always underlie it.

Fletcher begins his book with a description of three different approaches to the nature of moral decision making—legalism, antinomianism, and situationism. According to Fletcher,

> ...[The legalist] enters into every decision-making situation encumbered with a whole apparatus of prefabricated rules...Not just the spirit but the letter of the law reigns. Its principles, codified in rules, are not merely guidelines or maxims to illuminate the situation; they are *directives* to be followed....
>
> ...all major Western religious traditions have been legalistic....
>
> Statutory and code law inevitably piles up, ruling upon ruling, because the complications of life and the claims of mercy and compassion combine—even with code legalists—to accumulate an elaborate system of exceptions and compromise....It leads to that tricky and tortuous...business of interpretation that the rabbis called pilpul....
>
> ...With Catholics it has taken the form of a fairly ingenious moral theology that, as its twists and involutions have increased,...appears...to evade the very "laws" of right and wrong laid down in its textbooks and manuals. Love, even with the most stiff-necked of system builders, continues to plead mercy's cause and to win at least partial release from law's cold abstractions....
>
> Protestantism has rarely constructed such intricate codes and systems of law, but what it has gained by its simplicity it has lost through its rigidity, its puritanical insistence on moral rules.
>
> ...This is really unavoidable whenever law instead of love is put first....But even if the legalist is truly *sorry* that the law requires unloving or disastrous decisions, he still cries, "*Fiat justitia, ruat caelum!*" (Do the "right" even if the sky falls down). He is the man Mark Twain called "a good man in the worst sense of the word."...(pp. 19–20)

Antinomianism, on the other hand,

> ...is the approach with which one enters into the decision-making situation armed with no principles or maxims whatsoever, to say nothing of *rules*. In every "existential moment" or "unique" situation, it declares, one must rely upon the situation of itself, *there and then,* to provide its ethical solution.
>
> While legalists are preoccupied with law...[antinomians] are so flatly opposed to law—even in principle—that their moral decisions are random, unpredictable....(pp. 22–23)

The Situationist, however,

> ...enters into every decision-making situation fully armed with...ethical maxims... and he treats them with respect as illuminators of his problems. Just the same he is prepared in any situation to compromise them or set them aside *in the situation* if love seems better served by doing so. (p. 26)

In spite of Fletcher's initial attempt to distinguish the situational from the antinomian approach, his subsequent discussion makes the situational approach appear indistinguishable from the unprincipled antinomian one. In spite of Fletcher's claim that the situationist is "fully armed with ethical maxims," he does not enlighten us as to how situationists utilize these maxims, but talks, instead, about apprehending, in some apparently immediate and intuitive way, the dictates of love. For example, in describing the famous Sheri Fishbein abortion case of the early 1960s, Fletcher writes,

> When a lady in Arizona learned, a few years ago, she *might* bear a defective baby because she had taken Thalidomide, how was she to decide? She asked the court to back her doctor and his hospital in terminating the pregnancy, and it refused, to the judge's chagrin, since the law prohibits nonmedically indicated abortions without exception. Here husband took her to Sweden, where love has more control of law, and there she was aborted, God be thanked, since the embryo was hideously deformed. But nobody could know for sure. It was a brave and responsible and right decision, even if the embryo had been all right. (pp. 135–6)

Nowhere, however, does Fletcher give us any idea of which principles are relevant in deciding what the dictates of love are in this situation. Clearly, given his liberal sensibilities in the abortion issue, Fletcher focuses his loving concern upon Sheri Fishbein, the pregnant woman, but those who would strongly oppose her abortion will also perceive their opposition as stemming from loving concern, but, in their case, it will be for the unborn fetus. In a troublesome case such as this, one's moral choice should be illuminated and guided by moral principles. It is one thing to stress that moral principles are incapable of purely mechanical, computer-like application to complicated situations of moral choice, but it is something else to dispense entirely with their guidance, as Fletcher seems to do in the examples he uses. Given Fletcher's initial characterization of situation ethics, one would expect that the image of the situationist that will emerge from his discussion is one of a wise judge who uses his intuitive sense of justice or loving concern within the framework of existing rules and principles. Yet, this expectation is not satisfied.

As Fletcher himself initially perceived, such decisions, although not mechanically predictable, are not arbitrary either. A wise judge must always *justify* his decisions. His decisions about particular cases are not mechanically predictable, in the sense that more than one decision is often capable of justification. Yet, there are constraints, such as that of consistency, within which a wise judge must work. The present case must be examined within the backdrop of one's existing moral principles and rules, and on the basis of similar precedents. This is exactly the legalistic model that Fletcher holds in such little regard. The problem with religious legalism is not its legalistic procedure but its underlying otherworldly concerns and assumptions as to the source and unchallengeable status of precedents (such as revelation). Unless we accept the existence of a moral sense that enables us to see what is right in particular situations, without an appeal to moral principles, there is no recourse but to the legalistic method of principled justification that Fletcher so scorns. However strongly we may feel that a given action is right, if these feelings are to be more than prejudices, they must be justified in terms of general moral principles that one is willing to embrace in other situations. Since our moral principles, however complex, will never prove complex enough to solve all unforeseeable moral problems, the rational moral agent—like the legal judge—will find himself occasionally faced with special cases that require him to interpret, qualify, refine, and even at times abandon a moral principle. Such legalistic procedure may indeed be "tricky and tortuous" as Fletcher describes it, but it is essential if our moral decisions are to have a rational pattern and predictability.

Instead of the picture of a person constantly on the alert to interpret, modify, and enlarge his repertoire of moral principles, Fletcher, in his various examples, depicts the situationist as a person who, in some mysterious way, intuits the loving thing to do, without recourse to principles. The concept of love, as Fletcher's treatment of the abortion issue demonstrates, must be anchored to more specific moral principles. For example, in the context of the question of the morality of the Vietnam war (which was being waged as the book was written), Fletcher, disagreeing with both "doves" and "hawks," counsels us that the situationist's motto should be "Be not a dove, nor a hawk, but an owl." Who, however, will find any fault with such an uninformative claim. The problem untouched by Fletcher, resides in specifying the conditions that must be satisfied before one can qualify as an "owl"—and, one would hope, a moral one to boot! This is the problem. The rest is empty rhetoric. To tell us to let love decide as Fletcher seems to is to tell us nothing.

The question of the demands of distributive justice is cast aside by Fletcher who tells us that "*Love and justice are the same, for justice is love* distributed, nothing else." (p. 99). The principles by which love is to be distributed justly are, however, never hinted at by Fletcher, who thrusts the anchorless concept of love toward us in a sea of rhetoric leaving us to navigate for ourselves. Although Fletcher tells us that love should be thoughtful and "is a matter of intelligence, not sentiment," one is justified in claiming that it is sentiment more than intelligence that emerges in Fletcher's much too facile treatment of difficult moral issues. The Marxist criticism of utilitarianism as an incomplete amorphous system that can be bent into different shapes to suit the differing sensibilities of its adherents seems quite apropos as a criticism of Fletcher. Concern for others does not stipulate the direction this concern should take until we ask what in general is *the good for human beings;* this ultimate question is, however, never tackled in *Situation Ethics.* As Fletcher divulges his specific moral stands in the various examples he uses, his beliefs appear no different from those of many educated moral liberals of our day. He does not, however, attempt to justify his liberal stands, and therein lies the ultimate failure of his ethical outlook.

In addition to this basic failure of *Situation Ethics,* Fletcher is quite ambivalent in the statement of his thesis, at times claiming that it is the *motive* of loving concern, and at other times, the *maximization of beneficial consequences* to everyone concerned that makes an act right. For example, in discussing sexual ethics, Fletcher writes,

...if people do not believe it is wrong to have sex relations outside marriage, it isn't, unless they hurt themselves, their partners, or others. This is, of course, a very big "unless" and gives reason to many to abstain altogether except within the full mutual commitment of marriage. (p. 140)

Here Fletcher, as would a utilitarian, focuses his attention upon the consequences of our actions and not the motives behind them. Fletcher never resolves the basic tension in his position between its traditional utilitarian element and its reliance upon the motive of loving concern; it is, however, the latter view which is emphasized throughout Fletcher's book. Yet is it not much easier to deceive ourselves of the purity of our motives than it is to deceive ourselves of the probable consequences of our actions? At least when we focus upon the consequences of our actions we realize that our moral decisions require knowledge and foresight which may be lacking when we rivet our attention upon the immediate motive behind our actions. As history so amply demonstrates, opposing armies can easily convince themselves that it is on the basis of the motive of Christian love that they kill each other and innocent noncombatants. In a truly astounding claim, Fletcher tells us that President Truman's decision to drop atomic bombs on Hiroshima and Nagasaki were acts of love. This claim cries out for justification, yet Fletcher says not a word in its defense. One wonders how Fletcher arrived at this decision. Was it on the basis of Truman's professed motive in dropping the bombs—the saving of American lives? If so, we may ask Fletcher, if it was morally right for President Truman to focus all his "loving concern" upon Americans, to the exclusion of the Japanese, when the outcome of the war was not at stake. Furthermore in a case such as this, Truman's motive is not nearly as important for us to consider today as a consideration of the alternatives of action open to him and their probable consequences. Yet Fletcher does not mention that the utilitarian justification of Truman's action has been seriously questioned. Certainly, in those many situations, such as those found in the context of war, when we face a moral dilemma of hurting some to help others, we need facts and vision more than love or purity of heart.

Fletcher is much too sanguine about such sad moral choices as those faced in the context of a war. He makes it a point to tell us that we should not wallow in guilt for having chosen in accordance with the dictates of love. Yet when one feels forced to violate a moral principle which conflicts in a given situation with a more stringent one, one ought often to make one's choice only with a deep sense of regret and tension and even, at times, guilt. Without such feelings people are apt to become morally callous. In addition, since we must act in accordance with less than complete knowledge, momentous moral choices can sometimes only be made hesitantly in fear that the facts as they become known will prove us wrong. There is, however, no sense of moral tension, tragic loss and uncertainty conveyed in the examples Fletcher cites. For example, there is none in the case, heartrending to any loving parent, of a mother in the old American West who, convinced that the cries of her baby will alert the Indians as to the whereabouts of a wagon train of settlers, suffocates her child to save the rest of the wagon train. One may see the actions of such a woman, as Fletcher does, as one of heroic and loving sacrifice, but would we not drastically change our view of the moral character of this woman were we to discover that she could live her life after making such a decision without guilt and the deepest of regrets?

Another inadequacy of Fletcher's moral thinking is his tendency, frequently found in philosophers, to dwell upon the exceptional case rather than the more commonplace one. It is one thing to use special cases as a wedge to bring out the inadequacies of conventional moral principles or as a vehicle for generating critical thought, but it is something quite different when one presents some comprehensive moral view which is meant to guide people in everyday life. Here an over-reliance upon the exceptional is bound to cause a distortion in one's own view. This is the case with Fletcher.

For example, Fletcher relates the case of a German mother in a Russian prisoner of war camp who could gain release and rejoin her family only by having sexual intercourse with one of the prison guards. Many will agree with Fletcher that her decision was morally right in the circumstances, but what guidance does this rare case give to young people seeking a rational sexual morality? None at all. A more conservative sexual moralist than Fletcher can claim that the moral rule prohibiting extramarital sexual relations, which may have a justifiable exception in the case of the German woman, does not have exceptions when applied to the typical case of an extramarital affair.

Fletcher, in his preoccupation with the exceptional case, blinds himself to how disruptive of his own conception of proper human relationships his exceptional cases would be if they were to become the general rule. It would be very dangerous for a child to learn morality from Fletcher's book. How is a child, for example, to understand that it may be morally right to cheat in certain situations out of love for some classmate and not feel that it is equally right for him to cheat when he is simply not adequately prepared? Again the child, as indeed all of us, needs moral rules and principles as a necessary source of restraint, let alone as a guide in making the "loving choice."

DISCUSSION QUESTIONS

Do you think that the legalistic, situational, and antinomian points of view can be clearly distinguished? Is there, perhaps, some truth in all three views? Explain.

FURTHER READINGS

Joseph Fletcher's ethical theory is presented in his *Situation Ethics: The New Morality* (Westminster Press, 1966). *The Situation Ethics Debate* (Westminster Press, 1968) edited by Harvey Cox consists of a collection of essays and brief comments by Protestant theologians for and against situation ethics.

15. SOME REFLECTIONS ON THEORIES OF NORMATIVE ETHICS

The theories of normative ethics that we have critically discussed are inadequate to the task of providing specific directives toward the solution of moral problems. Given the vague nature of such principles as the categorical imperative and the principle of utility, philosophers committed to the same basic moral principle can arrive at different specific moral conclusions. For example, the principle of utility has been used by some as a justification for pacifism, while for others it has been used as a justification for the morality of war. The amorphous character of basic moral principles allows them to be used as rationalizations for particular moral judgments that are based on other considerations. For example, given the indefinite consequences of one's actions, hedonistic utilitarians can be quite adept at meeting the challenges of their critics by bending the principle of utility in the direction that they would like it to lead. When critics reply that a commitment to this principle, unsupplemented by other independent moral principles, is inadequate since it does not provide individuals with *rights* against having their individual liberty restricted in the name of social welfare or paternalistic benevolence, the utilitarian will often counter by claiming that the provision of rights of noninterference in human liberty is an essential condition for the maximization of human happiness. Behind such claims are often dubious psychological and sociological assumptions, such as the assumption that a human being is the best judge of how to maximize his own happiness (Mill's assumption) or that an unjust society will eventually prove to be an unstable one (the argument Taylor presents).

Realizing the slender threads by which human liberty is tied to the principle of utility, given the uncertainties of actual human desires and the world around us, the Kantian unsuccessfully attempts to detach the foundations of morality from these psychological and worldly uncertainties. The result is an abstract principle, such as the categorical imperative, which lacks any definite content. It is fine and well to claim, as Kantians do, that "similar cases must be treated similarly" or that "individuals should be treated as persons and not as things," but lacking any definite conception of what is to count as a morally relevant similarity or of what it is to treat someone as a person, such principles do not guide. Indeed, some utilitarians would claim that the notion of respect for persons implies nothing more than a relationship of involvement with others, such that our choices are governed by their aims and aspirations as well as our own. As such, these utilitarians will say, rather than being opposed to this notion, utilitarianism is built upon its very foundations and clarifies its meaning.

In reply, a Kantian would protest that one can be concerned about those one does not *respect* (such as animals). As the Kantian sees it, respect implies an acknowledgment of a person's *rational* status and *right* to *self-determination*. Nevertheless, the Kantian, like any reasonable person, would have to admit that human choices are not always rational or voluntary. One does not necessarily show disrespect for a person when one ignores his momentary nonrational or nonvoluntary wishes. For example, one is not necessarily showing disrespect for a person when one forcefully prevents him from committing suicide in the belief that *he himself will later repudiate this wish upon more rational consideration.* But given the ambivalence and flux of human desires, the notion of "what one would choose if one thought about it rationally" is indeterminate. As such, there will be a strong temptation for utilitarian notions of a person's best interests to be smuggled surreptitiously into one's notion of that person's rational or voluntary choices. For example, those who see suicide as against a person's best interests will be apt to refuse to see suicidal wishes as rational or voluntary wishes which reflect one's "true self." ("*You don't really want* to commit suicide; *you're just temporarily overpowered* by depression.")

The traditional utilitarian theory is, however, no less unclear and indefinite in application than the Kantian theory. Its apparent simplicity and unity are seen to be an illusion as the many unanswered questions it poses are brought to light. What, for example, does "pleasure" denote? How are we to measure and compare different degrees of it? Is it not the case that some individuals have the capacity for experiencing stronger pleasures (or have stronger desires) than others? If so, how is this to be taken into consideration in a utilitarian calculation of the maximization of human happiness? Similarly, how are we to take into consideration the fact that some people are unhappier than others, not because they experience less pleasure, but because their *expectation* of the pleasures they would like to be experiencing is greater? Are we to rank pleasures according to their quality as well as their quantity? If so, how do we determine the quality of a given pleasure and its importance relative to its quantity? Are we to be concerned with the distribution of pleasure as well as its aggregate maximization? Are we to be concerned about the pleasures of animals as well as of human beings, of future generations as well as the present generation? Is it right for us to create more and more people to inhabit this world as long as the total amount of pleasure experienced keeps increasing, or should we be concerned with maximizing the average pleasure experienced? As such questions crowd upon us, the clarity of the utilitarian vision grows dimmer. It is clear that the "utilitarian calculus," which Bentham believed would reduce morality to a type of "moral arithmetic," is a myth.

In addition, the utilitarian theory does not capture the complexity of moral reasoning which is often couched in the language of rights and specific obligations. For example, since as much harm can be caused by acts of omission as are caused by acts of commission, utilitarians often dismiss the relevance of common moral distinctions that place greater stringency on acts of commission than on acts of omission, sacrificing in the process, fundamental distinctions that most of us would be unwilling to abandon. These distinctions find their place in theories of justice and natural rights that can more adequately account for the distinctions we make between morally obligatory actions as opposed to those that are desirable, but not obligatory, some of which are supererogatory—i.e., "above and beyond the call of duty."

Given the inadequacies of traditional utilitarian and Kantian conceptions of morality which attempt to reduce our moral obligations to a single basic moral principle, other philosophers have turned to the ideal utilitarian or pluralistic deontological theories of such individuals as G. E. Moore and David Ross, which stress the existence of independent and possibly conflicting intrinsic goods or *prima facie* duties. Such theories, although more adequate to the realities and perplexities of moral choice, can no longer disguise the fact that they are incapable of generating determinate answers to specific moral questions. A morally perplexed person, faced with some moral dilemma, will be no more capable of resolving his difficulty after being exposed to such theories than he was before. He will have only learned how to formulate the nature of his moral perplexity in the more academic language of conflicts between *prima facie* duties or between intrinsic goods. The perplexity will remain unless one assumes that there exists some inner moral voice which can allow one to intuit the demands of morality in a given situation. How we are to distinguish this inner voice of moral truth from the promptings of psychological temperament and social conditioning is never made clear.

One must always be wary of abstract principles which are made to appear to provide more guidance than they really do. For example, in discussing sexual morality in his book *Thinking about Ethics,* Richard Purtill advocates the utilization of the golden rule—treating others as you would like to be treated in their place—as a guide for personal relationships. This is, however, a very indefinite guide. The function of such a principle is to point out that impartiality is a necessary condition of *any* adequate morality. The exact form this impartiality should take differs, however, from one specific conception of morality to another. The golden rule is a poor guide to sexual morality since it does not in any way tell us how to resolve conflicts of desire among different individuals and within oneself. I might very well know how I would like to be treated, were I Susan, and how I would want to be treated, were I Joan. But what if I cannot treat Susan the way she would like to be treated without treating Joan in a way that she would not like to be treated? Indeed, the concept of empathy is a philosophically puzzling one, for in the course of empathy one is supposed to remain oneself and yet become someone else. It may be logically impossible for an individual of a given temperament to empathize with an individual of a fundamentally different temperament. Even if one succeeds in vividly imagining what it would be like to see and feel the world with the emotions and thought structure of someone else, why should one feel a moral obligation to treat all individuals the way they would like to be treated? Is it not obviously the case that some individuals *ought* not to be treated the way they would like to be treated? There is a difference, after all, between understanding people and giving them their way. Purtill does not, however, point out these difficulties, creating the false impression that the golden rule provides guidance to the resolution of specific moral problems, which it does not.

While the theories of normative ethics we have discussed are incapable of providing determinate answers to specific moral problems, they can provide a conceptual framework for the resolution of these problems and by so doing function to organize one's moral thinking. Such conceptual frameworks can have the effect of pointing a person's thought in a particular direction and can consequently serve to narrow the field of morally relevant factors. For example, there is no guarantee how a person committed to the hedonistic utilitarian standpoint will resolve specific moral problems, such as those concerning the morality of adultery, euthanasia, and capital punishment. We do know, however, that such an individual will focus upon the consequences that such practices are likely to have on the happiness of individuals in this world, and this serves to narrow the scope of moral relevance. We know the direction of the hedonistic utilitarian's thought, if not the ultimate outcome. This is the case with other theories as well. Although one cannot predict how a Kantian will resolve a particular moral issue, one knows how he will organize his thoughts about this issue. For example, in the question of the justification of punishment, a Kantian will direct this justification *to the criminal himself,* attempting to show him why he *deserves* to be punished, while the utilitarian will direct this justification to *society as a whole,* attempting to show how punishment can act to *prevent* crime. While there is no unique utilitarian or unique Kantian way to resolve *specific* moral questions relating to punishment, one does have some idea of how utilitarians and Kantians will conceptualize and approach their moral questions in this area. As moral theories become more complex and pluralistic, the differences in approach may reside in no more than a difference in the relative emphasis that is placed on different morally relevant factors. For example, some deontologists and rule-utilitarians who emphasize acting on the basis of rules and not probable consequences of actions, add a "disastrous consequences" clause to their moral theory, allowing *prima facie* obligations to be overridden when the consequences of keeping them would be *disastrous.* If this notion is interpreted broadly, such a view may turn out to be indistinguishable in practice from a purely act-utilitarian theory which claims that, since there is great utility in the general following of important moral rules, they should be broken only in "very momentous circumstances."

As we proceed from the abstract conceptualizing characteristic of theories of normative ethics to a consideration of concrete cases of moral choice, very general and abstract principles as the categorical imperative and the principle of utility must give way to more specific moral principles. Each of us, in arriving at these specific moral principles and in determining how to balance them in cases of conflict, must refer to our deeply felt (and doubtlessly, at least to some extent, socially conditioned) beliefs about the morality of particular actions. This is the given frame of reference from which moral reasoning begins. From these particular moral beliefs we can then attempt to extract general principles that render these particular beliefs into a consistent and unified whole. These general principles can then be called upon as a guide to the solution of different moral problems. If some general moral principle to which we have up until now been committed leads us to a conclusion that goes counter to deeply felt moral sentiments in a new and unforeseen moral problem, one can either abandon this principle, or more likely, attempt to modify it in some way. On the other hand, when a general moral principle has proven itself to be a worthwhile guide to many different sorts of moral problems, one may cling to that principle when it seems to go counter to a nonreflective but deeply felt particular moral sentiment and reject that sentiment in favor of the reflective moral principle. For example, a person's initial view that homosexuality is wrong, might eventually give way to a growing commitment to a general principle of respect for human autonomy. As one's commitment toward this principle grows, one's immediate feelings of tolerance to divergent lifestyles is likely to grow as well.

This process of on-going mutual adjustment between general moral principles and particular nonreflective moral sentiments is very much like the sort of reasoning that can be found in judicial decisions in courts of law. Legal precedents play the same logical role for the legal judge as particular nonreflective moral sentiments do for the rational moral agent. Recognizing the inconsistencies of precedents or particular nonreflective moral sentiments the legal judge and rational moral agent accept the obligation *to act on principle,* even when their principles go counter to a deeply felt moral feeling that a particular case should be resolved in a particular way. They will attempt to modify their principles to accommodate these feelings or, if this is not possible, to abandon these feelings, but there is no guarantee that they will always be able to do this.

As we shall see in our discussions of some contemporary moral issues, the complexities of life often present us with unavoidable and painful choices between conflicting values and moral principles that cannot be resolved by an appeal to a higher value or moral principle. Faced with such dilemmas, we must choose, realizing that whatever we choose will exact a price and become a precedent for the future. It is no doubt psychologically easier to believe that there is some supreme moral authority that we can always turn to in times of moral doubt, be it God or some basic moral principle, which can generate uniquely correct moral answers, but this is an illusion. Ultimately, we must choose for ourselves how we want to live as indiviudals and as a society, but at least we can endeavor to choose rationally.

Rationality in moral choice in turn requires the wisdom that comes from an understanding of different moral perspectives, and a realization that even though there is no single source of moral enlightenment, the various theories we have discussed, all in their own way—especially in their criticisms of the excesses of other theories—shed light on the complexity of rational moral reasoning. We may find ourselves humbler at the end and less sure of the dictates of morality on specific issues than the passionate true believer who unrelentingly pursues a single source of moral light, but we will be wiser.

FURTHER READINGS

There are many excellent introductory texts which can supplement this text's discussions of the issues of ethical theory. The two I would recommend most to beginning students for their breadth of treatment and readability are James Rachel's *The Elements of Moral Philosophy* (Random House, 1986) and John Hosper's *Human Conduct,* second edition (Harcourt Brace Jovanovich, 1982).

The *Encyclopedia of Philosophy* and *Dictionary of the History of Ideas* are the best places to begin research on a particular area of philosophy. The *Encyclopedia of Bioethics* has an excellent 53-page twelve-part entry under the heading of *Ethics* on various general issues and viewpoints in ethical theory—the task of ethics, rules and principles, deontological theories, teleological theories, situation ethics, utilitarianism, theological ethics, objectivism in ethics, naturalism, non-descriptivism, moral reasoning, and relativism.

A pluralistic account of contemporary moral reasoning in tune with the viewpoint expressed in this book is found in Alasdair MacIntyre's *After Virtue* (Notre Dame Press, 1981). As MacIntyre sees it, the current moral landscape is not "an ordered dialogue of intersecting viewpoints," but "an unharmonious melange of ill-assorted fragments." Noteworthy too is MacIntyre's emphasis on virtues of moral character rather than on the formulation of general principles of right conduct—the predominant approach to studies of normative ethics from the days of Hume and Kant until the present. There are, however, a growing number of philosophers who have turned to a study of moral character rather than to moral action. For them the central question of morality is not "What should I do?" but rather "What should I be?" Consequently such views become intertwined with psychological theories of character development and moral education. A good introductory book in this spirit is Mike W. Martin's *Everyday Morality* (Wadsworth, 1989) which is enriched by its abundance of quotations from psychological, sociological, and literary sources. The book includes chapters on creativity, autonomy and moral growth, theories of virtue, harming oneself, self-deception, weakness of will, courage, prejudice, rudeness, envy, the parent-child relationship, friendship, and work. *Vice and Virtue in Everyday Life,* second edition (Harcourt Brace Jovanovich, 1989) edited by Christina and Fred Sommers is an excellent anthology of material on virtue ethics.

16. THE BOUNDARIES OF A MORAL COMMUNITY AND THE RIGHTS OF ANIMALS

> We have no right to treat a man like a dog.
> (Lester Maddox, Governor of Georgia 1967–71)

> Los Angeles police officers mourned the death of Marko, a German sheperd who helped collar 243 criminal suspects in his five years as a police dog before being stabbed in the neck last week by a car theft suspect. Marko was buried at a local pet cemetery.... "We're all pretty upset. It's like loosing a member of the family." [one officer] said. Officers had stood vigil inside a veterinary clinic, hoping for a miracle recovery for the 85-pound dog, which was on a life-support system. "Marko is not a human being, but he is about as close as you can get," [another officer] said.
> (L.A. Times, August 27, 1989)

The discussion of normative ethics in the preceding sections have centered on the issue of whether there is some basic principle or standpoint that can serve as a guide to members of a moral community. But who are the members of a moral community to whom moral principles are directed? Usually, we tacitly assume that they are human beings, while giving our assent to the principle that *all people should be treated equally.* Impartiality requires that we treat *all* people by the same standards, that no person should count more than anyone else. Yet, none of us live up to this ideal so central to universalistic views of morality. Instead, we all show greater concern to those with whom we have stronger feelings of identification. Parents, for example, naturally show greater concern for their own children than for the children of others. Similarly we naturally tend to feel greater concern for the poor among us than for the vaster number of even poorer people who live much further away. Are such distinctions capable of justification? Even if they are, such justifications would most likely be rationalizations, for the fact is that *feelings* of identification play a central role in determining our views of both the scope and stringency of our moral obligations. Only a callous moral monster would feel no guilt at eating at a luxurious restaurant while a small child, visible through a window, lies starving in the adjoining street. It is another matter, however, when the starving child is an invisible statistic somewhere else.

The utilitarian directive that morality demands that we strive for "the greatest happiness for the greatest number" is quite revolutionary, if it is meant to apply *equally* to all human beings. While the utilitarian principle is presented as universalistic in scope, it is rarely applied as such. Instead, the degree of sacrifice and concern we display and feel we ought to display is relative to the strength of our abilities to identify with the various communities to which we belong. This ranges from class, race, religion, nation, and then to the even broader community of all human beings, whether restricted to the presently existing or extended to future generations as well. But, what of animals? Are we guilty, as Peter Singer claims, of "specieism" if we neglect the rights of animals? Is our treatment of animals any more capable of justification than the institution of slavery, now so morally discredited? The natural feelings of shock and disgust elicited by the sight of suffering human beings appears psychologically indistinguishable from the feelings many of us have at the sight of suffering animals. At one time, we should not forget, human beings were treated in the callous way we now treat animals. Consider, for example, the ancient Romans who gleefully watched the spectacle of their gladiator slaves compelled to fight to the death. Or consider Black slave families split up and sold at auction to an unknown and possibly very cruel fate. Or, finally, consider the cruel medical experiments performed on inmates of Nazi concentration camps....Certainly, a morally sensitive person should shudder at the history of man's inhumanity to man. But are we not at least equally inhumane (notice the word) to animals today? Do animals have rights as the most lowly of human beings allegedly do?

According to Kant:

> But so far as animals are concerned, we have no direct duties. Animals...are there merely as a means to an end. That end is man....Our duties towards animals are merely indirect duties towards humanity. Animal nature has analogies to human nature, and by doing our duties to animals,...we indirectly do our duty towards humanity. Thus, if a dog has served his master long and faithfully, his service, on the analogy of human service, deserves reward, and when the dog has grown too old to serve, his master ought to keep him until he dies. Such action helps to support us in our duties toward human beings....If a man shoots his dog because the animal is no longer capable of service, he does not fail in his duty to the dog, for the dog cannot judge, but his act is inhuman and damages in himself that humanity which it is his duty to show toward mankind. If he is not to stifle his human feelings, he must practice kindness toward animals, for he who is cruel to animals becomes hard also in his dealings with men.

Are we justified in saying, as Kant does, that we do not have a duty to a dog and that decent behavior to a dog is merely practice for decent behavior toward human beings? Dogs may not be able to "judge," but neither are many human beings (consider children and the mentally retarded)—yet certainly we have duties to them. Is not the important question "Can that creature feel?" rather than "Is it rational?" Bentham thought so:

> The day *may* come when the rest of the animal creation may acquire those rights which never could have been withholden from them but by the hand of tyranny. The French have already discovered that the blackness of the skin is no reason why a human being should be abandoned without redress to the caprice of a tormentor. It may come one day to be recognized that the number of the legs, the villosity of the skin, or the termination of the *os sacrum,* are reasons equally insufficient for abandoning a sensitive being to the same fate. What else is it that should trace the insuperable line? Is it the faculty of reason, or perhaps the faculty of discourse? But a full-grown horse or dog is beyond comparison a more rational, as well as a more conversable animal, than an infant of a day, or a week, or even a month old. But suppose the case were otherwise, what would it avail? The question is not, Can they *reason*? nor, Can they talk? but, Can they *suffer*?

For Descartes there apparently was no necessity to choose between either rationality or the ability to feel pleasure and pain, for animals, according to Descartes, were not only incapable of rational thought, but devoid of consciousness as well![10] According to Descartes, human beings are distinguished from animals and complex machines (robots) by their unique capacities to use language in a spontaneous, nonparrot-like manner and to engage in conscious intellectual deliberation which can be utilized in diverse problem-solving activities. Apparently seeing intellectual perception as inseparable from all other states of consciousness, Descartes rejects the view that animals are conscious in the primitive sense of having sensations and feelings but are not capable of intellectual perception—a view held by Aristotle. Consequently, animals were for Descartes mindless creatures devoid of consciousness—mere automatons whose behavior was totally determined by the mechanical states of their physical organs. As one would expect, such a shocking view generated strong opposition from some of his contemporaries.

The views expressed by Descartes and Kant were greatly influenced by Judeo-Christian philosophy which, unlike Eastern religious philosophy, draws a sharp line between human beings and other animals. According to this perspective, only human beings can be treated as *free persons worthy of respect* rather than as *things*

[10]The reader probably wonders how a brilliant philosopher like Descartes could hold such an implausible view. First, in all fairness to Descartes, there is some verbal ambiguity in his position which has led some philosophers to suggest that Descartes denied, not that nonhuman animals feel, but that they think. Such a claim is, however, inconsistent with Descartes's metaphysical conception of the mind-body relationship. Unlike Aristotle, who attributed varying degrees of "souls" to living creatures, corresponding to their differing physical capacities, Descartes attributed souls only to human beings and assumed, furthermore, that all states of consciousness are states of the soul, considered as an immortal substance, and not states of a mortal physical body. Descartes's view was doubtlessly influenced by Christian theology, which promised a heaven for human beings but not for animals. It was also influenced by the scientific evidence that led him to see all animal behavior as physically determined, coupled with his religious desire to avoid a similar deterministic view of human behavior. As a result, Descartes felt logically compelled to draw the sharp distinction that he did between fully determined and unconscious animals and free and conscious human beings—whose freedom, he believed, was manifested by the interaction through the brain's pineal gland of a free soul with an otherwise determined physical body. Descartes, it would appear, was willing to give up common sense for theoretical consistency!

to be manipulated for the ends of others. Moral rights, in turn, can only be rightly conferred upon those worthy of respect—that is, only upon rational creatures who can freely choose between right and wrong. Many, like Bentham, have disagreed, claiming that from a moral point of view the similar capacities of animals to feel pleasure and pain should weigh more heavily than the rationality that supposedly separates human beings from animals. But are we not mistaken, as well, in assuming a uniquely human capacity for rational behavior? As Bentham provocatively suggests, "But a full-grown horse or dog is beyond comparison a more rational, as well as a more conversable animal than an infant of a day, a week, or even a month old." Many students of animal behavior would strongly second Bentham's claim that the higher animals are indeed rational creatures capable of rational behavior that is beyond the capacity of some human beings. Consider for example the widely publicized case of Washoe, the first chimpanzee to learn the American sign language for the deaf. Contrary to Descartes, Washoe and other chimpanzees apparently can learn to utilize language to express concepts of varying levels of generality and can use language to express their wishes (e.g., "Give Washoe Drink").

Those of us who have had the pleasure of having a cat or dog for a pet almost inevitably attribute higher emotional attributes to them, which some doctrinare philosophers and psychologists claim is an anthropomorphic mistake. For those who naturally love animals and can see the similarities that they share with human beings, words like "love," "caring," "stubbornness," and "courage"—with all their anthropomorphic implications—naturally come to mind. The capacity for moral understanding also comes to mind; for example, the relationship of a smart dog to his or her loving owner cannot be understood, as some have claimed it can, on a simple stimulus-response model. Those of us who have the ability to identify with the smart and loving dogs we own naturally come to see them as capable of moral understanding and of such feelings as guilt and shame. Consider, for example, a dog hiding his face, after doing something that he knows is wrong. But some will immediately retort, "They don't know it's wrong, they are just afraid of being punished." But that does not always appear to be the case, for even if the dog has no expectation of being hit or deprived of something, it may *feel* bad, it may feel ashamed at having let its master down and (in no doubt a very primitive way) recognizes that it has wrongly breached a reciprocal bond with its master that needs amending—i.e., it has a primitive sense of guilt. Such claims are widely shared by many students of animal behavior. The strong attachment so many of us make to the dogs we keep as pets comes from the fact that dogs can assume commitments to the forms and significance of our human needs and virtues. While other higher animals may be incapable of interaction with humans in the reciprocal manner of dogs, they do respond to the forms and significance of their own animal cultures. The intelligence of dolphins and their use of language, for example, is widely known.

Is our current treatment of animals then a prejudice, a form of "specieism" no less than the racism and sexism of the past that is now widely deplored? If so, how ought animals to be treated? Most of us would not be willing to go so far as to claim that they should be considered *equal* members of our moral community, for we do not have the same interactions with them that we have with human beings. But then again many of the limitations in our relations with animals are paralleled by limitations in our interactions with some human beings. Kant, for example, says (however mistakenly) that dogs cannot judge, but this is also true of small children and the mentally retarded, but who today would claim that such human beings have no rights and can be used *merely as instruments* for the satisfaction of others? How then can we justify the sweeping dichotomy we draw between the rights we attribute to human beings and the majority of us deny to animals? Do animals, for example, have a right to be protected from those who slaughter them for food and those who hunt them for sport? If such behavior toward animals can be justified,[11] how can we morally justify the cruel ways we treat animals both in raising them for food and utilizing them in medical experiments? Much has been written in this regard with the aim of raising our consciousness to the widespread abuse of animals. For example, books have been written on the abysmal conditions that exist in "animal factories," where animals are raised for food.[12] Similarly, much has been written by antivivisectionists about the cruel and sometimes gruesome experiments that are performed on animals (often without anesthesia!) for very dubious medical purposes. It is quite sad when the agonizing cries of experimental animals are euphemistically dismissed as vocalizations." Imagine using such language to describe the painful cries of human beings! Yet the self-deceptive use of language is rampant in our treatment of animals.

After a consideration of the widespread abuse of animals for medical experimentation, it is no wonder that so many famous people—for example, da Vinci, Tolstoy, Twain, Shaw, Jung, Gandhi, and Schweitzer—have criticized animal experimentation on humanitarian grounds (again notice the interesting word "humanitarian" in this context). Focusing on the abuses, many have (perhaps) gone too far in advocating no distress-causing experimentation with animals. As Shaw put it, utilizing an argument similar to Kant's, "The distinction is not between useful and useless experiments, but between barborous and civilized behavior. Vivisection is a social evil. . . . If it advances human knowledge, it does so at the expense of human character." Unlike Kant, however, antivivisectionists such as Shaw would have no hesitancy in attributing rights to animals. While we can

[11]Some have attempted to justify the raising of animals for food on the grounds that, unlike human beings, animals are not capable of the fear that comes with the expectation of death, for they are incapable of anticipating their death. With this as a premise, the argument goes on to assert that if we did not breed animals for food, they would never have lived and consequently never have experienced the pleasures of life. Better that their lives be intentionally cut short by human beings than that they never should have lived at all. In addition, in the wild most animals do not die of old age, but are killed by other animals. Consequently, so the argument runs, we are not doing animals a disservice by raising them to be eventually slaughtered for food.

[12]For example, chickens that are raised for food are typically packed so closely together that when they die there is not enough room for them to fall over. Crowded conditions also prevail in the breeding of veal calfs who do not have sufficient room to move their heads around. Prematurely separated from their mothers and fed liquid diets devoid of iron and roughage so that their meat can have the tender taste humans prize, they live in misery until death comes as a merciful release. Understandably, we do not think of such things, when we eat our meat!

reasonably disagree on the limits that ought to be placed on animal experimentation, there clearly should be greater restrictions than currently exist in animal experimentation and in animal factories which aim at supplying the greatest amount of meat for the dollar.

While we are often incapable of reciprocal interactions with the animals we use merely as means to our own ends, it seems inescapable that we should accept the legitimacy of our moral obligations to animals and their corresponding rights. But the fact is that most of us simply choose not to think about this unpleasant matter, just as many Germans choose not to think of what the Nazis were doing in their concentration camps. Those of us who, at least occasionally, do think about this, find it too easy to put such discomforting thoughts out of our minds, finding false moral security in the widespread acceptance of our callous treatment of animals. But in this are we any different from the Romans who watched their gladiators fight to the death or the slave owners who bought and sold their slaves like inanimate merchandise? Moral reason, devoid of the requisite feelings of psychological identification and concern cannot generate the motivation needed to change our behavior in such a fundamental way from the behavior of those around us. How many of us, for example, who would react with disgust at the thought of eating dog meat, however tasty, think nothing of eating pork? Yet pigs, we are told, are quite smart. The fact that they do not make good pets or are not cute should be morally irrelevant, but in fact such factors make a world of difference in our attitude toward animals, factors which, if utilized in distinguishing the rights of human beings, would be dismissed as gross immorality.

The question of the scope of our moral obligations and the correlative rights of other living creatures will come back to haunt us when we discuss the issue of whether a fetus is a person in the chapter on abortion. As we shall see, rationalizations prevail where reason proves incapable of justifying the lines we draw between those living creatures that have rights and those that do not.

DISCUSSION QUESTIONS

1. Should animals be considered to have rights? Which animals and which rights? Even if animals should have *moral standing,* should they have the same moral standing as human beings? Should there be differences in moral standing among animals?

2. What human needs are sufficiently important to warrant the infliction of pain and suffering on animals?

3. When is it right to kill animals for food? Given the present state of the world, are human beings morally obligated to adopt a vegetarian diet? Why?

4. Critically consider the merits of the following argument from Leslie Stephen:

   Of all the arguments for vegetarianism none is so weak as the argument from humanity. The pig has a stronger interest than anyone in the demand for bacon. If all the world were Jewish, there would be no pigs at all.

5. It has been claimed that rights should be extended to the general environment

as well as to conscious creatures. For example, Aldo Leopold, an adherent of this view, claims that the ultimate standard of right action should not be the satisfaction of the interests of conscious creatures, but whether actions "preserve the integrity, stability and beauty" of nature. Critically discuss.

6. It has been argued that the attempt to help the poor in overpopulated lands is ultimately self-defeating since such measures contribute to even greater overpopulation and resultant greater poverty. Critically discuss.

7. From a utilitarian standpoint, the philosopher Peter Singer, who is noted for his advocacy of the rights of animals, claims that the general moral principle that we should utilize in determining our responsibility to animals and to distant peoples is that "if it is in our power to prevent something very bad happening without thereby sacrificing anything of comparable moral significance, we ought to do it." Do you agree with Singer? Why? Does Singer's principle lead to a radical reappraisal of conventional morality?

8. In determining the boundaries of a moral community, it would seem that consideration must be given to the rights of future generations as well as to the presently existing one. Clearly, most of us would consider it callously immoral to deplete our natural resources and to lay waste to our environment, leaving a legacy of misery to future generations. But how can we weigh the rights or legitimate interests of future generations against the rights and interests of those of us who live today?

FURTHER READINGS

Peter Singer's *Animal Liberation* (New York Review, 1975) is the landmark book on animal rights. Singer's more recent article "Animals and the Value of Life" appears in *Matters of Life and Death* edited by Tom Regan (Random House, 1980). *Animal Rights and Human Obligations* (Prentice-Hall, 1976) edited by Regan and Singer is a good anthology of material on animals rights. The more general anthology *Ethics and Problems in the 21st Century* (Notre Dame Press, 1979) contains a paper by Singer on animal rights, one on the topic of the environmental rights of future generations, and three under the general heading of "broadening the concept of morality."

The quotation from Kant is taken from his essay "Duties Toward Animals and Spirits," in *Lectures on Ethics* (Hackett, 1963), pp. 239–40. The quotation from Bentham is taken from *The Principles of Morals and Legislation* (Hafner, 1948), p. 311, footnote 1.

Morality, Self-Interest, Free Will, and Moral Responsibility

3

In the next two sections we turn our attention to questions concerning moral responsibility and the relationship of morality to self-interest. "Is everyone really selfish?" "Why should I sacrifice my interests for others, if there's nothing in it for me?" "Is our behavior completely determined by environmental and biological factors, and, as such, in principle fully predictable by science?" "If so, can we be said to have free will and be morally responsible?" Such questions generate much popular debate. Many challenge the familiar distinctions that we make in characterizing individuals as selfish or unselfish, as free or unfree, and as morally responsible or nonresponsible. "We are all selfish," some say. "We are never free or morally responsible," others assert. As we shall see in the following two sections, these issues are partially *about words*—that is, what we mean or should mean by such concepts as "selfish behavior," "free choice," and "moral responsibility," and partially *about the underlying facts* that these concepts are meant to describe—that is, the facts of human psychology and the nature of the world we inhabit that lead us to distinguish people as selfish or unselfish, as free or unfree, and as morally responsible or nonresponsible.

17. MORALITY AND SELF-INTEREST

Psychological Egoism

Psychological egoism is a theory of human motivation, not an ethical theory. It is held today, as always, by many ordinary prople, and was once almost universally held to be true by philosophers. Today philosophers tend equally strongly to reject it. Whether they have good reasons for rejecting it is another matter, depending in part on the meaning we attribute to it. The following are some typical formulations of this theory.

1. All voluntary human acts are ultimately selfishly motivated.
2. People always act so as to promote their own self-interest.
3. People do things for others only because they expect something in return.

As is the case with most philosophical controversies, it is important that we attempt to extract the most plausible formulation of this doctrine before we pursue the question of its truth or falsity. The question at issue is not, as many have posed it, "Is psychological egoism true?" assuming that this doctrine has a single clear meaning; it is rather the more murky one, "Is there some fundamental insight about human nature that the above statements are getting at, and if so, what is the most enlightening and scientifically defendable way to formulate that insight?" The tenacity of the hold that psychological egoism has had on the minds of many may reflect some view of human motivation which goes beyond the imprecise formulations of this doctrine and the conceptually confused arguments that are often used in its defense.

Reasons for the Initial Plausibility of the Doctrine of Psychological Egoism

The widespread acceptance of psychological egoism can be given some degree of plausibility when one considers the prevalence of self-deception and the process by which we are taught to be moral or to be concerned about the interests of others. Let us briefly consider these factors.

Self-deception It is a sad fact of human nature that to some extent we all deceive others, as well as ourselves, as to the true nature of our motives. Who has not had occasion to realize that the apparently kindly, concerned, and unselfish attitude of others can be nothing more than a facade behind which lurks exclusively selfish desires? Although this deception may take the form of consciously intended duplicity, there are many occasions when people conceal their true motives from themselves. It is a short step for some from the realization that one's true motives can appear to be unselfish, while being in reality quite selfish, to the cynical view that this may always be the case. Behind every seemingly unselfish action the cynic will seek some underlying selfish concern. Politicians who loudly profess their love for the people will be seen as self-seeking power-hungry individuals, while the love of parents for their children will be seen as nothing more than ego-fulfillment or a source of vicarious selfish pleasure. Similarly, friendship will be seen as nothing more than the conscious or unconscious use of others to satisfy one's own desires. Nothing will be sacred from the piercing eyes of the truly convinced cynic. Religion, with its belief in heaven and hell, will be seen as a prime example of man's ultimate selfishness, for although we are told that we should worship and obey God because he deserves this response from us, we are motivated to so act by the security such action provides and by our fear of the undesirable personal consequences of doing otherwise. Conventional morality will be seen by the cynic to be, as Marx suggested, nothing more than a racket by which those in power attempt to maintain their position at the expense of the gullible. Charitable deeds will be seen as a source of self-congratulations on one's own good fortune or as a means of alleviating deep-seated guilt feelings which have been conditioned into us by the use of rewards and punishments. This claim brings us to the next important factor which has led people to the doctrine of psychological egoism.

Moral Education and Depth Psychology   According to almost all schools of psychology, moral educaiton draws upon associations with rewards and punishments. For example, the way behaviorists see it, since children are dependent upon their parents for the satisfaction of their inborn (primary) self-centered needs, such as food and security, they come to associate the satisfaction of these needs with the moral injunctions their parents utilize in rewarding and punishing them for their behavior. By such a process, children learn to consider the interests of others and to feel guilty when they do not. Such a view can be supplemented by psychoanalytic theory. As the psychoanalyst sees it, a child learns to be moral by a process of identification with his parents. By so doing, the child is made to feel safer. Instead of being terrified by a cold impersonal world upon which he is fully dependent for the sustenance of life, the child develops a sense of self-reliance. Normally, as the child's sense of self-reliance develops, he also stops seeing his parents as the powerful and awe-inspiring figures he once perceived them to be. They begin to be perceived as similar to him, having similar sorts of needs and feelings. The child is now able to identify with the feelings of his parents. Eventually the process generalizes and the child develops empathy with people in general. Nevertheless, concern for others is always integrally hooked-up with the maintenance of a sense of self-worth, which provides in subtle unconscious ways for a sense of security. As we delve into the unconscious depths and interrelations of human motives, a psychological egoist may contend, we will discover that behavior which is conventionally classified as unselfish is no different in underlying motivational structure from behavior which we would classify as selfish. Since all voluntary human action will turn out to be capable of being traced back to some purely self-regarding motivational component, such actions are ultimately selfish in nature, our psychological egoist will contend.

The Linguistic Ploy: Reducing the Doctrine of Psychological Egoism to a Tautology

Given the multitude of possibly selfish motives, a cynic can contend that underlying all apparently unselfish actions lurks some selfish motive, which may not be consciously perceived as such. For example, if a person sacrifices his life for someone else or for some cause, the cynical psychological egoist can claim that such an action was motivated by such selfish desires as the following:

a. to be rewarded in heaven for one's deed
b. to avoid guilt feelings
c. to be thought of highly by others
d. to escape from a meaningless life

In some cases, however, no concrete selfish desires, such as the preceding, seem to underlie an apparently unselfish action. For example, there are individuals who sacrifice their lives with no conscious desire to be rewarded in heaven (the agent might be an atheist) or to avoid guilt feelings (not everyone is troubled by strong guilt feelings and such feelings would have to be immense to outweigh all the satisfactions life might have to offer). As concrete selfish motives are suggested and dismissed in a given case, one begins to wonder what a psychological egoist is claiming when he says that all actions are "really selfish." Consider, for example, the following:

A: Cats are selfish. They want you only for the meal-ticket which you supply. But dogs will really sacrifice for you—they will starve at your feet rather than leave you, and they will travel a thousand miles, undergoing great hardship, just to be with you again.

B: I disagree with you. Even dogs are selfish. They won't do anything for you unless there's something in it for *them*. They want your love and affection more than they want food, and they fear insecurity more than hunger.

A: In the Artic some time ago an explorer was found who had been dead for three weeks. His dog lay starving at his feet, while his cat was eating his eyes out. Don't you consider that evidence for my position?

B: No. Both the dog and cat were selfish, but in different ways. And the same for human beings. They are always selfish too, but their selfishness more often includes a concern (selfish concern, of course) for the welfare of others.

A: I disagree once again. Dogs are less selfish than cats, and human beings *can* be more unselfish than either. Neither dogs nor cats act contrary to their own interests from principles of duty, but people do. Perhaps the dog finds it easier or less unpleasant to be with his master even if he himself is starving, but people often do the more difficult thing and the thing that they *don't* want. You have commanded the dog not to go oustide; although he wants to go out, perhaps he stays indoors because he fears punishment or loss of affection. But people sometimes do things for others without expecting anything in return—not even the satisfaction or security which the dog expects.

B: I think all three species are equally selfish, always. I grant that a person may act from a sense of duty, unlike the dog, but I don't believe he would do so if he didn't think he would derive more satisfaction (or avoid dissatisfaction) by so doing.[1]

This example is illustrative of two common faults of debates as to the truth of psychological egoism. First, it demonstrates the tendency of individuals to debate this issue without agreeing upon the definition that ought to be attributed to the

[1] John Hospers, *Human Conduct* (New York: Harcourt Brace Jovanovich, Inc., 1972), pp. 156–57. By permission.

concept of selfishness. Clearly, *A* and *B* do not share the same understanding of the meaning of this concept, and, as such, their disagreement is to some extent, a verbal one. Second, this example demonstrates the tendency that the doctrine of psychological egoism has of degenerating into a tautology. Let us see why this is so.

While it is unclear what definition *A* is attributing to the notion of selfishness, it is clear from *B*'s last remark that he rests his conviction that all voluntary human actions are selfish on the ground that such actions are always performed in order to "gain satisfaction or avoid dissatisfaction." On the surface, this claim seems clearly false. For example, what possible satisfaction is gained or dissatisfaction avoided by those who do what they believe is their moral duty in spite of their conviction that they would be much happier if they did not do so? Although people often experience guilt feelings when they fail to do their duty, this is not universally true, and at any rate the dissatisfaction they experience from doing their duty may seem to far outweigh the dissatisfaction that guilt feelings might bring. How then can the psychological egoist be so convinced that individuals who perform voluntary acts must get satisfaction out of their actions? What is the force of the "must" here? Certainly, there is no unique feeling of satisfaction (or dissatisfaction) that accompanies all voluntary action. What then does the psychological egoist mean by "satisfaction"? One ploy open to the psychological egoist is to claim that satisfaction simply means "satisfying one's desire." But if this definition of "satisfaction" is accepted, the thesis that "All voluntary actions are selfish" reduces to a tautology. This is so since the psychological egoist's reason for claiming that all voluntary actions are selfish is that such actions give one satisfaction and by "satisfaction" all he means is "satisfying one's own desire"—that is, "doing as one wants"—but this would appear to be precisely the definition of a voluntary act. Consequently, under such an interpretation, the claim that all voluntary actions are selfish, reduces to the claim, "Whenever an individual does as he wants, he does as he wants"—a tautology.

The initial appearance that psychological egoism was a profound observation of human nature—that things could have been otherwise, but alas are not—is a misinterpretation when this doctrine is turned into a tautology. Given the linguistic assumption that merely doing as one wants counts as a selfish action, the notion of a voluntary unselfish action—that is, an action where one does as one wants, but not as one wants—becomes self-contradictory. Under such an interpretation the doctrine of psychological egoism is not based on an *observation of the facts* of human nature but reflects a *linguistic decision* to use the notion of selfishness in an inflated and uncommon way. But if this inflated definition of "selfishness" is employed, no longer is it possible to contrast the notion of selfishness with that of unselfishness. Yet the notions of selfishness and unselfishness gain whatever meaning they possess in ordinary language precisely by virtue of the fact that they are used to describe contrasting actions within the class of voluntary actions. To assert that all voluntary actions are selfish would be informative only if we could contrast such actions with actions which could at least conceivably be unselfish.

Yet this can no longer be done when the doctrine of psychological egoism is reduced to a tautology.

The First Step in Resolving Philosophical Issues: Conceptual Clarification

As the preceding discussion indicates, if the doctrine of psychological egoism is not to be reduced to a tautology, it must be stated in terms which make its truth depend on the facts of human psychology and not on definitional fiat. It must be possible for us to imagine a state of affairs that would make it true as well as one that would make it false. With this objective in mind, how should we interpret the doctrine of psychological egoism? Let us return to the preliminary formulations of this doctrine.

1. All voluntary human acts are ultimately selfishly motivated.
2. People always act so as to promote their own self-interest.
3. People do things for others only because they expect something in return.

According to ordinary usage, these formulations are not equivalent in meaning. Let us consider the first one. In ordinary usage, the word "selfish" functions as a moral term which implies an *undue* disregard for the interests of others. Indeed, the notions of selfishness and unselfishness are used in ordinary language only in those contexts where an individual's interests conflict with the interests of others. A selfish person is one who unduly disregards the interests of others for the sake of his own interests, while an unselfish person is one who tends to act on the interests of others in disregard of his own perceived interests. In those contexts where the interests of others are not involved, it is inappropriate in ordinary language to speak of actions as being either selfish or unselfish. For example, if, upon dressing in the morning, I choose a blue shirt over a white one, one would be at a loss to understand what could be meant by calling such an action a selfish one. Similarly, although it is to my self-interest to have a well-balanced diet, it would seem inappropriate to call such a concern a selfish one. Consequently, if the notion of selfishness is given its ordinary meaning, the first formulation of psychological egoism would be trivially false, since there are many actions which can neither be said to be selfish nor unselfish. The second definition of psychological egoism fares no better when taken literally. Clearly, there are many people who habitually act contrary to their self-interest. This includes not only those individuals who fail to see what their self-interest demands, but also those of weak-will who knowingly act contrary to their own self-interest for some momentary satisfaction (such as smoking) or simply on impulse. Indeed, there are countless individuals whose actions reveal a self-destructive tendency, quite opposed to any of their rational self-interests.

The third definition of psychological egoism is the most promising. Unlike the other two, it does not attempt to specify a single motive that underlies all voluntary human actions, but instead attempts to rule out a particular type of motive—acting on the interests of others, without expecting something in return—that is, one never voluntarily acts to promote the interests of others as an end in itself. Let us call this motive the motive of *pure altruism*. According to the third definition of psychological egoism, pure altruistic actions do not exist. According to this thesis, one acts to promote the interests of others only as a means to the promotion of one's own interests. But, this thesis too appears false, since people at times do things for others without consciously expecting something in return. For example, people sometimes act impulsively to aid others without any thought of some reward.

At this point, the defender of the third definition of psychological egoism is likely to begin speaking of *unconscious expectations*. Yet one will find no support in psychological theory for the claim that one is always rewarded in some unconscious, if not conscious, way whenever one voluntarily acts on the interests of others—let alone that some type of reward is the *aim* of one's other-regarding actions. Consider, for example, the following: Walking home, Jones sees an old woman carrying a heavy package. Jones notices that it is clearly to the woman's interest to have someone carry that package for her. The woman is walking in the same direction as Jones and it is absolutely no trouble for him to aid her, and this he does impulsively, without giving it any thought. Is it not implausible to claim that Jones must be expecting some reward for such an easy and nonself-sacrificial action? Upon consideration of examples such as this, the psychological egoist may grant that one need not expect to be rewarded for every single other-regarding action. More plausibly, he could contend that although individuals do at times act on altruistic motives—not expecting or receiving anything in return for acts of benevolence to others—such a motive would not exist unless is were *associated with and generally reinforced* by some purely self-regarding interest.

Psychological Egoism and Behavioral Psychology

One can find support for this formulation of the doctrine of psychological egoism in the psychological theories of behavioral psychologists such as B. F. Skinner. According to Skinner, all human motives are either unlearned self-regarding ones, such as the desire for security, food, and sex, or "higher order" ones which derive from and are always dependent upon these primary self-regarding ones. These higher order motives, which include consideration for the interests of others, are dependent upon the primary self-regarding motives in that individuals would not indefinitely continue acting from them if they were no longer *in general* associated with the satisfaction of the primary self-regarding motives. In the more technical language of behavioral psychology, without reinforcement from the primary motives, the higher order ones would eventually become extinguished—that is, they are not functionally autonomous. Skinner's belief that higher order motives are not functionally autonomous has been rejected, however, by other psychologists. As some see it, although the higher order motives derive from the primary ones by a learning process of association and reinforcement, once learned, they no longer are dependent upon further reinforcement from the primary ones. There are other more complex possibilities. For example, even if altruistic acts always satisfy primary self-regarding motives, it is still possible that some altruistic acts are acts of self-sacrifice in which one gives more than one receives. One can also assume that people act from altruistic motives only if certain primary self-regarding needs like security and food are to some extent satisfied.[2] Once these needs are satisfied to a minimal extent, altruistic motives can flourish even if they are not in any way reinforced by the satisfaction of any primary self-regarding motives.

Psychological Egoism
and Depth Psychology

Even if it is true, as Skinner and other behavioral psychologists have suggested, that people usually get something in return for their other-regarding actions and would not perform these actions unless they generally did so, it may still be misleading to say that people are never "really unselfish." Would this not depend on exactly what people get out of their actions? Perhaps if one delved more deeply into underlying human motives, one would still want to distinguish some of the things one gets out of other-regarding actions as selfish and others as unselfish. Behavioral psychology is not rich enough to help us here, for behaviorists find no utility in delving into the rich underlayers of human motives. Psychoanalytic theory, on the other hand, does and thereby provides us with insight into the murky depths of human motives which can enable us to develop a more enlightening way of talking about the relative selfishness of people. Without this insight, statements that all people are or are not "really selfish" tend to be simplistic and misleading.

This is the case with most discussions of the doctrine of psychological egoism by philosophers who tend to dismiss it as either trivially false or logically confused. Even if they are right about this, given the ordinary language meaning of the concept of selfishness, perhaps the fault is not with psychological egoism but with the scientifically imprecise meaning attributed to the concept of selfishness in ordinary language. At times the vague concepts of ordinary language must be refined as a result of greater scientific understanding. Without this understanding, quick dismissals of the doctrine of psychological egoism by philosophers leave psychologically sophisticated people uneasy that not enough has been said.

For example, many philosophers today, in dismissing psychological egoism as stemming from linguistic confusion, claim that one must make a distinction between *the object* of one's desire and *the results* of satisfying one's desires. Even if it turned out that everyone did receive some satisfaction from their altruistic

[2]Such a view is supported by Colin Turnbull's description in his *The Mountain People* of an obscure tribe of African hunter-gatherers in Northern Uganda, the Ik. Given the constant struggle the Ik must maintain for bare survival, they live a life devoid of consideration for others. Love and generosity and all the various other ramifications of other-regarding concerns which we see as essential aspects of humanity and morality are nonexistent in the Ik's culture. As a result of his study of the Ik, Turnbull emphasizes the precarious and ultimately unstable nature of other-regarding motives. Turnbull's pessimistic picture of the human capacity under unfavorable circumstances to revert to primitive inhumane lack of concern for others is, however, not fully supported by our knowledge of how human beings responded to the chronic terror of life in Nazi concentration camps. Although many inmates lost any concern for the welfare of others, not all did so. Many could not kill to stay alive; they could not wish the other dead rather than themselves. Understandably, such people died more frequently than those who regressed into a more primitive and selfish way of seeing themselves and others, but while they lived they were perhaps able to maintain a better self-image than those who succumbed to their more primitive needs.

actions (in a sense that does not trivialize this into a tautology), this would not necessarily imply that one's (conscious) intention in acting altruistically must be the attainment of that satisfaction. We do not begin by desiring satisfaction and then attempt to figure out how to achieve it, but rather desire all sorts of other things—friendship, health, money, power, etc.,—and *because* we desire these things find ourselves deriving satisfaction when we obtain them. No doubt this is true and it is important to realize, for we see a moral difference between what a person directly intends and what he indirectly achieves.

Nevertheless, philosophers have often mistakenly assumed that people can be said to be selfish only when they do something with the (conscious) intention of obtaining pleasure or satisfaction for themselves. In so doing, they assume that the falsity of psychological egoism can be demonstrated without delving beneath the surface to the unconscious causes of our conscious intentions. According to these philosophers, if a person's conscious intention or desire is to aid someone else and is not to receive some satisfaction or pleasure from his action, such a person should, if one is to speak correctly, be said to be an unselfish person. Since such people clearly exist, psychological egoism becomes a trivially false doctrine. But a psychologically perceptive person would want to go beneath the surface of one's conscious intentions and desires, realizing that even if one consciously aims at the welfare of someone else, it is quite possible on an unconscious level that one's concern for others is never an end in itself. Although it is obvious that people often act on the interests of others, without consciously expected or wanting anything in return, it is not obvious that once we plumb the unconscious depths of human motives we will still want to say that such persons ought to be described as acting unselfishy. Perhaps, once we learn more about the hidden sources of human motives, a sceptic may claim, it will be discovered that in a much more enlightening sense "all motives are really ultimately the same" or that "truly unselfish actions do not exist." Such claims cannot be dismissed easily.

In order to obtain some insight into this matter, we must dig more deeply, as a psychiatrist would, into different personality types. Let us consider a few.

The psychopath: pure selfishness   Acting on the basis of the most primitive of human motives, the psychopath is exploitative and parasitic in his relationships with others. He is concerned about other people's feelings only insofar as the recipient of his concern can give him something concrete in return for that concern; if he perceives that this is not the case, he loses interest. Since he has no genuine concern for the feelings of others, he often commits acts injurious to others, and thus often finds himself in trouble with the law. While incapable of empathizing with others and caring about anyone other than themselves, psychopaths tend to have a higher than average shrewdness when it comes to knowing the motives of others and how to manipulate these motives to their own advantage. Projecting a facade of superficial charm, the psychopath hides his unreliability, insincerity and untruthfulness. Clinically, psychiatrists have observed that such individuals tend to be very insecure people who feel dependent upon others for their own security. When someone does not fill their needs, they feel panic and rage.

The oversolicitous mother: selfishness masked as unselfishness   The over-solicitous mother who sacrifices continually for her children while making sure that they know this, is an example of an individual whose apparently unselfish actions are tainted with an underlying self-regarding motive. By giving so much of herself, she is capable of inducing guilt and feelings of obligation in her children. As a result, she is often much more efficient in satisfying her desire for security than she would be were she to utilize the concrete and simple quid pro quo of the psychopath. In addition, by acting as she does, she feels self-righteous and this boost to her often fragile self-esteem can act as a powerful unconscious motive. Psychiatrists call her "the moral masochist," but whatever the name, the syndrome is quite familiar to them. On the surface, she is quite the opposite of the psychopath. When she comes to see a psychiatrist, she is suffering. Yet, she is reluctant to incur the expense of psychiatric treatment; perhaps her boy Joey needs a car and she says that despite her terrible depression she doesn't want to deprive him of it by indulging herself. She has spent her whole life, it soon appears, sacrificing herself for others—even now she doesn't want to sit in her psychiatrist's comfortable chair. ("Save the furniture for your other patients.") She seems, in fact, determined to sacrifice and suffer. How unlike the psychopath! How unselfish!

Yet, is she really responding to other people's needs or to her own? For example, during treatment, her psychiatrist becomes aware of how determined she is to suffer, and he begins to notice how, despite how intensely she complains, she rejects all his attempts to help. Finally, he brings Joey in for a visit and discovers that Joey, who has been given so much by mother, is an unhappy boy—one of his chief feelings being a feeling of inadequacy. It soon becomes apparent that mother doesn't know what Joey really wants from her. Joey needs to feel competent and capable, and does not enjoy mother's excessive concern. Yet he feels too guilty and inadequate to confront mother or to leave home.

Ultimately, the oversolicitous mother's motives do seem selfish—although in a different way from the psychopath's. Unlike the psychopath, she wants long-standing relationships with people, but she gets them by trapping people through unconscious feelings of inadequacy and guilt. Not only does she trap people, but she constantly boosts her self-esteem at the expense of others. On the surface, she seems the model of the unselfish person, but on a deeper level, she too can be seen as a manipulator who *uses others* as a means of satisfying her own needs. She can be said to be selfish because her needs so often motivate her actions instead of the needs of those whom she cares about and thinks she is helping. Unlike the psychopath, she cares deeply about others, but her concern is so wrapped up in her own self-regarding concerns that she is incapable of perceiving the true needs of those upon whom she showers her concern and upon whom she is so unknowingly dependent. Essential to her lifestyle is a mode of behavior toward her children that is oblivious to their need for growth, autonomy, and freedom from guilt. On the surface, she sacrifices for them; but on a deeper level, they are being sacrificed for her.

The empathic person: the psychological roots of unselfishness   If the notion of unselfishness is to be a viable concept, it must be one which finds its proper application in the sort of person who is capable of empathically comprehending and caring about the feelings of others. Such an individual does not respond to others as objects to be manipulated, but rather as persons whose feelings have worth in and of themselves. Although such a person may feel gratified by doing things for others, she does not expect some concrete reward for her altruistic acts. Simply seeing the recipient of her benevolence better off is reward enough. Nevertheless, a psychiatrist could claim that the unconscious motive reinforcing such actions is the same as that in the preceding examples—security and self-esteem. Indeed, consciously requiring and expecting less from others, the empathic and caring person usually gets much more in return. Others, perceiving her empathic concern, tend to trust her and respond to her in a similar way. Consequently, over the long haul, empathic concern is strongly reinforced and is most successful in satisfying one's self-regarding motives. Although one may call the capacity for empathic concern a secondary motive, such motives are very firm and difficult to disrupt in some people. Even the fear of death may not shake such motives, and a person may deliberately choose to die to help others without expecting anything in return. Are these motives, however, never fully autonomous, that is, would they eventually be extinguished if all (unconscious as well as conscious) rewards were to cease? Given the differences in psychological theories of human nature and the complexity of human motives, this question has no clear answer.

Concluding Comments:
The Plausibility of Psychological
Egoism

As we have seen, taken in the forms in which it is often presented, psychological egoism is a trivially false doctrine if the concepts in its definitions are used with their ordinary language meanings. On the other hand, these concepts can be so expanded in meaning as to render the doctrine into a tautology. Yet, there was a weaker version of the doctrine of psychological egoism which has some plausibility—a view which makes us focus upon the connection between other-regarding interests and self-regarding ones; this connection is one which psychologists would claim to be an important one. According to our weaker formulation of psychological egoism, people who consistently act on the interests of others would eventually cease to behave in such a manner if their own self-regarding interests were not generally satisfied by so acting. Yet, even if such a view were true, this is certainly a far cry from the view that everyone is selfish. To say that all people are selfish may enlighten in that it forces us to focus on the rewards that people get for their other-regarding actions, but it makes us neglect the vast differences in the nature of the rewards people receive. What it neglects is more important than what it emphasizes.

Only the psychopath in aiding others expects to get something very specific from the recipient of his other-regarding actions. What the empathic person may get—even though she may not be consciously seeking it—is a reinforcement of her sense of self and the love and concern of others. Ironically, if the psychopath could respond similarly, he would most likely be much more efficient in receiving the sorts of things he consciously strives to receive. The psychopath is a model of the truly selfish person—the person who does not care about anybody other than himself. If the oversolicitous mother is to be said to be selfish, her selfishness is quite different from that of the psychopath. Unlike him, she does genuinely care about other people, but like him, her needs motivate her actions and therefore she is often incapable of perceiving the desires of those whom she helps. To go further and call the empathic person selfish is to so expand the notion of selfishness as to make it a useless one for theoretical as well as ordinary purposes. Intuitively, most of us know that there are people totally wrapped up in their own concerns who don't seem to perceive the feelings of others and who never go out of their way for anyone. On the other hand, there are caring people who seem to feel the joy and pain of others. Among these are some who give us an uneasy feeling. They are going to want something specific back in return or they are going to exact a measure of guilt (by making us feel guilty, they can feel self-righteous). But others seem to give quite easily and with no strings attached. Clearly then, different people feel differently in a selfish-unselfish dimension. Since psychological theories of human behavior do not explain away this intuition, but rather serve to explicate it, it would serve no good purpose and can gravely mislead to dissolve this distinction by calling all human beings selfish. If we were to accept such a broadening of the concept of selfishness, we would very likely find the old distinction between selfishness and unselfishness creeping back into our language now in the guise of different sorts of selfish motives; such is often the case in philosophical attempts to dissolve conceptual distinctions that play an important role in ordinary discourse.

Can Self-Interest Alone Always Motivate A Person To Do the Right Thing?

The thesis that everyone is motivated only by self-interest has had a profound grip on many influential philosophers. Such a view was held, for example, by Plato, Thomas Hobbes, and Jeremy Bentham. Nevertheless, morality at times seems to demand that we sacrifice our own interests for the interests of others. Although we are often taught as children that following the dictates of morality always pays off in the end—that "honesty is the best policy" and that "crime does not pay"—we come to learn that there is no invariable connection between moral virtue and material prosperity, at least in this world. Immorality seems to pay off handsomely for some people, while following the dictates of morality often does not. If this is so, how can we reconcile the harsh realities of life in this world with the belief that following the dictates of morality will always be consistent with one's enlightened self-interest? The most famous attempt at such a reconciliation is to be found in Plato's most famous philosophical dialogue, *The Republic*, which is devoted primarily to the solution of this problem. Although Plato is willing to grant that material prosperity need not accompany the pursuit of morality, he argues that immoral people suffer from a psychic imbalance which precludes the possibility of happiness. Immoral people may be possessed of all sorts of material goods, but they will always lack the most important good of all—a "good soul" or "healthy psyche." The identification of virtue with psychic health was a central element in Plato's moral teaching. Let us consider this view.

Plato's Conception of Morality as Mental Health

Plato begins his discussion of morality and self-interest in *The Republic* by observing that it often pays to live a moral life since immoral individuals are not apt to obtain the cooperation and respect of others that is required for faring well in this world. Nevertheless, Plato realizes that if the only reason that can be given for being moral is the effect that such behavior has upon others, then it is not essential that one really be moral but merely that one appear to be so. If one could create the false impression that one were moral while secretly not giving any consideration to the interests of others and acting accordingly whenever one could with impunity do so, one could reap the beneficial consequences both of being thought moral as well as of actually being immoral. This argument is expressed by Glaucon, a participant in Plato's dialogue. The dictates of morality and law, Glaucon claims, are a compromise between one's basic immoral instincts and one's desire for security. (This view was to be echoed later in the philosophy of Thomas Hobbes.) The best sort of world for each of us would be one in which we could with impunity act immorally while others act morally. But since such a world does not exist, we are willing to compromise, binding ourselves to moral and legal restraints on condition that others do likewise. No rational person, however, who is capable of acting immorally with impunity would live up to such an agreement. In order to vividly illustrate his point, Glaucon relates the mythological story of Gyges who found a magic ring which enabled him to become invisible. Possessed of this ring, Gyges took what he wanted from others, untroubled by the demands of morality. All rational people in Gyges' place would have been moved by self-interest to act similarly, Glaucon asserts. If a person refused to employ Gyges' ring to wrong his neighbors with impunity when it was in his self-interest to do so, people would think him a miserable fool however much they might praise him in public. In order to show how injustice can pay off so much more handsomely in this world than justice, Glaucon asks us to imagine two men—one a perfect model of justice, the other of injustice. The unjust man, he tells us,

> ...must be like any consummate master of a craft...who, knowing just what his art can do, never tries to do more, and can always retrieve a false step. The unjust man, if he is to reach perfection, must be equally discreet in his criminal attempts, and he must not be found out...for the highest pitch of injustice is to seem just when you are not....we must allow him to have secured a spotless reputation for virtue while committing the blackest crimes; he must be able to retrieve any mistake, to defend himself with convincing eloquence if his misdeeds are denounced, and, when force is required, to bear down all opposition by his courage and strength and by his command of friends and money.

The just man, on the other hand,

...must be stripped of everything but justice, and denied every advantage the other enjoyed. Doing no wrong, he must have the worst reputation for wrong-doing...and under this lifelong imputation of wickedness, let him hold on his course of justice unwavering to the point of death.

Plato, through Glaucon's challenge, places before himself an extremely difficult task. He will cast aside all of the external rewards that morality often brings to those who accept its dictates and imagine a just man who is universally thought to be unjust, who is vilified by others and receives no material reward for his goodness. On the other hand, we are also to imagine a thoroughly immoral, but clever and rich, man who is the recipient of the lavish praise of others. Even in such a situation, Plato intends to show us, the moral man is far happier than the immoral one, for he alone possesses the inner peace and harmony of a healthy psyche or "good soul." Plato argues for this view on the basis of his psychological theory of the tripartite nature of the human psyche. In a mentally healthy person, Plato claims, the appetitive (bodily desires) and spirited (will or emotion) elements of the psyche are under the control of the third rational element. A mentally unhealthy person, on the other hand, is a person whose appetitive or spirited element is out of the control of reason. Such a person, lacking the inner harmony of an orderly psyche, is bound to be unhappy regardless of how great his external rewards may be. According to Plato's characterization of the immoral person, such a person is victimized by insatiable desires which his reason cannot control. To try to gratify such a person's desires, Plato claims, is like trying to pour water into a leaky vessel: the more water one pours, the greater the leak becomes because of the weight of the water; and the larger the leak becomes, the more rapidly one continues pouring, in the self-defeating attempt to compensate. A person who is victimized by insatiable desires, Plato claims, is incapable of happiness.

Although one may agree with Plato's assessment of such a person, there is no reason to believe that *all* immoral persons are of the type Plato describes. The person who threatens the prestige of justice is not the unreasoning sensualist or unchecked tyrant that Plato depicts, but rather the immoral person of moderation, the person whose reason restrains his vice today in the interests, not of virtue, but of vice, tomorrow. This is the person who praises virtue for what he can get out of it in the way of wealth, power, and reputation, and this is the person whose picture Glaucon so aptly paints. Such a person is not at all like the sick individual who passes on heedlessly from one action to the next without foresight. Nowhere in *The Republic* does Plato show that only those who follow the demands of conventional justice (such as, telling the truth and not stealing) have *harmonious psyches*. Contemporary psychiatrists would attest to the fact that psychic imbalance befalls the good as well as the bad and that bad people can be psychologically healthy. While a person totally devoid of a moral sense—that is, the psychopath—is a sick person who can never find long-lasting happiness, such individuals form only a small percentage of the immoral people in the world. At any rate, even if we accept the view that the acceptance of *some* moral obligation to others is a necessary condition of happiness, such a view does not specify the exact nature of these obligations and their stringency when they conflict with one's self-interest.

Total dishonesty or untrustworthiness may always be inconsistent with psychic health and happiness, but *moderate* dishonesty or untrustworthiness is not.

Concluding Comments

If Plato's attempt to draw an invariable connection in this world between the demands of conventional morality and self-interest is doomed to failure, one can appeal to the belief in an after-life where virtue will be rewarded and wickedness punished. To nonbelievers, however, this is a psychologically comforting myth that cannot be rationally justified. If so, what reasons can we give individuals for sacrificing their interests for the interests of others when morality demands it? Clearly, if a person is motivated only by reasons of self-interest, there is no reason we can give. But, as we have discussed, most of us are motivated by more than pure self-interest. A person genuinely concerned about others will often need no reason to behave morally other than the simple reason "because it will hurt someone else" or "because it is right."

Ethical Egoism

If individuals can be motivated to act contrary to self-interest should they do so? No, say *ethical egoists* who claim either that self-interest is the only justifiable motive for action or that it is one's foremost obligation. In the history of philosophy, the most forceful expressions of ethical egoism can be found in the writings of Niccolo Machiavelli (1469–1527), a political theorist of Renaissance Florence, and the German philosopher Fredrich Nietzche (1844–1900). In modern times, ethical egoism has found its strongest voice in the philosopher and novelist Ayn Rand (1905–82), a champion of individualistic capitalism. Unfortunately, this doctrine is often distorted by those who reject it. For example, one contemporary philosopher claims that "the pure egoist considers no one's feelings but his own. To value others' respect or friendship is not to be a pure egoist." Another assumes that an ethical egoist "doesn't care about other people" and that he does not accept "It would harm another person" as a reason not to do something. Consequently, this philosopher goes on, an ethical egoist is a person who "has no affection for friends or family," who "never feels pity or compassion, who is the sort of person who can look on scenes of human misery with complete indifference." If this is "ethical egoism," it has no reputable defenders! One does not have to be a psychiatrist to realize that complete indifference to other human beings usually, if not invariably, goes hand-in-hand with personal unhappiness and mental illness. Machiavelli, Nietzche and Rand were aware of this fact.

For example, Rand and her followers while advocating selfishness, do not advocate that we should not care about anyone other than ourselves. Although there is much ambiguity, and even inconsistency, in Rand's many expressions of her view, its essential theme is best seen in the quotation from her novel *Atlas Shrugged* that was utilized in our discussion of Kantian ethics (see p. 88). The underlying sentiment behind so much of Rand's writings is not that one should not care about others, but rather that one should not accept a moral obligation

According to Rand, one ought to act on the interests of others only insofar as these interests are one's own. For example, if one genuinely loves someone else, one will have a desire for (an interest in) the welfare of that person. If one were a person (or God) with the sentiment of universal benevolence that utilitarians advocate—a person for whom the interests of all other human beings are an integral part of one's own interests—then ethical egoism would coincide with universal benevolence. As Rand sees it, however, given human nature, universal benevolence is both unnatural and undesirable. Human beings who attempt to follow the utilitarian point of view, she claims, must of necessity restrict their desires out of an artificially created sense of moral duty which is incapable of rational justification. As Rand sees it, while utilitarians enjoin us "to love our neighbors as ourselves," love is "a profoundly personal and selfish value" that people "should have to earn by means of their virtues and which one cannot grant to mere acquaintances or strangers." As an example, Rand tells us to imagine a man who spends a fortune to cure a woman whom he passionately loves. It is absurd, she argues, to claim that this is a *sacrifice in her behalf,* for her welfare *is* his welfare. On the other hand, suppose that he lets her die in order to spend his money on saving the lives of ten other women, none of whom mean anything personally to him, as utilitarianism would advocate. This would be a *sacrifice.* But this is a sacrifice that we have no moral right to request of human beings, and that human beings cannot make without forfeiting their very individuality—that is, their integrity—as human beings, Rand passionately argues.

Philosophical Criticisms of Ethical Egoism

Many philosophers, in attacking ethical egoism, have claimed that it is incoherent *as a moral point of view.* For example, it has been claimed that it is to people's advantage to respect the rights and interests of others. Life in a society of ethical egoists pursuing their own uncurbed self-interest would be very insecure. Consequently, rational egoists would agree to abide by general laws which provide for mutual noninterference and cooperation and punishment for those who disobey. Nevertheless, if an egoist could with impunity disobey these laws he would, for he is bound to them not by respect but by fear. For an egoist, the best sort of world would be one where he can break the law with impunity but those around him cannot. On the basis of this consequence of ethical egoism, philosophers have argued that it is not a moral point of view. By definition, they have claimed, a moral point of view must be a *disinterested* one which requires that one be willing to universalize one's desires. Since the ethical egoist is unwilling to accept a disinterested point of view and would not want everyone to act as he wants to act, his position must be taken as a rejection of the moral point of view, it is claimed.

An ethical egoist could counter this objection, by rejecting the metaethical contention that all legitimate moral principles must be disinterested ones, for such a view assumes that moral people must be willing to submit themselves to a good other than their own, and this is simply not so, an ethical egoist may contend.

As we can see, the point of disagreement here is to some extent a *verbal* one concerning the proper use of the term "moral." However, it is more than just about words. As in most philosophical debates that hinge on the meaning that should be attributed to a key concept, underlying the verbal disagreement is a deeper and more substantial one—in this case, a disagreement over *the sorts of reasons that should be most binding on human beings.*

In ordinary language, we speak primarily of moral demands in the context of conflicts of interest with others and, as such, moral demands are social demands that involve a consideration of the interests of others. Nevertheless, we sometimes speak of individuals having moral obligations to themselves—for just as it is often very difficult to sacrifice self-interest for the interests of others, it is sometimes very difficult to accept the self-denial of momentary impulses that is often necessary for long-range happiness. There is a personal dimension to the moral point of view as well as the obvious social dimension. The critics of ethical egoism who claim that a moral principle must be disinterested, focus exclusively upon the social dimension, whereas ethical egoists focus exclusively upon the personal dimension. If the critics' view is to be accepted, purely personal commitments to a way of life, however seriously binding, are not to count as *moral* commitments. But the ethical egoist may disagree, arguing that any rational commitment to act in a particular way, in spite of external obstacles and internal temptations which move one to act otherwise, should count as *moral* commitments.

Even if ethical egoism is not *a moral point of view,* the ethical egoist would argue that it is *a reasonable* (or *the only reasonable*) point of view. People may agree that only other-regarding reasons should count as moral reasons but disagree on the substantive nonlinguistic issue of what sorts of reasons have rational weight or the strongest rational weight. This is the substantive issue separating the egoist from the nonegoist. As the egoist sees it, such reasons should be those of self-interest. Insofar as conventional morality counsels us to sacrifice our own self-interest to the interests of others, conventional morality is unreasonable and ought to be disregarded, the egoist claims. It is precisely because the notion of a moral reason carries for many the tacit implication of being the most binding of reasons for action that egoist and nonegoist alike will attempt to cling to this concept although offering different definitions of it. Any attempt to find the *real definition* of a key concept which is intertwined with other concepts whose meanings and interrelationships have shifted through the ages is bound to result in a stipulation as to how that concept ought to be used and therefore must reflect some philosophical commitment which goes beyond ordinary usage.

Whether or not moral views must, by definition be *disinterested,* an ethical egoist is not necessarily committed to rejecting the notion of *universalization,* for he may claim that everyone should act exclusively in terms of self-interest. Although he may very well not *want* others to do so, he may admit that, from their own point of view, they should. If the *universalizability principle* means that whatever principles one believes are right for oneself to follow should also be considered right for everyone else to follow, he may accept this principle as a necessary requirement of the moral point of view. If, however, a commitment to this principle is taken to imply that one must *want* others to accept the same principles as one accepts, then he may reject it.

Finally, an ethical egoist will reject the claim made by some philosophers that "ethical egoism is an inconsistent doctrine since it leads to inconsistent directives." According to this argument, if one is committed to the view that everyone ought to act exclusively in his own interest, then if doing X is in A's interest, A ought to do X. However, if doing X is contrary to B's interest, then B would correctly judge that X ought not to be done by A. Thus, we have two contradictory judgments—"A ought to do X" and "A ought not do do X"—which follow from the doctrine of ethical egoism. Consequently, it has been claimed, ethical egoism must be rejected as an internally inconsistent doctrine.

This argument is a confused one for the ethical egoist, for it will not make sense to him to speak of what morally ought to be done in an impersonal sense. As he will see it, judgments of what ought to be done *presuppose* and are *relative to* a given person's interests. Consequently, the alleged contradictory judgments are not, according to him, really contradictory if they are written in their complete form as "A ought to do X, from A's point of view" and A ought not to do X, from B's point of view." As the ethical egoist sees it, each person, from his own point of view, ought to attempt to emerge victorious from a conflict of interests with others. He may give this advice to others when asked, or, if his own interests are involved, he may remain silent or try to persuade others to accept an impersonal viewpoint. Such an attitude will be distasteful to most of us, but it is not incoherent.

Ethical egoism may not be incoherent, but is it reasonable? Is it reasonable to say that we ought never to act contrary to our own self-interest? Even if one defines "self-interest" broadly, as Rand does, to incorporate a natural (as opposed to morally induced) concern for others, given human nature, will it not be to one's self-interest at times to injure others in order to obtain what one desires? In reply to this question, an ethical egoist could concede the need for a *social* morality which acts to curb individual desires, but would maintain, nevertheless, that this social morality should be distinguished from one's *private* morality. As an egoist making this distinction would see it, it is to everyone's interest that social morality should act to curb the natural inclinations of individuals by giving individuals certain rights of noninterference. Such an egoist might well agree that individuals should be conditioned to internalize such obligations. Yet, he would recognize the possibility that one's private morality—that is, a general all-inclusive theory of conduct based on self-interest—may conflict with this social morality. When this happens, it would be his belief that individuals are always justified in sacrificing the demands of social morality for the demands of private morality. It will, of course, be to all our interests to have a strong criminal law that acts, through the fear of punishment, to make the demands of social morality coincide with the demands of private morality. Nevertheless, these demands will not always coincide and, no doubt, there will be occasions when a person can be reasonably assured that he will not be punished if he violates the legal rights of others. According to our ethical egoist, when this is the case, a wise person would violate the law.

Most of us would not, however, be willing to accept such a position. How many of us would be willing to accept the ethical egoist's apparent belief that one is justified in killing and stealing from others whenever one can be reasonably assured that this will be in one's ultimate self-interest? It would appear that even Ayn Rand doesn't hold such a view, since she places some curb on human selfishness by requiring that an individual's actions be consistent with *rational* self-interest. Although Rand does not spell this out, it would appear that she takes "rationality" as demanding that individuals be provided rights of noninterference from others. As she perceives it, the *rational* interests of human beings do not clash, since *rational* human beings (by definition) do not "desire the unearned," and treat other human beings as *traders,* "giving value for value." The principle of trade, she claims, is "the only rational ethical principle for all human relationships. . . . It is the principle of justice."

Rand advocates egoism within the background of a framework of rules which respect persons and property and which aim at maximizing human liberty and minimizing governmental interference. As such, Rand is committed to the moral position that individuals have an obligation not to violate the rights of others to their life and property, apart from the effect that such forbearance will have on their ultimate self-interest. Although Rand exhorts us not to accept a moral obligation to *aid* those whom we do not care about, she accepts obligations of *forebearance* (not harming). Consequently, Rand's commitment to one's *supreme* moral obligation to oneself is limited by other moral principles. Her ethical philosophy, in the last analysis, would seem to reduce itself to the more carefully spelled out libertarian philosophy of Robert Nozick that we briefly discussed.

As we have seen, Ayn Rand, the foremost contemporary advocate of ethical egoism, does not accept the doctrine that individuals have no moral obligations whatsoever to people other than themselves and should always act in their own self-interest regardless of the effect on others. Understandably, Rand and her followers do not claim that individuals are justified in doing anything they please to others—including robbing and killing them—as long as such action serves their long-range interests. If, as many philosophical critics of ethical egoism assume, this is what the doctrine of ethical egoism asserts, then Rand is not an ethical egoist. Although one can quibble over whether Rand should be called an ethical egoist, her moral point of view is much opposed to the utilitarian point of view. In essence, Rand is telling us that *our primary moral obligation is to ourselves* and that, although we have obligations of forbearance toward others, we do not have an obligation to help total strangers for whom we have no special feeling. We ought not, Rand tells us over and over again in her many writings, sacrifice ourselves or those we care about on the altar of universal benevolence.

This point of view has some plausibility and cannot be dismissed as confused or irrational. Is it not right sometimes to reproach a person for being *too* altruistic? Nevertheless, should we not reject Rand's view that we have no obligation whatsoever to help mere acquaintances or strangers? If Rand is right that an individual whose moral choices were always motivated by the utilitarian principle of universal benevolence would lack a very essential attribute of humanity, would not the same be true of a person who feels absolutely no empathy and inclination to help mere acquaintances or strangers? Shouldn't we accept the existence of purely self-regarding moral obligations as well as the more typical other-regarding moral obligations? The ancient Greeks believed this, emphasizing the purely personal moral virtues of prudence, self-courage, and temperance. How we weigh the moral demands of others against our own moral demands will reflect either the actual preferences we find within ourselves or those preferences by which we choose to be guided. We may shun, lock up, or kill, those who do not care for others as much as we think they should or who are willing to disregard the interests of others in ways we consider morally unjustified, but we cannot always hope to have a rational basis for proving that such individuals are wrong or irrational for not caring or not considering.

DISCUSSION QUESTIONS

1. Evaluate the following argument:

   The doctrine of psychological egoism is incompatible with true friendship. True friendship, by definition, involves a concern for the welfare of someone else as an end in itself. A concern for the welfare of someone else that is purely self-regarding is not true friendship. Yet the psychological egoist claims that all motives for action are self-regarding. Consequently, the psychological egoist rules out the possibility of true friendship.

2. Consider the following incident attributed to Abraham Lincoln:

   Mr. Lincoln once remarked to a fellow-passenger on an old-time mud coach that all men were prompted by selfishness in doing good. His fellow-passenger was antagonizing this position when they were passing over a corduroy bridge that spanned a slough. As they crossed this bridge they espied an old razor-backed sow on the bank making a terrible noise because her pigs had got into the slough and were in danger of drowning. As the old coach began to climb the hill, Mr. Lincoln called out, "Driver, can't you stop just a moment?" Then Mr. Lincoln jumped out, ran back and lifted the little pigs out of the mud and water, and placed them on the bank. When he returned, his companion remarked: "Now, Abe, where does selfishness come in on this little episode?" "Why, bless your soul, Ed, that was the very essence of selfishness. I should have had no peace of mind all day had I gone on and left that suffering old sow worrying over those pigs. I did it to get peace of mind, don't you see?"

   Do you agree with Lincoln that his action was a selfish one? Can you think of some test that would decide the issue?

3. In depicting a person who successfully feigns an unselfish concern for others, Glaucon imagines a thoroughly unjust person who cunningly deceives others into believing him just. Is it at all likely in the real world for a person to successfully practice such duplicity over the long haul? Are such dishonest people likely to be as happy as those who are motivated by a genuine unselfish concern for others? Explain.

4. Does a person always have a reason to act morally? Should a person always act as morality demands? Why?

5. Does it seem plausible to you that people will eventually stop acting in a particular manner if such conduct ceases to reinforce self-regarding interests? Why?

6. Aristotle claims that one develops a particular character trait by training oneself to act as that character trait demands. The good person for Aristotle is someone who habitually acts as morality demands. When people come to habitually behave in a particular manner do they eventually come to find that behavior satisfying? If this is not always true, is it true of moral behavior? Explain?

FURTHER READINGS

Plato's identification of morality with enlightened self-interest understood as psychic harmony is found in his book, *The Republic*. Glaucon's challenge is found in chapter 5. Of the various translations, I recommend the one by Francis Cornford, published in 1945 by Oxford University Press. Ayn Rand's version of ethical egoism is found in *The Virtue of Selfishness*, published in 1964 by the New American Library.

Burton F. Porter's *Reasons for Living* (Macmillan, 1988) has a good chapter on egoism, including long quotations from and critiques of the egoistic views of Plato, Hobbes, Machiavelli, Nietzche, Rand, and Fromm. The general introductory philosophy anthology *Reason and Responsibility*, 7th ed. (Wadsworth, 1989), edited by Joel Feinberg has a good collection of selections on egoism. Especially useful for introductory students is Feinberg's own analytic discussion of the tendency of psychological egoism to degenerate into a tautology. Feinberg's critical assessment of psychological egoism is followed by a more sympathetic discussion, a passage from *The Republic* which expresses Plato's egoistic viewpoint, a selection from Kant, defending his view that people can and should act out of duty and not self-interest, and a selection by Paul Taylor, arguing that a commitment to morality over self-interest cannot be decided by reason, but involves a choice as to the sort of person one wants to be. Baruch Brody's introductory philosophy text *Beginning Philosophy* (Prentice-Hall, 1977) has a clearly written chapter which discusses psychological egoism and answers to the question "Why Be Moral?"

18. DETERMINISM, FREE WILL, AND MORAL RESPONSIBILITY

As Kant emphasized, deeply a part of our conception of morality is a picture of human beings as free and morally responsible persons whose moral choices are justly the subject of judgments of moral praise or censure. Yet the picture science presents of human beings is quite different. As science tends to see it, human beings are complex machines whose actions are fully determined (caused) by environmental and genetic factors that make people behave as they do. Are these two pictures incompatible, as they appear to be? From the very first stirrings of the scientific spirit, people have pondered this question in perplexity. This is no less true of philosophers. "Are human beings *really* morally responsible?" philosophers have asked. "Is it *really* right that human beings should be punished and blamed for their wrongdoing?" they have wondered. Traditionally, these questions have centered on the compatibility of the notions of free will and moral responsibility, with the doctrine of *determinism*.

Determinism is the philosophical theory that everything in the universe, including human actions and choices, is entirely governed by causal laws of the sort that science attempts to discover. To put this thesis another way, determinism is the belief that for any event, E, in this universe, there is some cause, C. C, in turn, is called a *cause* of E, because there is a *law of nature* which asserts that "whenever C occurs, E will occur." According to determinism, then, nothing happens purely by chance, if "by chance" one means "without any cause." Although we often say that events happen "without any cause," if we accept the deterministic thesis such assertions cannot be taken literally. When we say, for example, that "Jones quit his job without any cause," the determinist will take such a statement to mean not that Jones' action was an uncaused one, but rather that we either do not know the cause of Jones' action or believe it to be unjustified. If determinism is true, every event that happens in this universe is in principle predictable if one knows the relevant laws of nature and the events leading up to that event. If there were a superscientist who knew absolutely everything that was happening in the universe at a given moment and every causal law, then he could predict the entire future of the universe from this moment on. This would be so, for any event E that will occur from this moment on will be related to some cause C through a law of nature that asserts that "whenever C occurs, E will occur"; and our superscientist will, according to our assumption, know of this law and of the existence of the event C which this law says will cause E

Although it is impossible to prove that determinism is true, for there are things that happen whose causes are at present unknown to us, this doctrine is, nevertheless, a fundamental feature of scientific method as well as everyday reasoning. Although there are many things whose causes we do not know, we rarely, if ever, consider the possibility that these events are uncaused, and consequently seek to discover a cause which we believe exists but is unknown. For example, doctors at present will admit that they do not know exactly how cancer is caused; we would be at a loss, however, if some doctor asserted that cancer, or some type of cancer, had no cause at all. Similarly, we tend to readily accept the claim that human physical characteristics are fully determined by biological and environmental factors.

Is it not equally true that human psychological characteristics and behavior are determined by causal laws which the science of psychology is in the process of discovering? If the science of psychology were as developed as the science of physics, could we predict the behavior of human beings just as we can now predict the motion of physical objects according to the laws of mechanics? Many philosophers and scientists have thought so, believing that a human being is a complex conscious machine whose feelings, thoughts, choices, and behavior are subject to scientific explanation no less than other parts of nature. Given the complexity of the human organism and the innumerable forces that act upon it in complex and ever-changing combinations, there will always be some element of uncertainty in the predictions scientists make about the behavior of human beings. Nevertheless, in principle, what a human being chooses or does is subject to scientific laws no less than is a pebble which, once thrown up in the air with a particular force and particular air resistance, eventually begins to fall at a velocity and rate of acceleration predictable by the science of mechanics, it has been claimed.

While we appear to assume the doctrine of determinism in our everyday judgments about so many different things, we also assume that individuals perform actions "of their own free will" in situations where they were capable of doing otherwise, and therefore are proper subjects of judgments of moral responsibility and blame. Yet many philosophers have found it impossible to reconcile the assumption that people act freely with the doctrine of determinism which seems to imply that every event that occurs is *the only one that could have occurred* in the circumstances. For example, assuming that determinism is true, if Jones kills Smith at time *T*, given the forces both internal and external acting on Jones just prior to *T*, his killing of Smith had to happen. Given the causal factors at work in this situation, as in all situations of human choice, nothing can happen except what does happen. Thus, it seems to follow that if determinism is true, human beings can never act differently from the way they do act—that what occurs must occur, given the causal factors involved—and that, consequently, people are not really morally responsible for their acts. Given the causal antecedents of their actions, they really have no choice but to act as they do. If determinism is true, the argument continues, then the feeling a person has that there are a number of alternative courses of action open to him is an illusion. Actually, only one of the imagined alternatives is possible—and indeed inevitable—given the causal law or laws involved.

Many philosophers and thinkers outside of the fold of professional philosophy have accepted the soundness of the preceding argument and have, as a consequence, argued that one must choose between the belief in universal determinism and that of the existence of human free will.[3] Others have disagreed and have held that any apparent conflict between determinism and human freedom is itself an illusion. Some who take this point of view assert that determinism is compatible with human free will and judgments of moral responsibility, while some go further, asserting that free will and judgments of moral responsibility presuppose the belief in determinism. Human freedom and moral responsibility, instead of being incompatible with determinism, they assert, is incomprehensible without it. There are, thus, three possible positions one can take on the determinism-free will issue and one can find influential supporters of all three.

First, there are those who, agreeing that determinism is incompatible with human freedom and moral responsibility, accept freedom and moral responsibility and reject determinism. Utilizing the generally accepted philosophical terminology, we shall call this the *libertarian* position. Most who take this position assert that the existence of free choice is a given fact of immediate experience. As the philos-

---

[3]There is no general agreement by philosophers over what can properly be said to be free (such as will, choice, or action). Although many philosophers use these concepts interchangeably (as we will), there are some philosophers who would consider them importantly different. For example, it has been said, that our actions are free when determined by our choices but that our choices are never free or are free when not determined or determined in a particular way. As in many philosophical controversies, an essential part of the philosophical issue at hand is to decide upon its very formulation.

opher Henry Sidgwick put it, "It is impossible for me to think (at a moment of choice) that my volition is completely determined by my formed character and the motives acting upon it. The opposite conviction is so strong as to be absolutely unshaken by the evidence brought against it; I cannot believe it to be illusory." Since free choice seems to be so intuitively certain and is incompatible with determinism—a doctrine that is unproven and believed on scientific faith—one should reject determinism. Many who take this point of view emphasize the feeling of freedom that we have when engaged in a moral choice. Our belief that we are moral agents, they say, presupposes that we have free choice. As Kant put it, "ought implies can" (that is, to tell a person that he ought to do something makes sense only when that person has the freedom to do that act or to refrain from doing it). If an abstract and unproven theory such as determinism conflicts with our consciousness of being moral beings, the scientific theory must be discarded, and not the immediate and strong testimony of our consciousness. Such a view has been defended by the American philosopher William James and the English physicist Sir Arthur Eddington, who believed that the ideas of contemporary quantum physics are incompatible with determinism. While James and Eddington were willing to identify freedom with chance, this is not true of all libertarians. For example, the twentieth century philosopher C. A. Campbell, who was influenced by Kant, insists that acts of will are neither capable of a full causal scientific explanation nor are they mere chance occurrences. According to this point of view, true freedom of choice implies the existence of an autonomous moral self (soul) that can transcend the biological, psychological, and social conditions of one's being. The essence of this version of libertarianism is not that a free act is uncaused, but rather that the decisions of this autonomous moral self are not themselves fully determined by biological, psychological, and social conditions that are studied by science and related to each other through causal laws. Those who take this position distinguish a person's *moral self* from his *empirical self,* which is subject to determination by such factors.

Second, there are those who, agreeing that determinism is incompatible with freedom and moral responsibility, accept determinism and reject freedom and moral responsibility. Following William James's terminology, such individuals are often called *hard determinists.*[4] According to this point of view, the constant advances in scientific explanation of phenomena, including human behavior, strongly favors belief in determinism. Any feeling we may have of freedom of choice that transcends causal determination by physical, psychological, and social conditions is a reflection of our ignorance of the causes that act through us. Human actions are the determined responses of complex machines subject to scientific understanding and control. Since we do not choose the biological and environmental factors that fully

[4]James called those determinists who believe that determinism and free will are compatible *soft determinists.* Although the terms James coined are currently used with no evaluative connotations, they were not intended as such. As a libertarian, James rejected the attempt to reconcile determinism with free will and, in calling those who attempted to do this soft determinists, James meant to imply that they were "soft-headed" thinkers who refused to accept the unpleasant, but inevitable, consequences of the belief in determinism. On the other hand, James believed, hard determinists were "hard-headed" enough to accept these unpleasant consequences.

determine our psychological makeup, which in turn determines our choices and actions, we are not ultimately morally responsible for what we do. We act as we do because we are what we are; but what we are is what our biology and environment has made us. In holding people morally responsible for their actions and in praising them for their good actions and blaming them for their bad ones, we like to think that people are morally praiseworthy or blameworthy for their actions; in doing this, we forget that those who do well are those who have been *lucky* enough to inherit desirable characteristics or to be exposed to environmental circumstances which cause them to develop the wherewithal to do well. This hard-deterministic perspective was held by the philosophers Hobbes, Spinoza, and Schopenhauer and also by the scientists Freud and Einstein, as well as by the novelists Thomas Hardy and Mark Twain. The famous twentieth century lawyer, Clarence Darrow, often expressed such a view, both in his writings and in his successful court pleas—in particular, in his defense of the kidnap-murderers Leopold and Loeb.

Third, *soft determinists* maintain that determinism is compatible with freedom and moral responsibility and that any appearance of conflict is a result of various philosophical confusions. According to this point of view, once we clearly consider what we mean—or ought to mean, if we are thinking clearly—when we call an act or choice "free," we shall see that we in no way imply that free choices or actions are uncaused. It is *specific types of causes* that make acts or choices unfree, not the mere fact that they are caused. Yet soft determinists disagree as to what these causes are and therefore disagree as to the proper analysis of the notion of free choice or free action.

Let us now turn to a critical discussion of some representative statements and defenses of positions on the free will-determinism issue. I will, then, briefly share with you my own reflections about an adequate resolution of this classic philosophical problem.

Hard Determinism: Darrow, Twain, and Hospers

The most sensational American crime of 1924 was the brutal kidnapping and murder of fourteen-year-old Bobby Franks by two brilliant students, eighteen-year-old Nathan Leopold, Jr. and seventeen-year-old Richard Loeb. The killers, both from wealthy Chicago families, had the distinction of being the youngest graduates of the University of Chicago and the University of Michigan. In order to demonstrate their contempt for conventional morality, the two planned to commit "the perfect crime." Their attempt, however, proved flawed; and captured, they confessed. The state demanded the death penalty, while the attorney for the defense, Clarence Darrow, already famous for his defense of unpopular causes, pleaded that the killers' lives be spared. For over twelve hours in his summation to the jury, Darrow passionately pleaded for mercy for the defendants. This plea proved successful and the defendants were sentenced to life imprisonment. Over and over again in his summation, Darrow implored that Leopold and Loeb were helpless victims of hereditary and environmental forces which they did not choose, but which, nevertheless, molded them into the murderers that they had eventually become.

> Nature is strong and she is pitiless. She works in her own mysterious way, and we are victims. We have not much to do with it ourselves. Nature takes this job in hand, and we play our parts. . . .
>
> What had this boy to do with it? He was not his own father; he was not his own mother; he was not his own grandparents. All of this was handed to him. He did not surround himself with governesses and wealth. He did not make himself. And yet he is to be compelled to pay. . . .
>
> To believe that any boy is responsible for himself or his early training is an absurdity. . . . If his failing came from his heredity, I do not know where or how. None of us are bred perfect and pure; and the color of our hair, the color of our eyes, our stature, the weight and fineness of our brain, and everything about us could, with full knowledge, be traced with absolute certainty to somewhere. If we had the pedigree it could be traced just the same in a boy as it could in a dog. . . .
>
> If it did not come that way, then . . . if he had been understood, if he had been trained as he should have been it would not have happened.
>
> If there is responsibility anywhere, it is back of him; somewhere in the infinite number of his ancestors, or in his surroundings, or in both. And I submit, Your Honor, that under every principle of . . . right, and of law, he should not be made responsible for the acts of someone else.

Similar sentiments were expressed by Mark Twain, when he wrote,

> Man is not to blame for what he is. He didn't make himself. He has no control over himself. All the control is vested in his temperament—which he did not create— and in the circumstances which hedge him round from the cradle to the grave and which he did not devise. . . . He is as purely a piece of automatic mechanism as is a watch, and can no more dictate or influence his actions than can the watch. He is a subject for pity, not blame. . . .

At the heart of the hard deterministic perspective shared by Darrow and Twain is the contention that we are never justified in holding a person morally responsible or blameworthy for his actions since "he didn't make himself." (Notice that Darrow and Twain use this same expression.) People may be free to act in accordance with their own desires, but since these desires are reflections of their character which has been molded by hereditary and environmental forces that they did not choose— they do not really have free will and are not really morally responsible. The notion that individuals are not morally responsible in a determined world since in such a world they do not "choose their own characters" is a central idea that one finds in expressions of the hard deterministic point of view. Yet the notion of choosing one's character is a puzzling one which seems to be self-contradictory, for in order to choose something, one would need to already possess some type of character. Although we can attach meaning to the notion of an individual who has a particular type of character choosing to change or develop certain personality traits, the idea of a type of characterless blob (which cannot be identified as a person) choosing its entire character from scratch seems to be nonsensical. It would seem to be as self-contradictory to talk about choosing one's (entire) character as it is to talk of a foursided triangle. Yet it seems to be this notion that hard determinists have in mind. Hard determinists, such as Darrow and Twain, bemoan the fact that since determinism is true, no one can choose his character; but even if determinism were false, it would appear that people would be equally incapable of choosing their character, for this notion appears self-contradictory. Consequently, it is misleading for a hard determinist to make it appear that the truth or falsity of determinism has any bearing on a person's free will or moral responsibility. The real problem here is to understand what possible sense can be attributed to this puzzling notion of choosing one's character.

Darrow and Twain, as well as other hard determinists, can also be criticized for their tendency to move imperceptibly from the idea that individuals do not make themselves to the idea that individuals are not morally responsible since they have no control over themselves. One can, however, admit that even though people do not make themselves (assuming we can attach some meaning to this expression), they often, nevertheless, have the power to control themselves and can therefore be held morally responsible for not exercising such control. For example, even though Jones may not have chosen to have the violent temper that he does, if he is not the victim of some type of "irresistible impulse," we expect him to control that temper. Assuming this to be true, even if Jones experiences himself as victimized by his violent temper which interferes with his normal personality and which inclines him to act against his value system, this should not alone excuse him from accepting responsibility for controlling that temper. Indeed, it is a fundamental psychoanalytic premise that the first step in controlling an "alien" desire is to accept responsibility for it—to recognize that we have the power to help direct and determine *the future course of our lives*. Without such an assumption, psychotherapy would be impossible. When people are treated as and look upon themselves as being *helpless* or as *not having control* or as being *acted upon by forces outside of themselves,* they tend not to exert the effort they have the power to command which would enable them to change themselves. As the philosopher Sidney Hook puts it,

> Far from diminishing the amount of needless cruelty and suffering in the world, I am firmly convinced that the belief that nobody is ever morally responsible, in addition to being false, is quite certain to have a mischievous effect and to increase the amount of needless cruelty and suffering. For it justifies Smerdyakov's formula in *The Brothers Karamazov:* "All things are permissible." One of the commonest experiences is to meet someone whose belief that he can't help doing what he is doing (or failing to do) is often an excuse for not doing as well as he can or at least better than he is at present doing.... We are responsible... for what it is in our power to do... In spite of the alleged inevitabilities in personal life and history, human effort can redetermine the direction of events.... It is not true that everything that happens to us is like "being struck down by a dread disease." The treatment and cure of disease—to use an illustration that can serve as a moral paradigm for the whole human situation—would never have begun unless we believed that some things that were did not have to be, that they could be different, and that *we* could make them different. And what we can make different we are responsible for.

Furthermore, is it not the case that our very dignity as human beings consists in our conception of ourselves as responsible beings? To consider oneself as a passive object or machine that is acted upon by forces that one cannot control is to rob oneself of one's dignity as a responsible and rational human being. One can well understand a person's plea that he *is* responsible and ought to be treated as such and not as a passive object of forces beyond his control. For this reason is it not a fundamental mistake to claim that people do not, at least to some extent, "make themselves" through the free choices they exercise?

With these criticisms in mind, let us turn to a defense of the hard deterministic point of view by the contemporary philosopher John Hospers, which is much more sophisticated than the defenses presented by Darrow and Twain. In his widely reprinted article, "What Means This Freedom," Hospers is quite willing to admit that for practical purposes we must hold people morally responsible for their actions and treat them as if they had free will. Nevertheless, when we reflect more deeply about the determinants of a person's behavior, we realize that in a deeper sense no one is ever morally responsible for his actions. Although we like to look down upon wrongdoers from a position of moral superiority believing them to be proper recipients of our moral feelings of righteous indignation and resentment, such feelings, Hospers argues, are out of place on deeper-level reflection. Since determinism is true, there is a causal chain stretching from conditions that existed before our birth to our present characters and present choices. This means that if we go back far enough we will find our characters to be causally determined by conditions over which we had no control. Thoughtful persons, Hospers contends, once recognizing this fact, will find feelings of moral superiority out of place.

> ...the more *thoroughly* and *in detail* we know the causal factors leading a person to behave as he does, the more we tend to exempt him from responsibility. When we know nothing of the man except what we see him do, we say he is an ungrateful cad who expects much of other people and does nothing in return, and we are usually indignant. When we learn that his parents were the same way and, having no guilt feelings about this mode of behavior themselves, brought him up to be greedy and avaricious, we see that we could hardly expect him to have developed moral feelings in this direction. When we learn, in addition, that he is not aware of being ungrateful or selfish, but unconsciously represses the memory of events unfavorable to himself, we feel that the situation is unfortunate but "not really his fault." When we know that this behavior of his, which makes others angry, occurs more constantly when he feels tense or insecure, and that he now feels tense and insecure, and that relief from pressure will diminish it, then we tend to "feel sorry for the poor guy" and say he's more to be pitied than censured. We no longer want to say that he is personally responsible.

As a famous French saying puts it, to understand all is to forgive all (tout comprendre, tout pardonner). But a critic is bound to reply, "this is certainly not always the case. Sometimes, the more I learn about a person, the more inclined I am to blame him for not making an effort to change himself. An individual is not simply passively acted upon by forces, but can exert the effort to change himself. Some individuals, alas, do not exert that effort and for that very reason should be blamed. Individuals who succeed often do so precisely because of *their* efforts and are not simply the lucky and passive recipients of forces acting upon them." Hospers has a reply to such a critic:

But, one persists, it isn't a matter simply of luck; it is a matter of effort. Very well then, it's a matter of effort; without exerting the effort you may not overcome the deficiency. But whether or not you are the kind of person who has it in him to exert the effort is a matter of luck....

The position, then, is this: if we can overcome the effects of early environment, the ability to do so is itself a product of the early environment. We did not give ourselves this ability; and if we lack it we cannot be blamed for not having it. Sometimes, to be sure, moral exhortation brings out an ability that is there but not being used, and in this lies its *occasional utility;* but very often its use is pointless, because the ability is not there. The only thing that can overcome a desire...is a stronger contrary desire; and many times there simply is no wherewithal for producing a stronger contrary desire. Those of us who have the wherewithal are lucky.

What are we to make of such sentiments? Is Hospers not right that there is a basic ambivalence in our attitude toward wrongdoers? On one hand, we feel inclined to blame and hold them morally responsible for the choices that stem from their defective characters. Yet, on the other hand, when we understand the causal factors that produced that defective character, we often find ourselves inclined to "feel sorry for the poor guy" and fortunate in having avoided the same causal influences. If we are good at empathy, we might be able to imagine ourselves turning out no different from the person we originally judged with feelings of moral superiority, saying, "there but for the grace of God, go I," or perhaps, more appropriately, "there, but for the grace of my causal antecedents, go I." When we see things this way, as so many of us can at times, the righteous indignation and resentment that we initially feel toward a wrongdoer undergoes a metamorphosis into a sort of cosmic sadness that the forces of the world created such a person. It is not the individual as a locus of responsibility to whom we direct our scorn but to those causes that molded him. "If only his physiology were different, or his early environment, or his parents,. .he would not have turned out as he did," we muse. And if there is anything at all that we find redeeming about this person, as we often will, we can imagine *him* existing without his bad qualities and direct our sorrow for the loss of what could have been at that good part of him we see before us.

Like Darrow and Twain, however, Hospers tends to confuse the notion that we are not morally responsible for our actions because they stem from qualities of character that can be traced back to causal antecedents over which we had no control, with the quite different thesis that we have no power to control our actions. For example, Hospers writes,

Let us suppose it were established that a man commits murder only if, sometime during the previous week, he has eaten a certain combination of foods—say tuna fish salad at a meal also including peas, mushroom soup, and blueberry pie. What if we were to track down the factors common to all murders committed in this country during the last twenty years and found this factor present in all of them, and only in them? The example is, of course, empirically absurd; but may it not be that there is *some* combination of factors that regularly leads to homicide?...When such specific factors are discovered, won't they make it clear that it is foolish and pointless, as well as immoral, to hold human beings responsible for crimes? Or, if one prefers biological to psychological factors, suppose a neurologist is called in to testify at a murder trial and produces X-ray pictures of the brain of the criminal; anyone can see, he argues, that the *cella turcica* was already calcified at the age of nineteen; it should be a flexible bone, enabling the gland to grow. All the defendant's disorders might have resulted from this early calcification. Now, this particular explanation may be empirically false; but who can say that no such factors, far more complex, to be sure, exist?

This passage is worthy of careful scrutiny. First, one should realize that even if a person would not commit a given crime if he had not eaten a certain combinatinon of foods or if he did not have a calcified *cella turcica,* it still need not be "pointless, as well as immoral" to hold such an individual responsible for his crime, as Hospers suggests, *if the individual had some control over the effects of these factors.* For example, if Jones would not have committed a crime had he not been in an agitated condition, and he would not have been in an agitated condition had he not eaten that particular combination of food, there is certainly a point in holding him responsible if he were conscious of his agitated condition and had the power to combat the desires that sprang from it. After all, we often find ourselves victimized by unexpected changes of mood—stemming from we know not where—which incline us to do things we normally would not; but clearly, this is precisely the time that it is important for us to accept responsibility for controlling the desires that we find imposing themselves upon us. Even though Hospers does not say this, he would appear to be assuming in the examples that he gives that the forces that *cause* a person to commit a crime do so in ways that bypass any conscious deliberation. Clearly, if certain combinations of food or a calcified *cella turcica* are in themselves *sufficient* to cause a crime, as Hospers seems to assume, then individuals are powerless victims of these forces. But there is no good reason to believe that human behavior is *fully* determined by such uncontrollable forces. As psychoanalysts point out, many actions which appear to be determined through conscious and rational deliberation are actually caused by unconscious factors over which we have no knowledge or control. Nevertheless, there is no good reason to believe that this is always or usually the case. The psychoanalytic insights Hospers so readily relies upon suggest not that actions are *never free,* but that they are *less free* than we originally thought. Indeed, the cornerstone of psychoanalytic thought is the belief that unconscious causes can be brought to consciousness and there be subject to control. From the psychoanalytic perspective it is in this that our freedom lies.

A newborn baby or a very young child is a fully passive recipient of environmental influences, but as the child grows older, he helps mold and direct that environment. If it could be shown that all or most conscious human deliberation over momentous personal choices is nothing but a rationalization for acting in ways that are fully determined by the unconscious effects of early childhood experiences, there would be justification for looking at individuals as mere pawns of fate, but there is no reason to believe that this is generally true. Indeed, agreed upon scientific laws relating early childhood experience to an adult's later capacity for conscious and rational choice are nonexistent.

Libertarianism

James: Freedom as Chance

William James (1842–1910), an influential philosopher and psychologist of the turn of the century and one of the key figures in the development of the school of American philosophy known as *pragmatism,* argues passionately for an acceptance of the libertarian point of view in his famous article "The Dilemma of Determinism." James begins his article by sketching the essential difference, as he sees it, between determinism and indeterminism. He writes,

> ...[Determinism] professes that those parts of the universe already laid down absolutely appoint and decree what the other parts shall be. The future has no ambiguous possibilities hidden in its womb....
> With earth's first clay they did the last man knead,
> And there of the last harvest sowed the seed.
> And the first morning of creation wrote
> What the last dawn of reckoning shall read.
> Indeterminism, on the contrary, says that the parts have a certain amount of loose play on one another, so that the laying down of one of them does not necessarily determine what the others shall be. It admits that possibilities may be in excess of actualities....Of two alternative futures which we conceive, both may now be possible; and the one become impossible only at the very moment when the other excludes it by becoming real itself. Indeterminism thus denies the world to be one unbending unit of fact. It says there is a certain ultimate pluralism in it;...

According to James, determinism is inconsistent with our unsophisticated view that "what has happened need not have happened." If determinism is true then our common intuitive experience that there are possibilities of action open to us must be an illusion. On the other hand, if this experience is not an illusion, then there must be some element of chance in the universe which makes complete scientific predictions of events impossible. From this perspective, James unhesitantly identifies freedom of action with acts due to chance. Nevertheless, James admits that we cannot be sure of the veracity of our intuitive feelings that there really are alternatives of action open to us; all we know is that this experience appears quite real to us.

As well as going against our immediate experience of freedom, the doctrine of determinism, James argues, is inconsistent with our deep moral feelings of regret that some things that happen need not have happened. He writes,

> I wish first of all to show you just what the notion that this is a deterministic world implies. The implications I call your attention to are all bound up with the fact that this is a world in which we constantly have to make what I shall, with your permission, call judgments of regret. Hardly an hour passes in which we do not wish that something might be otherwise; and happy indeed are those of us whose hearts have never echoed the wish of Omar Khayam—
> ...
> Ah! Love, could you and I with fate conspire
> To ment this sorry scheme of things entire,

Would we not shatter it to bits, and then
Remould it nearer to the heart's desire?

Thinking now of the story he had just recently read in the newspaper of a brutal murder in Brockton, Massachusetts, James reflects that in a determined world our feeling of regret that such a crime happened becomes irrational, for given the causes acting in the universe, such a crime was inevitable.

> But for the deterministic philosophy the murder, the sentence, and the prisoner's optimism were all necessary from eternity; and nothing else for a moment had a ghost of a chance of being put into their place. . . . If this Brockton murder was called for by the rest of the universe, if it had to come at its preappointed hour, and if nothing else would have been consistent with the sense of the whole, what are we to think of the universe? Are we stubbornly to stick to our judgment of regret, and say, though it *couldn't* be, yet it *would* have been a better universe with something different from this Brockton murder in it? . . . the judgment of regret calls the murder bad. Calling a thing bad means, if it means anything at all, that the thing ought not to be, that something else ought to be in its stead. Determinism, in denying that anything else can be in its stead, virtually defines the universe as a place in which what ought to be is impossible. . .

The acceptance of determinism, James claims, must lead to the very depressing conclusion that what is, however bad it might be, must be—that regret over particular events is irrational. (If regret makes any sense at all in a determined world, James goes on, such regret must be directed not to particular events, but to the "whole sorry scheme of things.")

There are many serious difficulties with James's view. First, it is doubtful that the introspective feeling of freedom that James relies upon supports his belief that our actions are not caused. According to the determinist, this feeling is nothing more than the feeling that one can do as one chooses. Although it is conceptually impossible for a person who is in the course of deliberating to know what the outcome of that deliberation will be, this does not mean that his act of deliberation is uncaused and could not be known beforehand by someone who was aware of all the conscious and unconscious factors influencing his decision. The fact that one is not aware of the causes of one's action in no way shows that there is no cause for that action. For example, it was Frued's contention that many apparently random slips of the tongue were quite significant revelations of unconscious mental processes that are capable of causal explanation.

Second, it seems unreasonable to identify free actions with those that are due to chance. If, for example, Jones's decision to murder Smith was due to chance—to, let us say, some random firing of certain neurons in his brain—how can we call such an action a free one for which Jones is morally responsible? As one soft determinist put it, "in proportion as an act of volition starts of itself without cause it is exactly, so far as freedom of the individual is concerned, as if it had been thrown into his mind from without—'suggested to him by a freakish demon!' " If, as James contends, our feelings of regret that a murder occurred would be inappropriate in a determined world, would they be appropriate in a world governed by chance? Certainly not. If undesirable events are due to chance, we would have no control over the future. On the other hand, if they are caused, we can learn how to prevent similar events from occurring *again*. Is it not the case that the intelligibility of feelings of regret resides precisely in the fact that the future is open to our control through a knowledge of causes?

Although an omniscient God would know beforehand of all the murders that ever will occur, the important thing for us as human beings who live at a particular point in time is that our actions can have some causal influence on the future. As soft determinists often point out, it is essential that one carefully distinguish—as James does not—the doctrine of determinism from that of fatalism. In a fatalistic world, human choices and actions are powerless to affect the future. Determinism, however, need not entail such a bleak view. The determinist is committed to the view that all events are caused, not that they will occur *in spite of* human actions to avoid them. Quite often, the nonfatalistic determinist would assert, human choices and actions can act as causes. While we cannot erase what has already happened, we can study the causes that made it happen and utilize this knowledge to create the causal conditions that will assure, or at least make less probable, its occurrence in the future. From such a perspective, human freedom resides in human control, which in turn presupposes a deterministic universe and not one ruled by chance.

Campbell: Freedom as Causation by a Nondetermined Moral Self

Given the implausibility of equating freedom with chance, most libertarians will grant that free acts are caused, but will insist that they are caused by a *self* whose actions are themselves not caused and, as such, are incapable of scientific prediction.

The most influential contemporary proponent of this point of view is C. A. Campbell (1897–1971). According to Campbell, the distinctive characteristic of human beings is that they are moral agents whose actions can transcend the promptings of *character* as formed by heredity and environment. Although the various states of consciousness and dispositions to behave in particular ways that comprise a person's character at a given moment are capable of scientific explanation and prediction, a person is more than just his character; he is also an autonomous *moral agent* (*self*) whose choices are *influenced* but not determined by the promptings of his character. The metaphysical picture Campbell presents of the nature of a moral self is quite in accord with the traditional Judeo-Christian conception of a soul as an immaterial substance whose distinctive characteristics are its free will and knowledge of right and wrong. According to this conception, scientific knowledge of a person's character and the external forces acting upon it will give us some idea of the degree of moral effort that the moral self will have to exert to make a certain choice. In addition, given our general knowledge of how human beings tend to respond, it is possible to develop scientific laws which can tell us that a certain percentage of human beings with a given type of character will act in a particular way in given circumstances. Consequently, it is possible to know beforehand what the *probability* is that a given person will so behave, but it is impossible for us to scientifically know with *absolute certainty* how a person will act since it is possible for the moral self to transcend the desires and tendencies toward action that comprise the promptings of character.

According to Campbell, most of our choices are fully determined and, as such, are not free. It is only in a situation of moral conflict, where our characters prompt us to do one thing and our sense of moral duty prompts us to do something else, that the moral self is capable of making a causally undetermined choice for which it is the sole author.[5] As Campbell puts it,

> Here, and here alone, so far as I can see, in the act of deciding whether to put forth or withhold the moral effort required to resist temptation and rise to duty, is to be found an act which is free in the sense required for moral responsibility; an act of which the self is sole author, and of which it is true to say that "it could be" (or, after the event, "could have been") "otherwise." . . .
> There is X, the course which we believe we ought to follow, and Y, the course towards which we feel our desire is strongest. The freedom which we ascribe to the agent is the freedom to put forth or refrain from putting forth the moral effort required to resist the pressure of desire and to do what he thinks he ought to do.
> But then there is surely an immense range of practical situations—covering by far the greater part of life—in which there is no question of a conflict within the self between what he most desires to do and what he thinks he ought to do. . . . over that whole vast range there is nothing whatever in our version of Libertarianism to prevent our agreeing that character determines conduct. In the absence, real or supposed, of any "moral" issue, what a man chooses will be simply that course which, after such reflection as seems called for, he deems most likely to bring him what he most strongly desires; and that is the same as to say the course to which his present character inclines him. . . .
> . . . the very function of moral effort, as it appears to the agent engaged in the act, is to enable the self to act against the line of least resistance, against the line to which his character as so far formed strongly inclines him. But if the self is thus conscious here of *combatting* his formed character, he surely cannot possibly suppose that the act, although his own act, *issues from* his formed character? I submit, therefore, that the self knows very well indeed—from the inner standpoint—what is meant by an act which is the *self's* act and which nevertheless does not follow from the self's *character*. . . . the "nature" of the self and what we commonly call the "character" of the self are by no means the same thing. The "nature" of the self comprehends, but is not without remainder reducible to, its "character"; it must, if we are to be true to the testimony of our experience of it, be taken as including *also* the authentic creative power of fashioning and refashioning "character."

[5]Campbell's view of free will is clearly influenced by, but not identical to, Kant's view. While it was the existence of conflicts between duty and inclination which led Kant to postulate the existence of free will, he did not believe that freedom existed only in such situations of conflict, as Campbell does. Furthermore, unlike Campbell, Kant believed that all human (externally observable) behavior was fully determined; what he thought was not fully determined was the human *will,* which in some mysterious way stood outside of the flux of events in the empirical world. From Kant's perspective, one can consistently look at human beings both from a purely scientific and deterministic standpoint and from another standpoint which assumes an autonomous moral self that can act on the basis of reasons rather than causes. In this respect, Kant can be seen as a soft determinist, but the complexity of Kant's view makes it misleading to classify him as such, since, unlike those who are usually classified as soft determinists, he makes no attempt to explain freedom but takes it as an unexplainable "postulate of practical reason" (in particular of moral reason). As usual Kant's view in this matter is insightful, but much in need of clarification.

There are many difficulties with Campbell's view. Without getting into the thickets of metaphysical reflection, which any complete treatment of Campbell's position would require, here are some of the main problems. First, it is difficult to understand what to make of Campbell's notion of a self as some type of a substantial entity that can be understood as being distinct from the various states of consciousness and dispositions to behave that comprise one's character. Indeed, many philosophers, following David Hume, have found this notion unintelligible. Although Campbell says that he can intuit the existence of this self, other philosophers would strongly disagree. Second, it is contrary to scientific teachings to believe, as Campbell does, that the choice between duty and desire is any less under the sway of causal determination than other choices between desires that Campbell is willing to grant are fully determined. Is Campbell not under the influence of an old religious metaphysics that has been discredited by modern science? Third, is it not implausible to maintain, as Campbell does, that although a person is free to choose between duty and desire, he is, nevertheless, not free in any other of the choices that he makes? Fourth, Campbell asserts that a person who struggles to overcome desires that lead contrary to the promptings of duty has free will, but if he gets to the point where doing his duty is the natural thing to do, he is no longer free. Does this make sense? Fifth, since Campbell claims that a person is only free when he consciously faces a choice between desire and duty, a very strange consequence of Campbell's view would be that a person is not free or morally responsible when he does not think about his duty. This, however, runs counter to our common practice of holding people morally responsible for not thinking of their duty when we believe that they had the power to do so.

Sixth, Campbell seems to imply that any choice between duty and desire is a free choice and, as such, one for which we can always hold people responsible; this is not true. For example, let us assume that Jones deliberates about whether to kill Smith with his gun (that which he desires) or by poison (that which he believes to be his duty), and, having the power to choose either way, he chooses one rather than the other. If Jones did not have the power to refrain from killing Smith in some manner, we would not consider his action a free one for which he is morally responsible. This would, in particular, be the case if Jones's conception of his duty appears to us to be irrational.

Finally, Campbell admits that the self is *influenced* by the promptings of character as determined by heredity and environment which can make it more or less difficult for the self to rise to duty. But, why isn't it possible that these promptings are so strong that the self is *powerless* to overcome them? Certainly, some people clearly see what they think they ought to do, try very hard to overcome desires that lead them to do otherwise, and fail. Are they free? Imagine, too, a person who is involuntarily "programmed" to consider his duty and to struggle fiercely to do it, and then to decide not to. Is he free? It would seem that whatever problems we initially had in explaining when a human being is free Campbell will have in explaining when a self is free. Campbell has not really solved our problem, he has simply side-stepped it. Before, we had the problem of when a human being is free; now we have the problem of when a self is free; we have gained nothing. In addition, since Campbell speaks of the self exerting more or less moral effort, ought he not to speak of *degrees of human freedom* and focus on the problem of how we are to compare and measure differences in the amount of moral effort individuals exert? Would it not be more reasonable to use this notion as the basis for assessing an individual's moral responsibility, and not rely upon the mysterious notion of a self that transcends scientific understanding?

Soft Determinism

The Belief that Determinism Is Incompatible with Free Will Is a Result of Conceptual Confusion

Although soft determisists do not agree upon what is, or ought to be, meant by calling human acts free in the sense required for justifiably holding individuals morally responsible, all soft determinists agree that the mere fact that acts are determined does not make them unfree. As they see it, acts are unfree only when they are caused *in particular ways*. Indeed, for many soft determinists, the notion of a free but causally undetermined act is logically incoherent. As the philosopher H. B. Hobart put it,

> An action which is not causally determined by the character of the agent (together with the situation in which he is acting) cannot be said to have stemmed from *him*, from the particular person that he is, and hence is not anything for which *he* can be held responsible. If it is causally determined by something independent of his character, it is not *his* act; while if it is not causally determined at all, it is a chance happening and, again, something for which he cannot be held responsible.

For most soft determinists, the widespread belief that determinism is incompatible with free will is a result of certain conceptual confusions and can easily be dispelled once those conceptual confusions are uncovered. Primary among those confusions, according to the soft determinist, is the tendency to confuse determinism with fatalism, which we have briefly touched upon. While freedom is incompatible with fatalism, it is not incompatible with determinism if the chain of causes that determine our actions operates through our desires and decisions.

As many soft determinists have seen it, the widespread tendency to equate the doctrine of determinism with the fatalistic belief that human actions are fully determined by forces that impose themselves unwillingly upon us stems from a confusion between *descriptive* laws of nature which merely describe how people *actually* behave and *prescriptive* man-made laws which prescribe how people *ought* to behave. While human beings often experience themselves as being under the *constraint* of prescriptive laws which *make* them behave in ways they would not naturally or freely choose without the existence of such laws, human choices and actions are not subject to descriptive laws of nature in the same sense. The laws of human behavior that behavioral scientists attempt to discover do not *constrain* us or *make* us behave in any particular way, but function as *explanations* of our behavior. Behavioral scientists attempt to uncover the patterns of connection that exist between our choices and the various physical and psychological factors upon which they depend. These physical and psychological factors, however, in free actions are not constraints which go contrary to our free will. They simply are the causal antecedents of that free will. If our free choices are determined, someone could, in principle, predict what we will choose, but this does not take away our freedom to choose. Indeed, do we not all, at times, find ourselves fully confident of our ability to predict the actions of those whose characters we know well? Yet this confidence in no way affects our belief that a person is acting freely and is morally responsible for his actions.

Soft Deterministic Analyses of Free Action

United in their belief that human acts can be said to be free even though they are fully determined and, as such, capable of scientific prediction, soft determinists diverge when it comes to the analysis they give of the sense of freedom they consider to be required for judgments of moral responsibility. There are four basic analyses that soft determinists have offered for the concept of free action:

1. *Freedom as the Absence of Compulsion:* According to this view, a person's actions are free when they are not a result of *compulsion* or, to put it in a positive way, when they result from the agent's own *unimpeded desire.*

2. *Freedom as Hypothetical Behavior:* According to this view, a human action is a free one as long as the agent *could (or would) have been able to do otherwise if he had chosen (or tried) to do otherwise.*

3. *Freedom as the Power to Choose and Do Otherwise:* This analysis of free action differs from the preceding one in that proponents of this view admit that it is possible that a person who could or would have done otherwise, if he had chosen otherwise or tried, might nevertheless still not be free if he did not have the power to choose otherwise or to try.

4. *Freedom as Capacity for Rational Action:* According to this view, only creatures capable of modifying their actions as a result of rational deliberation can be said to be free and morally responsible creatures. An individual is responsible for his actions when our responses to him—such as holding him morally responsible, blaming or praising him, and punishing him—can in some rational way influence him to make different decisions in the future.

Let us consider these views.

Freedom as the Absence of Compulsion   The identification of free action with the lack of external compulsion can be traced back to the ancient Greek philosopher Aristotle who, in drawing a distinction between voluntary and involuntary behavior, declared, "Those things, then, are thought involuntary, which take place under compulsion or owing to ignorance; and that is compulsory of which the moving principle is outside, being a principle in which nothing is contributed by the person who is acting...for example, if he were carried somewhere by a wind or by men who had him in their power." In more modern times, the philosophers Hobbes, Hume, Mill, Schlick, and Russell have defined freedom in terms of the lack of compulsion. For example, according to Schlick, "Freedom means the opposite of compulsion; a man is free if he does not act under compulsion, and he is compelled or unfree when he is hindered from without in the realization of his natural desires." According to this commonly accepted view, free acts are by definition those acts caused by the unimpeded desires of the agent, while unfree acts are caused by forces or conditions outside the agent.

A difficulty with this influential soft deterministic analysis of a free act resides in the conceptual obscurity that surrounds the notion of compulsion. There are clear cases of human behavior that we would all agree are due to compulsion and, for that reason, are unfree. For example, we would all agree than an epileptic is behaving under the influence of a compulsion and, consequently, is acting unfreely when he finds himself helplessly in the midst of a seizure. Similarly, if someone, by virtue of overpowering physical force, flings me across a room, I am under the physical constraint of the laws of physics as I fly through the room against my own free will. In these two clear-cut cases of unfree behavior, due to external physical compulsion, one should note that there is really no element of choice at all. Since this is so, many philosophers would refuse to describe such behavior as "actions," for according to their usage of this term, a human action must, by definition, involve some element of choice or intention. If one accepts this usage, since the examples we have given are not examples of actions, neither are they examples of unfree actions.

However one resolves this conceptual question, when we turn away from these clear-cut cases of involuntary behavior and turn to actions which involve some element of choice, it becomes difficult to understand exactly what we mean or ought to mean when we say that an action is due to external compulsion. An example often given of such an action is that of a person doing something under the threat of death—such as when someone points a gun at you and asks you to divulge some information. When a person acts as a result of such compulsion, it is said, such an act is an unfree one for which the actor is not morally responsible. This is, however, problematic. A person who chooses to divulge information rather than to face the clear and immediate prospect of his death could have chosen death rather than divulge the information if he had wanted to. Indeed, if the actor were a captured spy, we would consider it his obligation to choose death rather than to divulge any information that was vital to the interests of his country and as a result would consider him free to choose death and morally responsible if he did not.

The important conclusion that emerges is that our notion of what is to count as a compulsion is a reflection of what we are willing to excuse. Since in most circumstances we are willing to excuse, if not justify, an individual's choice to act in a particular way under the threat of death, we call such an act unfree. But is a person acting unfreely when he succumbs to the threat of a severe beating or the loss of his job or the loss of his reputation? Indeed, should a person be said to be acting under compulsion and for that reason unfreely if he does something he otherwise would not, in order to obtain a reward? Does it not depend on our perception of the relative magnitudes of his need for the reward and his duty to refrain from such action? For example, if a poor person insults someone to obtain money he desperately needs to feed his family, we may be willing to say that he acted unfreely, but say that he acted freely if he inflicts much greater injury on someone. Does not our inclination to call an action unfree vary directly with our belief about whether an individual *ought to succumb* to a particular temptation? It is precisely because people will disagree as to what we ought to accept as a good excuse or justification for a particular type of behavior that no clear answers exist for the questions we have posed. This fact is not recognized by those who present the notion of compulsion as if it were a purely *factual* notion that can be used to justify particular judgments about the freedom of action or moral responsibility of an individual. Since we are often faced with unpleasant choices that we perceive as being at least to some extent imposed on us from without, a decision must be made as to what type or degree of external constraint upon our behavior renders that behavior unfree and this decision is a *moral* one that cannot be resolved simply by looking at the facts.

For example, the attorney, F. Lee Bailey argued in defense of Patty Hearst that she was "brainwashed" into robbing a bank with members of a terrorist organization that kidnapped her. According to Bailey, the pressures under which Ms. Hearst was forced to choose whether or not to accept the wishes of her captors were so compulsive as to render her action an unfree one. No doubt, Ms. Hearst was in a very unpleasant situation when she allowed herself to be influenced by her captors to become the seemingly self-assured and proud terrorist that she became, but was she not also in a very unpleasant situation when she was influenced by her parents and her attorney to appear in court as a humble, timid girl who repentently became again the dutiful daughter she once was? If a choice made under the possible threat of death at the hands of her captors can justify calling Ms. Hearst's choice a compulsive one, why shouldn't a choice made under the threat of long imprisonment equally as well qualify as a compulsive one?

It is precisely because the answer to such a question requires a moral decision as to which factors ought to render one's action *unduly* caused that psychiatric experts on brainwashing find themselves in the unflattering position of so often disagreeing in their diagnoses. "Yes, she was brainwashed," "Yes, she did act under compulsion," some say. "No, she was not brainwashed," "No, she did not act under compulsion," others say. And though such a debate is often presented in courts of law as being over a purely factual issue for which psychiatrists are especially qualified to offer testimony, this is not the case. The fact is that psychiatrists, like the rest of us, do not agree on what *ought* to count as rendering an action so unduly caused as to justify calling it one due to compulsion and for that reason unfree. Two psychiatrists may agree on the nature of the pressures that a person faced and disagree over whether or not these pressures had compulsive force for they, like the rest of us, *do not clearly know what we mean by a compulsive force.* If we are to say, for example, that a person who makes a particular choice acts under compulsion only when he is under the influence of an *irresistible impulse,* we must have some way of distinguishing between impulses which are so strong that they *cannot be resisted* and those impulses that *can be resisted if sufficient effort is exerted.* This, as the law courts have discovered, is no simple task.

As we grapple with what it means to say that an act is due to compulsion, our heads may swim in a swirl of conceptual confusion. If acting under internal compulsion is to be identified with acting under an irresistible impulse, am I acting under compulsion when I run to help my small child who has severely hurt himself? Clearly, we do not want to say this, for we do not call actions compulsive when they are determined by internal states with which the actor identifies or approves. Consequently, the notion of choosing under compulsion carries along the suggestion of fighting against alien and strong desires which incline one to do something that does not fit in with one's normal personality or which goes against one's value system. Yet, one may wonder, why should a person's failure to identify himself with his desires be considered an excusing factor, for is not the decisive factor in the determination of moral responsibility whether an individual can control his desires and not that he consider them as parts of his normal self? After all, we all at one time or another find within ourselves very strong desires which seem alien to our nature, which seem as if they were imposed upon us from without. Yet as long as we have some degree of control over them, should we not be responsible for them? But as our minds continue swimming in philosophical confusion, we wonder how we can determine "the degree of control" individuals have over their desires. This becomes especially puzzling when we realize that a person can be a victim of an internal compulsion over which he is not even aware. For instance, he might be acting under the influence of a hypnotic suggestion. But if acting under a hypnotic suggestion renders one's action as due to internal compulsion and for that reason unfree, what if someone acts in a particular way because of some childhood experience or purely biochemical condition over which he is equally unaware; are these not unfree actions as well? If Freud and other psychiatrists are right, is it not the case that the sphere of compulsive actions is much wider than we thought? How wide is it? Are any of our actions ever totally free of internal unconscious influences that can be said to function as compulsive forces? Even if they sometimes are free of such forces, how can we ever know when this is so?

In addition, even if we could clearly agree upon a definition of that sort of internal or external compulsion that negates human freedom and could specify a range of human actions which is exempt from it, it still would seem to be wrong to claim that all acts which are performed free of compulsion may for that reason alone be said to be free actions which justify the ascription of moral responsibility. For example, the fact that small children can act without any internal or external compulsion does not render them free and morally responsible agents because they are not *rational* creatures who have a capacity for reasoned choice and moral reflection. Similarly, would we call a person free who acts as he chooses without any internal or external constraint but is incapable of perceiving and rationally weighing alternative courses of action? I would think not. Consequently, it would appear that individuals should not be said to act freely unless they are capable of rational action.

Freedom as capacity for rational choice   The identification of freedom with the capacity for rational choice also has a long philosophical history. According to the Greek philosopher, Plato, acting freely implies being rational and virtuous. A free man, for Plato, is a man who is ruled by reason, not by passions, and under the guidance of reason decides as he ought to decide. Furthermore, Plato conceived the rational and virtuous part of man's nature, and not his passionate nature, to be his true nature. Consequently, for Plato, the notions of freedom, rationality, virtue, and self-expression were interrelated. This classical Greek conception of freedom is well expressed by the philosopher Plotinus:

> When the Soul has been modified by outer forces and acts under that pressure so that what it does is no more than an unreflecting acceptance of stimulus, neither the act nor the state can be described as voluntary; so, too, when even from within itself, it falls at times below its best....But when our Soul holds to its Reason-Principle...only then can we speak of [a] voluntary act. Things so done may truly be described as our doing.

Saint Thomas Aquinas, the most influential of Christian philosophers, also closely associated the notion of freedom with that of rationality, as did the philosophers Descartes, Spinoza, Leibniz, and Kant. In contemporary times, the identification of rationality with free action was a central theme of the American philosopher John Dewey. The free man, for Dewey, is the man who, possessed of scientific knowledge of himself and the world about him, utilizes that knowledge to mold himself and his environment in ways that are more conducive to human fulfillment.

Contemporary soft deterministic philosophers who analyze the notion of free action in terms of the capacity for rational choice tend to assume a utilitarian moral perspective and, in particular, a utilitarian view of the nature and justification of punishment and reward. According to this perspective, we ask whether a person acted freely because we want to know whether to hold that person responsible and as a fit subject for judgments of moral praise or blame. In order to determine the answer to this question, supporters of this viewpoint would contend, the concept of moral responsibility should be seen as a forward-looking one. The question of whether individuals deserve reward or punishment should be taken as equivalent to the question of whether or not they should be rewarded or punished and that question should be answered on the basis of the probable consequences of rewarding or punishing them. A responsible individual, according to this perspective, is a person who is rational enough to be influenced by rewards and punishment. In holding individuals morally accountable for their behavior, we should not focus on the causal antecedents of their behavior, but rather on the best way to control their *future behavior*. While responsible people are capable of modifying their behavior as a result of rational considerations, nonresponsible people are not.

Such a view of responsibility is reflected in traditional utilitarian justifications of the insanity defense in the criminal law. Following Bentham, most utilitarians who have attempted to justify the existence of such a defense have claimed that the insane are mentally disordered human beings who are incapable of being deterred through the threat of punishment. The notion of deterrability is, however, no less exasperating to analyze than the notion of compulsion, for it is difficult to distinguish those who are *incapable* of being affected by the threat or infliction of punishment from those who are merely *indisposed* to be so affected. After all, there are some courageous free and responsible people who cannot be intimidated through the fear of punishment to change their behavior. For example, an incorrigible civil disobedient, such as Gandhi, would seem to be a model of nondeterrability, but he would not be considered a model of an unfree and nonresponsible individual. It is not clear, however, how we are to distinguish Gandhi, whom we want to say was *indisposed* to conform to the law from those individuals who are *incapable* of so conforming.

Freedom as hypothetical behavior   According to another commonly held soft deterministic analysis of "free action," an individual (X) acted freely in doing something (A) in situation (S) means that X was *capable* of acting otherwise *if* he had tried (or chosen) to. This statement has often been taken by soft determinists to be equivalent to "X would have done other than A in S if he had tried (chosen) to."

This analysis of "free action" has serious shortcomings. Since a person may try to do something and fail, and yet be thought to have been *capable* of it, the notion of what an individual is *capable* of achieving cannot be analyzed in terms of what he *would* achieve *on any given occasion*. As the philosopher J. L. Austin observed,

> Consider the case where I miss a very short putt and kick myself because I could have holed it. It is not that I should have holed it if I had tried; I did try, and missed. . . . Nor does "I can hole it this time" mean that I shall hole it this time if I try. . . for I may try and miss and yet not be convinced that I couldn't have done it; indeed, further experiments may confirm my belief that I could have done it that time although I didn't.

In addition, even if a person would be able to do something if he tried, he may not have the ability to try. This is especially the case if we take the concept of trying to involve the making of some strong effort. For example, if we deliberate over whether a criminal could have avoided his crime, our deliberation will rarely hinge on the question of whether that criminal could have done otherwise *if* he had tried, but rather over whether he was capable of trying. One's freedom, after all, may be severely limited by one's inability to realize all one could do, if only one tried.

Freedom as involving the power to choose or try   Given the inadequacies of the preceding analysis, it has been suggested that people are free if they "could have done otherwise if they tried and had the power to try." Let us call this "The Power To Do Otherwise." This leaves us with the difficult problem of specifying what is involved in having the power to do otherwise. The factors we most naturally focus upon in determining a person's power to do otherwise are the strength of one's desires and the amount of effort that would have to be exerted to overcome them. There are, however, other important factors which are relevant. For example, one's knowledge of alternative actions affects this power. A person who has little ability to think about the alternatives of action open to him or their consequences may have very little power to do otherwise; yet such a person does not yield to overpowering forces, nor does he try to overcome them and fail. Similarly, a person's power to do otherwise may be severely limited by his moral convictions or lack of them. A person who has a very strong moral sense may have very little power to do other than what he believes to be right, and a person who has little moral sense may have little power to attend to considerations that would lead him to do what we think is right. An individual whose character or moral convictions make it impossible for him to believe that behavior of a different kind would be desirable has no real choice between competing options of behavior. Such a person may clearly perceive the alternatives of action open to him and their probable consequences, but they will make no appeal to his emotional or moral nature. It is psychologically soothing for us to believe that great evildoers, such as Hitler, had the full power to do otherwise and as such were maximally morally guilty for their actions, but we often find that they were limited in their power to do otherwise by limited knowledge or moral understanding.

Since many concepts are packed into the notion of power to do otherwise, a person may be said to have a high degree of power to do otherwise from one perspective, but a low degree of power from another perspective. For example, a person may have great power to do something if he tries, but little power to attend to considerations which would lead him to realize why he ought to try. This makes comparisons of degrees of power to do otherwise conceptually uncertain. Nevertheless, we can make sense of the notion of full power to do otherwise which human beings seldom possess. To say that "X had full power to do $A2$ (a morally right action) rather than $A1$ (a morally wrong action) in S" can be analyzed as follows:

1. X fully recognized and appreciated the nature and relevant consequences of $A1$ and why it would be morally wrong for him to do $A1$ in S.
2. X fully recognized and appreciated the nature and relevant consequences of $A2$ and why it would be morally right for him to do $A2$ in S.
3. X did not try to do $A2$ instead of $A1$ in S although he realized that no effort or only a minimal degree of effort was necessary to do $A2$ rather than $A1$.

Once we depart from this concept of full power to do otherwise and attempt to measure its degree, we will find the different factors that go into this notion pulling us in different directions. At any rate, these factors are incapable of precise scientific definition and measurement. If such power can be determined at all, it is only on the basis of very imprecise generalizations about how roughly similar persons in roughly similar situations have been observed to behave.

The Hard Deterministic Rejoinder
to the Soft Determinist

Even if we could define "degrees of power to do otherwise" and had some scientific means for measuring and comparing such power, a hard determinist will argue that any distinction that a soft determinist makes between free and unfree actions is overly narrow in focusing its attention only on the present capacities of individuals without focusing on their causal antecedents. Consider, the hard determinist will say, that we are often willing to lessen our harsh moral judgment of individuals when we find that they suffered from environmental or biological disadvantages from which most of us have been spared. Indeed, the hard determinist will contend, if we attempt to trace back the causes of character, we will find that it is ultimately the product of factors over which people have no control, namely, heredity and early childhood experiences. Since people are not responsible for these factors, people cannot justifiably be held responsible for their actions, the hard determinist will protest. As the philosopher Schopenhauer put it, "A man can surely do what he wills to do, but he cannot determine what he wills." As we have seen, however, it would appear that there are no conceivable circumstances a hard determinist would count as justifying the ascription of moral responsiblity, for the notion of an individual fully forming his own character from scratch is unintelligible. Consequently, it would appear that the hard determinist should not be taken as asserting that free will is incompatible with determinism—tacitly implying that freedom would be possible if determinism were false—but should rather be taken to be asserting that this notion is meaningless.

Once we realize that people's acts can be traced back to hereditary and environmental causes belonging to a world that they had no part in making, we will realize, the hard determinist will say, that there is no distinction that can be made between free and unfree actions that can sustain the moral weight it is made to bear when we hold individuals morally responsible or nonresponsible for their actions. No doubt, the hard determinist will say, there can be a utilitarian justification for holding some individuals morally accountable for their actions as a way of affecting their future behavior, but, if we put aside any practical concerns about the future and try to rank individuals in terms of their moral responsibility for their actions, we will find that the distinction between free and unfree acts must be meaningless to an all-knowing God who can grasp the full network of causes that serve to explain why individuals behave as they do. For such a God, the feelings of righteous indignation and resentment that we as human beings so naturally feel toward those whom we perceive to have freely acted wrongly must be replaced by an understanding that transcends such feelings and makes it impossible to rank people in terms of moral worth. At the highest level of moral development, the notion of a type of divine justice where individuals are rewarded or punished in accordance with their "deserts" must be seen as unintelligible, the hard determinist will argue.

Some Reflections on the Free Will
Problem

As is often the case in philosophical problems, the free will problem is a quite tangled one that must be untangled before it can be solved. Each of the traditional solutions of this problem oversimplifies a multidimensional problem that involves the resolution of conceptual, scientific, and moral questions. For example, we must first decide upon the moral principles we are to use in making judgments of moral responsibility. With these principles in mind, we must then agree on the meanings to be attributed to key concepts in this controversy, such as "compulsion," "deterrability," and "trying." Once we settle on definitions of these concepts, we must attempt to answer such scientific questions as "How wide is the area of compulsive behavior?" "How deterrable, if at all, was this individual in this instance?" and "How much, if at all, did this individual in this instance have it in his power to try to do otherwise?"

While a complete solution of the free will problem is impossible without the resolution of issues such as these, there are certain observations that can be made about this problem that can serve to put it in a much clearer perspective. It seems that the soft determinists are right that although many things may interfere with a person's power to do otherwise, determinism is not one of them. If the distinction between free and unfree actions is to have any meaning at all, it must be understood in terms of the differences in the nature of the causes behind one's acts. Furthermore, we cannot obtain any solution to this problem by claiming that some causes are subject to scientific understanding and prediction and that others, in some mysterious way, are in principle beyond the reaches of such understanding and prediction as libertarians like Campbell claim. The problem with soft determinists, however, is that they tend to provide oversimplified analyses of "free action" that neglect the *many different and vague meanings* we attribute to this notion in ordinary usage. In particular, hard determinists are right that when we deeply reflect about people's responsibility—free of the immediate concern of trying to influence their behavior—we do not find ourselves focusing simply on current capacities, but consider it quite relevant to inquire into causal antecedents, considerations which are neglected by soft determinists.

The first step in resolving the free will problem comes with the realization that the real problem we are facing is not one of explaining whether or not free will is compatible with determinism, but rather of explaining what the concept of free will means. It is a mistake to begin this inquiry, as many philosophers do, with the tacit assumption that this notion has a single meaning in ordinary usage. There are many different things we mean when we say that a person acted freely. Judgments about freedom of action and moral responsibility are made from varying moral perspectives, reflecting different human concerns and attitudes. Who among us has not had occasion, when considering whether a person is morally responsible for his action, to feel torn between different perspectives, pulling us first this way, then that. "He should be held responsible," we say, "after all, . . ." but then we reflect "Maybe he really shouldn't be held responsible, after all, we have to consider . . .," coming at the end to no resolution. Consider, for example, the following imaginary dialogue:

A: I don't think that Bill was really responsible for his crime.

B: Come now! Bill knew what he was doing. He could have done otherwise if he had wanted to; he wasn't under any constraint to act the way he did.

A: I admit that and agree with you that Bill should be held legally responsible. After all, there is some chance that punishment might teach him a lesson. More important, his punishment will serve as a warning to others of the possible consequences of a similar act. What bothers me is that I don't think that he is *morally* responsible.

B: What do you mean?

A: Well, considering Bill's early environment—his drunken father and uncaring mother—one couldn't reasonably expect him to turn out any better.

B: Others have in similar circumstances.

A: Circumstances are never fully the same. If some other fellow turned out better than Bill, he must have been lucky enough to have had some advantage Bill did not have.

B: That's nonsense. The logical implication of a view such as yours would be that no one is ever responsible and I don't think you really want to say that. Furthermore, I think you are wrong to say it's only a matter of luck whether or not we turn out well. You make it appear that people are always the passive recipients of lucky or unlucky breaks. Doubtless, this is sometimes the case, but quite often things come or don't come to people only as a result of the effort they choose or choose not to exert and for which they deserve praise or blame. It's often a question of whether or not people have enough motivation and not simply a question of whether or not they have lucky breaks.

A: I see what you're saying about my view leading logically to the conclusion that no one is every really morally responsible, and I suppose that deep down that is what I believe. Remember I did say that Bill should be held legally responsible; it's just that I don't see how we can really blame him, thinking in the process that we're better than he. No, we're just lucky. According to you, it isn't just luck, it's also a matter of effort, but don't you see that whether or not a person has it within him to make that effort is itself determined by causes over which he has no control.

B: Boy, you really are confused over this whole matter.

A: I know I am, but I think your seeming clarity on this issue stems from your narrow-minded refusal to see the whole picture. By the way, as we were talking, something else occurred to me. I'm not so sure any more that I want to say as I did before that Bill knew what he was doing or that he wasn't acting under some type of a constraint.

B: What do you have in mind now?

A: Well, I'd grant that Bill knew that his act was wrong in the sense that he knew that society would condemn it and I suppose that his act was contrary to his own professed moral code, but I don't know how deep Bill's adherence to traditional morality goes. Sometimes, I think it's all just words with him—he simply doesn't *feel* deeply enough about the things that he should, and for this reason, I hesitate to say that Bill really knew what he was doing.

B: What about Bill acting under some type of constraint?

A: Well, you know sometimes people aren't aware of the constraints under which they act. Perhaps this was true of Bill. After all, he's got so many hangups that work their way through him without his being aware of them. Furthermore, by calling something a constraint, it seems to me all we mean is that it is something that limits one's options of choice, and Bill's options of choice are certainly limited by his environment and by his very way of thinking. Sure Bill isn't stupid. He can reason and judge consequences as well as you and I. He has the intelligence, no doubt, to make it in this world, if only he wants to. But it seems to me, his childhood experiences have provided him with an unrealistic picture of people and the world that makes it impossible for him to realize what possibilities of action are open to him and to care about the things you and I think are important. Isn't this a type of constraint?

B: You should change your major to philosophy and spend your time attempting to solve problems that arise out of your own conceptual confusion. Once you start playing this game of Bill didn't *really* know what he was doing or *really* acted under some type of constraint, I think you'll find yourself saying that every criminal either didn't really know what he was doing or really was acting under some type of constraint. Again, you'd be left with the absurd result that no one is ever responsible for wrongdoing. It seems to me that you are so inflating the meanings of the concepts of knowledge and constraint as to make them meaningless. You shouldn't misuse concepts that way.

A: I'm not so sure I'm misusing these concepts. Sometimes we use these concepts very broadly, the way I am. Anyway, I doubt that they have any clear meaning, and if you could settle on some simple definition of them, I think you'd want to say that some people are not morally responsible for their actions even though they knew what they were doing and weren't acting under any constraint. You'll just have to find other words to describe what I am describing under the heading of "lack of real knowledge" or the "presence of some constraining factor."

Perhaps neither *A* nor *B* has the full monopoly on truth here. *A* is right that his sentiments are indeed reflections of common ways of thinking about who is or is not morally responsible, and *B* is right that some of the common ways of thinking about this question will, if taken to their full logical conclusion, lead to conclusions most of us would be unwilling to accept. Perhaps the truth of the matter is that most of us work with all sorts of different ideas about moral responsibility—ideas which are not clearly spelled out in our minds and can, at times, pull us in different directions, and even generate outright inconsistencies.

Although philosophers have often made it appear that the question of whether an individual is free is a factual one that can justify ascriptions of moral responsibility, the fact is that a judgment of whether an individual is free *presupposes* some view of the conditions under which it is proper to hold individuals morally responsible. The resolution of the question of when an individual should properly be held morally responsible, however, involves taking a moral position and not simply uncovering the relevant facts, for it is our moral decision that will specify which of the facts are relevant. Consider, for example, a typical case of an individual acting under external compulsion. Smith is informed that if he does not assist in a particular crime his wife will be raped. Smith, acting under compulsion, commits the crime. Did he act freely? Did he have a choice? The answer we give to this question will depend *on what we are willing to excuse*. Those who want to excuse Smith will say, "he really didn't have a choice," or claim that his choice was forced and hence unfree. Those who do not want to excuse him will not call his choice a forced one, attributing it to a very unpleasant but nevertheless free choice. If the crime Smith was pressured to commit involved some horrid act like killing several people, most of us would say that he acted freely, but if the crime were a minor one, that he acted unfreely.

Similarly, consider a prisoner of war who is tortured into giving the enemy some intelligence. Did he have a choice? Did he act freely? "He was free to remain silent and suffer; he had a choice," some of us will say, while others will say, "he was not free; he had no choice." It is important to realize that what we say will depend on what we think a reasonable person ought to do in such circumstances. (If the prisoner were a spy, we would expect much more of him and consequently be much less inclined to excuse him by saying he acted unfreely.) Consider, too, the possible excuses of accident and mistake. It might seem that in such cases a person clearly has no choice—for one does not choose to be careless or to make mistakes. Assuming this to be the case (psychiatrists would say that it is not always the case), this is still not the whole story. Even though accidents and mistakes are not consciously chosen, we can still make a distinction between avoidable and unavoidable accidents and mistakes, as the law does. For example, if an intoxicated person is involved in an automobile accident, which would not have occurred but for his intoxication, the law will claim that his accident was avoidable, for he did not have to drink (that is, the law takes the view that even though an accident is not itself chosen, one can choose the events leading to it). Such an action is considered avoidable because we demand that reasonable people should refrain from driving when they are intoxicated. In general, whether an accident or mistake is said to be unavoidable in the law is decided on the basis of our judgment of whether it was a reasonable one, and what one considers reasonable depends upon what one is willing to excuse. Consider, too, the excuse of insanity. A person might say, "Jones was not morally responsible; he did not act freely as a result of his insanity." For such a person, the judgment that an individual is insane will often be seen as a factual psychiatric one that justifies the claim that an individual is not morally responsible. But the fact is that "insanity" is not a psychiatric term at all, but a legal one which is defined on the basis of an insanity rule. There is, however, much legal disagreement as to which insanity rule best picks out those who *morally ought* to be considered insane.

Since the decision as to whether or not an individual acted freely presupposes a moral standard under which the proper conditions for moral responsibility are defined, the question of whether a person acted freely reduces to the question of whether there is a single uniquely justifiable moral perspective from which judgments of moral responsibilty should be made. It is my opinion that there is not— that any single perspective will prove inadequate to achieve all reasonable human purposes and to express all reasonable human attitudes; as a consequence, we move from perspective to perspective as our shifting purposes and attitudes lead us. Indeed, philosophers have a tendency of overly intellectualizing the factors that motivate us to classify individuals as morally responsible or morally nonresponsible, neglecting the often unconscious factors that motivate us to make such discriminations and often reveal more about us than they do about those whom we judge.

For example, most of us will be inclined to excuse a kleptomaniac who steals valueless objects on the grounds that he is acting under the force of a compulsion. But what this means, we rarely ask. Certainly we cannot say that the kleptomaniac's desires are overpowering in the same sense that the epileptic's seizure is overpowering, for the kleptomaniac, unlike the epileptic, can refrain if he tries hard enough and often does refrain either because he is ashamed of his desires or fears apprehension. Can we claim, perhaps, that his desires, though not totally overpowering, are, nevertheless, sufficiently strong so as to make it unreasonable for us to hold him responsible for succumbing to them? Yet what does this claim really mean? It surely would not be unreasonable for us to hold him responsible if our sole concern were to maximize compliance with the law, for then we should say, as one jurist did, that "if an influence is so powerful as to be termed irresistible, so much the more reason why we should not withdraw any of the safeguards tending to counteract it." Do we, perhaps, mean that if an ordinary person were a victim of the desires of the kleptomaniac, he too would prove unable to control them? If so, how do we know this is true? And even if it is, there are surely some criminals whom we have no inclination to excuse who succumb to desires which the average person would also succumb to if he possessed them.

Why, for example, would many of us be willing to excuse the kleptomaniac, but not nearly as willing to excuse a thief who steals as a result of poverty. We surely have no reason for believing that the kleptomaniac's desires are invariably stronger (whatever this should be taken to mean) than those of the poor man. Indeed, why is it that when we find a rich man stealing valueless items, we are quite willing to assume, on the basis of no evidence at all, that he is the victim of a compulsion, but are, on the other hand, inclined to reject evidence which points to the great strength of the desires of others? We may assume that the kleptomaniac struggles against impulses which he rejects as alien and which generate much internal anxiety for him, and this may make his moral position seem more favorable than that of the thief who fully accepts his desires and feels no anxiety over them. Yet, we can just as easily assume that the poor man fights against his impulses and suffers much anxiety over them—impulses which he perhaps realizes are not in his ultimate self-interest.

The best explanation for our tendency to hold the poor thief morally responsible, but not the kleptomaniac, may be the classical psychoanalytical one. According to this view, we consider the thief to be an "ordinary" criminal and consequently feel justified in holding him responsible for his actions because he acts out of quite ordinary and understandable motives which we all find within ourselves at one time or another and have to control. After all, we often want things we cannot afford. Consequently, we naturally feel disposed to blame the thief who has not assumed the burden of control that we have; by punishing him, *we attempt to prove to ourselves* that crime does not pay. Similarly, we tend to exonerate the kleptomaniac because his motive for stealing appears to us to be so different from *the motives that we find within ourselves*. Although this is not always true, it is true more often than most of us would like to believe. Indeed, given the vagueness of the concept of power to do otherwise and our present inability to scientifically measure the various factors upon which it depends, it is inevitable that even those of us who attempt to dispassionately assess a person's power to do otherwise will be swayed by those factors which psychologically determine for us whether that person arouses our sympathy and understanding of our indignation and resentment.

DISCUSSION QUESTIONS

1. According to the Judeo-Christian tradition, God is an all-powerful (omnipotent), all-knowing (omniscient), and morally perfect creator of all else that exists. According to this tradition, human beings are free and morally responsible beings who will ultimately be judged by God for their action in this world.

   a. Which of the following attempts to reconcile the belief in God's omniscience with the conception of God as moral judge and of human beings as free and morally responsible before God do you find the most plausible?

      1. God does not have foreknowledge of our actions. This is not, however, a limitation on his omniscience, for it is logically impossible to have foreknowledge of the actions of free beings. Since human actions are free, they cannot be fully determined.

      2. God has foreknowledge of our actions and, since we are free beings, our actions cannot be fully determined.

      3. God has foreknowledge of our actions and, since we are free beings, our actions must be determined.

      4. God has foreknowledge of our actions and we are free. It is irrelevant whether our actions are fully determined or not.

   b. Are any of these positions acceptable to you? Assuming that God does have foreknowledge of our actions, can this fact be reconciled with the belief that God sees us as morally responsible individuals who deserve punishment or reward for our actions? If this reconciliation can be made as far as God's foreknowledge goes, can it still be made once one adds the fact that God is conceived as the omnipotent creator of all else that exists?

2. a. From Darrow's perspective, can anyone reasonably be held responsible for Leopold and Loebs's crime?

   b. How would Hook criticize this point of view?

   c. Can Darrow's position be defended against this criticism?

3. a. Is the feeling of freedom that libertarians emphasize inconsistent with the belief in determinism? Why?

   b. According to Campbell, free acts are acts in which "the self is sole author." What do you think this means? Is this condition ever satisfied?

4. Consider the following imaginary dialogue:

   A: I wish I could take a pill which would make me always want to do what I morally should.

   B: The cost of such a pill would be the loss of your freedom as a human being.

   A: On the contrary, it would provide me with the freedom I've always sought.

   What do *A* and *B* mean by freedom? Can a person ever be "forced to be free"? Explain.

5. In B. F. Skinner's utopian novel *Walden II,* children are conditioned by the methods of behavioral engineering to become happy and adjusted citizens of their community. The psychologist director of this program is a hard determinist (as is Skinner) who claims, "I deny that freedom exists at all. I must deny it—or my program would be absurd. You cannot have a science about a subject matter which hops capriciously about." How would a soft determinist reply? A libertarian?

6. How plausible is the psychoanalytic explanation of our tendency to excuse the kleptomaniac who steals valueless objects? Is there some other plausible explanation for this tendency? Under what conditions, if any, ought we to morally or legally excuse such an individual?

FURTHER READINGS

Free Will and Determinism (Harper & Row, 1966), edited by Bernard Berofsky, is an excellent comprehensive anthology of material on the free will/determinism issue. Another good anthology is *Determinism and Freedom in the Age of Modern Science* (Collier Books, 1961), edited by Sidney Hook, which consists of papers on the concepts of determinism, freedom, and responsibility that were given at a symposium in 1957 and comments by others on these papers. An excellent and comprehensive 16-page bibliographic essay describing the literature on the free will/determinism issue is inlcuded in the anthology *A Modern Introduction To Philosophy*, 3rd ed. (Free Press, 1973), edited by Paul Edwards and Arthur Pap, which also has a good selection of material on this issue.

A comprehensive critical analysis of contemporary perspectives on the free will/determinism issue directed to the more advanced student is provided by Harold Ofstad in his article "Recent Work on the Free Will Problem," which appeared in *American Philosophical Quarterly*, 4 (1967). Ofstad provides a more detailed analysis and survey of positions on this issue in his book *An Inquiry into the Freedom of Decision* (George Allen & Unwin, 1961).

William James defends his version of libertarianism in his article "The Dilemma of Determinism," which was originally presented as an address to Harvard Divinity students; it has been reprinted in many anthologies including Edwards & Pap and my *Perennial Philosophical Issues* (Prentice-Hall, 1984). Campbell's version of libertarianism is found in his book *On Selfhood and Godhood*, lecture IX (Macmillan, 1957). The quotation from Campbell in this chapter comes from this work. Campbell also defends his libertarian position and attacks soft determinism (in particular, Schlick's view) in his 1951 article "Is 'Free Will' a Pseudo-Problem," which is reprinted in the Edwards-Pap and Berofsky anthologies. Fyodor Dostoevsky's *Notes from Underground* is an insightful literary expression of the libertarian view that free human beings cannot see their actions and interests as scientifically, and indeed, even rationally, determined. This short existentialistic novel demonstrates both Dostoevsky's incisive powers of psychological anlaysis and the enduring psychological appeal of libertarianism.

Clarence Darrow's passionate, though philosophically unsophisticated hard-deterministic defense of Leopold and Loeb appears in "The Crime of Compulsion," in *Attorney for the Damned*, edited by Arthur Weinberg, and is reprinted in my anthology. Mark Twain, in his typically amusing fashion, presents in dialogue form another philosophically unsophisticated hard-deterministic picture of human nature in his article "What is Man?" included in the collection *What is Man? and Other Philosophical Writings* (University of California, 1973). John Hospers provides his provocative defense of the hard-deterministic viewpoint in "What Means This Freedom" which was first published in the Hook anthology and is reprinted in mine. The quotation from Hospers in this chapter comes from this work. Hospers takes a weaker stance in his earlier essay "Free Will and Psychoanalysis," which is reprinted in the Edwards-Pap and Berofsky anthologies.

Moritz Schlick's "When Is a Man Responsible?" contained in his *Problems in Ethics*, published in 1931, is a very clear nontechnical defense of soft-determinism. It is reprinted in the Edwards-Pap anthology and in mine. Schlick is especially concerned with uncovering what he takes to be the linguistic confusions that lead people to think that determinism is incompatible with freedom and moral responsibility. Schlick's contentions in this regard are challenged by Campbell in his article "Is 'Free Will' a Pseudo-Problem?" which follows the Schlick article in the Edwards and Pap anthology. In his article "Free Will as Involving Determinism and Inconceivable Without It," *Mind*, 43 (1934), R. B. Hobart argues that actions can be free only when they are determined. This article, which is directed to the sophisticated reader, is reprinted in the Berofsky anthology.

In his influential book *Free Action* (Routledge and Kegan Paul, 1961), A. I. Meldan argues that, while human *bodily movements* are caused, it is logically impossible for *actions* to be caused. In drawing a logical distinction between the domain of bodily movements, which can be explained in terms of causes, and the domain of actions, which can be explained only in terms of *reasons,* Melden's view of the free will/determinism relationship is similar to Kant's. Melden's point of view is criticized in D. Davidson's 1963 *Journal of Philosophy* article, "Actions, Reasons and Causes." Excerpts from both Melden and Davidson are included in the Berofsky anthology. This controversy is directed to the more advanced philosophy student.

In his influential article "Freedom of the Will and the Concept of a Person," *Philosophical Reveiw*, LXVIII, No. 1 (Jan. 14, 1971), Harry Frankfurt identifies freedom with rational action and downplays the challenge of determinism. Central to Frankfurt's analysis is the distinction between the desires one happens to find within oneself (first-order desires) and self-reflective judgments as to the sort of desires one would like to have (second-order desires). Frankfurt claims that the human capacity for reflective second-order desires is central to the concept of a *free person.*

II

SOME CONTEMPORARY MORAL PROBLEMS

Of one thing we may be sure. If inquiries are to have any substantial basis, if they are not to be wholly in the air, the theorist must take his departure from the problems which men actually meet in their own conduct. He may define and refine these; he may divide and systematize; he may abstract the problems from their concrete contexts in individual lives; he may classify them when he has thus detached them; but if he gets away from them he is talking about something his own brain has invented, not about moral realities.

JOHN DEWEY AND JAMES TUFTS

Pretend what we may, the whole man within us is at work, when we form our philosophical opinions.

WILLIAM JAMES

Out of the crooked timber of humanity no straight thing was ever made.

attributed to IMMANUEL KANT

Sexual Morality and the Enforcement of Morals

4

.... *It is evident*... *that every emission of semen, in such a way that generation cannot follow, is contrary to the good for man. And if this be done deliberately, it must be a sin....Likewise, it must also be contrary to the good for man if the semen be emitted under conditions such that generation could result but the proper upbringing would be prevented.... [S]ince the needs of human life demand many things which cannot be provided by one person alone... it is appropriate to human nature that a man remain together with a woman after the generative act, and not leave her to have relations with another woman. ... [T]he society of man and woman of the human species, which we call matrimony,... should endure throughout an entire life.*

SAINT THOMAS AQUINAS

....*the only purpose for which power can be rightfully exercised over any member of a civilized community, against his will, is to prevent harm to others....*

JOHN STUART MILL

....*society is...something that is kept together by the invisible bonds of common thought....A common morality is part of the bondage.... and mankind, which needs society must pay its price....*

PATRICK DEVLIN

Given the importance of sex in our lives, it is understandable that sexual morality is a topic of universal concern. Since sex is connected with the bringing of children into the world, it is inevitable that sexual behavior, however private and intimate in itself, must be a concern of our social morality as well as of our own private moralities. There are many people, however, who believe that, as long as children are not involved, private consenting adult sexual behavior should be beyond the scope of legal prohibition or moral criticism. As they see it, while individuals can rightfully be condemned for such things as the dishonesty, selfishness, or exploitiveness that accompanies their sexual behavior, they cannot rightfully be condemned for their sexual behavior alone, however repulsive or unnatural it appears to the majority. Underlying the views of such individuals, one will find a strong commitment either to hedonistic utilitarian or libertarian principles. Secular utilitarians, focusing upon the consequences of different sexual practices, are considerably less apt to accept rigid moral principles in this area than those who derive their sexual morality from religious tradition. Aware that the science of anthropology testifies to large variations in patterns of sexual behavior in different cultures, such individuals are apt to be tolerant of divergent sexual lifestyles.

Their conservative opponents, on the other hand, will be considerably less tolerant. From their perspective, certain deviant sexual practices threaten the very fabric of our collective way of life. Such individuals will discard the anthropological findings of diverse sexual practices as morally irrelevant. Most who accept this perspective will appeal to some view of natural law or divine revelation as the source of their moral condemnation of certain sexual practices. However, not all moral conservatives on sexual matters base their view on the belief that there is a single correct sexual morality which derives its ultimate justification from natural law or from the revealed word of God. As we shall see in this chapter, there are moralists who attempt to justify a conservative attitude toward sexual morality on the basis of a utilitarian concern for the maximization of human happiness. As they see it, certain *conventions*, however arbitrary, as to proper sexual behavior are necessary to maintain the cohesiveness that is essential for social living and, in turn for human happiness.

The first part of this chapter will be devoted to critical discussions of the morality of nonmarital sex, homosexuality, contraception, and artificial reproduction. Since the burden of moral persuasion should be on those who would have us interfere with or morally condemn others for their behavior, our primary concern will be with the arguments that have been offered for a restrictive conservative attitude toward sexual morality. As we shall see, these arguments tend to collapse on careful analysis. Nevertheless, specific permissive liberal attitudes towards sex—as exemplified, for example, by the *Playboy* philosophy—are equally incapable of proof. The open-marriages and freedom from sexual guilt that sexual liberals often advocate have their benefits, no doubt, but they also have their price. In particular, the permissive view of the virtues of sex without marriage that flourished in the late '60s through the mid-'80s has recently been overshadowed by the ominous threat of AIDS. As the specter of death hovers menacingly as a price for nonmonogamous sex, casual sex has lost much of its appeal. Caution now is the smart word in sexual matters and monogamous relationships its natural expression. Yet the "new morality" of sexual permissiveness was already on the decline as the flower children of the '60s found themselves approaching middle age and often discovering that the sexual freedom they once loudly heralded as a sign of their emancipation was nothing but a detour on the road to long-range happiness. Inundated by nudity and graphic sexuality in the various mediums of communication, many of us look back wistfully to the day when sex was linked more strongly with romance and sexual activity was imaginatively suggested rather than graphically displayed. The freedom from guilt that so animated the sexual revolution of the late '60s, it was widely discovered, could leave one emotionally impoverished and adrift. Yet while sex alone cannot, for most of us, provide the emotional salvation we seek, we are inundated by conflicting messages on the relationship of sex and marriage and the moral propriety of certain sexual practices. In addition, we find ourselves in the midst of crosscurrents of conflicting pronouncements as to the legitimate limits of a society's right to enforce its predominant and pervasive moral values upon members who reject these values. This issue shall occupy us in the second part of this chapter.

NONMARITAL SEX

With its Christian heritage, western culture is among the more repressive of societies in its conception of proper sexual morality. Early Christian sexual morality, greatly influenced by the sexual asceticism of Saint Augustine and Saint Paul, was especially negative in its evaluation of the value of sexual behavior. Total sexual abstinence was presented as the ideal to which humans should strive. (Because of this conception, even today, we tend to associate the notion of a virtuous woman with that of a chaste one.) However, given man's strong animal nature, it was granted that such an ideal was too difficult for the average man who was permitted to indulge his sexual desire within the sacrament of marriage. While contemporary western religious moralists are more positive in their attitude toward sex, the intimate connection between sex and marriage is still loudly proclaimed. Although we should not be ashamed of our natural sexual desires, it is now said, these desires should involve the whole person and be connected with feelings of love and affection; they should also have procreation as their ultimate purpose, the more conservative add. The love and affection which expresses itself through sexual behavior, conservative sexual moralists proclaim, must furthermore be of an exclusive sort which finds its rightful place within marriage. As they see it, our social and affectional natures can find their maximal fulfillment only within the institution of marriage and the family structure that it embraces. The limitation of sex to marriage, it is argued, is a necessary condition for forming and maintaining stable family units; for such a limitation will encourage people to get married and to stay married, and the impermissibility of sex outside marriage will tend to strengthen the marriage.

The liberal sexual moralist, on the other hand, will challenge one or both of the assumptions of his conservative opponents—that sexual passion should always be connected with feelings of love and affection, and that it should be directed to one person at a time. For some, although human sex should not be promiscuous and loveless, it need not be restrictive. Just as a parent can find gratification in the love of several children, one can carry on meaningful love affairs simultaneously with more than one person. Adherents to such a view will argue that it is often considerably better for a person to have sex with more than one person over some long period of time than to engage in less deep and more fleeting successive sexual liaisons which take place within the alleged sanctity of the marriage bed.

For other sexual liberals it is not only the exclusiveness of sex that should be rejected, but also the assumption that it should always be connected with feelings of love and affection. According to this viewpoint, now that reliable contraceptives are readily available, one should see sex as the purely pleasurable physical experience that it can be. Just as one can enjoy good food in a variety of settings without investing such enjoyment with the burden of moral solemnity, so one can enjoy a casual sexual experience with someone without any feelings of love or special affection. Most adherents of this position would be quite willing to grant that love tends to enhance sex with greater meaning. Nevertheless, they will claim, most people at some point in their lives find themselves sexually intersted in individuals for whom they feel little or no love. Indeed, there are many people who have no capacity for affection or love at all, although they possess normal sexual desires. It is much more conducive to human happiness, it will be claimed, that such individuals be permitted to obtain whatever gratification they can from their sexual desires, without the burden of moral guilt, as long as they do not impose their sexuality involuntarily, hurtfully, or deceitfully upon others.

Premarital Sex

With these general sketches of the differing perspectives on sexual morality in mind, let us consider the philosopher Carl Wellman's case for the undesirability of both casual and premarital sex in his book *Morals and Ethics* (1975). Clearly by the very use of the term "premarital," Wellman is directing his attention upon the typical young college age student that a university professor is likely to encounter in his undergraduate classes, the majority of whom will one day marry. Wellman writes:

> The pleasantness of casual premarital sex is often reduced by certain unpleasant aspects of the experience. Unless the lovers have ready access to some fairly suitable and completely private place, the sex act is likely to be performed hurriedly and uncomfortably. Even if both partners feel no guilt, each is apt to feel anxiety about participation in a socially forbidden practice. . . . Reduced pleasure is still pleasure, of course, but it is important to note that in the case of casual premarital sex it is almost inevitably trivial pleasure. That is, the act of sexual intercourse lacks full meaning or significance for the partners because it lacks the full context of past shared activities, present joint life, and future commitment that marriage can give. . . .
> Some of the likely consequences of casual premarital sex . . . often make it

undesirable. The sharp rise in the incidence of venereal disease in the teenage population of this country suggests that sexual promiscuity has its very real dangers....
Moreover, the danger of an unwanted pregnancy is always there. The existence of
modern contraceptive devices makes it all too easy to ignore this possibility, but
no device is completely effective. The real danger, however, lies not so much in
the defectiveness of the device as in the fact that it may not be used properly or
used at all....In the absence of any established relationship or genuine love, neither
partner may care enough to take precautions to protect the other....Finally, both
the insistence of sexual desire and the ideal of spontaneous love making tempt casual
sexual partners to throw caution to the winds....It seems to me that the values
of casual premarital sex are too slight to be worth its very real dangers.

It is less clear that stable premarital sexual relationships are undesirable. The
existence of an established personal relationship and mutual love give the experience
of stable sex a significance and meaning that the experience of casual sex lacks,
and these same factors eliminate or reduce such negative factors as anxiety or the
danger of venereal disease. At the same time, premarital sex within a stable relationship presents a danger of its own; it threatens to damage or impair the relationship between the sexual partners....

Premarital sex threatens to damage a stable personal relationship in at least three
ways. First, it tends to overemphasize sexual activities...at the expense of other
activities....This danger is not limited to premarital sex. Some married couples
probably share very little of their lives except the sex act itself. But this danger
is less within marriage, where the sex partners have usually had an extended period
to grow as persons and to learn to share many parts of their lives, and where
husband and wife necesssarily participate in many joint enterprises concerning the
home and family....

Second, premarital sex tends to overcommit the sexual partners to each other....en-
gaging in sexual intercourse usually intensifies the emotional involvement of the sex
partners and may lead them to become too deeply committed to their personal relationship too quickly....It may even cause a mismatched couple to get married....

Third, premarital sex, whether casual or stable, destroys one precious future
possibility—the possibility of sharing in marriage something unique to that marriage.
Although I do not believe that divorce is always wrong, I do firmly believe that
the completeness and finality of the commitment to each other in marriage is essential to the lasting health and social value of that institution. I also think that the
knowledge that sexual intercourse has been reserved for marriage gives added
significance to marital sex....

Wellman's familiar arguments against premarital sex are quite weak. As is often
the case with arguments in the area of sexual morality, it is plausible to believe
that Wellman started with his position and then worked backwards to find
arguments to support it, i.e., he rationalizes.

First, one should note that some of the undesirable consequences of premarital
sex that Wellman fears can be rendered obsolete by new developments which can
eliminate or greatly reduce these undesirable consequences—specifically, fully
reliable contraceptives and the elimination of the threat of venereal disease—and
AIDS, which was not a problem when Wellman wrote. Although Wellman is right
that all existing contraceptives are subject to failure and, consequently, that individuals who have no plan to marry and raise children stand some risk of pregnancy, it could be said in reply that today's methods of contraceptives make such
a risk quite small if reasonable precautions are taken as they should be. If those

who engage in premarital sex do not take reasonable precautions to avoid pregnancy, it could be said, such individuals should be faulted not for their sexual behavior but for their negligence in not taking these precautions. Similarly, given the threat of AIDS, it is essential that young people be taught the need to use condoms to prevent infection from sexual contact. As all knowledgable people realize, education in sexual matters is essential and it belongs in the schools, however much it can be supplemented at home with moral instruction. It is a sad commentary on our culture that many influential people resist explicit public education on sexual matters. But they are simply wrong. Education as to the facts of sexuality and its attendent dangers, contrary to what they say, does not lead to promiscuity.

If one is afraid that young lovers will (to use Wellman's expression) "throw caution to the winds," one need not jump to the conclusion that they should abstain from premarital sex for this reason alone, but can instead insist upon the necessity of teaching young people to be more careful and responsible in their sexual relations. In addition, one could argue that mature and responsible young people who engage in premarital sex should have the right to decide whether or not to take the small risk of an undesired pregnancy. In reply, many will contend that an unwanted pregnancy is not a purely personal decision since the welfare of the third party—the unborn fetus—should be considered. As we shall see in our discussion of the abortion issue, for those who see an early fetus as "merely a mass of tissue" or, at least, as "nonhuman," such considerations will be rejected as irrelevant. To such individuals, an abortion, though not a preferred mode of contraception, is, at least in early pregnancy, a morally unobjectionable one. Others will strongly disagree, claiming that all abortions involve the killing of innocent "persons."

From such a perspective, the possibility of an unwanted pregnancy will provide a reason for some individuals to refrain from premarital sexual behavior. It does not, however, provide a reason why all people should avoid premarital sexual experience. Such a consideration would, for example, have no bearing upon a couple who are planning to get marrried and would gladly accept the birth of a child. Similarly, it would have no bearing when one or both of the potential parents would be willing to raise the child themselves or give the baby up for adoption to one of the many childless couples who would want so much to adopt it. One might think that in many cases the possibility, let us say, of a young unmarried woman or man raising a child alone is not ideal, but is that any reason for condemning it as *immoral* if the child's welfare will not be damaged by such an arrangement? It may be foolish for people to engage in sexual behavior, willingly accepting the possibility that certain personally disruptive and undesired consequences may occur, but some other reason must be given for calling such people immoral if they are willing to accept the responsibility for reasonably dealing with those consequences should they occur. After all, it is usually thought to be a person's own affair whether or not he is prepared to accept some measure of personal discomfort as the possible price of the gratification of his desires.

Wellman's claim that the pleasure of casual premarital sex is reduced by the difficulty of finding "some fairly suitable and completely private place" and by the anxiety that is apt to accompany such behavior is similarly very weak. Such difficulties, when they occur, after all, follow from the stigma of immorality that is often perceived to attach to premarital sex and would not exist if this behavior were considered fully acceptable. If this were the case, private places would become readily available and the anxiety of participating in a socially forbidden practice would disappear. Wellman's remarks here, though relevant to a particular person's decision to engage in premarital sex *given* a background of social disapproval of such behavior, is no argument at all for the desirability of that social attitude.

Even if one accepts Wellman's contention that casual sex is less worthwhile than sex within marriage, one may still claim that the pleasure it provides is far from trivial. Assuming that such pleasure is less worthwhile than affectionate sex within the confines of a deeply loving personal relationship, such pleasure may be quite fulfilling relative to what is available. One can, after all, enjoy the pleasure of casual premarital sexual experience and can consider such experience as very worthwhile while looking for someone with whom one can have a deeper and more fulfilling sexual relationship.

Wellman's criticisms of stable premarital sexual relationships are equally weak. His claim that those who have such relationships tend to become preoccupied with sexual activities to the exclusion of other activities is a curious one. Such an objection can be made to cut in exactly the opposite direction, for it could be said that the prohibition of premarital sex has the effect of causing those whose natural sexual desires are not offered an outlet to become overly preoccupied with thoughts of sex to the exclusion of other possible shared experiences one can have with members of the opposite sex. In claiming that those who enter stable premarital sexual relationships are apt to become "overcommitted" to each other, Wellman seems to beg the question at issue of whether deep affection and sex should be reserved for marriage (that is, he assumes precisely the point he was supposed to establish). Liberal sexual moralists would retort that Wellman is much too sanguine about the prospects of happiness that await those who enter into marriage without any sexual experience. Rushing into marriage so as to experience the sexual pleasures that are uniquely in its domain, such individuals may find, once that experience has been savored, that there is little else of value to hold that marriage together.

Adultery

As a springboard for our consideration of morality of adultery, let us turn to the popular newspaper advisor Abigail Van Buren ("Dear Abby"). Consider the following from her daily newspaper column:

> DEAR ABBY: You told a woman who was in love with a married man, "Send him home to his wife and children..."
> Abby, this is 1977. Why didn't you tell her to ask her married lover to be honest with his wife about her, and try to develop an "open marriage" that would include the girl friend too?
> A marriage doesn't have to be exclusive to be good. Each of us can love more than one person. Why be hypocritical? If there were fewer "either/or" ultimatums, there would be fewer divorces.

After 28 years of a monogamous marriage, my wife and I decided to "open" our marriage to include others. I now encourage and help my wife to have outside relationships with other men, and she does the same for me with other women. Our open marriage has revitalized us and strengthened our marriage.

OPEN AND HAPPY

DEAR OPEN: I didn't suggest an "open marriage" because I wouldn't advise anyone to do what I myself wouldn't do. Marriage is (or should be) a sacred covenant between two persons, and to "open" it to include others is a violation of that covenant.

It may be possible to love more than one person, but in a civilized society, it's one at a time. The "group" thing, which includes many partners, is not a "love feast"—it's a sexual smorgasbord.

While Abby does not attempt to justify her brief reply, it would be instructive to subject it to scrutiny. To begin with, one should notice that when Ms. Van Buren begins her reply with the assertion that "I didn't suggest an 'open marriage' because I wouldn't advise anyone to do what I myself wouldn't do," the impression is created that she is presenting her view as a statement of personal preference, without any implication that such a position is the only rational or moral one. This impression is, however, shattered when she goes on to say that "in a *civilized* society, it's one at a time." It becomes clear at this point that Abby considers her position *correct*. Can her conventional view of marriage be shown to be superior to the "open marriage" advocated by the letter writer? Clearly, many people do not think that marriage should be described as a sacred covenant or have different conceptions as to the terms of this sacred covenant. Indeed, one wonders exactly what Abby has in mind by using such a term. Since she is not against divorce, it would appear that she believes that although this sacred covenant demands that one limit one's sexual relations to "one at a time," it does not prohibit sexual relations with one after the other—that is, not "until death do us part," but until "divorce do us part"! Although western religious tradition has considered the marriage covenant to include a promise of exclusive sexual fidelity, those who open their marriage to include others may never have agreed to such a contract or, if they had, they might have felt justified in openly rescinding it. Abby does not tell us why such individuals are unjustified in refusing to commit themselves to sexual exclusivity, as she claims they should. Whatever defects open marriages may possess, they are at least free of the complex web of deceit that often accompanies an adulterous relationship. This often proves more of a destructive force to a marriage than the adulterous relationship that led to it. Aware of this, some couples include the acceptance of marital infidelity into their self-composed marriage vows.

In addition, even if an adulterous relationship takes place behind a cloak of deceit or the breaking of a commitment, such actions may be capable of a utilitarian justification. It is possible in some situations that all parties, including the deceived one, would be better off were an adulterous relationship not brought out in the open. Realizing this, some married individuals make it clear that they would prefer not to be told, and even lied to, if their spouse were unfaithful. As unpleasant as it may be to admit, there are probably many marriages that are saved or made more bearable *to both parties* by the practice of adultery.

Anthropological data testifies to the broad spectrum of sexual practices that seem, as far as can be discerned, to contribute equally well to the satisfaction of the basic human sexual drive. There are and have been many societies which are or have been tolerant of adulterous relationships in various degrees and circumstances. Similarly, there are many societies which reject the view, fundamental to so many in our society, that sexual behavior should always be preceded by deep affection and commitment.[1] It may be our culture's ideal that sexual behavior ought to be exclusive and deeply embedded within a broader framework of affection and commitment, but such an ideal cannot be shown to be the only one that maximizes human happiness in this world. One should always be wary of those who say otherwise, for their conceptions of human happiness will turn out to presuppose specific and challengeable cultural conceptions of the proper ends of sexual behavior.

This is the case, for example, when adultery is condemned on the grounds that such behavior is destructive of the institution of marriage and the family, for even if this is true, such a view tacitly assumes that the traditional western conception of marriage and child rearing within a nuclear family is worthy of preservation. As obvious as this assumption may appear to some, it can be challenged. One may, for example, reject western society's conception of a monogomous marriage and the family unit, while advocating a system in which women have sexual relationships with many men (and vice versa) while the children of such unions are brought up in communal nurseries. Many of us will find such a scheme distasteful, but that may simply be a reflection of our cultural conditioning. Most advocates of adultery, however, would not go so far as to challenge the very pillars of western ideas of marriage and family life but will instead argue that these ideas are compatible with the notion of a sexually nonexclusive marriage. For example, it will be argued that, although sexual relationships need not take place only within marriage, children should be raised in a traditional family setting and the tolerance of sex outside marriage need not undermine such a setting.

Furthermore, even if it could be shown that those who do not desire extramarital sexual relationships tend to have the most satisfying sexual lives, this would not establish that those who do desire extramarital relationships would generally be happier if they repressed their desire or terminated their marriage prior to having sexual relations with someone else. Finally, even if one could establish that the maximization of human happiness requires that one's sexual relations be confined

[1] This is true in the Polynesian island of Mangaia. The Mangaian male is not expected by the Managaian female to demonstrate his personal affection for her prior to sexual intimacy. On the contrary, the Mangaian girl takes an immediate demonstration of sexual virility as the first test of a man's desire for her and as a reflection of her own desirability. Personal affection may or may not result from acts of sexual intimacy, but the latter is the first step to the former, exactly the reverse of western society's ideal of the relationship of sex and affection. The man who sexually excites a Mangaian girl and then "wastes her time" with too much preliminary talking or "fooling around" is likely to be pushed away and called "uri paruparu" ("limp penis") by the irate and insulted girl.

to a single marriage partner and a traditional western family structure, this does not provide a good reason, in and of itself, to condemn those who fall short of this idea as being immoral rather than foolish. Clearly, those who are deeply committed to such an ideal and perceive deviations from it as deviations from a moral standard do not derive their sexual morality from a secular utilitarian framework. The acceptance of this ideal stems instead from traditional Judeo-Christian morality and the biblical command that "Thou shalt not commit adultery." As we have mentioned before, however, the authority of a given bible and the proper interpretation that ought to be placed on its pronouncements is always open to challenge.

Nevertheless, in our culture, the desire for an adulterous relationship is frought with danger. As many psychotherapists would see it, such a desire is practically always, if not always, a symptom of a deeper need. Clearly, both individual and marital counseling is desirable to sort out the underlying unfulfilled needs and to provide the self-knowledge required for making momentous personal decisions. At times, the pursuit of an adulterous relationship which initially promises great fulfillment proves at the end to lead only to destruction, leaving the roots of the dissatisfaction untouched. In this regard, consider another letter to "Dear Abby":

> DEAR ABBY: Regarding letters from "the other woman": So far you have printed only letters from women who were dumped. How about a letter from a "winner"? My married lover left his wife for me!
>
> I was told that I wasn't breaking up anything; his marriage was dead long before he even met me. His wife had gotten fat. I was married, too, but I assured him that my marriage was also over—my husband had gotten dull and boring.
>
> So I divorced my boring husband and he divorced his chubby wife. Oh yes, we both had children, but we explained that we were in love and when they were older they would understand.
>
> Our marriage was a dream come true. No more lying and sneaking around. At long last we were legally man and wife for all the world to see.
>
> Our apartment was filled with modern furniture and old-fashioned guilt. And plenty of doubt and mistrust.
>
> Two years later he was meeting someone new. I told him he was a liar and a cheat. He said it took one to know one.
>
> And by the way, he's gotten a little dull and boring, and I've put on a little weight.
>   A WINNER

Nevertheless, many adulterous relationships do eventually lead to self-discovery and to the realization that the unhappy marriage that prompted the adulterous relationship was a mistake. More aware of the frailty of human psychology, the mistakes we often make in those whom we marry, and the limited choices that reality often imposes on us, psychotherapists who deal with the problems that arise from unhappy marriages tend to be considerably less inclined than others to make judgments as to the wrongness or wisdom of adulterous relationships. Furthermore, they recognize the disutility of confessions as to adulterous affairs. Such confessions may alleviate guilt, but they rarely have a positive influence on a troubled marriage. It would be nice if there were some simple principle we could appeal to in deciding what is right in the complicated and twisted matters of the heart, but there is not.

ROMAN CATHOLIC NATURAL LAW
VIEWS CONCERNING CONTRACEPTION
AND ARTIFICIAL REPRODUCTION

As we have discussed, Roman Catholic moral teaching, with its natural law foundation, faces the formidable difficulty of justifying its view of the essential elements of human self-realization. Nowhere is this difficulty more manifest than in the controversial pronouncements of orthodox Catholicism on sexual matters—a controversy that has caused a schism in the Church between liberal Catholic moralists and the more influential conservative hierarchy in Rome. As we have seen, according to Thomistic natural law, procreation is one of the basic inviolable values of human nature. According to this view, while people do not have a duty to procreate, they do have a duty not to utilize their sexual organs in an unnatural way that is inconsistent with the purpose of procreation. From this perspective, masturbation is considered morally wrong—a view universally rejected by secular moralists. Of greater social concern, traditional Catholic moral teaching is adamantly opposed to *unnatural* methods of contraception. This opposition is expressed in the following papal pronouncement:

> Christian doctrine establishes, and the light of human reason makes it most clear, that private individuals have no other power over the members of their bodies than that which pertains to their natural ends; and they are not free to destroy or mutilate their members, or in any other way render themselves unfit for their natural functions, except when no other provision can be made for the good of the whole body. ("Costi Connubil," 1930)

According to prevailing Catholic doctrine, while procreation is the primary function of sexual intercourse, it is legitimate in some situations to engage in a sexual act within marriage as an expression of love and affection even though it is known that a pregnancy cannot occur. According to this view, although the affectional and companionable end of sexual intercourse is a secondary end, it is legitimate when the primary end is unattainable either from natural causes—such as when one of the parties is sterile, after menopause, or during the "safe period"—or as a result of treatment that was justifiable on its own account and not performed in order to preclude the possibility of pregnancy—such as if a treatment for painful periods has rendered a woman temporarily sterile. Liberal Roman Catholic theologians are attempting to undercut such a doctrine by rejecting the view that procreation should always be taken as the primary end of sexual intercourse and are claiming that the affectionate and companionable function of sex, at least within the confines of marriage, is fully legitimate and need not be subject to the restrictions mentioned above. The more conservative, however, have held fast to this doctrine and its unclear logic. According to this doctrine, although one cannot legitimately choose to sterilize oneself or to use mechanical or chemical means of contraception with the aim of preventing a pregnancy, one can legitimately aim to avoid pregnancy through the restriction of intercourse to the safe period. This is legitimate, it is said, because one is not employing an *artificial* means to interfere with a *natural* process. The fact that such a contraceptive technique is not all that safe for some and that there are much more effective and less sexually frustrating methods of contraception is considered morally irrelevant.

As we shall discuss in greater detail in the context of the morality of homosexuality, the notion of what is natural in sexual matters is unclear both in meaning and in moral relevancy. Indeed, rather than dispensing with this cloudy notion, some liberal Catholic theologians have attempted to bend it to their own moral purposes. Some, for example, have argued for the acceptability of the pill as a contraceptive measure on the grounds that this method—but not the condom or diaphragm—utilizes a "natural physiological system of fertility control" that is employed by the human body. As one person put it, "The pills provide a natural means of fertility control such as nature uses after ovulation and during pregnancy." The condom or the diaphragm, on the other hand, it is claimed, are *extraneous* devices and, as such, are illegitimate as are "wholly artificial chemical action." Others, however, have found the extraneous character of the condom or diaphragm as a point in their favor and counting toward their "naturalness." Clearly, reference to the notion of naturalness in such claims serves only to obscure the issue.

The inadequacy of traditional Roman Catholic teachings on sexuality is reflected in the Church's 40-page document "Instruction on Respect for Human Life in Its Origins and on the Dignity of Procreation," which was released in March 1987 and carries the weight of the Church's official teaching authority for the world's 825 million Catholics. While useful in its prophetic warnings of the dangers of the uncharted waters of the technology of artificial reproduction which for many call forth images of the excesses of Huxley's *Brave New World,* the Church, in its insistence upon naturalness in sexual matters, offers a dubious justification for its condemnation of artificial reproductive techniques. According to the report, "human procreation can rightfully occur only through the sex act performed by married partners," thus ruling out artificial insemination with a donor's sperm, surrogate motherhood, and in vitro fertilization (in a laboratory dish), even when the married couple provide their own sperm and ova. Part of the objection to in vitro fertilization stems from the fact that such procedures usually require that a number of ova be fertilized and cultivated in a laboratory dish, resulting in embryos that perish. Given the Roman Catholic insistence that embryos from the moment of conception are human beings worthy of the same protection as a fully developed person, such concerns are understandable. Nevertheless, the Roman Catholic objection to in vitro fertilization goes much deeper. In defense of its condemnation of in vitro fertilization (and surrogate motherhood), the report declares:

> Fertilization achieved outside the bodies of the couple remains by this very fact deprived of the meanings and values which are expressed in the language of the body and the union of human persons.

What this means, I do not profess to know; yet upon its unclear foundation, potential parents who can supply the requisite ova and sperms to produce a child are to be deprived the opportunity to do so on the sole basis of whether or not fertilization occurs within the mother's body. As is often the case when papal pronouncements cut too deeply into the needs of people, some have already attempted to soften the blow through a liberal reading of the papal pronouncement: "Human procreation can rightfully occur only through the sex act performed by married partners." Father Bartholomew Kiely, for example, who teaches moral theology in Rome and who helped the author the document claims that the doctrine allows for a particular medical technique called GIFT (gamete intrafallopian transfer) which was developed by Dr. Richardo Ash of southern California. In this technique, a woman's eggs and a man's sperm are injected into the fallopian tubes, where conception occurs. According to Ash, with the concurrence of Kiely, couples who wish to respect Catholic morality are allowed to collect sperm for the GIFT procedure during intercourse. (Recall that masturbation is morally wrong, according to Catholic doctrine.) During intercourse, the husband wears a perforated condom-like device that retains seminal fluid for use in the GIFT technique. The sperm is placed in a catheter next to eggs taken from the wife's ovaries. But the sperm is separated from the eggs by an air bubble so that there is no opportunity for unions to occur outside of the body. The eggs and sperm are then injected into the fallopian tubes where conception "naturally" occurs. According to Kiely, in order for such a procedure to be morally justified it is essential that the union not occur outside the mother's body. But why in the world should this matter? Assuming that the chances for a healthy child are greater if the union occurs prior to insertion into the fallopian tubes, are couples morally required to take the greater risk, and if so, what value are they preserving? Father Kiely does not address this hypothetical question, but he should. Granted that current techniques of artificial reproduction, such as surrogate motherhood, raise troubling moral questions, the official Roman Catholic stand on these matters clouds the already murky and uncharted waters created by advancing medical technology that we must learn to navigate. Fortunately, however, there is much internal debate in the Church today and one can hope that the reformers ultimately prevail.

HOMOSEXUALITY

The Factual Background

According to anthropological data, there are and have been many societies in which homosexual behavior has been considered to fall within the range of normal sexual behavior. Some societies actually encourage such behavior. For example, in some societies young boys are introduced to sex through homosexual unions with older men at puberty and continue their homosexual conduct among themselves until they have become sufficiently mature in the eyes of their elders to have sexual relations with women. Homosexual behavior was also quite openly accepted in the ancient Greece of the famous philosopher Plato. Many a student has been surprised to find upon reading Plato's dialogue "The Symposium" that as Plato expounds upon the nature of love his attention seems to be riveted upon a young man, for Plato, it would appear, was himself a homosexual. Homosexual behavior has, however, been subject to the gravest moral and legal condemnation in Christian cultures.

As recently as 1961, all states had sodomy laws making certain sexual practices (such as anal and oral sex and sex with an animal) illegal. Currently, however, about half the states—including California—have repealed such laws and have, as a result, legalized private homosexual activity between consenting adults.[2] Western society's strong condemnation of homosexuality can be traced to several biblical condemnations of homosexual acts. For example, the Bible tells us that homosexuality is an "abomination" (Leviticus 18:22) and that homosexuals will not "inherit the Kingdom of God" (I Corinthians 6:9–10). In addition, it is widely assumed that the destruction of Sodom and Gomorrah mentioned in the Old Testament was a result of the general licentiousness, especially homosexuality, of these communities. Many moral theologians still adhere to a strict condemnation of homosexuality. For example, the official Roman Catholic view is that although "the particular inclination of the homosexual person is not a sin," homosexual acts are "an intrinsic moral evil, intrinsically disordered, and self-indulgent." The number of theologians who challenge this view is growing. Many challenge it by attributing the unmistakable biblical condemnation of homosexuality to faulty cultural interpretation. For example, it has been said by some theologians that the sins of Sodom and Gomorrah were not the sins of sexual licentiousness and abuse but those of pride and inhospitality to strangers. Similarly, Norman Pittenger of the Cambridge University School of Divinity attributes Paul's strong condemnation of homosexuality in the New Testament to the fact that the homosexuality of Paul's era "was often just licentious, not in any way a noble and moral affair as it had been among the Greeks of, say, Plato's time." The contention that homosexual behavior can be moral is also echoed by the Quakers who maintain that the standards of judgment applied to homosexuals should be no different from those that apply to heterosexuals, and that "it is the nature and quality of a relationship which matters. . . . Homosexual affection can be as selfless as heterosexual affection and therefore we cannot see that it is in some way morally worse." Other theologians, in their attempt to soften the traditional Judeo-Christian moral condemnation of homosexual behavior, distinguish between voluntary and involuntary homosexuality. According to the Dutch Catechism (a liberal wing of Roman Catholicism), for example, "the very sharp strictures of Scripture. . .must be read in their context as a denunciation of a fashion that was spreading to many who were quite capable of normal sexual sentiments." The Catechism then goes on

---

[2]In June 1987, the Supreme Court in a 5–4 decision ruled that states have the constitutional right to punish homosexual acts that occur between consenting adults in the privacy of their homes. As the majority of the Court saw it, the constitutional right to privacy—the foundation of recent contraception and abortion decisions—does not encompass homosexual relations. The case at issue involved a Georgia statute making sodomy a crime. While this law, and others like it, applies to heterosexuals as well as homosexuals, the Court restricted its attention to homosexual activities, and did not address the contention that sodomy laws are unjustly discriminatory in almost always being applied exclusively to homosexuals.

to tell us that those homosexuals who are "incapable of normal sexual sentiments" should not be subject to censure.

Psychological Theories
of the Causes of Homosexuality

There is no consensus as to the causes of homosexuality. It is, however, generally conceded that homosexual behavior is far more common in our society than was previously believed. Kinsey, for example, in his famous survey of American sexual behavior, found that 4 percent of white male adults were exclusively homosexual for their entire life, 10 percent had been exclusively homosexual for at least three years, and that as many as 37 percent had engaged in homosexual activity to the point of orgasm on some occasions. This would especially be the case, for example, with predominantly heterosexual people who find themselves in environments (such as prisons or armies) which preclude the possibility of heterosexual activity for long periods of time.

The classification of people as homosexuals or heterosexuals is made cloudy by contemporary psychological theory and the existence of bisexuality. Many psychologists follow Freud in claiming that there is a basic sexual duality in human beings. The problem of sexual classification is further complicated by the biological fact that external genitals need not always correspond to genetic programming or internal sexual organs. The victims of one of the most common forms of such disorders are born with penises and an empty scrotum, but are nevertheless "girls" with respect to chromosomes (XX) and internal sexual organs and hormones. Such "girls" are usually labeled male at birth, raised as boys, and brought in for treatment when their breasts start developing at puberty. There is a male equivalent of this disorder—male in chromosomes (XY), internal gonads and hormones, but having a blind vagina and two lumps in the groin where undescended testicles are located. There are other kinds of "hermaphroditism," combining various degrees of ambiguous biological sexual components. Given such biological sexual ambiguity, the classification of behavior as homosexual or heterosexual becomes unclear. Are different copulatory organs alone the only necessary feature of heterosexual relations, or are different gonadal structure or genes necessary? Although such a question will strike some as pointless, it must be faced by those who condemn all homosexual acts as immoral.

However ambiguous the biological signs of gender may be, researchers have found that gender identity (that is, how one classifies oneself sexually) almost always agrees with rearing and sex assignment. In other words, whatever people are labeled and are raised to be is what they think they are and live as—no matter what the genes, gonads, or genitals indicate to the contrary. Considering the primacy of learning in gender identity, the choice of sex-object, most researchers believe, must also be learned. Consequently, the generally accepted view is that homosexuality, as well as many other elements in human sexuality, is not *fully* determined by physiological factors. For example, it seems clear that while changing the amount of male or female sex hormones in a person's body will affect that person's sexual excitability, it will not in itself change one's gender identity or choice of sex object, nor will it make the very shy or inhibited sexually aggressive.

Nevertheless, there are many researchers who emphasize the physiological factors that contribute to at least some types of homosexuality. For example, it has been suggested that the homosexuality of effeminate men who, from early childhood, were classified as "sissy little boys" is determined by prenatal factors. As this theory has it, there is a critical point in the development of male mammals—and in humans it is while the fetus is still in the uterus—at which the brain must be sensitized by male hormones. If not, the male will behave in an effeminate way. Those who emphasize the bearing of genetic factors on homosexuality often point to studies which seem to indicate that fraternal twins (who do not have identical genes) do not tend to be as concordant on sex-object preference as identical twins (who have identical genes). The reliability and significance of such studies have, however, been challenged.

Among researchers who accept the predominance of learning upon the development of homosexual tendencies, the predominant approach is to look for the cause of homosexuality in distorted family relationships. According to one influential theory, a large percentage of male homosexuals were, as children, treated by their fathers in a detached, hostile, and unaffectionate manner, while their mothers reacted to them in a very warm but sexually provocative manner. Arousing them to sexuality, such women would be puritanical in repressing any expression of it. It has been claimed that such boys upon maturity tend to be unconsciously afraid of any heterosexual impulse, for such impulses are associated in their minds with the incestuous sexual conflicts that were instilled in them by their dominating and seductive mothers. Many researchers, however, doubt that this theory or any other single theory of the cause of homosexuality can ever be found; the truth, they suggest, is probably that there are diverse forms of homosexuality produced by complex intertwining biological and cultural factors. Some researchers who share this point of view think that it is a mistake to assume that homosexuality and heterosexuality are two distinct categories having distinct causes. Sexuality, they say, should be perceived as a continuous line between the poles of exclusive heterosexuality and exclusive homosexuality. Some have gone on to assert that all of us are to some degree bisexual, although the homosexual component remains latent in most of us.

Are Homosexuals Sick?

Just as psychologists disagree on the cause or causes of homosexuality, they also disagree on the normality or mental health of the homosexual. To some, homosexuality is a way of life which can be as satisfying and conducive to mental health as a heterosexual one. Supporters of such a view will grant that homosexuals are often unhappy, guilt-ridden, and maladjusted, but will attribute this to society's reaction to them and not to the inherent inadequacy of their sexual preference. Such a view is, however, hotly contested by those who believe that homosexuality in and of itself is, or at least tends to be, a sign of some underlying psychopathology which limits a homosexual's capacity for a full satisfying life.

Much of the disagreement over the mental health of homosexuals stems from differences in scientific beliefs about the nature and causes of homosexuality. Nevertheless, this disagreement is, to some extent, also of a conceptual nature in that individuals who share the same factual beliefs about homosexuality can disagree as to whether or not these facts justify the ascription of the label of "mental health" or of "mental illness" since they attribute different meanings to these concepts. Quite often, psychologists who utilize these concepts in a particular way are unaware of the fact that their usage reflects a *moral commitment* to the desirability of behavioral patterns which cannot be decided merely by a consideration of the scientific facts. It is no mere coincidence that morally liberal psychologists who are less willing than their more conservative counterparts to condemn lifestyles as immoral are also much less willing to label them as mental illnesses.

The conceptual fog surrounding the meaning that should be attributed to the concept of mental illness (or disorder) was reflected in the widely publicized decision of the American Psychiatric Society in 1973 to remove homosexuality from its official list of mental disorders. Many psychiatrists, however, strongly dissented from this decision. For example, Dr. Charles W. Socarides, a leading authority on homosexuality, declared that "It is quite wrong for homosexuals to be treated as criminals, but it is scientific folly for psychiatry to normalize homosexual relations as if they had no psychopathology. . . . Homosexuality is a devastating disease of psychological origin." On the other hand, those who claim that homosexuality should not per se be considered a sign of mental disorder claim that psychiatrists who generalize about the psychopathology of homosexuality tend to mistakenly assume that all homosexuals are like the troubled ones who come to them for help. As such, they have no experience of those adjusted homosexuals who lead normal and, indeed, often quite distinguished lives in every other respect.

Arno Karlen in his extensive study of homosexuality claims that (male) homosexuals tend to suffer from an underlying sexual insecurity over their masculinity, which gives rise to a compensating tendency toward hostility and verbal bickering, "a kind of verbal wrestling for who is on top." It is not, however, clear that the implication of this view is, as Karlen suggests, that homosexuality, in and of itself, causes these psychological characteristics. Perhaps such characteristics are nothing more than a reflection of the *normal* human reaction to being perceived as a deviant. This is the contention that would be made by many students of the sociology of deviance who see the very stigmatization directed toward a person who is labeled as homosexual as driving that person further into his deviant career. According to this view, homosexuals, because they are labeled as perverse or deviant, tend to identify with their own subculture and return the majority's hostility in a bitter, mocking, and supercilious way. One way to show this hostility, it is claimed, is to flaunt one's stigma by living up to the very stereotype that society has provided for you.

Can Homosexuals Be Cured?

Mental health professionals also disagree on whether or not homosexuals can be cured. Again, part of the disagreement is conceptual in nature and reflects different conceptions of what is to count as a cure. Although there are some psychiatrists and clinical psychologists who would claim that homosexuality cannot be cured, many claim that they can obtain complete change in about one-third of their homosexual patients and partial change in another third through psychotherapy (that is, talking therapy). Behavioral psychologists have, however, claimed up to 80–90 percent cure rate in their treatment of homosexuals through behavioral conditioning.[3] This claim is hotly contested by psychoanalytically oriented therapists who claim that such treatments do not resolve the underlying psychic conflicts from which homosexuals suffer. There is also disagreement among therapists as to the ultimate aim of "successful" therapy for homosexuals. Some aim at the total eradication of a patient's homosexuality, while others aim not at changing the homosexual but at getting him to accept himself for what he is. Other therapists take a middle stand, attempting to aid the homosexual not in repressing his attraction to members of the same sex, but in widening his field of sexual attraction to include members of the opposite sex. From this therapeutic standpoint, the problem of homosexuality is not attraction to members of one's own sex, but a flight from members of the opposite sex. Supporters of this viewpoint often believe that when a homosexual's underlying fear of members of the other sex has been removed and heterosexual relationships are established, this new form of satisfaction will make the old one obsolete and unnecessary.

The Morality of Homosexuality

It is the belief of many people in our society that homosexuals are not only sick, but immoral as well. On the face of it, this is a paradoxical claim, for usually people who are described as sick are assumed to be victims of some involuntary affliction and, consequently, are not seen as fit subjects for judgments of moral blame. Certainly, if we believe that homosexuals are sick, in that they are victims of a condition that precludes a fully satisfying life, we should not subject these individuals to the added burden of being classified as immoral social outcasts without some strong justification. If, as is generally conceded, a homosexual does not voluntarily choose to be a homosexual, it would be unfair to blame him for his condition. Similarly, it would be unfair to blame a homosexual for not overcoming or working to overcome his homosexual tendencies if one believes, as many do, that homosexuals have little or no control in changing their homosexual tendencies and can choose not to act on these inclinations only at the heroic cost of accepting a life of great frustration and lack of fulfillment. Unfortunately, these considera-

---

[3]According to behavioral psychologists who accept the "learning theory" point of view, homosexual behavior is behavior that develops according to the same psychological laws of learning or association as those governing the development of normal behavior and can be extinguished through a reconditioning process. The learning therapist, unlike his psychotherapeutic counterpart, does not seek to remove the underlying causes of homosexuality nor to provide the homosexual with insight into his condition. Instead, he arranges a program of reconditioning in which new reinforcements are instituted in order to condition the homosexual into heterosexuality (or bisexuality). A technique often utilized to achieve this aim is aversion therapy in which the therapist aims at setting up an associative process between unpleasant stimuli and the thought of homosexuality.

tions are rarely considered by those who condemn homosexuals as immoral. Let us turn to the arguments that have been offered in defense of this claim.

Homosexuality Is Offensive

No doubt, many people find the homosexual lifestyle a highly offensive one, but even if the vast majority of people in our society felt this way, this would not justify the moral condemnation of homosexuality as a way of life. This is so since people may find behavior offensive without good reason or for nonmoral reasons. For example, most of us would find it very offensive to be in the presence of someone who never washes and emits the strongest of body odors. Such a person, short as he may find himself of friends, would not normally be considered an *immoral* person. Some reason apart from the mere offensiveness of a person's conduct must be given for its moral condemnation.

Nevertheless, it is generally agreed that a society has a right to shield itself through legal sanctions from conduct which the vast majority of its citizens finds offensive, even if that conduct is not in itself immoral. For example, even though it is not immoral for a husband and wife to have sexual intercourse, most of us would find it highly offensive were we to come across a married couple in the midst of an act of sexual intercourse while we strolled with our family through a public park. We would believe that such *public conduct* ought to be legally prohibited since we, and so many others, find it offensive. Although we might very well feel that the voluntary sexual practices of people in private is no business of the law, their public behavior, we think, is. It would seem that even the most liberal of supporters of free expression would be willing to limit public behavior that a vast majority of citizens find offensive when such behavior is thrust upon them unwillingly. Such a stand is reflected in laws relating to "public nuisance." This is one of those areas in the law in which principles to which we give some degree of allegiance clash and consequently call for balancing. In this case, we find a person's right to freedom of expression conflicting with another individual's right to privacy and noninterference by others. At times, drawing a balance between these conflicting considerations is a difficult matter. For example, just as practically all of us would feel justified in making public heterosexual intercourse illegal in public places which can be avoided only with unreasonable inconvenience by those who would be offended by such conduct, we would feel justified in making homosexual intercourse illegal in similar circumstances. But what about less flagrant displays of homosexual affection? Clearly, most of us would be much more tolerant and less apt to be offended by public displays of heterosexual affection. Even if one is willing to admit that one ought not to make such a discrimination, the fact is that most of us do—however culturally conditioned this discrimination is—and cannot easily change our feelings in this manner. Does our right to shield ourselves from offensive public behavior override a homosexual's right of freedom of expression? Reasonable people will give different answers to such a question. To some, even if most people find certain displays of homosexual, but not heterosexual, affection highly offensive, that is still not sufficient justification for restricting the homosexual's right to freedom of expression. Supporters of this position may go on to suggest that we would be healthier psychologically if we were not offended by such conduct and that exposure to it might make us more tolerant of it. On the other hand, there are those who draw the balance sheet in favor of the offended majority and who feel justified in restricting displays of homosexuality to the privacy of one's home or private homosexual meeting places.

Homosexuals Are Dangerous

It is often claimed that homosexual behavior ought to be morally condemned since such behavior is in some respect dangerous to other individuals or to society as a whole. At times, the grounds given for such a claim are quite ludicrous. For example, it is often argued that "homosexuality is immoral because the existence of such behavior encourages others to do the same and if everyone or large numbers of people were to become homosexuals, there would no longer be any human race." Underlying such a claim would appear to be the fear that countless people would turn to homosexuality if such behavior were free of moral condemnation[4]—so many, in fact, that the very existence of the human race would be put in jeopardy. Certainly, one should have more faith in the heterosexuality of human beings! This should especially be the case if one believes, as most opponents of homosexuality do, that a homosexual life is not as satisfying as a heterosexual one. Furthermore, in an overpopulated world, one would think that homosexuality would be quite desirable. Finally, a preference for homosexuality is not inconsistent with procreation. One can easily imagine a society of people devoted to a homosexual way of life who enter brief heterosexual unions, produce a socially required number of children, and then devote the rest of their sexual lives to homosexuality. Indeed, with the advent of artificial insemination and artificial wombs, such individuals would not have to engage in heterosexual activities at all.

It has also often been suggested that homosexuality is dangerous and, as such, is immoral in that such conduct tends to undermine the family unit and that this, in turn, tends to lead to a general moral breakdown. In the next part of this chapter we shall scrutinize the many unclear and questionable assumptions implicit in such a claim when we discuss a society's right to enforce its prevailing moral standards upon nonconformists. It will suffice now to simply point out some of these questionable assumptions. First, such an argument assumes that the traditional heterosexual family unit, as found in contemporary western culture, is worthy of preservation. Second, it assumes that homosexuality poses a dangerous threat to this family unit. Those who take this view, however, are usually silent in their condemnation of divorce, nonmarital sexual relations and the easy availability of con-

---

[4]According to Freud, such underlying assumptions are often not brought to consciousness since they are rationalizations for our own fears of becoming homosexuals ourselves. The condemnation of homosexuality, on this view, helps strengthen our own heterosexuality by repressing the homosexual element that lies hidden within our unconscious.

traceptives which has contributed to the growing number of childless heterosexual marriages. Yet they would appear to provide a much greater threat to the traditional western family unit. Third, even if the tolerance of homosexuality would pose some substantial threat to the existence of the traditional western family unit, it is not at all obvious that this would, in turn, lead to other fundamental revisions in our current moral standards which should, if they were to occur, be described in the negative judgmental terms of "moral breakdown" rather than in the neutral terms of "moral change" or the positive-sounding terms of "moral evolution."

In addition to such general and abstract defenses of the dangerousness of the homosexual way of life, a much more concrete argument is often heard that homosexuals are dangerous since they tend to molest children and in general to impose their sexual preferences unwillingly on others. There is, however, no evidence to support the general belief that this is true of a greater percentage of homosexuals than heterosexuals. The fact that such claims are so often made with no evidence at all would seem to indicate that they are used as rationalizations either for less easily articulated reasons or for deeper unconscious fears or conflicts.

Today, the widespread fear of homosexuality is closely identified with the fear of AIDS. The danger here, however, is primarily to the homosexual community itself. Even if, as the present evidence indicates, homosexuals are at greater risk in contracting this disease than heterosexuals, this does not imply that homosexuals are acting immorally, if they *act responsibly* in their sexual behavior, as all people should. Clearly, if a particular disease were contracted only by heterosexual activity, we would not, for this reason alone, condemn such activity as immoral.

Homosexuality Is Unnatural

Homosexuals are often subjected to moral criticism on the grounds that they practice an *unnatural* form of behavior. Unfortunately, those who make such a claim rarely attempt to clarify the meaning they wish to attribute to the notion of unnatural behavior, nor do they argue for the moral relevance of such a notion— that is, why unnatural behavior is *immoral* behavior. Indeed, it would appear that the claim that "homosexuals are immoral *because* they engage in unnatural behavior" is often utilized in a tautological manner where the notion of unnatural behavior is used synonymously with that of immoral behavior. When this is so, critics of homosexuality may give others, as well as themselves, the mistaken impression that they are giving a reason why homosexuals are immoral when they are not.

What then are we to take the notion of unnatural to mean in this context? Clearly, if by natural behavior all one means is behavior that is found in nature, then homosexuality is natural. (In this sense the concept of unnatural is synonymous with that of supernatural.) Similarly, if we take the notion of unnatural to mean uncommon, the studies of Kinsey and others would indicate that homosexuality is not at all unnatural to human beings. More important, however, even if homosexual behavior were uncommon, this would not be a good reason for morally condemning such behavior. Running a four-minute mile is uncommon, but it is not immoral. It would seem that those who claim that homosexual behavior is unnatural are asserting that such behavior goes contrary to either the purpose assigned by God for the proper utilization of the sexual organs or to the proper biological and psychological role of sexuality in human beings. Let us consider these contentions in turn.

Those who claim that homosexual behavior is contrary to divine purpose assume that this world and everything in it was purposefully designed by God for some good purpose. As they see it, homosexuality is contrary to the divine purpose ordained for the use of the sex organs. Since it is assumed on this view that procreation is the only legitimate purpose for the utilization of the sex organs, it would seem to logically follow that the very great number of heterosexuals who use contraceptives or engage in oral intercourse are as immoral as homosexuals. Even if one believes that God created the sexual organs and made sexual acts pleasurable in order to assure that these organs be utilized for procreation, this would not entail that it is contrary to God's will that these organs be utilized in other ways as well. For example, if one believes that God created the human eye to enable human beings to see, this would not entail that a woman is acting contrary to divine purpose when she uses her eyes in a flirtatious manner. Just as we would assume that God does not object to this, why should he object to the nonprocreative utilization of the sex organs as a mode of expressing love or merely as a means of obtaining pleasure when this is done in a nonharmful and freely chosen manner? And if it is true that he does not object in the case of heterosexuals, simple justice would seem to demand that he not object in the case of homosexuals. Unless one is content, as a thinking person should not be, to accept at face value those passages in the Bible which express God's supposed moral condemnation of homosexuality but which provide no explanation for this condemnation, one must seek some justification for the special wrath that God supposedly reserves for homosexuals. Yet, I cannot see how such a justification can be given.

Not all, however, have sought their justification in the alleged will of God for the claim that homosexuality is unnatural; from a purely secular perspective, some have attributed the unnaturalness of homosexuality to the alleged inability of this mode of behavior to satisfy human needs or to the alleged fact that such a sexual orientation is not found in other animals. Let us consider these claims more fully. First, even if it were true that homosexuality is inherently unsatisfying, this provides no good reason for subjecting homosexuals to criticism, let alone moral criticism, for their choice of lifestyle. It might very well be, for example, that although the homosexual life would be quite unsatisfying to the majority of human beings, it is still the best or only form of sexual gratification available to homosexuals. More important, however, even if homosexuals have a "free choice" of being heterosexual and would be happier if they made this choice, why should they be subject to moral condemnation for such a choice? After all, people make all sorts of foolish choices which are not subject to moral condemnation.

Similarly, if one classifies homosexual behavior as a form of unnatural behavior on the grounds that other animals are never exclusively homosexual, such a fact, if it is a fact[5] would appear to provide no grounds at all for the moral condemnations of the homosexual way of life. Homosexuality in humans, it might turn out, results from a unique human capacity to go beyond rigid biological sexual programming and to invest sexuality with a complexity and psychological meaning that is beyond the capacity of animals. It is indeed ironic that those who are often the loudest in proclaiming the uniqueness of human beings among the animals of this world are often the very same people who comdemn homosexuals on the alleged fact that they are not sufficiently like other animals!

Homosexuals and the Law

One can believe, as many do, that although consenting adult homosexual conduct is immoral or undesirable, it ought not to be subject to legal prohibition. From

[5]Some researchers in animal behavior have claimed that although animals may participate in what would appear to be homosexual activities, such behavior results either from a lack of heterosexual outlets or is nonsexual—for instance, a male may mount another male not in order to obtain sexual gratification but as a sign of friendship or as a method for asserting control. This view, is, however, a minority one. According to the majority view, homosexual behavior is widely found in the animal kingdom. For example, bulls begin to mount each other when they are ripe for breading, and consequently a young bull is sometimes used as a "teaser" to induce mounting and ejaculation when semen needs to be collected from a breeding bull for purposes of artificial insemination. Indeed, the sight of domestic dogs mounting each other and making copulatory movements is a very familiar spectacle. Among primates, even when the situation permits access to the opposite sex, unmistakable sexual behavior among members of the same sex commonly occurs. In males, such behavior usually occurs between a mature dominant male and a juvenile. The dominant male mounts his partner, clasping and thrusting with the pelvis, at times to ejaculation. In the case of females, homosexual behavior commonly takes the form of genital licking.

While the preceding examples can be seen as pointing towards bixesuality rather than homosexuality, permanent homosexual animal bonding has been observed to occur among animals segregated among their own sex. Such animals come to prefer their own sex even after heterosexual opportunities have been restored. In addition, male rats, given electric shocks whenever they copulate with females, have been conditioned by experimenters into becoming exclusively homosexual. Homosexual pair-bonding also occurs spontaneously in nature. For example, Konrad Lorenz writes:

> The capacity for homosexual behavior is part of the normal makeup of many animals....In geese, falling in love and pair-bonding can be as dissociated from copulation as it can be in man. You may find a very strong homosexual bond between two male geese who behave like a pair though they cannot copulate. They never do—they always forget that the other refuses to be mounted and they try again every spring. Each goose behaves in a perfectly normal male way and, if he could speak, he would say, "I love my wife very much but she's definitely frigid."
>
> Homosexual male pairs rise very high in the rank order of a goose colony because the fighting potential of two males is superior to that of a heterosexual pair. Therefore, they are admired by unmarried females. Often when they fail to copulate because each wants to mount and neither will crouch, a loving female will crouch between them and is copulated by one or by both. This female is gradually accepted by the two males, but she gets no respect. If she succeeds in getting a nest and laying, she may awaken the parental response in both males and they may guard the nest and accept the babies. Then you have a *ménage à trois* in which two males love each other and the female loves one of them.

It is interesting to note that Lorenz apparently conceives of his "homosexual" geese as being unaware of the proper sexuality of their mate ("I love my wife...but she's...frigid"). As such, it is open to a critic to contend that such geese are not really homosexuals but are instead confused heterosexuals. This would be true only if one incorporates an intellectual awareness of the sexuality of one's mate into the definition of homosexuality. If this awareness is understood to involve an intellectual conceptual awareness that only human beings possess, it would follow that animals are actually *incapable* of true homosexuality.

this perspective, when an act such as a homosexual one is private, between consenting adults and where no one is subject to physical danger, it ought not to be punishable. Such a position is a widespread one. The influential American Law Institute in its 1955 Model Penal Code, for example, made homosexual acts criminal only when they involved force, fraud, or a minor. Such a view is becoming more and more popular in the United States as is evidenced by the growing number of states that have changed their laws to make consenting adult sexual behavior legal, including homosexuality. In other states, the old penalties for "sexual perversion" are being lightened. For example, North Carolina's sodomy law which prohibits anal intercourse and "all kindred acts of bestial character whereby degrading and perverted desires are sought to be gratified" originally called for up to 60 years imprisonment for such an offense, but when a man was sentenced in 1962 to 20 to 30 years for a private consenting, homosexual act under this law, enough of a public outcry was aroused that the law was revised, reducing the sentence to 4 months to 10 years.

Many critics of the laws which make homosexual conduct per se illegal point with disgust to the manner in which the police in various cities enforce the laws relating to homosexuality. Since it is understandably difficult to obtain evidence against consenting homosexuals, "vice squads" are often forced to use decoys to lure homosexuals into making advances and to engage in the surveillance of places in which homosexual behavior is likely to take place (such as in public bathrooms).[6] Such conduct has itself been loudly condemned as more morally degrading than the behavior it is meant to deter. Such a view is reinforced by skepticism as to the effectiveness of criminal prohibition in deterring individuals from homosexual behavior.

Nevertheless, there are many who are opposed to the decriminalization of homosexuality. According to such individuals, the law should not only protect people from the unwelcome harm or unfairness of others but should also strive to make people virtuous. For example, in the television program *60 Minutes,* James J. Kilpatrick, in reply to Shana Alexander's claim that "I would remove the penalties from all victimless crimes," argues as follows:

Up to a point, Shana, I share your libertarian theories. I too believe an individual has a right to mess up his own life, so long as he does no harm to others. But there is such a thing as society or community or the commonwealth—a body of moral conviction developed over many centuries out of law and religion—and I believe it cannot wisely be disdained. In libertarian theory, laws against prostitution should be repealed. A woman's body is her own, and she can sell it if she wants to. But I believe society has a right to say prostitution is wrong, it's degrading; and if it can never be eliminated it should not be implicitly approved. It's the same with hard-core pornography. As a writer, I'm troubled by legal censorship. I don't like it. But I believe the community has a right to say hard-core pornography is wrong,

---

[6]While the courts have generally considered entrapment a defense to criminal prosecution, they have disagreed as to the definition and specific behavior that counts as entrapment. According to the most popular definition, entrapment occurs "when the criminal design originates with the officials of the government, and they implant in the mind of an innocent person the disposition to commit the alleged offense and induce its commision in order that they may prosecute."

it pollutes, and it subtly eats at the fabric of our life. You make persuasive arguments for legalized heroin, but maybe society has a right to say, out of its collective wisdom and experience: Heroin is a terrible evil; we ought not to make it easy for the weak to surrender to addiction. What I am suggesting, Shana, is that we should not flinch from setting standards of right conduct, of virtue, of public good and public evil. And we ought to shun the notion that the drunk, and drug addict, and the whore, even if they do not demonstrably harm others, do not affect others—for they do. For better or for worse, a community is influenced by each of its members. Saints and sinners, we are touching atoms. So, ask not for whom the bell tolls, Shana, it tolls for thee and me, and for all of you out there. (*Used with permission*)

Prominent among those who share Kilpatrick's sentiments are moral absolutists who believe that there is a uniquely correct set of moral standards that can be discovered through reason or religious revelation. Convinced that they possess the only true morality, and often convinced as well that it is more important to protect people's character from moral harm than to protect their body from physical harm, such individuals will consider it irrational for the law to protect individuals from physical but not moral harm. It is not true, however, that only ethical absolutists are sympathetic to Kilpatrick's sentiments. As is the case with Patrick Devlin, whose views we shall soon subject to scrutiny, some who believe that a society is justified in using the law to discourage consenting adults from voluntarily engaging in conduct which is considered immoral according to the prevailing moral standards of that society are ethical relativists who grant that the morality they wish to enforce is not uniquely justifiable. Accepting Durkheim's claim that morality is the cement that holds members of a society together, supporters of this viewpoint assert that without a strong, generally accepted morality or way of life, a society tends to disintegrate. From this perspective, it is the cohesive power of a morality, and not its quality, that matters. Let us now turn our attention to this view and the traditional libertarian one to which it stands in marked opposition.

LIBERTY AND THE ENFORCEMENT
OF MORALITY

The Classical Liberal Position:
John Stuart Mill's On Liberty

The classical libertarian position on the legitimate scope of governmental interference with individual freedom is expressed by John Stuart Mill in his famous essay *On Liberty* (1859). In the beginning of this essay, Mill states his position, writing:

The object of this Essay is to assert one very simple principle, as entitled to govern absolutely the dealings of society with the individual in the way of compulsion and control, whether the means used be physical force in the form of legal penalties, or the moral coercion of public opinion. That principle is that the sole end for which mankind are warranted, individually or collectively, in interfering with the liberty of action of any of their number, is self-protection. That the only purpose for which power can be rightfully exercised over any member of a civilized community, against his will, is to prevent harm to others. His own good, either physical or moral, is not sufficient warrant. He cannot rightfully be compelled to do or forbear because it will be better for him to do so, because it will make him happier, because, in the opinion of others, to do so would be wise, or even right. These are good reasons for remonstrating with him, or reasoning with, or persuading him, or entreating him, but not for compelling him, or visiting him with any evil in case he do otherwise. To justify that, the conduct from which it is desired to deter him must be calculated to produce evil to someone else. The only part of the conduct of anyone, for which he is amenable to society, is that which concerns others. In the part which merely concerns himself, his independence is, of right, absolute. Over himself, over his own body and mind, the individual is sovereign.

Underlying Mill's defense of his thesis was his fear of the tendency toward the suppression of individual freedom that he saw growing in the democracies of his day. It was Mill's belief that democratic social theorists, such as John Locke, in their attempt to defend majority rule over the power of an absolute monarchy, failed to place sufficient safeguards upon the possible tyranny of the majority. It was essential, Mill believed, that the rights of minorities to unconventional styles of living and to freedom of expression should be protected, however offensive such styles of living and beliefs might be to the dissenting majority. As well as being afraid of the possibility of repressive laws, Mill was even more afraid of the indirect power of societal pressure directed against nonconforming minorities— pressures which can be strong enough to deprive people of the right to a job, to live where they choose, and to teach what they believe. Without such rights, Mill believed, a democracy would merely exchange the tyranny of absolute monarchy for the potentially even greater tyranny of the majority.

Mill's defense of individual freedom hinges upon his distinction between self-regarding and other-regarding actions. Although a society has a right to interfere with a person's conduct when it "affects others," it has no right to interfere with that part of his conduct "which merely concerns himself." Underlying Mill's un-compromising defense of his position is his utilization of the idea of "the free market-place of ideas." Borrowing the contention of the laissez-faire economists of his day that the best interests of the consumer can only be satisfied in a free economy which allows an unfettered competition of economic products, Mill argues that the on-going search for truth and happiness requires an unrestricted competition among differing ideas and lifestyles. As long as people do not interfere with the liberty of others, they should be allowed the right to be idiosyncratic and to live their lives as they choose. Since we have not obtained perfection, Mill argues, the maximization of human happiness requires that individuals be allowed the freedom to form their own "experiments in living" and not be forced into a stifling "tendency to conformity which breeds only withered capacities."

Some Difficulties with Mill's Position

Mill's classical defense of a person's right to act as he so chooses in that domain of his life which "concerns only himself" has been subjected to much criticism. First, while Mill speaks of this right being unlimited, this is not his actual position, for he concedes that

> ...this doctrine is meant to apply only to human beings in the maturity of their faculties. We are not speaking of children, or of young persons below the age which the law may fix as that of manhood or womanhood. Those who are still in a state to require being taken care of by others must be protected against their own actions as well as against external injury. For the same reason, we may leave out of consideration those backward states of society.... Despotism is a legitimate mode of government in dealing with barbarians, provided the end be their improvement, and the means justified by actually effecting that end. Liberty as a principle has no application to any state of things anterior to the time when mankind have become capable of being improved by free and equal discussion.

As this passage and others demonstrate, Mill intended to restrict his principle to human beings "in the maturity of their faculties." As such, the principle was not to apply to children, irrational people, barbarians, and those under the influence of temporary irrational passion.[7] This is, however, a very open-ended qualification. Although Mill wrote in an era which proclaimed the basic rationality of most human beings, we do not live in such an era today. Given the pessimistic twentieth century emphasis upon the irrationality of human beings, we are much less apt than Mill to accept his assumption that each individual is the best judge of his own interests. As the success of modern day advertising seems to confirm, it is not necessarily the best products that sell or the truth that always wins out at the end, but rather the best packaged product or that version of the truth which best appeals to the subliminal and often irrational desires of the masses. Given such a pessimistic view of human rationality, a person who accepts Mills' proviso that his principle applies only to rational and mature individuals may go on to assert that this, unfortunately, excludes most of us.

It is interesting to note in this regard that Mill believed that a commitment to the maximization of human happiness would lead in turn to a commitment to a principle allowing broad tolerance of individual freedom. The link between these principles was, for Mill, the assumption that individuals are generally the best judges of their own interests. Without this assumption, there is no assurance that a commitment to the principle of utility will lead us to embrace the wide guarantees of individual freedom that Mill advocated. Instead, many would argue, a government devoted exclusively to the maximization of the welfare of its citizens would be forced by its citizens' lack of rational foresight to pass many paternalistic laws, which attempt to protect people from themselves. The choice between the principle of utility and principles of individual freedom is one of the foremost political questions of our day. In our country today, it is those who are classified as liberals who emphasize the value of social welfare, while those who are classified as conservatives emphasize the value of individual freedom. For example, it was the

---

[7]One should note that Mill was writing during the British colonial period when Britain asserted much control over the individual freedoms of the inhabitants of the colonies. Many would today loudly protest Mill's ethnocentricity in assuming that the inhabitants of the colonies were barbarians who were incapable of judging their own best interests while the English were not.

liberals in Roosevelt's New Deal days who, accepting Mill's basic commitment to the maximization of human happiness, argued for the necessity of compulsory social security laws, while the conservatives, accepting Mill's commitment to individual freedom, were opposed. While the argument in Mill's *On Liberty* would have been that each individual should be free to make his own arrangements for life, old-age and disability insurance through voluntary savings or insurance plans, the liberals of the Roosevelt era would not accept Mill's belief that allowing people to make their own free decisions on this matter would ultimately work out in their best interests. They realized that those who need social security protection the most would be just those who would find it most difficult to put aside money for some indefinite "rainy day" when it could be so easily put to use immediately. As modern day conservatives are wont to proclaim, a commitment to social welfare in the twentieth century has gone hand in hand with an abridgment of individual freedom.

There are few people today who would not be committed to some degree of paternalistic legislation which attempts to protect people from themselves. Existing laws that make suicide or euthansia or driving without seat belts illegal or that refuse to accept consent as an excuse to assault (that is, *X* cannot be excused for killing *Y* simply on the grounds that *Y* asked him to) are motivated primarily, if not exclusively, by the paternalistic principle that society has some legitimate right to tell individuals what is for their own good.

Mill's defense of individual freedom has also been challenged on the grounds that the basic distinction between self-regarding and other-regarding actions that underlies this defense cannot be made clear. As Mill's critics have pointed out, the consequences of human actions can rarely, if ever, be isolated to one person. If, for example, a person through the use of drugs allows his body or mental capacities to deteriorate, he harms not only himself but those who care for him or rely upon him for support. Even if such a person's action does not cause direct harm to others, it may affect others by the corrupting example it provides. Mill is not insensitive to such a criticism. He writes:

> I fully admit that the mischief which a person does to himself may seriously affect, both through their sympathies and their interests, those nearly connected with him, and, in a minor degree, society at large. When, by conduct of this sort, a person is led to violate a distinct and assignable obligation to any other person or persons, the case is taken out of the self-regarding class. . . . If, for example, a man, through intemperance or extravagance, becomes unable to pay his debts, or, having undertaken the moral responsibility of a family becomes from the same cause incapable of supporting or educating them, he is deservedly reproached, and might be justly punished; but it is for the breach of duty to his family or creditors, not for the extravagance.

According to Mill, then, in determining what is to count as an exclusively self-regarding action, one must first know the scope of a person's obligation to others. Mill does not seem to realize, however, that people can have very different conceptions as to how broad or narrow one's obligations to others ought to be. For example, Mill would have accepted as legitimate one's obligation not to physically hurt other people, but would have rejected as illegitimate one's obligation not to offend others by one's private behavior. It is problematic, however, that such a position can be justified on purely utilitarian grounds, since being offended sometimes causes a person more pain than being physically hurt. While Mill, no doubt, would have said that consenting private adult homosexual behavior does not "affect the interests" of disapproving heterosexuals, and consequently should not be subject to legal sanction, the fact is that many disapproving heterosexuals do indeed "take an interest" in such behavior—behavior which many of them see as a moral abomination, contrary to the will of God. For such individuals, the presence in their community of homosexuals may cause greater pain than a physical blow. Furthermore, they will certainly consider the possibly corrupting influence of homosexuals as affecting their own vital interest in their community and especially in the bringing up of their own children. As many of them see it, the extravagance of homosexuality is a contagious one that poses a substantial *risk* of harm to others.

Whether or not homosexuals "violate a distinct and assignable obligation to any other person or persons" and consequently, according to Mill, whether their behavior should be seen as other-regarding will depend on the obligations we *choose* to place upon homosexuals. This in turn will depend on the importance of the social interest we see threatened by homosexuals and the degree of the risk we see them posing to this interest. As such, the distinction between self-regarding and other-regarding actions is not at all, as Mill made it appear, a morally neutral one that can be called upon to form the foundation of a simple moral principle that can guide us in deciding when to limit human freedom. On the contrary, this distinction *presupposes a moral position* on the scope of the *legitimate,* legally enforceable interests individuals can take in the actions of others. A "self-regarding action," as Mill uses this term, is one that is not *rightfully* subject to legal coercion. Consequently, Mill's claim that self-regarding actions ought not to be subject to legal coercion is a tautology.

In the final chapter of *On Liberty,* devoted to applications of his principle, Mill implicitly repudiates his initial claim that there is "one very simple principle [that is] entitled to govern absolutely the dealings of society with the individual in the way of compulsion and control." For example, although Mill originally restricted governmental interference to presenting actions that harm others (let us call this "the harm principle"), he accepts in this chapter a society's right to prohibit publicly offensive behavior, writing,

> Again, there are many acts which, being directly injurious only to the agents themselves, ought not to be legally interdicted, but which, if done publicly, are a violation of good manners and, coming thus within the category of offenses against others, may rightly be prohibited. Of this kind are offenses against decency: on which it is unnecessary to dwell...

As this quotation indicates, given the reserve of his era, Mill chose not to dwell upon these matters. Nevertheless, they must be dealt with when it comes to setting the limits of a society's tolerance of offensive behavior. Mill quickly passes over major modifications of the harm principle in other sections of *On Liberty*. For example, committed to the utilitarian goal of the maximization of the general welfare, Mill allows for a society's right not only to *prevent harm* to others, but also to compel its citizens to *provide benefits* to others, through such things as redistributive taxation. But, again, he does not elaborate as to the limits of such a principle. Similarly, troubled by the self-destructiveness of certain behavior, Mill grants society the right to use selective taxation to make it more difficult to obtain personally harmful substances (e.g., liquor) and to place restrictions on business activities that cater to the vices of human beings. In this regard, while Mill would grant individuals the freedom to gamble or to engage in prostitution, he would allow for the prohibition of gambling houses and pimps. He admits that he is troubled by this concession to freedom of choice, but he makes it nevertheless.

Mill also further complicates his position when he discusses the following example:

> If either a public officer or anyone else saw a person attempting to cross a bridge which had been ascertained to be unsafe, and there were no time to warm him of his danger, they might seize him and turn him back, without any real infringement on his liberty; for liberty consists in doing what one desires, and he does not desire to fall into the river.

Mill does not, however, specify the general principle that is to rule in such cases, for one can desire something under one description, but not under another and our desires are often fickle and unclear. In addition, greater understanding or changes of mood often lead to changes in desire. Are we to say then, as many psychiatrists would, that many people who consciously desire suicide do not desire this at a deeper level and would come to reject their suicidal wishes if their thought were not distorted by their depressive mood? In such cases, would people be right in interfering with suicide attempts on the same grounds that Mill would interfere with the man attempting to cross the unsafe bridge?

Speaking of the bridge example, Mill remarks:

> Nevertheless, when there is not a certainty, but only a danger of mischief, no one but the person himself can judge of the sufficiency of the motive which may prompt him to incur the risk; in this case, therefore (unless he is a child, or delirious, or in some state of excitement or absorption incompatable with the full use of the reflective facility), he ought, I conceive, to be only warned of the danger; not forcibly prevented from exposing himself to it.

This, however, does not tell us what to do in those cases where there is great probability of some self-destructive outcome nor does it come to grips with how we are to distinguish those who act rationally from those who are "in some state of excitement or absorption incompatable with the full use of the reflective faculty."

At one point, Mill remarks that an individual should not have the right to sell himself into slavery, for, by so doing,

> he abdicates his liberty; he forgoes any future use of it beyond that single act. He therefore defeats, in his own case, the very purpose which is the justification of allowing him to dispose of himself. . . . The principle of freedom cannot require that he should be free not to be free.

After making this claim, Mill goes on to concede that the principle, involved has wider application than the case at issue, but he does not dwell upon the new complexity he has introduced. Can one, for example, prohibit suicide, no less than slavery on the grounds that a person should not "be free not to be free," for the choice of suicide, no less than the choice of slavery precludes any further freedom of choice? Can one prohibit less immediate freedom-limiting behavior such as smoking and drugs? Where is the line to be drawn? It is to Mill's credit that he recognizes the complexities, but he does not resolve them, leaving us, at the end with a jumble of qualifications of the harm principle which can lead us in many different directions.

The conflict between Mill's implicit recognition of the cogency of different moral considerations and his desire for intellectual unification through some comprehensive general moral principle is deeply reflected in his writings on ethics. We have already had occasion to discuss the inadequacies of Mill's qualitative hedonism which, contrary to his desire, served to toally undercut Bentham's ethical theory. In a similar vein, Mill was unable to reconcile his deep commitment to individual freedom with his growing commitment to socialism. While originally committed to laissez-faire capitalism, as he grew older he grew more sensitive to the futility of political freedom without economic opportunity and security. At the end of his life, Mill had become a socialist. Yet unlike other idealistic socialists of his day, Mill's advocacy of socialism was tempered by his fear of the tendency of socialism to go hand-in-hand with the suppression of individuality—a fear which the triumph of communism in Russia and China in the twentieth century would later prove to be justified. As Mill's commitment to socialism grew, he became more and more hopeful that this tendency could be avoided. Yet, in his later writing, most notably his later editions of his *Principles of Political Economy,* one notes a tension between his commitment to the value of liberty and to that of economic equality. While he remained steadfast in his advocacy of the right of individuals to lead their *private* lives as they see fit, he came to view the scope of a person's private life more narrowly than he did as a younger man. For example, believing in the great power of education to reduce the poverty and misery of the masses, he came to advocate *compulsory* education and the legitimacy of *compelling* parents to provide for the education of their children.

Similarly, occupied throughout his life with the belief that overpopulation was one of the greatest sources of human misery and vice in this world, Mill's initial reliance upon the efficacy of education as a tool for voluntary family planning slowly gave way to a pessimistic belief in the need for governmental intervention.[8] Such issues as the need for education and the control of population, Mill eventually came to believe, could not be left to the uncertain outcome of "experiments in living" and to the freedom of parents to educate their children as they see fit. On the issues that Mill saw as most critical, he came to favor the direct intervention of the state. Moving even closer to the views of those who advocate social indoctrination of the masses, Mill came to advocate refashioning the minds of human beings away from selfish concerns toward public purposes. In such refashioning, he wrote, "lies assuredly the course of future progress." This socialistic concern with leading people to act in concert and to have equal access to the world's resources came to overshadow Mill's fear of the "tyranny of society over the individual" expressed so elegantly in *On Liberty*. Doubtlessly, at least in part, as a result of his experience as a member of the English Parliament, Mill's writings indicate his implicit, if not explicit, recognition of the conflicting demands of legitimate moral values, irreconcilable by reliance upon a "simple principle" such as the harm principle he presents at the outset of *On Liberty*.[9] While one should question the concepts and arguments Mill employs in defending his plea for individual freedom—as Mill himself did—Mill's own passionate conviction of the value of individual freedom tends to engender a similar passion in his readers. As indicated by the many people who quote from it, nowhere in the English language can a stronger and more elegant defense of the value of individual freedom be found than in *On Liberty*—Mill's most enduring philosophical legacy to his generation and to generations to come.

The Philosophy of Community:
Devlin's The Enforcement of Morals

Opposed to Mill's libertarianism is the conservative philosophy of the political philosopher Edmund Burke and the sociologist Emil Durkheim, who emphasize

[8]In his autobiography, Mill tells us that this belief was percipitated by a walk with his father through the streets of London. Along the way, the young Mill saw the dead body of a newly born infant, wrapped in rags. Further along, he passed the hanging bodies of several criminals. As he walked, the young Mill was struck with the realization that both of these sad sights were connected with overpopulation. Overpopulation, he came to believe, is one of the greatest causes of misery and vice in this world. This misery and vice, he thought, could be prevented if people were educated to realize the need for voluntary family planning—a topic too indelicate for the sensibilities of the English citizens of his day. From that moment on, Mill became firmly committed to the importance of a public education that could undercut the unthinking attitudes and ways of life of the masses. This belief, in turn, led Mill, as a 17-year old youth, to be arrested for distributing birth control information—a case of civil disobedience.

[9]For over half of his life (1823–58), Mill held responsible administrative posts with the East India Company, eventually becoming the head of one of its departments. (The East India Company was a royally chartered company responsible for increasing British trade and influence in India.) While so employed, Mill devoted his spare time to writing. Upon retirement from the East India Company, Mill was proposed as a Liberal Party candidate for Parliament. Even though he refused to campaign, he was elected to office. In office, he consistently sided with the liberal forces for social equality and individual freedom. William Gladstone, the British Prime Minister, once said of him, "He had the good sense and practical tact of politics, together with the high independent thought of a recluse. He did us all good."

the human need to enfold oneself within the structure of values provided by an established community. According to this view, the liberty and individuality which Mill celebrates tend to lead to individual unhappiness. Freed of the meaning and warmth that shared values provide, most individuals find themselves alone, anchorless and adrift in a sea of unstructured desires. Individual reason proves incapable of unifying these desires into a coherent whole and the quest for individuality tends to lead, not as Mill thought it would, to an invigorating feeling of freedom, but rather to the cold, barren feeling of isolation. When this feeling of isolation from shared values becomes widespread in a society, the society loses its reason for existence as a collective unit and disintegrates from within.

This conservative perspective was given fresh expression in 1958, when Patrick Devlin, an English judge, gave a lecture before the British Academy in criticism of a report (the Wolfenden Report) made public the year before by a committee that was commissioned to study the justification for subjecting homosexuality and prostitution to criminal sanction. Accepting Mill's general libertarian perspective, the committee recommended that homosexuality and prostitution should not, in and of themselves, be illegal. Although not questioning the immorality of homosexuality and prostitution, the committee asserted that "there must remain a realm of private morality and immorality which is, in brief and crude terms, not the law's business." According to Devlin, however, there is no way of specifying or defending a clearly defined realm of private behavior that should remain immune from punishment. Devlin's lecture aroused great interest and controversy and led him to write a series of supporting and amplifying essays which were published in 1965 in a book entitled *The Enforcement of Morals*. This book, in turn, generated much comment and criticism in both Great Britain and the United States. Perhaps, as Devlin himself suggested in the preface of his book, the great interest in his ideas was due in large measure to the fact that they were "an expression of orthodox views on a subject in which orthodoxy is more seldom found in print than it is in common behavior" and because his ideas were expressed at a time which found growing numbers of people uncertain as to the sexual values of an older era. There can be no doubt that Devlin expressed in these essays ideas often acted upon by others who either lack the inclination or capacity to articulate them. It is for this reason above all that Devlin's argument deserves careful attention and analysis.

Devlin's Statement of His Position

Devlin begins his inquiry by posing the question that will be the focus of his concern: "What is the connection between crime and sin and to what extent, if at all, should the criminal law of England concern itself with the enforcement of morals and punish sin or immorality as such?" In defending his conclusion that society can properly "punish immorality as such," Devlin begins by defining a society as a collection of people who share a common morality. He writes,

> [a] society means a community of ideas; without shared ideas on politics, morals, and ethics no society can exist. . . . If men and women try to create a society in which there is no fundamental agreement about good and evil they will fail; if, having

based it on common agreement, the agreement goes, the society will disintegrate. For society is not something that is kept together physically; it is held by the invisible bonds of common thought. If the bonds were far too relaxed the members would drift apart. A common morality is part of the bondage. The bondage is part of the price of society; and mankind, which needs society, must pay its price. (p. 10)

As an example of the implication of such a claim, Devlin considers the institution of marriage, writing,

Whether a man should be allowed to take more than one wife is something about which every society has to make up its mind one way or the other. In England we believe in the Christian idea of marriage and therefore adopt monogamy as a moral principle. Consequently, the Christian institution of marriage has become the basis of family life and so part of the structure of our society. . . . It has got there because it is Christian, but it remains there because it is built into the house in which we live and could not be removed without bringing it down. The great majority of those who live in this country accept it because it is the Christian idea of marriage and for them the only true one. But a non-Christian is bound by it, not because it is part of Christianity but because, rightly or wrongly, it has been adopted by the society in which he lives. It would be useless for him to stage a debate designed to prove that polygamy was theologically more correct and socially preferable; if he wants to live in the house, he must accept it as built in the way in which it is. (p. 9)

The next step in Devlin's argument is his claim that every society has a right to use the law to preserve its underlying morality which is essential for its very existence. He writes,

. . . an established morality is as necessary as good government to the welfare of society. Societies disintegrate from within more frequently than they are broken up by external pressures. There is disintegration when no common morality is observed and history shows that the loosening of moral bonds is often the first stage of disintegration, so that society is justified in taking the same steps to preserve its moral code as it does to preserve its government and other essential institutions. (p. 13)

Nevertheless, Devlin is willing to admit that the rights of the individual must be balanced against society's right to "punish immorality as such." No simple principle capable of mechanical application can, however, be given for this balancing. Although "there are no theoretical limits to the power of the state to legislate against immorality," there are, Devlin asserts, three "elastic principles" supporting the rights of the individual against the state. These principles are as follows:

There must be toleration of the maximum individual freedom that is consistent with the integrity of society. . . . Nothing should be punished by law that does not lie beyond the limits of tolerance. . . . As far as possible privacy should be respected. (pp. 16–18)

How are the moral judgments of a society to which individual liberty must at times give way to be ascertained? Devlin writes,

It is surely not enough that they should be reached by the opinion of the majority.
...English law has evolved and regularly uses a standard which does not depend
on the counting of heads. It is that of the reasonable man. He is not to be confused
with the rational man. He is not expected to reason about anything and his judgment may be largely a matter of feeling. It is the viewpoint of the man in the street.
(p. 15)

A Critique of Devlin's Argument

There is an unresolved tension in Devlin's argument between an extreme view
that strong popular feeling alone suffices to justify making behavior criminal and
a more moderate one which claims that behavior can be made criminal to prevent
injury to society as a whole, as well as to specific individuals.

The moderate thesis   According to the more moderate position that can be
extracted from Devlin's writings, there is no single rule which should be relied upon
to tell us when the state has the right to limit the freedom of its citizens. Each case
must be considered separately and decided on the basis of the balancing of principles of individual freedom against principles which attempt to prevent practices
that are injurious either to specific individuals or to society as a whole. Although
the right of the state to interfere in the actions of its citizens is limited by various
principles, it is not limited in accordance with Mill's distinction between self-regarding and other-regarding actions. The law, Devlin asserts, exists not only to protect
individuals from injury or annoyance, but also to protect the "community of ideas,
political and moral, without which people cannot live together." As a result, Mill
was wrong when he claimed that an individual cannot rightfully be compelled by
a society "to do or forbear because it will be better for him to do so, because it
will make him happier, because, in the opinion of others, to do so would be wise,
or even right."

Moralistic language permeates the law. For example, incest and homosexuality have often been moralistically described in the law as "unnatural" and
"depraved." Similarly in the test routinely utilized in obscenity cases prior to 1957,
American courts asked "whether the tendency of the matter charged as obscenity
is to deprave and corrupt those whose minds are open to immoral influences."
In discussing the rationale for distinguishing degrees of homicide, the California
courts routinely spoke of "the quantum of moral turpitude." The strong condemnation of euthanasia in western countries also stems primarily, but not exclusively,
from concerns about the immorality of suicide.[10]

Devlin is quite right that there is no simple principle we can appeal to in
deciding upon the limits of the criminal sanction. As we have seen, Mill's pivotal

---

[10]It is an evasion to assert, as H.L.A. Hart does in his *Law, Liberty, and Morality* that many
legal prohibitions of voluntary behavior such as that pertaining to suicide should be seen not as attempts
to "enforce morality as such" but as paternalistic measures directed to protecting people from harming themselves. The problem here, neglected by Hart, is that practices may be seen as harmful precisely
because they are perceived as immoral. The notion of harm—especially of the psychic variety—can
be a very slippery notion and must be clarified if it is to serve in a useful way in a liberty-limiting principle.

distinction between other-regarding and self-regarding actions presupposes some view of the socpe of a person's *legitimate* legal obligations to others. Furthermore, while Mill was adamant in restricting governmental interference with individual liberty to those actions which harm *specific* identifiable individuals, the very distinction between criminal and tort liability hinges on the distinction between public and private harm. When Devlin says that crimes are offenses "not merely against the person who is injured but against society as a whole," he is expressing the very essence of the distinction between the *punishment* we feel is appropriately applied to criminals and the *compensation* that we believe is due to those who wrongfully suffer private injury. Even if one insists that the concept of social harm must be reducible to specific harm to individuals, questions crowd in upon us as to the meaning of individual harm and the degree of it that justifies the use of the criminal sanction. For example, can the criminal law legitimately protect us from "psychic harm" or the "harm of being offended," as well as from physical harm and harm to property? How likely must the risk of that harm be? (Consider the problem of gun possession.) How direct or immediately connected to one's action must that risk of harm be? (Consider the problem of criminal attempts.) When should failing to provide benefits to others count as harm to others? When, if ever, should people be protected from the harm they would inflict upon themselves? If paternalistic protection should be restricted, as Mill suggests, to actions that are not "fully voluntary," how is this notion to be interpreted? As well as coming to grips with such questions, we must balance the harm we hope to prevent against the degree of infringement on the *rights* of individuals the prevention of such harm will entail. For example, even if it could be shown that pornography leads to sex crimes, some would argue that it is more important to protect the right to freedom of expreession than to prevent this harm.

Devlin does not, however, throw any light on how the rights of the individual are to be balanced against a society's right to preserve certain moral standards and consequently he gives us no way to determine whether or not specific laws attempting to enforce moral standards, such as those relating to euthanasia and homosexuality, are justifiable ones. In particular, the three fundamental moral principles he supplies, which aim at protecting the individual from the moral judgment of society, suffer from a degree of elasticity that would appear to rob them of any meaning whatsoever. For example, lacking any definition of what is to count as "the integrity of society," Devlin's claim that "There must be toleration of the maximum individual freedom that is consistent with the integrity of society" tells us nothing. Similarly, lacking any clarification of what "lies (or should lie) beyond the limits of tolerance," Devlin's principle that "Nothing should be punished by law that does not lie beyond the limits of tolerance," gives us no guidance. If all Devlin means to assert here is that people should only punish behavior they are *as a matter of fact* not willing to tolerate, this is trivial and clearly not a principle protective of individual freedom. If, on the other hand, Devlin's assertion is taken to mean that people should punish only that behavior which lies beyond the limits of *legitimate* tolerance, this claim reduces to a tautology (that is, we ought to punish only those things that ought to be punished). Devlin's third principle that "As far as possible privacy should be respected" suffers from the same indeterminacy as the others. No one, from the most tolerant to the most repressive of individual freedom, will deny that privacy should be respected *as far as possible*. They will, of course, greatly differ as to how far that is.

The extreme thesis   Devlin's moderate position is overshadowed in his writings by a more extreme one, according to which, strong popular sentiment against certain behavior is in and of itself sufficient to make that behavior criminal. In this vein, Devlin writes,

> ...before a society can put a practice beyond the limits of tolerance there must be a deliberate judgment that the practice is injurious to society. There is, for example, a general abhorrence of homosexuality. We should ask ourselves in the first instance whether, looking at it calmly and dispassionately, we regard it as a vice so abominable that its mere presence is an offence. If that is the genuine feeling of the society in which we live, I do not see how society can be denied the right to eradicate it. Our feeling may not be so intense as that. We may feel about it that, if confined, it is tolerable, but that if it spread it might be gravely injurious; it is in this way that most societies look upon fornication, seeing it as a natural weakness which must be kept within bounds but which cannot be rooted out. It becomes then a question of balance, the danger to society in one scale and the extent of the restriction in the other. (pp. 17–18)

As we see in this passage, Devlin appears to equate behavior that is "injurious to a society" with behavior which elicits strong feelings of disgust in most members of that society. While one would have thought that a determination of whether a given form of behavior is injurious to a society would require some inquiry into the actual consequences of that behavior, this does not seem to be true for Devlin when he expresses his extreme thesis. According to this position, strong general feelings of disgust are alone sufficient to make behavior criminal, without either any inquiry into the consequences of prohibition or a balancing of conflicting principles. The balancing of conflicting principles, it would seem, is supposed to take place only when popular feelings are not too strong.

Morality and popular sentiment   Although Devlin is right in emphasizing that moral notions grew out of strong human feelings, he neglects the rational component of morality. No coherent concept of what counts as a moral principle emerges from Devlin's writings. It will not do, for example, to equate judgments of immorality with strong feelings of revulsion, as Devlin seems to, for there are many things we feel revulsion toward that are not moral matters. By neglecting a consideration of any factors other than the depth of popular disgust, Devlin makes it impossible to evaluate moral positions on rational grounds and consequently dissolves the distinction between rational and irrational moral beliefs.

Devlin does not seem concerned that popular sentiment may prove to be inconsistent on various issues. For example, he tells us that homosexuality may properly be made illegal if it elicits strong enough feelings of disgust in the average person who accepts Christian sexual morality. What then of other sexual practices, such as adultery, which are equally contrary to Christian sexual morality? Why shouldn't they be equally subject to the strong feelings of members of our society and equally subject to their moral and legal condemnation? Devlin replies that "the fact that adultery, fornication, and lesbianism are untouched by the criminal law does not prove that [male] homosexuality ought not to be touched." Why male and female homosexuality should not elicit the same degree of revulsion Devlin does not attempt to explain, but he suggests that adultery does not elicit the degree of revulsion that homosexuality does simply because it is more common. For this reason, he tells us, it is "generally regarded as a human weakness not suitably punished by imprisonment." This is quite unconvincing. Drunk driving is also a very common human weakness, but it is still a crime. Certainly, the best reason for not punishing adultery stems from the recognition that making such behavior illegal is unlikely to lead to happy marriages. Similarly, it is unreasonable to believe that making homosexuality illegal is likely to lead to the creation of adjusted and happy heterosexuals or celibates.

Anyone who has any respect for civil liberties would have to reject, out of hand, a society's contention that it has the right to make behavior illegal merely on the grounds that the average citizen finds that behavior disgusting. Although Devlin tells us that such judgments of disgust ought to be given weight only when they are made "calmly and dispassionately," it is not at all easy—if not downright conceptually impossible—to imagine a person arriving at a description of a form of conduct as an abominable vice after calm and dispassionate reflection. According to Devlin, it would appear, the homosexual must subject himself to the vicissitudes of popular feeling, while those who judge him need not subject their feelings to the scrutiny of scientific understanding of the nature and consequences of homosexuality and the efficacy of the prohibition of such conduct. Clearly, popular feelings often need to be subjected to guidance and not always taken for granted. As Bentham put it,

> But ought the legislator to be a slave to the fancies of those whom he governs? No, between an imprudent opposition and a servile compliance, there is a middle path, honorable and safe. It is to combat these fancies with the only arms that can conquer them—example and instruction. He must enlighten the people, he must address himself to the public reason; he must give time for error to be unmasked. . . . It is to be observed, however, that too much deference for prejudices is a more common fault than the contrary excess.

One wonders, furthermore, how Devlin can be so sure of societal feelings; he clearly is not basing his observation on surveys. Perhaps a survey would reveal that, while the average person feels some degree of distaste or discomfort towards homosexuality, the knowledge of its voluntary and private practice by others does not disgust him nearly as deeply as Devlin seems inclined to believe. One cannot be faulted for suspecting that Devlin might be projecting his own prejudices upon others rather than inquiring into people's actual beliefs. Again, as Bentham puts it,

> [Popular prejudice] serves oftener as a pretext than as a motive. It is a convenient cover for the weakness of statesmen. The ignorance of the people is the favourite

argument of . . . [cowardliness] and indolence, while the real motives are prejudices from which the legislators themselves have not been able to get free. The name of the people is falsely used to justify their leaders.

Furthermore, one should not neglect the effect that legalization of a particular form of behavior has on leading to greater toleration of it. If, as previously argued, no justifiable reason can be given for the strong revulsion so many of us feel toward homosexuals, exposure to homosexuals, who would no longer fear to identify themselves as such, may awaken us to the fact that our initial stereotype of them is sadly mistaken and that they are, as a whole, no less moral than the rest of us. By making human feeling the sole yardstick of legality, as Devlin does, our prejudices can be insulated and protected from a possibly disrupting clash with the facts.

A society's right to preserve itself   Devlin's extreme thesis hinges on the following two claims:

1. A society consists by definition of a group of people who live under a common morality or way of life. (a conceptual claim)
2   A society has the right to preserve its existence and to use the criminal law to enforce the common morality which is essential for its existence. (a moral claim)

Let us consider these claims. Devlin's definition of a society as a group of people who share a common morality or way of life is not an arbitrary one, but reflects one common usage of this term. For example, it is this definition of a society that we employ when we say that Czarist Russia was *a different society* from Communist Russia. Nevertheless, this same fact can be expressed as well by saying that *the same* Russian society was at one time Czarist and at another time Communist. The fact is that the concept of a society does not have a single clear meaning. Much of the force of Devlin's argument stems from the manner in which Devlin trades upon this ambiguity in his argument. The plausibility of Devlin's moral claim that a society has "a right to preserve its existence" resides in the fact that such a claim tends to make us think of a society preserving itself from physical violence and internal anarchy. Devlin trades upon this association when he speaks of a society "disintegrating" or of its members "drifting apart."

Nevertheless, it is clear that Devlin means to include much more than the mere minimum core of law and order, which is required for the existence of any society, in his conception of those aspects of morality which are required for "the existence of a given society." Therefore, when Devlin speaks of a society having a right to preserve its existence, his claim must be taken as asserting that a society has the broad right to preserve its distinctive way of life and not merely that it has the narrower right to protect itself from violence and anarchy. The failure to enforce this broader right need not, however, lead inevitably to the need to enforce the narrower right, for a society's distinctive way of life can undergo gradual or abrupt change without accompanying violence or anarchy, and, therefore, without anything that should be called disintegration or the drifting apart of its members.

If "the continued existence of a society" is to be taken to mean living according to some specific shared moral code, then it will follow, by definition alone, that whenever this moral code undergoes change, a society has ceased to exist. It is intolerable, however, to assert, as Devlin seems to, that a society has the right to use the criminal sanction to prevent this change, however peaceable.

In addition, one should realize that some changes in the morality of a society are much less threatening to the fabric of moral ideas and attitudes that comprise its style of life than are others. While Devlin admits that not all deviations from a society's common morality threaten its existence, he appears to assume that, as one critic aptly put it, a person's morality is "a seamless web" and, as such, a change in any part of this fabric is bound to affect other parts. As Devlin himself asserts, "most men take their morality as a whole." As a description of the facts, this might be true. As a prescription, however, of how people ought to take their morality, such a view should be rejected as contrary to the discriminating and refining attitude of mind that is essential for the development of good moral principles. There is no reason to believe, for example, that a person who challenges a society's sexual morality will challenge other parts of that morality as well.

Finally, Devlin is much too facile in his utilization of the notion of "the common morality" of a given society. In the Middle Ages, one could speak of feudal morality or Christian morality as the common morality of large groups of people, but today in many democratic countries, where one finds all sorts of different moralities coexisting, this makes very little sense. A clear consensus of opinion on many deeply felt moral issues will rarely be found in morally pluralistic societies like our own. In such instances, Devlin's notion of the moral feelings of "the average man" becomes a myth. If one accepts the libertarian perspective of Mill's *On Liberty*, such a fact is to be applauded. For, according to this perspective, the tolerance of divergent moral ideas and lifestyles is more conducive in the end to human happiness and development than that attitude of mind which refuses to tolerate any deviation from a single scheme of moral ideas. One will search in vain through Devlin's writings for any argument directed toward a refutation of this point of view.

DISCUSSION QUESTIONS

1. Val, a character is Marilyn French's novel *The Women's Room,* advocates the separation of sex from love., Erotic love, Val claims, is "the taking over of a rational and lucid mind by delusion and self-destruction." Under the grips of erotic love, she continues, "you lose yourself, you have no power over yourself, you can't even think straight." Nevertheless, Val delights in the pleasures of loveless sex. As French writes:

    > Val slept with people the way other people go out for dinner with a friend. . . .She rarely expected anything from it beyond the pleasure of the moment. At the same time, she said it was overrated: it has been so tabooed, she claimed, that we had come to expect paradise from it. It was only fun, great fun, but not paradise.

    Critically comment.

2. What does "true (erotic) love" signify? Is this a hopelessly subjective con-
    cept, reflective of rationally irreconcilable differences in views concerning
    what should count as the most desirable erotic love relationship? At least
    for you, what are the most desirable features of an erotic love relationship.
    Consider here the relative importance of passion, caring, unselfishness,
    understanding, equality, and rational choice. Do you think that it would be
    possible for you to *truly* erotically love two people at the same time? Why?
    If it were psychologically possible, is such a condition usually, or always,
    undesirable from a moral point of view? Why?

3. What commitments are basic to traditional marriage? Are these commitments
    reasonable? What commitments should be required and how binding should
    they be? In particular, is it reasonable that they should involve lifetime
    promises that involve psychological attitudes?

4. In his book, *Having Love Affairs,* Richard Taylor argues that surreptitious
    extramarital love affairs need not threaten good marriages. Indeed Taylor
    can be interpreted as suggesting that whenever love affairs threaten a
    marriage, the marriage must, by definition, have some deficiency. Critically
    discuss.

5. What is your reaction to the claim made by some that sexual fidelity fosters
    "a possessive attitude that interferes with self-realization"?

6. Consider the following imaginary dialogue:

    A: Although I don't think that adultery is always wrong, I do think that it is wrong
    more often than not. It seems to me that today's permissive sexual attitude
    has a stiff price. It tends to vulgarize sex and to detach it from deeper human
    feelings. People who previously might have worked harder to make their
    marriages work find it too easy to seek gratification elsewhere. Unfortunately,
    however, the little romp in the motel room rarely solves their problems. Indeed,
    it often leaves them more alienated than they were before. It wasn't sex they
    really wanted; it was the warmth and meaning of a caring and sharing human
    relationship, but such a relationship is difficult to achieve when it is accom-
    panied by the guilt and dishonesty of most adulterous relationships.

    B: I'm sure that what you say is often true. Nevertheless, it seems to me that many
    affairs are much more than mere romps in motel rooms. While some people
    are lucky enough to find a spouse with whom they can share all that is impor-
    tant to them, most people cannot. Consequently, married people often look
    for someone else with whom they can share dimensions of experience they
    cannot share with their spouses. Even when this is not the case, an affair can
    serve as an act of self-discovery. Frustrated people who remain faithful to their
    spouses because of moral principle tend to take their frustration out on their
    spouses—often blaming them for problems whose source lies within themselves.
    People often discover this is the course of an affair. Having to face the new
    set of personality problems of a lover can make one more appreciative of one's
    spouse and the value of one's marriage. People, it seems to me, often need
    to experiment before they can discover what they really want. I think this is
    true about sexual relationships after marriage as well as before.

    C: I think that both of you are overintellectualizing this matter. Adultery is often
    simply an escape from boredom. The very illicitness of an adulterous affair
    tends to make it exciting—a refreshing break from the monotony and staleness
    of a boring life or a boring marriage. People may speak of the meaning or

sharing of experience that can be obtained from adulterous relationships, but it is primarily good old-fashioned repressed lust that makes adultery an exciting and often rejuvenating experience.

What do you think? What bearing do these different views have on the morality of adultery?

7. Critically consider and evaluate the following claim:

    While the rigid sexual morality of my day caused much frustration and guilt, it seems to me that today's permissive sexual morality exacts a much heavier price. With today's permissive attitude, many young couples who live together claim there is no need to bother with the legal technicality of marriage, conveniently refusing to make the *commitment* that marriage entails. Hand-in-hand with our permissive sexual morality, has come a much more selfish attitude toward life. This is reflected in today's widespread preoccupation with such things as "self-realization" and "self-growth" and the proliferation of psychological movements which reflect this concern. Preoccupied with self-fulfillment, couples do not work as hard as they did in my day to make their marriage work. The sad results are increasing divorces and the unhappy children of so many of these divorces. Preoccupied with finding their own private meaning, many people fail to appreciate the meaning that comes from enveloping oneself in a fabric of shared values and responsibilities. In spite of its shortcomings, the rigid sexual morality of my day was part of such a fabric. Our current self-indulgence is reflected in so many of today's books. For example, in a book I just read, a couple traces the course of their marriage—his discovery of desires for men, her shock and anger, their therapy sessions, her discovery of desires for women, etc. Throughout the book, the couple rehashes the selfish blather we hear all the time about the joys of sex and self-realization. Ironically, while one hears more talk today about one's right to personal happiness, one was more likely to find that happiness when our moral principles were more rigid and less self-centered.

8. Is society justified in limiting the rights or job opportunities of individuals on the basis of their homosexuality? If so, how and why?

9. In *Petit v. State Board of Education* (1973), the Supreme Court of California ruled 5–2 that the State Board of Education had the right to fire a female teacher of retarded elementary school children for several acts of oral copulation with different men at a private "swingers club." The acts of the teacher in question were observed by an undercover policeman who infiltrated the private club. Apart from this episode of sexual activity, which the Court conceded, the teacher was unlikely to repeat, there was no evidence of her unfitness to teach. Nevertheless, her teaching credential was revoked on the grounds that her conduct involved moral turpitude and demonstrated her unfitness to teach. How would you resolve such a case?

10. Can you think of any actions that would generally be considered highly immoral that are not prohibited by law? Should they be? Why?

11. Which of the following reasons for compelling the use of seatbelts in cars do you find most satisfactory?

    A: It is in the best interests of motorists. Motorists should not have the right to make the irrational decision not to use seatbelts. I see no problem in sacrificing a person's freedom of choice whenever this is clearly in his self-interest.

    B: Laws requiring motorists to wear seatbelts should not be seen as infringements of freedom, but as an attempt to prevent people from making capricious choices which do not reflect their own rational desires. When we tell motorists that they are required by law to wear seatbelts, we are only telling them to do what they would choose to do if they rationally reflected on the matter.

C: It is to the best interest of society to compel motorists to wear seatbelts. This requirement prevents injuries that are costly to society. For example, if motorists without adequate insurance suffer severe injury or death in automobile accidents, they or their dependents may become public charges. At any rate, the cost of accidents is reflected in general insurance rates which are absorbed by all of us. Consider, as well, the psychic injury of involvement in an automobile accident that causes severe injury to someone else that could have been avoided if a seatbelt had been utilized.

12. What is your position on the current controversy concerning the legalization of drugs. If you favor legalization, what would you legalize and how would you make it available? If "hard drugs" (e.g., cocaine and heroin) should be made available without a doctor's prescription, should tranquilizers, like Valium, be treated in the same manner?

13. Which of the following should be illegal? Why?
   a. gambling
   b. polygamy
   c. prostitution
   d. The desecration of the national flag
   e. the mistreatment of a corpse, including the use of a corpse for medical experimentation without prior consent
   f. copulation with an animal

14. Beginning in 1957, the Supreme Court has struggled over whether obscene material, which it equates with pornography is protected by the Constitution's guarantee of free speech. According to a minority of the shifting members of the court, such material should be so protected, even though there may be legitimate state interests in regulating their distribution, so as to protect children, unwilling audiences, and neighborhoods from unwanted intrusion. According to the majority, however, obscene materials are not, in general, protected by the First Amendment (or any other provision of the Bill of Rights). The most recent Supreme Court decision in this matter, *Miller v. California* (1973) held that legally prohibited obscene material must be,

   1. restricted to works that depict or describe sexual conduct
   2. such that "the average person applying contemporary [local] contemporary community standards would find that the work, "taken as a whole, appealed to prurient interests" and was "patently offensive"
   3. "taken as a whole, lacking in serious literary, artistic, political, or scientific value"

Critics have contended that the Miller test is unworkable. Do you agree? How would you handle what legal scholars have come to call "the intractable obscenity problem"?

15. In *Stanley v. Georgia* (1969), the Supreme Court held (9-0) that the First Amendment protects a person's right to possess and view pornographic materials in the privacy of his or her home. Yet in *Paris Adult Theatre v. Slaton* (1973), the Supreme Court held (5-4) that states have the constitutional right to prohibit the exhibition of pronographic motion pictures in

adult-only theatres. Do you agree with the Supreme Court's decision in these two cases? Why?

16. A group of neo-Nazi white supremacists wearing swastaka pins gathered together at an Octoberfest celebration in a German restaurant in Torrance, Calif. Asked by the restaurant's owner to remove their pins, they refused. Asked at this point to leave the restaurant, they again refused. The police were called and they were arrested. The group, with the help of the American Civil Liberties Union, sued the restaurant owners. As this is written, the case is pending in the courts. How do you think the law should handle such a case?

17. Consider the following general principles for restricting an individual's behavior:
    a. to prevent physical harm to others
    b. to protect the property of others and to enforce contracts
    c. to prevent psychic injury or offense to others
    d. to protect social institutions
    e. to benefit others
    f. to prevent that person from making involuntary choices
    g. to prevent harm to that person
    h. to benefit that person
    i. to prevent or punish immorality or sin
    j. to preserve human dignity

    Which of these principles would you accept? How, if at all, would you attempt to limit them? Do you think that some of the principles on this list have the same practical implications?

18. Critically consider and evaluate the following:

    A: Judged on the basis of the purely utilitarian goal of maximizing the general welfare, the Communists have succeeded spectacularly in transforming Chinese society. Nevertheless, a very stiff price in terms of individual liberty has been paid to make these achievements possible. Molded into preset collectivistic roles, the Chinese people lack the individuality and commitment to liberty that is an essential aspect of human dignity. Communism, no doubt, promises the Chinese people greater security, but only at the morally unjustified price of the forfeiture of their freedom and individuality.

    B: Your sentiments are an expression of a bourgeois capitalistic ideology. The freedom you so extol turns out, in practice, to be the freedom to be selfish and exploitative. True human fulfillment, and yes, human dignity, comes not from the lonely pursuit of individual pleasures but rather from the willingness to share and sacrifice for the common good. Western philosophers may speak of liberty as "the first virtue of social institutions," but for the ordinary person that virtue is protection or security—a virtue that can best be achieved through a commitment to collectivistic goals that transcend our purely selfish desires.

FURTHER READINGS

Sexual Morality

Conservative

In "The Human Venture" in *Sex, Love, and Marriage* (Associated Press, 1949), Peter A. Bertocci presents a defense of traditional Christian sexual morality addressed primarily to young people contemplating premarital sex. As Bertocci sees it, unmarried young people are apt to lose much more psychologically by indulging their sexual appetites then by restraining them. Sex, he claims, provides its most enduring and enriching satisfaction when it is a "symbolic expression of other human values," which gives it human significance. According to Bertocci, the human significance of sex is inseparable from feelings of love and should be restricted to marriage. He develops the idea of a "love progression," whereby love naturally leads to marriage and to procreation. The same point of view is expressed in Bertocci's 1967 book *Sex, Love, and the Person* (Sheed and Ward). I would, however, recommend the earlier book as the better of the two.

Roger Scruton's *Sexual Desire: A Moral Philosophy of the Erotic* (Free Press, 1986) is a defense of traditional Christian sexual morality from an Aristotelian natural law perspective. Like Bertocci, Scruton argues against premarital sex. Carl Wellman presents a very clear discussion of the arguments for and against premarital sex in the first edition of his *Morals and Ethics* (Scott, Foresman, 1975). As we saw in this chapter, Wellman himself sees premarital sex as generally undesirable. A similar viewpoint is presented in Vincent C. Punzo's *Reflective Naturalism* (Macmillan, 1969). The fundamental premise of this book is that marriage is constituted by mutual and total commitment.

An interesting, though, in sections dated, treatment of sexual morality is found in C. H. and W. M. Whiteley's *Sex and Morals* (Bratsford, 1967). The book begins with a chapter entitled "Why Is There Sexual Morality?" This is followed by three chapters devoted to the patriarchal, puritan, and romantic attitudes toward sex. Chapter 5, "Unfruitful Sex," is the most interesting chapter of the book. In this chapter, the Whiteleys (husband and wife) consider forms of sexual activity that cannot lead to procreation, such as masturbation and homosexuality. A serious drawback of this otherwise good book is the Whiteley's disconcerting tendency to make unsupported, factual assertions, some of which are not generally accepted.

Liberal

A good analytic treatment of the topics of "free love," divorce, homosexuality, contraception, and artificial insemination from a liberal perspective is found in Ronald Atkinson's *Sexual Morality* (London: Hutchinson and Company, 1965). The discussion of these topics is preceeded by a general discussion of ethics and of the specific sorts of arguments encountered in the area of sexual morality (such as prudential and utilitarian arguments, arguments relating to justice, to human nature, or to natural law).

In *Sex Without Love* (Prometheus, 1980), Russell Vannoy defends the value of sexual enjoyment without love. In this break from traditional views of sex and love, Vannoy argues that humanistic and fulfilling sex is best found when it is enjoyed for its own sake and is separated from notions of love. While many will reject Vannoy's arguments, his book contains insightful discussions of the views of others and such notions as sexual perversion, good sex, and love. The concept of erotic love, Vannoy claims is "riddled with contradictions that set up conflicting desires within the lover and cause endless mental torture." "Sex with a humanistic lover," he claims, is "far preferable to sex with an erotic lover."

Another very permissive view is defended in Richard Taylor's *Having Love Affairs* (Prometheus, 1982). Taylor claims that extramarital love affairs "can be more meaningful than the fulfillment of monogamous marriage," and "above all . . . they are not in any significant sense immoral." While one can justifiably quarrel with Taylor's methodology and generalizations based on questionnaires filled out by adulterers, his discussions and abundant quotations from these questionnaires are thought-provoking. Not at all hesitant to advocate deceit, Taylor presents a list of do's and don'ts for those who engage in extramarital affairs which aims at minimizing harm.

Moderate

The most psychologically sensitive books on sexual morality present moderate views. Two are highly recommended: Shulamith Firestone's *The Dialetic of Sex: The Case for Feminist Revolution* (Morrow, 1970) and Robert C. Solomon's *About Love: Reinventing Romance for Our Times* (Simon & Schuster, 1988). Presenting a view of ideal erotic love as an intermingling of the personal identities of two equal partners, Firestone, a feminist, claims that, given the present vulnerability of women to men, ideal erotic love is difficult to achieve, since it requires equality of status. Solomon's central thesis is that "love is an emotional process that not only takes time but also reaches into the future and builds its own foundation." Consequently, one must see it "as a process rather than a passion." "Love is best when cultivated from friendship rather than propelled with great force from some initial explosion of passion." Embracing Firestone's view which echoes that of Plato, Solomon advocates the view of love as a merging of two people into a unified whole. Love, he claims, is a finding of oneself, and, as such, is an ongoing creative process—i.e., it is constantly "reinvented."

A clear and highly recommended discussion of sexual morality from a moderate perspective is found in part four of Mike W. Martin's applied ethics text, *Everyday Morality* (Wadsworth, 1989), which contains discussions of the positions of contemporary philosophers, including Scruton, Vannoy, Taylor, Firestone, and Solomon. The topics of homosexuality and pornography are also discussed and enriched by literary, factual and psychosocial references.

Anthologies

The Philosophy of Sex, edited by Alan Soble (Rowman & Littlefield, 1980), and *Philosophy of Sex*, new revised edition, edited by Robert Baker and Frederick Ellison (Prometheus, 1975), are anthologies devoted to the topic of sexual morality. The selections in the Baker-Ellison anthology were chosen for their accessibility to nonphilosophers and it contains a very imformative introduction by the editors which explores the history of western philosophers' views on sexuality. The specific topics covered in the selections are love and feminism, the morality of adultery, marriage, contraception, and conceptions of sex. Soble's selections are more analytically technical and, as such, will be difficult for beginning philosophy students. Soble precedes his selections with a 54-page introduction in which he summarizes their contents and presents his own unconventional view that human sexuality is naturally bisexual and that the traditional family unit and liberal capitalism are oppressive and not conductive to the desired development of bisexuality.

All the popular general philosophy anthologies of contemporary moral issues have chapters on sexual morality. The one I would recommend the most is Thomas A. Mappes and James S. Zembaty (eds.), *Social Ethics,* third edition (McGraw-Hill, 1987), which contains a chapter on pornography and censorship, as well as one on sexual morality. The chapters and selections in this anthology are preceeded by useful editorial introductions. The chapter on sexual morality begins with the Vatican's 1976 "Declaration on Certain Questions Concerning Sexual Ethics." Following this selection is Mappes' liberally oriented "Sexual Morality and the Concept of Using Another Person" which is followed by Vincent Punjo's conservative attack upon premarital sex. Included too are U.S. District Court opinions in a 1976 Virginia case which rejected a suit brought by homosexuals to declare unconstitutional a Virginia statute making sodomy a crime. The pornography and censorship chapter contains excerpts from Burger's majority and Brennan's minority opinions in the Supreme Court's 5–4 decision in *Paris Adult Theatre v. Slaton* (1976) which upheld a court action to prohibit the showing of two pornographic movies at an adults-only public theatre.

Another good collection of material on sexual morality is found in Richard Wasserstrom's *Today's Moral Problems,* third edition (Macmillan, 1985). Especially worthwhile for the beginning student is Wasserstrom's own article "Is Adultery Immoral?" and excerpts from the 1973 California Supreme Court's (5–2) majority opinion and its two dissents in *Petit v. State Board of Education,* which upheld the California State Board of Education's decision to revoke an elementary school teacher's license to teach on the grounds that her acts of sexual conduct (oral copulation at a private "swinger's club") was evidence of her unfitness to teach. Other selections deal with incest, homosexuality and the notion of "better sex."

Other good selections of material on sexual morality can be found in James E. White (ed.), *Contemporary Moral Problems,* second edition (West, 1988) and John Arthur (ed.), *Morality and Moral Controversies,* second edition (Prentice-Hall, 1986). The White collection contains the Vatican's 1976 declaration, Wasserstrom's article, and excerpts from Vannoy and Taylor's books. Arthur's collection contains excerpts from the majority and minority opinions in the Paris Adult Theatre and Petit judicial decisions, as well as the Wasserstrom article and an excerpt from Taylor's book. Also included is Kant's conservative view on sexuality, expressed in his *Lectures on Ethics,* along with a liberal article on the morality of homosexuality which refers to Kant's view. It also contains a critique of radical feminist views that claim that men's sexual attitude toward women fails to treat them as persons, and that women should not cater to this by trying to appear attractive to men.

Liberty-Limiting Principles

John Stuart Mill's *On Liberty,* which was originally published in 1859, is reprinted by Bobbs-Merrill (1982) and Hackett (1978). The Hackett edition has a brief historical and analytic introduction by

Elizabeth Rapaport which would prove more helpful to beginning students than the one supplied by Currin Sheilds for Bobbs-Merrill. A good discussion of *On Liberty* in the context of Mill's other writings, especially in support of socialism, is found in Gertrude Himmelfarb's *On Liberty and Liberalism: The Case of John Stuart Mill* (Knopf, 1977). Patrick Devlin's critique of Mill is found in his collection of essays, *The Enforcement of Morals* (Oxford University Press, 1965), whose key essay is "Morals and the Criminal Law." Devlin is, in turn, criticized by H.L.A. Hart in his *Law, Liberty, and Morality* (Random House, 1963).

Joel Feinberg's four-volume *The Moral Limits of the Criminal Law* (Oxford University Press, 1984–88) is a comprehensive study of the issues raised by Mill. Dividing his study into a consideration of Harm to Others (vol. 1), Offense to Others (vol. 2), Harm to Self (vol. 3), and Harmless Wrongdoing (vol. 4), Feinberg defends a liberal perspective that is faithful to Mill's spirit. Feinberg contends that the only legitimate reasons for criminal prohibitions are to either prevent harm or offense to others. In defending his position, Feinberg provides detailed analyses of such concepts as harm, offense, autonomy, voluntariness, and morality which draw him into a web of related concepts—e.g., interests, wrongs, causes, consent, rationality, choice, and community. The book is by far the most thorough treatment of the legitimate limits of the criminal law's infringement on individual freedom. Although the book is directed to an analytically sophisticated audience, Feinberg's clear writing style and the detailed table of contents make this four-volume set accessible to beginning students, who will be rewarded with Feinberg's expert ability to mix philosophical theorizing with considerations of actual and hypothetical examples.

Richard Wasserstrom (ed.), *Morality and the Law* (Wadsworth, 1971) is an excellent anthology of material on the issue of liberty-limiting principles for the criminal law. Included are excerpts from Mill's *On Liberty*, Devlin's "Morals and the Criminal Law," and discussions of the issues raised by the Devlin essay by the philosophers H.L.A. Hart, Ronald Dworkin, and A. R. Louch; a discussion of the justification of paternalistic laws by the philosopher Gerald Dworkin; a discussion of the American Law Institute's treatment of moral offenses in its 1962 draft of its Model Penal Code by Louis Schwartz, a law professor; and exceprts from judicial opinions in four cases involving the enforcement of morality.

Another good collection of material is found in Tom Beauchamp and Terry Pinkard (ed.), *Ethics and Public Policy* (Prentice-Hall, 1983), which contains two articles on the right to privacy, a selection from Devlin followed by an opposing one from Hart, and a selection from G. Dworkin's defense of paternalistic laws, followed by an opposing article by Beauchamp.

Citations

The Quaker view of sexual morality can be found in Alastair Heron, ed., *Towards a Quaker View of Sex*, published in 1964 by the Friends Home Service Committee. Arbo Karlen's extensive study of homosexuality is found in his 1971 book *Sexuality and Homosexuality*, published by Norton. The quotation from Konrad Lorenz relating to the homosexuality of animals can be found on p. 5 of Richard I. Evans collection of interviews with influential psychologists, *The Making of Psychology*, published in 1976 by Knopf.

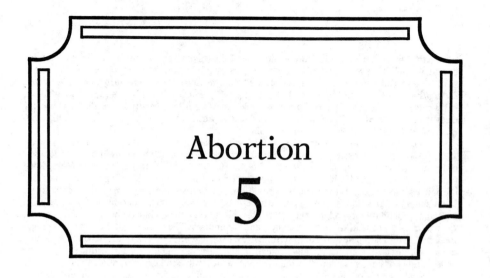

Abortion
5

As to [abortion]...however much we may pity the mother whose health and even life is gravely imperiled in the performance of the duty alloted to her by nature, nevertheless what could ever be a sufficient reason for excusing in any way the direct murder of the innocent?

POPE PIUS XI

[A] being with a human genetic code is man....[O]nce the humanity of the fetus is perceived, abortion is never right except in self-defense.

JOHN T. NOONAN, JR.

...[G]enetic humanity is neither necessary nor sufficient for establishing that an entity is a person. Some human beings are not people, and there may well be people who are not human beings....[A] fetus, even a fully developed one, is considerably less personlike than is the average mature mammal....[N]either a fetus's resemblance to a person, nor its potential for becoming a person provides any basis for the claim that it has any significant right to life....

MARY ANNE WARREN

INTRODUCTION

In no contemporary moral issue can one find the passionate conviction and advocacy surrounding that of abortion. On one hand, many proponents of the women's liberation movement rally round this issue, seeing restrictive abortion laws as one of the many instruments of female subjugation. A woman, they exhort, should have absolute right to control her own body. On the other hand, there are those, often of a deeply religious persuasion, who see abortion as an act of wanton murder of the most defenseless of human beings. Given such widely divergent perceptions of abortion, antagonists rarely speak directly to their opponents' arguments, rejecting their fundamental assumptions as unworthy of serious discussion. Seekers and holders of political office are besieged to take a stand by those passionately committed to this issue. Yet the stands that politicians take are usually unreflective ones that serve to pander rather than to educate an emotionally aroused electorate.

For example, as this is written, a new President, George Bush, has just been inaugurated and has pledged his support to antiabortionists. Abortion, he says, is only justified when the life of the mother is at stake or the pregnancy results from rape or incest. In all other cases, he says, "adoption is the answer." Is it really? More fundamentally, since abortions are performed for many reasons, what is the question to which adoption is the answer? The President doesn't say, but echoes the sentiments of right-to-lifers whose perceptions he has come to share. Yet, if, as he now believes, an abortion is murder, is it any less of a murder when a fetus is conceived as a result of rape or incest? If abortions should be legally permitted in such cases out of consideration for the feelings of the mother, what about her feelings when she discovers that she is carrying a gravely ill or defective child or one destined, as Tay-Sachs babies are, to an inevitable and painful early death? If considerations of a mother's feelings are relevant in the cases of rape and incest, should they not be relevant here? Furthermore, is it not plausible to argue that abortion of some gravely abnormal fetuses is actually in their interest, while it is not in the interest of those normal fetuses that, through no fault of their own, carry the social stigma of having been conceived in nefarious circumstances? Does the right to abortion in cases of rape derive not from a consideration of the mother's feelings, but from her lack of responsibility for her condition? If so, can the same reasonably be said of incest? In addition if abortion is to be legally permitted only in cases of rape and incest, would not many young women—some in their early teens—either resort to illegal abortions or opt to keep babies for whom they cannot adequately care? Should the law be blind to such considerations? The President does not publically address himself to such questions, and one wonders if he even addresses them to himself in private.

In spite of the loud political rhetoric and widespread interest in the abortion issue, there is little attempt at principled justification and conceptual clarity. Very rarely do the antagonists come to grips with the fundamental questions that lie at the core of the abortion issue. What, for example, do we mean when we call something a *human being* or a *person*? Is a fetus a *person*? If so, when does it become one? How do we weigh the rights of the unborn against the rights of those already born? Does a fetus, perhaps, have a right not to be born because of some severe physical abnormality? In what situations is it morally justifiable to kill the innocent? Before we grapple with these issues, let us briefly consider the biological facts and the historical and legal background of the abortion issue.

THE BIOLOGICAL FACTS

The union of the human ovum and sperm forms a single-celled zygote, having a full genetic blueprint for further development, half from each parent. The zygote begins a process of cellular divisions doubling the number of cells each time. As it continues to divide and grow, it slowly moves through the fallopian tube to be implanted in the uterine wall. This occurs about seven days after fertilization at about the same time that segmentation takes place—the process by which the various individuals in a multiple birth are separated. At this point the zygote is now called a conceptus. From the end of its second week, when it consists of an inner and outer layer of cells, until the eighth week, it is called an embryo. At about the third week, the various organ systems begin to form, so that by the eighth week, the embryo, which is now called a fetus, begins to look human.[1] It is also at this time that brain waves can be monitored (actually there is primitive brain activity from about the sixth week on). The next important milestone (at least psychologically) in the developing pregnancy is the mother's experience of quickening—the feeling of fetal movement. This occurs by about the eighteenth week. When the fetus's organ systems have developed to such an extent that it is capable of surviving outside its mother's womb and grow to maturity (with the assistance of medical technology), the fetus is said to be viable. With current medical technology, viability usually occurs around 24 weeks.

At present, pregnancy cannot be diagnosed for at least ten days after the failure of the onset of menstruation. A suspected pregnancy may, however, be terminated by a "morning after" pill which prevents the implantation of the zygote into the uterine wall. Up to the twelfth week of pregnancy, abortions are usually performed by a suction technique or by the technique of dilitation and curettage (D & C). In the suction procedure the cervix (mouth of the uterus) is dilated (stretched) until a tube can be inserted which is attached to a suction apparatus. The embryo or fetus is sucked out, being crushed or badly torn in the process. In the dilitation and curettage method, a sharp loop-shaped instrument (curette) is inserted into the dilated uterus, and the embryo or fetus is scraped out.

After the twelfth week of the pregnancy (the end of the first trimester), abortions become more complex and more dangerous to the mother.[2] Various procedures are used for second and third trimester abortions. Most common today

---

[1]In this chapter, we will employ the standard practice of using the term "fetus" broadly to include reference to a zygote, conceptus, and embryo as well.

[2]The death rate among women undergoing late abortions is 12 per 100,000, compared with fewer than 2 per 100,000 in first-trimester abortions.

is the technique of dilation and evacuation (D & E), which is least traumatic to the pregnant woman, but is the bloodiest and most unpleasant for the doctor. In this direct assault upon the fetus, the pregnant woman's cervix is dilated and then, while she is under anesthesia, the fetus is dismembered inside her uterus and removed with forceps. Until recently, saline abortions were the most common procedure for late abortions and this procedure is still widely used. It consists of the insertion into the mother's womb of a needle which extracts about eight ounces of amniotic fluid, replacing it with a highly concentrated salt solution which usually terminates the life of the fetus. Then 8 to 72 hours later, the mother goes into labor and expels it. Occasionally, however, the fetus survives the salt solution and emerges alive. A major drawback to the use of this method is the chance that the needle may accidentally penetrate one of the mother's blood vessels, permitting the salt solution to enter her blood stream, which can cause convulsions and death. For this reason, many doctors choose to avoid this procedure, injecting a hormone-like substance called prostaglandin that causes strong uterine contractions. Only a small amount of this substance is required, so it does not necessitate the removal of any amniotic fluid. Furthermore, it is harmless, should it find its way into the mother's blood stream. This method does, however, have the unfortunate consequence of making it much more likely that the fetus will be born alive, although gravely harmed. Hysterotomy, the least often used method of late-term abortions, poses the greatest danger to the mother and is the most likely to result in a live fetus. The surgeon makes an incision similar to that for a caesarian delivery, only smaller, and extracts the fetus. Where sterilization is desired, the physician performs a hysterectomy, removing the uterus itself with the fetus inside.

Clearly, if an abortion is to be performed, it should be done as early as possible. Nevertheless, there are some women who do not realize their condition until well along in their pregnancy. Others find themselves unable to come to an early decision. At times, the situation changes as the pregnancy develops (such as when the father abandons the pregnant mother or loses his job). Late abortions are also the result of the discovery that the fetus is mongoloid or suffering from some other grave defect. At present, this knowledge can only be obtained by a procedure done after the fourteenth week, called amniocentesis, in which amniotic fluid is removed and tested; approximately three weeks is required to complete the laboratory analysis. This technique is utilized for diagnoses of genetic abnormalities. In addition, computerized ultrasound machines which translate sound waves into pictures are utilized in the diagnoses of the physical conditions of developing fetuses.

The diagnostic techniques of amniocentesis and ultrasound, as well as the growing ability of doctors to intervene in fetal development can create difficult moral dilemmas when abnormalities are detected. Should potential parents' wishes to have a normal child justify abortions when the abnormality is minor or medically treatable after birth? Since amniocentesis allows a diagnosis of the sex of a fetus, should potential parents be allowed, as they have, to abort a healthy fetus on the basis of their displeasure with its sex? Should potential parents be encouraged to abort severely abnormal fetuses who will most likely either die soon after birth or live pitiful lives? Does it matter if the potential parents cannot financially or emotionally afford the cost of care for a severely abnormal child? Should doctors intervene to save fetuses that would be naturally aborted, regardless of considerations as to the quality of life that await them should they survive? If not, where is the line to be drawn? No easy answers are possible and doctors routinely make difficult moral choices, guided by their uncertain appraisal of the medical consequences of these choices and, often, unarticulated moral values.

HISTORICAL AND LEGAL BACKGROUND

There have been many societies in which abortion, and even infanticide, were considered morally proper. This was true, for example, in ancient Greece and Rome where deformed babies or unwanted female babies were often left to die. The early Judeo-Christian view of abortion, which was greatly influenced by Aristotelian metaphysics, was also permissive. As Aristotle saw it, the characteristic that made a physical body human was the human soul, but he did not conceive the soul, as we do now, as a *substance* that occupies a body. Instead, Aristotle saw the soul as the *function* of the body. A body possessed a human soul, he believed, when it was capable of performing the functions that were unique to human beings. As he saw it, this was possible only when a body possessed a human shape and human organs. Accepting this view, and assuming that human fetuses did not possess a human shape or human organs until well along in the pregnancy, early Judeo-Christian thinkers believed that while immature human fetuses are alive, they are alive in ways no different from the ways in which plants and other animals are alive. In Aristotelian language, an immature human fetus possessed a vegetative or animal soul, but not a human soul. This was, for example, the view held by the Christian Medieval philosopher Thomas Aquinas. The Catholic Church officially adopted this position in 1322 and as a result forbade the faithful from baptizing any premature births which did not have a definite human shape.

Under the influence of erroneous scientific reports, the Church in the early seventeenth century accepted the view that a human fetus has a human body from the very moment of conception (the preformation theory). According to this view, the develoment of the fetus simply consists of a continuous increase in size of organs and bodily structures which were assumed to be fully present in microscopic form from the moment of conception. With the acceptance of both the preformation theory and the Aristotelian view of the soul, it could be assumed that the human soul was present in a human fetus from the moment of conception. The preformation theory, however, was eventually rejected as was the Aristotelian view of the soul, which gave way as the Cartesian dualism of Descartes (1596–1650) gained influence. According to the Cartesian picture, soul and body are two radically different sorts of substances, capable of existing independently. A human being, as Descartes saw it, is a combination of these two radically different and interacting substances. The soul, from this perspective, is an immortal, conscious substance that occupies or animates a body for a period of time. When this animation or ensoulment took place was an open question. Originally, it was assumed to take place on the fortieth day for males and on the eightieth day for females. Consequently, it was only after this period that abortions became a mortal sin, justifying the eternal torment of hell. An eternity of the deprived existence of limbo awaited the unbaptized fetus, tainted now forever with original sin. In 1869, Pope Pius IX decreed that all fetuses should be considered to be ensouled from conception.

There is no single moral attitude toward abortion that can be described as the Jewish position. According to the most prevalent tradition, a fetus does not become a full person with full moral rights until it is born. Some rabbis who accept this view have advocated abortion on demand, while others have claimed that although abortion is not technically murder, it is still "akin to homicide" and "allowable only in grave cases." There is no consensus, however, among those who take this view as to what is to count as a "grave case." While some use this term narrowly, others use it broadly. There are some rabbis who are opposed to liberal abortion laws, not on the grounds that it is akin to homicide, but on the grounds that such laws would have such undesirable social consequences as encouraging promiscuity, adultery, and childless marriages. In spite of the very different attitudes toward abortion in Jewish morality, there is a strong consensus that the welfare of a pregnant woman is more important than that of the fetus she is carrying. From this perspective, some rabbis have advocated the abortion of defective fetuses on the grounds of the anguish their births would cause their mothers rather than out of concern for the fetus.

In the United States, prior to the landmark Supreme Court decision in *Roe v. Wade* (1975), states were unlimited by constitutional restraints in the formulation of their own abortion laws. Consequently, some states had much more restrictive abortion laws than others. Arguments have been made, however, both by those in favor of and those opposed to abortion, that states should be limited in their right to formulate abortion laws by certain provisions of the Constitution. It has been claimed, for example, that a fetus should be considered a person, whose right to life is protected under the Fourteenth Amendment. On the other side, the argument has been presented that a fetus should not be considered a person under the Constitution, and that a pregnant woman has a right to privacy derived from the Bill of Rights which renders unconstitutional all state laws prohibiting abortions.

In *Roe v. Wade,* the United States Supreme Court came to grips with the constitutionality of abortion. According to this 7–2 decision, fetuses are not "full legal persons" and women do indeed have a right to privacy which gives them the right to abortion on demand during the first trimester. During the second and third trimesters when abortions become more risky, the Court declared, the states have a "legitimate interest in preserving and protecting the health of the woman," and, consequently, the right to regulate abortions, requiring, for example, that they be performed in fully equipped hospitals rather than in a doctor's office. Only in the last trimester did the Court recognize that an "important and legitimate interest in potential life" might outweigh the mother's rights and wishes. Giving no constitutional guidelines as to how these rights should be weighed, except to say that the state cannot forbid abortion in the third trimester when it is "necessary to preserve the life or health of the mother,'' the Supreme Court left the matter to the individual states.

The majority decision in *Roe v. Wade* is unstable since its pivotal distinctions are a function of an ever-advancing medical technology. As abortion methods become more advanced, the risk to the health of the mother may be eliminated and, consequently, the state's interest in the health of the mother and the relevance of the second trimester could drop out of consideration entirely. Similarly, the moment of viability could conceivably be brought back to conception. Yet, according to the majority decision, it is viability which presently occurs at approximately the beginning of the third trimester that marks the point where the state's interest in potential life can justify restricting abortion in the interests of the developing fetus. Thus, the Supreme Court decision would seem to allow the point where a fetus is given the right to life to be constantly moved back toward conception as techniques of artificial incubation become more sophisticated.

Roe v. Wade stirred great controversy. Conservative legal scholars accused the court of usurping the political process in extending the right to privacy to include the right to abortion. Some went further, claiming that there was no constitutional warrant for a general right to privacy. Liberal legal scholars came to *Roe's* defense. As the years passed, the composition of the Supreme Court became more conservative. Given the Supreme Court's reluctance to overturn precedents, the court's initial impetus was not to overturn *Roe* entirely, but to limit it. The first step in this direction was a 1977 ruling that states do not have a constitutional obligation to pay for the abortions of women on welfare whose medical care would be paid for if they continued their pregnancy. The direction of the Supreme Court in limiting *Roe* in the '80's was best exemplified by the sole woman on the court, Sandra Day O'Connor who, while unwilling to deny a woman a constitutionally guaranteed right to abortion, was willing to allow states the right to make abortions more difficult to obtain as long as such restrictions do not become "unduly burdensome," a term she left undefined.

In the summer of '89, the nation eagerly awaited the Supreme Court's decision in a Missouri statute limiting the right to abortion—*Webster v. Reproductive Health Services.* How would the court go? Blackmun, Brennan, Marshall and Stevens stood solidly for the maintenance of *Roe,* while Rehnquist, Scalia and White were for overthrowing it entirely. The newest member of the court, Anthony Kennedy's position remained unknown and O'Connor sat on the fence. Unable to obtain a majority for overturning *Roe,* the court's majority decision proved to be very limited in scope—merely validating Missouri's right to prohibit the use of public employees and facilities to perform abortions not necessary to save the mother's life. With Kennedy among them, 4 justices were willing to "narrow" *Roe* by extending the state's right to protect potential life before viability. Surprisingly, O'Connor, who explicitly rejected the trimester framework in previous cases, was unwilling to make the plurality decision a majority one. Perhaps, as some have suggested, she did not want to be seen as the deciding vote in an issue so sensitive to women. Blackmun wrote a passionate dissent, claiming that while the plurality decision does not explicitly repudiate *Roe,* it "is filled with winks, and nods, and knowing glances to those who would do away with *Roe* entirely" and that it "turns a stone face to anyone in search of what the plurality conceives as the scope of a woman's constitutional right to terminate a pregnancy." As a result, the liberal justice concluded, "the signs are evident and very ominous, and a chill wind blows."

While supporters of abortion shared Blackmun's diagnosis, antiabortion groups were encouraged. Perhaps, their campaign begun after the passage of *Roe* for a constitutional amendment banning abortions would prove unnecessary. Meanwhile in Congress, Representative Henry Hyde and Senator Jesse Helms have proposed the following congressional declaration:

> For the purpose of enforcing the obligation of the States under the 14th amendment not to deprive persons of life without due process of law, human life shall be deemed to exist from conception.

It is controversial, however, whether Congress has the Constitutional power to enact such a bill. On the other side of the abortion debate, some proponents of abortion have argued that a fetus should have a legal right not to be born into a life which has no reasonable prospect of being a life worth living. There have been several civil suits which have been based on this alleged right, but until now they have all been rejected by the courts.

Several doctors have been tried for the homicides of fetuses born alive after abortion attempts on the grounds that they did not make sufficient attempts to save the lives of the fetuses they had a legal right to abort. At least two were convicted. Such cases raise the troublesome question of whether a pregnant woman has a right only to detach herself from a dependent fetus or has the right as well to procure its death in those situations where an ever-advancing medical science has the means to keep it alive outside her womb. The most poignant case in this regard is one of rape. One can certainly understand a woman's desire to secure the death of a fetus conceived in such circumstances. Similarly, if the fetus is gravely deformed and an abortion is desired, the desire will amost always be that the fetus die.

THE CENTRAL PHILOSOPHICAL ISSUE: IS A FETUS A PERSON?

The philosophical issue of the moral status of a fetus lies at the very heart of the abortion issue. Some claim that a fetus never attains the status of a person and that at least an early abortion is nothing more than "the removal of a piece of tissue from the woman's body." Others, however, accept the official Roman Catholic position: "Every unborn child must be regarded as a human person with all the rights of a human person from the moment of conception." Others straddling the line between these opposing positions describe the fetus as a "potential person," possessing from conception some rights, but not the rights of a "full person." Others say that a fetus becomes a person somewhere along its gradual and continuous development within its mother's womb. While others suggest that a newborn baby, like an unborn fetus, should not be considered a person and, consequently, should not be afforded a right to life.

Without a resolution of the fundamental question of whether a human fetus should be considered a person, possessing the same rights as living human beings, many of the arguments used by proponents of abortion miss the mark. For example, it is often argued that the state has no more right to interfere with a woman's freedom to choose whether or not to complete a pregnancy than it does to interfere with her religious freedom. A woman who is opposed to abortion, has the right not to obtain one, but she should not have the right to impose her beliefs on those who disagree, it is said. To those who see the fetus as a person, however, the question of abortion is not a question of one's freedom to choose one's own private beliefs and practices, but one of minority rights—the right of a defenseless innocent human being to life itself. Certainly, none of us who deplore the immorality of racism would afford the racist the freedom to victimize those whom he sees as inferior. To those who see the fetus as a person, the situations are morally identical.

Similarly, if the fetus is a person, arguments which relate to the undesirable consequences of an unwanted pregnancy seem callously out of place. Most of those who support very liberal abortion laws would be aghast at the proposal that the aged, deformed, retarded, and senile be put to death when the cost of caring for them becomes burdensome. Again, for those who see the fetus as a person, the situations are morally identical. As one "pro-lifer" put it, "You must eliminate the problems people have, not the people themselves." Similarly, pro-lifers will reject as morally irrelevant the undeniable fact that, should abortion be made illegal, many women would turn to illegal abortions and risk their own deaths. This is an undesirable consequence, they will admit, but one does not justify the murder of innocent people this way! Indeed, many pro-lifers would want abortion made illegal, even if this does not have an effect on the abortion rate, for they would argue that the state should not sanction the immorality of murder.

How does one decide whether a fetus is a human being or a person? Indeed, should these terms be used interchangeably, as many use them, or should we attach different meanings to them, as some have suggested? In resolving these quesitons, it is essential that one realize that these terms do not have a single agreed upon factual meaning; two people may agree on the biological characteristics of a developing organism and disagree on whether it ought to be called a human being or a person, since they take different positions on the *moral* relevance of these characteristics. The decision to call a fetus a person, for example, clearly has moral implications. One will not use this term to describe an organism unless one is willing to ascribe rights to it—in particular, the right to life. One cannot, for example, dispose of persons without weighty reasons.

Now, while one may utilize the concept of a human being interchangeably with that of a person, it is more useful and consistent with common usage to utilize the notion of a person as a moral concept and that of a human being as a biololgical one. In this usage, to be a person is to be the sort of creature who is considered an appropriate bearer of rights, and, as such a member of a moral community. To be a human being, on the other hand, is to be a member of the biological species *homo sapiens.* If we accept this usage, useful distinctions become possible. We may now speak of nonhuman persons (such as God or an advanced extraterrestrial life form) and of human nonpersons (a human being born without a cerebrum or one in a coma).

In resolving the issue of whether a fetus is a person, we must grapple with the issue of the appropriate requirement for membership into a moral community, an issue which we have already touched upon in Part I of this book. What are the essential characteristics that make the ascription of personhood possible? Do human fetuses have these characteristics? If so, what is the scope of the rights they should possess? Let us turn to a critical discussion of answers that have been given to these questions.

A Person at Conception

It is often argued that a fetus is a person from the moment of conception. Given the continuity of gradual development, it is claimed, any other dividing line is arbitrary. The moment of conception, however, marks a radically discontinuous step from what existed before. Of those who mark the humanity of a fetus at the very moment of conception, some do so on the basis of the fetus' alleged possession of an immortal soul and others on its genetic completeness and capacity to develop into an adult human being. Let us briefly consider these positions in turn.

A Fetus Has a Soul

According to the Roman Catholic position, a fetus becomes a person when it is infused with an immortal soul. Although it is generally conceded now that this moment cannot definitely be known, one must assume that it is the moment of conception itself. Opponents of this position will point to its unverifiable nature, many claiming that the very notion of a soul is without meaning. The antagonists, of course, have reached a metaphysical impasse. Yet, even if we grant, for the sake of argument, that a soul is infused into the zygote at conception, what are the theological consequences of an abortion? Some have argued that if a fetus is aborted, its immortal soul, now forever incapable of receiving the salvation only baptism can provide, will be resigned to an eternity in "limbo," never to experience the joys of heaven. The quick and, to my mind, decisive objection to this view is that it seems incomprehensible that the infinitely powerful and good traditional Judeo-Christian God would allow such a thing to happen. One must realize that if baptism is required for salvation, many human souls would be deprived of salvation through no fault of their own; this would include all those children whose parents do not believe in baptism, as well as all those countless fetuses that die as a result of natural or induced abortions or whose mothers die before delivery. Certainly God should not penalize people for things they are powerless to control. If the ensouled fetus was put in this world to face a moral test with the possibility of a heavenly reward, does it not seem reasonable that God should give that individual another chance and recycle it into some other body?

The Right to Life Based
on Genetic Potentiality

In defense of a fetus' right to life from the moment of conception, many have pointed to the fact that it is at this moment that a complete genetic blueprint is formed that determines the future development of a specific organism. It is this point and this point alone, it is claimed, that can be marked as the beginning of an organism's life. From this perspective, it is not a fetus' *current* characteristics that justify its right to life, but its genetic *potentiality* to become a person. But what is the moral significance of this potentiality? Can it not equally as well be said that an unfertilized egg or sperm has the potentiality of developing into a human being? Certainly, they cannot develop into a human being alone, but neither can the fertilized egg.[3] Granted, too, that the natural probabilities of an egg and sperm becoming part of a causal chain leading to the birth of a human being are vastly smaller than that of a fertilized egg, why should a fertilized egg be considered entitled to the rights of a human being until it actualizes its potentialities? An acorn, for example, has the potentiality of becoming an oak tree, but it is not an oak tree. If one considers it wrong to abort a fetus simply because of its potentiality, then ought not one be opposed to all methods of contraception which prevent unfertilized eggs and sperms from developing the potentialities they would otherwise possess? If potential life has a right to be actualized, where are we to draw the line? Clearly, we do not want to say that fertile celibates are acting immorally by not attempting conception.

Furthermore, even if one accepts the view that a human fetus has a right to life based on its potentiality to become a person, some human fetuses may not possess that potentiality due to severe genetic abnormality. The notion that human fetuses should possess rights on the basis of their potentiality to become persons presupposes a position on what counts as being a person. For example, if consciousness or some minimum mental ability is essential to being a person, then not all human fetuses possess that potentiality.

Implications of the View That
a Fetus Is a Person at Conception

The view that a fetus has the right to life at the very moment of conception has implications which should be considered. On this view, those who successfully

---

[3]Clearly, however, most of us believe that while it is reasonable to call a fertilized egg a potential person, it is not reasonable to use this term to describe an unfertilized egg or sperm. Why is this so? I think there are two main reasons for this attitude. First, the union of a sperm and an egg is naturally seen as the beginning of a causal sequence which contains all the important causal ingredients—that is, the genes—for the development of a human being. On the other hand, an unfertilized egg or a sperm contains only part of these essential causal ingredients, and as such neither can reasonably be picked out as the beginning of a causal series that can lead to the formation of a human being. Second, as a matter of brute biological fact, a much greater percentage of fertilized eggs become persons in the natural course of events than do unfertilized eggs or sperms. It is interesting to note in this regard that if female reproduction were such that, instead of eliminating ova that are not fertilized in a short period of time and releasing new ones every month, a woman would retain the same unfertilized egg until it became fertilized before forming (and not simply releasing) a new one, we would be much more apt to call an unfertilized egg a potential person than we are now.

use the "morning-after" pill, which causes expulsion of a fertilized egg are guilty of intentional homicide. The same would be true of a woman who successfully employs the abortion pill developed in France which has proven capable of inducing abortions in 85 percent of pregnant women. The pill, taken ten days after the first missed menstrual period, acts to block the release of a hormone, without which the fetus dies. This abortion technique has been heralded by some as a momentous alternative to contraceptive devices. Similarly, a woman who uses an intrauterine device which most likely works like the morning-after pill to prevent uterine implantation of fertilized eggs is responsible for the creation of a homicidal risk, and one who negligenty causes herself to miscarry is responsible for a negligent homicide.

Consider too that when eggs and sperm are artificaly joined in vitro (in a test tube), a much smaller percentage of these unions survive than do those that occur naturally in a woman's body. Since this is the case, should such extra-uterine fertilization be legally prohibited as wanton reckless homicide? If you say no, must you not reject conception as the point at which a fetus obtains the right to life? Indeed, if extra-uterine fertilization (with, let us say, 10 percent chance of survival) became very common, would we not naturally begin to place less importance on the moment of fertilization and more importance on what happens afterwards?

Mental Activity and Physical Appearance

Like the influential philosopher René Descartes, we tend to associate ourselves with our states of consciousness (that is, our thoughts, memories, feelings, and emotions) and not with our physical bodies. If our mental life were to come to a final end, so would we. Since this is so, should we not claim that a fetus has no moral significance or is not a person until it becomes conscious? Many philosophers have thought so. The existence of a primitive level of fetal brain activity probably begins about the sixth week of the pregnancy. The point at which brain activity gives rise to consciousness is, however, open to question. Nevertheless, some physiologists suggest that it is improbable that a fetus has the capacity to experience sensations, such as pain, until about the twenty-fourth to the twenty-eighth week, when its nerve endings develop their fatty myelin sheaths which seem to play some role in the transmission of nerve impulses.

Even if we knew the point at which a fetus first becomes conscious, there are grave difficulties in identifying this point as that at which a fetus becomes a person. One must realize that the level of mental activity that exists at the first dawn of human consciousness is quite primitive, and no different from the mental activity of the fetuses of other mammals, such as dogs or chimpanzees. Indeed, one may assume that this is true throughout a pregnancy. If we are then to afford a right to life to a human fetus by virtue of the existence of primitive states of consciousness, ought we not give an equal right to the fetuses of other mammals? Conversely, if we are not to give other fetuses such a right, how can we justify giving it to a human fetus? Clearly, what leads many to attribute the right to life to a human fetus, but not to a dog or chimpanzee fetus resides not in the level of its mental activity, but in its external physical resemblance to a human being.

As the pictures of fetuses pro-lifers are wont to show amply demonstrate, the thought of aborting a creature that looks like a little baby, is quite disturbing to many of us, as is the thought of cutting it to pieces or tearing it apart in an abortion procedure. I must admit that this has an emotional impact on me, but is it morally relevant? Is it not reasonable to claim that it should be mental activity, and not physical appearance, that confers personhood upon an organism? An extra-terrestrial creature and a greatly deformed human being may have very little external resemblance to a human being, but would they not be considered persons if they had the mental capacities of persons? Conversely, is it not proper to consider a seriously brain-damaged individual who looks like a human being, but is unconscious or conscious on a very primitive level, as a "mere vegetable," and not a person?

If the mere existence of a primitive level of consciousness or the external physical resemblance to a human being does not confer personhood on a fetus, where are we to draw the line? What mental capacities must a fetus possess before it becomes a person? A developing fetus can have pleasant and painful experiences, but it cannot reason, have human emotions, or enter into the human socialization process. Are we then to say that a fetus is never a person, and perhaps go so far as to say that this is also true of a newborn baby, implying that neither has a right to life? This is the position of the philosopher Michael Tooley who claims that a creature should not be considered a person unless it "is capable of desiring to continue existing as a subject of experiences" and furthermore "possesses the concept of a self as a continuing subject of experiences and other mental states, and believes that it is itself such a continuing entity."

Tooley develops this idea in his involved book *Abortion and Infanticide,* published in 1983. He argues, on purely conceptual grounds, that if an entity, X, has a right to something, Y, X must have an *interest* in Y which, in turn, requires that X have a capacity to *desire* Y. In order to have an interest in a continuing existence, he claims, an entity must *understand* this notion which necessitates *a concept of personal identity* and the ability to *envision* and *desire* its continuation. To have a concept of personal identity, in turn, requires "the sort of unification of consciousness over time that makes something a subject of non-momentary interests," he claims. This requires, among other things, the having of *thoughts* which, he claims, requires conceptual ability lacking in fetuses and the newborn. Realizing that his notion of a person admits of degree, Tooley introduces the concept of a "quasi-person," which he defines as "a being that possesses the properties required for being a person at a very low degree," and consequently, a being that has *some degree* of a right to life. When do humans become quasi-persons? "If forced to speculate, the age of three months might be as reasonable a guess as any," he tentatively asserts. Exactly what the rights of quasi-persons are, Tooley does not say, but they are less than those of persons. Nevertheless, since new-born humans are not even quasi-persons, infanticide is permissible, he confidently concludes.[4]

---

[4]As an interesting corollary of his view, Tooley is willing to admit that adult animals may be persons and consequently entitled to a right to life. If this is true, Tooley suggests, "one may

Tooley's position is frought with difficulties, for the conceptual connections upon which he builds his argument are problematic. For example, it is problematic that one cannot have a right to something without being able to desire it or that one cannot desire something without being able to conceptualize what one desires. Animals may not have a concept of death, but their *behavior* in avoiding it can be taken as evidence for their desire to live. Tooley's chain of arguments are intricate, but their links are weak. Although Tooley is correct in claiming that the standard for personhood should involve some minimal consciousness and mental capacity, it seems implausible to single out the complex sense of personal identity as the sole standard. Perhaps a good way to focus upon the characteristics essential for personhood is to imagine ourselves faced with complex extraterrestrial life form or man-made robots of the future. What would such creatures have to be like to be called persons? Certainly, it would be essential that they were considered to be conscious beings, capable of having feelings and emotion. This is not, however, sufficient. In classifying something as a person, we would be concerned with such mental qualities as its problem-solving abilities, its capacity for reasoned self-directive activity, its capacity for introspective self-awareness and self-identity through time, and its capacity to communicate and relate to others. Although no definite answer can be given as to the relative weights that should be placed on these mental capacities in judging the personhood of a creature, as the number and degree of these capacities increases, our natural inclination to classify a creature as a person will increase. From this perspective, personhood is based not on a single characteristic but on a cluster of imprecisely defined ones which admit of distinctions as to degree, making it possible to speak of *the degree* of a creature's personhood. In addition, our *actual* tendency to classify creatures as fellow persons will also involve the degree of fellow-feeling we have for these creatures. After all the facts are in, we will have to decide whether we *choose to afford these creatures rights which reflect our concern and respect.*

Viability and Birth

Many have suggested that viability or birth should be considered the point at which a fetus becomes a person and consequently is entitled to the right to life. Those who take this perspective claim that while a fetus is dependent upon its mother for its existence, it is not a separate and independent person. It becomes so, they claim, either when it no longer is dependent or need be dependent upon its mother. This position is inadequate. Granted that a fetus is dependent upon its mother in a unique way and would die if it were severed from that relationship prior to viability, this does not mean that the fetus is not a separate organism from its mother. After all, a newborn baby is also dependent on others for its very life.

---

find himself driven to conclude that our everyday treatment of animals is morally indefensible, and that we are in fact murdering innocent persons." In addition, Tooley suggests that although a fetus or newborn does not have a right to life, it may have, by virtue of its capacity to feel pain, a right not to be tortured. Tooley does not, however, develop this idea or consider its moral implications when a method of abortion will cause a fetus pain.

When a fetus is born, the nature of the environiment it depends upon undergoes a radical change. Instead of being dependent upon only one, its needs can now be satisfied by many, but it is still at the mercy of others just as much as it was before. The mere fact that a child is dependent upon its parents in no way negates its right to life. If it seems morally monstrous to even suggest such a thing, is it any less morally monstrous to claim that the mere fact that a fetus is dependent upon its mother robs it of its personhood and right to life? Similarly, can one reasonably suggest that the mere *capacity* for independence from its mother's womb confers personhood on an organism that otherwise would not possess this characteristic? Assuming, for example, that medical science will one day be able to keep a three-month-old fetus alive in an artificial incubator, could one reasonably suggest that while it has no right to life now—and can be aborted for any reason—it would then have such a right? Similarly, can one reasonably suggest that if two fetuses having the same level of consciousness differ only in lung development, making one viable and the other not, that the first, but not the second, has the right to life?

As a rational principle, the mere independence or capacity for independence of a fetus from its mother must be rejected as morally irrelevant to its personhood or right to life; as a psychological factor, on the other hand, one cannot doubt that the fact that a fetus is *hidden* within its mother's womb makes it psychologically easier for us not to see it as a person that has rights. Similarly, a woman may not perceive a fetus to be a person until she feels its movement, but no one would suggest that a fetus that suffered from some type of motor paralysis, making it incapable of movement, would be less of a person than an otherwise identical fetus that could move.

THE RIGHTS OF A FETUS
V. THE RIGHTS OF ITS MOTHER

A Woman's Right to Refuse the Use
of Her Body to a Dependent Fetus

Although one may be unjustified in using viability or the moment of birth as the moment at which a fetus becomes a person, one may plausibly argue that, while dependent upon the use of its mother's body, a fetus does not have a right to the use of that body in certain circumstances and its mother has no obligation to afford it that use. This is the position of Judith Thomson in her widely reprinted article "A Defense of Abortion." Granting for the sake of argument that a fetus is a person,[5] Thomson claims that in cases where the mother's life is at stake or where she has been raped, or has engaged voluntarily in sexual intercourse but has taken reasonable precautions to avoid pregnancy, she has no obligation to accept the

[5]Thomson confesses to the difficulty of determining when a fetus should be considered a person and offers no suggestion as to where that line should be drawn. She does, however, express her view that a fetus is not a person at conception and is one "well before birth."

inconvenience of a pregnancy.[6] To make it a woman's obligation to accept these inconveniences when she is not responsible for her pregnant condition is, according to Thomson, to force her to be "a Good Samaritan" which the law does not force other people to become.

Assuming that a fetus is a person entitled to the *full* rights of live persons, Thomson attempts to convince us that a mother's right to decide what shall happen to her own body may override the fetus's right to life through the use of an example which she claims is morally analogous. She tells you to imagine yourself waking up one morning in bed with a famous unconscious violinist whose circulatory system has been plugged into yours, so that your kidneys can be used to extract poisons from his blood stream. Having discovered that only you have the right blood type to save the ailing violinist from otherwise certain death, the Society of Music Lovers has kidnapped you and plugged you up to the violinist without your consent. You are told that the violinist will require the use of your body for nine months, after which time he will have recovered from his ailment and can be safely unplugged from you. It is clear to Thomson that the violinist has no right to the use of your body. Indeed, according to Thomson, even if the violinist needed the use of your body not for nine months, but only for an hour, you would have no moral *obligation* to afford him the use of your body and would not be acting *unjustly* if you refuse that use. Nevertheless, Thomson admits, if the violinist needed your body only for such a short period of time, you would be "callous" and "indecent" to refuse.

Thomson's description and moral appraisal of the violinist case is Kantian in nature. The refusal to afford the use of one's body in this situation is not unjust since it is not a violation of one's (perfect) duty, but rather a refusal to provide benevolent assistance to someone to whom one has no special obligaiton. Reflecting the Kantian view that laws should function to assure justice and not to provide for benevolence, existing laws do not, Thomson points out, attempt to force one into becoming Good Samaritans or indeed even into "minimally decent Samaritans" (when the sacrifice is small).

Counting on you to accept her moral judgment of the violinist case, Thomson believes that cases of unintentional pregnancy due to rape or even resulting from the nonnegligent failure of contraceptive methods are analogous, in every morally relevant respect, to the violinist case. Consequently, she claims, just as you would have no special obligation to keep the violinist alive by affording him the use of your body, a pregnant woman in situations of unintentional and nonnegligent pregnancy has no obligation to afford a fetus the use of her body.

Thomson's argument is very strong in the case of a pregnancy due to rape. But even here, one could suggest that a woman who allows a fetus resulting from rape to develop within her womb for a certain period of time has tacitly assumed an obligation toward it. Leaving aside the case of rape, however, greater difficulties

---

[6]In these cases, it is Thomson's position that the mother only has the right to refuse the use of her body; she does not have the right to secure the death of the unborn fetus, if it is possible to detach it alive. This is true, she claims, even in cases of rape.

arise when one turns one's attention toward unintentinonal pregnancies that result from voluntary indulgence in sexual intercourse. Thomson's position here is that a pregnant woman has no responsibilities toward the fetus as long as she took reasonable precautions to avoid pregnancy. Many, however, would disagree. Unlike the violinist case and the analogous case of a pregnancy due to rape, the "victim" has some degree of responsibility for her condition. Even if one is willing to grant along with Thomson that a pregnant woman has a responsibility to a fetus only if she has failed to take reasonable precautions to prevent pregnancy, there will be disagreement as to the standard that should be used to make this determination. At any rate, even if we were to agree on what counts as a "reasonable precaution" to avoid pregnancy, it would be quite impractical to obtain verification that such precautions were taken, and, consequently a workable law distinguishing justifiable from unjustifiable abortions cannot be based on such a distinction. Since pregnancies due to rape are comparatively rare, Thomson's inadequate treatment of other types of unintended pregnancies makes her defense of abortion quite tenuous. Adequate arguments for a broadly liberal abortion policy must center on a denial that a fetus is a full person and as such is not entitled to the full legal and moral rights afforded to living human beings, but this is precisely the question Thomson attempts to sidestep.

DIRECT ABORTIONS ARE NEVER
MORALLY JUSTIFIED: THE ROMAN CATHOLIC RESPONSE

Diametrically opposed to Judith Thomson's position that a woman's right to her body can in many circumstances outweigh a fetus' right to life is the controversial Roman Catholic position which, based on the principle of the double effect, claims that a pregnant woman never has a right to *directly* intend (either as an end or as a means) the death of the fetus she is carrying. As we have seen, however, the distinction between the direct and indirect intentions of an act is unclear, since the same act can be described in more than one way. For example, in applying this doctrine, Roman Catholic moralists have claimed that while it is permissible to remove the cancerous uterus of a pregnant woman, thereby *indirectly* killing the fetus, one morally cannot perform a crainiotomy, in which the skull of a fetus in the process of being born is crushed, since this would be a *direct abortion*. Yet, as we previously remarked (see p. 69), with some verbal dexterity, the crainiotomy can be redescribed as an indirect abortion, no less than the removal of the cancerous uterus. Even if we assume, however, that reasonable people would agree in most cases on how the principle of the double effect is to be properly applied, many have challenged its moral importance. Consider, for example, a woman whose egg is fertilized in one of her fallopian tubes. If it is allowed to develop, it will rupture the tube, killing both the mother and fetus. According to the Roman Catholic position, it would be permissible to remove her fallopian tube (an indirect abortion—just like the removal of the cancerous uterus), but it would be impermissible to directly kill the fetus through a D & C procedure. Does this make any sense? Must we condemn the pregnant woman to sterility and to an intrusive surgical procedure to avoid acting wrongly, even though the much more drastic surgical procedure will result in the death of the fetus just as the D & C procedure will? For many, the answer is a resounding no. The no becomes even more resounding to the Roman Catholic stance that it would be wrong to directly kill a fetus when this is necessary to save a mother's life, even if both mother and fetus will die if nothing is done and no indirect abortion is possible. Is this not beyond moral justification? Yet the typical Catholic response in this situation would be that it is better for both innocent persons to die as a result of an act of God than for some human being to directly intend the death of one, even if, by so doing, he can save the other. (Consider the case of the overcrowded lifeboat in our list of moral dilemmas.) This may appear especially morally unjustified in the early weeks of a pregnancy when Catholics concede that one cannot be sure that a fetus is a person ("ensouled"). How, one may ask, can we justify allowing a woman to die, who can be saved, on the mere *chance* that by saving her we will be killing a person who will die in a short time anyway?

Some Catholic moralists have attempted to avoid this tragic result on the basis of the principle of forfeiture (see p. 68), claiming that the fetus in such situations is an aggressor on the life of the mother, even though morally innocent, and consequently the mother has a right to use lethal force to repel this aggressor, as long as the aggression cannot be stopped by any lesser means and the direct intention goes no further than stopping the assault (that is, it does not include the desire to kill the fetus). This position is, however, a minority one, since the general consensus among Catholic moralists is that the principle of forfeiture applies only to non-innocent aggressors.

SOME REFLECTIONS

It is, unfortunately, much easier to bring out the inadequacies of other people's positions on the abortion issue than to offer a cogent position of one's own. The continuous development of a fetus renders untenable all attempts to objectively justify any specific time as the point where a fetus becomes a person and, as such, a bearer of moral rights. Any point we focus upon in the continuous development from conception to fetus to baby seems arbitrary and open to telling objections. Yet we quite rightfully feel a need to draw a line somewhere and the thought that all such lines are ultimately arbitrary is too difficult for most of us to accept. So we construct our arbitrary lines and try to find some justification for them, but we never really succeed. The reasons we give for our positions on the abortion issue are often rationalizations that we conveniently construct to hide from ourselves how *feelings of identification* more than reason motivate us in this issue. For some this feeling of identification focuses naturally on the developing fetus, while for others it focuses on the suffering or wishes of the expectant parents. For the former abortion is naturally *felt* to be immoral, while for the latter it is *felt* to be moral. Reasons are given to justify these feelings, but they prove inadequate. Those of us who, like myself, feel identification with both the developing fetus and the expectant parents, struggle to draw some reasoned intermediate position, but reason fails us no less than it fails our absolutist opponents. If one says, as I do, that it is consciousness that bestows personhood upon a fetus, one finds oneself incapable of specifying in any definite way the degree of consciousness that is required. The definite line that we seek in separating persons from nonpersons proves to be disturbingly arbitrary. Given the significance of this matter, however, we refuse to allow people to draw their own lines, free of legal restraint. Instead, we fight it out, debunking the inadequacies of our opponents' positions but conveniently overlooking the inadequacies of our own.

I do not profess to have any easy answers to the abortion issue, but let me share with you some of my reflections on this issue. First, I am willing to categorically state that a fetus is not a person until it becomes conscious—that consciousness is an essential condition for personhood. I realize that I am open to the objection that if consciousness is essential for personhood, then individuals in a dreamless sleep or in a reversible coma are not persons. I am willing to accept that, but would say that they should have rights nevertheless since they are capable of regaining consciousness. This answer, I recognize, is not in itself satisfactory, for fetuses too are usually capable of gaining consciousness if they are left alone. But there seems to be a morally relevant difference in these two cases. Fetuses never were persons, whereas those asleep or in a coma were, and for that reason should have rights that the former need not be given. I am quite aware, however, that to many this difference in the two cases is not strong enough to bear the moral weight that I impose upon it.

Since I see the presence of consciousness as a necesary condition for the personhood of a fetus, I would say that a fetus is not a person before it develops a functioning brain. Consequently, I would see no moral dilemma in affording a woman an absolute right to dispose of a developing fetus prior to this point. I would, however, begin to feel uneasy about abortions after the eighth week, feeling that the loss of a fetus at this point is more than the mere removal of unwanted tissue from a woman's uterus, as some have described it. I must admit that I have no effective reply as to how I can justify having moral regrets over the loss of an 8- to 12-week-old human fetus, but not the fetuses of other animals whose levels of brain activity are indistinguishable. As we have seen, I do not think it is adequate simply to say that a human fetus is worthy of more respect since it looks like or is potentially a human being. Nevertheless, my feeling still persists, which indicates that these considerations do move me. However, psychologically understandable my attitude may be, I find it incapable of rational justification. I think I should be less concerned about mindless fetuses that look like human beings or can be envisioned as developing into persons and should be more concerned about animals that are more like persons.

Certainly a human fetus during the last trimester of development should have a claim upon our moral sensibilities. Nevertheless, I would not afford it the *full rights* of a human being. I would, for example, feel no moral hesitancy in choosing the life of a normal pregnant woman over the life of a fetus, however developed. I do not hesitate to say that the mother's life is a more valuable one that that of the fetus. The fetus, unlike its mother, does not have an already developed personality, nor has it established relationships of affection and social responsibility with others. As well as giving the claims of a fetus less weight than those of the already living, I would also afford a fetus a right not to be born, if it possesses certain clearly defined severe abnormalities; parents should be permitted to claim that right on behalf of their unborn.

Critics of abortion are likely to protest strongly that one should never attempt to weigh the relative worth of human life, for this mode of reasoning will eventually lead us down a slippery slope of moral reasoning which first justifies early abortions, then later ones, and eventually infanticide and the involuntary euthanasia of such individuals as the feeble-minded and senile who are seen as not fully human or as having no prospect of a meaningful life. I have two replies to this claim—one factual, the other philosophical. As a factual matter, those countries—such as Sweden and Denmark—which have long-standing liberalized abortion laws have not, as a matter of fact, found themselves going down that slippery slope. Indeed, the practice in Sweden and Denmark is to give the best of care to all living individuals, including the physically deformed, mentally retarded, and senile. On a philosophical level, however, one cannot dismiss the claim that the logic of a position which distinguishes the relative worth of human life transcends the abortion issue. This is indeed true, but the relevance of this notion to such issues as infanticide and euthanasia cannot be determined before a detailed consideration of the differences as well as similarities in these issues. One must consider each issue on its own merits. Reasonable people committed to the relevance of considerations relating to quality of life can disagree as to the moral permissibility of various *specific* proposals relating to abortion, infanticide, and euthanasia. Certainly this concept is capable of application in ways that most of us would find morally reprenhensible. This does not, however, distinguish it from many other moral concepts (such as utility) which can be misapplied equally as well. As I have suggested in our discussion of ethical theory, moral values provide us with guides, not with mechanical answers. In the hands of morally insensitive people, the best of moral guides can lead us astray.

The critics are right, however, that a consistent adherence to my mode of reasoning will have logical consequences which appear morally repugnant to some. For example, since I would consider late-term abortions morally permissible when a fetus is discovered to be severely deformed, and since I do not think that the act of birth should confer special rights to a fetus that it did not possess just prior to birth, I should in all consistency, be willing to grant the moral permissibility of infanticide in certain circumstances. I am so willing.

Many philosophers who contend that a fetus is not a person, entitled to moral rights, throughout the gestation period, have been unwilling to advocate infanticide. The justifications provided for such a position are inadequate rationalizations. For example, the well known contemporary philosopher Joel Feinberg claims that the prohibition of infanticide is supported by utilitarian reasons, arguing that,

> Nature has apparently implanted in us an instinctive tenderness toward infants that has proven extremely useful to the species, not only because it leads us to protect our young from death, and thus keep our population up, but also because infants usually grow into adults, and in Benn's words, "if as infants they are not treated with some minimal degree of tenderness and consideration, they will suffer for it later as persons." One might add that when they are adults, others will suffer for it too, at their hands. Spontaneous warmth and sympathy toward babies then clearly has a great deal of social utility, and insofar as infanticide would tend to weaken that socially valuable response, it is, on utilitarian grounds, morally wrong.

What Feinberg has in mind here is that if we treat babies as expendable, this, to quote from the contemporary philosopher S. I. Benn to whom Feinberg refers, "might well lead us into a callous unconcern for others too"—e.g., toward such people as the gravely deformed, retarded, and senile. This argument is reminiscent of Kant's argument for treating animals kindly (see p. 135). It is not that they *deserve* such treatment, but that such treatment is good practice for our relations with those that do. If this is so, is it not also possible that a permissive view of abortion also leads us into a callous unconcern for others? Many, after all, think it does. Looking at it from the opposite point of view Feinberg and Benn conveniently neglect the fact that there have been societies that practiced infanticide without becoming callous to others. For example, the 19th-century author Robert Louis Stevenson wrote to a friend that he was surprised upon visiting Polynesia that although the people on these islands practice infanticide, they "love their children far more than Europeans do." The instinctive tenderness that nature has implanted in us is socially variable. For some, it encompasses fetuses, and, for some, it encompasses animals. Some societies do not encourage this instinctive tenderness until a baby reaches a certain age. For example, in some societies where natural infant mortality is high, it is only after a period of time (e.g., a year) that children are given names, which establish them as members of the group, entitled to full moral and legal rights. Such societies are not generally more callous than those societies that confer the rights of societal membership upon the newborn. By drawing the line of societal membership at the moment of birth, Feinberg and Benn display, but do not justify, typical contemporary liberal moral sensibilities on the abortion issue. As we have discussed in the section on the rights of animals, advocates of animal rights would contend that these typical moral sensibilities are not nearly as progressive as they ought to be, for if we are to be concerned with callous unconcern for others, we should be concerned with our current treatment of animals as well as with proposals for infanticide. The question of infanticide is indeed troubling, but so should be the question of abortion and the rights of animals. A *principled* advocacy of infanticide need not be a symptom of callousness, but rather can go hand-in-hand with the advocacy of restrictions on abortions and our present treatment of animals. The knife of critical reflection in this matter cuts in more than one direction.

DISCUSSION QUESTIONS

1. Under what conditions, if at all, would you consider (direct) third-trimester abortions morally justifiable? Would you consider infanticide morally justifiable under the same conditions? Would you be willing to grant parents the legal right to abortions and infanticides you consider wrong? How far would you be willing to go in allowing parents the legal right to make their own choices in this area? Consider the following situations:
   a. the fetus has severe brain damage which makes it certain that it will never gain consciousness.
   b. the fetus has severe brain damage which makes it unlikely that it will ever gain consciousness.
   c. the fetus has severe brain damage. Although it will grow to be conscious of its environment, it will suffer from grave physical, emotional, and intellectual retardation and will most certainly require supervision for the remainder of its life.
   d. the fetus has the Down's syndrome genetic disorder (mongoloidism) which will result in mental retardation of uncertain degree. There is no specific reason to believe that it will have any other defects, but a statistically significant number of mongoloid babies are born with other severe defects.
   e. the fetus has a genetic defect which results in Tay-Sachs disease. Although at birth and early childhood, it will develop normally, eventually it will slowly lose muscle control, become blind, deaf, paralyzed, and retarded, and will most likely die by the age of 5. There is *no chance* that it will reach adulthood.
   f. the fetus has a 50 percent chance of developing a painful and crippling neurological disease, accompanied by severe mental retardation that will most likely kill it before it reaches adulthood.
   g. the fetus has no legs and arms, but is otherwise normal.
   h. the fetus is normal, but it is unwanted by its parents who are financially and emotionally incapable of caring adequately for a new child.
   i. the fetus has been discovered by amniocentesis to be developing into a normal female baby. The parents desire an abortion so that they may try again for a boy.

2. According to a Supreme Court decision (*Planned Parenthood v. Danforth*, 1976), a pregnant woman need not get the father's consent before having an abortion performed. Does this seem fair to you? Are there any situations where a man's desire to have and raise his own child should be sufficient to compel a woman not to have an abortion to which she would otherwise be entitled? If not, should the law at least require the woman to inform the father that she is having an abortion?

3. In June 1977 the Supreme Court of the United States ruled that although *Roe v. Wade* gives a woman the unrestricted right to an abortion during the first trimester of her pregnancy, it is constitutional for the states to place restrictions on the use of welfare funds to pay for the abortion of women on Medicaid. Federal law, the Court declared, allows, but does not require, the states to provide elective abortions under their Medicaid plans. There has been much controversy over this ruling. Do you think this ruling was right? Why? What are your reactions to the following argument in defense of this ruling?

During the first trimester of pregnancy, women have a right to obtain an abortion: the state may not make it a crime to perform such abortions. But there is no accompanying right to elective abortion at public expense.

Analogies spring to mind. I have a right of free press. Does this mean that the government must buy me a newspaper? Every citizen has a right to free speech. Must the taxpayers hire him a hall? We have a right to the free exercise of religion. It is not contended that the Treasury must finance churches and synogogues so that the right may conveniently be exercised. There is a right to keep and bear arms. Do we have a right to free rifles?

Let us move closer to the status of those on public welfare. Every indigent person has a right to travel. Such a person may want to visit Hawaii, indeed he may "need" to visit Hawaii; but for want of money it may be difficult or impossible for him to pay his own way. It is fatuous to argue that the taxpayers . . . therefore must buy the indigent a round-trip ticket to Honolulu. Yet, in principle, this is what the petitioning pregnant women have demanded in the abortion cases. (James J. Kilpatrick, *reprinted by permission.*)

4. Although President Bush claims that women should have the legal right to obtain abortions in cases of rape and incest, he is opposed to public funding for abortions in such cases for woman on welfare. Can a coherent justification be given for this position?

5. As this is written, thirty-two states require some form of parental notification in the abortion of minors. The Supreme Court has upheld the constitutionality of such requirements, deferring the issue to the states. For example, in their 1990 term, the Supreme Court upheld by a 6 to 3 vote, a state's requirement that at least one parent be notified, unless the pregnant minor obtains a court ruling that the notification may be bypassed. At the same time, the court upheld, 5 to 4, a Minnesota requirement that both parents must be notified, again with the proviso of a judicial bypass. Indeed 4 of the 5 justices who upheld this requirement would not have required the bypass, even in those cases where a parent does not live with or support the pregnant minor. (Justice O'Connor was the justice who required the bypass.) How would you handle this issue?

6. There have been occasions when doctors have successfully aborted one defective fraternal twin (usually a mongoloid fetus), without harming the normal twin. Nevertheless, such procedures create a risk of an unintended abortion of the normal fetus. How should such cases be handled?

7. About 50 percent of fertilized eggs fail to implant themselves in the uterine wall and are naturally aborted. If a fetus is a person having full moral status, is it not incumbent upon us to attempt to develop methods to reduce this vast number of spontaneous abortions? Yet, if we do, many more severely abnormal children would be born, since abnormal fetuses are considerably less likely to successfully implant than normal ones. Critically discuss.

8. Hemophilia, a genetic disorder characterized by excessive bleeding and diagnosable at birth, affects 50 percent of a female carrier's sons, but not her daughters. While the sex of a fetus is detectable by amniocentesis, this disorder is not. Consequently, many carrier females who choose not to have a hemophiliac son, have amniocentesis and if they are carrying a boy, abort, risking a 50 percent chance of losing a nonaffected son. If abortions are to

be continued to be permitted in such cases, would it be better to allow infanticide, thereby saving nonaffected males? Critically discuss.

9. Consider the following dialogue:

    A: A 3-month-old human fetus is not a person; it's more like a lump of tissue or a human organ. Since it is not a conscious organism at this point, it has no moral worth.

    B: But it looks so human! Just like a little baby! All the organ systems, you know, are already formed. Clearly such a being has moral worth, by virtue of what it is and what it could become. More moral worth than the fetuses of animals and indeed more moral worth than adult animals.

    A: That's pure emotion. I thought we were trying to discuss this issue rationally.

    B: I'm not sure we can. I wonder how rational you are about this matter yourself. Assuming that an aborted 3-month-old human fetus could be prepared as a gourmet's delicacy, would you eat it, the way you eat suckling pigs?

    A: Heavens no!

    B: But why? After all, you say that a 3-month-old human fetus has no moral worth. Is your reaction to the thought of eating a human fetus rational?

    Does *A* have an effective reply?

10. If it were possible to safely remove from its mother's womb and to artificially incubate a fetus that is a month old, in what situations, if at all, should a woman have the right not only to free herself from a dependent fetus but also to have that fetus destroyed?

11. Assuming, as Thomson does, that a fetus is a person, possessing the same moral rights as its mother, what would your reaction be to the following defense of abortion made by a young woman?

    I've been lucky enough to be admitted to medical school in the fall and if I continue with this pregnancy I won't be able to attend and most likely will never have another chance. The impact of having a child will be devastating upon my life prospects. Don't I have a moral right to protect myself against this sort of injury? My fetus is innocent, but so am I; I took every reasonable precaution to avoid getting pregnant. An abortion in a case like mine should be seen as an act of self-defense. If I can protect myself against physical injury, why can't I protect myself from having my life ruined?

12. Some philosophers have attempted to undermine Thomson's argument for the right to an abortion, even in the case of rape, by undermining her anology with the violinist. It has been said, for example, that if one unplugs oneself from the violinist, one has simply *let* the violinist *die,* and has not *killed* him; but in an abortion, the fetus is killed. Others have claimed that while the intent in an abortion is to kill the fetus, this is not the intent in the violinist case. Critically discuss.

13. What do you think of the following argument?

    It is absurd to say that abortion is contrary to the will of God since about two-thirds of conceptions result in natural abortions or stillbirths. If God were opposed to abortions, he would not have allowed nature to work in this manner. Is it not more reasonable to say that God allows natural abortions—such as the natural abortion of a fertilized ovum that is incapable of successfully implanting itself on the uterine wall—as a means of weeding out possible defective organisms. On this analogy, the decision of parents to abort a genetically defective fetus is quite natural.

14. Your author claims that the life of a third-trimester fetus is less valuable than the life of a normal pregnant woman. Underlying his view, is the position that a fetus, however fully developed, should be seen as less of a person than a normal adult human being. Do you agree? If so, does this mode of thinking logically lead to the view that old senile people are not full persons, and that their right to life is consequently less than it was when they were younger? Would you accept such a conclusion?

15. If consciousness is an essential condition of personhood, can any reasonable justification be given for refusing to grant the right to life to fetuses before they become conscious, but to grant this right to adults who are in a dreamless sleep or reversible coma?

16. What do you think of the following argument?

It was right for the Joneses to abort their severely physically deformed fetus several years back. If they hadn't done this, I know they wouldn't have had any more children, and healthy, happy Johnny would never have been born. Certainly, it is better that they waited to have Johnny than to have had a defective child that would not have had the potential for a happy and healthy life that Johnny has.

FURTHER READINGS

Books and Articles

A conservative perspective on the abortion issue is found in chapters 6 and 7 of Germain Grisez, *Abortion: The Myths, The Realities, and the Arguments* (Corpus Books, 1970), which also discusses the factual and historical aspects of abortion. Another conservative view is found in John T. Noonan, Jr., "An Almost Absolute Value in History," which originally appeared in his anthology of essays on the abortion issue, *The Morality of Abortion: Legal and Historical Perspectives* (Harvard University Press, 1970) and has been reprinted in many anthologies. In this clearly written article, Noonan, a law professor with an allegiance to Roman Catholicism, argues that any being with a human genetic code is a human being, and consequently, the destruction of a fetus is morally wrong except when its continued existence threatens its mother's life. All other standards for drawing the line as to the moral status of a fetus, Noonan forcefully argues, are logically arbitrary.

For a contrasting extreme liberal position, one should turn to Michael Tooley whose refined and comprehensive treatment of the abortion issue is found in his 441-page book, *Abortion and Infanticide,* published in 1983 by Oxford University Press. In this book, Tooley develops the theme first expressed in his landmark 1972 article of the same name that appeared in the philosophy journal *Philosophy and Public Affairs* (Vol. 2, No. 1). Tooley's book is quite analytically technical in its consideration of the positions of others and in the depth at which it delves into the thickets of conceptual issues in philosophical psychology and technical science. Fortunately, for the general reader, Tooley clearly and nontechnically summarizes his position at the end of chapter 12, connecting his view of the morality of abortion with the issues of infanticide and the rights of animals.

A clear nontechnical defense of the liberal view that a fetus is not a person, and, consequently, does not have a right to life is found in Mary Anne Warren's "On the Moral and Legal Status of Abortion," which originally appeared in the January 1973 issue of *The Monist* (Vol. 57, no. 1). Distinguishing a biological and moral sense of the concept of a human being, Warren criticizes Noonan's view. She also critically discusses Thomson's view. This article has been reprinted in many anthologies, along with her postscript on infanticide.

Judith Thomson's influential paper on the abortion issue, "A Defense of Abortion," which appears in many anthologies, originally appeared in the very first issue of *Philosophy and Public Affairs* (1971). A stimulating extension of Thomson's perspective is found in Jane English's "Abortion and the Concept of a Person," which first appeared in Vol. V, No. 2 of the *Canadian Journal of Philosophy* (Oct. 1975). Moderating the conservative view, she argues that even if a fetus is a person, abortion can be justified in terms of self-defense when the continuation of the pregnancy will cause the mother "serious" physical, psychological, economic, or social harm. Moderating the liberal view, she claims that even if a fetus is not a person, as its physical resemblance to human persons increases so does its moral value. In the late months of pregnancy, even if a fetus is not a person, she writes, "abortion seems to be wrong except to save a woman from significant injury or death."

A moderate view on the abortion issue anchored in utilitarian theory is presented by L. W. Sumner in his book, *Abortion and Moral Theory* (Princeton Univ. Press, 1981). Dismissing extreme liberal and conservative views, Sumner claims that the threshold of consciousness constitutes the boundary where fetuses obtain moral status. Pre-threshold abortions should be seen as private acts, while post-threshold abortions should be permitted only on therapeutic or eugenic grounds. While the bulk of this book is rather technical, especially in its discussion of ethical theory, Sumner's presentation of his own view in chapter 4 is clear. The beginning student is advised to focus on this chapter, while browsing over the rest.

A skeptical view of the possibility of solving the abortion issue, very much in tune with the viewpoint expressed by your author, is found in Roger Wertheimer's "Understanding the Abortion Argument," which first appeared in Vol. 1, no. 1 (Fall 1971) of *Philosophy and Public Affairs*.

Anthologies

John T. Noonan (ed.), *The Morality of Abortion: Legal and Historical Perspectives* (Harvard University Press, 1970) consists of selections representing theological and generally conservative perspectives on the historical, legal, and moral aspects of abortion.

The most comprehensive collection of material on the moral and legal aspects of the abortion issue is found in Joel Feinberg (ed.), *The Problem of Abortion,* second edition (Wadsworth, 1984). Many of the selections included are analytically technical. Among the less technical ones are selections from Noonan, Sumner, Warren, Thomson, and Wertheimer, all previously mentioned in this bibliography. Also included is an article by Tooley which was written just prior to the publication of his book. Excerpts from the majority opinion and a dissent in *Roe v. Wade* also appear. The anthology begins with a clear introduction by the editor and ends with a comprehensive bibliography.

A less analytically oriented collection of selections is found in Robert L. Perkins' *Abortion: Pro and Con* (Schenkman, 1974) whose editorial introduction contains literary and historical references.

All of the major anthologies on contemporary moral issues have selections on abortion. The one I recommend most for beginning students seeking readable analyses of the abortion issue from diverse viewpoints is Thomas A. Mappes and Jane S. Zembaty (eds..), *Social Ethics,* third edition (McGraw Hill, 1987). Included are the articles from Noonan, Warren, and English that were previously mentioned, and an article by Daniel Callahan defending a moderate view of the abortion issue which criticizes efforts to eliminate the moral tension involved in abortion decisions. Also included are excerpts from the majority opinion and a dissent in *Roe v. Wade,* and Sandra Day O'Connor's dissenting opinion in a 1983 abortion decision in which she takes a skeptical view of the logic of *Roe v. Wade.* Each selection is preceded by a brief editorial introduction and the chapter on abortion itself begins with a good editorial introduction.

James White (ed.), *Moral Problems,* second edition (West, 1988) also contains a good selection of material on the abortion issue, including the writings of Noonan, Warren, Callahan, and English, as well as excerpts from *Roe v. Wade.* It also contains a chapter introduction and introductions to selections. Another good collection is Richard Wasserstrom (ed.), *Today's Moral Problems,* third edition (Macmillan, 1985) but it does not have editorial introductions. It contains the articles by Noonan, Thomson, Warren, and English, and excerpts from Brennan's majority opinion, Douglas' concurrent opinion, and White's dissent in *Roe v. Wade.*

In addition to anthologies on contemporary moral issues, there are many anthologies on medical ethics, all of which have selections on abortion.

General Reference Source

The Encyclopedia of Bioethics (Macmillan, 1978) has a very good entry on abortion by several contributors on medical, religious, and legal aspects of abortion.

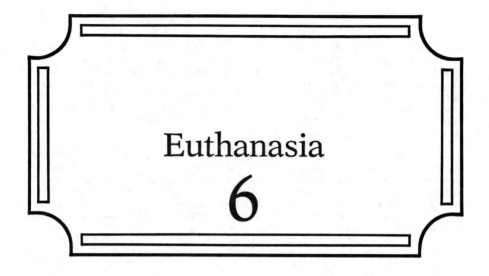

Euthanasia

6

I see there is an instinctive horror of killing living things under any circumstances whatever. For instance, an alternative has been suggested in the shape of confining even rabid dogs in a certain place and allowing them to die a slow death. Now my idea of compassion makes this thing impossible for me. I cannot for a moment bear to see a dog, or for that matter any other living being, helplessly suffering the torture of a slow death. I do not kill a human being thus circumstanced because I have more hopeful remedies. I should kill a dog similarly situated because in its case I am without a remedy. Should my child be attacked with rabies and there was no helpful remedy to relieve his agony, I should consider it my duty to take his life.

MAHATMA GANDHI
Young India
November 18, 1926

THE CONCEPT OF EUTHANASIA

Death inevitably awaits us all. To some it comes unexpectedly and peacefully, while to others it comes in pain and dreadful anticipation. In cases of painful terminal illness or severe physical defect, is it right for human beings to take it upon themselves to choose the moment and mode of death, attempting to make it as painless and dignified as possible? This is the question at the heart of the euthanasia debate.

The concept of euthanasia is used today with varying meanings. In its original Greek meaning, "euthanasia" meant no more than an easy and painless death (*eu* = well; *thanatos* = death) and was later extended to refer to the work of a physician in alleviating as far as possible the suffering of dying. Today, however, "euthanasia" is often used synonymously with that of "mercy killing" and as such entails the bringing about of death. *The American Heritage Dictionary* (1975) defines "euthanasia" as "the action of inducing the painless death of a person for reasons assumed to be merciful." As this definition demonstrates, central to our current concept of euthanasia is the idea that such an action be motivated by a desire to be merciful to or to do good to the recipient. As such, when most people are asked to think of a case of euthanasia they imagine a person who is dying of a painful terminal illness, such as cancer, and is given some lethal drug or injection that is meant to "put him out of his misery."

Is it *euthanasia,* however, if doctors purposely refrain from treating a terminally ill patient in the belief that treatment would merely prolong the agony of dying? Many people would say no. As they use the term, euthanasia must involve some *positive* action; mere *refusals to save* or decisions to *let die,* they would say, are not *acts* of euthanasia. Since the question of the relevance of the active-passive distinction is central to the euthanasia debate, it is best to use the notion of euthanasia broadly to include intentional acts of omission (such as the refusal to connect a person to a respirator) as well as acts of commission (such as giving a patient a fatal injection). Most commentators on the euthanasia issue have made this linguistic decision and consequently distinguish between *active euthanasia* and *passive euthanasia.* Straddling the line between active and passive euthanasia are those actions which involve the termination of life-support measures (such as unplugging a patient from a respirator).

Euthanasia (like abortion) can also be distinguished as *direct*—where the intent is to kill—and *indirect*—where death is not intended but accepted as a by-product of an act motivated by some other concern. For example, it would be indirect euthanasia if a patient died as a result of a massive dose of a narcotic administered not to kill, but to alleviate pain. Since one can intend the death of a person by an act of omission as well as commission, the active-passive distinction cuts across the direct-indirect distinction. In addition, euthanasia can be distinguished as either *voluntary* or *nonvoluntary.* An act of voluntary euthanasia would require the voluntary consent of the recipient, whereas nonvoluntary euthanasia would encompass both those cases where consent cannot be obtained (such as when the patient is comatose) or where euthanasia is applied contrary to the wishes of the recipient (such as euthanasia of the irrational, retarded, and senile).[1] It is only the latter type of nonvoluntary euthanasia which should properly be said to be involuntary, although both are often so described.

While the motive of acting for the sake of the patient is central to our contemporary concept of euthanasia, it is quite questionable that this motive is behind

---

[1] One should note that in cases where consent is denied, it will be very difficult (some would say impossible) to show that the act is a *kindly* one and consequently an act of euthanasia.

the often-made decision not to utilize life-support measures for those in hopeless comas. Yet deaths resulting from such decisions are often cited as examples of euthanasia. If we are to accept this common usage, euthanasia should be defined as an act of inducing or permitting death to occur, when death, if not a benefit, is at least not an evil, to the recipient. (Notice, too, that we have deleted reference to a *painless* death in the preceding definition since individuals who are allowed to die—that is, passive euthanasia—often die in pain.)

MEDICAL AND LEGAL REALITIES

The rapid progress in the development of ever more sophisticated means of life support poses an acute moral dilemma for today's doctors. A generation ago, a patient died when his heart stopped and extraordinary treatment consisted of an injection of adrenalin. Today, however, with the advent of such means as respirators, heart-lung machines, and organ transplants, patients who would otherwise have died, can be kept alive much longer, and maybe before long indefinitely. Given the possibility of prolonging life, doctors must make painful choices. To some, a doctor's hippocratic commitment to the treatment and cure of disease necessitates that he always do all in his power to prolong life. Others, emphasizing instead the hippocratic commitment to the relief of suffering, see the prolongation of life in some cases as nothing more than the futile and cruel prolongation of suffering. Others, of a practical bent, focus upon the vast potential cost of the absolute commitment to the prolongation of human life. Is it worth the immense cost, they wonder, to connect 1,000 people to a respirator for long periods of time when the chances are that only one might—just might—survive? Could not this immense amount of money if spent on medical research be of much greater long-range value to the ideal of lessening human suffering and prolonging human life?

The utilization of passive euthanasia in hospitals is widespread. Physicians routinely decide whether treatments should be applied or life supports utilized or withdrawn. It is common procedure in hospitals, for example, for doctors to indicate (in code) on the charts of terminally ill patients that they should not be resuscitated should their hearts stop beating. In some cases, decisions to withhold treatment are made in a very circuitous manner. For example, instead of unplugging a hopelessly ill person from a respirator, a physician may order that antibiotics not be used if the patient develops some infection, like pneumonia. Wary of the possible legal consequences of their actions or seeking to soothe their own consciences, some doctors employ devious plots to accomplish their benevolent purposes. Instead of switching off the respirator, they may order instead that the oxygen tank not be replaced when empty. Other doctors, hardened by their constant exposure to death and dying, can be quite callous in the choices they make, allowing patients to die whenever the effort to save them becomes personally burdensome.[2]

---

[2]"Do you mind if this patient dies?" the doctor asked of one emergency case. "The respirator's on the fifth floor and the nurse says it's a pain in the ass...." (quoted in *Newsweek,* November 3, 1975, p. 67)

An especially difficult decision that doctors must face is that of withholding treatment from a patient who is unable to express his or her wishes. Such decisions are particularly controversial in the case of infants born with severe mental or physical defects. The decision to withhold treatment from a newborn infant is made most easily in cases of extreme mental defect—the most extreme of which is anencephaly, the complete absence of a cerebral cortex. As Dr. John Freeman of Johns Hopkins put it, "With the best of care they live for only a few months, so many of us believe it is acceptable to withhold feeding and treatment of infections." There have, however, been cases of infants born with severe mental defects whose parents were forced to avail themselves of the lifesaving techniques of medical science. Among these cases was that of David Patrick Houle, who was born without a left eye and ear canal, various neurological disorders, and a stomach disconnected from the esophagus. Admitting that if David should live he probably would be blind, deaf, palsied, and might never have gained consciousness "as we know consciousness," the hospital in which he was born sued his parents after they refused to allow corrective surgery. Siding with the hospital, the Maryland court ordered the operation, saying that parents "have no right to withhold such treatment and that to do so constitutes neglect in the legal sense. The basic right enjoyed by every human being is the right to life itself." The surgery, which consisted of the implantation of a food tube in David's stomach, was performed. A second operation, to connect the baby's esophagus to his stomach, was to have been performed, but David died—15 days after he was born.

Courts have also ordered corrective surgery in cases of mongoloid infants (Down's syndrome). Many of these infants are born with gastrointestinal or cardiac defects that would be fatal unless surgically repaired. Although doctors have often accepted parents' decisions not to operate in such cases, there is growing opposition to this practice and court cases have resulted. Of course, for each court case, there are countless noncontested decisions that parents and doctors make every day. Many infants whose potentiality for normal mental development is unimpaired are refused medical treatment for physical abnormalities which are capable of surgical correction. Dr. Jordan Weitzman of the University of Southern California School of Medicine recalls the case of a child born with no genitals, intestines, or bladder who was left to die even though his condition was treatable. According to Weitzman, "Nobody said a word." This was so, he reflects, "because we live in an era of the Body Beautiful, so the sight of a kid with almost nothing below the waist gave everybody pause."

There is much controversy among doctors on the appropriate treatment for infants born with spina bifida—an opening in the spine. In serious cases, (about 2 per 1,000 live births), the infant is born with a protruding unclosed sac in the lower back which contains nerve tissue and cerebrospinal fluid. As a consequence of the spinal cord deformity, the infant has no bladder and bowel control and is usually paralyzed from the waist down. Such infants are also often born with hydrocephalus (water on the brain) which, if not treated, will lead to severe mental retardation. For some doctors, the appropriate medical response to such unfortunate infants is aggressive medical intervention, including many operations. Yet even with such vigorous intervention, more than 50 percent of such children die before they are 16, and some are even made worse by complications of surgical intervention. Those who survive usually have low IQ's and face the pitiful prospect of continued operations, full or partial paralysis, severe problems of incontinence, and recurring urinary infections. Furthermore, such children tend to create great strain on their families. In many cases, their parents forgo having further children so that they can devote themselves more fully to their defective child. Focusing on the personal cost of aggressive medical intervention, some doctors strongly advocate doing nothing. As they see it, it is better for both the spina bifida child and its parents for "nature to take its course" in such cases. With no medical intervention, they point out, approximately 90 percent of such children will die before their first birthday. On the other hand, advocates of aggressive medical intervention point to the fact that the 10 percent that do survive without intervention will usually have a much lower quality of life as a result of not being treated. Furthermore, while most treated infants face the bleak prospect of retarded intellectual development and gross physical defects, not all do. If we are to do nothing to help children born with severe spina bifida, other doctors have pondered, would it not be kinder to directly kill them? If nature is to be allowed to take its course, they ask, is it not best that nature be helped to take her course more quickly? Other doctors focus on the vast economic cost of treatment for such children and ponder over its social utility. How, so many doctors wonder, are we to weigh the unclear and conflicting demands of morality in such cases?

As we turn from the nonvoluntary euthanasia of the newborn to the voluntary and nonvoluntary euthanasia of adults, we also find great controversy. For example, state courts have taken conflicting positions on the right of patients to refuse lifesaving treatments. While the courts have generally respected competent adults' wishes that treatment be withheld in their own cases, they have not always done so. Nevertheless the trend of cases is moving in this direction. Such a trend is supported by the American Medical Association, which takes the position that doctors should be allowed to withhold medical treatment, including food and water, from competent terminally ill patients who request it and from the irreversibly comatose, when this is requested by their family. Such sentiments were echoed by a commission authorized by President Reagan to make recommendations concerning legislation related to medical ethics. In several states laws have been passed allowing competent adults to authorize someone to act as their proxy in decisions relating to treatment, including the withholding of treatment, should they become incompetent to do so themselves.[3] With or without prior authorization to withhold treatment, the trend of legal decisions in the U.S. reflects the AMA's stance. For example, in the widely publicized case of comatose 21-year-old Karen Quinlan, the New Jersey Court allowed Karen's doctors, with the consent of Karen's parents, to disconnect her from a respirator. Although she was expected to die as a result, she lingered on for 10 years, while being fed intravenously. In spite of the difference many feel between intravenous feeding and artificial respirators, in California

---

[3]The legal instrument for accomplishing this is called a "durable power of attorney for health matters."

the legal right to stop food and water for adult patients was recognized in 1983 in a case in which two physicians were cleared of murder charges for halting intravenous feeding of a comatose patient who had already been disconnected from a respirator.

In spite of the widespread belief that relatives should be allowed to act as proxys in decisions to cease treatment of the comatose, the Supreme Court, in its first venture into the issue of the right to die, ruled in July 1990 that there is no constitutionally protected right for such proxy decisions. The case at issue involved a young Missouri woman, Nancy Cruzan who, as a result of an automobile accident, persisted for seven years in "a persistent vegetative state." Speaking for a 5 to 4 majority, Chief Justice Rehnquist regretfully rejected Nancy's parents' plea, already rejected by the state of Missouri, that Nancy be disconnected from an abdominal food tube and allowed to die. Nevertheless, Rehnquist did accept a constitutionally protected right for a patient to refuse treatment. Denying that this right derives from an implicit constitutionally protected right to privacy which the Supreme Court had used in the Roe v. Wade abortion decision, Rehnquist derived this right from the due-process clause of the Fourteenth Amendment which proclaims that states may not "deprive any person of life, liberty or property without due process of law." Given the long legal tradition of protecting people from unwanted incursions upon their bodies (the crime of *battery*) "a competent person has a constitutionally protected liberty interest in refusing unwanted medical treatment," Rehnquist declared. In this pronouncement, Rehnquist had the support of all the justices but Scalia, who, consistent with his position in the Webster abortion case, declared that the federal courts "have no business in this field." The rub for Nancy's parents was that the Rehnquist majority was unwilling to grant relatives the right to substitute their judgments for a comatose person, lacking "clear and convincing evidence," to be determined by the individual states, that this would have been the patient's desire. While Rehnquist refrained from imposing a limitation on a state's right to impose its judgment of the best interests of a patient and its general "interest in the preservation of life" over the objections of family members who claim to be better judges of their relatives interests, O'Connor, in her concurrence, indicated her willingness to accept a comatose person's previously expressed wishes in a living will or durable power of attorney.[4] Adding her vote to that of the four dissenters, there was then a clear majority for this position. The dissenters would have gone further. As they saw it, lacking any specific evidence to the contrary, relatives, and not the state, are the best judges of a patient's wishes and interests, the decisive issue in cases involving medical treatment. As O'Connor saw it, however, further extensions of the right to die should be worked out by legislators in "the 'laboratory' of the states."

[4]A *living will* is the notion used to refer to a signed statement indicating one's wish to be allowed to die in certain situations. It is typically formulated in very general terms, requesting that *mechanical,* or *artificial,* or *heroic* life-support measures be withheld or discontinued in *terminal conditions* or when there is *no hope of recovery*. Since such claims are subject to varying interpretations, they do not provide clear guidance. To avoid such uncertainty, more specific living wills are available. For example, Harvard Medical School ethicist Linda Emanuel has published a detailed document which requires individuals to check 48 boxes specifying exactly what treatments they would desire under specific circumstances.

The message that emerged from the Supreme Court's decision in the Cruzan case is that Americans should determine their feelings about the right to die and either attempt as best they can to anticipate under what conditions they would prefer to be allowed to die, or, since all such situations cannot be anticipated, delegate someone else to act as one's proxy in situations of mental incapacity. The fact that most people, understandably, put such unpleasant matters off or that the educated and affluent are more likely to do this than the uneducated and poor was left unaddressed by the court. While the legal trend in this country has been to respect competent adults' wishes to be allowed to die, the courts have often intervened to ensure that minors be given lifesaving treatments in spite of their own and their parents' objections, even when based on religious grounds. For example, the courts have intervened against Jehovah's Witnesses who have refused blood transfusions for their children. The courts are, however, united in their opposition to active euthanasia (mercy killing) which is legally classified as an unjustifiable homicide. Nevertheless, there have only been two cases of doctors coming to trial in the United States for active euthanasia. In 1949, Dr. Hermann Sander of New Hampshire was accused of injecting air into the veins of a cancer patient and, in 1973, Dr. Vincent A. Montemaro of New York was charged with giving a cancer patient a lethal dose of potassium chloride. Sympathetic juries acquitted both.

There have been about a dozen cases of lay individuals being brought to trial for the active (both voluntary and nonvoluntary) euthanasia of relatives. In the majority of these cases, the defendant was either acquitted or found temporarily insane by jurors who were guided more by their sympathies than by the law. While jurors in the U.S. often are forced by their sympathies for the defendant to ignore the law in euthanasia cases, many European countries, unlike the U.S., permit a reduction of the level of homicide in mercy killings, allowing, in most cases, for a suspended sentence. The Uraguayan penal code is more direct, allowing the motive of mercy to be a complete excuse to homicide in certain cases. According to this code, "The judges are authorized to forgo punishment of a person whose previous life has been honorable where he commits a homicide motivated by compassion, induced by repeated requests of the victim." Active euthanasia is also legally condoned in Holland. As this is being written, the Dutch government is expected to propose legislation to formally legalize euthanasia, absorbing into statute law, practices that are now permitted by the Dutch courts.

Although there are probably many physicians in the United States who have participated in active euthanasia, there are many more who use circuitous methods of avoiding this charge. Many, for example, administer increasing doses of narcotics to terminally ill patients with the full knowledge and intention that the drug will not only relieve pain, but will also kill. Sometimes, doctors simply leave pills for patients with the warning, "I have something for your pain. If you take too much, it will be harmful," allowing the patient to make his own deicison. Dr. Joel Posner of Pennsylvania describes the case of a man on a respirator who was so sick that the respirator tube would slip out of his throat several times a day, causing him to turn blue from near suffocation. Seeing the man's suffering, Posner decided that further care on the respirator was pointless and that it would be better for him if he died. Although Posner would have had no legal problem if he simply turned off the respirator, he perceived this course of action as a cruel one since it might take the patient a half a day of choking before he died. Since morphine to put him to sleep and suppress his respiration would be active euthanasia, Posner decided to turn off the respirator, while administering pure oxygen to the patient. The effect was the same, yet, as Posner puts it, "somehow more legal."

THE RELIGIOUS CASE AGAINST EUTHANASIA

Suicide

While, as we shall see, liberal euthanasia policies have been rejected on the basis of their alleged dangerous consequences (disutility), the most forceful, and historically most influential, objections to euthanasia come from the traditional Judeo-Christian condemnation of suicide as a grave sin. Some religions and societies, however, have perceived certain suicides as honorable and brave actions. The Greeks and Romans took this view as do many Eastern religions. Actions such as "suttee" in which a wife throws herself on the funeral pyre of her dead husband and "hara-kiri" invest suicide with honor and embellish it with ritualistic dignity.

Stoic and Epicurean philosophers of the ancient world considered the choice of the time and mode of one's own death as the ultimate expression of human freedom, dignity, and rationality. For example, the Roman stoic Seneca (4 B.C.?–65 A.D.) wrote,

> As I choose the ship in which I will sail and the house I will inhabit, so I will choose the death by which I leave life. In no matter more than in death should we act according to our own desire. . . .
> If I can choose between a death of torture and one that is simple and easy, why should I not select the latter? Why should I endure the agonies of disease when I can emancipate myself from all my torture? I will not depart by death from disease as long as it may be healed and leaves my mind unimpaired, but if I know that I will suffer forever, I will depart, not through fear of pain itself, but because it prevents all for which I live.

Western religion's condemnation of suicide can be traced to the conception that we are God's property and that the physical world we briefly inhabit is a testing ground provided by God for the development of our moral virtue. As such, we have no right to take it upon ourselves to leave this world and consequently to leave unfinished the tasks God intends for us. In the words of the philosopher John Locke,

> . . .men being all the workmanship of one omnipotent and infinitely wise Maker; all the servants of one sovereign Master, sent into the world by His order and about

His Business; they are His property, whose workmanship they are made to last during His, not another's pleasure.... Every one... is bound to preserve himself, and not to quit his station willfully....

Kant echoes the same sentiments, writing,

We have been placed in this world under certain conditions and for specific purposes. But a suicide opposes the purpose of his creator; he arrives in the other world as one who has deserted his post.... Human beings are sentinels on earth and may not leave their posts....

Relating such sentiments directly to the euthanasia issue, a contemporary Catholic writes,

...euthanasia is murder and as such can never be permitted... it must be resolutely refused to the sick person... however intense his suffering, however small the hope of recovery. God alone is lord over life and death. It is not God's will and is neither permitted to us mortals, nor indeed possible for us, to strip death of all its terror and pain; death is meant to be the last and greatest test we have to undergo here on earth.

Such statements have been reaffirmed by the present pope, John Paul II, who claims that the suffering of the terminally ill is "an unavoidable element of the human condition" and part of "God's saving plan." These sentiments are unconvincing and cruel in their implications. If one consistently believed that all life's sufferings are a necessary part of an omnipotent and benevolent God's plan, would it not follow that all human attempts to alleviate suffering are an unjustified interference with that plan?[5] If we say, with the mainstream of Western religious thought, that it is God's will that we alleviate suffering, how can one be convinced that God totally prohibits human beings from "quitting their stations" when life offers them nothing but suffering? How can anyone who has witnessed the slow, painful, and hopeless physical and mental wasting away of a human being plausibly claim that in such cases the victim is undergoing his last and greatest test. What is the point of such a test and what is required to "pass" it?

If God condemns all suicides, he should have good reasons for his condemnation. But one can search in vain through the writings of Locke and Kant for plausible reasons for this condemnation. The first sustained Christian condemnation of suicide can be traced back to Saint Augustine (354–430) who claimed that such action was a violation of the divine Commandment that "thou shalt not kill." Historically, Augustine's stand against suicide can be seen as a reaction to the suicidal tendencies of many Christians of his day. Given Christian theology, such tendencies were quite understandable. Since, for the Christian, this world was

---

[5]This sort of reasoning has been used by those who have opposed the use of anesthetics and other medical treatment. Since God has made us suffer, they argue, such suffering must be essential for some greater good and consequently any alleviation of that suffering, while immediately beneficial, is bound, in the long run, to be detrimental. Believers in an all-powerful, all-knowing, and perfectly good God must give some plausible reason why God would approve of our alleviation of suffering, while he himself allows this suffering to exist. This sort of question poses a serious challenge to the traditional Judeo-Christian God.

merely preparatory for the afterlife, providing a moral testing ground to sort out those who would ultimately go to heaven or to hell, the supreme personal aim for each Christian was to assure that he pass this test. Since the way to accomplish this end was by avoiding sin, and since the world and one's natural desires made it all too easy to sin, many Christians committed suicide for fear of succumbing to temptation. Some accomplished this by purposely provoking infidels to martyr them, while others did it more directly by casting themselves from cliffs. If suicide were not itself ruled out as a sin, Augustine recognized, such action would be quite reasonable. Indeed, the most logical course of action for those singularly bent on assuring their own place in heaven would be to commit suicide right after a sin-cleansing baptism. Augustine's assumption that there was an absolute divine prohibition of suicide served to deny the validity of this line of reasoning.

The most influential Christian condemnation of suicide is found in the following passage from the Medieval philosopher Saint Thomas Aquinas's (1225?-1274) *Summa Theologica:*

> It is altogether unlawful to kill oneself, for three reasons. First, because everything naturally loves itself, the result being that everything naturally keeps itself in being. . . . Wherefore suicide is contrary to the inclination of nature. . . . Hence suicide is always a mortal sin, as being contrary to the natural law. Secondly, because every part . . . belongs to the whole. Now every man is part of the community, and so, as such, he belongs to the community. Hence by killing himself he injures the community. . . . Thirdly, because life is God's gift to man, and is subject to His power, Who kills and makes to live. Hence whoever takes his own life sins against God, . . . as he who usurps himself judgment of a matter not entrusted to him. For it belongs to God alone to pronounce sentence of death and life.

We have already touched upon the inadequacy of Aquinas's third reason. If, as Aquinas claims, only God can rightfully decide when a human life should come to an end, could not one argue as well that one is usurping God's province when one decides to prolong one's life as well as to shorten it? Such a view, as Hume pointed out in his essay "Of Suicide," would imply that "If I turn aside a stone which is falling on my head, I disturb the course of nature and I invade the peculiar province of the Almighty by lengthening out my life beyond the period, which. . .he has assigned to it." In addition, one can construct an argument for the morality of suicide which is analogous to Aquinas's, as the Roman scholar Pliny (23-79) did. As Pliny put it, the existence of poisonous herbs with which one may so easily kill oneself, is a benevolent gift from God. Clearly, Aquinas would reject such a view, claiming that we are usurping the province of God when we act to shorten our life but not when we act to preserve it. As Aquinas would see it, God gives us life, an instinct for survival, and a moral injunction that it is wrong to take one's life. When, despite our efforts, he takes us, it is his doing, not ours; but when we fail to avert danger, etc., it is our abuse. This is, however, simply a statement of a position, and not an argument for it.

The same is true of Aquinas's contention that suicide is contrary to natural law. Taken literally, all suicides would appear to be refutations of Aquinas's claim that everything naturally keeps itself in being. At any rate, Aquinas would not say that we ought always to do what we are most strongly inclined to do. (Consider in this context the Catholic requirement that priests be celibate.) Like all natural law theorists, Aquinas is selective in choosing which inclinations are natural, utilizing this concept in an evaluative way which equates it with proper inclinations. But lacking a means of identifying proper human inclinations apart from the alleged commands of God, Aquinas's first reason reduces itself to his third, which is itself anchorless.

Aquinas's second reason is a purely secular one based on a person's moral obligation not to injure his community. Yet Aquinas does not tell us how suicide injures a community. Although a person may have a moral obligation to tolerate great personal suffering if this is a necessary condition for the fulfillment of a specific social obligation, it would appear absurd to say that all suicides injure the community as Aquinas (echoing Aristotle) declares. While many suicides are selfish actions which cause great suffering to those who loved the suicide victim, it can by no stretch of the imagination be reasonably claimed that most suicides hurt society as a whole in any appreciable way.

Aquinas's classic discussion of suicide in the *Summa Theologica* also suffers from his failure to settle on a clear definition of this concept. In this discussion, Aquinas seems to be employing a broad definition of suicide as intentionally doing or omitting to do something that results in one's death, either with the desire that one die or the knowledge that one's death is a very likely consequence of this action which is chosen as a means to some other end. If this definition is accepted, however, all acts of heroic self-sacrifice would become instances of suicide. For example, a soldier who sacrifices his life for his comrades, a spy who swallows a lethal pill in order not to divulge vital information under torture, and a person who steers his automobile over a cliff and toward his almost certain death in order to avoid killing a group of children in its path, would all have to count as suicides under this definition. Aquinas seems willing to accept the characterization of such acts as suicidal and hence unjustified, for he does explicitly claim that the heroic self-sacrifice of Samson was a suicide and was not a sin only because he was acting under a command of God. While Aquinas seems unbending in his characterization of acts of heroic self-sacrifice as suicides which can be justified only by command of God, he does not take the same line in his subsequent discussion of the morality of killing the innocent. In this discussion, Aquinas employs the principle of double effect that has been an integral part of Christian moral thinking, with its roots in natural law theory. Contemporary religious moralists, utilizing the doctrine of the double effect would define "suicide" more narrowly as an act whose direct intention is the taking of one's life; as such Samson's act would be described as a nonsuicidal one since his direct intention (purpose) was not to take his life, but to thwart the actions of his enemies. As we have seen, however, the distinction between direct and indirect intention is unclear.

While one should approach the question of the morality of suicide with an open mind that allows for the possibility that some acts of suicide may turn out to be rational, justifiable, and praiseworthy, many religious moralists approach this question burdened by the unchallengeable dogma that suicide is wrong. They may try, as Aquinas did, to argue for such a view, but, ultimately, they accept it on faith. Yet, like the rest of us, there are acts of heroic self-sacrifice that they want to praise (such as Samson's act). So they either turn to unverifiable assumptions as to God's commands in particular situations, as Aquinas did, or attempt to find some definition of suicide that makes the actions they want to praise non-suicidal, and hence not subject to automatic censure. The principle of the double effect is supposed to do that job, but it doesn't do it well. For example, religious moralists, like the rest of us, tend to recoil at the thought of censuring the brave action of Captain Oates, a member of Robert Scott's last fatal expedition to the South Pole, who walked into the Antarctic snow to die because his frostbitten legs made him a life-threatening handicap to the rest of Scott's party. As Scott himself wrote of Oates in his journal,

> He slept through the night. . .hoping not to wake; but he woke in the morning. . . .It was blowing a blizzard. He said, "I am just going outside and may be some time." He went out in the blizzard. . . .We knew that poor Oates was walking to his death, but although we tried to dissuade him, we knew it was the act of a brave man. . .

Did Oates commit suicide? Some moralists have said no. He did not kill himself, they say, the blizzard did. Since he did not directly intend his death, his act is not a suicide. But is this true? Clearly, Oates knew that his act would lead to his death and this is precisely what he chose as a means of freeing his comrades from the burden he created. He knew his action would cause his death as much as a self-inflicted series of bullets to his head. Yet the same moralists would feel compelled to describe Oates's action as a suicide if he shot himself and hence would feel compelled to morally condemn it. But the blizzard is supposed to be different. If one says that the difference resides in whether Oates walked into the blizzard desiring to die or simply to separate himself from his comrades, the reality is probably that he desired both, for why would he want to prolong his walk to death?

Euthanasia: Killing and Letting Die

As we turn from western religion's general condemnation of suicide to its more specific condemnation of euthanasia, one surprisingly finds that the distinction between direct and indirect killing, which plays a central role in religiously oriented discussions of the morality of self-induced death is left in the background, while the distinction between active and passive killing becomes the focus of discussion. At its simplest, the claim has been made that while active euthanasia is never justified, passive euthanasia (allowing to die), where essential life suport is not offered, can be justified. In such cases, it is said, the *cause* of death is not a human action, but the disease or condition from which the victim suffers. This simple characterization is inadequate. In some cases an *intentional* omission which results in death can be seen as an *act* that *causes* death, no less than an intentional shooting or poisoning, and consequently one's moral responsibility for deaths resulting from acts of omission are not necessarily less than those from acts of commission. For example, the decision to refuse feeding a newborn baby should be described strongly as an *act of killing* the infant and not one of merely *permitting it to die*. No justification can be given for claiming that one is less responsible for the death of a child through starvation than through a lethal injection, if in both cases one acts or omits to act with the intention that the child die. Indeed, since death is as inevitable through starvation as through a lethal injection, it is morally better to give the injection since this is much quicker and less distressful to the infant.

The distinction between *killing by some positive action* and *refusing to save by some omission* also proves inadequate as a morally relevant distinction in those cases of euthanasia involving a decision to terminate an already initiated life-support measure. A doctor, for example, who unplugs a respirator from a pain-racked terminally ill patient has certainly *done* something. Yet when death follows such an action, many of us refuse to describe the doctor's action as one of *killing* his patient. No, we tend to say, the doctor did not *kill* his patient, his underlying condition did that; the doctor simply decided no longer to try to *save him* and *let him die*. Clearly, the fact that the doctor did rather than omitted to do something plays no part in the widespread hesitancy to describe his action in the active terms of killing rather than the passive terms of letting die or not saving.

Most of us recognize that there is no justification for giving a doctor the right to refuse to connect a patient to a respirator and to refuse him the right to disconnect a patient already so connected. It would be absurd to suggest that if respirators, by some chance, required periodic recharging, a doctor would have the right in certain circumstances not to recharge the respirator—an omission— but would not have the right in the same circumstances to unplug a continuously operating respirator—an action. Seeing no morally relevant difference in such actions and omissions, we describe them equally as instances of refusals to save individuals or of letting them die, and not as instances of killing them. As commonly used in the context of the euthanasia issue, the notion of *allowing to die* or *refusing to save* may involve something other than a failure to act. Just as we tend to describe the act of unplugging a respirator as one of refusing to save rather than of killing, so we tend in certain circumstances to call the act of moving a patient out of an intensive care unit a refusal to save rather than an act of killing even though we may well know that such an action is bound to result in a patient's death. In spite of the element of *action* in these cases, we tend to classify them as *refusals to treat* patients rather than as *acts of killing* them. Although doctors have a moral obligation, we tend to believe, to provide *ordinary* assistance to their patients (such as feeding a newborn baby), they do not have a moral obligation to render *extraordinary* (or *heroic*) assistance in all cases. Since we consider doctors responsible for providing *ordinary* assistance, when it is not provided we describe that failure to act as one of *killing*. On the other hand, when the failure to act is one of not providing *extraordinary* assistance, we tend to call it an act of *not saving* or *letting die,* and attribute whatever deaths result from such failures to act to the patient's underlying condition rather than to the action or omission of the physician.

It is this often invoked distinction between ordinary and extraordinary or heroic means of life support that the late Pope Pius XII relied upon in his influential discussion of the euthanasia issue in a speech before a group of doctors and medical students. The Pope claimed that while we have no moral right to omit the utilization of ordinary means of life support (and to do so would be equivalent to killing), we do have such a right when it comes to extraordinary life-support measures (and to refuse to use such measures is not killing, but simply permitting to die). In explaining the meaning of an extraordinary lifesaving measure, the Pope claimed that such a measure is one that "cannot be obtained or used without excessive expense, pain, or other inconvenience for the patient or for others, or which, if used, would not offer a reasonable hope of benefit to the patient." The Pope's distinction between ordinary and extraordinary life-support is widely utilized in discussions of the morality of euthanasia. Yet the meaning of the key concepts in this widely used distinction are usually left without clarification. The key notions here are "excessive inconvenience" and "reasonable hope of benefit to the patient." To begin with, we should notice that if the Pope's statement is taken literally, one has no obligation to avail oneself of means which *either* are excessively inconvenient *or* do not provide a reasonable hope of benefit to the patient.

Let us now consider each of these two key notions separately. First, the notion of "reasonable benefit to the patient" is open to both liberal and conservative analyses. To those who support a liberal euthanasia policy, any life-support measure that leaves a patient without a meaningful or dignified life would qualify as being without benefit. On the other hand, to the very conservative, any measure which improved any condition or disease from which the patient suffers in however limited a degree could count as a benefit. Without any clarification as to what is to count as "a reasonable benefit to a patient," the use of this notion does not offer any guidance. The same can be said of the other key notion, "excessive inconvenience." Although the cost and potential pain a lifesaving method may entail are indeed factors that we implicitly use in our determination of its excessiveness, it would seem that the condition of the patient and certainty and scope of the effect of the treatment are also relevant to whether a lifesaving measure ought to be used. Certainly, most of us would feel a strong moral obligation to use expensive and inconvenience-causing methods that are likely to enable a person to live a normal or close-to-normal life and would for that reason alone hesitate to call it an extraordinary life-support measure. At any rate, what is to count as an excessive means of life-support cannot be determined without first determining what is to count as a reasonable benefit—i.e., the two clauses of the principle are logically interdependent and implicitly evaluative in nature.

It is important to realize that while such factors as the cost, scarcity, probable pain, certainty, scope of result, and possible side effects of a treatment are all relevant in judging the extraordinariness of that treatment, reasonable people can weigh these factors differently. The description of a treatment as extraordinary does not justify our judgment that doctors have no moral obligation to utilize it, but rather is often used as a mere vehicle for expressing that judgment. As often utilized, "an extraordinary treatment" simply means "a treatment that we have no moral obligation to provide." When so used, the claim that "we have no moral obligation to provide extraordinary treatments" is a mere tautology. We do not tend to first decide whether a mode of treatment involves ordinary or extraordinary measures, without the utilization of any moral considerations, and then use this nonmoral determination as the standard for justifying the imputation of moral obligation. On the contrary, our decision as to the standards to be utilized in determining what is to count as an extraordinary as opposed to ordinary life-support measure is often itself based upon some moral judgment. For example, the decision as to whether or not intravenous feeding of terminally ill patients should count as extraordinary treatment involves taking some moral stand as to what one ought to do in such circumstances.

In addition to the implicit moral judgments that often go into the determination of whether a given mode of treatment in a given situation is extraordinary, it is important to realize that for many a mode of behavior is considered extraordinary only when it is perceived as something which interferes *artificially* with the familiar pattern of events. As such, the perception of a medical technique as being extraordinary tends to vary inversely with one's exposure to that technique and its availability. Years ago, antibiotics were widely perceived as extraordinary since they were a new introduction into the arsenal of medical treatments. Today respirators and dialysis (kidney) machines may be considered as such by laypersons, but are less apt to be considered so by physicians who are more used to them. In the future, especially if their cost goes down relative to newer methods, they will tend to be seen as ordinary and the newer methods as extraordinary. There is no reason, however, to believe that the ever-shifting popular conception of which specific treatments are extraordinary and which are ordinary is at all a coherent one from a moral point of view. For example, people appear to classify mechanical devices, such as respirators and dialysis machines, as extraordinary much more readily than they do drugs; there is no good reason, however, to believe that such a distinction can provide a rational basis for distinguishing those treatments that ought to be utilized from those that need not be.

As we have seen, the commonly invoked distinctions between killing and letting die and between ordinary and extraordinary life-support measures are quite unclear. Although one can attempt to clarify them in a manner that makes them morally relevant, these distinctions cloud the moral waters rather than clear them. As our discussion of existing medical practice indicates, doctors attempting to adhere to these notions often act in circuitous ways for which no moral justification can be given. For example, it seems the height of moral insensitivity to claim that Posner would have been morally justified in unplugging the respirator from the terminally ill patient, but not in giving him the morphine, *even if his intention in both cases was exactly the same.* Clearly, if in both cases, Dr. Posner's intent was to shorten life, than the only morally relevant distinction is that the giving of morphine is kinder and, as such, morally preferable. Similarly, if one is motivated by a desire that a terminal patient die as quickly as possible and not suffer the anguish of a slow death, is it not cruel and morally pointless to avoid directly giving the patient a wanted injection that will peacefully kill him but to wait instead until he inevitably contracts some infection and then not treat it, if the only reason for refusing to treat the infection is a desire that the patient die?

The only reasonable moral basis for allowing Posner to unplug the respirator but not to kill with morphine comes not from the active-passive distinction but from a consideration of Dr. Posner's motives. Since considerations of autonomy lead us to grant a patient a right to refuse intrusive medical intervention, if Dr. Posner unplugged the respirator, not to kill, but in response to the pleas of his patient (or his family or legal surrogate), one would be inclined to say that the patient's condition rather than Dr. Posner was responsible for the death that ensued. Similarly, if Posner unplugged the respirator with the sole purpose of alleviating pain, and merely accepted death as an inevitable byproduct of his action, we again would be inclined to say that the patients' condition, and not Dr. Posner, was responsible for the patient's death. Consequently, the distinction between the direct and indirect intentions of one's act seems to play the key role here, not that between acts of commission or omission.

In the United States and Great Britain today, there are facilities called hospices for the terminally ill which are committed to passive euthanasia but which shun active euthanasia. A spokesman for the idea of hospices, Dr. Richard Lamerton of Great Britain, was in Los Angeles in April of 1976. Lamerton is reported by the *Los Angeles Times* (April 21) to have told an audience of health professionals at the U.C.L.A. School of Public Health that regular hospitals do not treat terminally ill patients appropriately. Giving an example of the appropriate treatment for a terminally ill patient, Lamerton related the case of a young man with cancer of the neck who suddenly hemorrhaged because the cancer had eroded the tissues in his neck and had exposed a major blood vessel. Most doctors and nurses would have attempted to stop the bleeding, but, according to Lamerton, such care would have been inappropriate. Stopping the bleeding would not alter the patient's terminal condition and the hemorrhaging would inevitably have recurred within a few days, causing the patient and his wife to face the ordeal a second time. The correct treatment, Lamerton claimed, was to cover the patient with a blanket so that nobody would see the bleeding and to sit with him until he died. As I read this in the *Times,* my immediate reaction was to wonder how long the bleeding would take, hoping that the ruptured blood vessel was indeed a major one and that death would be rapid. As I thought about this case, I had a morbid picture in my mind of a man slowly bleeding to death and of some nurse routinely changing the blankets. Fortunately, in this case, death would most likely come peaceably as the patient slowly loses consciousness from the loss of blood. But what of those cases where refusals to treat prolong the agony of death? It is precisely at this point that Lamerton's implicit premise that doctors should never actively kill through a lethal injection will be challenged by advocates of euthanasia, who challenge the moral relevance of the often invoked distinction between killing and letting die.

For example, consider the notorious case at John Hopkins of an infant born with Down's syndrome and duodenal atresia (a closure in the upper part of the small intestine). While the atresia could have been corrected easily surgically, the child's parents refused and the infant was allowed to slowly starve to death over a period of 15 days. Clearly, such an action was an evil to the poor child and as such was not an act of euthanasia. But leaving aside this linguistic point, and assuming that parents should be given the legal right to refuse treatments for certain congenital defects of their mongoloid offspring, is it not clear that when such a refusal will cause a slow, painful, and inevitable death, morality demands that we make death quick and painless through active euthanasia?

If the distinction between killing and letting die does not serve as an adequate moral guide in the euthanasia issue, why then are these distinctions so commonly invoked? No doubt, there is a psychological factor involved here. People simply do not *feel* as responsible for their omissions as they do for their actions. This feeling is capable of a general justification. Any practical morality must limit one's sphere of responsibility and hold people to higher standards of responsibility within their special spheres. While one can encourage and praise people for helping those to whom they are not bound by special responsibilities, it is too much to morally require individuals to render aid to others in all situations where the principle of utility would require it. An important way we attempt to limit people's responsibilities to others is by drawing a distinction between one's responsibilities for acts and for omissions—a moral distinction that is also reflected in the law. For example, while Jones has a legal obligation not to strike Smith, unless he has some special responsibility toward Smith he generally has no legal obligation in our society to render him aid. Indeed, this would be true even *if* Jones knew that rendering that aid would require no effort or sacrifice on his part and that without it Smith would die. Although practically all of us would consider such an omission morally reprehensible, we do not make it punishable. This is not unreasonable, however, for if the law accepted a general obligation to render aid to strangers in need, such an obligation might prove too vague and diffuse to be practical. As one group of British legal commentators put it,

> It is true that the man who, having abundance of wealth, suffers a fellow creature to die of hunger at his feet, is a bad man—a worse man, probably, than many of those for whom we have provided very severe punishment. But we are unable to see where, if we make such a man legally punishable, we can draw the line. If the rich man who refuses to save a beggar's life at the cost of a little copper is a murderer, is the poor man just one degree above beggary also to be a murderer if he omits to invite the beggar to partake of his hard earned rice? Again: if the rich man is a murderer for refusing to save the beggar's life at the cost of a little copper, is he also to be a murderer if he refuses to save the beggar's life at the cost of a thousand rupees? . . .
>
> It is indeed most highly desirable that men should not merely abstain from doing harm to their neighbours, but should render active services to their neighbours. In general, however, the penal law must content itself with keeping men from doing positive harm and must leave to public opinion, and to the teachers of morality and religion, the office of furnishing men with motives for doing positive good. It is evident that to attempt to punish men by law for not rendering to others all the services which it is in their duty to render to others would be preposterous.

Given such considerations, the law attempts to limit a person's obligation to "be his brother's keeper." In general, the law says that we have obligations to render aid only to those to whom we stand in special relationships of responsibility—such as our children, parents, spouses, charges, and those whom we have harmed. For example, our "callous passerby," Roger Smith, in our list of moral dilemmas, would generally have no legal obligation in our society to rescue the teenage boy. (Whether he should have is, of course, another matter.) On the other hand, in a case that went before the Indiana Supreme Court in 1942 (*Jones v. State*), a defendant was held responsible for the murder of a twelve-year-old girl whom he had raped. The girl, distracted by pain and grief, fell or jumped into a creek where she drowned. The defendant abstained from rescuing her although he could have done so at no risk to himself. The Supreme Court of Illinois, affirming a conviction of second degree murder, declared, "Can it be doubted that one who by his overpowering criminal act has put another in danger of drowning has a duty to preserve her life?" If a person dies as a result of the neglect of that duty, the Court implied, such neglect can be said to be *the cause* of the resultant death.

So, we see, the law does not, as a matter of fact, consider the distinction between acts and omissions relevant in those cases where the person who omits to act has a special responsibility to the person who requires his aid. Clearly, this is the relationship of a doctor to his patient. To some extent, the commonly invoked distinction between acts and omissions in the euthanasia issue stems from an uncritical importation of a general moral and legal doctrine to an area where it should have no application. Should the decision not to stop the young man's bleeding made in Lamerton's hospice have been perceived as a decision to *kill* that young man as much as the decision of the rapist not to rescue his victim or of a mother not to feed her baby? Indeed, while the rapist may be said not to have intended the death of his victim, this cannot be said of those who refrained from stopping the man's bleeding in Lamerton's hospice. Clearly, they *wanted* the poor man to die in this instance. If, by some chance, the bleeding had stopped by itself this time, they would have been disappointed for, as they would have perceived it, this would have been simply a cruel postponement of the inevitable fatal hemmorhage.

THE CASE FOR ACTIVE EUTHANASIA

Underlying the pleas that have often been made for active euthanasia is the belief that it is not mere human consciousness that has value but the quality of that consciousness. As the advocates of active euthanasia see it, in many terminal illnesses the physical and mental anguish that often accompanies a slow death can strip life of any remnant of promise or beauty, making consciousness a personal injury and death a benefit. As many opponents of active euthanasia see it, however, there is always the possibility that beauty and meaning will be found in human consciousness, however filled with suffering. The supporters of active euthanasia will dismiss such romantic sentiments as, at times, quite unjustified, claiming that meaning and beauty is rarely found as a pernicious disease eats away at one's body and mind. Nevertheless, such a claim is not apt to convince their opponents who accept a much more optimistic attitude toward the value of human consciousness, in and of itself. We have reached at this point the moral bedrock of deep subjective feeling and commitment that rational argument builds upon but cannot easily alter. It is for this reason that arguments as to the personal benefit to be derived from acts of euthanasia tend to founder as divergent moral standpoints come into conflict.

The strongest case to be made for active euthanasia must be sought not in the notion of utility, but in the Kantian notion of rational self-determination. Those who believe that they can find meaning in the suffering of a terminal illness or who believe that consciousness itself is a thing of precious beauty should not be prevented from seeking that meaning or beauty, but neither should terminally ill individuals be forced to seek a meaning or beauty that they believe cannot be found. The immorality of refusing to accept a rational patient's voluntary plea to be afforded active euthanasia comes from the fact that we have no right to make him endure the physical and mental anguish of a terminal illness against his will, and from the cruelty of refusing to render him assistance in painlessly taking his life when he is incapable of doing it himself.

A NONRELIGIOUS CASE AGAINST EUTHANASIA

Professor Yale Kamisar of the University of Minnesota School of Law would object strongly to the preceding plea for voluntary active euthanasia. In a clearly written and cogently argued article, Kamisar grants that "as an ultimate philosophical proposition, the case for voluntary euthanasia is strong."[6] As far as the patient is concerned, voluntary euthanasia, Kamisar admits, would be a morally justified course of action if the "person is *in fact* (1) presently incurable, (2) beyond the aid of any respite which may come along in his life expectancy, suffering (3) intolerable and (4) unmitigated pain and of a (5) fixed and (6) rational desire to die." Although Kamisar does not deny that such cases exist,[7] nevertheless, "abstract propositions and carefully formed hypotheticals are one thing; specific proposals designed to cover everyday situations are something else again!"

The problem, as Kamisar sees it, is two-fold. First, although one can imagine cases of terminally ill patients for whom voluntary euthanasia would be the preferred mode of response, any law which attempts to specify the conditions under which euthanasia can be practiced is bound to be vague and subject to mistakes and abuse, resulting in the morally unjustified utilization of euthanasia in some instances. In order to protect potential victims of vague euthanasia laws, Kamisar is willing to sacrifice those who "*in fact* have no desire and no reason to linger on." Secondly, Kamisar fears that laws allowing for voluntary euthanasia will most likely lead to laws allowing the involuntary euthanasia of the feeble-minded, insane, and senile. Acceptance of the principal behind voluntary euthanasia that there is such a thing as a life not worth living tends to brutalize us, Kamisar claims, mak-

---

[6]Kamisar does not make a distinction between active and passive euthanasia in his article.

[7]He does not, on the other hand, explicitly affirm that they do. Taken literally, it is doubtful that cases fitting Kamisar's standard will be found. With the availability of pain-killing drugs, it is doubtful that anyone will suffer "unmitigated" pain. In addition, in most cases, one cannot rule out the possibility that "a respite may come along" during the patient's lifetime, although the chances of this happening are often close to nil. Kamisar does not, however, adhere too strictly to his standard and admits more loosely, that there are individuals who "have no desire and no [rational] reason to linger on."

ing it easier for us to "dispatch" all whom we find troublesome—as the Nazis did in their comprehensive euthanasia program. Let us consider these objections in greater detail.

First, Kamisar is quite skeptical of the standards that would be utilized to determine when a patient's decision to choose euthanasia is a voluntary and rational one. In this context, Kamisar quotes with approval someone else's claim that those who advocate voluntary euthanasia expect the decision to be made "only if the victim is both sane and crazed by pain." Kamisar asks,

> By hypothesis, voluntary euthanasia is not to be resorted to until narcotics have long since been administered and the patient has developed a tolerance to them. When, then, does the patient make the choice? While heavily drugged? Or is the narcotic relief to be withdrawn for the time of the decision? But if heavy dosage no longer deadens pain, indeed, no longer makes it bearable, how overwhelming is it when whatever relief narcotics offer is taken away, too?...
>
> Even if the patient's choice could be said to be "clear and incontrovertible," do not other difficulties remain? Is this the kind of choice, assuming that it can be made in a fixed and rational manner, that we want to offer a gravely ill person? Will we not sweep up, in the process, some who are not really tired of life, but think others are tired of them; some who do not really want to die, but who feel they should not live on because to do so when there looms the legal alternative of euthanasia is to do a selfish or cowardly act? Will not some feel an obligation to have themselves "eliminated" in order that funds allocated for their terminal care might be better used by their families or, financial worries aside, in order to relieve their families of the emotional strain involved?

In addition, Kamisar is skeptical of a patient's and his doctor's decision that his case is hopeless. Under any euthanasia law, Kamisar believes, there are bound to be victims of euthanasia whose conditions would have improved had they lived. But even if laws could be precisely formulated to protect individuals from becoming unjustified recipients of euthanasia, Kamisar fears that such laws are likely to be but the "first wedge" leading to measures to which he is firmly opposed. Realizing that the wedge argument that something which is, in itself, not bad will lead to something worse and then to something worse yet is often an unwarranted one, Kamisar believes that the argument should not be taken too lightly in this instance since the "parade of horrors" that constituted the Nazi euthanasia program began with a program of the euthanasia of incurables.

> Even before the Nazis took chage in Germany, a propaganda barrage was directed against the traditional nineteenth-century attitudes toward the chronically ill, and for the adoption of a utilitarian....point of view....Lay opinion was not neglected in this campaign. Adults were propagandized by motion pictures, one of which... deals entirely with euthanasia . This film depicts the life history of a woman suffering from multiple sclerosis; in it her husband, a doctor, finally kills her to the accompaniment of soft piano music rendered by a sympathetic colleague in an adjoining room. Acceptance of this ideology was implanted even in the children. A widely used high school mathematics test...included problems stated in distorted terms of the cost of caring for and rehabilitating the chronically sick and crippled. One of the problems asked, for instance, how many new housing units could be built and how many marriage-allowance loans could be given to newly wedded couples

for the amount of money it cost the state to care for "the crippled, the criminal, and the insane. . . ." The beginnings at first were merely a subtle shift in emphasis in the basic attitude of the physicians. It *started with the acceptance of the attitude, basic in the euthanasia movement, that there is such a thing as life not worthy to be lived.* This attitude in its early stages concerned itself merely with the severely and chronically sick. Gradually the sphere of those to be included in this category was enlarged to encompass the socially unproductive, the ideologically unwanted, the racially unwanted, and finally all non-Germans. But it is important to realize that the infinitely small wedged-in lever from which this entire trend of mind received its impetus was the attitude toward the nonrehabilitatable sick.

A Critical Reply

Kamisar's criticisms against voluntary euthanasia are helpful in making us focus upon the pitfalls of an overly zealous rush into the legalization of euthanasia, but they do not justify the total prohibition of laws allowing euthanasia that he advocates. First, Kamisar's skepticism over the possibility of formulating laws which require the voluntary and rational consent of a potential recipient of euthanasia is overdrawn. While his hesitancy in counting as truly voluntary the pleas for euthanasia of a pain-racked patient are understandable, he does not give adequate consideration to the possibility that the pain-racked patient before becoming ill may have signed a statement requesting euthanasia if he contracts an incurable disease or develops a totally disabling condition. In reply to the claim that "where a pre-pain desire for euthanasia is reaffirmed under pain there is the best possible proof of full consent," Kamisar has only the following to say:

> Perhaps. But what if it is alternately renounced and reaffirmed under pain? What if it neither is affirmed nor renounced? What if it is only renounced? Will a physician be free to go ahead on the ground that the prior desire was "rational" but the present desire "irrational"?

After raising his questions, Kamisar lets the matter drop, nowhere amplifying the "perhaps" admission he made prior to raising his questions. These questions serve to sidestep us from the issue at hand which is the bearing on the voluntariness of a terminal patient's decision for euthanasia *when* such a decision serves to reaffirm a similar prior decision.[8] Whatever we are to make of Kamisar's enigmatic answer of "perhaps" to the question of whether such a decision should count as a truly voluntary one, certainly such a decision should at the very least strongly *count toward* the voluntariness and rationality of a person's death-bed decision.

Furthermore, Kamisar is quite unjustified in his caricature of the patient who opts for euthanasia as "sane, but crazed with pain." With modern drugs, pain is rarely constantly "intolerable and unmitigated." Even while in pain, terminal

---

[8]Kamisar's questions are subject to straightforward answers. If the prior decision is renounced or alternately renounced and reaffirmed, euthanasia should not be permitted. If the prior decision is neither affirmed nor renounced, one would assume that the patient must (because of unconsciousness or some mental disability) be incpable of doing either. If this is the case, the prior decision should be respected.

patients can often show a lucidity and keenness of judgment that is often lacking in those embroiled in the mundane cares of life. More fundamentally, Kamisar is wrong in suggesting that euthanasia could only be the appropriate mode of response for those suffering intolerable and unmitigated pain and consequently in concluding that modern pain-killing drugs have to a large extent obviated the need for euthanasia.[9] Although modern drugs often can eliminate pain for long periods, they do so at high cost—the cost of living long periods in a twilight state of wakefulness and drugged stupor, while suffering various side effects of the drugs such as severe nausea and vomiting. Ironically, the most effective pain-killing drug which induces a euphoric, nonsedative state, without the typical adverse side effects, is heroin. But this drug is illegal, even for terminally ill patients! Fortunately, a bill legalizing heroin for the terminally ill is presently being sponsored by several congressmen. The use of marijuana for the alleviation of nausea is fortunately already available for the terminally ill. In addition to these side effects, there are other miseries associated with terminal illnesses. For example, many terminal cancer patients have to endure foul smelling malignant fungus-like growths on their bodies and have to endure as well such miseries as incontinence, obstruction of the bowels, severe difficulty in swallowing, coupled by severe dehydration and uncontrolled itching and fatigue. Bed sores develop, as the dying patient, desirous of movement, finds himself without the strength to move in a bed which has become a cage. The process of slow death by illness, is, unfortunately, often a very ugly business. If severe physical pain is capable of justifying euthanasia, these agonies should justify it too, especially when they are coupled with the mental anguish that comes from the realization of one's hopeless plight and the loss of human dignity that they bring in their wake. Is it inappropriate, as Kamisar suggests, for patients whose lives must continue at such personally costly prices to consider it an unjustifiable financial or emotional burden to impose upon their families? In addition, Kamisar neglects the much more common situation of terminal (but not pain-racked) patients choosing to die rather than to continue with the extensive and debilitating treatments they have suffered through (such as cancer-leukemia patients). While some people would consider such refusals to continue with treatment justifiable since they involve passive and not active euthanasia, Kamisar does not draw this distinction.

The best protection against the unjustified self-sacrifice to euthanasia of those who are not hopelessly ill is the provision that concomitant to a patient's consent should be the judgment of several doctors that he is indeed suffering from such a disease or condition. Indeed, both the English and American Euthanasia Societies provide elaborate safeguards in their euthanasia proposals to insure, as much as possible, that the patient's consent is both informed and voluntary and that his condition is truly hopeless, given current medical knowledge. The American Euthanasia Society, for example, provides that a person over 21,

---

[9]Kamisar does not mention that patients develop tolerances to narcotic pain-killing drugs, necessitating larger and larger dosages for the same result. Sometimes the dosages required will considerably speed up the death of the patient or induce it immediately. Some doctors are unwilling to administer such massive dosages.

suffering from severe physical pain caused by a disease for which no remedy affording lasting relief or recovery is at the time known to medical science" petition for euthanasia in the presence of two witnesses and file same, along with the certificate of an attending physician, in a court of appropriate jurisdiction; said court to then appoint a committee of three, of whom at least two must be physicians, who shall forthwith examine the patient and such other persons as they deem advisable or as the court may direct and within five days after their appointment, shall report to the court whether or not the patient understands the nature and purpose of the petition and comes within the act's provisions; whereupon, if the report is in the affirmative, the court shall—unless there is some reason to believe that the report is erroneous or untrue—grant the petition; in which event euthanasia is to be administered in the presence of the committee, or any two members thereof.[10]

Surprisingly, Kamisar, although quoting the provisions of both the American and English Euthanasia Societies, does not take a stand as to whether they provide sufficient safeguards against the mistake and abuse he fears. His main criticism is directed instead toward Glanville Williams' proposal for euthanasia as described in his book *The Sanctity of Life and the Criminal Law*. According to Williams, the safeguards of the Euthanasia Societies are too drawn-out and cumbersome in operation, and should be replaced by a much simpler proposal. According to Williams,

The reformers might be well advised...to abandon all their cumbrous safeguards... giving the medical practitioner a wide discretion and trusting to his good sense. ...The essence of the bill would then be simple. It would provide that no medical practitioner should be guilty of an offense in respect of an act done intentionally to accelerate the death of a patient who is seriously ill, unless it is proved that the act was not done in good faith with the consent of the patient and for the purpose of saving him from severe pain in an illness believed to be of an incurable and fatal character. Under this formula it would be...for the prosecution to prove that the physician acted from some motive other than the humanitarian one allowed him by law.

Certainly, Kamisar is right that Williams' proposal is fraught with the danger of mistake and misuse. As Kamisar suggests, one's personal physician may not be "a sufficient buffer between the patient and the restless spouse or overwrought or overreaching relative, as well as a depository of enough general scientific knowhow and enough information about current research developments and trends, to assure a minimum of error in diagnosis and anticipation of new measures of relief." One would expect that after dismissing Williams' proposal as being too apt to be misused, Kamisar would turn his attention to the particular provisions of the English and American Euthanasia Societies, but he does not. The legal

[10]Notice that the American Euthanasia Society, by requiring that a patient be "suffering from severe physical pain," does not make provision for those terminal patients whose pain can be deadened by pain-killing drugs, but only at a personally unacceptable cost or for those comatose patients who have suffered irreversible and major brain damage but have previously made their wishes for euthanasia in such a situation known. Cases such as these are also not included in the proposal of the British Euthanasia Society, which requires that a patient should be "suffering from a disease involving severe pain and of an incurable and fatal character."

machinery provided by these societies would appear to provide ample safeguards and are sufficiently quick and potentially easy in operation. Indeed, the period of time (about one week) that would be required from the moment a patient gives his consent to the actual implementation of euthanasia is desirable in providing a period for reconsideration. The added pain and anticipation of death that potential euthanasia patients will face during that week is well worth the price.

A bill such as that proposed by the American Euthanasia Society is also the best protection against the possibility that a cure might exist or be found for a patient's apparently hopeless condition. One would expect that the doctors on the euthanasia committee would have full access to information as to any new medical research which might have some bearing on a euthanasia applicant's case and this knowledge would be communicated to the patient and his doctors. Of course, as opponents of euthanasia are wont to stress, there is always the chance that a recipient of euthanasia could have been saved from some painful and terminal condition by a medical breakthrough that was not known at the time he was subjected to euthanasia. We should not, however, exaggerate this possibility. In the final stages of a terminal illness, it will practically always be too late for a treatment to be effective, especially a new one in the experimental stage. At any rate, is it not unjustified to refuse the pleas of the vast number of people whom we would be condemning to needless pain, for the sake of the few whose lives would be unnecessarily taken, if euthanasia were made legal? Is not such a gamble best left with the patient? For some, one chance in a thousand or even a million of a lifesaving breakthrough may be worth the wait, while for others, one chance in a hundred or even ten may not be worth the certain agony that the wait entails.

Let us turn now to Kamisar's contention that all proposals for voluntary euthanasia should be rejected, since, if enacted, they are likely to lead us down a "slippery slope" toward the involuntary euthanasia of the senile, retarded, and insane and, finally, the useless and unwanted. One must always be skeptical of slippery slope (wedge) arguments such as this, many of which are fallacious. For example, during Roosevelt's New Deal days, Social Security was often criticized on the grounds that it would lead to greater and greater socialism, until the United States became a completely socialistic state. This does not seem to be happening, however. The "slip" from one socialistic measure to another is far from inevitable. The United States has proved to be much less inclined to embrace the socialistic measures that other western democracies such as Great Britain and the Scandinavian countries have, and there is every reason to believe that in the foreseeable future the economic choice for the United States will not be that of pure capitalism versus pure socialism, but rather one of proper balance in a mixed economy.

No doubt, as Kamisar claims, euthanasia laws would always be subject to misuse and overextension. This, however, is the case with all laws. For example, existing laws allowing for the civil commitment of the dangerously mentally ill and laws allowing for voluntary human experimentation are capable of grave misuse and overextension, and have, as a matter of fact, been misused and overextended. Yet few would suggest that such laws should be eliminated.

Although a slippery slope argument is often the last refuge of the doctrinaire conservative, such arguments cannot be dismissed out of hand and each must be considered on its own merits. Kamisar's impassioned invocation of a slippery slope argument in the context of the euthanasia issue derives its force from the association of euthanasia with the Nazi experience. There are no good reasons, however, to think that contemporary proposals for voluntary euthanasia are at all likely to lead to the Nazi horrors. The Nazi program of "euthanasia" was motivated from the start solely by cold-blooded considerations of social utility, often perceived on purely economic terms. Untroubled by any concern for individual rights, the Nazis had no principled objection to involuntarily taking the lives of the socially troublesome and useless. On the other hand, current-day advocates of voluntary euthanasia who perceive such action as a benevolent response to suffering individuals which, by requiring their voluntary consent, acts to maximize human freedom, would have to abandon their moral principles of individual justice and benevolence in order to embrace the Nazi practices of involuntary merciless killings. Granted that the Nazis often hid their merciless principles of social utility behind the cloak of benevolence, and that kindness, especially when divorced from consent, can often turn to cruelty, the horrors of the Nazi experience, rather than providing a path for us to follow, should act as a beacon bidding us to be more vigilant in establishing safeguards to prevent us from slipping away from principles of justice and kindness. The best safeguard for this is the informed consent of the euthanasia recipient.

Nevertheless, as Kamisar warns, if (active and intentional euthanasia) is legalized and becomes widespread, the *personal right* to euthanasia can slowly and perniciously be transformed into a generally perceived *social obligation* not to selfishly cling to the last remnants of life. "Informed consent" may, consequently, become infused with subtle and potentially chilling social pressures that will lead people in the future to act "voluntarily" in ways they presently would not. This effect would be most troubling with the gravely disabled and with the increasing number of elderly people who suffer from debilitating, but nonterminal, conditions such as Alzheimer's disease. Given scarce medical and economic resources, difficult moral choices as to who is to be saved and who is to be allowed to die already face us. If indeed, we do one day come to give legal recognition to the principle that "some lives are not worth living," one can well imagine a growing social cry that scarce resources not be wasted on "useless lives" and that "some people are better off dead." This is indeed a chilling prospect and not one to be easily dismissed as a mere scare tactic of the doctrinare conservative.

The greatest danger of slipping into the Nazi pratice of sacrificing human lives for nebulous and short-sighted visions of the common good comes from nonvoluntary euthanasia. As we have seen, the nonvoluntary euthanasia of defective newborn infants is not a threat that lurks in the future; it is, rather, an actuality. The law at present deals with this problem primarily by overlooking it. When it is forced by litigation to look, its decisions are not guided by adequate moral principles. For example, was it not wrong for the law to compel surgery on David Houle against his parents' wishes? On the other hand, was it not wrong for the law not to intervene in the Johns Hopkins case either to compel surgery or, at the very least, to compel that the child be killed directly and mercifully rather than indirectly and cruelly? While divergent moral sentiments in this area make it unreasonable to expect any general consensus as to when nonvoluntary euthanasia is morally appropriate, consensus is much more likely on the extreme cases, and that is where we must begin.

Slippery slope arguments to the contrary, strong advocates of active voluntary euthanasia may change sides when it comes to a consideration of *particular* proposals for nonvoluntary euthanasia—for there are ethically relevant differences in the two cases. Given the need to observe the implications of our proposals in action and the widespread opposition that the thought of active euthanasia engenders in the minds of many, it is unwise to attempt to answer all questions at once. The answers to some questions are best left to the future, while we move cautiously forward a step at a time, ready to learn from experience and to adjust our ideas accordingly. Although the future will always be filled with pitfalls for the uncautious and self-deceived, our concern and fear of the possible future effects of our actions should never drive us into a paralysis of action that often seems to be the strict logic of many slippery slope arguments.

Let us also not lose sight of the fact that doctors, who are not especially trained in moral matters, are, as a matter of fact, presently making daily under-the-counter decisions concerning who should live and who should die. These decisions and the moral principles that are used to justify them should not be hidden from public scrutiny as they presently are, but discussed and debated in the open. The result of this process of public debate should be the creation of a law relating to euthanasia that doctors can respect and appeal to as a guide for their actions. The present widespread divergence between medical practice and professed moral and legal principle is a sham. Certainly, the current practice of surreptitious and conscience-salving actions of doctors should be replaced by an honest reliance on uniform legal principles, arrived at after careful public discussion and debate. Decisions relating to euthanasia may be easier when they are swept under the rug or delegated to doctors who often make their decisions behind closed doors, but this is a very poor way of arriving at good decisions.

If active euthanasia should be made legal, we must ask ourselves why. Are we afraid, as Kamisar is, of the vagueness of possible euthanasia laws and the difficulties of their practical administration? If so, are such difficulties worse than the difficulties that now face us? If we are afraid, as Kamisar is, of introducing a principle into the law that "some lives are not worth living," we must face the fact that such judgments, as a matter of fact, implicitly come into play in decisions as to the extraordinariness of a given treatment. If we have a principled objection to active euthanasia that goes beyond these practical difficulties, we must scrutinize the rational basis of this objection. If our objection is a religious one, based on the belief in a divine prohibition against suicide, we must inquire as to its meaning and justification. (Is a person committing *suicide* when she refuses lifesaving treatment?) Even if we can find, as I think we cannot, some rational religious basis for an absolute moral prohibition against active euthanasia, we must ask ourselves if we have a right to impose our religious beliefs in this matter upon those who disagree. Does the value of human autonomy override whatever harm active euthanasia is likely to bring in its wake? If not, how should we react to those heart-rending cases where people motivated by pure benevolence engage in active euthanasia? Should they be legally prosecuted? They often are not, as authorities turn a blind eye to those whom they do not blame. If they are prosecuted, should grand juries indict? Again they often do not, and when they do, trials in the heart-rending cases usually end in acquittal by juries guided by sympathy and not by the letter of the law. If, on the other hand, the law should be enforced, should leniency come in the sentencing stage? But do we want kind people who have agonized and suffered over their act of euthanasia to suffer the added agony and cost of a trial and the ignominy of being labeled a convicted felon? Such are the questions that must be tackled if we are to come to a reasoned resolution of the euthanasia issue.

DISCUSSION QUESTIONS

1. Which of the following acts would you label as suicide? Why?
   a. a soldier falls on a grenade to save his comrades (would it matter if such an act were instinctive or deliberate?)
   b. having the option of retreating, a soldier fights against overwhelming odds, realizing that by so doing, he is bound to die (would it matter if the soldier were under orders to remain or had the military discretion to retreat?)
   c. blinded, but with his strength regained, Samson brings the pillars of the Philistine temple down upon his enemies and himself with the intent of destroying his enemies, but not himself. He realizes, however, that his act will cause his death.
   d. the Captain Oates case (see p. 279)
   e. rather than being force-fed, Socrates, sentenced to die, takes the poison himself and drinks it
   f. a person kills himself in a game of "Russian roulette" (does it matter why he was playing this game?)
   g. a daredevil stuntman attempts a very dangerous feat, knowing that there is high probability of death and dies
   h. a person jumps in a rapidly moving river intending to kill himself, but alive in the water, he changes his mind. Swimming to safety, against rapid currents, he dies.
   i. a person, wondering whether his life has meaning, asks God for an omen. He jumps into a dangerous river and swims as best he can. If he survives, he will take this as a positive omen from God. He dies, however.
   j. a person steps out on a ledge with the intent of jumping. He hesitates, while he musters the courage to make the plunge. Losing his balance, he slips, falling to his death.

2. Do you believe that a physically healthy individual's decision to commit suicide can be a full voluntary and rational one? Consider, in particular, the possibility that someone very dear to you decides to commit suicide. Under what circumstances, if any, would you be willing to accept such a decision as voluntary and rational?

3. If you believe that the suicides of physically healthy individuals can be voluntary and rational, is it justifiable, nevertheless, that people be trained to believe

that they have a moral obligation not to commit suicide and consequently develop a natural disposition to feel guilty when they contemplate suicide?

4. Consider:

A: Infanticide is best capable of justification in the case of the very severely mentally retarded, for such individuals are not, and never can become, persons.

B: I don't agree. As long as such human beings are physically healthy, it is implausible to claim that death will be more of a benefit to them than their limited life. While you and I might prefer to be dead rather than to become severely mentally retarded, since we know the value of the mental capacity we would be losing, we have no right to claim that a severely mentally retarded person who knows nothing else would prefer death to life. On the other hand, I think infanticide is much more capable of justification in the case of mentally normal infants born with severe physical abnormalities. In such cases, death can be a benefit to an infant who faces the bleak prospect of lifelong physical suffering, made all the worse by her recognition of her sad fate.

What do you think?

5. Consider the following moving description of the agony hospital staffs endure when they are forced to watch the slow death of newborn infants whose parents refuse to consent to lifesaving surgery:

> ...When surgery is defined [the doctor] must try to keep the infant from suffering while natural forces sap the baby's life away. As a surgeon whose natural inclination is to use the scalpel to fight off death, standing by and watching a salvageable baby die is the most emotionally exhausting experience I know. It is easy at a conference, in a theoretical discussion, to decide that such infants should be allowed to die. It is altogether different to stand by in the nursery and watch as dehydration and infection wither a tiny being over hours and days. This is a terrible ordeal for me and the hospital staff....(Shaw, A., "Doctor, Do We Have a Choice?" *The New York Times Magazine,* January 30, 1972, p. 54).

Do you think hospital staffs would feel less agony if such infants were quickly and painlessly put to death by some lethal injection? Is this the right thing to do in such situations? Why?

6. In cases where the state will incur the cost of lifesaving treatment for a newborn infant as well as the cost of lifelong institutionalization should it survive, do you think the state should ever have the right to refuse to pay for such treatment even if the parents want it?

7. Joseph Fletcher, a Protestant spokesman for voluntary euthanasia writes,

> A commission of American Protestants recently concluded that the mass extermination of civilians by atom bomb blasts can be 'just,' although many members of the commission would hesitate to agree that fatal suffering could be ended righteously for one of the victims burned and charred externally and internally, not even as a response of the victim's pleas.

Fletcher thinks that such a view is morally absurd. How do you think the commission members would have defended their view? Do you find this defense plausible? Why?

8. Consider:

A: It would have been so much better if the doctors had given dad a lethal injection to end his misery. We all knew that there was no hope. The cancer had spread too far. Instead, he was left to die a slow, painful, and undignified death.

B: If the doctors had given him a lethal injection, it would not have been the cancer which killed him, as it did, but the injection they administered. It's one thing not to interfere with a disease process that is killing a person and consequently to let that person die, but it is quite different to initiate a death-producing causal process. You can't expect doctors to play the role of executioners.

A: If doctors are to be perceived as executioners when they give terminally ill patients lethal injections, they should be seen as executioners when they refuse to act to prolong a terminally ill patient's life out of a desire to spare him the additional agony that the prolongation of his life would entail. At any rate, if dad's doctors did not want to take the responsibility of directly killing him, they should have left some lethal pills for him to swallow himself, with our aid.

B: While I am willing to admit that there are cases where active euthanasia is preferable to passive euthanasia, it would be too dangerous to accept a general practice of active euthanasia. Such a practice runs too great a risk of undermining respect for human life.

A: I admit that the acceptance of a general legal rule, permitting active euthanasia in particular circumstances, is fraught with difficulty and the potential for misuse, but it seems to me that there is as much difficulty and potential for misuse in attempting to hold fast to the absolute prohibition of active euthanasia. In our overriding desire to avoid active euthanasia, we attach more weight than we should to the distinction between active and passive euthanasia. Consider, for example, the Mongoloid infant who was denied a simple operation and was allowed to starve to death.

B: Clearly, one needs to restrict the range of legally permissible passive euthanasia, but this is much easier than attempting to restrict the range of legally permissible active euthanasia. You are quite right that these are cases where active euthanasia is justifiable and even more cases where it is excusable, but these are still relatively exceptional cases. It is quite important that we see these cases as exceptional ones that *defy our normal moral universe.* As jurists have often observed, "hard cases make bad law." In these hard cases, juries often rightfully refuse to punish those who engage in mercy killings, in spite of what the law says. That's the way it should be.

A: While juries often find those who commit mercy killings temporarily insane, this is usually dishonest. A verdict of this sort is simply a convenient way of refusing to apply an overly broad general rule. Rather than countenance this dishonesty, it would be better to modify the general rule.

Critically discuss.

9. Do you think voluntary euthanasia should be restricted to those who are dying from some terminal illness or should it be allowed in other situations as well? If so, when?

10. Which of the following legal alternatives do you favor? Why?

   a. Doctors should be legally permitted in certain circumstances to actively kill their patients.

   b. Doctors should not be legally permitted to actively kill their patients, but should be allowed to provide patients who are terminally ill and mentally competent with the means to take their own lives.

   c. Doctors should be legally prohibited from assisting suicide but should not have a legal duty to take precautions to prevent terminally ill and mentally competent patients from committing suicide (such as by making it difficult or impossible for the patient to disconnect his oxygen bottle).

   d. Doctors should have the legal duty to take precautions to prevent patients, even if terminally ill and mentally competent, from committing suicide.

11. Do you favor the American Euthanasia Society's proposal for active euthanasia? Would you modify it in any way?

12. Consider:

A: In 1971, Delores Heston, 22 and unmarried, was severely injured in an automobile accident in New Jersey. While incoherent herself, her mother informed the hospital that Delores was a Jehovah's Witness and would be opposed to a blood transfusion but not the surgery the doctors said was necessary. In spite of the lack of consent, the hospital successfully petitioned to get legal permission for the transfusion. The surgery and transfusion were performed and Delores recovered. On appeal (*John F. Kennedy Memorial Hospital v. Heston*), the New Jersey Supreme Court affirmed the lower court decision on the grounds that "there is no constitutional right to choose to die." As the court saw it, a Jehovah's Witness who refuses a lifesaving blood transfusion is attempting suicide. Since attempted suicide is a crime in New Jersey, the court reasoned that Jehovah's Witnesses do not have a right to refuse blood transfusions. The court saw no relevant legal or moral distinction in "passively submitting to death and actively seeking it." This was a mistake. Miss Heston did not want a blood transfusion, but *she did not want to die.* Consequently, her act should not be seen as suicidal.

B: I don't think it's as easy as that. In a sense, one could say that practically all those who attempt suicide would prefer to live *if only the prospects of their lives were better.* Mrs. *X*, for example, may decide to take her life after her husband has died and her children have abandoned her, only because life under such conditions appears unbearable to her. Nevertheless, she would not want to die if she felt there was somebody who really cared. Just as Miss Heston did not want to live at the price of a blood transfusion, so Mrs. *X* does not want to live at the price of being alone. You and I may think that Mrs. *X*'s act is irrational, but this is a purely subjective statement of personal preference; Mrs. *X* has as much right to her opinion as we do to ours. If Jehovah's Witnesses should be allowed to choose death rather than life at an unbearable price, so should those who base their choice on nonreligious grounds.

C: There is a morally relevant difference in the two cases. In Mrs. *X*'s case, death is actively chosen, whereas in the case of Miss Heston, it was simply accepted as a byproduct of the intention to avoid doing evil—remember the principle of the double effect.

D: I think we also make a distinction in the two cases because we believe there is a good chance that we can—and should try to—get through to Mrs. *X* and persuade her to see things differently. Consequently, we tend to see her as blinded by depression and see her suicidal choice as not a truly voluntary one. On the other hand, we are willing to take Miss Heston's choice as a voluntary expression of her true self and do not feel justified in trying to dislodge her religious convictions.

E: I'm not at all sure what Miss Heston really wanted. I remember reading that deep down, many Jehovah's Witnesses really want to be forced to submit to lifesaving blood transfusions. This way they can both live and be free of the responsibility of making what they take to be a sinful choice. Consequently, they are relieved when doctors take the burden of responsibility off their shoulders. This is a possibility we should not lightly dismiss.

Critically discuss.

13. Should lifesaving blood transfusions be imposed on Jehovah's Witnesses with dependent children on the grounds that they have an obligation to care for their children? Why?

FURTHER READINGS

Suicide

For a liberal view turn to David Hume's "Of Suicide" in his *Essays, Moral, Political, and Literary* (Oxford University Press, 1963). Hume is especially concerned with refuting the view that suicide is a crime against God, but he also argues that it need not be a violation of one's duty to society or to oneself. For a contrasting conservative view turn to Immanuel Kant's "Suicide" in his *Lectures on Ethics* (Hackett, 1963). Counting as a suicide only acts done with "the intention [purpose] to destroy oneself," Kant claims that suicide is always wrong. For the classic Roman Catholic view turn to Saint Thomas Aquinas's *Summa Theologica,* part II, question 64: "Of Murder" (London: Burns, Oates and Washborne Ltd., 1929).

    Ethical Issues in Suicide by M. Pubst Battin (Prentice-Hall, 1982) is a study of different views concerning the morality of suicide which is rich in factual detail. *Suicide: The Philosophical Issues,* edited by M. Pabst Battin and David J. Mayo (St. Martin's Press, 1980) is an excellent analytically oriented anthology on the historical conceptual, psychiatric, legal, and moral dimensions of suicide. Especially recommended are the various articles on the concept of suicide, Battin's article "Manipulated Suicide," and James Bogin's "Suicide and Virtue."

Euthanasia

Three Books and Articles

    In chapters 7 and 8 of his book *The Sanctity of Life and the Criminal Law* (Knopf, 1957), Glanville Williams, a legal scholar, clearly and nontechnically discusses the historical and legal background and moral arguments relating to suicide and argues for its decriminalization, along with the unselfish encouragement of others to commit suicide. A contrasting conservative view is found in the religious moralist Paul Ramsey's *Ethics at the Edges of Life,* Part II (Yale University Press, 1978). Like much of Ramsey's writings on medical ethics, this book is incisive and thought-provoking, but, at times convoluted and vague. Secular moralists will also find Ramsey's underlying religious moral perspective too dogmatic. In addition, the general reader will be disconcerted to find that much of Ramsey's discussion is directed to criticisms of the writings of others. Nevertheless, one can learn much from Ramsey.

    Yale Kamisar's influential and clearly written article against the legalization of euthanasia "Some Non-Religious Views Against Proposed 'Mercy-Killing' Legislation" first appeared in the *Minnesota Law Review*, 42 (1958). In the next issue, Glanville Williams presents a rejoinder. Both of these articles are reprinted in the Beauchamp-Perlin and Abelson-Friquegnon anthologies.

    Elizabeth Kubler-Ross, a psychiatrist who has specialized in psychotherapy with dying patients, reports her observations on the psychological processes of the terminally ill in her book *On Death and Dying* (Macmillan, 1974). Reading Kubler-Ross's description of the despair that terminally ill patients often experience as they learn of and eventually accept their fate will act to undercut Kamisar's unfair caricature of such patients as "pain-crazed."

Anthologies

There are several anthologies devoted exclusively to the euthanasia issue which are interdisciplinary in content, containing selections from theologians, lawyers, and doctors, as well as philosophers. Among them are Marvin Kohl (ed.), *Beneficient Euthanasia* (Prometheus, 1975), T. Beauchamp & S. Perlin (eds.), *Ethical Issues in Death and Dying* (Prentice-Hall, 1978), and J. Behnke & S. Bok (eds.), *The Dilemmas of Euthanasia* (Anchor, 1975). John Ladd (ed.), *Ethical Issues Relating to Life and Death* (Oxford University Press, 1979) consists of essays by contemporary analytic philosophers on the conceptual and moral issues of euthanasia, most of which are directed to the philosophically sophisticated. Less difficult and highly recommended for those concerned with the conceptual dimensions of the euthanasia issue is Bonnie Steinbock (ed.), *Killing and Letting Die* (Prentice-Hall, 1980). Steinbock's introduction to this collection provides a good map of the selections that follow.

    Chapters on the euthanasia issue can be found in T. Mappes and J. Zembaty (eds.), *Social Ethics,* third edition (McGraw-Hill, 1987); J. White (ed.), *Contemporary Moral Problems,* second edition (West, 1988); J. Arthur (ed.), *Morality and Moral Controversies,* second edition (Prentice-

Hall, 1986); and R. Abelson and M. Friquegnon (eds.), *Ethics for Modern Life,* third edition (St. Martin's, 1987). In addition, there are many anthologies available on medical ethics, all of which contain selections on euthanasia.

General Reference Source

The Encyclopedia of Bioethics (Macmillan, 1978) has useful articles on the topics of suicide, death and dying: euthanasia and sustaining life, death: attitudes toward, and the right to refuse medical care.

Citations

The quotation from Dr. Joel Posner comes from *Newsweek,* Nov. 3, 1975, p. 67. The quotation from Locke is found in the *Second Treatise of Government* (Bobbs-Merrill, 1952), pp. 5–6. The quotation from Kant is found in *Lectures on Ethics* (Hackett, 1963), pp. 153–54. The Catholic condemnation of euthanasia is from Everhard Welty, *A Handbook of Christian Social Ethics* II (London: Nelson, 1963), pp. 130–31. The quotation from Aquinas comes from the *Summa Theologica,* Vol. II, Part II, question 64, article 5. The quotation from Robert Scott concerning Captain Oates is found in *Scott's Last Expedition,* 2nd ed. (Dodd, Mead, 1964), p. 155. The quotation from Pope Pius XII relating to extraordinary life support is found in "Papal Allocation to a Congress of Anaesthetists," 24 November 1957, *Acta Apostolicae Sedis,* 1027–33. The argument against a general legal requirement to render aid to strangers was presented by Macauley and other Indian Law Commissioners in 1837. The quotation from Glanville Williams comes from pp. 339–40 of his *Sanctity of Life and The Criminal Law.*

Racial and Sexual Discrimination and the Problem of "Reverse Discrimination"

7

My view has long been that race-conscious classifications designed to further remedial goals... [are morally required and constitutionally permissible]....A profound difference separates governmental actions that themselves are racist, and governmental actions that seek to remedy the effects of prior racism.... The majority today retreats from the Court's long standing solicitude to race-conscious remedial efforts.... I profoundly disagree with the cramped vision of the Equal Protection Clause which the majority offers today.... The battle against pernicious racial discrimination is nowhere near won....

> Supreme Court Justice
> THURGOOD MARSHALL
> in his dissenting opinion
> in *Richmond v. Croson* (1989)

The difficulty of overcoming the effects of past discrimination is as nothing compared with the difficulty of eradicating from our society the source of these effects which is the tendency...to classify and judge men and women on the basis of their country of origin or the color of their skin....[T]hose who believe that racial preferences can help to "even the score" display, and reinforce, a manner of thinking by race that was the source of the injustice and that will, if it endures within our society, be the source of more injustice still....

> Supreme Court Justice
> ANTONIN SCALIA
> in his concurring opinion
> in *Richmond v. Croson* (1989)

The civil rights movement of the 1960s has served to bring the question of discrimination to the fore of the American consciousness. Blacks, women, and other groups who perceive themselves as oppressed, cry out for the equality that the American dream promises but does not seem to deliver. Their pleas often strike a sympathetic chord upon the consciences of white affluent males who share their equalitarian ideals and admit that the future should see a much greater participation of women and minority groups in occupations that have up until now been almost exclusively the domain of white males. Rather than complacently accepting the fruit of generations of discrimination, they are willing to make amends. But how is this to be done? What does our society owe to groups who have been treated unjustly in the past and carry the legacy of that injustice today? Should they be compensated for the injustices of the past? If so, what form should that compensation take, how great should it be, and how long should it last? Is it right to compensate people at the price of temporary injustice to others? Is it right for a white man to be penalized today for the injustices perpetrated against women and the nonwhite in the past, even though he himself may not have participated in or profited from those injustices himself? Can preferential treatment of individuals who are victimized by the lingering effects of prior discrimination be squared with the constitutional provision for equal treatment? Can we sacrifice some degree of present equal treatment for a greater equality in the future? Is that fair? If it isn't, can the social utility that may result from efforts to eliminate discrimination outweigh the injustice of those efforts? Such is a sampling of the questions that face us today as we ponder the advisability of affirmative action programs, as their proponents tend to call them, or reverse discrimination, as their opponents tend to label them. As is often the case in debates over complex moral issues, positions on this matter tend to be defended by appeal to moral principles which, though reflecting legitimate strands of our collective moral common sense, seem to point us in conflicting directions. Uncritically accepting our own moral principles and neglecting those of our opponents, we fail to come to grips with their meanings, implications, and presuppositions. It is this essential task which will occupy us in this chapter.

THE EQUALITARIAN IDEAL: EQUALITY OF OPPORTUNITY

In its most basic form, the concept of justice is associated most closely with that of equality. The central idea here is that justice demands that we *treat like cases alike.* Since any given case will resemble other cases in some respects and differ from them in others, until it is established what resemblances and differences are *relevant,* the command to treat like cases alike remains merely the empty form of a principle, devoid of specific content. As the current debate over the relevance of race or sex in deciding who is to be admitted into certain professional schools or occupations indicates, people can strongly disagree as to which characteristics are relevant and which are irrelevant.

Deeply a part of the American ethic, however, is the belief that justice requires equality of opportunity. At the core of this ethic is the view that competition for the most desirable positions in our society should be a fair and open one in which all participants are afforded equal access to educational opportunities and other social benefits. When this is so, we believe, it is only fair that individuals should go as far as they can and be rewarded differentially in accordance with their *individual merit.*

There are, however, serious difficulties with this basic equalitarian ethic. First, as is often pointed out, the ideal of equal opportunity is not a reflection of the social realities of our society. Although we proudly proclaim the equalitarian ideal of equal access to educational and social benefits, it is clear that the rich reap much more of these benefits than the poor. As such, a great deal of competition in our society is unfair. Since the advantages of inherited wealth or the disadvantages of inherited poverty create gross inequalities in opportunities to compete, it is unfair to expect persons from deprived, poverty stricken backgrounds to compete equally with those from affluent, highly advantaged backgrounds. This commonplace criticism is at the very heart of the arguments utilized by those who support affirmative action programs. Less obvious, however, is the problem of *natural,* as opposed to socially induced, inequalities, for just as poverty can work against an individual, so too can innate biological handicaps.

The question of the relative influence of nature and nurture in developing one's personality and abilities has been a perennial philosophical one. Nevertheless, it would be generally conceded that the contribution of inborn abilities or predispositions cannot be fully discounted and that these inborn characteristics which depend on "the luck of the genetic draw" create advantages for some and disadvantages for others. Given the undeserved inequalities of environment and inborn abilities, is it not unfair to base financial rewards on achievement? The proper indicator of one's individual merit, it has been said, should be effort, not achievement. From this point of view, a truly just society which cannot eliminate the inequalities of genetic or environmental factors would have to reward people not on what they accomplish, but on how hard they work to accomplish what they do.[1] For example, Edward Bellamy, in his novel *Looking Backward* (1889) imagines a society where all workers receive the same salary for doing their best, regardless of what they actually accomplish. Just as citizens today of Communist China or of an Israeli kibbutz, the citizens of Bellamy's imagined community are motivated to do their best not by the promise of higher financial rewards but by their devotion to the common good, by feelings of patriotism and pride and by the desire for recognition. Karl Marx, too, envisioned a society where reward would not be based on achievement. For Marx, however, the principle of proper distribution in such a society was not to give each person the same share of the benefits of that society, for some people needed those benefits more than others. The proper principle of distribution, he believed, was that each person should receive in proportion to his

---

[1]But even this, some will claim, is not just since the effort people exert is itself dependent upon hereditary and environmental conditions which one does not choose. (Recall our discussion of the hard deterministic view in the chapter on free will.)

need. As Marx put it, "from each according to his ability, to each according to his need."

As Bellamy and Marx realized, the often quoted equalitarian view that people *deserve* to be rewarded in accordance with achievement is built on the presuppositions of equal environmental opportunity and equal natural ability. If either of these two presuppositions is denied, it becomes reasonable to deny that justice or fairness demands that one be rewarded in accordance with one's achievement. From this point of view, it is plausible to think that justice demands that people should in some way be compensated for their undeserved disadvantages which prevent them from fairly competing with others. As we shall see, such a claim is often made by those who defend affirmative action programs where the focus is on environmental disadvantage. One should not forget, however, that individuals also suffer from inherited disadvantages as well. If a person can rightfully demand compensation for being poor, can he not also rightfully demand compensation for being born a moron? Is this not equally a demand for justice? Similarly, if we have a moral obligation to eliminate as best we can environmental inequalities that contribute to differing abilities, do we equally have a moral obligation, once genetic engineering becomes technically possible, to eliminate genetic differences which contribute to differing abilities?

Another grave difficulty with the view that justice demands that individuals be rewarded in terms of their merit lies in the fact that one's conception of meritorious qualities is culture-bound and dependent upon shifting social needs and desires. What would be considered meritorious qualities in one society may not be so considered in another society. For example, Kareem Abdul-Jabbar's undeniable merit as a basketball player would have gone unrecognized at the Court of Versailles. Consequently, "having merit," at least to some extent, implies being lucky enough to be in the right place at the right time. As the products, services, and forms of entertainment of a society change, so too do those qualities which are deemed meritorious and, for that reason, subject to special reward. One's conception of merit, especially in a free enterprise system, is especially vulnerable to the vicissitudes of supply and demand.

RACIAL AND SEXUAL DISCRIMINATION

Since justice demands that individuals be treated equally unless some *relevant* difference exists which can justify their unequal treatment, if individuals are treated differently on the basis of irrelevant differences, an injustice has been committed. While it is often claimed today that it is unfair to deny jobs to individuals simply because of their race or sex, this statement is too strong. For example, we would not think it unfair to restrict parts in some play or movie to people of a particular race or sex. Similarly, sex is clearly decisive in determining who should be hired as a wet nurse. In addition, some would claim that while individuals cannot rightfully be excluded from desirable positions simply on the basis of their race or sex, *as a matter of biological fact* the race or sex of an individual often has an important bearing on his or her ability to perform well in these positions. For example, according to Aristotle, it is man's nature to rule, while it is woman's nature to be ruled.

Sexual Equality: The Argument from Nature

Aristotle's sexist view is still shared by many people. For example, it is not uncommon to hear people say, "No woman should ever be President of the United States; women are too emotional for such responsibilities." Such a claim reflects the still common belief that the sex of an individual is highly correlated with psychological characteristics and, as such, may be used as an indicator of an individual's capacity to perform certain tasks. As a result of this belief, women are often treated unequally in our society.

This belief is the subject of controversy. On one side are those who, like Aristotle, believe that there are various psychological differences between the sexes which are biologically caused and make women by their very nature unequal to men in significant respects. On the other side, there are those who, like John Stuart Mill in the nineteenth century, deny either that such sexual psychological differences exist, or if they do exist, that they are inborn.[2] According to the latter claim, whatever psychological differences exist between the sexes is caused by environmental factors. From this point of view, if it is true that women tend to be considerably less aggressive than men, this is a result of the fact that society encourages or pressures women to accept passive roles while men are encouraged or pressured to accept more aggressive roles. Therefore, these differences are artificially induced and are not based on any natural sexual inequalities.

Such a claim is challenged by those who argue for the existence of fundamental biological differences in the sexes which result in differing psychological attributes. For example, according to psychoanalytical views, a person's experience of his or her own body has an important affect on personality development. Some psychiatrists have drawn analogies between genitals and sex roles. Since a vagina, they say, is passive and a penis is aggressive, this naturally leads women to see themselves as passive, while men see themselves as aggressive. The argument has also been made that hormonal differences in the sexes make men inherently more aggressive than women. For example, Steven Goldberg defends this thesis in his book *The Inevitability of Patriarchy*. As Goldberg sees it, man's inherent greater aggressiveness guarantees male domination of the high status roles in society. Furthermore, if society did not attempt to socialize women away from competing with men for such roles, then although some women would be aggressive enough to succeed in the competitive struggle, the vast majority of them would be failures—socialized to desire high-status positions but incapable of achieving them.

---

[2]Mill was an early strong defender of women's rights. While a member of the English Parliament, he submitted the first bill on the enfranchisement of women to the House of Commons. His essay "The Subjection of Women" is a classic feminist defense.

There are many problems with Goldberg's argument. First, he uncritically assumes that the level of *physical* aggressiveness that one may reasonably assume is correlated with the level of the male hormone testosterone is the only sort of aggressiveness that is required for success in the struggle for high status positions—a highly dubious assumption. If it is indeed true, as Goldberg assumes, that aggressiveness is (always or usually?) a requirement for success in high-status positions, the notion of aggressiveness, it would appear, must be taken to encompass more than the physical aggressiveness upon which Goldberg implicitly focuses. Let us, however, leave this central difficulty aside and see how Goldberg proceeds with his argument. He writes:

> . . .one need merely consider the result of society's *not* socializing women away from competitions with men, from its *not* directing girls toward roles women are more capable of playing than are men or roles with status low enough that men will not strive for them. No doubt some women would be aggressive enough to succeed in competitions with men and there would be considerably more women in high-status positions than there are now. But most women would lose in such competitive struggles with men. . .and so most women would be forced to live adult lives as failures. . . . Now I have no doubt that there is a biological factor that gives women the desire to emphasize maternal and nurturance roles, but the point here is that we can accept the feminist assumption that there is no female propensity of this sort and still see that a society must socialize women away from roles that men will attain through their aggression. For if women did not develop an alternative set of criteria for success their sense of their own competence would suffer intolerably.

Even if we assume that Goldberg is right that there are hormonal differences between the sexes which account for significant psychological differences, he does not establish his point that our society *should enforce the acceptance of sex roles* where women are socialized to be passive and not aggressive. Even if one assumes with Goldberg that women will *tend* to lose out in the competitive struggle with men for high-status positions, it does not follow that women would *on the whole* be happier if they were socialized away from the desire to compete for these positions than they would be if they were encouraged instead *to make their own choices* as to the roles they would like to follow, free of social pressure. If there are significant inherent psychological differences in the aggressiveness of the sexes, as Goldberg claims, it is natural to expect that women would tend to freely choose the less aggressive roles in our society, without any external force having to be applied. Indeed, Goldberg concedes this point, but he does not seem to perceive the possibility that nature itself will see to it that those women who are most likely to lose out in the competitive struggle for high-status positions would not choose to enter that struggle without social pressure. As Mill so aptly put it in "The Subjection of Women," "The anxiety of mankind to interfere in behalf of nature, for fear lest nature should not succeed in effecting its purpose, is an altogether unnecessary solicitude."

One should not lose sight of the fact that if there are natural psychological differences in the sexes which make women on the whole less aggressive than men, this will not be *universally* the case. Although women *may on the average* be less aggressive than men, there will be some women who are quite capable of successfully competing with very aggressive men for those roles in our society which require such attributes. It is far from clear that society has a right to systematically deny these roles to those women who would be capable of winning a free competitive struggle for them for the benefit of those women who would not be so capable. First, one could argue that even if Goldberg is right that women as a whole would be worse off if they were not socialized away from competition for these positions, it is unfair, and for that reason wrong, to penalize those women who would succeed in the competitive struggle for the benefit of the greater number who would not (that is, one could assume a deontological standpoint where the value of justice outweighs the disutility of a social practice). From this perspective, justice demands that each individual be judged on the basis of individual merit and not on the basis of the average psychological makeup of that individual's sexual group.

Furthermore, Goldberg's utilitarian claim that the lack of socially enforced sex roles is apt to result in a lesser quantity of happiness for women as a whole than would be obtained were these sex roles socially promoted is more complex than he makes it appear. According to Goldberg's utilitarian argument, in order to maximize the happiness of women a society would have to encourage women to accept the view that it is their nature to be less aggressive than men and, consequently, that it would be unwise for them to compete with men for the high-status positions in our society. Goldberg's conclusions would follow, however, only if one assumes that the happiness that would be gained by socializing women away from unsuccessfully competing with men for high-status positions would be greater than the happiness that would be lost to those women who are socialized away from entering a competitive struggle they could have won and otherwise would have entered. There is, however, no evidence that would support (or refute) such a claim. Goldberg's argument seems to rest more on an act of faith than on any scientific fact, and as such tends to lend support to the contention that arguments from nature for male dominance in our society function as myths for making this dominance acceptable to male and female alike. At the very least, our commitment to the value of individual autonomy should be strong enough to require that any person who advocates restricting free choice on utilitarian grounds should have the burden of providing strong evidence that the consequences of such a restriction would indeed contribute to the greatest good for the greatest number. This is a burden that has not been met when it comes to encouraging social acceptance of sex roles

Racial Equality: The Nature versus Nurture Question

Like those who defend male dominance, those who defend racial subjugation point to alleged innate differences to account for the alleged superiority or inferiority of certain races. For example, the typical justification for Negro slavery in this country rested on the belief that Negroes suffered from a genetically inherited racial inferiority which accounted for their childlike and irresponsible natures. Given this widely accepted stereotype of the essential nature of the Negro, slavery could be perceived as a benevolent institution which provided the Negro with the fully protective environment that was essential for his survival in a civilized society. This view of genetic Negro inferiority was the predominant one among educated as well as uneducated whites in the United States until the early twentieth century. Its influence began to wane, however, as the environmentalism of the developing behavioral sciences gained influence in educated circles in the late 1920s and 1930s and became the predominant view in these circles in the 1940s and 1950s. The tendency, during this period, was to deny the validity of the typical "Sambo" personality of the black man as docile and loyal but irresponsible and lazy; humble but chronically given to lying and stealing. Instead an emphasis was placed on the black man's courage and rebelliousness against strong odds. By the 1950s and 1960s, it was generally taken as beyond questions that the innate inferiority of the Negro had been fully discredited by modern science and that blacks differed at birth from whites only in color pigmentation. As Kenneth Stampp put it in his influential study of slavery, *The Peculiar Institution* (1956), "Negroes are, after all, only white men with black skins, nothing more, nothing less."

Not, all, however, shared Stampp's view that the Sambo personality was a myth created to justify Negro subjugation. Given the environmental intellectual temper of the times, scholars who believed that the Sambo personality was not a pure myth but reflected some truth about the typical Negro personality during and after slavery in this country turned to environmental explanations of its source. It was claimed, for example, that this personality type was a direct result of the savage environmental conditions of African tribal life. Yet anthropological observations of the energy, resourcefulness, and dignity of African tribal life undercut such a perspective. In addition, although such noble Negro qualities did tend to be crushed for those Negores who became slaves in the United States, this did not seem to be the case in Latin America and the West Indies. Why was this? According to Stanley Elkins in his influential book *Slavery* (1959), it was the American slavery system itself which created the "Sambo" type. Borrowing the sociological concepts of "role theory," Elkins claimed that the American Negro during slavery, unlike his Latin American counterpart, tended to display the typical "Sambo" characteristics because in the United States, unlike in Latin America, this was the only role the Negro would be rewarded for playing. Since he was rewarded for playing up to the role of a person who was incapable of being trusted with the full privileges of freedom and adulthood, the American Negro tended to display these characteristics which could then in turn be used as evidence for his inherent inferiority and as a justification for his continued subjugation.

Throughout the 1960s, the view that there was a genetic base for differences in the abilities of various races was almost universally rejected in academic circles. In 1969, however, Arthur Jensen published an article which asserted that blacks as a group have lower I.Q.s than whites. In this and later articles, Jensen elaborated his view that the mean black I.Q. is about 15 points below that of whites. Heredity, Jensen claimed, accounts for some 80 percent of I.Q. variance, while environment (including prenatal environment) accounts for only 20 percent. Since such a claim struck at the very heart of the equalitarian liberalism of the 1960s, Jensen's article was widely and vehemently denounced in academic circles. Yet Jensen too had his supporters,[3] and a new round in the nature versus nurture debate began in the 1970s.

There are good reasons for one to be skeptical of the claims that are now being made again about the inherent intellectual inferiority of blacks. Similar claims were made not long ago about other minority groups, only to be refuted. For example, in the early days of I.Q. tests, immigrant Poles, Russians, and Jews were found to score on the average about 25 or 30 points lower on these tests than the Nordics from Northwestern Europe. Such a fact fueled the belief that there was a genetic reason for such differences. But as these various supposedly intellectually inferior minority groups became assimilated into American culture, the I.Q. differences disappeared. As environmentalists have charged, standard I.Q. tests may be culturally biased ones that are slanted to favor abstract thinking that is a product of the environmentally enriched home.

Nevertheless, it is important that we realize that there are competent people who strongly take issue with the standard liberal assumption that a society that provided equal environmental opportunities to all would be a society in which all racial and ethnic groups would be represented in the different sectors of our economy in proportion to their percentage of the total work force. This is questionable not only on genetic grounds but also on the basis of cultural differences in values and styles of living. Such cultural differences can be greatly diluted in the United States melting pot, but they do not tend to disappear fully. Since many people who have the opportunity to assimilate themselves into the more diffuse mainstream of American culture often voluntarily choose to remain faithful to their older cultural traditions, it is doubtful that mere equality of opportunity would eliminate these cultural differences and whatever other differences they bring in their wake.

However, even if different racial or ethnic groups would naturally gravitate to different sectors of the economy, it would be unjust to deny particular individuals equal environmental opportunities and the chance to compete for particular positions on such grounds. However much heredity or cultural differences account for differing abilities, there will be some members of all racial and ethnic groups who would succeed in the competitive struggle if they were given a chance. As Jensen himself declares,

> I'm a strong advocate and always have been of equal opportunity, of civil rights. I've been opposed to racial or social class segregation. I believe in treating people

---

[3]In particular, William Shockley and R. Hernstein. Shockley, Hernstein and Jensen's concerns are, however, quite different. Jensen's main concern has been with ways of changing the educational system. Shockley has been concerned with what he calls dysgenics—that is, the genetic downbreeding of the population. As he sees it, the less able elements in society tend to breed faster than the more able elements, producing more and more offspring who cannot take their productive place in a technological society. Hernstein's concern has been with the implications of the equalitarian ideal of providing equal environmental opportunities to all. As Hernstein sees it, if all environmental inequalities were removed and individuals freely competed for the best jobs on the basis of *individual merit,* then occupational level and social class level would ultimately be determined solely by the genes, resulting in a *meritocracy* of inherited social class based on genetics.

in terms of their own individual characteristics, rather than in terms of their group membership....every person is a unique combination of genes. Your genetic background can produce so many different combinations even within one family... that you have to think of yourself in terms of what you, yourself, are and not in terms of your origins. I think it's racist thinking to think of yourself in terms of your group or your ancestry: What about a Japanese fellow, say, who's six feet three inches. Should he worry about the fact that the Japanese population as a whole is shorter than, say, the Scandinavian population as a whole? He's six feet three inches, which is tall enough to be a basketball star. Now if he were five feet four inches, he'd never make it as a basketball star, not because he's Japanese, but because he's five feet four inches. It's the same thing in the intellectual realm.

Jensen's analogy is misleading, however. A person's height is an obvious physical characteristic, observable to all. This is not true of a person's native intelligence. The belief that blacks are generally less intelligent than whites is apt to make blacks feel inferior and be looked upon as inferior, preventing them from achieving their potential and helping to create racial intellectual differences that will be attributed mistakenly to genetic causes. Since we should not allow general racial perceptions to distort equal environmental opportunity, it is plausible to question the wisdom of research into genetic racial differences in native intelligence. Jensen may indeed be committed to equal opportunities for all racial groups, as he says, but he should realize that his pronouncements do not support this goal.

THE QUESTION OF "PREFERENTIAL TREATMENT" FOR VICTIMS OF SOCIAL INJUSTICE

Introduction

As a result of the Civil Rights Act of 1964, affirmative action programs have been initiated which aim at eliminating discrimination and improving the condition of disadvantaged minorities in our country.[4] At first, these programs aimed at eliminating deliberate barriers which denied to some the opportunities that were afforded others. In addition, there was an attempt to root out the more subtle types of discrimination that are often not recognized as such. For example, it has been claimed that standards which are good predictors of performance for members of one group are poor predictors of performance for other groups. Similarly, attention has been directed to the unfair utilization of beliefs that race and sex are correlated with other features that would seem to justify discriminatory practices. For example, it has been said that it is unfair to discriminate against a woman on the grounds that, unlike a man, she would be likely to eventually have child care or other domestic responsibilities which would limit the time she could devote to her job.

[4] As we shall later discuss, the meaning of "disadvantaged minority" and the groups it refers to is a subject of debate. As this term is usually used, it is taken to refer to blacks, Spanish Americans, American Indians, and, at times, women. Often no distinction is made as to the relative degree of disadvantage of individuals within these groups; instead, merely belonging to one of these groups is taken to qualify an individual for a special affirmative action program.

In addition to the attempt to eliminate explicit and more subtle discriminatory practices, there was a widespread belief that certain minority groups should be compensated for the environmental disadvantages that made it impossible for them to equally compete with others who were provided greater opportunities. Fairness dictated that minorities that were denied equal opportunities in the past be provided these opportunities now. Such was the underlying sentiment behind the federal affirmative action program launched by Lyndon Johnson in 1965. As President Johnson put it,

> You do not take a person who, for years, has been hobbled by chains and liberate him, bring him up to the starting line of a race, and then say, "You are free to compete with all the others," and still justly believe that you have been completely fair.

Educational programs were instituted, such as the federal Headstart program, which attempted to provide prekindergarten learning experiences to economically disadvantaged children, and the New York State Seek program, which provided free college preparatory courses and allowances for economically disadvantaged high school graduates who were judged capable of doing college work but would not ordinarily gain admittance to colleges in New York on the basis of their grades and test scores.

Since such remedial programs did not have an appreciable and immediate effect, some governmental programs encouraged the hiring of members of minority groups or their admission into educational programs on the basis of criteria other than those normally used. This generated widespread criticism. It was unfair, the critics protested, to attempt to remedy the injustices of the past by utilizing unfair discriminatory practices in the present. Individual merit, they protested, should be the only standard utilized in deciding who should receive jobs and educational opportunities. Just as it is wrong to prevent people from obtaining positions simply because they are members of some minority group, it would be wrong, they argued, to favor certain minorities at the expense of more qualified candidates. It was especially wrong, such critics affirmed, to guarantee groups a set number of places in some trade or educational institutions. Affirmative action goals, they asserted, had the tendency in practice to become unfair quotas. The idea of racial quotas, seemed especially immoral to many members of other minority groups, such as Jews, who were themselves in the past penalized by quotas. If some individuals are to be rewarded on the basis of quotas, they argued, others must necessarily be unjustly penalized as a result of these quotas.

On the other hand, those who defended preferential treatment for minority groups saw such programs as morally justified for various reasons. For some, such programs were seen as a just way of compensating individuals or groups for past injustices or for present disadvantages stemming from past injustices. Others saw the requirements of justice in a forward-looking light. While willing to admit that such programs are unjust to those who are forced to pay the price of the creation of a more equalitarian society, they saw the price as a temporary one that a just society should bear. Still others saw such programs as justifiable on purely utilitarian grounds. As they saw it, such programs were required as a means of bringing about certain future goods, such as providing for diversity of ideas in the various professions or as a means of providing role models for disadvantaged minorities to help break the grip of self-fulfilling expectations that they cannot succeed in certain areas.

The conflict over what justice or utility requires in the setting of standards for allocating scarce jobs and educational opportunities has become a politically explosive one which fuels the passions of both those who demand their fair share of the American dream and those who see themselves as unjustly threatened on the basis of their race or sex. Such treatment, they argue, is contrary to the equal protection guaranteed every American by the Fourteenth Amendment of the Constitution. It is precisely this claim that was put before the Supreme Court in a series of cases that began in 1971 when Marco De Funis filed a lawsuit against the University of Washington Law School, claiming that he had been unfairly and unconstitutionally denied admission on the basis of the fact that he was a white male. The constitutionality of alleged reverse discrimination against white males was raised again in the famous 1978 case of Allan Bakke who was denied admission to the medical school at the University of California at Davis, and in the 1979 case of Brian Weber who was passed over at Kaiser Aluminum and Chemical Corporation for a training program which reserved half of its openings for blacks. These cases, and those that followed them have generated much controversy and have divided groups that pride themselves on their commitment to justice for minority groups. Let us turn to a consideration of these cases.

The DeFunis Case (1971)

In his lawsuit against the University of Washington Law School, DeFunis contended that he had been denied admission to the law school while minority applicants, defined on racial standards, who were less qualified by virtue of lower college grades and lower Law School Admission Test scores were admitted. This, he claimed, was contrary to the Fourteenth Amendment which provides that "[No state may] deny to any person within its jurisdiction the equal protection of the laws." The Washington trial court that heard DeFunis's case ruled in his favor and granted an injunction enabling him to enroll in the University of Washington Law School. On appeal, however, the Washington State Supreme Court reversed the lower court decision, ruling in favor of the University of Washington Law School's admission policy.

In defending this judgment, the court contended first that it was quite reasonable for a law school to depart from a mechanical consideration of test scores and grades when considering minority applications, for this

> ... does not always produce good indicators of the full potential of such culturally separated or deprived individuals, and that to rely solely on such formal credentials could well result in unfairly denying to qualified minority persons the chance to pursue the educational opportunities available at the University.

Although the test scores and grades of minority applicants admitted to the Law School were generally lower than those of many rejected applicants, their records, nevertheless, showed that they were qualified to compete in the law school program, the court declared. In addition, the court continued, the University did not violate DeFunis's right to equal protection under the Fourteenth Amendment by granting preferential treatment to certain racial categories of applicants. In defense of this claim, the Court pointed out that according to Supreme Court decisions, racial classifications are not always unconstitutional. Indeed, according to *Brown v. Board of Education,* there are times when race must be utilized by public educational institutions as essential to bringing about racial balance in the schools.[5] While a racial classification is a "suspect classification" subject to "strict scrutiny," such a classification is legitimate constitutionally when its utilization is essential to some "compelling state interest."[6] The utilization of racial classifications in the admission policy of the University of Washington Law School was indeed essential for a compelling state interest, the court declared, asserting,

> It can hardly be gainsaid that the minorities have been, and are, grossly under-represented in the law schools. . . . we find the state interest in eliminating racial imbalance within public legal education to be compelling. . . .
>
> The legal profession plays a critical role in the policy making sector of our society. . . . That lawyers, in making and influencing those decisions, should be cognizant of the views, needs, and demands of all segments of society is a principle beyond dispute. The educational interest of the state in producing a racially balanced student body at the law school is compelling.
>
> Finally, the shortage of minority attorneys—and, consequently, minority prosecutors, judges, and public officials—constitutes an undeniably compelling state interest. If minorities are to live within the rule of law, they must enjoy equal representation within our legal system.

In reply to the claim that a minority admissions policy is not necessary for the achievement of these objections, the court replied,

> It has been suggested that the minority admissions policy is not necessary, since the same objective could be accomplished by improving the elementary and secondary education of minority students to a point where they could secure equal representa-

[5]In this momentous 1954 decision, the Supreme Court addressed itself to the question of whether "segregation of children in public schools solely on the basis of race, even though the physical facilities and other 'tangible' factors may be equal, deprive the children of equal educational opportunities." Claiming that segregated schools are "inherently unequal" and consequently contrary to the equal protection clause of the Fourteenth Amendment, the Supreme Court answered, yes.

[6]As interpreted by the courts, the equal protection clause of the Fourteenth Amendment limits the types of classifications states can utilize in determining how to distribute their various benefits and burdens. In most cases, as long as there is some "rational relationship" between the classification utilized and a permissible legislative purpose, the courts, in deference to the legislative judgment of the states, have allowed classifications to stand, even when there might be good evidence that some other type of classification would better serve their purpose. However, when a classification infringes on a basic constitutionally guaranteed right, the courts look harder at whether a legitimate purpose exists and whether the classification serves that purpose. In such cases, the classifications are said to be "suspect" and subject to the "strict scrutiny" test. According to this test, a state has the burden of showing that its classification "is the least restrictive means toward furtherance of a compelling state interest." As far as the issue at hand is concerned, some claim that the racial and ethnic classifications utilized in special admissions programs should be subjected to the "rational relationship" test, while some claim that they should be subjected to the stiffer "strict scrutiny" test. Yet others claim that some intermediate standard of appraisal should be utilized.

tion in law schools through direct competition with nonminority applicants on the basis of the same academic criteria. This would be highly desirable, but 18 years have passed since the decision in *Brown v. Board of Education*. . .and minority groups are still grossly underrepresented in law schools. If the law school is forbidden from taking affirmative action, this underrepresentation may be perpetuated indefinitely. No less restrictive means would serve the governmental interest here.

DeFunis appealed the Washington Supreme Court's decision to the United States Supreme Court which heard the case in 1974 and in a 5 to 4 decision declared the case moot since DeFunis was, at that time, in his last quarter at the law school and as such did not stand to gain from a favorable verdict.

The Bakke Case (1978)

In 1973 and again in 1974, Alan Bakke, a white, thirty-six-year-old civil engineer, applied for admission to the medical school at the University of California at Davis, but was rejected. Since Davis, during these two years had accepted minority students whose college averages and test scores were considerably lower than his, Bakke went to court, claiming that the University of California had denied him admission, while granting admission to less qualified students, solely on the grounds that he was white. This, he charged, was a violation of the equal protection clause of the Fourteenth Amendment. In particular, Bakke claimed, it was unconstitutional for the U.C. Davis Medical School to put aside a quota of 16 out of its 100 places in its first-year student body for minority group applicants.[7]

The University of California filed a cross-complaint, asking the court to determine that their special-admissions program was valid. Minority group status, the University contended, was only one factor out of several in the selection process. In particular, minority students were considered for admission under the special

---

[7]Applicants to medical schools are required to take the Medical College Admissions Test which consists of four tests (verbal, quantitative, general information, and science). Alan Bakke's scores on the tests and his average were quite high relative not only to "minority" admittees, but also to regular admittees. For example, in 1973:

	Overall GPA	Verbal	Quantitative	Science	General Information
Alan Bakke	3.51	96	94	96	72
Averages of Regular Admittees	3.49	81	76	83	69
Averages of Special Admittees	2.88	46	24	35	33

While test scores and grade point averages were by far the most important factors considered for nonminority applicants, the Davis Medical School's Admissions Committee also took into consideration an applicant's extracurricular and community activities, his work experience, his personal comments on his application, and the two letters of recommendation that each applicant is required to have submitted on his behalf. After considering these factors, the Admissions Committee determined whether the applicant showed sufficient promise to warrant a personal interview. (Bakke was interviewed both years that he applied. It has been claimed that his age was a strong factor in his rejection.) In addition to the regular admissions procedure, the university operated the special admissions program which, although described as one whose aim is to "increase opportunities in medical education for disadvantaged citizens," had been used only to aid specific minorities (black, Chicano, American Indian). Such students were placed in a separate admissions pool to compete only against each other for the 16 places reserved for them. (A similar procedure was utilized at that time at all the University of California medical and law schools.)

minority program only when they suffered from financial disadvantage. Granting that some minority admittees may have been less qualified than nonminority rejectees such as Bakke, the University asserted that this program nevertheless served a compelling state interest. This was so, the University argued, in that the minority program served to promote diversity in the student body, to expand the opportunities for medical education to minorities who came from economically and educationally disadvantaged backgrounds, to provide for greater representation of minorities in the medical profession, and to increase the number of doctors serving the minority community. Since such purposes, the University contended, served a compelling state interest, the special admissions policy instituted to achieve them did not violate the equal protection clause of the Fourteenth Amendment. Furthermore, the University contended that racial classifications should be seen as suspect classifications requiring strict scrutiny only when they result in invidious discrimination. Using the courts' own standard of "invidious discrimination" as the utilization of a method of classification which "excludes, disadvantages, isolates, or stigmatizes a minority or is designed to segregate the races," the University contended that white applicants denied admission were not so stigmatized.

In September 1976, the California Supreme Court ruled (6–1) that the University of California's special admissions programs for minorities at the Davis Medical School was unconstitutional. The court ordered the program abolished and that Bakke be admitted to the Davis Medical School. The California Supreme Court, which at that time was considered one of the most liberal in the country, declared that the equal protection clause of the Fourteenth Amendment is incompatible with granting preferential treatment to individuals on the basis of their race.[8] Agreeing that the use of racial criteria in the University of California special admissions programs would be constitutional if a "compelling state interest can be demonstrated and there are no viable nonracial alternative methods available," the court ruled that the University of California had not, as a matter of fact, exhausted alternative methods of achieving its legitimate goal of greater minority enrollment. Among such alternative methods, the Court suggested, would be more aggressive recruitment of fully qualified minority applicants, remedial educational programs, lessening the emphasis on grades for all students, or increasing the number of medical school places. If such methods should, however, prove inadequate, it would be permissible for the University to grant preferential treatment to students on the basis of educational and economic disadvantage, but not race, the Court declared.

It was abundantly clear, the Court declared, that whites suffered a grievous disadvantage when they were excluded from the University's Medical School on racial grounds. The fact that they were not also invidiously discriminated against

[8]In the sole dissenting opinion, Justice Matthew O. Tobriner upheld the university's position, claiming that the court ought to distinguish between invidious and benign racial classifications. "Our society cannot be completely color blind in the short term if we are to have a color-blind society in the long run," he wrote. The benign racial classifications utilized by the special admissions program were used not to exclude any particular racial group "but to assure that the qualified applicants of all racial groups were actually represented in the institution." Consequently, they were not a violation of the Fourteenth Amendment, Tobriner argued.

in the sense that a stigma was cast upon them because of their race was irrelevant. In reply to those who claimed that racial classifications may be used for benign or favorable purposes, the Court replied that the special admissions program was not benign to Bakke and other nonminority applicants who were denied admission as a result of it. There should only be one standard utilized for all 100 places at the Davis Medical School, the Court contended. Because he was white, Bakke was unable to compete for the 16 places reserved for minority applicants. This was wrong, the Court declared. Bakke was entitled to have his application evaluated without regard to his race or the race of any other applicant.

Given the California Supreme Court's ruling on Bakke's behalf, the University of California appealed to the United States Supreme Court. Let us turn to a brief summary of the arguments presented by the University of California and by Bakke to the Supreme Court and to the Supreme Court's resolution of this case.

The University of California's Position

Utilizing the same standard that it presented to the California Supreme Court, the university claimed in its brief to the U.S. Supreme Court that the Fourteenth Amendment does not prohibit "race-conscious state action that is neither hostile or invidious, and which is closely tailored to achieving a major public objective." Even though the Davis Medical School provides quotas on the number of white students it admits, it does not discriminate against them in a manner precluded by the Fourteenth Amendment, for such quotas do not stigmatize them as inferior. The special admissions program, furthermore, is not unfair, as some have contended, allowing unqualified students to enroll at the expense of qualified ones, but simply exercises discretion among groups of qualified students who differ by degree. No persons are admitted under the special minority admissions program unless they are deemed qualified to succeed in their professional schools.

If increasing minority enrollment is a legitimate public objective, as the California Supreme Court conceded, there simply is no way to achieve this goal other than through the use of racial classifications, the University of California argued. In particular, the California Supreme Court's suggestion that it should open its special admissions program to all disadvantaged students regardless of race, "founders on the rock of reality," the University contended. The problem is that far more low-income whites apply for medical and law schools than low-income members of minority groups. For example, the University cited a study by the Association of American Colleges showing that in 1976, of medical school applicants from families earning less than $10,000 annually, 71 percent were white and 29 percent were members of minority groups. Indeed, if the University of California were to open its special enrollment program to all disadvantaged students, the figures would be even more strongly slanted against minority groups, as the University would find itself swamped with the applications of an "enormous number of whites who do not now apply because they know their grades are too low." In addition, disadvantaged whites only far outnumber disadvantaged minorities, but also tend to outperform them in grades and admission test scores.

Attributing the lower academic performance of blacks to the inferior and segregated schools they are often forced to attend, the University argued that being black should not be equated for moral purposes with being poor, for it is blacks and not the poor who "have been compelled by unconstitutional laws to attend segregated and inferior schools."

Bakke's Position

The arguments presented to the Supreme Court supporting Bakke fell into two groups. First, there were those who claimed that the Fourteenth Amendment requires state-run professional schools to choose among their applicants solely on the basis of their individual qualifications, without any consideration being given to their race or ethnic background. Bakke was denied his Fourteenth Amendment right to be considered on his merits as an individual since the Davis Medical School admitted minority students who were clearly less qualified than he, as evidenced by Bakke's far superior academic credentials.

Not all who supported Bakke, however, claimed that only the most qualified, as judged by academic credentials, should be admitted to medical and law schools. For example, Reynold H. Colvin, a Bakke attorney, in oral argument before the Supreme Court, conceded under questioning that, in his opinion, the Davis Medical School's special admissions program would be constitutional if it aimed at aiding all disadvantaged students and not only those who are members of minority groups. According to this line of reasoning, considerations of *compensatory justice,* can override the principle of rewarding people according to *individual merit* based on academic credentials, but the equal protection clause of the Fourteenth Amendment prohibits the direct utilization of racial standards in any admissions policy. What general category of "disadvantage" then should warrant compensation? For most who took this point of view, including Colvin, the relevant category was that of economic disadvantage, while for others, this category should be conceived more broadly, to include the disadvantages that result from racial segregation and racial prejudice as well, as long as such factors are not considered exclusively.

The Supreme Court's Decision
on the Bakke Case

On June 28, 1978, the Supreme Court of the United States presented its ruling in the Bakke case. First, it ruled 5–4 that the admissions program at Davis was unlawful and ordered Bakke admitted. Second, it ruled 5–4 again (but with a different majority) that race may properly be considered a factor in admissions programs. Justice Lewis Powell had a pivotal role in this decision, joining Justices Stevens, Rehnquist, Stewart, and Burger in striking down the Davis program and in ordering Bakke admitted, but leaving their fold to join Justices Brennan, Blackmun, Marshall, and White in permitting universities to consider race as an element in their admissions policies.

As Stevens, Rehnquist, Stewart, and Burger saw it, there was no need to consider the constitutionality of Davis' admissions program under the equal protection clause of the Fourteenth Amendment since this program was unlawful under

Title VI of the Civil Rights Act of 1964. Although the words of the Fourteenth Amendment may be open to different interpretations, the directive of Title VI, they declared, "is crystal clear" in forbidding federally funded universities from "excluding individuals on the grounds of race, color, or national origin." Since the University of California could not meet the burden of proving that Bakke was not excluded on the basis of his race, he should be admitted, the Stevens-Rehnquist-Stewart-Burger bloc declared.

On the other side, Justices Brennan, Blackmun, Marshall, and White claimed that the Davis admissions program was legal under both Title VI of the Civil Rights Act and the equal protection clause of the Constitution since it was an essential means for remedying societal discrimination against blacks and other minorities. As these justices saw it, university admissions policies which place some weight on an applicant's racial or ethnic background are unlawful only when they serve to stigmatize or stamp as inferior a particular group of people. This, they declared, is not the case with the admissions policy employed at Davis, which legitimately attempts to overcome "the handicap of past discrimination" and to remedy the "substantial and chronic underrepresentation of minority groups in medical school."

Justice Powell began his opinion with a discussion of Title VI of the Civil Rights Act. Believing that the types of racial classifications prohibited under Title VI are exactly those prohibited under the equal protection clause of the Fourteenth Amendment, Powell then turned his attention to the equal protection clause. He began by rejecting the view that this clause should be taken as directed only to certain minority groups who are deserving of more protection than others, declaring that "the guarantee of equal protection cannot mean one thing when applied to one individual and something else when applied to a person of another color." On this basis, Powell rejected the University of California's argument, accepted by the Brennan, Blackmun, Marshall, and White bloc, that the Court should adopt the view "that discrimination cannot be suspect [of a violation of the equal protection clause of the Fourteenth Amendment] if its purpose can be characterized as benign [that is, if it does not stigmatize and serves some legitimate purpose]." The equal protection clause is not framed in terms of "stigma," he stated:

> [This notion] reflects a subjective judgment that is standardless. All state-imposed classifications that rearrange burdens and benefits on the basis of race are likely to be viewed with deep resentment by the individual burdened. The denial to innocent persons of equal rights and opportunities may outrage those so deprived and therefore may be perceived as invidious. . . . One should not lightly dismiss the inherent unfairness of, and the perception of mistreatment that accompanies, a system of allocating benefits and privileges on the basis of skin color and ethnic origin.

Powell then went on to point out that the white majority is itself a collection of minorities, many of whom were themselves subjected to a history of prior discrimination at the hands of the state and private individuals. There is no principled basis, he declared, for deciding which groups should merit "heightened judicial solicitude" and which should not under a special minority admissions program.

Davis, for example, was unable to explain why it had signaled out only those minority groups that it did. Powell noted.

Nevertheless, Powell was not willing to rule out consideration of race and ethnic status entirely. Instead, he took the view that although the Constitution protects all individuals from discrimination on the grounds of race and ethnic background, it is still possible for universities to utilize such classifications as a factor in their admissions programs. Such classifications, he claimed, are suspect ones, which require strict scrutiny.[9] Powell then went on to consider the various goals proposed by the University of California as justifications for its special minority admissions program, rejecting as unconstitutional all but the goal of obtaining a diverse student body. Universities have a "countervailing constitutional interest" to select those students who will contribute the most to the "robust exchange of ideas," he declared.

Powell did not, however, accept the view that the goal of a diverse student body can be constitutionally achieved by the utilization of racial and ethnic quotas which, he believed, place too much emphasis upon race and ethnic background to the exclusion of other relevant factors. Racial and ethnic origin is but a single element in the far broader array of qualifications and characteristics that contribute to academic diversity, he asserted. As examples of these other qualities, Powell mentioned unique work experience, leadership potential, maturity, demonstrated compassion, and a history of overcoming disadvantage. Although race may properly be considered by universities in judging who should be admitted, a university must "adhere to a policy of individual comparisons" as opposed to a method that results in a systematic inclusion of certain groups. In such an individualized, case-by-case process, "the file of a particular black applicant may be examined for his potential contribution to diversity without the factor of race being decisive when compared, for example, with that of an applicant identified as an Italian-American if the latter is thought to exhibit qualities more likely to promote beneficial educational pluralism," Powell wrote. Since the Davis admissions program "prefers the designated minority groups at the expense of other individuals who are totally foreclosed from competing for the 16 special admissions seats," it is unconstitutional, Powell declared. Powell then went on to commend the Harvard College admissions program which attempts to recruit a diverse student body without setting any racial or ethnic quotas. At Harvard, Powell approvingly pointed out, "the race of an applicant can tip the balance in his favor, just as geographic origin or life spent on a farm may tip the balance in other candidates' cases." Such a program, unlike the one employed at Davis, Powell noted, does not insulate "the individual from comparison with all other candidates for the available seats."

Powell's opinion in the Bakke case is a logically fragile one. While Powell sees a major difference between the admissions program employed at Harvard College, which utilizes race and ethnic background as *a factor* to be weighed in

---

[9]The Brennan-White-Marshall-Blackmun bloc rejected both the strict scrutiny and rational relationship standards, utilizing instead the intermediate standard that racial and ethnic classifications "must serve important governmental objectives and must be substantially related to achievement of these objectives."

a university's admission policy, and the admissions program employed at Davis which utilizes racial and ethnic *quotas*, this difference is at best, as Justice Blackmun described it, "a thin and indistinct one." Indeed, Justice Brennan suggested that it is entirely illusory, writing:

> There is no sensible and certainly no constitutional distinction between, for example, adding a set number of points to the admissions rating of disadvantaged minority applicants as an expression of the preference with the expectation that this will result in the admission of an approximately determined number of qualified minority applicants and setting a fixed number of places for such applicants. . . . there is no basis for preferring a particular preference program simply because, in achieving the same goals that the Davis Medical School is pursuing, it proceeds in a manner that is not immediately apparent to the public.

Brennan has logic on his side. There is no justification for saying, as Powell does, that admissions programs that utilize racial quotas violate *individual rights,* while this is not true of admissions programs that consider race as a factor. Clearly, in the latter programs, as long as race counts, nonminority students, who would otherwise have been admitted, will lose places to minority students. As such, race will be an admissions handicap to nonminority students. Until one knows how much race is to count in such programs, one will be unable to determine whether nonminority students will be better off under such programs where their race is a handicap for all positions than they would be under programs where it will be no handicap for a smaller number of positions. If admissions programs which consider race as a factor do not necessarily violate the individual rights of applicants, as Powell claims, then neither should racial quotas.

In its self-description of its admissions program, Harvard College declared:

> a truly heterogeneous environment. . .cannot be provided without some attention to numbers. . . . 10 or 20 black students could not begin to bring to their classmates and to each other the variety of points of view, backgrounds, and experience of blacks in the United States. Their small numbers might also create a sense of isolation among the black students themselves. . . .Consequently, when making its decisions, the Committee on Admissions is aware that there is some relationship between numbers and achieving the benefits to be derived from a diverse student body, and between numbers and providing a reasonable environment for those students admitted.

So numbers do matter at Harvard College after all! Does Harvard then do covertly what Davis does overtly? Although Justice Powell concedes the possibility that flexible university admissions programs can be utilized to disguise racial and ethnic quotas, he is willing, he tells us, to presume that universities will operate on "good faith." But what this means when the standard they are supposed to use is terribly vague he does not at all suggest. It is clear, however, that Powell is concerned with *what appears to be just* to the general public as well as with what actually is just. After telling us that the Davis admissions policy "will be viewed as inherently unfair by the public generally, as well as by applicants for admissions to the state university," Powell goes on to quote from the late Supreme Court Justice

Frankfurter that "Justice must satisfy the appearance of justice." Is the great virtue of the Harvard program, then, not that it *is* more just than the Davis program, but that it merely *appears* that way to the general public?

The Weber Case (1979)

On June 27, 1979, a year after its Bakke decision, the Supreme Court spoke again on the issue of reverse discrimination in the case of *United Steel Workers of America v. Brian F. Weber.* In this less heralded, although more significant case, a majority of the Supreme Court ruled that private employers are acting within the law when they utilize racial quotas to "eliminate conspicuous racial inbalance in traditionally segregated job categories," even though they are not guilty themselves of racial discrimination.

The Weber case had its roots in a 1974 agreement between Kaiser Aluminum & Chemical Corporation and the United Steelworkers of America to initiate on-the-job skilled-craft training programs at 15 Kaiser plants, open to unskilled Kaiser workers. Prior to these programs, Kaiser hired as skilled workers only those who had prior craft experience. Because they had long been excluded from craft unions, few blacks had such experience and consequently were greatly underrepresented among Kaiser's skilled workers. For example, in the plant in Gramercy, Louisiana, where Weber was employed as an unskilled worker, only 2 percent of the skilled craftsmen were black, even though blacks comprised 39 percent of the local work force. The Kaiser training programs were initiated to overcome this racial imbalance. Black craft hiring goals were set for each Kaiser plant equal to the percentage of blacks in the respective local labor forces. In order to achieve this goal, each training program was to reserve 50 percent of its openings for blacks (until the goal was met), with black and white applicants to be selected on the basis of their relative seniority within their racial groups. When Kaiser announced that it was offering a total of 9 positions in three of these on-the-job training programs at the Gramercy plant, Weber applied for all three programs, but was not selected. When he learned that 2 of the 5 successful black candidates had less seniority than he, Weber brought suit in the U.S. District Court of Louisiana, alleging that use of the 50 percent minority admission quota to fill vacancies in Kaiser's craft training programs violated Title VII of the Civil Rights Act. The section of Title VII that speaks directly to this issue provides that:

> It shall be an unlawful employment practice for any employer, labor organization, or joint labor-management committee controlling apprenticeship or other training or retraining, including on-the-job training programs to discriminate against any individual because of his race, color, religion, sex, or national origin in admission to, or employment in, any program established to provide apprenticeship or other training.

Both the U.S. District Court and Appeals Court agreed with Weber prohibiting further use of Kaiser's racially based training program. As these courts saw it, while employers who have themselves utilized racially discriminatory employment or promotional policies may be compelled by a court to compensate the victims of these discriminatory policies, Title VII forbids employers who are not guilty of racial discrimination from using race as a factor in deciding whom to employ or promote. A majority of the Supreme Court disagreed.

Since the Weber case did not involve state action, the Supreme Court did not turn, as it had in the Bakke case, to a consideration of the Fourteenth Amendment's equal protection clause. Instead, it turned to the narrower legal question of whether Title VII prohibits the use of Kaiser's racially based training program. In a 5 to 2 decision, the Supreme Court ruled that it did not. (Justices Powell and Stevens excused themselves from this decision.) Justices Brennan, Marshall, Blackmun, and White who took the position in the Bakke case that the utilization of racial quotas in universities is constitutional were joined by Justice Stewart. While Justice Stewart, along with Justices Burger, and Rehnquist, had claimed in Bakke that the Civil Rights Act prohibits the use of *state imposed* racial quotas, Stewart's position in the Weber case indicated that he did not see the Civil Rights Act as prohibiting private employers from voluntarily utilizing racial quotas to redress racial imbalance. Burger and Rehnquist strongly disagreed.

The Supreme Court's Weber decision came as a relief to many large companies who were unsure of the legality of their affirmative action programs. On one hand, they found themselves pressured by the federal government—through the fear of loss of federal contracts—to increase the number of their minority employees. On the other hand, the district and appeals court in Weber ruled that they could not grant special preferences to underrepresented groups unless they had discriminated against these groups in the past. If they did not admit to this discrimination and proceeded, nevertheless, to grant special racial preferences, they invited legal suits for reverse discrimination from passed-over whites. Yet, if they admitted prior discrimination, they invited suits from the alleged victims of their previous discrimination. Clearly this situation was intolerable.

Justice Brennan wrote the majority opinion in the Weber case. While admitting that a literal interpretation of Title VII would prohibit the Kaiser training program, Brennan claimed that such an interpretation would be inconsistent with the spirit behind the Civil Rights Act—the advancement of blacks in the American economy. In defense of his contention that Congress did not intend that Title VII prohibit employers with racially imbalanced work forces from granting preferential treatment to racial minorities, Brennan pointed to the fact that Title VII does have a section which explicitly provides that nothing contained in Title VII "shall be interpreted to require any employer. . .to grant preferential treatment to any [racial] group." If Congress intended not to *permit* as well as not to *require* employers to grant preferential treatment to underrepresented racial minorities, it could easily have said so. Since it did not, Brennan argued, "[t]he natural inference is that Congress chose not to forbid all voluntary race-conscious affirmative action."

Rehnquist began his sarcastic 37-page dissent (about three times the length of Brennan's majority opinion) by comparing Brennan's reading of Title VII to George Orwell's *1984* where government officials distort the meanings of words to make them conform to shifting government policies. While Kaiser's racially discriminatory admission quota is flatly prohibited by the plain language of Title VII, and as such should make it unnecessary to inquire into the usually murky question of legislative intent, in this case, however, Rehnquist claimed, "the legislative history of Title VII is as clear as [its language]. . . and it irrefutably demonstrates that Congress meant precisely what it said. . . .—that *no* racial discrimination in employment is permissible under Title VII. . . ." The bulk of Rehnquist's opinion is devoted to a very detailed review of the legislative history of Title VII, including an abundance of direct quotations from Congressmen who participated in the debate over passage of the Civil Rights Act. As Rehnquist convincingly demonstrates, while the clause prohibiting the imposition of racial preferences was motivated by the fear of many Congressmen that federal officials might interpret any racial imbalance in a work force as a sign of racial discrimination, many supporters of the 1964 Civil Rights Act argued that federal agencies could not *require* racial preferences *since* Title VII clearly *prohibited* them.

While it is difficult to speak of "the intent of Congress" since the intent of the members of Congress who pass a given bill may be quite different, the devastating force of Rehnquist's direct quotations makes it clear that even if there were some members of Congress who assumed that Title VII did not prohibit the voluntary utilization of racial quotas to help underrepresented racial minorities in private industry, many clearly thought that it did. Equally clear, in 1964, there would have been no chance for the Civil Rights Act to pass if it were generally assumed that this act would later be used, as it was, by the federal government as a prod to *encourage* private employers to embark upon *voluntary* affirmative action programs giving special preferences to racial minorities. This is quite understandable, for in 1964 the goal of supporters of the Civil Rights Act was to put a stop to the explicit racial discrimination that prevented blacks from having *equal access* to jobs. It was only later that the belief became widespread that the cause of racial assimilation required more.

While Rehnquist is right in his reading of the general congressional intent in 1964, he does not mention, however, that as America's perception of the relevance of race has changed, so has that of Congress. Even though Congress has had ample opportunity to resolve the issue of whether the Civil Rights Act should be taken to mean what it seems to be saying, it has chosen not to do so. Indeed, rather than making it clear that this act prohibits the granting of racial preferences as a means of remedying racial discrimination, Congress passed a public works program in 1977 which requires racial preference. In this program, Congress mandated that at least 10 percent of grants for local public works projects should be spent for "minority business enterprises" defined as businesses 50 percent of which are owned by "Negroes, Spanish-speaking [Americans], Orientals, Indians, Eskimos, and Aleuts." Clearly, it would appear that the congressional intent in 1964 was not the intent in 1977. As a matter of legal principle, Rehnquist and Burger may be quite right that if the 1964 Civil Rights Act should not be taken now to prohibit the granting of racial preferences, it should be Congress, and not the Supreme Court, that says so. If the Supreme Court had upheld the Appeals Court's decision in the Weber case, however, it would have been intolerable to employers engaged in affirmative action programs if Congress did not come to grips with this issue quickly. Whether they would have been able and willing to resolve this politically explosive question is another matter.

1980–86 Cases

Fullilove (1980)

In a 6–3 decision in 1980 (*Fullilove v. U.S.*), the Supreme Court upheld the Congressional law, mentioned above, which set aside at least 10 percent of local public works projects for minority contractors. As Chief Justice Burger who wrote for the majority put it, "We reject the contention that in the remedial context, the Congress must act in a wholly 'color-blind' fashion." Guided in this decision, at least in part, by deference to Congress, the Supreme Court left unclear whether its decision applied to other governmental agencies as well.

Memphis Firefighters (1984) and Jackson Board of Education (1986)

While willing to accept the constitutionality of minority preferences in hirings and university admissions, the Supreme Court came down against such preferences in the issue of layoffs. In two decisions, one relating to Memphis firemen and the other to teachers in Jackson, Michigan, a majority of the Supreme Court held that it is unconstitutional to disrupt seniority systems in order to save newly hired blacks. Affirmative action, the Court was now saying, was appropriate for hiring, but not for firing. The primary difference, as the Court saw it, is that while the burden of affirmative action in hiring "is diffused to a considerable extent among society generally," this is not true with firings which impact on specific individuals.

New York Sheet Metal Workers (1986)

In this case, the Supreme Court upheld the constitutionality of a court imposed order that the New York Sheet Metal Workers adapt a 29 percent minority membership goal. Two general rules emerged in this case. First, a court may order a union to use quotas if this is necessary to overcome a history of "egregious discrimination." Second, minority members who themselves were not victims of past union bias can benefit from such quotas. In this regard, the Court rejected the position of the Reagan Justice Department that affirmative action quotas are constitutionally permissible only when the benefited minorities were themselves victims of prior discrimination.

Johnson vs. Transportation Agency of Santa Clara (1987)

In this (6–3) ruling, the Supreme Court, for the first time, specifically upheld job preferences for women. The case at issue involved a suit by Paul Johnson who was passed up for a position as a road dispatcher in favor of Diane Joyce. While in previous cases the Court had upheld affirmative action hiring programs only in those cases in which an employer or union had previously engaged in intentional ("egregious") discrimination, the Court was willing in this case to embrace the more sweeping principle that employees and unions are constitutionally permitted to engage in affirmative action solely on the basis of forward-looking considerations of distributive justice that aim at proportionate representation of women and minorities in the labor force. In a scathing dissent, the newest Supreme Court justice, the judicial conservative Antonin Scalia, who replaced retiring Chief Justice Burger, accused the Court's liberal faction of being more interested "in the alteration of social attitudes than in the elimination of discrimination." Claiming that the majority decision ignores both the letter of the law and the sociology of the sexes, Scalia chided, "It is absurd to think that the nationwide failure of road maintenance crews. . .to achieve the agency's ambition of. . .female representation is attributed primarily, if even substantially, to systematic exclusion of women eager to shoulder pick and shovel."

The Johnson decision has often been read as an affirmation of the principle that it is constitutionally permissible to give employment preferences to women over more qualified men; this reading is, however, dubious. While a higher court is bound to accept the factual findings of lower courts, the Supreme Court largely ignored the lower court finding that Johnson was better qualified than Joyce. This position was quite understandable since seven people, including Joyce and Johnson, were deemed eligible for the job, based on experience and interviews. According to established civil service procedure, any of these seven eligible applicants could be legitimately selected for the position. On the basis of an oral interview score of "73," Joyce was ranked third, Johnson and another man with interview scores of "75" were ranked second and first, respectively. Considering that no woman had ever occupied any of the 238 "skilled craft" positions in the Transportation Agency of Santa Clara and that most of these positions, unlike that for road dispatcher, involved the operartion of heavy equipment, one can understandably wonder if there were at least some latent bias in the *all male* interviewing committee's perception that Joyce was not the most qualified applicant. Indeed, obvious bias can be inferred by one interviewer's description of Joyce as a "rabble-rousing, skirt-wearing person."

Richmond v. Croson Co. (1989)

The promise of the Johnson decision proved short-lived. Written by Brennan, its sweeping pronouncement, that affirmative action was justified solely by the social engineering goal of the creation of a more integrated society, commanded the explicit support only of Marshall and Blackmun. Pointedly, Justice Sandra Day O'Connor, who was herself a victim of sexual discrimination as a young Stanford law school graduate, could not subscribe to Brennan's reasoning. Although rejecting Johnson's suit, she did not join Brennan in his opinion. In a brief comment, concurring with Brennan's decision, O'Connor claimed that the opinion should have been narrower in scope and restricted to the facts of the

Johnson case. Brennan's defense of his decision, she wrote, follows "an expansive and ill-defined approach" to affirmative action that goes beyond the law.

O'Connor's more restrained response to the demands of affirmative action would, however, soon command a majority of the Court. As a new conservative Supreme Court justice, Anthony Kennedy replaced the often pivotal Powell, the court would soon render another decision in its zigzag path through the thickets of affirmative action, with Justice O'Conner this time writing the majority opinion.

In this 6–3 decision, the court struck down a Richmond, Virginia plan that guaranteed minority groups at least 30 percent of that city's construction contracts. Casting doubt on governmental affirmative action programs, the decision, in defence to Congressional power, let stand the Fullilove decision which upheld a Congressional statute requiring a lesser quota for federally funded construction contracts. Also left standing were prior decisions allowing nongovernmentally imposed agreements concerning minority quotas and the right of courts to impose quotas that are necessary to overcome a history of egregious discrimination. The retreat centered on the right of cities or states to impose quotas on allegedly remedial grounds, while lacking specific evidence of governmental or private discrimination and the efficacy of the quotas in alleviating that discrimination.

As O'Connor saw it, to justify minority quotas in industry, local governments must provide evidence that the groups favored were victims of specific discrimination in gaining access to industrial opportunities. To establish specific discrimination as distinct from general and amorphous societal discrimination, it would not suffice, O'Connor wrote, to compare the percentage of minorities in a city or state; instead "the relevant statistical pool for purposes of demonstrating discriminatory exclusion must be the number of minorities qualified to undertake the particular task." On this question the city of Richmond had offered no evidence, O'Connor observed. If a relevant statistical disparity between the proportion of qualified minority contractors and the proportions of funds or contracts received by such contractors could be established, this would be prima facie evidence of discrimination and could justify governmental remedial attempts, including racial preferences. Such a remedy, however, O'Connor claimed, should be subject to strict scrutiny and rejected if a racially neutral method can serve the same remedial purpose.

In arguing that "an amorphous claim that there has been past discrimination in a particular industry cannot justify the use of an unyielding racial quota," O'Connor was troubled by the fact that the 30 percent minority quota in the Richmond case was imposed by a city council of which 5 of the 9 members were black. Nevertheless, the fact is that although 50 percent of Richmond, Virginia is black, only three-quarters of a percent of the city's construction contracts went to minorities in the five-year period preceding the enactment of the Richmond Ordinance. (The Richmond Ordinance defined a "minority" in the same manner as the federal government did in its minority set-aside program.) As O'Conner doubtlessly correctly perceived, such a wide discrepancy was due in large part to the very low percentage of minority contractors in Richmond, Virginia. Yet affirmative action quotas are often imposed precisely to remedy such discrepancies by creating strong incentives to attract minority participation. As such, these programs are tools for overcoming traditional minority under-representation by opening up tightly knit industries that perpetuate patterns of minority exclusion. Such patterns are rarely traceable to specific and identifiable discrimination, but rather reflect the quite understandable human tendency to do business with those with whom one is familiar and to be skeptical of newcomers. Consequently, the three most liberal members of the court—Brennan, Marshall, and Blackmun—claimed that the practical force of O'Connor's decision would be to preclude the use of affirmative action programs to overcome the most profound racial discrimination that afflicts our nation.

Yet as the twisting path of affirmative action decisions has indicated, this issue is far from being settled by the Supreme Court. Although the Court has decidedly turned to the "right" in the Richmond decision, only Scalia and Kennedy indicated in their concurring opinions in this case that they opposed affirmative action in nearly every instance. Rehnquist and White joined O'Connor in giving government the power to undertake affirmative action in narrowly defined circumstances. How narrow remains to be seen. Stevens, too, sits on the fence, accepting as O'Connor does, the legitimacy of the weighing of conflicting principles in the resolution of affirmative action cases. So, the resolution of future cases is unpredictable. As this is written, however, the trend is ominous for liberal supporters of affirmative action.

An Analysis of the Moral Arguments

The Demands of Compensatory Justice

Two different senses of the notion of compensatory justice are often appealed to as a justification of affirmative action programs. For some, this notion is a purely backward-looking one that demands that individuals be paid back for the unfair burdens they have suffered in the past. In this view, compensation is the payment of a *debt* rightfully *owed* to those who were wronged by those who were either responsible for that wrong or who profited from it. On the other hand, some see the demands of compensatory justice from a forward-looking perspective. As they see it, affirmative action programs are attempts to alleviate unfair or undeserved disabilities, whatever their source, that prevent people from competing on equal terms. In this view, it is not the unfair burdens individuals *have suffered* which in themselves justify compensation, but rather *the effect* these unfair burdens have had in preventing people from competing on equal terms. From this perspective, compensatory justice is an attempt to neutralize the *present* competitive disadvantages caused by unfair burdens so as to *create* a more equalitarian society.

Those who rely on the notion of compensatory justice also disagree over whether groups as well as individuals should be granted compensation. If blacks as a group have been victimized in the past by injustice, does compensatory justice demand that blacks as a group be compensated for this injustice, or does it require instead that only those who were victimized by this injustice be compensated? One will find supporters of both positions. For example, many of those who see compensation as a backward-looking debt assume that this debt is one owed by continuing groups (such as whites) to other continuing groups (such as blacks). If one accepts the idea of group responsibility and group entitlement to compensation for the injustices of the past, one must come to grips with the thorny question of how far back in the past one should go in one's attempt to compensate for injustices. Furthermore, since we cannot eliminate all the injustices of the past, which ones should we attempt to erase? Is it not impossible to erase some injustices of the past, without creating new injustices?

While some see the compensation of individuals for the injustices suffered by their group as just, others do not. Beneficiaries of compensatory justice, they believe, should themselves be victims of the injustices for which they are being compensated. For example, although one cannot deny that blacks as a group have been and continue to be victims of unjust discrimination, there is no invariable connection between being black and suffering from unjust discrimination. Should a middle class black who himself has not suffered the injustices suffered by blacks as a group be given preferential treatment in the name of compensatory justice over a white person who has suffered great economic injustice (such as a person who fought his way out of the grinding poverty of Appalachia)? Many have thought not.

Any system of affording preferential treatment only to members of particular minority groups is bound to be unfair to those victims of severe injustice or undeserved disadvantage who happen not to fall into any of these groups. For example, in September 1977, a California lower court enjoined the University of California at Davis to admit Rita Clancey to its medical school. Ms. Clancey, like Bakke before her, had brought suit against the University of California, charging that she was denied a place in the 1977 first year class at the Davis Medical School as a result of their special admissions program and that this program violated the equal protection clause of the Fourteenth Amendment.

Ms. Clancey, number one on the U.C. Davis Medical School's waiting list, on any reasonable standard, was a victim of far greater undeserved disadvantage than many of the students who were admitted as disadvantaged minorities. Indeed, at one point, officials at the Medical School considered her for their special program, but in the end rejected her since she was white and as such did not qualify as a disadvantaged *minority*. Ms. Clancey, an A – psychobiology graduate from U.C.L.A., was born in Russia to parents who had survived imprisonment in concentration camps. She came to the United States at fourteen able to speak only Hungarian and Russian. After the Clancey's emigrated, Rita's father, a bookkeeper, was incapacitated by brain surgery. The family then went on welfare and Rita worked her way through school. If members of certain minority groups can justly demand compesnation for previous unfair disadvantage, why shouldn't Ms. Clancey have this right too? In reply, some have defended restricting special admissions programs to specific minority groups on the basis of the high correlation between being a member of these groups and having suffered from injustice.

It would be too difficult administratively, they have claimed, to attempt to make such discriminations on an individual basis.

Restricting special admissions programs to members of particular minority groups generates the problem of deciding which groups should qualify as disadvantaged minorities and how membership in these groups should be defined. For example, given the large number of interracial offspring, it is not clear what should count as being "black." Similarly, if special preference is to be afforded "Spanish Americans," how is membership in this group to be defined? Persons with Spanish surnames, for example, may have little or no Spanish cultural heritage.

Furthermore, if individuals can justly demand compensation on the grounds of environmental disadvantage, can they justly demand compensation on the grounds of hereditary disadvantage? For example, if Mr. Jones can demand compensation on the grounds that he was the victim of poverty and racial discrimination, then should Mr. Smith also be able to demand compensation on the grounds that he was born with an inferior intellectual capacity? Although hereditary handicaps can be as unfair to their possessor as environmental ones, they are not created by societal actions and consequently we do not feel as much of a societal responsibility to compensate people for them. It is not, however, obvious that such a fact can justify the basic fairness of affording compensation to those who suffer from environmental injustices but not from hereditary disadvantages.

As well as disagreement as *to whom* compensation is justly due, there is disagreement over the question of *from whom* this compensation should be exacted. For example, many opponents of affirmative action programs have argued that it is unfair to place the burdens of remedying the injustices of the past upon the shoulders of young white males who are attempting to enter careers, while those who are already established in their careers are not expected to make similar sacrifices. Indeed, some who are asked to bear the cost of compensation may not have contributed to the injustices for which they are being made to compensate. In reply, it has been said that even though those who shoulder the burden of affirmative action programs may not have been responsible for the injustices that some minority groups have suffered, they nevertheless have profited from them. If these injustices had not existed, they would have found themselves facing much keener competition from members of these minority groups. According to this view, individuals who have suffered from injustices can exact from those who have not a compensation commensurate with their unfairly lost ability to compete on equal terms. Some who accept such a point of view have contended that compensatory justice demands that minority groups who have been denied a fair opportunity to compete with others should be given the number of places in professional schools that they would have fairly won *had they been given an equal opportunity to compete*. There is, however, no reasonable standard that can be utilized to determine what this hypothetical number should be. In addition, there clearly must be some threshold level of minimum competence which limits the utilization of such a principle of justice. It will not do, for example, to admit a minority candidate to medical school who lacks the requisite academic qualifications, on the grounds that he would have had them if he had been given a fair chance.

It is for this reason that a forward-looking notion of compensatory justice which aims at providing equality of opportunity and not to pay debts for the actions of the past is a much more inviting view. As many who accept a forward-looking view of compensatory justice see it, the way to achieve compensation is not through occupational or educational quotas but through special training, remedial education, and scholarships to victims of injustice or undeserved disadvantages at general taxpayer expense. After such compensation is afforded, they claim, the demands of compensatory justice have been met and one can then allow a fair and open competition to decide upon the relative representation of different groups in occupations and educational institutions.

But a critic is sure to reply, "such remedial programs cannot erase a lifetime, or indeed generations, of unfair discrimination or economic injustice, and, as a result, it will still be unfair, even with such programs, to subject those who have in the past been victimized by grave injustice to the same standards that we apply to those who have not been victimized by grave injustice." But even if one accepts this view, it does not necessarily follow that the proper way to compensate victims of injustice is by making it easier for them to gain admission to colleges or to obtain scarce jobs, especially when such a policy of compensation may place unfair burdens upon those who are displaced by such a policy. Instead, one might argue that Congress shuld pass legislation granting tax exemptions or governmental allowances to the victims of injustice. At least such a policy would have the virtue of spreading the burden of compensation fairly upon the general taxpayer and not unjustly upon certain individuals.

The Demands of Distributive Justice

If compensatory procedures which go beyond providing special training and educational programs are required to redress the injustices of the past, how are we to determine when such compensatory procedures should come to a halt? Many tacitly assume that such procedures should continue until the goal of "reasonable representation of minorities" in our economy is achieved. From this point of view, affirmative action programs should aim at providing for a more just distribution of the goods of our scoeity among different groups. Since some groups do not share in the goods of our society in a manner proportionate to their percentage of the general population, it is often assumed that this must be the result of the fact that they have not received their fair share. For many who accept this point of view, the goal of achieving *social justice in the future,* which requires that the goods of our society be justly distributed, can morally justify the tolerance of a certain level of *individual injustice in the present.* From such a perspective, while it is individually unjust both that some are made to accept a special burden of redressing the injustices of the past and that others are given advantages that they may not individually deserve, such results are required for the advancement of particular groups as social justice demands.

Although programs which aim at providing particular groups with percentages of the goods of society in proportion to their numbers seem fair to some, to others the logical consequence of such programs would be the creation of quotas which unfairly restrict the shares of other groups. If, for example, fairness dictates that 12 percent of the doctors in our country be black since blacks form 12 percent of our population, then it would seen to be unfair as well that the percentage of Jewish doctors in our country is far greater than would be justified on the basis of their percentage of the general population. Is it right then to restrict the number of new Jewish doctors? Such a proposal would be greeted with widespread moral abhorrence. While we may be willing to use quotas to help specific minorities gain greater opportunities, we do not want to use quotas to restrict the opportunities of specific minorities. Is this not because we realize that certain minority groups may deserve more of certain positions in our economy than their percentage of the population would indicate? Do we not implicitly accept the possibility that there are deeply ingrained cultural differences in lifestyles and general value commitments among different minority groups that would exist even if all groups were given the same access to environmental opportunities?

The view that the goal of affirmative action programs is to obtain for minority groups their proportionate share of the goods of our society also founders when we attempt in some principled way to determine which groups can rightfully demand their fair share. In particular, if every racial or ethnic group can make such a demand, why shouldn't other groups that cut across racial or ethnic lines (such as orphans or ghetto residents) be allowed to make similar demands. But since people fall into overlapping classes, individuals will necessarily opt for that classificatory system which gives them the greatest share. For example, although Jones may be a white male, he may also be the first generation son of immigrants. If a black man can point to the indisputable fact that blacks are vastly underrepresented in proportion to their percentage of the population in prestigious professional schools, why can't Jones point to the equally indisputable fact that the same is true of first generation children of immigrants? Indeed, such individuals may be even more underrepresented than blacks.

In addition, it is important to realize that there is great variance in the average age of members of different racial and ethnic groups. For this reason, it is a mistake to assume, as many do, that a minority group's percentage of the general population can reasonably be used as a basis for determining what its percentage in the work force ought to be. Furthermore, the percentages will differ from one geographical area to another. Understandably, each minority will use that geographical area that is most favorable to itself. For example, at a 1972 Berkeley minority student caucus attempting to arrive at a fair distribution of minorities at the University of California at Berkeley's law school, blacks looked to national population figures. Chicanos to California ones, and Asian-Americans to the San Francisco Bay area. Together, they demanded, in the name of justice, about half the places in Berkeley's entering law class.

Who Is a Qualified Applicant:
The Utilitarian Underpinnings
of the Notion of Individual Merit

According to the most often heard argument against affirmative action programs, the very notion of affording any group special preferences is incompatible with the basic principle of justice that people should be rewarded solely on the basis of *individual merit*. A scarce job or opening in a college should go to the most qualified applicant regardless of his or her racial or ethnic background or any other group affiliation, it is often said. But how is "merit" to be determined? In the case of university admissions, critics of affirmative action claim that grades and test scores are the only standards that can properly be used to determine who *as individuals* merit admission. But, since some people find it much easier to accomplish some things than others, achievement is not a good indicator of *moral merit*.

We are interested in grades and test scores not primarily as indicators of what individuals deserve for what they have done, but rather as predictors of how they are likely to perform in school and in their professions. A decision to admit only those with the highest grades and test scores reflects the belief that this *group* of individuals is most likely to succeed. The question as such is not one of individual versus group rights, but rather what type of groups should be admitted. Should it be solely the group of those with the highest grades and test scores or should some other classification system be employed? Since tests and grades are used primarily as predictors of performance, it has been argued that performance should often be measured on a broader yardstick. Supporters of this view have argued that grades and test scores, though clearly relevant, should not be decisive in deciding who are, for example, the most qualified to become good doctors and lawyers.

It has often been suggested that the Law and Medical School Admissions Tests are unfair indicators of the abilities of minority students. Such tests, it is said, put a premium on accumulated knowledge that has limited bearing on competence. One should realize that being a good doctor or lawyer involves more than doing well on tests; it also involves the ability to serve one's clients in ways that require human qualities as well as the abstract knowledge of law and medicine which is tested in medical and law schools. In a society in which racial and ethnic identities play an important role in everyday life, it has been suggested, a lawyer's or doctor's racial or ethnic background may have an important bearing on his ability to serve his client. Many of the tasks, for example, that lawyers perform for their clients require an understanding of the social context in which their clients' problems arise. Given the distinctive subcultures within our society, it is said, it is essential that lawyers be trained who understand the problems of their clients and "speak their language." Such qualifications for a good lawyer are most likely to be found, it is claimed, among lawyers who share their clients' racial or ethnic identity. Similarly, a good doctor for a minority community would have to be able to communicate with his patients and both understand and empathize with their special physical and psychological problems.

Utilitarian Arguments for Preferential Treatment of Minorities

Many supporters of affirmative action programs, conceding that such programs create some individual injustice, claim that they are nevertheless justified as the essential or best means for bringing about certain future goods. For example, those who desire the creation of a society where economic goods and political power are more evenly distributed, tend to see these programs as essential to the eradication of racial and sexual discrimination, which stands in the way of the creation of a just society. For such individuals, the future good of the creation of a just society may be of sufficient importance to justify short-term measures which cause injustices to particular individuals who find themselves displaced by less qualified members of minority groups. However, as we have seen, not all supporters of preferential treatment programs for minorities would take the view that those admitted under such programs are less qualified than those who are admitted under different standards.

Other supporters of affirmative action do not appeal to the goal of creating a more just society in the *future* as a justification for such programs but to the desirable *current* benefits of such programs. For example, it is claimed that:

1. Integration of the classrooms can provide for a diversity of ideas and values and as such for a broader and more valuable educational experience. This would be especially the case in law schools where minority members may bring valuable perspecvtives on the functions of law in society. The representation of minority members in the student bodies of professional schools and then in the professions will act to create a much more widespread awareness among professionals of the needs of the minority community.

2. The integration of minorities into the larger economic and political framework which will result from their integration into the professions and skilled trades will act to widen or alter the perceptions of other members of society, making them more aware and responsive to the special needs of minority communities and less apt to think in terms of unflattering stereotypes.

3. Minority lawyers or doctors are more likely than others to serve their own minority communities which are often badly in need of their services and to take an interest in their special legal and medical problems. Furthermore, minority lawyers and doctors are likely to have the greatest rapport with members of their minority communities and thus can best serve them.

4. The existence of minority professionals can provide role models to young people in minority communities, demonstrating to them that they too can overcome environmental handicaps.

Utilitarian Arguments Against Preferential Treatment of Minorities

The critics of preferential treatment programs for minorities also use utilitarian arguments to justify their position. For example it has been claimed that:

1. Rather than tending to eradicate racism, such programs will make us classify ourselves and others in racial or ethnic terms. Such programs tend to cause racial friction as different minority groups vie to catch the public eye and to play the game of power politics in order to gain special consideration for themselves. Since there is no agreed-upon standard for determining which minority groups should be granted special preferences, the result will be claims and counterclaims by various groups which are incapable of principled resolution. In pleasing some groups by granting them special consideration, we will displease those who are denied this special consideration and now perceive themselves as victimized by unjust discrimination. Therefore, the policy of granting special consideration to certain minority groups is apt to be an unstable one which generates widespread dissatisfaction.

2. Admitting minority applicants to professional schools whose academic credentials are considerably lower than those of nonminority admittees is apt to result in a general erosion of academic standards. For example, minorities, enrolled under special affirmative action programs, who would otherwise have been rejected, tend to cluster at the bottom of their medical or law school classes. In addition, they tend to fail certification exams in much greater proportions than graduates who were admitted under normal admissions policies that are based on grades and test scores. Unable to dispute the relevance of the significant percentage of affirmative action admittees who fail medical board specialty exams, some defenders of affirmative action have taken on the state bar exams, claiming that they are unfair since they favor those who can "think, act, and react from a white, middle-class mold." Such claims are rationalizations for failure. Bar exams are usually quite fair and favor those who can think, act, and react as good lawyers. If thinking like a good lawyer is defined as a type of middle class thinking, then the charge that bar exams have a middle-class bias is trivially true and not to be morally condemned. If, however, we are to accept this claim in a nontrivial way, how is the middle class bias of bar exams to be removed? Are we to have two bar exams just as we now have two admissions policies, or are we to lower the passing grades? Although the first proposal may be more in line with the logic of special minority admissions programs, the second seems to be the direction in which we are moving. Both proposals, however, are bound to result in a general erosion in the quality of legal services.

3. The utilization of special minority preferences for admission to professional schools and skilled trades will tend to perpetuate the discrimination and stigmatization that it is meant to eliminate. The unmistakable impression will be created that certain minority groups are inferior and cannot make it on their own.

4. Many of the utilitarian arguments for special minority admissions policies are unsound. The goal of the truly equalitarian society that we should be striving toward is not one with black doctors and lawyers for blacks, Chicano lawyers and doctors for Chicanos, etc., but a society where *good* professionals are available to all. It is untrue that minorities are so culturally insulated that outsiders cannot "speak their language." The way to attract doctors and lawyers to minority communities and the problems that especially concern them is not through the very

indirect and unpredictable method of setting aside a certain number of places for minority candidates in medical and law schools, but rather through the more direct way of making government financial subsidies available to all qualified doctors and lawyers who are willing to work where there is a special social need for them. This objective can also be achieved if governmental scholarships are made available to all needy, but academically qualified, students who, regardless of race and ethnic origins, are willing to make a pledge to work a certain number of years under a general governmental public service program that assigns lawyers and doctors to those areas where their services are especially needed.

Some General Reflections on the Justification of Preferential Treatment of Minorities

Given the moral and factual complexities surrounding it, the issue of "reverse discrimination" is an exceedingly difficult one to satisfactorily resolve. It is precisely those who are most convinced of the rightness of their positions who so readily utilize such notions as *racist, individual merit* and *qualified applicant* with no sense of their problematic meanings. For example, opponents of special minority admissions programs in medical and law schools often take it as obvious that those who benefit from these programs are less qualified than those they displace, giving no thought to the possibility that grades and test scores may not always be the best indicator of an applicant's potential to be a good doctor or lawyer. On the other hand, supporters of such programs tend to dismiss their opponents much too glibly as racists, while they do not reflect that it is they and not their opponents who support the use of racial categories. The concepts that we so easily bandy about are rarely clarified in the heat of moral arguments that touch upon the raw nerves of self-interest or deep ideological commitment. While I am not certain of my own answers to the questions we have been discussing, let me share my general reflections with you, with the hope that they will help to clarify your own.

While the strongest pleas for preferential treatment for minorities are made on behalf of the demands of compensatory justice, when we attempt to apply this concept to the issue of preferential treatment, we find ourselves facing a morass of unanswerable questions in deciding which individuals should be granted compensation, what form that compensation should take, how much it should be and at whose expense it should be exacted. The notion of compensation can be most easily applied in those cases where both the victims and responsible parties to an injustice are easily identifiable and the degree of injury is measurable. All of these elements are, however, quite unclear in the issue at hand.

First, it is not clear what principles should be used in determining those who merit compensation. Clearly, those who are born in poverty suffer from an undeserved disadvantage, but so do those who are born retarded or ugly or of uncaring parents. Where is the line to be drawn? I cannot draw it. Second, it is not clear who should pay that compensation. For example, if Jones, a black, can exact compensation for the injustices of slavery that continue to be his legacy today, should the children of immigrants have to pay a portion of that compensation? Finally, it is not clear how we are to determine the amount of compensation due. While the law conceives compensation as an attempt to restore a person to the position held prior to suffering an injustice or misfortune, in the case at hand we are attempting to compensate people for what they, because of social injustice, never were or had in the first place. Consequently, there is no norm we can appeal to in determining how much compensation is required.

It is also not obvious that this compensation should take the form of jobs and university positions. It is important to realize that such a method of exacting compensation aids only those minority members with marketable skills, leaving unaffected those who are perhaps most deserving of compensation. Furthermore, it exacts that compensation usually from young and lower-middle-class whites entering the job market, while it leaves both the more established and more affluent whites unaffected.

In addition, many who defend special admissions programs for minority groups on the basis of compensatory justice assume that such programs are necessary either for the elimination of racial discrimination or to prevent the lingering debilitating effects of racism from being passed on to generations yet unborn. I am not so sure, however, that this is true. No doubt, as Justice Marshall claimed in his opinion on the Bakke case, the ideal of racial equality should be "a state interest of the highest order." The question at issue, however, is that of means. Given the conflicting sociological views of the underlying factors interfering with the realization of the ideal of racial (and ethnic) assimilation and the likely effects of various remedies, one cannot be too sure of how this ideal can be best achieved. That there are deep racial injustices in our society, however, we should not deny. As Justice Marshall passionately relates in his opinion in the Bakke case:

> A Negro child today has a life expectancy which is shorter by more than five years than that of a white child. The Negro child's mother is over three times more likely to die of complications in childbirth. . . . The median income of the Negro family is only 60 percent that of the median of a white family, and the percentage of Negroes who live in families below the poverty line is nearly four times greater than that of whites. . . . For Negro adults, the unemployment rate is twice that of whites, and the unemployment rate for Negro teenagers is nearly three times that of white teenagers. . . . Although Negroes represent 11.5 percent of the population, they are only 1.2 percent of the lawyers and judges, 2 percent of the physicians, 2.3 percent of the dentists, 1.1 percent of the engineers, and 2.6 percent of the college and university professors.
>
> The relationship between those figures and the history of unequal treatment afforded to the Negro cannot be denied. At every point from birth to death the impact of the past is reflected in the still disfavored position of the Negro. . . .
>
> The dream of America as the great melting pot has not been realized for the Negro; because of his skin color he never even made it into the pot.

While it may not be true that a just society would see blacks represented in the various sectors of our economy in direct proportion to their percentage of the general population, there can be no doubt that much of the statistical discrepancy Marshall mentions must be attributed to racial injustice. One's perception of the social realities of being black in America should not, however, be uncritically projected upon other groups that are often classified as disadvantaged minority groups in affirmative action programs.

The strongest case for affirmative action programs rests not on the backward-looking assertion that specific groups deserve a certain compensation or percentage of desirable places in our economy, but rather on the forward-looking assertion that such programs are required to achieve an integrated society in which people are not denied opportunities simply on the basis of their racial, ethnic, or sexual background. The notion of diversity that Justice Powell made the focal point of his decision in the Bakke case cannot suffice to replace the most morally compelling reason for affirmative action programs which the Brennan-Marshall-Blackmun-White bloc in that case rightly saw as the attempt to remedy the effects of past societal discrimination. It is questionable, after all, that Powell's notion of diversity has as much place in scientifically oriented medical schools as it does in law schools and liberal arts colleges whose curricula are more value-laden. Similarly, the notion of diversity cannot reasonably be used to justify the preferential hiring and promotion of members of minority groups in private industry. If we want racial diversity, for example, in the construction trade, it is not because this diversity leads to better constructed houses, but rather because we hope it will lead to a better constructed society.

It is important that we see affirmative action programs as attempts to remedy social and not individual injustice. Since it is impossible for us to alleviate all individual injustices, we must of necessity restrict ourselves to the alleviation of those injustices we see as important social problems and whose alleviation we hope will contribute to the creation of a more just society, less troubled in the future by that type of injustice. It is not individual desert that justifies the preferential treatment of specific groups, but the utility that preference promises for the achievement of a more integrated society in the future.

In addition, we should not lose sight of the fact that the notion of who is most qualified or who merits admission to professional schools cannot be separated from utilitarian judgments as to who can best fulfill the goals of our society. As such, the brightest as measured by grades and test scores are not necessarily the best. Even though the first step in any adequate academic admissions program should be to screen out those candidates who do not meet certain minimum standards of academic achievement as measured by grades and test scores, the fact that there are so many more applicants for law and medical schools than there are places for them has raised these minimum standards in some schools to unreasonably high levels which tend to screen out a high percentage of disadvantaged students who might make the very best of lawyers or doctors. Clearly, there are innumerable reasons why an applicant with a lower grade-point average and test scores than some other applicant may still be considered the more promising law or medical student. In particular, the disadvantages with which a student had to contend, be they the disadvantages of poverty, or racial discrimination, or of a physical disease, can themselves be predictors of his chances of succeeding, since a person's academic achievement is measured not only by how high he stands but also by how far he had to climb to get to where he is. Nevertheless, it is quite important that we do not overly downplay the importance of grades and test scores, as many supporters of affirmative action programs do. Unfortunately, the academic discrepancies between regular and special admittees often turn out to be substantial and not easily discounted.

Perhaps the principal strength of Powell's decision in the Bakke case is its avoidance of squarely facing the issue of how much race and ethnic background should count in a university's admissions program. But do we really want a definite answer to this question, and if we do, can it be answered any way other than in terms of the numbers of specific racial and ethnic minorities we desire to be admitted? Indeed, as long as considerations other than grades and test scores are to be considered relevant to university admissions, race and ethnic background will be considered relevant, indirectly if not directly, regardless of what the courts say. The black student who is admitted to a university seeking diversity in its student body may not be said to be admitted because he is black, but rather because he has, let us say, special interests or special perspectives, but it will be his blackness that makes us attribute these interests and perspectives to him. Such individuals as farmers, the physically handicapped, and homosexuals, after all, also have special interests and special perspectives, but one doubts that as much weight will be placed on such types of diversity as will be placed on *racial* diversity. There is no rational basis in a society such as ours, where race and ethnic background are important social forces, to exclude considerations of a university applicant's racial and ethnic background while considering such things as his geographical background in attempting to achieve diversity in a student body.

As we turn from the university to the workplace, we should focus on the importance of affirmative action programs in breaking down widespread, and often unconscious, unwarranted stereotypes that perniciously underlie many highly subjective judgments as to who is most qualified. For example, unwarranted stereotypical thinking most likely played a role in the judgment of the interviewing committee that judged Diane Joyce as less qualified than Paul Johnson—and led one interviewer to describe her as a "rabble-rousing, skirt-wearing person"—a remark which suggests much about that man's sexist prejudice about the role of women and nothing about Joyce's qualifications. It is such stereotypical thinking that makes us feel uneasy with those whom we perceive as different and too ready to rationalize our uneasiness, often bred of ignorance, to some inherent flaw in personality or ability. Given the subtlety and often unconscious nature of these prejudices, we, unfortunately, often have to be nudged to accept those whom we would otherwise reject on the unfounded grounds of their relative unworthiness. Affirmative action programs can provide that necessary nudge. The delicate question here, incapable of exact answer, is how great that nudge should be.

In the debate over preferential minority treatment, the choice before us is not one between a right and a wrong, as so many disputants make it appear, but one of the proper balance between conflicting moral values. The quest for social justice, unfortunately, often requires unfair moral burdens and unpleasant social turmoil. This may be the case with the goal of ending racial and sexual discrimination. The ideal of racial and sexual assimilation deserves the taking of some risks and the imposition of some temporary unfair burdens. In deciding how far preferential treatment should go, we must balance our vision of justice tomorrow with our conception of the needs and rights of individuals today. As is the case with all conflicts of basic values, there is no uniquely reasonable and right way of weighing these values against each other.

DISCUSSION QUESTIONS

1. Evaluate the following imaginary dialogue:

    A: What people deserve depends on what they would have achieved if they were given a fair chance.

    B: Even if we could agree on what is to count as "a fair chance" and had some basis for determining what individuals *would have achieved* under different circumstances, I still would not accept your moral principle. While Jones may have been capable of achieving more than Smith, if he were given the same environmental opportunities, the fact of the matter is that Smith has worked much harder and accomplished much more than Jones and consequently *deserves* more for *what he has done*. Indeed, because of his extra opportunities and his response to them, Smith has developed a more meritorious character than Jones. We don't live in hypothetical worlds but in this one.

    A: Smith may have a better character than Jones but that's only because he had more undeserved environmental opportunities. Consequently, he doesn't *deserve* to be rewarded for his character.

    B: In your sense, no one will ever deserve anything.

2. Evaluate the following claim:

    The ideal of complete equality of opportunity conflicts with the ideal of individual autonomy. For example, it is the ideal of individual autonomy which justifies allowing parents to choose how many children they should have. In makinng this choice, parents realize that the more children they have, the less they will have to give each child. If complete equality of opportunity is our prime goal, would it not follow that family size should be strictly controlled? Furthermore, while one may, through strict social controls, equalize the financial opportunities parents can provide for their children, there is no way one can hope to equalize the vast differences in opportunities for psychological and intellectual growth that parents provide their children within the setting of the traditional family unit. The ideal of complete equality of opportunity, then, would seem to be achievable only in a social system where children are raised in communal nurseries. Yet how many of us would welcome such a scheme?

3. How would you reply to the following plea of Jones, a lower-middle-class white?

    I grant that I have indirectly benefited from the injustices of racial discrimination at the expense of blacks, but then again, whites born of rich parents have benefited from the injustices of differential wealth and the inheritance of wealth at my expense. Consequently, if I owe blacks a debt, rich whites owe me one.

4. In what respects do the disadvantages women have suffered as a result of sexual discrimination differ from the disadvantages blacks have suffered as

a result of racial discrimination? Are blacks more deserving of special preferences than women?

5. Your author claims that Rita Clancey "was a victim of far greater undeserved disadvantage than many of the minority students who were admitted [under the Davis special admissions program] as 'disadvantaged minorities'." Is this true? In what morally relevant respects, if any, do the disadvantages Rita Clancey suffered from differ from those suffered by the various minority groups that are usually included in preferential admissions programs?

6. Evaluate the following claim made by Professor Thomas Sowell, a black professor of economics:

> the actual harm done by quotas is far greater than having a few incompetent people here and there—and the harm that will actually be done will be harm primarily to the *black* population. What all the arguments and campaigns for quotas are really saying, loud and clear, is that *black people just don't have it,* and that they will have to be given something in order to have something. The devastating impact of this message on black people—particularly black young people—will outweigh any few extra jobs that may result from this strategy. Those black people who are already competent, and who could be instrumental in producing more competence among the rising generation, will be completely undermined, as black becomes synonymous—in the minds of black and white alike—with incompetence, and black achievement becomes synonymous with charity or payoffs.

7. Evaluate the following argument:

> The sad truth is that without an affirmative action program for minorities at the UCLA Law School, we would have absolutely no black or Chicano students. This is, however, morally intolerable for a publicly supported law school located in an area which contains such a high percentage of blacks and Chicanos. It is very important that minorities participate in the legal process which now often neglects, demeans, and discriminates against them. At every turn of the legal process, criminal justice is to a large extent discretionary. Police exercise discretion in deciding whom to arrest or search, prosecutors in pressing or dropping charges, juries in finding facts, judges in sentencing, wardens in awarding time off for good behavior, and parole boards in granting parole. In every discretionary step, however, racial bias may, and often does, play some role. For this reason, there is some justification for the widespread minority perception of the law as an instrument of white oppression. The only way to remedy this is by a race-conscious attempt to increase minority representation in the legal community. Lawyers, we must realize, wield enormous political power in the United States. For example, most legislators are lawyers. The almost total exclusion of minorities in the legal profession must come to an end, and soon.

8. Evaluate the following imaginary dialogue:

> **A:** I'm just as concerned as you with eradicating the lingering effects of racial discrimination. In the past, when universities and industries employed racial quotas to exclude certain groups, we were both against them. We agreed that it was wrong to base employment and admissions policies on an applicant's race. But you seem to forget all this now, when you favor today's policy of preferential treatment toward members of particular races. You're being inconsistent. If racism was wrong before, it is wrong now.
>
> **B:** It was racism before, but it is not racism now. We were both opposed to racial policies before because they were part of a social system which aimed at un-

justly excluding individuals from the mainstream of our society simply on the basis of their race. The situation is quite different, however, in the case of those white individuals who are excluded on the basis of preferential treatment programs that favor racial minorities. It is absurd to say that they are being oppressed by such policies. It is unfortunate that qualified white people are being bypassed as a result of these programs, but they are being bypassed in order to create a more just society and not to perpetuate injustice. That's why it's absurd to call such programs racist.

9. Is it right to compare the admissions policy of an undergraduate liberal arts college with that of a medical school as Justice Powell does in his opinion in the Bakke case? Does the same apply to law schools? Why?

10. Is Powell's notion of "diversity" any less subjective and standardless than the notion of "stigma" which he rejects? What do you think Powell would say to a university that decides to restrict the number of Jewish medical students on the grounds that the goal of diversity demands such restriction? What would you say?

11. Consider and evaluate the following argument for utilizing quotas in some industry:

Unlike the universities, there are no natural standards for evaluating the qualifications of people seeking apprentice positions. Formerly, those with pull were those who got in. Since those in the industry were almost exclusively white, their friends were almost exclusively white too. Indeed, even those whites in positions of influence who prided themselves on their lack of racial prejudice naturally tended to choose other whites as the most "promising" employees, simply because they, without realizing it, were socially conditioned to see as most promising those who looked and acted like themselves. The enforcement of minority quotas is the only way to break the subtle and self-perpetuating grip of racism in our society.

12. What do you think of the following claim?

It is ludicrous to assert that Bakke was no more qualified to be admitted to the Davis Medical School than the minority student who was admitted in his place. The discrepancy between Bakke's test scores and those of the special minority admittees is so glaring as to dim into insignificance any other possible factor. Especially glaring is Bakke's 96 percent score on the science test as compared to the average 35 percent score for the minority admittees. It is quite unreasonable to think that such a discrepancy does not really matter. Patient rapport and empathy may be among the qualities one would expect of a good doctor, but they are not nearly as important as scientific knowledge. Bad bedside manners may make us feel uneasy and even aggravate our conditions, but they rarely kill us, while ignorance does.

FURTHER READINGS
Sexual Equality

John Stuart Mill's classic essay "The Subjection of Women" (1859) can be found in *Essays on Sex Equality,* edited by Alice S. Rossi (University of Chicago Press, 1970). The collection consists of this essay, along with Mill's wife Harriet Taylor Mill's "Enfranchisement of Women" (1851) and "Early Essays on Marriage and Divorce" (1832) by both. The editor's introduction discusses the interesting story of the Mills' relationship. Those interested in the history of feminist thought should turn to Rossi's collection of *The Feminist Papers* (Bantam, 1974).

The January 1973 issue of *The Monist* (57, no. 1) and the fall and winter 1973–4 issues of *The Philosophical Forum* (V, nos. 1 & 2) are devoted to articles by contemporary philosophers on the oppression and liberation of women.

Shirely Weitz's *Sex Roles* (Oxford University Press, 1977) is a well-balanced and informative survey of the causes, nature, and future of sex roles by a social psychologist who claims that cultural as well as biological factors contribute to the maintenance of sex roles. Weitz critically considers various different theories of sex roles, the connection between sex roles and the family, and the contribution of symbolism to the maintenance of sex roles. In the final chapter she provides a cross-cultural look at several societies (U.S.S.R., China, Israel, and Sweden) that have instituted sex role changes in this century and discusses the history of feminist thought in the U.S.

A good collection of philosophical writings on the issue of sexual equality is found in Jane English (ed.), *Sex Equality* (Prentice-Hall, 1977). Classical philosophical positions are represented (Plato, Aristotle, Locke, Mill, and Engels) as well as contemporary philosophical arguments and expressions of popular points of view. The issues of natural sex differences, sex roles, the role of the family, equal opportunity, and reverse discrimination are discussed. An excerpt from Steven Goldberg's *The Inevitability of Patriarchy* (Morrow, 1973) is included. English also edited along with Mary Vetterling-Bragin, *Feminism and Philosophy* (Rowan & Littlefield, 1977), which consists of selections dealing with sexism, preferential hiring, marriage, rape, and abortion.

Racial Equality

Those interested in the topic of prejudice against blacks in the United States should turn to two articles by Irving Thalberg, both published in 1972. In "Visceral Racism," which first appeared in the October 1972 issue of *The Monist* (56, no. 4). Thalberg uses the term "visceral racism" to refer to the unacknowledged attitudes that lead whites who pride themselves on being unprejudiced to misrepresent "social inequalities which are glaringly evident to black observers." Thalberg attempts to uncover the "protective cocoon of ignorance and distortion" with which visceral racists structure events. In his article "Justification of Institutional Racism," which first appeared in the winter 1972 issue of *The Philosophical Forum* (Vol. 3), Thalberg criticizes those who are opposed to changes which he takes to be necesary to provide blacks with equal economic and political status.

Arthur Jensen's controversial view of race and intelligence is found in his "How Much Can We Boost IQ and Scholastic Achievement?" *Harvard Educational Review,* 39. William Schockley's view is found in his "Dysgenics, Geneticity, Raceology," *Phi Delta Kappan,* January 1972 and Richard Hernstein's in *I.Q. in the Meritocracy* (Little Brown, 1973). The quotation from Jensen in support of equal opportunity is found in Richard I. Evans, *The Making of Psychology* (Knopf, 1976), p. 65.

Preferential Treatment

There are two excellent anthologies devoted to the topic of preferential treatment: M. Cohen, T. Nagel, and T. Scalon (eds.), *Equality and Preferential Treatment* (Princeton University Press, 1977) and Barry Gross (ed.), *Reverse Discrimination* (Prometheus, 1977). Of the various articles on this topic, Richard Wasserstrom's "Preferential Treatment," which appears in his *Philosophy and Social Issues: Five Studies* (University of Notre Dame Press, 1980), is especially good for introductory students. In this clearly written article, Wasserstrom distinguishes the logical, empirical, andf moral arguments relating to preferential treatment and defends such treatment as a necessary means for the creation of a just society.

All of the major anthologies of readings on contemporary moral issues contain a chapter on preferential treatment and many also contain a chapter on sexual equality. The one I would recommend most, both for its selections and useful introduction, is T. Mappes and J. Zembaty (eds.), *Social Ethics,* third edition (McGraw-Hill, 1987), which covers both topics, and contains an excerpt from Goldberg. An equally good collection, but one without introductions, is Richard Wasserstrom (ed.), *Today's Moral Problems,* third edition (Macmillan, 1985). Another good collection is Richard Purtill's *Moral Dilemmas* Wadsworth, 1985). A briefer collection of selections is found in James E. White (ed.), *Contemporary Moral Problems,* second edition (West, 1988). John Arthur (ed.), *Morality and Moral Controversies,* second edition (Prentice-Hall, 1986) also has a collection of articles on affirmative action which is noteworthy for its inclusion of material from the general media—two William Buckley *Firing Line* television discussions, and discussions from *The New York Review of Books* and *The New Republic.* This anthology also contains excerpts from the Weber and Memphis firefighter Supreme Court affirmative action cases. The Mappes and Zembaty and the Wasserstrom collections include excerpts from the Bakke case.

Punishment and Rehabilitation

8

Punishment is punishment, only where it is deserved. We pay the penalty because we owe it, and for no other reason; and if punishment is inflicted for any other reason whatever than because it is merited by wrong, it is a gross immorality....

F. H. BRADLEY, *Ethical Studies*

What is past is but one act; the future is infinite. The offense already committed concerns only a single individual; similar offenses may affect all. In many cases it is impossible to redress the evil that is done; but it is always possible to take away the will to repeat it; for however great may be the advantage of the offense, the evil of the punishment may be always made out to outweigh it.

JEREMY BENTHAM, *The Theory of Legislation*

"He is a delightful man," continued the interpreter, "but he has suffered terribly from" (here there came a long word which I could not quite catch, only it was much longer than kleptomania) "and has but lately recovered from embezzling a large sum of money under singularly distressing circumstances; but he has quite got over it, and the straighteners say that he has made a really wonderful recovery; you are sure to like him."

SAMUEL BUTLER, *Erewhon*

INTRODUCTION

Questions concerning crime have perennially generated widespread public debate. There is more involved in this concern than intellectual curiosity; moral questions relating to such issues as abortion or euthanasia, though personally agonizing for some, are not as universally pressing as crime. Who has not had the experience of hearing about some ghastly crime and shuddering with the feeling of personal vulnerability? We are frightened and skeptical about the effectiveness of our system of criminal justice. Our fear and distrust is amply justified by a look at the bleak statistics. In the bigger cities, the law-abiding feel compelled to arm themselves and barricade their homes, fearful of the invisible menace outside. Fearful of our own safety, we feel that something is seriously wrong when we become aware that so few criminals are apprehended and fewer still punished. We react with disgust when we learn of clearly guilty criminals being released because of some legal technicality. We are annoyed at the slow movement of a criminal justice system which often seems more concerned with the rights of criminals than with the control of crime. The price of such justice, many of us believe, is increased crime, and we suspect that the price is too high—that not enough attention is being given to the rights of the victims or potential victims of crime.

As well as criticisms directed to the effectiveness of our criminal justice system in controlling crime, there is widespread dissatisfaction at the unfair results of the practical workings of the law to those criminals who are eventually punished. For example, there is widespread dissatisfaction with the great and unguided discretion afforded judges in the setting of sentences and to its resultant injustices. Similarly, there is widespread dissatisfaction with the practice of plea bargaining, where a defendant pleads guilty to a lesser offense for fear of being found guilty of a greater one; such a practice, it is clear, has very little to do with justice and much to do with the practical pressures facing overworked courts.

Dissatisfaction with our punishment system, however, goes much deeper than a skepticism over its effectiveness and the nature of the justice which it, as a matter of practice, dispenses; the very foundations of our criminal justice system have been challenged by those who speak out against the immorality and ineffectiveness of traditional conceptions of retributive punishment which they see as a barbaric and useless relic that merely satisfies our urge for revenge. Most who take such a point of view attack the very philosophical foundation of our criminal justice system on hard deterministic grounds. Our criminal justice system, they contend, based as it is on the illusions of moral responsibility and free will is incapable of moral justification. The progress of the deterministic sciences, they claim, has made such concepts obsolete. The behavior of a human being is simply the determined response of an object to the forces which act upon it. The relationship of these stimuli and responses can be studied and controlled scientifically. Instead of attempting the philosophically impossible task of measuring the fault connected with some act in the past, we should turn our attention to the future rehabilitation of the criminal and to the prevention of crime. These sentiments are often expressed by saying that a system of *treatment* ought to replace our present *punishment* system.

THE CONCEPT OF LEGAL
PUNISHMENT

"Punishment," in general, may be defined as "a penalty imposed for wrongdoing" and "legal punishment" as a "penalty imposed by a legal sysem for a crime." If we take a penalty to be the intentional infliction of some unpleasant consequence for some action or condition, not all legal penalties are forms of punishment. For example, the involuntary quarantine of the physically contagious and the civil commitment of the dangerously mentally ill involve the penalty of forfeiture of liberty, but such procedures are not considered forms of punishment since they are not criminal in nature. Similarly, a person who is forced to pay a penalty for a breach of contract would not be said to be punished, for again no crime is involved. When, then, is a legal penalty a punishment—i.e., a *criminal* penalty? While philosophers of law would disagree on the precise characterization, it would appear that two elements are required to make a legal penalty a punishment. First, the offense being punished must be perceived as an offense against the legal system as a whole and not merely against specific individuals. Second, the offense must be perceived as a breach of duty that is worthy of moral censure. Consider, for example, a mentally ill person who is involuntarily civilly committed to a mental hospital where he is subjected to involuntary confinement and treatment. While this is a penalty, according to the definition above, it is normally not considered punishment since we do not normally see the mentally ill as morally responsible and blameworthy. It is for this reason, that even though such people may be intentionally and involuntarily subjected to unpleasant experiences, such unpleasantness is not the aim of our treatment of the mentally ill. The aim, rather, is that of providing help or, at the very least, of containing a dangerous or potentially dangerous person in as humane a manner as we deem practically possible.

The idea that punishment is essentially a vehicle for the expression of community judgments of moral disapproval and feelings of righteous indignation is central to modern sociological and psychological views of punishment. For example, according to the sociologist Emile Durkheim in his classic study *The Division of Labor in Society* (1893), every society is bound together by a collection of moral beliefs and feelings which he called "the common conscience." As Durkheim saw it, it is "the common conscience" that provides a society with "the social solidarity" that binds it together as a group. Punishment, in his view, was a passionate reaction to offenses against the common conscience. Its prime function, he claimed, was to provide a socially accepted ritualistic channel for the expression of community feelings of hostility and outrage toward those who have violated the common conscience, feelings which, if not expressed, would result in the breakdown of social solidarity. As Durkheim wrote,

> ...we must not say that an action shocks the common conscience because it is criminal, but rather that it is criminal because it shocks the common conscience....
> ...whenever a directive power is established, its primary and principle function is to create respect for the beliefs, traditions, and collective practices; that is, to defend the common conscience....And in truth, punishment has remained, at least

in part, a work of vengeance. It is said that we do not make the culpable suffer in order to make him suffer; it is none the less true that we find it just that he suffer. Perhaps we are wrong, but that is not the question. We seek...to define punishment as it is or has been, not as it ought to be....

Punishment, thus, remains for us what it was for our fathers. It is still an act of vengeance since it is an expiation. What we avenge, what the criminal expiates, is the outrage to morality....It is sufficient, moreover, to see how punishment functions in courts, in order to understand that its spirit is completely passionate, for it is to these passions that both prosecutor and defense-attorney address themselves. The latter seeks to excite sympathy for the defendant, the former to awaken the social sentiments which have been violated by the criminal act....

According to many psychiatrists following Freud, punishment is a moralistic response brought about by the internal conflicts of the law-abiding. Since the desires that the criminal has dared to act upon are present in the ordinary citizen, he is a source of hidden envy, for he has done what we would have done had our instinctual desires had their way. As Freud put it,

The human code of punishment...rightly presumes the same forbidden impulses in the criminal and in the members of society who avenge his offense. Psychoanalysis here confirms what the pious were wont to say, that we are all miserable sinners.

Faced with similar latent criminal desires ourselves, Freud and his followers tell us, we react with moral indignation and resentment toward those who dare to act on these desires; furthermore we feel it necessary to prove to ourselves that crime does not pay. As Flugel writes,

...the criminal by his flouting of law and moral rule constitutes a temptation....it is as though we said to ourselves, "if he does it, why should not we?" This stirring of criminal impulses within ourselves calls for an answering effort on the part of the super-ego [our conscience], which can best achieve its object by showing that "crime doesn't pay." This in turn can be done most conveniently and completely by a demonstration on the person of the criminal. By punishing him we are not only showing him that he can't "get away with it" but holding him up as a terrifying example to our own tempted and rebellious selves....

In addition, psychiatrists have claimed that punishment provides an outlet for aggressions which can be hidden behind a facade of morality. It has been claimed that limitations upon this expression of aggression may cause the aggression to be expressed in criminality itself. According to this view, a punishment system represses dangerous expressions of aggression and channels them into the punishment of the criminal. Indeed, in punishing the criminal there may be an opportunity of vicariously committing the very crime that it is to be punished. As Frued claimed, "...punishment will not infrequently give those who carry it out an opportunity of committing the same outrage under colour of an act of expiation."

The insights of Freud and Durkheim have been incorporated into contemporary sociological views of punishment which see the punitive reaction to crime as growing out of the moral indignation of the public. Punishment, according to such views, is a ritual expression of the sentiments which uphold the institutionalized values the criminal has violated. This ritual expression serves to consolidate those sentiments and to strengthen them in that part of the population which has latent criminal tendencies.

The preceding psychoanalytic and sociological views of punishment stress two important, often neglected, facts. First, one of the aims of punishment, as the philosopher Nietzsche (1844–1900) saw, "is to improve him who punishes." Second, criminal punishment presupposes the existence of a community of individuals who identify with each other within a background of mutual cooperation. Within such a community, a violation of certain community interests by members from within is seen as a moral issue since the offender of these interests is seen as having a moral obligation to respect these interests. For this reason, a community's reaction to a criminal carries with it a judgment of moral censure and is unlike the mere hostility directed to a source of danger from without (such as natural forces, animals, and, often, prisoners of war) who are not seen as having any moral obligation to the community whose interests they threaten. The criminal is not seen merely as an enemy, but as a traitor to the community to which he is tied by the bonds of moral obligation.

PHILOSOPHICAL THEORIES
OF PUNISHMENT

The Retributive Theory

As Freud and Durkheim emphasized, central to the concept of legal punishment is the idea that a criminal has exacted something unfairly from the law-abiding and therefore owes them something in return. In punishing a criminal, we say that he is paying his debt to society or getting what's coming to him, that is, we see punishment as something that a criminal *deserves*. The notion that punishment is essentially a debt deservedly exacted from a criminal for his wrongdoing is the central idea of *retributive* theories of punishment. (The concept of retribution has its etymological roots in the Latin *retribuere* = to repay.) Although, as scientists attempting to understand the underlying psychological and sociological meaning of the practice of legal punishment, it was not Frued and Durkheim's task to justify this practice, those who accept the retributive theory of punishment attempt precisely this. For the retributivist, punishment is not simply something that ordinary people tend to see as deserved; it is something that *ought* to be so seen.

While all retributivists share the belief that a society's right to punish derives from a principle of justice and not utility, there is no single retributive theory of punishment. Retributivism is often described in the philosophical literature as the view that punishment is justified purely on the grounds that *wrongdoing merits punishment,* that it is *morally fitting that a person who does wrong should suffer in proportion to the degree of his moral blameworthiness* (or to use a California court's stronger language, "moral turpitude"). Such a view, however, was not held by Kant, who is considered the best example of a retributivist. As we have seen in our discussion of Kant's ethical theory, for Kant, political societies exist not to maximize utility, nor to proportion reward and punishment to moral desert, but to maximize liberty. As such, the way Kant saw it, criminals should be punished not for their *wickedness,* but for their *injustice*—that is, for upsetting a balance of benefits and burdens which is essential for the maximization of freedom in a community. However bad a person may be, a state has no right, Kant firmly believed, to punish him unless he *intentionally acted* to upset that balance. If the state were to attempt to punish for moral blameworthiness (which depends ultimately on one's motives) as well as injustice, liberty would not be maximized—indeed it would be greatly restricted as the state attempted to discover the underlying motives of individuals as well as their intentions and actions. Furthermore, Kant was very skeptical of the possibility of discovering the underlying motives behind individual actions. For this reason, Kant, in spite of the highly moralistic tone in much of his writings, was surprisingly hesitant about ultimate judgments of moral worth—judgments which, he believed, can be made reliably only by God.

Retributivists are deontologists who see morality as the fulfillment of obligations and duties. Living in a society requires mutual cooperation which in turn demands regulation of conduct involving self-restraint, for one's personal interest at a particular moment often conflicts with one's obligation to do what is in the ultimate interest of all. A legal sysem, in the retributive view, is a reciprocal affair in which individuals gain the benefits of noninterference by others at the cost of self-restraint. The criminal, in this view, is a parasite who has accepted the benefits of a legal system while refusing to pay the price of self-restraint. Such a person owes the law-abiding a debt and is a proper object of resentment, for he has gained an unfair advantage over them. Matters are not even until this advantage is erased. Punishment, for the retributivist, is the means of exacting that debt and is a demand of justice—the restoration of a condition of equality between the law-breaker and society.

Furthermore, for retributivists, the severity of punishment should be proportional to the social importance of the duty violated and the ease with which that duty might have been fulfilled. Though for some retributivists, such as Kant, just punishment is unconditionally binding and not to be mitigated by any utilitarian consideration, a retributivist can consider the disobedience of a law as creating a right, but not an inescapable duty, to punish and may even consider it desirable to punish only when it is useful. Nevertheless, it will always be a criminal's desert which provides the upper bound of morally permissible punishment. It is only because punishment is recognized as deserved, the retributivist will claim, that the notions of forgiveness and mercy are deeply a part of the language of punishment, for to be merciful or to forgive is to let an offender off of part or all of his deserved punishment. The law, the retributivist will argue, should always treat individuals as sources of rightful claims and never merely as instruments for the promotion of utility. The only people who can justly be punished are the guilty, that is, those who have shirked an obligation of reciprocity justly demanded of them. Punishment of those who are not guilty is wrong, not because it results in more unhappiness than happiness, but because it does not treat such individuals justly.

Kant is the most influential of all retributivists. Since criminal punishment is a severe infringement of human liberty, it can, for Kant, only be rightfully inflicted on a criminal who has unjustifiably interfered with the liberties of others. In punishing the criminal, we attempt, as best we can, to do to him what he has done to others. In Kantian terms, we attempt to demonstrate to him the implications of the universalization of the maxim under which he has acted. As such, for Kant, the justification of punishment is directed to the criminal himself who is to be shown that he has "brought his punishment upon himself." We do this, according to Kant, by applying the criminal's maxim of action to the criminal himself. If he murders, he must be executed; if he steals, he must be stolen from, etc.

Kant's retributive sentiments are best expressed in the following often-quoted passage:

> Judicial punishment can never be used merely as a means to promote some other good for the criminal himself or for civil society, but instead it must in all cases be imposed on him only on the ground that he has committed a crime; for a human being can never be manipulated merely as a means to the purposes of someone else... He must first be found to be deserving of punishment before any consideration is given to the utility of this punishment for himself or for his fellow citizens. The law concerning punishment is a categorical imperative, and woe to him who rummages around in the winding paths of a theory of happiness looking for some advantage to be gained by releasing the criminal from punishment or by reducing the amount of it.... If legal justice perishes, then it is no longer worthwhile for men to remain alive on this earth. If this is so, what should one think of the proposal to permit a criminal who has been condemned to death to remain alive, if, after consenting to allow dangerous experiments to be made on him, he happily survives such experiments and if doctors thereby obtain new information that benefits the community? Any court of justice would repudiate such a proposal with scorn... for... justice ceases to be justice if it can be bought for a price.
>
> What kind and what degree of punishment does public legal justice adopt as its principle and standard? None other than the principle of equality (illustrated by the pointer on the scales of justice), that is, the principle of not treating one side more favorably than the other. Accordingly, any undeserved evil that you inflict on someone else... is one that you do to yourself. If you vilify him, you vilify yourself; if you kill him, you kill yourself. Only the law of retribution (*jus talionis*) can determine exactly the kind of punishment.... All other standards... cannot be compatible with the principle of pure and strict legal justice.

There are three basic points that Kant makes in this passage, all of which are integral parts of his retributive theory. First, the only acceptable reason for punishing a person is that he is guilty of a crime, and, therefore, deserving of punishment. Although Kant is adamant that utility cannot justify either the infliction of punishment or its degree, once a criminal's punishment and its degree are justified on the basis of desert, this punishment may then be utilized in order to serve utilitarian goals. However, it is never these utilitarian goals themselves, Kant insists, that confer upon us *the right to punish;* only criminal desert can do that. Second, the only acceptable reason for punishing a person in a given manner and degree is that the punishment inflicted is equal to the crime which the criminal has committed. Third, it is not only wrong to punish people who do not deserve punishment or to punish them more than they deserve; it is also wrong to let a person off his justly deserved punishment or some measure of it, even if such punishment can be given no utilitarian justification. A person's guilt *demands* punishment and if we refuse to exact that demand, we "may be regarded as accomplices in this public violation of legal justice," Kant declares.

The Utilitarian Theory

Whereas the retributivist will see the practice of punishment as justifiable independent of its consequences, utilitarians, such as Bentham, have considered it a painful necessity, justified only by its ability to prevent crime. From this point of view, the retributive insistence upon seeing punishment as deserved, apart from any consideration as to its consequences, is dismissed as nothing more than an intellectual rationalization for a primitive and morally unjustified desire for revenge. The end of legal punishment, as the end of all justifiable legal institutions, utilitarians such as Bentham have declared, must be "to augment the total happiness of the community." From this perspective, the justification of legal punishment is not directed, as it is by the retributivist, to the criminal himself, but to the personally uninvolved citizen whose aim is to live in a society where the general happiness is maximized. Crime, according to this perspective, is a form of *mischief* which interferes with the general happiness, and *punishment* is a specific *remedy* for the suppression of this mischief. As Bentham saw it, punishment is one of four remedies for crime: (1) *preventive,* (2) *suppressive,* (3) *satisfactory,* (4) *penal remedies* or *punishment.* A *preventive remedy* would be one which attempts to prevent crimes from ever happening by eliminating some of their essential causes (such as the confiscation of weapons that can be used for the commission of crimes, and reeducating people away from possible criminal lives). A *suppressive remedy,* on the other hand, would be one utilized after a criminal act has been initiated but not completed (such as grabbing a would-be killer's gun from him). Once the crime has been completed, a *satisfactory remedy* would be one which consists of reparations or compensations to the victims of crime. Finally, *punishment* may be inflicted upon a criminal who has committed an offense. For Bentham, *punishment* differs from *satisfactory remedies* for crime in that its purpose is not one of compensating the victim, but rather "to prevent like offenses, whether on the part of the offender or of others." He writes,

> ...punishment which, considered in itself, appears base and repugnant to all generous sentiments, is elevated to the first rank of benefits when it is regarded not as an act of wrath or vengeance against a guilty or unfortunate individual who has given way to mischievous inclinations, but as an indispensable sacrifice to the common safety.

The aim of the crime prevention, Bentham claims, can be achieved through the incapacitative, deterrent, and rehabilitative power of punishment. First, punishment provides an incapacitative function by temporarily (such as by imprisonment) or permanently (such as by death) making it physically impossible for the criminal to commit again the same or similar actions. Second, punishment acts as a deterrent by giving the criminal himself a motive (fear of being punished again) to refrain from similar criminal activities in the future (specific deterrence). And most important of all, for Bentham, the punishment of the criminal can act as a source of intimidation to the rational self-seeking potential offender who requires the fear of punishment as a restraint on his own behavior (general deterrence). Finally, punishment can serve its rehabilitative function when its imposition can so change the desires or values of a criminal that he no longer desires to commit similar criminal actions. Unlike the deterred offender, a rehabilitated offender has undergone a personality change which makes the external restraint of fear of criminal punishment unnecessary.

Since, for Bentham, punishment is in itself, apart from a consideration of its beneficial consequences, an evil, it would be wrong to inflict it in any situation where its infliction would likely cause more harm than good or where that good could be achieved at a *cheaper rate* (that is, at less of a utilitarian cost). Once the infliction of punishment is justified on utilitarian grounds, its manner and degree must also be so justified. For example, Bentham argues that it is necessary to set penalties in such a way that a person will have more motivation to commit a crime which produces less harm rather than one that produces more.

While Bentham saw general deterrence as the chief end of punishment, contemporary utilitarians are often quite skeptical of the value of punishment as a deterrent. As they see it, this view rests on the mistaken assumption (made by Bentham) that most people rationally decide whether to be criminals—balancing its possible dangers against its possible rewards. Such a view of human beings, they claim, has been refuted by the psychological and social sciences. Skeptical of the value of deterrence, such utilitarians emphasize the rehabilitative aim of punishment. Since many who emphasize rehabilitation over deterrence see the justification of criminal rehabilitation at least as much in terms of the betterment of the offender as in terms of the goal of crime suppression, and, furthermore, tend to assume, as Bentham did not, that retributive notions are essential to the concept of punishment, defenders of this viewpoint often advocate the elimination of punishment and its replacement by a fully forward-looking treatment-oriented mode of dealing with criminals. (For the sake of clarity, let us refer to those utilitarians who accept such a viewpoint as *rehabilitationists.*)

Not all contemporary utilitarians, however, dismiss the effectiveness of punishment as a deterrent. As some see it, a belief in deterrence is compatible with contemporary psychological views which downplay the role of rational calculation and emphasize the emotional and unconscious factors that influence human behavior. As we have briefly discussed, current sociological and psychoanalytic theories of the nature of punishment emphasize the power of punishment as an unconscious deterrent. It is by means of a ritualistic law which is deeply connected with moral feelings, Durkheim, Freud, and their followers have claimed, that the moral impropriety of criminal behavior is emphasized and internalized by the general community. Specific punishments may have little immediate deterrent effect, but the pratice of punishment may have a long-run general deterrent effect upon the suppression of criminalistic tendencies, it has been suggested.

Some Reflections on Utilitarianism and Retributivism

As we have seen in our discussion of normative ethics, utility and justice are both essential moral values. Utilitarians and retributivists emphasize one of the two values at the expense of the other; by so doing, they achieve a uniformity of theory which is inadequate to the complexities of the moral life. It is a mistake to insist upon one theory at the expense of the other. If, on one hand, we insist upon a purely retributive theory of punishment, unlimited by any utilitarian considerations, we will be unable to clearly distinguish our unrelenting demand for retribution from the primitive urge for revenge. Similarly, if we insist upon perceiving the principle of equality of crime and punishment as a principle which can be applied without any appeal to utilitarian considerations, we will be incapable of distinguishing this principle from the primitive principle of "an eye for an eye, and a tooth for a tooth" and will be at a loss, at times, to know how to apply such a principle at all. For example, what do we do to the rapist, the embezzler, the mass murderer, or a person who is responsible for a reckless or negligent homicide?

If, on the other hand, we insist upon a purely utilitarian theory of punishment, unlimited by principles of individual justice, there can be no principled objection to subjecting individuals to unjust punishment whenever this can serve the aims of crime prevention. In particular, as retributivists have pointed out, there can be no principled utilitarian objection to punishing an innocent person in certain circumstances. For example, let us assume that there is a widespread outbreak of a particular crime and that none of the guilty parties can be found. Nevertheless, there is a pressing need for someone to be punished to serve the aim of general deterrence. Why, then, should we not sacrifice an innocent person, if the harm of his punishment is less than the harm of the crime that his punishment can serve to deter? Even if, as utilitarians have suggested, *a systematic practice* of punishing the innocent would, in the long-run, cause sufficient insecurity and general disrespect for the law as to outweigh the short-term good of such unjust punishments, it is false to assert that the punishment of innocent individuals could never be justified on purely utilitarian grounds *in certain special circumstances*—such as in those situations where there is every reason to believe that the knowledge of the punished person's innocence can be kept quiet and thereby not tend to subvert general respect for law or generate mass insecurity. (Recall our criticism of rule-utilitarianism.)

If laws aimed only at utility, legislators would be justified in passing laws requiring strict liability (liability without fault) which are presently resisted out of a sense of their injustice. Similarly, the utilitarian legislator may have good reason to punish negligent manslaughter caused by drunken drivers much more severely than most premeditated murders, for the former is generally more deterrable and dangerous to more people than the latter. Yet the murderer is punished more severely since he, unlike the drunk driver, intended to kill. It is our sense of justice and not a utilitarian calculation that instinctively assumes that guilt should depend upon intent as well as the effect produced. In addition, if utilitarian considerations were the sole judicial concerns, it would be perfectly proper in some situations to allow the sentence for a given crime to be constantly adjusted in accord with the shifting demands of general deterrence—for instance, whenever there is a general outbreak of a particular crime, its punishment would be made more severe. Again, it is our sense of justice that recoils at the thought of using the criminal *merely as a means* for promoting the good of others and of allowing his punishment to be varied according to the vicissitudes of social need, without any relation to his degree of fault.

Nevertheless, must we not agree with the utilitarian that it is wrong to punish criminals simply because they deserve it, even when the general welfare would be better served by not doing so. While such individuals may owe us a debt, is it right for us to exact it regardless of the consequences? It is, after all, one thing to say that only the guilty *may* be punished and something quite different to say that the guilty *must* be punished, as Kant does. In addition, the utilitarian is justified in rejecting the Kantian view that the penalty appropriate for a given crime should be determined apart from a consideration of consequences. On the contrary, our notion of the appropriateness of penalties must ultimately reflect our conception of the relative seriousness of crimes which can either be understood in terms of the purely psychological notion of the degree of revulsion they generate in the minds of the law-abiding or in terms of the relative harm they produce. Certainly, the degree of revulsion people feel toward specific crimes should be subject to appraisal according to some rational principle; this principle should be the utilitarian one of grading crimes according to the degree of harm they are likely to cause.

Although utility and justice may be competing values, they are not mutually exclusive. Punishment is always best when it is both useful and just. Nevertheless, there are times, in both the legislative and judicial realms, where these values conflict and we must choose between them, depending upon our own ultimate moral preferences. For example, a judge must often weigh the competing values of justice and utility against each other, trying not to blind himself to one value or the other. Yet, in the end, he must often choose, guided to some extent by precedent and to some extent by his own moral preferences. As such, some judges tend to see themselves more as stern balancers of the scales of justice, whose responsibility it is to give people what they *deserve* and not primarily what is *best,* while other judges see themselves more as social engineers, who, working within the constraints of the laws they are sworn to uphold, attempt to accomplish as much good as possible in particular cases. Even though such different perceptions of one's role as a judge often generate differences in particular sentencing policies, this is not always the case, for quite often both justice and utility can be seen as pointing toward the same resolution of a particular problem. For example, both retributivists and utilitarians have justified punishing individuals more for crimes involving deliberation than for those done in the heat of passion. For the retributivist, this will be seen as justified in terms of the greater moral culpability of a person who acts with deliberation, while for the utilitarian, this will be seen as justified in terms of the greater deterrability or dangerousness of those who deliberate over those who do not.

Those with liberal political leanings often dismiss retributivism as nothing but a rationalization for revenge. This is a mistake. As we shall see in our discussion of the dangers of a purely rehabilitative approach to crime, the retributive model may be the only protection a criminal can have against a utilitarianism gone mad, for this model, unlike the utilitarian one, treats individuals as *free agents* who have *rights* protecting them from being completely at the mercy of someone else's conception of *the common good* or of what it is to be an *adequate* human being. A complete devotion to the utilitarian model, unlimited by principles which distribute rights to individuals and which aim at minimizing the state's interference in the liberty of its citizens cannot help but invite the worst horrors of Orwell's *1984* or Huxley's *Brave New World*.

On the other hand, on grounds of political philosophy, I prefer emphasizing utilitarian principles rather than retributive ones, for I fear that an emphasis upon the concepts of justice and desert can generate a smug self-righteousness which considers the practice of punishment as being immune from scientific support or criticism and does not look for more efficient and humane ways of reducing crime. As the philosopher John Dewey once claimed,

> No amount of guilt on the part of the evildoer absolves us from responsibility for the consequences upon him and others of our way of treating him, or for our continuing responsibility for the conditions under which persons develop perverse habits.

I am also led away from the retributive view on more substantial philosophical grounds. The retributive model of a rational offender who receives his deserved punishment for upsetting a justly balanced scale of benefits and burdens, though reflecting a model of human beings and society as they ideally ought to be, cannot be made to fit human beings and society as they actually are.

Punishment as retribution makes sense in a community of equal individuals bound together by freely and commonly accepted legal rules. It is for this reason that the retributive view has often been associated with a commitment to a social contract theory of the grounds of legal obligation which looks upon society as if it were based upon a pact between rational individuals who have assented to subject themselves to a system of mutually beneficial rules. These rules are to be imposed and enforced so impartially and fairly that no person subject to them can justifiably claim that he is being victimized. As such, the retributivist is open to the Marxist challenge that existing societies, with their crime-breeding economic and social injustices, do not live up to this requirement. Certainly, in this country, those minority groups that are most given to crime do not have the same social benefits as the more affluent majority. A retributivist may agree with this criticism, claiming that the retributive model is an ideal to which existing society ought to strive.

The retributivist is, however, open to the more serious challenge that no society can, on psychological grounds, ever live up to his ideal. Surely, if a given legal system is to be fair, all who are punished should be capable of conforming to the law and should be punished to a degree proportionate to their degree of power to so conform. Although such power varies greatly among individuals, the retributivist, as well as existing legal codes, assume that most citizens have roughly equal powers to conform to the requirements of law. It is on the basis of this assumption that the retributivist and existing legal systems tend to attribute the characteristics of a mythical average man to criminal offenders, in spite of the fact that this is often not the case. Quite often, a skeptic will claim, criminals tend to have far less power to conform to the law than the law-abiding. Consequently, the retributivist is unjustified in his assumption that the criminal is *morally worse* than the rest of us, since we have exercised self-restraint, whereas he has not, for often exercising that self-restraint was simply easier for us. As we learn more about the causes of human behavior, our skeptic will say, we will begin to realize that most offenders have much less power to do otherwise than the retributivist is willing to admit. The moral distinctions the retributivist insists upon are merely a function of our empirical ignorance and will disappear once that ignorance has been dispelled.

One's position on the free-will issue has a great influence on one's position on the justification of punishment. A person who believes that people are not free to act otherwise than they do will reject the retributive view and maintain that one can with no more justification speak about just retribution against a criminal than one can speak about just retribution against a dangerous dog. Though those with such sentiments will not themselves look upon punishment as a deserved infliction of suffering upon the morally guilty, they may be forced, on purely utilitarian grounds, to advocate a system of punishment like our own in which retributive notions have an important place. Realizing that retributive feelings are a fundamental part of most people's natures, such utilitarians may see the retributive language as serving a social purpose. While the general community will see retributive punishment as morally called for, they will see it as an orderly outlet for the desire for retribution which either cannot be suppressed or can only be suppressed at the cost of dangerously lessening in the general populace the largely unconscious behavior controls provided by feelings of guilt, remorse, and indignation.

THE ASSAULT UPON THE NOTION
OF CRIMINAL LIABILITY

Introduction: The Concept of a Crime

Our criminal justice system has for some time been caught up in a wave of ideological criticism directed toward its fundamental philosophical foundation. "Treat criminals, do not punish them," the critics exhort. We must, they say, uproot the notion of retributive punishment with its emphasis upon the *moral guilt* incurred by a *free agent* who *deserves* to be punished in a particular manner and degree for his criminal act; instead, our response to crime should be flexible and oriented toward the differing needs of the criminal. The criminal, they say, should not be seen as a *responsible* and *blameworthy* individual who is paying his debt to society, but rather as a *sick* individual who needs to undergo some "therapeutic regime for personal betterment."

Among those who hold such a position, there is much dissatisfaction with the manner in which our existing criminal law attempts to distinguish legally responsible from legally nonresponsible offenders and attempts to distinguish varying degrees of legal responsibility. Before we inquire into the nature of this dissatisfaction, let us briefly see how the law presently defines "crimes" and "criminal liability."

Traditionally, a "crime" has been defined as a voluntary act or omission (in Latin, an *actus reus*) accompanied by some mental element which renders the offender blameworthy (in Latin, *mens rea* = guilty mind). In applying this definition, the law counts all acts as voluntary as long as they are chosen, regardless of how forced that choice may be. From this perspective, the law would count as involuntary behavior (for which there can be no criminal liability) conduct occurring while one is asleep, unconscious, or in a state of "automatism," but would count as voluntary an act performed under extreme coercion. It is the *mens rea* requirement of criminal liability which attempts to distinguish blameworthy voluntary acts from nonblameworthy ones. For some crimes, the *mens rea* requirement is that the voluntary act was done purposely (that is, the actor knew what would happen and wanted it to happen), or knowingly (that is, the actor knew what would happen), or recklessly (that is, the actor knew that there was a good chance that the result would occur and unreasonably disregarded that risk), or negligently (that is, the actor was not aware of the possibility of the result, but a reasonable person in his situation would have been aware). For other crimes, a more specific *mens rea* may be required (such as premeditation for first degree murder). In this century, however, there has been a growing tendency in the criminal law to dispense with the *mens rea* requirement and to subject blameless people to criminal liability. For example, it is common now to punish individuals for manufacturing, distributing, or selling adulterated foods, even if they did not know nor could not have reasonably been expected to know that those foods were adulterated.

Even if all the defining elements of a crime are present, a person's act is not a crime if it is capable of justification or excuse. In calling an act justifiable, the law asserts that under the circumstances it was the right thing to do, while in excusing an act the law asserts that even though it was wrong, it would be improper to punish it. For example, if a policeman kills an armed robber in self-defense, this would be a justifiable homicide, while if the policeman nonnegligently kills an innocent bystander while attempting to shoot at a fleeing killer, this would be an excusable homicide. While there is disagreement as to its definition and extent, the criminal law accepts a principle of "necessity" which affords a general justification for conduct that would otherwise constitute an offense. In its broadest formulation (such as that formulated in the American Law Institutes Model Penal Code), such a principle of general justification can be utilized whenever a person's action is necessary to avoid a greater evil. More commonly, however, such a justification is limited to the avoidance of specific grave evils, such as death or bodily injury.

Nevertheless, if a person is faced with a choice of unpleasant alternatives and makes a choice which the law considers to be wrong, he may still be legally excused if his choice was made under the influence of such duress (coercion) that "a person of reasonable firmness" in his situation would have been unable to resist.

The Insanity Defense

Recognizing that there are persons who, on any common sense notion of justice, are not morally blameworthy for their actions, not because of specific external pressures, but rather because of their grossly abnormal personalities, the law also accepts the excuse of insanity (the insanity defense). Although the plea of duress is directed to average citizens who are assumed to be capable of accepting the obligation to obey the law as a rational one and to have roughly similar capacities to reason, to judge consequences, and to exercise self-restraint, the insanity defense is directed to individuals who are so different from the rest of us that we do not consider them as members of our moral community. If they do something that adversely affects our interests, we try to stop them, very much as we would stop animals or small children whom we do not morally blame for their actions.

Although utilitarians have attempted to justify the existence of the insanity defense on the grounds that some individuals are nondeterrable and consequently there is no utilitarian justification in punishing them, such a view is fraught with difficulties. First, even if some individuals are nondeterrable, the acceptance of such an excuse would encourage persons who are deterrable to either simulate such an excuse or to deceive themselves into thinking that they are powerless to act rationally (that is, punishing the nondeterrable might have a beneficial effect upon general deterrence). More fundamentally, however, if we accept the principle that only deterrable criminals should be punished, this would seem to lead us to the paradoxical conclusion that ordinary incorrigible criminals should not be punished, even though most of us would want to say that such individuals *deserve* their punishment, whereas the insane do not. In addition, the common assumption that the insane cannot respond to threats of punishment seems to be refuted by the fact that those committed to mental hospitals for their insanity are quite often capable of responding to the suspension of privileges, ridicule, corporal punishment, and unpleasant jobs no less than "ordinary criminals."[1]

It would appear that utilitarian considerations are really not what lead us to accept an insanity defense; it is rather our sense of the injustice of punishing the innocent that retributivists so strongly insist upon. Recognizing this fact, contemporary rehabilitationists have often strongly denounced the justification of the insanity defense. The confusion surrounding the principles presently utilized to distinguish insane from sane offenders, they claim, amply demonstrates the impossibility of distinguishing the sick from the bad or the nonresponsible from the responsible. The insanity defense, they say, must be abolished and, along with it, the traditional retributive insistence upon the moral guilt of criminal offenders.

---

[1]See, for example, Erving Goffman, *Asylums: Essays on the Social Situation of Mental Patients and Other Inmates* (Doubleday, 1961).

The insanity rule utilized in Great Britain and in most states in the United States is the famous M'Naghten rule which was formulated in Great Britain during the reign of Queen Victoria in the mid-nineteenth century. According to this rule,

> ...To establish a defense on the ground of insanity, it must be clearly proved that, at the time of the committing of the act the party accused was labouring under such a defect of reason, from disease of the mind, as not to know the nature and quality of the act he was doing; or if he did know it, that he did not know he was doing what was wrong.

In spite of the fact that the M'Naghten rule has become a focal point in the contemporary controversy surrounding the insanity defense, there has been little judicial interpretation of its meaning. For example, even though psychiatrists and psychologists often disagree as to what, if anything, the concept of mental illness (disease) means, the courts have not taken a definite stand as to what is to count under M'Naghten as "a defect of reason from disease of the mind." The generally accepted view among legal commentators has been that this notion should be taken as synonymous with the psychiatric notion of a psychosis. Unfortunately, however, the standards for distinguishing psychoses from neuroses or for distinguishing cognitive from affective and motivational defects are far from clear. Although it is common for people to assume that the distinguishing difference between a psychosis and a neurosis is that only the former results in a defect of reason, such an assumption is not in accord with psychiatric usage. For example, the elaborate rationalizations of many neurotics are often described by psychiatrists as defects of reason.

The interpretation to be given the phrase, "he did not know he was doing what was wrong" has been the subject of much controversy in the debate over the M'Naghten rule. The critics, mainly psychiatrists, have tended to assume that according to this rule the mere emotionally detached ability to recognize that one's action would be condemned by others as wrong qualifies one as sane, even though one may have an extremely inadequate understanding of the moral and physical implications of one's act and no emotional appreciation of it (such as feelings of guilt, shame, or inner moral conflict). The critics often distinguish this narrow concept of knowledge from a broader psychiatric one which involves having some insight into the nature and implications of one's act and some degree of emotional appreciation of it. In spite of the widespread assumption that the law imposes a narrow interpretation of "know," this is mistaken. In most jurisdictions, the jury is simply given the words of the rule, without explanation, and left to give it their own common-sense interpretation. Those jurisdictions that do address themselves to the question have tended to favor rather broad interpretations of "know." Some courts have taken the "nature and quality" clause as supporting a broad interpretation. This clause is, however, rarely treated by the courts as if it adds anything to the "know...wrong" clause; indeed, some courts omit this phrase entirely. While many courts are willing to assume that "knowing one's act is wrong" requires some insight and/or emotional appreciation of one's action, they have not attempted to specify how much of this broader knowledge is required for criminal responsibility nor have they offered any rationale as to why only those who lack this broader knowledge as a result of "a defect of reason, from disease of mind," should be exculpated, while "ordinary" criminals should not.

Since M'Naghten is directed only to those offenders who lack knowledge of the nature or consequences of their actions and, since it is widely assumed that a person who has such knowledge might still be incapable of controlling himself, in many states in the United States M'Naghten is supplemented by some type of "irresistible impulse" rule. This often-used term is misleading in mistakenly suggesting that such rules require that actions be a product of sudden impulses. There is no single irresistible impulse test; indeed, most tests do not utilize this term at all, directing themselves to whether an offender "was capable of controlling himself" or whether he had "freedom of choice." As we have seen, however, in our discussion of the free-will issue, such phrases have no agreed-upon meaning. As with M'Naghten, their interpretation is usually left to the common sense of the jury. The only precise interpretation of these phrases has been supplied by the military courts which require conduct which would not be prevented even by a "policeman at the elbow" of the defendant. Yet the only acts which probably satisfy this strong requirement are acts which the law would recognize as involuntary and hence acts which would make an insanity plea unnecessary.

As we have seen, the meaning of the M'Naghten and irresistible impulse rules are unclear. Since many, if not most, criminals either lack insight or emotional appreciation of their actions and their consequences or are very limited in their capacity to do otherwise, the application of the insanity defense is limited primarily by the requirement that offenders be mentally ill. Who then is mentally ill? Mental health professionals do not agree. Indeed for some the classification of people as mentally ill simply reflects *a decision* to look upon them as people who need help. Since mental health professionals are trained to help people, it is not surprising that many of them are tempted to see all deviant behavior as a sign of mental illness. Although the concept of mental illness was once largely restricted to those severe psychological disorders that required hospitalization, today it has been so extended that it is often taken to include individuals who experience problems in social adjustment or vague feelings of dissatisfaction, lack of fulfillment, or lack of a sense of self-identity.

The courts, in their attempt to restrict the insanity defense to those who suffer from a mental illness, have learned that this notion is subject to conflicting psychiatric interpretations. In an important insanity trial in the District of Columbia (*Blocker v. United States,* 1959), for example, psychiatrists first testified that psychopaths did not suffer from a mental disease; then, after a weekend of reflection, decided that they did. Though the basis for this decision was not given, one can be assured that it was not a result of a new medical discovery. This sorry state of affairs prompted the appeal judge, Warren Burger (who later became Chief Justice of the U.S. Supreme Court) to remark, "This is reminiscent of Lewis Carroll's classic utterance, 'When I use a word,' Humpty Dumpty said, in rather a scornful tone, 'it means just what I choose it to mean—neither more nor less,' " and he could have added with Alice, "The question is. . . whether you can make words mean so many different things."

When psychopaths are described by those who have studied them as "antisocial, aggressive, highly impulsive individuals who feel little or no guilt and who are unable to form lasting bonds of affection with other human beings," this would seem to confirm their classification as wicked people. Yet psychiatrists would claim that the psychopath is not only mentally ill but seriously so.[2] Indeed, the psychopath, given his impulsiveness and lack of internal moral restraints, would seem to be the very model of a nondeterrable individual who lacks any emotional appreciation of the significance of his acts. Consequently, under a broad interpretation of the M'Naghten rule or under an irresistible impulse rule, he would seem to qualify as insane. Yet to the general community, such a judgment will appear quite unjustified—for the psychopath appears so normal and so bad.

For the hard determinist, this inconsistency is quite understandable. For once we delve into the causes of the behavior of even the most seemingly wicked of criminals, we will ultimately come to some cause for which he cannot reasonably be held responsible. This is true, the hard determinist would say, not only for those whom the ordinary person would perceive as mentally ill, but also for those apparently mentally healthy individuals who are victims of any one of the many unfortunate unlucky breaks of life, such as that of being born poor or into a subculture that rejects the values of the predominant majority. Such individuals also often grow up incapable of accepting or appreciating the moral standards that form the foundation of our law and incapable of feeling the sort of guilt, shame, and inner moral conflict that the ordinary criminal is supposed to feel when he commits a crime. Since such individuals did not choose to be brought up as they were, why should they be considered any more responsible for their actions than those whose actions result from what would commonly be called a mental illness, our hard determinist will rhetorically ask. His question is one that cannot easily be answered.

Indeed, psychiatrists who do not challenge the insanity defense on general hard-deterministic grounds have posed fundamental questions concerning the justification of assuming, as insanity rules tacitly do, that there is something special about mental illness that tends to rob persons of their free will. Today, there are many psychiatrists who would consider this assumption quite mistaken.[3] From their point of view, one should reject the typical medical model of mental illness as some type of psychic cancer which involuntarily invades and afflicts people and is responsible for the abnormal patterns of thought, feeling, and behavior that

[2]See, for example, H. Cleckley's *The Mask of Sanity* (Mosby, 1964). According to Cleckley, the psychopath suffers from an *inability* to care about others or to empathize with their plight, which is so severe that he is incapable of understanding the "ultimate significance and intention of words and phrases," and is consequently unable to "integrate and appreciate his experience"; this, Cleckley claims, is a "psychosis." Indeed, many psychiatrists have claimed that the distinctive uncaring, impulsive, and remorseless attitude of the psychopath is not really his fault, but is the result of the deprivation of parental love suffered in early childhood.

[3]See, for example, Thomas Szasz, *The Myth of Mental Illness* (Dell, 1961) and R. D. Laing, *The Divided Self* (Penguin, 1960).

form the symptoms of the disease from which they suffer. Instead, they claim, one should see most mentally ill patients as free agents whose illnesses may be seen as chosen strategies for living. For such psychiatrists, it is not the model of non-responsibility and victimization, which is reflected in the insanity defense, that threatens to swallow up the ordinary criminal, but it is rather the traditional legal reliance upon responsibility and free choice that threatens to swallow up the insanity defense. For example, the psychiatrist Bernard Diamond (who testified on behalf of Sirhan Sirhan, the assassin of Robert Kennedy) has suggested that in some cases people *choose to become psychotic* in order to commit crimes which they want to do but otherwise would lack the courage to do. Are we then to hold people responsible, at least in some cases, for choosing to become mentally ill? As psychiatrists ponder such questions, the distinction between those who should and those who should not be considered morally responsible for their actions fades into obscurity.

Objective versus Subjective Liability

Until recently, if a mentally ill offender wanted to utilize his psychological abnormality as a factor in his defense, he would generally be able to do so only through a plea of insanity. This has been the result of the widespread adoption of the objective theory of criminal liability, which assumes that the differences in the psychological capacities of noninsane adults should be disregarded in the determination of the existence and degree of criminal liability. For example, most jurisdictions require, for a successful plea of self-defense, both that the defendant honestly believed at the time of his act that his life was in immediate danger and that this belief was reasonable in the circumstances, where the standard of "reasonableness" is objective (that is, the relevant question is whether *the reasonable man*—who is not assumed to have the defendant's psychological incapacities— would have thought that his life was in danger). However, in some jurisdictions, the objective theory of liability is giving way to a subjective theory of liability, which inquires into a defendant's actual psychological capacities. For example, a few jurisdictions now permit a jury to take some of the defendant's psychological characteristics into account in deciding what the reasonable man would have done in the defendant's situation. The movement away from the objective theory of criminal liability has, however, been most noticeable in those jurisdictions which allow evidence of mental illness to reduce the degree of certain crimes—most notably in homicide cases, through what has come to be known as a plea of diminished responsibility (capacity). In California, this plea was widely used until the legislature stepped in to put a halt to it in 1981 after the widely publicized case of Dan White who successfully used this plea to have a murder charge reduced to voluntary manslaughter in the killings of San Francisco Mayor George Moscone and Supervisor Harvey Milk. Ridiculed in the press as "the Twinkie defense," the legislature responded to widespread public indignation in allowing White "to get off" with manslaughter in what was generally perceived as clearly premeditated murder on the dubious grounds that his mental faculties had been impaired by a steady diet of junk food.[4]

THE REHABILITATIVE IDEAL: THE ELIMINATION OF PUNISHMENT

Until recent years, the direction of reform in the determination of the criminal responsibility of mentally abnormal offenders has centered on broadening the insanity defense and allowing evidence of mental abnormality to reduce the degree of homicide. Today, however, there are critics who believe that this trend of reform is misdirected. The practical and theoretical difficulties involved in developing an insanity defense and in attempting to correlate the degree of punishment with an offender's moral guilt, these critics contend, cannot be patched up, since they are ultimately tied to the illusion of human free will. The remedy is not in better tests of insanity or degrees of diminished responsibility, but rather in completely discarding the traditional retributive insistence that only the morally guilty should be punished and that individuals should be punished in accordance with their degree of moral guilt. It is these principles that are the motivating force behind the insanity defense and the movement toward subjective liability, which the critics see as incapable of a utilitarian justification. In particular, the critics see the movement toward subjective liability (such as, the doctrine of diminished responsibility) as inconsistent with the important utilitarian aim of punishing individuals in accordance with their degree of dangerousness. Unlike a successful plea of insanity, which often calls for indefinite commitment until cured or no longer dangerous, a subjective approach to the determination of criminal liability is bound to have the undesirable utilitarian consequence of reducing the length of imprisonment of persons who have difficulty in restraining themselves and are, consequently, particularly dangerous. As the critics see it, it is quite often precisely those whom psychiatrists are apt to describe as suffering from some mental abnormality which substantially impairs their responsibility who are the most dangerous offenders. The aim of the law, they argue, should not be the impossible one of attempting to proportion punishment to moral guilt, but rather that of social protection and individual rehabilitation.

As the critics see it, all crimes should require strict liability. Since actions attributable to negligence, accident, or innocent ignorance can be as dangerous as the most premeditated and malicious of actions, the law's traditional concern with the moral blameworthiness of offenders serves no useful purpose. The tradi-

---

[4]Prior to the legislative action, the California courts had held that the premeditation and deliberation required to justify a first degree murder conviction do not refer merely to the extent of time "during which the thought must be pondered before it can ripen into an intent which is truly deliberate and premeditated" but must also "include consideration of a defendant's ability to *maturely and meaningfully* reflect upon the gravity of his contemplated act. In addition, the courts had held that the "malice" required for a murder (as opposed to manslaughter) conviction is not present when a defendant "because of mental defect, disease, or intoxication. . . is unable to comprehend his duty to govern his actions in accord with the duty imposed by law."

tional notion of *mens rea*, they claim, should be uprooted from the law. All dangerous actions should be subject to criminal control, regardless of the perceived moral culpability of the offender. All inquiries into a defendant's mental state at the time of his crime should be reserved for *a post conviction* dispositional analysis of how an offender can best be treated so as to prevent a recurrence of the forbidden act.

United by their rejection of both the retributive insistence upon viewing criminals as morally blameworthy individuals who must pay for their wrongdoing and the traditional utilitarian insistence that general deterrence is the main justification for punishment, the critics emphasize the rehabilitative goal of punishment. The common slogan, "treat the criminal, not the crime," best captures the essence of the rehabilitationist philosophy. Although there are important differences in the views of different supporters of this general point of view, there are certain interrelated principles that seem to form the core of the rehabilitationist philosophy. First, rehabilitationists tend to be hard determinists who assume that since all human actions are fully determined, free will and moral responsibility are illusions. As the psychologist B. F. Skinner put it in his popular book *Beyond Freedom and Dignity,*

> The concept of responsibility is particularly weak when behavior is traced to genetic determiners. We may admire beauty, grace, and sensitivity, but we do not blame a person because he is ugly, spastic, or color blind. Less conspicuous forms of genetic endowment nevertheless cause trouble. Individuals presumably differ, as species differ, in the extent to which they respond aggressively or are reinforced when they effect aggressive damage, or in the extent to which they engage in sexual behavior or are affected by sexual reinforcement. Are they, therefore, equally responsible for controlling their aggressive or sexual behavior, and is it fair to punish them to the same extent? If we do not punish a person for a clubfoot, should we punish him for being quick to anger or highly susceptible to sexual reinforcement?...The concept of responsibility offers little help. The issue is controllability. We cannot change genetic defects by punishment....What must be changed is not the responsibility of autonomous man but the conditions, environmental or genetic, of which a person's behavior is a function.
>
> Although people object when a scientific analysis traces their behavior to external conditions and thus deprives them of credit and the chance to be admired, they seldom object when the same analysis absolves them of blame....The mistake...is to put the responsibility anywhere, to suppose that somewhere a causal sequence is initiated. (pp. 70–72)

Second, since criminals are not ultimately morally responsible for their actions, they should be seen as unfortuante people who require help in becoming productive members of society. Since the behavior of human beings is subject to scientific understanding and control, this help should be provided by experts in the behavioral sciences. Third, our response to offenders should be directed not primarily to the nature of the crime and the aim of general deterrence, but to the suppression of criminalistic tendencies, and, if this is not possible, to physical restraint. Fourth, since one should reject the retributive view that criminals must pay a particular price for their crime, proportionate to the moral gravity of their crime and their guilt in committing it, and since our response to criminals should be oriented instead to their needs for rehabilitative treatment, the nature and length of a criminal's sentence should be left primarily in the hands of correctional experts. Ideally, sentences should be indeterminate in length, criminals being released only when cured or no longer dangerous.

Is commitment to the rehabilitative ideal the hope of a scientific and humane future less victimized by the threat of crime, as its supporters claim, or is it the latest threat to human dignity and freedom, as its detractors warn? As with other moral issues that have caught the mood of our time, although passionate rhetoric abounds on this issue, careful analysis and well-thought-out proposals are rare. It is easy to point out the glaring inadequacies of our current system of criminal justice, but much more difficult to suggest a practical way of overcoming them. Ironically, those who cry out loudest against our current dealings with crimnals have the least to offer in concrete proposals. Their suggestions for change are described in a very sketchy manner which generates many unanswered questions.

If offenders are to be subjected to treatment, for example, what will its ultimate aim be? Will it be educative or will it be directed to methods of behavioral conditioning which bypass the intellectual processes? If behavioral conditioning is to be used, will it be isolated to extinguishing particular socially undesirable learned behavior or will it aim at fundamental personality reorganization? Will the aim not only be to develop socially desirable behavior controls but also to create greater effectiveness and personal comfort for the offender? Can this be accomplished in a context of forced deprivation of liberty? Will limits be placed on the type of treatment that may be inflicted upon an offender? Will criminals have a right to refuse a treatment that promises to change their personality and to request punishment instead? How are the demands of general deterrence to be weighed against the demands of individual rehabilitation? If sentences are not to reflect guilt and are to be indeterminate, what standards are to be used to determine when an offender is cured or no longer dangerous and should consequently be released? What are we to do when the offense is minor and the treatment long or nonexistent? Let us turn to some of these questions. By so doing, we will come to realize the importance of subjecting the rehabilitative ideal to the restraints of a just law.

The Criminal as Sick
and Nonresponsible

The concept of responsibility is more deeply a part of our conception of human beings than rehabilitationists such as Skinner would have us believe. As hard determinists often do, Skinner confuses the notion that we are not ultimately responsible for the desires we find within ourselves with the quite different notion that we are incapable of modifying these desires or controlling them. Clearly, there is a difference between having a clubfoot and being quick to anger or highly susceptible to sexual reinforcement. When Skinner raises his rhetorical question: "If we do not punish a person for a clubfoot, should we punish him for being quick to anger or being highly susceptible to sexual reinforcement?" the proper reply is, "We don't punish a person *for being susceptible* to outbursts of anger or to sexual reinforcement, but for *succumbing* to that susceptibility when he has the power to refrain." Although we cannot change genetic defects by punishment, as Skinner claims, this does not mean that we cannot change human behavior that is *not fully determined* by genetic defects through punishment.

One should not neglect the fact that the act of holding some people morally responsible can act as a causal determinant in their behavior. Inanimate objects do not respond to being held morally responsible, but most human beings do. Perhaps, if the law were to give official support to the idea that people are not morally responsible for their actions, this would have a highly detrimental effect upon the behavior of individuals who have a certain disposition to criminality but, by accepting responsibility for their actions, are capable of controlling themselves. Must we not be concerned with such people? What if, as many psychiatrists suggest, a majority of us are like this? As we shall see, although behavioral psychologists, such as Skinner, would treat criminals by employing conditioning techniques which bypass their sense of responsibility and capacity for reasoned self-determination, this is not the case with the methods of psychotherapy (talk-therapies) that other critics of punishment and moral responsibility advocate. Psychotherapists recognize that the help that they have to offer people is dependent upon their acceptance of responsibility for what has happened to them and what will happen to them in the future. Psychotherapeutic patients are told that they can control their future by their own educated choices and should not see themselves as helpless objects, fully controlled by forces beyond their control.

Rehabilitation as the Sole Response to Crime

Supporters of a rehabilitative nonpunitive response to criminal behavior tend to totally neglect the general deterrent aim of the criminal law. Some critics have claimed that punishment does not deter. But there is no evidence for this claim, clearly contrary to common sense. It would appear that the critics of deterrence mistakenly direct their attention only to those criminals who have already committed criminal acts and have consequently not been deterred, rather than to the much greater number of people who refrain from criminal activities possibly because they have been deterred. It is one thing, after all, to claim that a great portion of crime is committed in situations where deterrence is not effective; it is an entirely different matter when one reflects on what the crime rate would be if we approached the situation from a purely nonpunitive point of view which looks solely at the rehabilitative needs of the criminal, while neglecting the demands of general deterrence. For example, a battered wife who is responsible for the premeditated murder of her brutal husband may not be a dangerous woman in need of rehabilitation. While we may feel great sympathy for such a woman, we hesitate to let her off, for we want to discourage others from acting as she did.

The supporters of rehabilitation also neglect the connection that should exist between the crime committed and the length of involuntary confinement. Many have claimed that criminals should be subject to indeterminate sentences and released only when *no longer dangerous* or when *cured*. They do not, however, tell us how these concepts are to be applied. What shall we do, for example, to a petty offender whose criminal action (such as exhibitionism or disturbing the peace by singing in the middle of the night) is caused by a personality disturbance which is either incurable or subject to cure only through long and drastic methods of personality change?

They are also silent about the connection that should exist between one's state of mind in committing a criminal act and the sort of personality deficiencies that should be subject to treatment. Will a person who is convicted of negligently causing an accident be subjected to psychological testing only for the purpose of ascertaining accident proneness or will the inquiry be broader in scope? What are the authorities to do if they find that a person who negligently committed a minor crime has homicidal tendencies? Do we subject him to treatment for these tendencies? If so, why restrict inquiry only to those who through some fortuity find themselves in the clutches of the law? Would it not be more reasonable to require that all citizens should undergo periodic examinations to determine whether they are dangerous and need to subject themselves to some type of "compulsory regime for social protection and personal betterment." Indeed, as long as the treatment which is imposed upon an offender is conceived as a personal benefit as well as a means of social protection, there will be a natural tendency toward a not too rigorous standard for potential dangerousness and great pressure toward not requiring any overt act at all.

If, on the other hand, some inherent connection is to be made between the state of mind of an offender at the time of the crime and the scope of the inquiry into dangerousness and treatability, will we not have to begin speaking again of one's *guilt* in committing a crime? It would appear that if we are not to totally neglect the demands of justice, we must inquire into precisely the issues that critics of punishment tell us we should avoid. The critics, in their dedication to the ideal of rehabilitation, do not seem at all concerned with the dictates of justice. Indeed, Karl Menninger says,

> The very word *justice* irritates scientists. No surgeon expects to be asked if an operation for cancer is just or not. No doctor will be reproached on the grounds that the dose of penicillin he has prescribed is less or more than *justice* would stipulate. Behavioral scientists regard it as equally absurd to invoke the question of justice in deciding what to do with a woman who cannot resist her propensity to shoplift, or with a man who cannot resist an impulse to assault somebody. This (to the scientist) is a matter of public safety...not of justice. The question...is not what would be *just*...but what would be effective in deterring them!

This is a truly astounding claim. Can one seriously say that *involuntarily* inflicted treatments should never be judged just or unjust? If the shoplifter were *stopped* by the coercive use of mind-altering drugs that drastically numbed and interfered with her intellectual and emotional processes, would not one say that she had been treated unjustly? Would not Menninger say so, if she were his wife or daughter? Is it not the case that treatment can be quite *effective* in the limited sense of successfully eliminating or deterring criminalistic tendencies, but quite *ineffective* from a broader perspective? Effectiveness, after all, can only be measured relative to some purpose—a purpose whose moral worth cannot be discovered simply by scientific investigation. Although notions of justice are not scientific in nature, they need not be inconsistent with the findings of science. If a scientist finds himself irritated by such notions, then he ought not to be addressing himself to the question of the *morality* of punishment, as Menninger does.

Methods of Rehabilitative Treatment

The most serious question left unanswered by the proponents of the rehabilitative ideal concerns the methods of rehabilitation that should be employed and the rights, if any, a criminal should have to refuse certain treatments. Let us consider the possible forms the rehabilitation of criminals might take.

Psychotherapy and Vocational Training

The least morally troublesome type of rehabilitative treatment would consist of some form of psychotherapy (talk-therapy) and vocational training. In such a scheme, criminals would be subjected to an educative process, learning about both themselves and some marketable skill. While this type of treatment of criminals is the one most widely suggested by the critics of punishment, it is the most ineffective. Given the high cost of individualized psychotherapy, group psychotherapy, where groups of inmates are given an opportunity to talk out their problems in the presence of a therapist who may exert much or little control on the reflections of the group, is all that can be provided. Such sessions for criminals are already established procedure in many progressive states. Unfortunately, the results are not impressive. Indeed, it has been claimed that even individualized psychotherapeutic sessions are generally ineffective as a method of rehabilitating criminals.

First, the effectiveness of such treatment is dependent upon the voluntary cooperation of its participants. Second, the generally understood purpose of the various methods of psychotherapy is self-knowledge which does not guarantee the abstention from further criminal behavior. For the psychoanalyst, for example, what is important is that offenders free of unconscious fears, anxieties, and repressions, should make their *own* rational and informed decisions as to whether to continue their criminal activities. Given environmental limitations, criminal activity may in some situations be quite rational. Furthermore, even if the problem of crime could be controlled by a combined program of psychotherapeutic education and vocational training, it is the height of injustice and disutility to provide psychotherapeutic and vocational services to criminals that are not provided to the law-abiding. Consequently, those who advocate such services for criminals ought to concern themselves with making these services freely available to all those who may want to avail themselves of them. Understandably, those who loudly demand these services for criminals, do not direct their attention to the vast cost of these services if they are to be made available to all who need them, nor to the political reality of the general unwillingness of voters to incur such costs. If psychotherapy were a clearly effective method for eliminating much of crime, the cost would be well worth it; unfortunately, there is no reason to believe that this is so.

Behavioral Conditioning
(Aversion Therapy)

It would seem that if rehabilitative treatment is to become the prime justification for what is now called punishment, with the realistic hope that it can be effective in controlling crime, criminals will be *made to undergo* methods of treatment which aim at changing their desires, emotions, and attitudes in ways which do not require their consent.

Presently, the most widely used method of nonpersuasive therapy is aversion therapy. Such treatment is based on a conditioning process where an association is set up between unpleasant or painful experiences and the behavior which it is designed to eliminate. Aversion therapy is used today in many state prisons and mental hospitals, and is fictionally depicted in *A Clockwork Orange*.

Surgical, Biochemical,
and Electrical Methods of Control

The most fascinating and morally troublesome methods of rehabilitation involve the use of various surgical, chemical, and electrical methods of control. During the 1950s, for example, psychosurgical procedures such as the now generally discredited frontal lobotomy were widely used methods for controlling undesirable behavior. Today, those uncontrollable patients who would have previously been candidates for frontal lobotomy and electroshock treatment can be kept sedated by the use of various powerful tranquilizing drugs. The art of psychosurgery, where laser beams may soon replace the surgeon's scalpel, has become increasingly advanced since the 1950s. The sophisticated practices of brain mapping and electrode implantation described in Michael Crichton's *The Terminal Man* are not science fiction. Hundreds of men and women have had up to a dozen or more needle-thin electrodes implanted into their brains. These electrodes can trigger various behaviors. One famous practitioner of this technique, Dr. Jose Delgado of the University of Madrid, has publicly demonstrated this technique by stopping charging bulls in midflight.

Electronic monitoring devices have been developed which are capable of the constant surveillance of individuals. In addition to monitoring a person's location, the device is capable of monitoring voice, blood pressure, heartbeat, and other physiological activities. Electrode implantation and electronic surveillance fit together well and could lead to the ultimate in aversion therapy. Researchers have envisioned a sophisticated system where dangerous criminals who are allowed to walk the streets are monitored by transmitters which report their location and physiological reactions to some central computer which decides upon the appropriate response, including the activation of implanted electrodes (or drugs) which can calm emotions such as hostility or send pleasurable or unpleasurable "messages" to the criminal. Supporters of these techniques claim that their use would be cheaper and safer for society than the present prison system. Some have suggested that these techniques should be provided only as a voluntary alternative to prison. On the other hand, critics have suggested that these techniques would be immoral since have suggested that these techniques would be immoral since they would rob the criminal of his human dignity, turning him into a nonmoral agent who cannot be praised or blamed for his conduct.

Rehabilitation and the Rights of the Criminal

Given the morally awesome power that the rehabilitative techniques of the future may provide, one should react with alarm when Menninger writes,

> Do I believe there is effective treatment for offenders, and that they *can* be changed? *Most certainly and definitely I do.* Not all cases, to be sure; there are some physical afflictions which we cannot cure at the moment. Some provision has to be made for incurables—pending new knowledge—and these will include some offenders. But I believe the majority of them would prove to be curable. The willfulness and the viciousness of offenders are part of the thing for which they have to be treated. These must not thwart the therapeutic attitude. It is simply not true that most of them are "fully aware" of what they are doing, nor is it true that they want no help from anyone, although some of them say so.

The implications of such a remark are shocking. One wonders, for example, how political dissenters would fare in such a system. Are all who disagree with those who have political power to be looked at as sick and then compulsorily cured of behavior which they believe to be right? (Consider the Soviet practice of committing political dissidents to *mental hospitals* to be *cured* of their *unhealthy* political views.) Surely, a person should have a right not to be forcibly turned into what he does not want to be. Without specific guarantees as to the rights a criminal will have against rehabilitative techniques, one can justifiably fear that a wholesale acceptance of the rehabilitative point of view cannot help but allow the revengeful, brutal, callous, or merely frightened among us to sacrifice human liberty to the demands of social protection. As Supreme Court Justice Louis Brandeis once perceptively warned,

> Experience should teach us to be most on our guard to protect liberty when government's purposes are beneficent. Men born to freedom are naturally alert to repel invasions of their liberty by evil minded rulers. The greatest dangers to liberty lurk in insidious encroachment by men of zeal, well meaning but without understanding. (*Olmstead v. U.S.,* 1928)

It is unjust that we are willing to grant that detention which is conceived as penal must be limited, yet, at the same time, are willing to assume that detention which is conceived as "therapeutic" need have no limits at all. We must be on guard against the self-deception inherent in the utilization of the language of therapy to justify the taking of preventive measures which would be rejected as unjust if seen as punitive. As Sol Rubin puts it,

> The constitution gives the defendent in a criminal case certain enumerated rights. . . embraced under the heading of due process of law, without observance of which

he cannot be convicted and his liberty cannot be encroached. The law evades...these requirements by calling the procedure...noncriminal, hence not requiring criminal due process. How is this accomplished? Only by the magic word formula. We go after the criminal, and process him without the final declaration that he is a criminal....Meanwhile we skip some of the procedural protections he would have if he were dealt with as a criminal, and then we proceed to punish him more severely than we could under the criminal law—a longer term of incarceration, lessened eligibilty for probation or parole, no better treatment.

As Rubin so aptly puts it, while quoting the words of the King from Rogers and Hammerstein's *The King and I,* "If allies are strong with power to protect me, might they not protect me out of all I own?" One can well understand a criminal's plea to be afforded a just retributive punishment instead of being "helped" in ways that he does not want.

Some Reflections

The American political landscape of the 80's has proved hostile to the rehabilitative ideal, but the political winds may blow in the rehabilitationists direction in the future as the effectiveness of techniques of behavior modification increases. What the future calls for is not a passionate commitment to slogans, but the practical wisdom to proceed cautiously with moral sensitivity. Instead of urging us toward an evanescent panacea, supporters of the rehabilitative ideal should seek to develop the concepts and standards that such a commitment entails. They must face the questions we have posed. Is it right, for example, that petty criminals should be involuntarily subjected to a longer and more unpleasant mode of rehabilitative treatment than the offender who has committed a much more serious crime? Does not justice demand that we maintain some upper bound on the length of involuntary treatment that may be imposed on an offender? Should criminals always be given the right to refuse treatments and the use of monitoring devices and to accept a fixed jail sentence or, perhaps, even death instead? If criminals are to be allowed to refuse certain treatments, what is to count as *informed* and *noncoercive* consent? Are prisons and mental hospitals inherently coercive? Do people have a right to refuse treatment on the basis of a constitutional right to keep their personality inviolate to involuntary change—do criminals, to put it bluntly, have a right to be bad, if they so choose? How are we to weigh the demands of general deterrence against the needs of individual rehabilitation? The questions abound; yet careful answers are nonexistent. Without answers to these questions, substituting the euphemistic notion of treatment for that of punishment may lead a society to feel justified in interfering with behavior which it finds offensive but would find too unjust to punish. Let us hope that our desire for crime control never becomes so strong that we are willing to completely ignore the ideals of a free society in our attempt to achieve it.

DISCUSSION QUESTIONS

1. It is a general legal practice to punish people more for a completed crime than for an attempt to commit that crime. This is true even if the criminal

has done everything in his power to commit that crime and fails as a result of some unforeseen circumstance (for example his gun jams). Can a utilitarian justification be given for this practice? A retributive one?

2. Critically discuss the issue involved in the following dialogue:

    A: While retributivists are right that moral guilt is a necessary condition of punishment, utilitarians are right that it is not a sufficient condition. Punishment should be inflicted only when it has a utilitarian justification.

    B: I don't agree. The guilt of a criminal is often itself a sufficient condition for punishment. Eichmann, for example, deserved to be punished, even though his punishment had no utilitarian justification. It would have been unjust for him not to have been punished.

3. What justification would a utilitarian give for the legal practice of punishing negligent behavior less than intentional behavior? How would the retributivist see it? What do you think?

4. Should the direction of penal reform be more toward strict liability (that is, liability for harm done with no concern for individual blameworthiness) or toward greater subjective liability (that is, liability based on the actual blameworthiness of individuals which reflects their individual psychological capacity to conform to the law they have violated).

5. Assuming that we had reliable tests for determining which individuals were prone to certain types of criminality, how would a utilitarian analyze the problem of the desirability of involuntarily subjecting people to such tests? How would a retributivist analyze the problem? What do you think?

6. Is it realistic to hope that we may someday find a method or methods for curing most criminals? Can criminals be cured on a large scale without general societal reform?

FURTHER READINGS

Classical Material

Bentham's utilitarian theory of punishment is presented in his *An Introduction to the Principles of Morals and Legislation,* chapters XIII–XVII and in *The Theory of Legislation* (pp. 239–472) which overlap considerably. These technical discussions are not directed to the general reader. Nevertheless, the detailed table of contents in both books make them good reference sources on the classical utilitarian theory of punishment.

Kant's most thorough treatment of punishment is contained in his *The Metaphysical Elements of Justice* (pp. 99–107 and 131–33, Bobbs-Merrill). Nevertheless, Kant has things to say about punishment in his other writings, not all of which seem to be consistent with his official theory in *The Metaphysical Elements of Justice.* For example, in his *Lectures on Ethics* (Harper & Row, pp. 55–56), Kant, sounding very much like a utilitarian writes, "All punishments imposed by governments are pragmatic. They are designed to correct or make an example. Ruling authorities do not punish because a crime has been committed, but in order that crimes should not be committed."

General Discussions

There are several excellent general discussions of the nature and justification of punishment. *The Rationale of Legal Punishment* by Edmund L. Pincoffs (Humanities Press, 1966) is an excellent analytic study of the nature of retributive and utilitarian justifications for legal punishment, from a philosopher who himself offers an integrated theory. Also included is a chapter on the punishment vs. treatment issue.

Punishment and Responsibility (Oxford University Press, 1968) consists of a collection of the famed twentieth-century philosopher H.L.A. Hart's essays on punishment, criminal responsibility, and the rehabilitative assault on punishment. Especially recommended are Hart's essays "Prolegomenon to the Principles of Punishment" and "Legal Responsibility and Excuses." In these articles, Hart considers the meaning, justification, and proper scope of criminal punishment. As he sees it, utilitarians are right that punishment must be justified in terms of its beneficial consequences. However, he sees the traditional retributive (Kantian) concern with the maximization of freedom as a limiting condition on the proper scope of criminal punishment.

In *The Limits of the Criminal Sanction* (Stanford University Press, 1968), the late Stanford University Law Professor Herbert Packer presents a discussion geared to the general public of the rationale, processes, and limits of criminal punishment.

An insightful discussion of the notion of punishment is found in Joel Feinberg's essay "The Expressive Theory of Punishment," which originally appeared in the July 1965 issue of *The Monist* (52) and was reprinted in Feinberg's collection of essays *Doing and Deserving* (Princeton University Press, 1970). Feinberg contends that punishment is by definition "a conventional device for the expression of attitudes of resentment and indignation, and of judgments of disapproval." It is only by realizing the expressive aspect of punishment, Feinberg argues, that some of the functions of punishment and some of the conceptual problems it raises can be made intelligible. After describing some of the expressive functions of punishment, Feinberg relates these functions to the constitutional problem of defining criminal punishment and the problem of strict criminal liability. He also argues against that form of the retributive theory of punishment which insists that the ultimate justification of punishment is "to give each criminal offender exactly that amount of pain the evil of his offense calls for, on the alleged principle of justice that the wicked should suffer pain in exact proportion to their turpitude." As Feinberg sees it, such a view turns out, on analysis, to be incoherent, its incoherence resulting from its failure to distinguish between the hard treatment aspect of punishment and its expressive function. The article is clearly written and highly recommended for beginning students.

Punishment and Rehabilitation

In *Erewhon and Erewhon Revisited* (Modern Library), Samuel Butler satirizes the traditional view of the criminal as morally responsible by imagining a society where criminals are considered to be victims of disease and subject to treatment by "straighteners," while those with physical illnesses are considered to be morally blameworthy individuals rightly subject to punishment.

Rehabilitationist views are defended in Karl Menninger's *The Crime of Punishment* (Viking, 1968) and B. F. Skinner's *Beyond Freedom and Dignity* (Bantham, 1971). Both books are directed to a wide lay audience. A more detailed proposal for a rehabilitationist approach to crime is found in Barbara Wooton's *Crime and the Criminal Law* (London: Steven and Sons, 1963). In this nontechnical short book, Wooton, an English lay magistrate, argues for a rejection of the traditional retributive elements of punishment and advocates a system of strict liability. In her proposed system, individuals will be held criminally liable for all of their dangerous actions, however faultless. Once a person has been convicted of some dangerous act, he will be turned over to a team of behavioral scientists who will determine the kind of treatment he should receive in the interests of crime prevention. (Excerpts of this book can be found in the Murphy and Wasserstrom anthologies.) Wooton's proposal is criticized in H.L.A. Hart's "Changing Conceptions of Responsibility" which appears in his *Punishment and Responsibility.*

Forceful criticisms of the rehabilitationist ideal, from a retributivistic perspective are found in C. S. Lewis's "The Humanitarian Theory of Punishment," *6 Res Judicatae* (1953) and Herbert Morris's "Persons and Punishment," *The Monist*, 52, no. 4 (Oct. 1968). Lewis's article is quite passionate, but not as substantive as Morris's which delineates the features of our present punishment system—with its retributive underpinnings—and compares this system to a therapy sysem which sees crime as a symptom of disease. Morris then argues, in the Kantian tradition, that retributive punishment, unlike treatment, respects the dignity of human beings. A good article to follow Morris's is Jeffrie Murphy's "Marxism and Retribution," *Philosophy and Public Affairs,* 1973. Believing that "retributivism can be formulated in such a way that it is the only morally defensible theory of punishment," Murphy also accepts the Marxist view that, given the social injustices of most existing societies, such a theory is largely inapplicable. The radical conclusion Murphy draws is that "modern societies lack the moral right to punish." Also highly recommended for a critique of the rehabilitationist ideal is Sanford Kadish's "The Decline of Innocence," 26 *Cambridge Law Journal* (1968) which focuses primarily on Barbara Wooton's proposal.

A forceful critique of the possible tyranny implicit in the rehabilitationist ideal is found in the psychiatrist Thomas Szasz' *Law, Liberty, and Psychiatry* (Macmillan, 1963). Szasz is especially concerned with uncovering what he sees as the tendency of psychiatry to promote moral and political values which are mistakenly presented as value-free health values. The psychiatric treatment of criminals and those who are civily committed should be seen, Szasz argues, not as medicine but as social engineering which can be, and has been, used to suppress individual freedom and dissent. In his controversial article "The Myth of Mental Illness," Szasz argues that there is no such thing as mental illness. What are now commonly called "mental illnesses," he claims, should be seen instead as problems in living. This essay has generated much controversy in psychiatric circles. It is included in the Murphy anthology and Szasz's collection of essays of *Ideology and Insanity* (Anchor, 1970), which criticizes psychiatry for dehumanizing people into nonresponsible beings.

The Insanity Defense

Those interested in a historical and analytic study of the insanity defense should turn to Abraham Goldstein's *The Insanity Defense* (Yale University Press, 1967). One should realize, however, that since the publication of this book, a growing concern about the scope and justification of the insanity defense has caused many states to tighten their definition of insanity and that several states have changed the plea of "not guilty by reason of insanity" to "guilty, but mentally ill." It remains to be seen, however, if these conceptual changes will have a significant practical effect.

Anthologies

Jeffrie Murphy (ed.), *Punishment and Rehabilitation* (Wadsworth, 1973) is an excellent anthology of selections on punishment and rehabilitation by classical and contemporary philosophers, lawyers, psychiatrists, and psychologists. It contains excerpts from Kant and Marx on punishment, Morris's "Persons and Punishment," and excerpts from Menninger, Skinner, and Wooton advocating the rehabilitationist ideal. It also contains John Rawls' influential article "Two Concepts of Rules" which contends that it is important to distinguish the justification for the institution of punishment from the justificaiton within that institution for punishing individuals. As Rawls sees it in this article, utilitarian arguments are appropriate in justifying the practice of punishment, while retributive arguments fit the application of particular rules to particular cases.

Herbert Morris (ed.), *Freedom and Responsibility* (Stanford University Press, 1961), is an excellent anthology of interdisciplinary material representing the fields of philosophy, psychiatry, sociology, and law on the issue of moral and legal responsibility. *Philosophical Perspectives on Punishment,* edited by Gerturde Ezorsky (State University of New York Press, 1972), is another good anthology of selections on the philosophy of punishment.

Chapter 5 of Joel Feinberg and Hyman Gross (eds.), *Philosophy of Law* (Dickenson, 1975) has a good selection of materials on punishment, including a selection from Bentham, and the articles by Morris and Rawls previously mentioned. Richard Purtill's *Moral Dilemmas* (Wadsworth, 1985) contains C. S. Lewis's retributive denunciation of the rehabilitative ideal and a utilitarian defense by J. R. Lucas of the deterrent aim of punishment, coupled with a criticism of retributivist and rehabilitationist views.

Citations

The quotation from Emile Durkheim comes from *The Division of Labor in Society,* 2nd ed. (Free Press, 1960), pp. 88–90. The quotation from Sigmund Freud comes from *Totem and Taboo* (Routledge & Paul, 1950), p. 12. The quotation from John C. Flugel comes from *Man, Morals, and Society* (International Universities Press, 1945), p. 174. The quotation from Kant comes from *The Metaphysical Elements of Justice* (Bobbs-Merrill, 1965), pp. 100–101. The quotation from Bentham comes from *The Rationale of Legal Punishment* (Humanities Press, 1966), p. 22. The quotation from John Dewey comes from *Human Nature and Conduct* (Holt, Rinehart & Winston, 1922), p. 18–19. The quotations from Karl Menninger comes from *The Crime of Punishment* (Viking, 1969), pp. 17–18, 261–62. The quotation from Sol Rubin comes from his *Psychiatry and the Criminal Law* (Oceana, 1965), pp. 154–55.

The Death Penalty
9

If...he has committed a murder, he must die. In this case, there is no substitute that will satisfy the requirements of legal justice.

IMMANUEL KANT

...the uncertainty...[of its deterrent power] favors the death penalty as long as by imposing it we might save future victims of murder....we have no right to risk additional future victims of murder for the sake of sparing convicted murderers.

ERNEST VAN DEN HAAG

For there to be an equivalence, the death penalty would have to punish a criminal who had warned his victim of the date at which he would inflict a horrible death on him and who, from that moment onward, had confined him at his mercy for months. Such a monster is not encountered in private life.

ALBERT CAMUS

To identify before the fact those characteristics of criminal homicide and their perpetrators which call for the death penalty, and to express these characteristics in language which can be fairly understood and applied by the sentencing authority, appear to be tasks which are beyond present human ability.

Supreme Court Justice
JOHN MARSHALL HARLAN

Among all the issues of penal policy, none generates the storm of controversy that surrounds capital punishment. In the strongest of words, its adherents have praised the death penalty as an essential instrument of justice and the prevention of crime, while in equally strong terms, its opponents have condemned it as inhumane, unfair, and useless, if not actually harmful. Millions of words have been written, arguments stated and restated; yet, the issue of capital punishment remains clouded in moral and empirical uncertainty.

THE LEGAL BACKGROUND

The number of executions in the United States has steadily declined through the years. In the 1930s, the annual average of executions was 166; in the 1940s, 127; in the 1950s, 71. The number of executions continued to decline during the 1960s and came to a halt in 1967, as the states awaited a Supreme Court decision on the constitutionality of capital punishment, which finally came in 1972. At that time, 39 states had a death penalty, 5 of which restricted it to exceptional cases, such as murder of police officers or prison guards or for second offenders. The methods of execution employed by the states were electrocution, lethal gas, and hanging. In Utah, a person condemned to execution had the option of choosing death by a firing squad as an alternative to hanging. This was the dramatic method of execution chosen by Gary Gilmore, who was executed in January 1977, the first person executed since 1967.

The constitutional objection to capital punishment stems from the Eighth Amendment which prohibits the federal government from inflicting "cruel and unusual punishment."[1] Since there is substantial legal authority to the effect that the Eighth Amendment is incorporated within the due process clause of the Fourteenth Amendment, which applies to the various states, the prohibition against cruel and unusual punishment is applicable to the states as well as to the federal government. In June 1972, the Supreme Court in *Furman v. Georgia* made its long-awaited decision concerning whether the death penalty is cruel and unusual punishment. In a 5–4 ruling, with each justice writing his own opinion, the death penalty was declared unconstitutional in the state of Georgia. Given the differing arguments of the majority, however, the implications of this decision were not clear. Only Marshall and Brennan argued that capital punishment was unconstitutional in all circumstances. Marshall, appealing to his reading of the popular will, claimed that the death penalty is cruel and unusual since "It is morally unacceptable to the people of the United States at this time in their history." For Marshall, the test of moral acceptability did not rest on prevailing opinion, "but on whether people who were fully informed as to the purposes of the penalty and its liabilities would find the penalty shocking, unjust, and unacceptable."

[1] Although the Eighth Amendment speaks of "cruel *and* unusual punishment," judicial interpretations of this phrase indicate that it is actually taken as a disjunction, prohibiting "cruel *or* unusual punishment." This, indeed, is the phrase used in the California Constitution.

As Brennan saw it, the cruel and unusual clause "prohibits the infliction of uncivilized and inhuman punishments." Such punishments, he claimed, are those that do not treat persons with respect or comport with human dignity. The death penalty is such a punishment for several interrelated and converging reasons, he declared. First, it is excessive. A punishment is excessive, he wrote, when it is "unnecessary... when it is nothing more than the pointless infliction of suffering." This is the case, he claimed, with the death penalty since there is no reason to believe that this severe penalty serves any justifiable penal purpose more effectively than does the less severe punishment of long imprisonment. Second, it is arbitrarily applied. Third, as evidenced by its infrequent use, its "rejection by contemporary society is virtually total." Fourth, it is too severe a punishment, since "the deliberate extinguishment of human life by the State is uniquely degrading to human dignity." This is so, he claimed, given the irrevocable nature of the death penalty and the physical and mental anguish it causes. The severity of the death penalty would in itself be sufficient grounds for judging it cruel and unusual punishment were it not for its long-standing usage, Brennan claimed. Believing that it is the convergence of the features of severity, excessiveness, arbitrariness, and popular rejection that make the death penalty unacceptably degrading to human dignity, Brennan turned to the complex principle that "It is a denial of human dignity for the State arbitrarily to subject a person to an unusually severe punishment that society has indicated it does not regard as acceptable, and that cannot be shown to serve any penal purpose more effectively than a significantly less drastic punishment." On the basis of this principle, Brennan concluded that "death is today a 'cruel and unusual' punishment."

The other three members of the majority, Douglas, White, and Stewart, were more guarded in their opposition. It was not the punishment of death itself they objected to, but its erratic and discriminatory method of application. The death penalty, Douglas emphasized, operates in a cruel and unusual fashion because it gives judges and juries the discretion to decree life or death, which they use in an arbitrary manner, unjustly applying it in many cases to members of minority or unpopular groups, while others, equally deserving, escape. Stewart and White, interpreting the notion of cruelty as the unnecessary infliction of suffering, argued that the death penalty was a cruel punishment since, given its seldom use, it could not serve as a credible threat or deterrent. It was unusual, they claimed, by virtue of its capricious application. To be sentenced to death, Stewart declared, is essentially, like being struck by lightning. The dissenters in this decision were Burger, Blackmun, Powell, and Rehnquist. Their objections rested on two grounds. First, it is the task of the legislatures, who are more in touch with the will of the people, and not the courts, to decide which penalties best serve the ends of penology. Second, the majority's objection of erratic infliction of the death penalty could be overcome if legislatures would provide clear and unequivocal standards for juries and judges to follow in applying the death penalty.

As most interpreters of the Furman decision saw it, states could now maintain the death penalty only by making it mandatory for certain specifiable categories of offenders in certain states. Several states changed their laws to accomplish this end. In California, for example, in a referendum posed to the voters, a measure to reinstate the death penalty passed by a 2–1 margin. As a result, the state legislature designed and passed a death penalty statute that made the death penalty mandatory in certain circumstances, which included, among others, murder for hire, killing a police officer, murder to prevent a witness from testifying, killing during a commision of a robbery, kidnapping or a rape, and a prior conviction of murder.

The prevalent belief that the Supreme Court would require mandatory death penalties was, however, proven wrong when the Supreme Court reconsidered the capital punishment issue in various cases argued before the bench in July 1976. In some cases, the death penalty was upheld, while in others it was rejected. Nevertheless, the swing was clearly toward upholding the death penalty, as was evidenced by the 7–2 majority votes in upholding the death penalty provisions of Georgia, Florida, and Texas. The guiding principle behind the reasoning of the majority in these decisions was that the states could not make the death penalty mandatory and consequently go too far in curtailing discretion, nor could they go too far in the opposite direction by allowing so much discretion so as to make the decision a capricious one. Exactly how much discretion a jury should be given, the Court did not say. The justices generally thought that Georgia's law concerning the death penalty was the best of the cases they had before them. The discretion of the jurors was, in this state, Stewart claimed, effectively channelled by requiring them to consider mitigating as well as aggravating circumstances and requiring the existence of at least one aggravating circumstance before conviction. (Georgia follows the American Law Institute's proposal in its 1959 Model Penal Code in this regard.) In addition, it was required that the state Supreme Court scrutinize every capital case and be prepared to overturn a death sentence when this sentence was not applied in previous similar cases. In the Texas case, Stevens declared that any sentencing system that allowed a jury to consider only aggravating circumstances and not mitigating ones would be too mandatory and hence unconstitutional. In light of this Supreme Court decision, the California high court declared unconstitutional the California death penalty statute passed after Furman which did not allow for mitigating circumstances. As a result, the California legislature refashioned and overwhelmingly passed a new death penalty statute.

The constitutionality of the death penalty was reaffirmed by the Supreme Court in 1987 in a case which again involved the state of Georgia. In this 5–4 decision, a majority of the Court rejected the argument that the death penalty should be declared unconstitutional on the grounds that it is contaminated by racism. The case involved the death sentence of a black man convicted of killing a white policeman. Rejecting the constitutional relevance of a statistical study that found that murderers were 11 times more likely to receive the death sentence in Georgia if the victim were white rather than black, a majority of the Supreme Court said that while the statistics are troubling, they do not prove that race dictated the death penalty in the case at issue.[2] Far stronger proof of purposeful discrimination is

___

[2]The study also revealed that the death penalty in Georgia was dealt to 1% of blacks convicted of murdering other blacks and 3% of whites convicted of murdering blacks. But when the victims were white, the death penalty was dealt to 8% of white murderers, but to 22% of black murderers.

required, the Court declared, before it would invalidate a death sentence on the grounds of racial discrimination. What the Court was willing to count as the far stronger proof it required, it did not say. Two of the dissenters—Brennan and Marshall—again reaffirmed their objection to the death penalty, even if it could be freed of bias in its application. The other two dissenters—Blackmun and Stevens—claimed that Georgia officials should be forced to explain the apparent unfairness in their system, and if possible, revise their laws and procedures to eliminate racial bias. In another 5–4 decision in 1987, the Supreme Court upheld the application of the death penalty to "major accomplices" of murder, who, while not themselves intending to kill, display "a reckless indifference to life." The conservative trend of the Supreme Court in death penalty cases continued in 1989, when the court again ruled 5–4 that states are not barred by the Constitution in imposing the death penalty on mentally retarded offenders and on 16-year-olds.

Let us turn our attention to the arguments for and against the death penalty. We shall proceed by first sketching the arguments on both sides of the issue and then shall subject these arguments to analysis.

THE ARGUMENTS FOR THE DEATH PENALTY

Justice Demands the Death Penalty for Certain Criminals in Certain Crimes

Although retributive arguments for the death penalty are not fashionable today in academic circles, it is still generally believed that death is the appropriate response to certain criminals in heinous crimes. Many of a religious persuasion quote passages of the Bible as divine authority for the unique appropriateness of the death penalty. The death sentence meted out by the Israelis to the Nazi war criminal Adolf Eichmann in 1962 was clearly motivated not by utilitarian considerations, such as general deterrence or societal protection, but by the feeling that this man *deserved* to die, that to allow him to spend his life in prison was to give him less than he deserved, to somehow cheat the dictates of justice. Seldom clearly articulated, this feeling runs deep.

The Death Penalty Is Needed as a Deterrent

The strongest case that can be made for the death penalty is that it is required as a deterrent for certain crimes. For example, Burton Leiser writes,

> . . . certain major crimes cannot possibly be deterred by any penalty but the death penalty. The revolutionary or terrorist who contemplates blowing up a school bus

or an airliner in order to terrorize the population and gain notoriety for his organization and its cause is not likely to be deterred by the threat of life imprisonment, for he believes that even if he is caught, he will be released and be given a hero's welcome by his comrades and supporters. Similarly, the potential traitor in wartime will not be deterred from betraying his country by the fear of life imprisonment, for he believes that when his country is "liberated" by the enemy, his imprisonment will be brought to an end. The same must be true of criminals who are already serving life sentences. The threat of yet another lengthy sentence is meaningless and can have no effect upon the lifer who contemplates killing his cellmate or the guard on duty in his cell block. If anything at all will deter such men from the crimes they are contemplating, it will be nothing less than the death penalty.

According to many who deal directly with criminals, captured criminals have admitted that after committing offenses punishable by life imprisonment, it was only the fear of capital punishment that induced them to refrain from murder, even though such action would have increased their chances of escape. It is this same fear, criminals have also admitted, that caused them to refrain from carrying deadly weapons in the serious crimes they have committed. If the death penalty were abolished, it is urged, it would be to the self-interest of a criminal who has already committed a crime subject to life imprisonment, such as kidnapping or rape, to kill any witnesses to his crime. The death penalty is also essential, it has been claimed, for repeat murderers for whom imprisonment has proved an insufficient deterrent and who might otherwise kill guards and fellow inmates in prison with impunity. This claim leads us to the next argument.

Some Criminals Are Too Dangerous to Be Allowed to Live

Some supporters of the death penalty do not argue that some criminals deserve to die or can be used to deter others, but rather argue on the basis of the social utility of eliminating dangerous individuals who cannot reasonably be expected to be rehabilitated. As Jacques Barzun puts it,

> It is all very well to say that many of these killers are themselves "children,"
> ...Doubtless a nine-year-old mind is housed in that 150 pounds of unguided muscle. Grant, for argument's sake, that the misdeed is "the fault of society," trot out the broken home and the slum environment. The question then is, What shall we do, not in the Utopian city of tomorrow, but here and now. The "scientific" means of cure are more than uncertain. The apparatus of detention only increases the killer's antisocial animus. Reformatories and mental hospitals are full and have an understandable bias toward discharging their inmates. Some of these are indeed "cured"— so long as they stay under a rule. The stress of the social free-for-all throws them back on their violent modes of self-expression....
>   As in all great questions, the moralist must choose, and choosing has a price. I happen to think that if a person of adult body has not been endowed with adequate controls against irrationally taking the life of another, that person must be judicially, painlessly, regretfully killed before that mindless body's horrible automation repeats....
>   ...what are we to say of the type of motive disclosed in a journal published by the inmates of one of our Federal penitentiaries? The author is a bank robber who

confesses that money is not his object:

> My mania for power, socially, sexually, and otherwise, can feel no degree of
> satisfaction until I feel sure I have struck the ultimate of submission and terror
> in the minds and bodies of my victims. . . . It's very difficult to explain all the
> queer fascinating sensations pounding and surging through me while I'm holding
> a gun on a victim, watching his body tremble and sweat. . . . This is the mo-
> ment when all the rationalized hypocrisies of civilization are suddenly swept
> away and two men stand there facing each other morally and ethically naked,
> and right and wrong are the absolute commands of the man behind the gun.

This confused echo of modern literature and modern science defines the choice
before us. Anything deserving the name of cure for such a man presupposes not
only a laborious individual psychoanalysis, with the means to conduct and sustain
it, socially and economically, but also a re-education of the mind, so as to throw into
correct perspective the garbled ideas of Freud and Nietzche, Gide and Dostoevski.
. . . Ideas are tenacious and give continuity to emotion. Failing a second birth of
heart and mind, we must ask: How soon will this sufferer sacrifice a bank clerk
in the interests of making civilization less hypocritical? And we must certainly question the wisdom of affording him more than one chance.

The recidivism rate is too high, it has been said, to afford us the luxury of
allowing certain dangerous criminals to live. Even life imprisonment, without the
possibility of parole does not eliminate the risk that these dangerous criminals provide to other criminals and to guards.

A death penalty is also required, it has been said, for certain political criminals
who, if allowed to live, might become a focal point for dangerous revolutionary
agitation. As Sidney Hook puts it,

> There is an enormous amount of historical evidence which shows that certain political
> tyrants, after they lose power, become the focus of restoration movements that are
> a chronic source of bloodshed and civil strife. . . . I did not approve of the way
> Mussolini was killed. Even he deserved due process. But I have no doubt whatsoever
> that had he been sentenced merely to life imprisonment the Fascist movement in
> Italy today would be a much more formidable movement, and that, sooner or later,
> many lives would be lost in consequence of the actions of Fascist legitimists.

It Is Too Costly to Keep Prisoners
in Jail for Long Periods of Time

Some supporters of the death penalty see it not only as a way of permanently
eliminating very dangerous people from our society, but as a measure of cold-
blooded economics. It simply costs too much money, they say, to keep criminals
in jail for very long periods of time, especially if the criminal is a violent or mentally unstable one who requires special psychiatric or custodial facilities. Prisons
are too overcrowded already and we ought to alleviate this overcrowding by using
the death penalty on nonreformable criminals who would otherwise be sentenced
to life imprisonment. The countless thousands of dollars that will be required to
imprison a person like Charles Manson over a long period of time could be better
spent on more socially desirable causes, such as the attempt to eradicate the

sociological and psychological roots out of which such individuals as Manson grow, it is claimed.

THE ARGUMENTS AGAINST
THE DEATH PENALTY

The Death Penalty Is Inhumane

Just as most of us would reject torturous punishments as inhumane even if it could be shown that such punishments are a better deterrent than imprisonment or relatively painless death, so too should we reject the intentional and cold-blooded killing of a criminal as inhumane. When we kill a criminal who has killed someone else, we, along with him, have contributed to a cheapening of the value of human life. Instead of reinforcing society's concern for the sanctity of human life, we have struck a blow against this most central of moral principles.

If the infliction of death itself is not inhumane, the drawn-out procedure of appeal, reappeal, and postponement that accompanies a sentence of death certainly is. The average time between the imposition of the death penalty and execution is almost four years—four years of uncertainty of the most agonizing nature. This is a type of torture that no civilized society should allow, it is claimed.

The Death Penalty Is Unjustly Applied

A study of case histories of individuals sentenced to death shows the vast injustice of the process by which we decide who shall live and who shall die. Professional killers, the rich and powerful, are, when infrequently caught, able to get lesser sentences through astute criminal representation. Those who are perceived as "wild beasts" generally escape death through a judgment of insanity. This, however, is not always the case. Some whose horrid crimes make the public cry out for vengeance are executed as ruthless criminals instead of being perceived as the sick and helpless victims they really are. If a defendant facing the death penalty has the money, however, he can employ psychiatrists who can paint a sympathetic picture of him. But, if he is poor, he is at the mercy of the psychiatrists the state chooses to supply. In addition, he is always at the mercy of the prejudices of the jury that will decide his fate. If he is poor or black or a member of some unliked minority group, the odds are greatly increased that the jury will not find the same sympathy for him that they are apt to find for other criminals. There is no greater injustice than taking the life of one man and sparing the life of another, no more deserving, simply because he happens to be richer, more powerful, or white. Yet, this happens regularly.

The Death of Innocents

Inevitably, if there is to be a death penalty, some individuals will be executed for crimes they did not commit. There are many case histories of evidence clearing an innocent individual being found too late to save him from execution. There is no way, given the irreversible nature of death, for us to attempt to compensate an executed man for our error. The death penalty must be abolished to prevent an innocent person from ever being executed again, it is claimed.

The Death Penalty Does Not Deter
More than Long-Term Imprisonment

As practically all official government studies on capital punishment, both in this country and others, have found, the death penalty is not a greater deterrent than long-term imprisonment. Statistical studies have confirmed this time and time again. Common sense also indicates that we should not expect it to be a more effective deterrent. As most penologists have emphasized, the deterrent power of a given penalty depends more upon the likelihood of its application than it does upon its harshness. If a person thinks that there is an excellent chance that he will escape punishment, no punishment, however harsh, is apt to deter him. Yet that is precisely the situation today, as most criminals escape apprehension entirely. A rational offender will also often realize that even if he is apprehended there is a good chance that he will escape a death sentence since the percentage of individuals who are actually executed will be small compared to the numbers of individuals who commit similar crimes. Consequently, if the criminal is a rational offender who carefully deliberates over his course of action, the mere existence of a death penalty is not apt to play any appreciable role in his deliberations.

As well as failing to frighten the rational, the death penalty will clearly fail to deter the unpremeditated homicides which are often committed by either mentally unstable people or individuals in the grip of temporary passion. Yet most homicides are of this nature. It also clearly will not deter those criminals who do not care if they die or who actually want to die. Yet there are many criminals like this. Indeed, the very existence of the death penalty might incite mentally unstable people who want to die to commit capital crimes with the hope that the state will take their lives for them. For example, some individuals accused of capital crimes have admitted that before committing their crime, they attempted, or lacked the courage to attempt, suicide. Other mentally unstable individuals commit capital crimes as a way of achieving some degree of recognition—even if it must be of notoriety— from a world that has up until now ignored them.

When one subtracts all those individuals for whom the death penalty cannot reasonably be expected to function as a deterrent, one is left only with those who are sane and cautious enough to weigh the risk of punishment against the anticipated gain from crime and then decide that the risk is worth taking if the penalty is long imprisonment, but not if the penalty is death. It is unreasonable to assume that any appreciable numbers of such people exist, if any, it is claimed.

The Existence of the Death Penalty
Has a Profoundly Disturbing Effect
upon the Administration of Justice

The sensational aspects of many capital crimes attract a press eager to publicize details of capital crimes which make a fair trial difficult, if not impossible, to obtain. Capital trials are exceedingly wasteful of time and money. The process of empanelling a jury for a capital case is a prolonged and difficult affair. Given the practice of apealing and reappealing death sentences, a sentence of death results in a drawn out process of litigation which has caused the average length of time spent under sentence of death to steadily increase through the years while the actual numbers of individuals executed decreases. There are only two ways to avoid this unacceptable consequence. We may either abolish the death penalty or reduce the due process afforded a criminal subject to execution. The latter alternative is unacceptable, for we should not tamper with the rights of a person subject to a death sentence. The abolishment of the death penalty is then our only recourse, it is claimed. The United States stands alone among Western democracies in maintaining the death penalty. This is a dubious distinction for a nation that prides itself for its respect for individual life, it is claimed.

ANALYSIS OF THE ARGUMENTS

Justice Demands

Underlying the view that justice at times demands the death penalty is the principle central to retributive theories of punishment that punishment should fit the crime. The simplest formulation of this principle is found in the ancient code of Hammurabi which prescribes "an eye for an eye and a tooth for a tooth." As critics have pointed out, however, there is no way to justify which punishment "fits" or is "equal to" a given crime. For example, what is the punishment fitting rape? We may feel that death is the appropriate penalty for certain murders but that can, of course, be explained by our attachment to tradition and not by any principle of reason. If death is the fitting penalty for single murders, what is the punishment fitting mass murderers? Even if we could in some way measure the degree of suffering a criminal has caused his victims, most of us will react with moral revulsion at the thought that justice demands that we sadistically kill a sadistic murderer so that he be made to suffer to the degree that he made others suffer. While many of use feel this way in moments of passion, most of us would shudder to live in a society where these sentiments are reflected in law.

The retributive principle of the equality of punishment to crime is not, to be sure, an entirely empty notion, but reflects a fundamental principle of justice that one's punishment should reflect one's degree of guilt and not be allowed to vary depending on the vicissitudes of utilitarian considerations, such as deterrence (for instance, we should not punish X at time A more than Y at time B simply because there was a greater need to deter offenders at time A than at time B). The idea behind this principle is that our ranking of punishments from the harshest at one extreme to the most lenient at the other should be made to directly correspond to our perceived ranking of the moral gravity of a crime. This principle does not tell us, however, as some retributivists would have us believe, how harsh or lenient our scale of punishments should be. In the past, simple death was considered an inappropriately lenient punishment unequal to the gravity of certain offenses. Elaborate and brutal tortures often awaited a condemned man who would cry out for the release of death. Justice demands that the worst criminals get the worst punishments, but our notion of humaneness helps determine what that punishment is.

Given our present moral sensibilities, the torturous executions of the past are ruled out as inhumane, regardless of their possible utility or instinctively felt sense of appropriateness. Should the same be true of the death penalty? It is no doubt true that many of us *feel* that justice would be denied if there were no special punishment, qualitatively different than imprisonment, for certain heinous criminals. Even life imprisonment, without the possibility of parole, will not suffice to satisfy the widespread feeling that these moral monsters be punished in some special way. One can understand such feelings, but they are feelings that can never be fully satisfied. Even if we were to set aside a special qualitatively different punishment for the gravest of crimes, among these crimes some will still appear immeasurably worse than others and will consequently call forth the feeling that some special penalty be applied in their cases. This reasoning can then be applied ad infinitum, as we seek harsher and harsher penalties to reflect the unbounded human capacity for evil.

The Death Penalty Is Inhumane and Results in the Death of Innocents

Those who cry out about the inhumanity of capital punishment and speak of the sanctity of human life are often silent when it comes to opposing wars which result in far greater loss of human lives and, in this case, of innocent ones. Since most opponents of capital punishment are not morally opposed to all use of lethal force, such as in situations of self-defense, their invocation of the principle of "the sanctity of human life" in the context of the death penalty issue rings hollow. The acts of criminals sentenced to death for murder are the clearest examples of inhumanity. If capital punishment is a superior deterrent to imprisonment for these acts of criminal inhumanity, and if the number of people that are deterred from these acts exceeds the number of people executed, then capital punishment should be perceived as a measure of social self-defense which aims not at the destruction of human life, but at its preservation. Our concern for the loss of convicted criminals' lives should not blind us to the lives of the innocent victims of crime we could save if capital punishment is indeed a superior deterrent to long-term imprisonment.

Similarly, although we should do everything within our power to avoid executing an innocent people, we must weigh these lost innocent lives against the potentially much greater number that would be lost if we were to abolish the death penalty and it turned out to have deterrent value. There are many more substantial risks of the death of innocent people that we are willing as a society to take. For example, we license people to drive automobiles, knowing that a number of them will kill innocent victims. We try to screen out the bad risks, but we do not stop driving cars.

Although the death penalty is loudly condemned as inhumane and irreversible, it is not clear that long-term prison sentences are more humane and reversible. One can certainly sympathize with a criminal who, out of pride for his *dignity*, prefers death to the subhuman condition of long-term imprisonment that might be awaiting him in a given prison. Although the critics of capital punishment often offer imprisonment without the possibility of parole as a humane alternative to death, they will rarely be willing to allow the criminal the right to choose which of these two penalties he would prefer. Imprisonment without the possibility of parole may be easier on the critics' consciences, but not necessarily more compatible with the human dignity of the criminal. In addition, what could possibly suffice as compensation for a person whose innocence has been established after his having served ten or twenty years of his sentence? Yet this, too, sometimes happens. Such is the price we must pay for the fallibility of the judicial fact-finding process.

The Death Penalty Is Unjustly Applied

There is no doubt that prejudice plays a role in death sentences. This is, however, not a sound criticism against the death penalty itself, but against the basic principles of the administration of justice and, in particular, the jury system. Sentences of long imprisonment are no less apt to be motivated by the prejudice of jury members than the sentence of death. In order to minimize miscarriages of justice involving the death penalty, we should insist that all death sentences be subject to very careful higher-level scrutiny. But, given the uniqueness of each case of murder, no judicial review, however careful, can be expected to eliminate all bias. Again, this is the inevitable price we must pay for the fallability of the judicial process Furthermore, while one should look with regret at the large percentages of minority group members who are sentenced to death, one should not forget that their victims are often minority group members as well. It is for this reason that an Illinois State Senator, who is himself black, once refused to vote for a moratorium on the death penalty in Illinois, declaring, "I realize that most of those who face the death penalty are poor and black.... I also realize that most of their victims are poor and black...and dead."

It Is Too Costly to Keep Prisoners in Jail for Long Periods of Time

It is not clear that society reaps any financial savings by having a death penalty. First, there are many lifers who settle down to productive jobs that more than pay for their upkeep. Second, there is great financial cost associated with capital punishment, including the cost of prolonged trials, appeals and special facilities in prisons, including the various instruments of execution. It is quite questionable that these costs are less than the cost of prolonged imprisonment. Indeed, Governor Mario Cuomo of New York, who is opposed to the death penalty on noneconomic moral grounds, has claimed that, given the high cost of litigation, it costs the State of New York approximately three times as much money to execute a criminal than to incarcerate him for the remainder of his life.

If financial cost is to be one of our prime concerns, we should give serious consideration to the various methods of psychophysical control and rehabilitation that were discussed in the previous chapter. If a person's behavior could be subjected to change or control to such an extent as to render him no longer a threat to society, some will argue that such a person should be freed from the constraints of prison and allowed to live and work outside, perhaps paying a percentage of his earnings to the families of his victims or to society as a whole. As was mentioned in the previous chapter, if individuals are to be given the right to refuse having their personality changed against their will, a person could be given the option of choosing this sort of treatment in lieu of long imprisonment or a death sentence, if capital punishment is to be retained. The problem, however, of deciding when a choice of this sort is truly voluntary and informed would, however, prove vexing. Although some civil libertarians would oppose a movement in this direction on the basis of their concern for criminal rights, others will be concerned that methods of behavioral control be unpleasant enough to serve the retributive objective of giving a criminal what he is perceived to deserve and the utilitarian objective of furthering general deterrence. Consequently, such methods, to be generally accepted, would have to be perceived as undesirable enough to be a credible deterrent and a just retribution, but not so undesirable that no rational person would voluntarily choose it as an alternative to long-term imprisonment or death. Developing legal principles which reflect this requirement would be formidable indeed.

Some Criminals Are Too Dangerous to Be Allowed to Live

Again, one response to dangerous criminals is the use of the various techniques of behavioral control. Drugs have already been utilized on an involuntary basis in prisons as a method of control. Such treatment has generated judicial litigation and legislative debate. Leaving aside the vexing question of behavioral modification, the fears that lead many to envision murderers as exceedingly dangerous individuals whose recidivism rate is higher than that of other offenders is without justification. This is borne out by the statistics as well as the first-hand observations of correctional officials.[3]

It is important to realize that the closer one comes to the image of a murderer as a crazed and uncontrollable wild beast, the closer one comes to the image of

[3]See, for example, Sara R. Ehrmann, "The Human Side of Capital Punishment," in *The Death Penalty in America*, Bedau, ed., pp. 492–519.

insanity. Yet, our current punishment system with its retributive roots in notions of moral guilt leads us to the acceptance of an insanity defense which attempts to weed such individuals out of the criminal process. While our current criminal law considers it morally inappropriate to treat such individuals as dangerous animals to be exterminated, this is the sentiment behind Barzun's proposal. In essence, he proposes that capital punishment should be perceived not as a retributive measure, but rather as the preventive execution of potential murderers. Such an idea was defended by George Bernard Shaw in his 1922 essay "The Crime of Imprisonment." As Shaw put it, "persons who give more trouble than they are worth will run the risk of being. . .returned to the dust from which they sprung."

Some will protest that human beings should never be treated in such a manner and robbed of their dignity as persons. I would not, however, take this line myself. Regretfully, I must admit that some creatures who possess the bodies of human beings should indeed be perceived more as "beasts" than as persons who can reasonably be expected to be part of a moral community. If there is no possibility of turning these creatures into moral agents, I feel a strong pull toward Barzun and Shaw's view. However, since we do not at present know how to make reliable predictions as to a person's potential dangerousness, and will not be able to do so in the foreseeable future, such a view is fraught with the potential for misuse. At best, one could reasonably claim that the state should have the option to use capital punishment (or behavioral modification) on those who, after being sentenced to prison for murder, murder again either upon release or while serving their sentence. The determination of the appropriateness of utilizing that option should center not on the degree of such a person's guilt, but rather upon the risk society takes in allowing him to live.[4]

The Question of Deterrence

Some who claim that the death penalty does not deter rest their claim on the more general assertion that all punishments fail to deter. This is false. The question is not whether the death penalty deters, for it most certainly does, but whether it deters more than long-term imprisonment for those crimes we deem most serious. (Obviously, a death penalty would be a very effective deterrent for parking violations!) Also not at issue is the question of whether there are more effective deterrents than the death penalty (such as death preceded by torture). Given our current moral sensibilities, such punishments would be ruled out as too inhumane, regardless of their deterrent efficacy.

What are we to make of the conflicting claims as to the deterrent power of the death penalty? Both sides rely on conflicting pronouncements of common sense

[4]Consider, for example, the case of Joseph Morse of San Diego, who was sentenced to death for killing his mother and sister but given life imprisonment following a retrial. While awaiting transportation back to prison, he killed a fellow inmate over a few packs of cigarettes for which he again was sentenced to death; but it was reduced again to life imprisonment when California's death penalty statute was declared unconstitutional. What, one may reasonably ask, other than death, complete isolation, or drastic behavioral modification, is to prevent such a man from killing again?

and conflicting readings of statistical studies. Some of these studies have compared the homicide rates in states that do and do not have the death penalty. Such studies are of doubtful value since even if states which have death penalties tend to have significantly lower homicide rates, this may not be a result of the death penalty, but of underlying socioeconomic conditions.

More meaningful statistical studies have restricted their comparison to the following:

1. adjacent states, having roughly the same socioeconomic conditions, one (or more) of which has the death penalty for murder, and one (or more) of which does not.
2. homicide rates in a given state before and after abolition.
3. homicide rates in a given state before, during, and after a capital trial and/or execution.

These studies are also beset with problems of interpretation. First, most are studies of general homicide rates and make the questionable assumption that this rate directly corresponds to the rate of capitally punishable homicides. Secondly, the causes of crime and of homicide in particular are quite complex. One cannot simply look at the figures to arrive at reliable interpretations. If, for example, the homicide rate in state X drops after it abolishes the death penalty, an abolitionist might interpret this as offering evidence for the assertion that the existence of a death penalty actually incites people to homicide rather than deterring them. This, however, could be false; it is quite possible that the drop in the homicide rate in state X is causally independent of the abolition of the death penalty (for instance, perhaps when state X abolished their death penalty, other penal reforms were also instituted which account for the drop in the homicide rate). Similarly, if X's homicide rate increases after abolition, retentionists are apt to interpret this as evidence of capital punishment's deterrent efficacy. Again, this need not be the case; perhaps X's homicide rate would have increased anyway due to other factors, regardless of the existence or nonexistence of the death penalty. Indeed, it is possible that even though the homicide rate has increased in state X, the abolition of the death penalty has served to reduce it, for if the death penalty had been maintained, the homicide rate would be even higher.

The general consensus of those who have analyzed these statistical studies has been that they are inconclusive and give no evidence to support the view that capital punishment is a superior deterrent to imprisonment for the crime of murder. Some have gone further, asserting that the statistics *establish* or *support* the view that capital punishment is no better a deterrent than imprisonment for the crimes for which it is used as a penalty. Some have even gone so far as to assert that the statistics indicate that capital punishment actually incites more to violence than it deters. Largely on the basis of these statistical studies, the vast majority of governmental studies of the desirability of the death penalty have concluded that there is no good reason to assume that the death penalty is a superior deterrent to long-term imprisonment. This conclusion is, however, denied by Professor Isaac Ehrlich of the University of Chicago who in a study concluded that between 1933 and 1967, "an additional execution per year...may have resulted (on the average) in seven or eight fewer murders." Ehrlich's statistical methods, however, have been strongly contested, and the debate continues. Given such conflicting pronouncements, it is best for us to discount these statistical studies entirely. It might very well be that the death penalty has such a negligible effect upon the general homicide rate as to prove statistically insignificant.

Leaving aside the ambiguity of the statistics, what can we say of the various common sense arguments concerning the deterrent efficacy of the death penalty? First, the abolitionists are correct that it is unreasonable to expect that many individuals who would not be deterred by the threat of long imprisonment will be deterred by the remote threat of death when they most likely think they will not be caught. Second, Leiser's claim that revolutionaries and terrorists provide prime examples of individuals who can be deterred by the threat of death but not of long imprisonment does not seem reasonable. Revolutionaries would seem to be the best example of individuals who may be so committed to their cause as to be nondeterrable by any punishment that can be inflicted upon them. The same is often true of the idealistic terrorist or traitor. The less idealistic, one would suppose, act in the belief that they will escape any punishment. Third, Leiser's claim that the death penalty is the only deterrent for criminals who are already serving a life sentence is false. There are many rewards and punishments that can be utilized on those sentenced to life imprisonment that can act as deterrents, including the possibility of early parole, solitary confinement, and the forfeiture of some of the conveniences that make prison life more bearable, such as the privilege of having visitors.

However, we should not easily discount, as many abolitionists do, the testimony of captured criminals to law enforcement officials that the threat of death deterred them either from killing a potential witness to a crime already punishable by life imprisonment or from carrying or using a lethal weapon which would have increased their chances of escape. For example, one can easily imagine a cold-blooded kidnapper who refrains from killing his victim only because of his fear of the death penalty. No doubt, as abolitionists claim, such a cold-blooded criminal would most likely never have embarked upon his criminal activities if he believed that there was a substantial risk of being caught. Nevertheless, if the kidnapping does not go as planned, the criminal's concern over the risk may greatly increase.

Nevertheless, as abolitionists point out, criminals who tell law enforcement officials that they were deterred from murder by the existence of a death penalty are often telling these officials what they want to hear and these officials often, like everyone else, hear what they want to hear. This has been supported by prison wardens who report that criminals have often admitted to them that they lied when they made those remarks. Consequently, some skepticism must be employed in weighing the value of the pronouncements of law enforcement officials as to the important deterrent effect of capital punishment, but we would be rash to fully discount their pronouncements.

The moral choice we must face is whether we should risk abolishing the death penalty and risk losing the lives of those innocents who would otherwise be spared should it prove to be a better deterrent to murder than long imprisonment. This is a choice each of us must ponder for ourselves. Certainly, however, our sympathy for those who are condemned to capital punishment and whose plight is visibly presented to us should not blind us to the invisible victims of murderers who are possibly saved through the special deterrent power of the death penalty. On the other hand, if we are to opt for capital punishment in the hope that it proves a superior deterrent, weighing against our wager will not only be the lives of those guilty of the most serious crimes, but some innocent individuals as well—those who are unjustly executed and those who die at the hands of those who are incited to crime by the existence of the death penalty. Do we have a reasonable basis for assuming that their numbers will be less than the numbers of innocent lives saved which can be attributed to the superior deterrent efficacy of capital punishment?

If we decide to maintain the death penalty, gambling on the belief that the death penalty is a superior deterrent to murder than long imprisonment, we should realize that it is a gamble and not a certainty with which we are dealing; and we should not exaggerate the possible deterrent value of capital punishment as many law enforcement officials do. It is easy to mask one's frustrations at controlling crime by a passionate commitment to capital punishment, but the existence of such a penalty cannot be expected to have a significant effect upon the incidence of crime and certainly it should not blind us, as citizens, to the causes of crime, whose eradication will have a profoundly greater effect upon crime control.

DISCUSSION QUESTIONS

1. Do you believe the death penalty is unjustified? Why?
2. What do you think of the following argument:

    Individuals have a moral right to kill in self-defense. If individuals have a moral right to kill in self-defense so does a nation. *The death penalty is a measure of national self-defense.* Therefore, it is right to use the death penalty.

3. Do you think the death penalty has a brutalizing effect on society as some claim? If so, how important is this factor relative to the possible beneficial consequences of the death penalty?

4. Which of the following arguments do you find more convincing? Why?

    A: The most basic of human rights is the right to life. It is purely speculative whether the death penalty has a deterrent value and as such can save lives. The utilization of capital punishment, on the other hand, is a clear infringement on that most basic of human rights. One is never justified in violating a person's right to life on the basis of a purely speculative good. Therefore, the death penalty is unjustified.

    B: It is unclear whether more lives are saved or lost with capital punishment, but since the life of a potential victim of crime should be valued more than the life of a convicted murderer, the death penalty is justified.

5. Assuming that an insane killer poses a substantial threat of killing again and can only be contained through physical restraint or biochemical or electrical

intervention with his mental processes which will reduce him to a zombie-like existence, should either of these means be utilized or would it be better that such an individual be painlessly put to death?

6. Do you think the execution of a terrorist murderer can be justified on the grounds that her imprisonment is likely to cause other terrorists to threaten the death of innocent hostages as a price for her release? Would this be justifiable if the terrorist had committed a lesser crime?

7. Should the death penalty be allowed as a voluntary alternative to life imprisonment without the possibility of parole? As a voluntary alternative to some lesser penalty?

8. Argue for or against Justice Brennan's claim that "the deliberate extinguishment of human life by the State is uniquely degrading to human dignity."

9. Do you think the Israelis were right in executing Adolf Eichmann for his responsibility in the extermination of the Jews? How would you have treated him? Why?

10. a. According to legal practice, if a criminal who is sentenced to death becomes physically ill, he is treated for his physical illness and then killed at the appointed time of his execution. Do you find this practice justifiable? Why?

    b. Similarly, do you find any justification for the legal practice of postponing the execution of those criminals who "go out of their mind" in jail until they are of "sound mind"?

11. Some Supreme Court justices have claimed that the constitutional prohibition of cruel and unusual punishment should be taken to prohibit only those punishments that the framers of the Constitution would have considered to be cruel (such as the thumbscrew and the rack, but not whipping). Most Supreme Court justices, however, have taken the position that this prohibition should be interpreted in terms of evolving moral standards. Supporters of this point of view are divided as to how the courts should determine these standards. Some justices think the courts should rely on legislative enactments and the sentencing behavior of juries as the standard of what punishments *are as a matter of fact found acceptable* under contemporary standards of decency. On the other hand, some justices have taken the view that the standard of cruelty should be a *normative* one. For example, Justice Marshall takes the view that the courts should turn not to what people will as a matter of fact say about a given punishment, but rather to what they would say if they *were fully informed*. Which of the above views do you find most acceptable? Why?

12. Several states have substituted painless lethal injections for the standard and more dramatic forms of capital punishment. If the death penalty is to be maintained, do you think that this is advisable? Why?

FURTHER READINGS

Individual Works

In *Capital Punishment: The Inevitability of Caprice and Mistake* (Norton, 1974), Charles L. Black, a law professor, argues for the abolition of the death penalty on the grounds that it is impossible to eliminate arbitrariness and mistake in its application. In *Death Penalties* (Harvard University Press, 1982), Raoul Berger, also a law professor, claims that declaring the death penalty unconstitutional under the Eighth Amendment would be contrary to "the intent" of the framers. In *The Courts, the Constitution, and Capital Punishment* (Heath, 1977), Hugo Bedau, an abolitionist, discusses legal issues surrounding the death penalty. In *For Capital Punishment* (Basic Books, 1979), Walter Berns argues that the death penalty can be justified on retributive grounds. In the course of this defense, he discusses a broad spectrum of issues surrounding the morality of the death penalty.

"The Jurisprudence of Death: Evolving Standards for the Cruel and Unusual Punishment Clause," 126 *University of Pennsylvania Law Review* (May 1978) by Margaret Jane Radin is a study of the principles utilized by various Supreme Court justices for determining whether capital punishment is cruel and unusual punishment. Radin defends the abolitionist point of view.

Those interested in the issue of the effectiveness of the death penalty as a deterrent should turn to the debate by Ernest Van der Haag (for) and Hugo Bedau (against) which appeared in the philosophy journal *Ethics*. The first article in this debate was Van der Haag's "On Deterrence and the Death Penalty," *Ethics*, 78, no. 4 (July 1968). Bedau's criticism follows in "The Death Penalty as a Deterrent," *Ethics*, 80, no. 3 (April 1970). Van der Haag provides a brief and heated rebuttal in "Deterrence and the Death Penalty: A Rejoinder," *Ethics*, 81, no. 1 (Oct. 1970), and Bedau briefly replies in "A Concluding Note" in the same issue.

A clear (29-page) discussion of the death penalty is found in chapter 7 of Burton M. Leiser's *Liberty, Justice, and Morals*, third edition (Macmillan, 1986). The quotation in this chapter appears on p. 250.

Anthologies

Hugo Bedau (ed.), *The Death Penalty in America*, revised edition (Doubleday, 1967) is the best and most comprehensive interdisciplinary anthology of material on the pros and cons of the death penalty, representing religious, philosophical, sociological, law enforcement, legal, and psychological perspectives. The anthology begins with a presentation of the historical background of the death penalty and ends with a presentation of case histories of people sentenced to death which Bedau, an abolitionist, selected to demonstrate "the inhuman side of capital punishment in America." Included in this anthology are Sidney Hook's "The Death Sentence" and Jacques Barzun's "In Favor of Capital Punishment" which were referred to in this chapter. Bedau criticizes Hook and Barzun in his own article "Death as a Punishment." (The quote from Barzun in this chapter can be found on pp. 159–60 of this anthology, and the one from Hook on p. 151.)

Capital Punishment in the United States (AMS Press, 1975), which Bedau edited along with Charles M. Pierce, is a good supplement to *The Death Penalty in America*. This anthology consists of material on psychological and sociological research on the death penalty that has appeared since the 1972 Supreme Court ruling in *Furman v. Georgia*. James A. McCafferty (ed.), *Capital Punishment* (Lieber-Atherton, 1972) is an anthology of selections on the pros and cons of the death penalty by philosophers and those involved in the administration of the criminal law.

T. Mappes and J. Zembaty (eds.), *Social Ethics*, third edition (McGraw-Hill, 1987), J. White (ed.), *Contemporary Moral Problems*, second edition (West, 1988), and R. Purtill, *Moral Dilemmas* (Wadsworth, 1985) have selections on the death penalty. The Mappes, Zembaty and the White books include excerpts from the 1976 Supreme Court case of *Gregg v. Georgia*, concerned with the constitutionality of the death penalty.

The Morality
of War
10

Appeal to human beings as human beings, remember their humanity and forget the rest.

ALBERT EINSTEIN

THE TRAGIC AND IRRECONCILABLE
CLASH OF MORAL PRINCIPLES
INVOLVED IN WARS

The question of the morality of war is a deeply troubling one. For some, the very notion of a moral war is a contradiction in terms, for war, as they see it, is by definition a brutal struggle for survival which reduces human beings to a primitive amoral level of existence whose only guiding principle is that of self-preservation. For others, questions relating to the morality of war, however practically difficult they may be to resolve, are at least in principle resolvable, given sufficient factual information and moral understanding. For still others, like myself, who accept the possibility of irreconcilable conflict between basic moral principles, questions relating to the morality of war bring home, in an acutely disturbing way, the potentiality for tragic and unresolvable moral conflict.

For the utilitarian, the brutality of war, and in particular the killing of innocent human beings that it involves, can be morally justified whenever such a measure is an essential means for securing a greater good. For the Kantian, however, who sees the demands of justice in absolutist and immediate terms, war must be condemned as the very model of immorality. What better example is there of treating individuals as mere means—which Kantian ethics forbids us ever do to—than to intentionally drop bombs that one knows will kill innocent civilians, including children, for some utilitarian purpose. When one thinks of the death and horror inflicted on so many innocent people in wartime, a morally sensitive person must feel some pull toward the Kantian view that some things are wrong, regardless of the consequences. If one would consider it wrong to shoot an innocent child at point-blank range, even if this were essential as a means to some greater good, how can one consider it right to drop bombs that will kill thousands of innocent children, as the Allies did in their obliteration bombing of German cities and in the American nuclear bombing of Hiroshima and Nagasaki in World War II? Doubtlessly, it is *psychologically easier* to drop bombs than to fire a gun point-blank at the head of a helpless child whose little frightened face one cannot help but see. The bomber pilot may not see the countless little frightened children, but he has killed them nevertheless. Although one's moral horror over the results of one's actions may vary inversely with one's distance from that horror, one's moral responsibility does not. If one focuses on the immense human horror of modern war, on the colossal forfeiture of human rights that it involves, one may understandably feel strongly inclined toward the view that modern wars are always morally wrong. Better that we should die or be victimized by the injustices of others than that we should intentionally will such stupendous injustices. Such a moral view may not be best suited to assure our survival or happiness in this world, but it is essential, one may feel, if we are to maintain our humanity as moral beings.

Nevertheless, the utilitarian pull is also very strong, for few of us believe, as Kant did, that justice must be done even "if the heavens are about to fall." While many wars and the means utilized in waging them cannot be justified on utilitarian grounds, some can be. For example, when one thinks of the possibility of the triumph of Nazism and the vast inhumanity that such a triumph would have assured, can one so easily say that the vast numbers of innocent civilians killed by the massive Allied bombing of German cities was unjustified *if* it was required for defeating the Nazis? As Einstein and other scientists who urged that our country undertake the construction of an atomic bomb believed, in spite of one's moral revulsion at the thought of using such a bomb, its use would be morally justified *if there were no other way* of winning the war against Hitler. In order to preserve the value of justice and of human life for this and future generations, justice and human lives would have to be sacrificed.

It is precisely because most of us are responsive to both the utilitarian and Kantian ways of moral thinking and are at times subject to their irreconcilable demands, that the question of the morality of war is an especially difficult one. The ultimate moral tragedy of war is that it produces choices that our utilitarian moral intuitions tell us we must make and our Kantian intuitions tell us we never can. As the contemporary philosopher Thomas Nagel puts it in his sensitive essay "War and Massacre," when we squarely face the question of the morality of war, we also come squarely face to face with the possibility "that these two forms of moral intuition are not capable of being brought together into a single, coherent moral system, and that the world can present us with situations in which there is no honorable or moral course for a man to take, no course free of guilt and responsibility." As Nagel sees, whatever decision we make in such situations must be made with a sense of tragic loss, guilt, and agony over the cost of one's decision. A totally committed utilitarian or Kantian who sees morality as being built on a single basic moral principle need not feel any moral guilt or regret as long as he observes that basic moral prinicple, but for those of us who accept a plurality of independent and possibly conflicting basic moral principles, there is always the possibility of having to face a moral dilemma, all of whose options involve choosing something which violates a basic moral principle and for which we will feel deep guilt and regret for the remainder of our days. Such is the tragic condition of life in this world—a tragic condition that cannot be escaped by any morally sensitive person who attempts to assess war in moral terms.

MORAL REASONS FOR WAR
AND MORALITY IN WAR

Since the waging of war involves grave injustices, unlike anything we are willing to condone in any other context, many would question the very possibility of assessing war in moral terms. For example, Bayard Rustin remarks,

> I have said to these young men that they make too much of American brutality. The Viet Cong is equally brutal. Whether one is among the battling Pakistanis and Indians, or in Watts, or in warfare anywhere, the law of violence is such that each side becomes equally vicious. To try to distinguish which is more vicious is to fail to recognize the logic of war.

According to Rustin, it would appear, it is not simply that human beings as a matter of fact refuse to subject the means used in waging war to principles of moral assessment, but that the very logic of war makes this assessment impossible. From this perspective, although one may distinguish between moral (or just) and immoral (or unjust) reasons for waging wars, it makes no logical sense to speak of morality or justice in the waging of war. The distinction between the justice of war (*jus ad bellum*) and justice in wars (*jus in bello*) was a central one for medieval moralists who reflected on the morality of war. It was, they believed, very important for us to morally appraise both the reasons nations have for waging war and the means they adopt in waging it. For Rustin, however, a distinction between moral and immoral ways of waging war cannot be meaningfully drawn. As the familiar saying goes, "All's fair in love and war"—that is, any kind of deceit in love and any kind of violence in war. Although Rustin's claim is psychologically comforting to those who share responsibility for waging war, it flies in the face of the fact that we often do make the distinction between moral and immoral ways of waging war.

For example, many of us condemned as immoral the Pakistani way of waging war in Bangladesh in 1971. Whether or not Pakistan had any justification for attempting to repress Bangladesh's movement for autonomy, their *manner of repressing* that movement for autonomy was loudly morally condemned. It was wrong, so many of us said, to turn an army loose to massacre innocent civilians as Pakistan did. It was beyond moral justification for an army to rampage freely, burning, raping, and killing as it saw fit. It was wrong for it to compile death lists of political, cultural, and intellectual Bangladesh leaders and then to systematically slaughter them. Although the entrance of India on the side of Bangladesh was, at least in part, motivated by India's own strategic interests, many who cared little or nothing about these interests rallied on the Indian side, seeing their action as called for by a humanitarian concern to stop the Pakistanis from waging a type of war that was beyond the pale of moral justification.

Just as it is possible for a just war to be fought justly, it is possible for an unjust war to be fought justly. For example, although Rommell was fighting for the unjust cause of Nazi Germany, he, unlike so many other German generals, adhered to some basic principles of morality in waging his war. For example, he burned the Commando order issued by Hitler which laid down that all enemy soldiers encountered behind the German lines were to be killed at once.

Although one can often separate the question of the morality of a nation's reasons for waging war from the question of the morality of its means of waging war, these questions are intertwined. From a utilitarian perspective, a war waged for morally justified purposes may become immoral when the means of waging that war is likely to cause more harm than the good that can be achieved by it. Such a situation often arises when a foreign influence finds itself fighting guerrillas that have local support. As Michael Walzer puts it,

> Foreigners fighting local guerrillas are likely to find themselves driven to justify, or rather to attempt to justify, virtually every conceivable action against a hostile population—until they reach that climactic brutality summed up in the orders issued by General Okamura, Japanese commander in the struggle against Communist guerrillas in North China during World War II: "Kill all! Burn all! Destroy all!
> At this point, the question of morality in war and of the morality of a particular war come together. Any war that requires the methods of General Okamura, or anything approaching them, is itself immoral, however exalted the purposes in the name of which it is being fought.

Conversely, from a utilitarian perspective, the more morally justified one's reasons for waging war, the more individual injustice one should be willing to tolerate to win that war. For example, considering the clear and pressing moral justification for defeating Nazi Germany and the far from clear and pressing need to defeat the Viet Cong in Vietnam, the United States might have been justified in the obliteration bombing of German cities, but not in the bombing of Vietnamese villages and cities.

THE UTILITARIAN VIEW OF THE MORALITY
OF WAR: THE NOTIONS OF PROPORTIONALITY
AND MILITARY NECESSITY

For a utilitarian, in deciding upon the morality of waging a particular war in a particular way, one must weigh the harm that is likely to be caused as a result of waging this war against the good that is likely to be achieved by waging it. In principle, then, it becomes possible that the harm likely to be produced through the waging of a war can exceed whatever good consequences a country hopes to achieve by waging and winning that war. If this is the case, such a war is wrong from a utilitarian perspective.

In practice, however, nations tend to assume that the utility of their aims is so immense that any means can be justifiably utilized from a utilitarian standpoint to achieve them. This is especially the case when nations see their enemies as incarnations of evil who must be crushed at any cost and see themselves as waging a war for some supreme ideal—such as "making the world safe for democracy" or "waging a war to end all wars"—that far overshadows in utility the immediate suffering and death that individuals will be forced to endure in a war to achieve this ideal. Although history attests to the fact that these supreme ideals are elusively unachievable through the horrors of war, we cling to this illusion, nevertheless, for with it we can escape the essential utilitarian need to weigh the utility of our means in waging war against the utility of our objectives.[1] Instead we assume that our objective is of such overriding importance that it can justify whatever means are essential to achieve it. From such a perspective, the utilitarian question reduces itself to that of choosing those means essential for achieving one's objective at the cheapest utilitarian price. Nations are rarely willing to grant that the undesirable consequences of waging a war are likely to be greater than the good consequences that are achievable through that war. Unwilling to accept this possibility, nations assume they can do *anything* they must to win, as long as what they do is actually related to winning. This view is captured in the notion of military necessity, which is a key notion in the various international laws of war which attempt to specify the scope of a nation's legitimate means for waging war. In essence, the laws of war which allow nations to do everything militarily necessary to win their war rule out only purposeless or wanton violence. This is not, however, a small achieve-

---

[1]The psychological processes by which human beings convince themselves, often without any adequate justification, of the importance of their ends is considered by Ralph K. White, a social psychologist, in his insightful book *Nobody Wanted War: Misperception in Vietnam and Other Wars* (Doubleday, 1968). In his book, White describes the typical, recurrent misperceptions that often make war possible, even when on both sides there is an urgent desire to avoid it. Paramount among these misperceptions, according to White, are the recurring tendencies to see one's enemy as some type of devil ("The Diabolical Enemy-Image") and to see oneself as motivated by the highest of unselfish and noble motives ("The Moral Self-Image"). In addition, White asserts, the desire to avoid humiliation and to be seen as strong is often a very strong-motivating force in a nation's decision to wage war ("The Virile Self-Image"). In many wars, governments are acutely conscious of the danger of backing down or seeming to back down, while they are much less aware of the pain and death of the countless human beings who will have to pay the price of their virile self-image ("Selective Inattention" and "Absence of Empathy").

ment, for much of the violence of war does not serve any useful purpose. Military history, unfortunately, is a sad tale of wanton brutality beyond the bounds of any plausible utilitarian justification.

Our moral intuitions (and the various laws of war which reflect them), however, go beyond the utilitarian notion of proportionality and military necessity. However entitled countries may be to win their wars, we do not believe that they are entitled to do anything that contributes to this objective. Certain things, many of us believe, are wrong regardless of the beneficial consequences they are likely to achieve. For example, it has been said that the prospect of plunder and rape is "a spur to the courage of the troops." The plausibility of such a claim would be strongest in the case of mercenaries who are hired to aid a country in fighting a war. Now although one can argue on utilitarian grounds with great plausibility that the license to rape is an inefficient spur to masculine courage, the point is that even if such a spur were an essential means to motivate an army to fight on, most of us would loudly condemn such means, regardless of its beneficial consequences. As Kant before us, we would say that it is wrong to offer an innocent woman as a sacrifice to some soldier's lust, for to do so is not to treat her as a person but as a mere object—a mere prize of war. This is a morally unjustifiable violation of her rights and dignity as a human being. The only alternative to the slippery and overly permissive utilitarian notion of proportionality, it has often been said, is the position that there are certain prohibitions against types of violence that can never have any rightful exceptions, regardless of the consequences. Paramount among these prohibitions is the prohibition against using (and especially killing) the innocent. Let us critically consider this view.

THE KANTIAN CASE FOR
THE IMMORALITY OF WAR:
THE KILLING OF THE INNOCENT

The strongest case for an absolute moral condemnation of war in the modern era of sophisticated military technology comes from the vast numbers of innocent human lives that are inevitably lost in modern wars. Although the question of who is truly innocent in times of war is open to debate (for instance, are civilian supporters of a government waging war innocent?), most of us make a basic distinction between those people—such as soldiers, government officials, and workers in munitions factories—who are directly involved in the waging of war and those who are not and as such have done nothing that can justify the violation of their right to be left alone. However we make the distinction between the innocent and the noninnocent in times of war, everyone would agree that there are some people in any country who clearly are innocent by any reasonable standard, for example, defenseless children. In the days when the means for waging war were more primitive—such as bows and arrows or swords—one could wage a war with the realistic hope and expectation that innocent lives could be spared. Modern military technology, however, makes it impossible to limit the sphere of death and destruction. Inevitably, when we drop our bombs and shoot our guns from great distances, we know that innocent people, including children, will die as a result of what we do. For those fully committed to the Kantian way of thinking, such actions appear to be incapable of moral justification, regardless of how essential they are as a means to achieve a noble end.

Just as we would be morally outraged at the prospect of sacrificing the lives of a few innocent children to medical experiments which promise to save the lives of a much greater number of children, we should be morally outraged at the thought of sacrificing children for whatever beneficial consequences we hope to achieve through the waging of war, it has been said. Indeed, even if we were absolutely convinced that the only way to save thousands of potential victims of a childhood disease would be by the sacrifice of only a very few innocent children, our sense of justice would lead most of us to loudly condemn such an action as immoral. If we are to accept such a moral perspective in this case, consistency would seem to demand that we morally condemn as well all wars that we know will result in the deaths of innocent human beings.

For those who take such a point of view, one can only remain morally pure by refusing to dirty one's hands with the injustice of modern wars which inevitably cause the death of the innocent. The grave difficulty with this view, however, is that our utilitarian instincts pull us to accept our responsibility for the consequences not only of our actions, but also of our *failure to act* to defend our values from violation by others. For example, can a pacifist committed to "the sanctity of human life" remain morally pure when by his refusal to fight a war he allows others such as Hitler to flagrantly violate this value? If one were sure that the only way to prevent Hitler from engaging in a worldwide program of genocide would be by waging a war to stop him, a war which would doubtlessly cost innocent human lives but far fewer lives than would be lost if this war were not waged, what should a person who values innocent lives do? Surely, those of us who would consider it morally justifiable to wage war against Hitler must accept responsibility for those innocents who will die as a result of our decision, but must not those who refuse to wage war accept responsibility for those innocent lives that one might have saved? To assume that one remains morally pure by refusing to use evil means is to assume that one cannot be morally responsible for *letting people die* as long as one does not *kill them* oneself, and this squarely conflicts with our utilitarian moral intuitions. If the moral purity that many who absolutely condemn war seek is a way of acting for which one should feel no moral regret or guilt, then moral purity is sometimes impossible to achieve in this imperfect world.

WAR AND THE DOCTRINE OF THE DOUBLE EFFECT

Although there have been Christian pacifists who have condemned all wars as immoral on the grounds that evil may not be done as a means of achieving good, the classical Christian position toward war is reflected in the writings of Thomas Aquinas and other Catholic moralists who, by means of the prinicple of the double effect, attempt to reconcile the prohibition against killing the innocent with utilitarian considerations. As we have discussed, according to this classical doctrine, it is morally permissible to peform an action likely to have evil consequences (such as killing of the innocent) provided that one does not directly aim at these evil consequences (either as an end or as a means) but instead aims at morally acceptable consequences (such as the killing of enemy soldiers or the destruction of military installations). Furthermore, one must believe that the likely good effects of one's actions are sufficiently good to compensate for allowing the evil effect. On the basis of such a principle, contemporary Catholic moralists have justified aerial bombardment. Even though this inevitably results in the death of innocents, it is nevertheless justified, they have said, as long as these deaths are not directly aimed at and the bombing has a utilitarian justification. Such a position, however, can lead us to judgments that most of us would find morally unacceptable.

Even if the distinction between the direct intentions of our actions and their foreseen, but unintended, consequences should have some moral relevance, it is implausible to give it decisive relevance. Is it better to drop bombs that one knows will unintentionally kill *thousands* of innocent persons than to intentionally kill *a few* innocent persons who are involuntarily or unwittingly contributing to the enemy's cause? Yet according to the doctrine of the double effect, the latter action is absolutely immoral, whereas the former one is capable of moral justification. No doubt, it will often prove more psychologically difficult for us to intentionally kill innocent persons than to direct our intention exclusively toward some good consequence of our action, while accepting the deaths of innocents that one knows will inevitably result from one's action, for it is much easier not to think about these deaths this way; but this does not show that the latter action is a more morally justifiable one. It will, after all, hardly matter to our victims. As the sorry spectacle of apologists for the U.S. war in Vietnam amply demonstrated, the doctrine of the double effect can simply justify too much. For example, it was common American military practice to subject areas which harbored enemy soldiers to devastating aerial bombardment. Such bombardment could be seen as having a double effect—enemy soldiers were killed, but so were many innocent civilians who happened to be in those areas. It was not the intention of those who ordered such actions to kill those civilians, of course, for they were acting out of a concern for their own soldiers. Yet such actions should not be complacently accepted as being morally justified, even if they could be justified on utilitarian grounds. Such a position does not do justice to our deep moral feeling that a soldier must accept certain risks to himself and indeed to the very cause for which he fights in order to preserve the rights of those innocent people who are caught up in a war, *regardless of the apparent disutility* of such a concern in particular circumstances.

There are many situations in the context of a war when we expect soldiers to take personal risks in order to save innocent civilians without calculating utilitarian costs. For example, consider the following from Frank Richards' memoirs of his experiences as a soldier in World War I:

> When bombing dug-outs or cellars, it was always wise to throw the bombs into them first and have a look around them after. But we had to be very careful in this village as there were civilians in some of the cellars. We shouted down to them to make sure. Another man and I shouted down one cellar twice and receiving no reply were just about to pull the pins out of our bombs when we heard a woman's voice and a young lady came up the cellar steps. . . . She and the members of her family. . . had not left [the cellar] for some days. They guessed an attack was being made and when we first shouted down had been too frightened to answer. If the young lady had not cried out when she did, we would have innocently murdered them all.

If Richards and his fellow soldiers felt morally restrained only by the dictates of military necessity, it would have been prudent for them to throw their bombs without any warning, for if there had been German soldiers in the cellar, they might very well have rushed out, firing as they came. Yet Richards would have considered such a course of action wrong, regardless of its immediate disutility. Even if he were convinced that a policy of bombing without warning in situations such as this would in the long run be justified on purely utilitarian grounds, he, like so many of us, would most likely consider such an action an *unjustified murder*. Yet according to the doctrine of the double effect, Richards would have been justified in bombing without warning if he thought such an action were justified on purely utilitarian grounds. If such actions were required as an *essential* means for winning a just war, most of us would agree, but we would not agree simply if their utilitarian gains outweighed their utilitarian costs. Yet it is precisely this type of utilitarian calculation that supporters of the doctrine of the double effect would have us use in those situations where we do not *directly intend the death of innocents*. Such a moral doctrine makes the moral choices that soldiers inevitably face too easy, for it does not give sufficient weight to the immense injustice that innocent people suffer in war.

SOME GENERAL REFLECTIONS

Even if there is no unified moral theory that we should rely upon to resolve questions relating to the morality of war, this does not mean that correct answers cannot be given to such questions. When one attempts to appraise war in moral terms, one commits oneself to a mode of discourse, governed by indefinite and at times conflicting rules that often allow us to offer plausible moral justifications for conflicting moral positions; but it does serve to limit the sphere of things that can be said and may force those attempting to justify their actions to say things that are false. For example, although people can reasonably argue over who was the aggressor in many wars, there are some wars where all reasonable and informed people would agree as to which side merits this label. Hitler's invasion of Poland, for example, was clearly an aggressive act by any reasonable definition of this term. It was precisely because this was the case that Hitler invented an elaborate charade to disguise his naked aggression.[2] The truth in this situation simply could not be clothed in moral garb.

The assumption that it is impossible to subject one's decision to wage war to moral appraisal makes it much too easy for us to desensitize ourselves to the horrendous price we often choose to pay for our military victories. If one allows oneself to empathize with the countless victims of war, one cannot help but realize how difficult it is to morally justify most of the wars that crowd upon us through the pages of history. For some, this price can never be rightfully paid. But even if one believes that it can be, history amply testifies to the fact that it is paid much more than it should. Nations have often been willing to pay unjustifiably high prices for their victories precisely because they have refused to subject their military decisions to the constraints of moral criticism.

Refusing to subject their ends and the means that are essential to achieve them to moral criticism, government officials can allow themselves to do things in the name of political realism that they would never do in the name of morality. Such an amoral point of view is, for example, implicitly advocated in Henry Kissinger's *A World Restored*. Rejecting "a faith in universal values," Kissinger advocates a "cold-blooded and unsentimental submission of our values to the facts." National leaders, he tells us, must attempt to "harmonize the just with the possible." Although he does not explicitly tell us what this cryptic phrase means, in context it would appear to mean that national leaders should choose whatever means are essential to their ends, untroubled by the restraint of universal values. It is this manner of thinking that made it much too easy for government officials in the United States to accept the immeasurable human cost of the death and destruction that our military technology brought to Vietnam as an acceptable price for the lofty ends we professed. In their minds, a concern for the victims of their military decisions took second place to more abstract speculations about the future of democracy and communist containment. This in turn led to a much too facile tendency to rely upon coldblooded and abstract calculations of future goods to justify very concrete charred human bodies. A moral person should, however, shudder as he thinks of the *certain* massive sacrifice of innocent persons that political leaders and civilians alike have often been willing to accept with no apparent sense of guilt and anguish on the basis of nebulous utilitarian calculations that such actions would *probably* lead to some greater good in the future. We are much too apt, it would appear, to trade certain evils for speculative future goods which often prove to be more difficult to obtain than we expected. Although no precise formula is possible here, a certain evil should always weigh much more heavily in our minds than a greater but speculative future good. Yet the game of international power politics that political leaders so readily play seems to lead them to act on the very opposite principle, weighing their conception of the future good much more heavily than the certain evil they often employ as means to achieve these goods.

---

[2]According to this charade, Germans were dressed up as Polish soldiers who then staged a mock attack on a number of German border outposts creating a pretext for the invasion of Poland.

The assumption that a nation's ends are of such momentous value as to outweigh whatever evil is essential to achieve them is psychologically comforting to those who so often unthinkingly make this assumption. With it, one can maintain one's moral self-image as one chooses whatever means are essential to achieving one's ends, regardless of their price. Unwilling to contemplate the possibility that this price may be too high, we tend to close our minds to moral arguments, as too many of our government officials did during the Vietnam war. Seeing their responsibility to their country's vital self-interests as overriding all their other obligations, such government officials could perceive themselves as conscientious civil servants who must muster the courage to do their duty. In this, they were no different from the Nazi Eichmann whose central role in the extermination of the Jews is perceptively depicted in Hannah Arendt's *Eichmann in Jerusalem: A Report on the Banality of Evil*. Of course, as we become increasingly used to such a mode of thought, we tend to make ourselves callous to the evil we cause, as we more and more coldbloodedly attempt to accomplish our ends in the most efficient manner, untroubled by nagging moral questions concerning our responsibility to values that transcend our national borders.

Although questions of morality are unwelcome intruders to our peace of mind and self-esteem when we contemplate the megadeath of modern war, it is through them that we are forced to examine the ultimate justification for our actions and in the process are often forced to bring to consciousness the many implicit assumptions that underlie our perception of our situation and motivate us to resort to war as an arbiter of our international conflicts. Similarly, by subjecting our decision to wage war to moral scrutiny and debate, we are much more apt to empathize with the motives of our antagonists and often forced to come to the psychologically disturbing recognition that we are motivated by no more loftier interests and ideals than they. If a peaceful resolution to our conflict is not now possible, our recognition of the ambiguities of our situation should make it much more difficult for us to justify our decision to wage war. That is the way it should be, for the moral justification for waging war should never be an easy matter. If we decide to opt, as most of us will, for an essentially utilitarian solution to our moral dilemmas concerning war—weighing more heavily our vital national interests than the rights of those who stand as obstacles to it—we must not be free of guilt for what we do. A moral theory that allowed us to make the decision to wage war, without any guilt for violating the rights of the innocent, might be easier to live with and be more coherent; but it would not do justice to our moral sensibilities which often lead us to want to say both yes and no to the moral choices that face us when it seems that we have no choice but either to allow others to interfere with our legitimate interests or to fight for them and in the process kill and maim those with whom we have no right to interfere.

The Morality Of Nuclear Deterrence

Mankind has never faced a peril as ominous as the threat of nuclear annihilation. More people died in the firebombing raids of Tokyo than in the nuclear bombings of Hiroshima and Nagasaki, but hundreds of planes and bombs were involved in these raids. With just one plane and one bomb, however, close to 100,000 Japanese people were killed in Hiroshima, many within an instant of the bomb's impact. The peril did not, however, end when the immediate dead were counted, for it continued in an invisible form as the radioactive fallout of the two mushroom clouds exacted their toll among the survivors. Yet the atomic bombs dropped on Japan had only a small fraction of the destructive power of the nuclear bombs we have today, and we have tens of thousands of them. The unleashing of only a small percentage of this massive arsenal threatens the very survival of the human race. Scientists tell us that less than one percent of the world's present arsenal of nuclear weapons could trigger a catastrophic nuclear winter in which temperatures could drop more than 50 degrees. Consequently, even if humanity survives the initial destructiveness of a nuclear war, longer range perils, greater in magnitude than any we have experienced before, lurk in the aftermath. Unlike a conventional war, the destructiveness of a nuclear war cannot be expected to be contained within the borders of the belligerents. Unlike a conventional war, too, the quickness and massive destructiveness of nuclear missiles allows little or no time for reconsideration and negotiation. In a nuclear war, soldiers on battlefields give way to technicians behind consoles, far removed from the center of hostilities. A nuclear war would be qualitatively different from any war previously fought, yet we carry on as we did before, threatening war as the final arbiter of international conflicts.

As Einstein perceptively warned, "The unleashed power of the atom has changed everything save our modes of thinking, and we thus drift toward unparalleled catastrophe." And yet the reality is that for many years we have lived in the shadow of the bomb and the catastrophe has not yet come, even though our nuclear arsenals have continued to grow. As this is writtten, the Russian threat has abated and with it the threat of massive nuclear war, but the future, as always, remains uncertain. Can we work together finally to avoid nuclear catastrophe or is the chance of human or technological error too great? Have we unleashed a monster that we can no longer control? These are the thoughts that gnaw at us as we contemplate the nuclear weapons that we continue to build and constantly keep ready for immediate deployment. Given the magnitude of the peril of nuclear war, we are united in our condemnation of it, but divided on how best to prevent it.

In the 1950s, the philosophers Bertrand Russell and Sidney Hook debated the question of unilateral nuclear disarmament in the nuclear age. The question at issue in this debate was whether it would be morally preferable to die in a nuclear war or to surrender and live under Soviet domination—that is, "Is it better to be red or dead?" According to Russell, life under almost any kind of political system was preferable to death. Since, as Russell saw it, nuclear war promised the end of the human race or a significant part of it, he opted for unilateral disarmament, while Hook strongly disagreed. If the only alternatives were living under a highly oppresive political system or fighting a war which would destroy one quarter to one half of our population, most of us would most likely, agree with Russell, but such a choice is not a forced one, since we hope, through a policy of nuclear deterrence, to avoid both alternatives. The threat of nuclear slaughter, it is hoped, can provide a balance of terror which prevents belligerents from ever having to use their nuclear weapons. As Churchill put it at the close of World War II, with nuclear weapons, we hope that "safety will be the sturdy child of terror, and survival the twin brother of annihilation." This is the doctrine of nuclear deterrence, the cornerstone of our nuclear policy.

Assuming that nuclear wars were unwinnable, the policy that prevailed, until recently, was one of "mutual assured destruction," or MAD, for short. According to this policy, both the United States and the Soviet Union attempt to deter the other side from initiating nuclear hostilities by threatening a nuclear counterattack that would be so devastating in its magnitude as to result in a total destruction of the enemy's society. Consequently, according to the logic of MAD, deterrence is the only justification for nuclear weapons. Such weapons, consequently, are built never to be used. This creates an apparent paradox for, according to the logic of MAD, we threaten a devastating nuclear retaliation which *can serve no rational purpose.* If deterrence fails, all we can do is destroy our enemy; we cannot prevail. The attempt to resolve this apparent paradox is at the center of contemporary philosophical discussions of the morality of nuclear deterrence.

In a widely discussed 1983 pastoral letter, United States Catholic bishops proclaimed,

> Under no circumstances may nuclear weapons or other instruments of mass slaughter be used for the purpose of destroying population centers or other predominantly civilian targets. Retaliatory action which would indiscriminately and disproportionately take many wholly innocent lives. . .must also be condemned. . . .We do not perceive any situation in which the deliberate initiation of nuclear war, on however restricted a scale, can be morally justified. . . .Our examination of [the issue of limited nuclear war] makes us highly skeptical about the real meaning of "limited." One of the criteria of the Just-War teaching is that there must be a reasonable hope of success in bringing about justice and peace. We must ask whether such a reasonable hope can exist once nuclear weapons have been exchanged. . . .We hope that leaders will resist the notion that nuclear conflict can be limited, contained, or won in any traditional sense.

Nevertheless, the bishops found the policy of nuclear deterrence morally acceptable "as a step on the way toward progressive disarmament." The bishops did not, however, face the apparent paradox of claiming, as they did, that it is morally permissible to threaten the use of nuclear weapons whose actual use they have ruled out as immoral. According to the bishops, one can threaten to retaliate with nuclear weapons, but one cannot intend to act on that threat, if deterrence fails. Moral deterrence then becomes a bluff. Once the enemy has launched his missiles, a moral leader must, according to the logic of the bishops' position, absorb the strike without retaliating, for retaliation would be an act of senseless immorality. Obviously, however, if the bluff is to work, our enemy must be made to think that we intend to use our nuclear weapons. This is easy to accomplish, for once nuclear weapons have been launched, we enter a realm of decision making which, in the words of former Secretary of Defense Robert McNamara, is "a vast unknown."

In this vast unknown, one cannot rule out the possibility of a national leader unleashing a retaliatory strike in defense of a nation which in a few minutes will essentially cease to exist. While one may shudder, in abstract reflection, at the thought of a leader who demands an eye for an eye in responding to a nuclear aggressor, the psychological power of the retributive desire that an enemy should be made to pay for his aggression is likely to be quite strong and the time for decision short. In the atmosphere of panic likely to exist at the moment of such a decision, one may not focus on the thought of the millions of innocent people who will be killed as a result of a retaliatory nuclear strike in a war that was lost the moment the enemy's missiles were launched against us. The weakness of MAD is that if deterrence should fail, we are left with no policy. Recognizing this, officials of the United States government have embraced the notion of a winnable limited nuclear war, making nuclear war a thinkable option and creating a greater peril of the drift to "unparallelled catastrophe" of which Einstein warned.

Since the knowledge and materials for making nuclear weapons are facts of today's world, there is no way we can completely eliminate the threat of a nuclear catastrophe; realistically, we can only hope to minimize it. There is, unfortunately, no panacea to our perilous plight. Unilateral disarmament leaves us completely vulnerable to the nuclear blackmail of others, including fanatical world leaders and terrorists of the future. Mutual complete disarmament between the Soviet Union and the United States also does not solve the problem of nuclear weapons in the hands of others. Furthermore, mutual pledges of complete disarmament, without mutual trust, may ironically prove destabilizing since it makes conventional war more likely and increases the strategic significance of cheating. Unless nations choose to give up their sovereignty and the right to protect it to some world government, conflicts are bound to arise which create a threat of a resort to force. In such an atmosphere, there might be a great risk of a rush to produce nuclear bombs motivated by a fear of the possible nuclear capacity of one's enemy. Such quickly constructed bombs will not have the elaborate safety features that are built into today's sophisticated weapons. Consequently, even though we may one day find ourselves with only a minute fraction of today's nuclear arsenals, accidental nuclear war may be more likely. As before, the greatest threat of nuclear holocaust will be, not in the cold-blooded aggressive acts of a superpower, but in a preemptive strike out of panic or in a human mistake or technological accident. Clearly, disarmament must proceed hand-in-hand with improvement in international political conditions, especially between the United States and the Soviet Union. Our common awareness of mutual peril must act as a beacon leading us to a common understanding and trust that can, through gradual disarmament and international controls, move us slowly away from the brink of nuclear disaster.

DISCUSSION QUESTIONS

1. What standard should be used for distinguishing the innocent from the non-innocent in time of war? Are all civilians innocent? What of workers in muni-

tions factories, writers of propaganda, and farmers, all of whom contribute in some way to the war cause (for instance, farmers supply the food that soldiers must eat)?

2. It has often been said that a nation has a right to wage war *only* in self-defense to repel acts of aggression by other countries. What do you think the notions of self-defense and aggression should be taken to mean when applied to the actions of nations? Can one, for example, speak meaningfully of economic, political, or ideological aggression or self-defense? If so, how would you define these notions? Assume that nation *A*, fearful that nation *B* might obtain the advantage of striking the first blow, preemptively strikes that first blow itself. Is nation *A* acting in self-defense or aggressively in such circumstances? If you think this depends on more specific circumstances, on what exactly do you think it depends? Assuming that Hitler posed no threat to any other country and had the full and open support of a majority of German citizens in his extermination of the Jews and other groups of people, would a country be acting aggressively if it dropped its own armed paratroopers on German soil to rescue large numbers of intended victims of the Nazi extermination program who were waiting to die in Nazi concentration camps, and then destroyed those camps?

3. Do you think that any reasonable principle can be given for distinguishing between moral and immoral weapons of war? For example, can some reasonable grounds be given for claiming, as some have, that biological weapons are not moral, whereas chemical ones are? Is the use of napalm and antipersonnel shrapnel, as was used in Vietnam, immoral? What of bombs such as the controversial neutron bomb that have the special capability of killing people without destroying property? (Such a bomb, it has been suggested, could be especially useful in repelling an invading Soviet army in Western Europe.)

4. "Obliteration bombing" has been defined as follows:

    It is the strategic bombing, by means of incendiaries and explosives, of industrial centers of population, in which the target to be wiped out is not a definite factory, bridge, or similar object, but a large section of a whole city, comprising one-third or two-thirds of its whole built-up area, and including by design the residential districts of workingmen and their families.

    Such bombing was carried out on a massive scale by the Allies during World War II against German cities. Its intent was not only to destroy military targets but also, by its sheer massiveness, to terrorize civilians and undermine their morale. Some claimed that it was essential for victory, while others claimed that even though the war could be won without it, it would hasten the war's end and minimize the final count of war dead. Still others disagreed, arguing that such bombing was not likely to have any appreciable effect on the war. Indeed, some claimed that obliteration bombing would stiffen the resistance of the Germans just as the German bombing of England had stiffened the resistence of the English and would make the German people so hateful toward the Allies that it "might engender...a volume of hatred which not even the peace will be able to assuage." Some also argued that the economic and social problems likely to result from the terror bombing of large German cities would prove to outweigh, in the long run, whatever possible good such bombing would achieve in the short run.

Let us assume, however, that it was reasonable to believe that such bombing would be likely to shorten the war and minimize the ultimate number of war dead, even though the war could be won without it. If this were so, do you think that the decision to utilize such bombing against densely populated German cities was a morally justifiable one? Would it make any difference in your mind (as it would to those who accept the doctrine of the double effect) whether the death of innocent civilians was essential if such bombing were to achieve its intention of undermining German morale? What would be your reaction to a supporter of the doctrine of the double effect who said the following:

The intent of such bombing was not to kill civilians in their homes but merely to destroy their homes. Even though we knew that innocent civilians would doubtlessly be in their homes when their homes were destroyed and would consequently be killed themselves, it was not our intent to kill these civilians. Since we merely foresaw their deaths and did not intend them, our act was a morally justifiable one, but it would not have been morally justified if we intended to kill civilians.

5. In offering his justification for using the atomic bomb against Japan, President Truman declared in an address to the American people on August 12, 1945:

We have used [the bomb] against those who attacked us without warning at Pearl Harbor, against those who have starved and beaten and executed American prisoners of war, against those who have abandoned all pretense of obeying international laws of warfare. We have used it in order to shorten the agony of war.

On the surface, Truman, in claiming that the atomic bomb was "used in order to shorten the agony of war," seems to be offering a straightforward utilitarian justification of this action. If this is the case, why does he refer to Japan's alleged "war crimes" in justifying his action. Does he mean to assert that since the Japanese, but not we, were to blame both for beginning the war and for disobeying the laws of war, we were not morally obligated to subject our manner of waging this war to as rigid a moral appraisal as would otherwise have been required? Does he believe that, given the Japanese aggression in beginning the war and in waging that war in an illegal manner, Japanese civilians can rightfully be deprived of basic rights with less moral justification than would otherwise be required? Do you see any plausibility in such a claim? If, by some chance, we were losing the war and it was the Japanese who had the bomb, what do you think Truman would have said had they used it on American cities, killing tens of thousands in order to shorten the agony of war? Would Truman not have considered such an act as another one of Japan's war crimes? If so, can Truman's sentiments be rendered into any reasonable moral principle?

6. Let us now consider the dominant utilitarian strand of Truman's argument. As the story has it, the choice facing Truman was whether to utilize the atomic bomb or to prepare for an invasion of the Japanese islands which would meet fierce Japanese resistance and would be far costlier in both American

and Japanese lives.[3] Churchill, for example, described the atomic bomb as "a miracle of deliverance" which promised to "avert a vast, indefinite butchery... at the cost of a few explosions." There is, however, possibly a serious flaw in this utilitarian argument, for the Americans were apparently unwilling to accept anything less than an unconditional surrender of Japan. If less than this were asked of the Japanese, they might very well have surrendered without either an invasion or the use of the atomic bomb. Assuming this to be the case, was it morally justifiable for the Americans to refuse to accept anything less than an unconditional Japanese surrender? What undesirable consequences of a conditional Japanese surrender would outweigh, on a purely utilitarian moral ledger, the vast human costs of utilizing the atomic bomb against Japan?

7. Consider the following hypothetical case:

Either an invasion of Japan or the use of atomic bombs will be necessary to obtain even a conditional Japanese surrender. Either way, the defeat of Japan is assured. If atomic bombs are dropped, about 150,000 Japanese civilians will perish. No Americans, however, would die. If an invasion is chosen, about 5,000 American soldiers will die, as well as 10,000 Japanese soldiers, and 20,000 Japanese civilians.

Since victory is assured in either case, a utilitarian American military strategist would seem to have to be committed to choosing to invade Japan, on the grounds that Japanese lives should count no less than American lives. Doubtlessly, however, American officials would consider themselves as having a greater responsibility to save American lives than to save Japanese ones. If this is so, how are American lives to be weighed against Japanese lives? Is it right, for example, to sacrifice one hundred Japanese soldiers to save one American soldier, when the outcome of the war will not be affected by such a choice? Where would you draw the line? Would it make any difference to you if the choice were one of sacrificing Japanese *civilians* or sacrificing American *soldiers*?

8. Is there a logical flaw in the policy of deterrence since we threaten a second strike which has no sensible justification?

[3]This story is not universally accepted as true. According to the revisionist historian Charles Mee, Jr., in his *Meeting at Potsdam*, (M. Evans, 1975), neither an invasion of the Japanese islands nor the use of the atomic bomb was necessary to obtain the unconditional surrender the Americans demanded. Why then was the atomic bomb used? According to Mee, the major reason for its use was political: "to make Russia more manageable in Europe," as then Secretary of State Byrnes put it. With an atomic bomb that "worked potently on the imagination," Truman felt that he could intimidate the Russians into dealing with him in a more conciliatory manner in the resolution of post-war questions concerning the future of Europe and the Far East. As Mee puts it,

The psychological effect on Stalin was twofold: the Americans had not only used a doomsday machine; they had used it when, as Stalin knew, it was not militarily necessary. It was this last chilling fact that doubtlessly made the greatest impression on the Russians. (p. 299)

According to Mee, many military figures did not want to use the atomic bomb against Japan. For example, General Eisenhower said that Japan was already so utterly defeated that the bomb was "no longer mandatory as a measure to save American lives," and to drop it was "completely unnecessary." Admiral King and Generals Arnold and LeMay also agreed. Admiral Leahy, Mee tells us, "was at a loss to explain the determination to use the bomb and thought it was 'because of the vast sums that had been spent on the project.'" With its use, Leahy asserted, Americans "had adopted an ethical standard common to the barbarians of the Dark Ages."

9. Under what conditions, if any, are the use of nuclear weapons justified?

10. Should all nations pledge never to initiate nuclear hostilities? The United States has refused to make such a pledge on the grounds that, given the present imbalance of Soviet conventional forces in Europe over Nato forces, the threat of a Nato nuclear counterattack is a necessary deterrent to a possible Soviet invasion of Europe. If, as it now appears, the threat of a Soviet European invasion is unrealistic, does the refusal to pledge never to initiate nuclear hostilities still serve the aim of deterrence?

FURTHER READINGS

Individual Works

Just and Unjust Wars (Basic Books, 1967) by the Princeton political theorist Michael Walzer is an excellent general study directed to the general reader of the morality of war. Also directed to the general reader are Jonathan Schell's *The Fate of the Earth,* which originally appeared in *The New Yorker,* and its sequel *The Abolition* (Alfred A. Knopf, 1982 and 1984). In *The Fate of the Earth,* a book which more than any other aroused general public debate on the issue of the morality of nuclear deterrence, Schell first describes the devastating effects of a nuclear attack on human life and the earth as a whole. He then argues that total disarmament enforced by a world government is the only way out of the abyss created by the threat of nuclear war. Retreating from his pessimistic belief in *The Fate of the Earth* that the renunciation of national sovereignty is the only adequate solution to the threat of nuclear war, Schell argues in *The Abolition* for the abolition of nuclear weapons, without world government.

Anthologies

Richard Wasserstrom (ed.), *War and Morality* (Wadsworth, 1970) is an excellent anthology of material on the morality of war, representing diverse viewpoints. Other anthologies are Robert Ginsberg (ed.), *The Critique of War* (Regency, 1969), which discusses causes, justifications, and alternatives to war, and Nigel Blake and Kay Pole (eds.), *Objections to Nuclear Defense* (Routledge & Kegan Paul, 1984) which discusses the morality of nuclear deterrence. Especially recommended in the latter collection is Anthony Kenny's article "Better Dead Than Red." Like Bertrand Russell before him in his debate with Sidney Hook, Kenny disagrees.

   War and Moral Responsibility (Princeton University Press, 1974), edited by M. Cohen, T. Nagel, and T. Scanlon, is an anthology of articles by philosophers, lawyers, and political scientists that originally appeared in the philosophical journal *Philosophy and Public Affairs.* The first part of this anthology contains articles on the general problem of the moral restraints that should be placed on wars. The second part consists of articles discussing the special circumstances of World War II, the justifiability of the Nuremberg Trials, and selective conscientious objection.

   The October 1973 edition of *The Monist* (57, no. 4) is devoted to the topic of the morality of war. The April 1985 issue of *Ethics* (Vol. 95) consists of discussions on nuclear deterrence by philosophers and professional weapons strategists which are preceded by a useful introduction.

   The following anthologies on contemporary moral issues have chapters on the morality of war: T. Mappes and J. Zembaty (eds.), *Social Ethics,* third edition (McGraw-Hill, 1987); R. Wasserstrom (ed.), *Today's Moral Problems,* third edition (Macmillan, 1985); R. Purtill (ed.), *Moral Dilemmas* (Wadsworth, 1985); J. White (ed.), *Moral Problems,* second edition (West, 1988); and J. Arthur (ed.), *Morality and Moral Controversies,* second edition (Prentice-Hall, 1986).

   The Mappes and Zembaty and the Purtill anthologies contain the Catholic bishops pastoral letter. The White anthology contains an excerpt from Schell's *The Fate of the Earth* and Michael Walzer's discussion of nuclear deterrence from his *Just and Unjust Wars.*

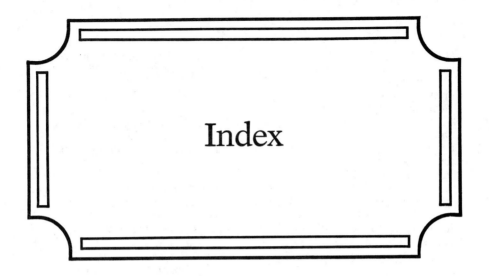

Index